21st Century Goth

21st Century Goth

MICK MERCER

R·H

REYNOLDS & HEARN LTD
LONDON

Thanks

Aimee, Asako Honma, Blue, Gerard Bumanglag,
Stéphane Burlot, C, Cynds, Derekandclive, Disco Max,
Doi Pollas, Don, Gary, Peri Godbold, Joan, Joe Two Words,
Julie, Keiko, Chris Limb, Lina A'rel, Lindy, Stéphane Lord,
Lurkerama Pete, Lynda, Marcus Hearn, Mark Moran,
Martin Dench, Michelle Matzke, Miss Pamela GTO,
Miss Scarlett, Miss Take, Mistress McCutchan, Mothburner,
Mr Jolly, Ms Lovely, Nikola Prevot, Paul Not That Paul,
Richard Reynolds, Sean, Shannon, Trudie, Vamp Girl,
Yuko Tsukamoto.

Publisher's Note

The entries in this book are listed alphabetically. Sometimes a decision regarding where to place a particular entry has been problematic, particularly when dealing with bands, zines and so on whose names begin with 'A' or 'The'. If we believe the indefinite or definite article to be an inseparable part of the title (as, for example, in 'A Perfect Circle') then we have listed the entry under 'A'. If not, then look for the entry under the first letter of the second word (as with 'The Autumns'). Individuals are listed under their surnames – but as even this can sometimes be ambiguous, it's worth searching around!

The internet changes all the time. Sites come and go, existing sites establish new links or change out of all recognition. Every effort has been made by the author and publisher to check that all sites mentioned in this book are functional at the time of going to press, and offer relevant content. We are not, however, responsible for sites or links from sites that are irrelevant, disagreeable or may even contravene local laws and by-laws in particular countries, states or regions.

First published in 2002 by
Reynolds & Hearn Ltd
61a Priory Road
Kew Gardens
Richmond
Surrey TW9 3DH

A CIP catalogue record for this book is available from the British Library.

ISBN 1 903111 28 5

Frontispiece photo © Stéphane Burlot
Contents page photo © Lord Heathcliff

Designed by Peri Godbold.

Printed and bound by Biddles Ltd, Guildford, Surrey

Contents

Introduction

It's that time again, when the myopic Mercer emerges blinking into the light, having sacrificed another ungodly period of time in writing like a mad thing inside his gloomy quarters. Once again I am prepared for outcry and criticism – *plus ça change* – but this *is* for you, whether you like it or not. Inevitably, there will be things you'll expect to find but won't. It is not a perfect world. Given that I have taken a Net-based concept, and as Goth is such a broad genre now, there simply isn't room for everything, so tough choices had to be made.

You will already have dozens of favourite sites bookmarked, naturally. By the end of this book you may have hundreds. That is the idea. I have honestly done my best to include all the basics, with sufficient resource sites to cover all areas, into which you'd spin off at will anyway. Obviously it is important to up the band count as high as possible and if you were wondering how An Old-Fashioned Book can hope to compete with the Internet, you simply won't find a website anywhere which will have as many URLs for bands as I provide here. Fact. Similarly, I give a better all round perspective of other areas than big sites do.

Goth was the first and biggest scene to take to the Net, when ignorant music media (apart from in Germany) decided that nothing was to be found worth writing about it, other than traditional snide cynicism. That in itself deserves a book, but the way Goth's net presence can now transport people into the heart of a new world requires commemoration.

I've tried to introduce new elements, particularly highlighting exposure of Asian developments. Some of you won't find that interesting, because you don't actually love Goth *itself*, you just like what suits you, having already decided where your interests lie, and 75% of this book fulfils your needs, by offering standard material. For the *dedicated* Goth explorer there is much here to unearth. Goth has always been about subtle drama and visual style, and that is provided throughout Japan and S E Asia, no problem. Those of you who simply prefer to investigate the American, European or UK scenes go ahead, see if the rest of us care. You may notice that there is now far more Canadian, New Zealand and Australian info than I was able to offer last time round. That is the beauty of the Net. Delve deep and eventually you can find anything – which is why I hope the book will help, in that it also saves you time.

previously 2 **Daisy Chainsaw**

As usual, everyone has a cross to bear, or else everyone seems cross. Should Goth be traditional, should it make way for Cyber, and just where do you place Manson, other than blindfolded in front of an oncoming bus? It was interesting to read Scorpion's brilliant words (see Goth People), about changes within the American Goth atmosphere, which clearly matches the mid-eighties aggravation in the UK when the audiences found more oafish individuals joining... but this is only stasis in evidence. Everything changes, as it should. Scorpion is right to advocate taking a stand, not just against boorish genre-hoppers who suddenly bring their sullen presence to bear, but also in criticising the arrogant elitists who only foster bigotry.

Personally I am only disgusted by the laughable cretins who mock my work on the grounds that I have had the temerity to write about their music, *their* scene. Yes, you witless wonders, here I am once again spending a year of my life, online 16 hours a day, to bring this to you, because I *obviously don't care*! Instead of imagining how dreadful it is that I may be trying to popularise the genre, try using the smattering of your grey cells still functioning to realise that books on Goth sell

Inkubus Sukkubus

to Goths, and no-one else. These do not reach the mainstream and have no effect on it. They are for people whose imagination and desire, and *appreciation* of Goth, leads them to want to explore further. That is why I do them, because I know that some people enjoy them. For the snooty or crass apologists who Know What They Like, which includes slagging me off, when they have consistently failed to understand any of my previous predictions or observations, I say only this: you are not to going to enjoy the rest of this intro.

Ironically, as expressed on some surly newsgroups and message boards a few years ago, people think it odd that I haven't had a website, or hadn't when they were snickering. The answer is simple. From '93 – '97 I was using cyber cafés (when they still allowed smoking), and Goth sites were rubbish. It's as simple as that. I'd tried interesting UK publishers in doing a Net magazine just after my second book came out at the end of '91 but nobody understood what I was on about. I *realised* the long-term potential. Later, I also saw the reality. Well that has now all changed. The Internet has teemed with brilliance for several years. Unfortunately, with an excess of journals, things have gone so text heavy with domain/project overloads, that you sometimes can't find anything to enjoy, merely absorb. Just as the early sites were fundamentally boring and simplistic, so the new breed of journal and webcam infestation is the higher level of drudgery for the visitor.

I didn't want to do anything with a site, because I didn't see what people would want, and I had too many ideas that I wished to explore. My text files ideas of doing things of depth was relevant, but dismissed by many, although similar ideas have been put to great financial use by companies these days. Some didn't appreciate that doing a text files service on disk was a way people who couldn't afford to go online could be included. In the last three years the Net has got more in-depth, intelligent, academic, and fun, and general costs have come down. The variety is quite dazzling. And so Mercer will only add to the joyous mess, of which more later.

To the farcical clowns who decry my dedication to the genre, shame on you! None of you would willingly spend a year doing something like this, and I'm not going anywhere, so get used to it. Yes, I have been into this music since before some of you started school (that being the way many of you petulantly defend your scene 'status' against newbies I believe?) and no, the chances of your interest outliving mine is pretty unlikely, wouldn't you say? So when I do something you should accept that it is actually done for the *same* reasons as you profess devotion to this music. That said, stop your whimpering and settle down to enjoy the book.

To the normal Goth devotee, I need make no apologies or offer any explanation, as you will already understand the relevance of this book, and the fun that lies in store when you start investigating certain sites. Or if you don't, at least you realise *why* I do it – for everyone to enjoy. You will find more new material to ponder in just a few weeks of following leads through here than you would in haphazardly following what links remain alive on most sites over a period of months. I have also avoided the boring sites, but included a few creaky antiquities, to shock you. Regrets? I've had a few, but mainly that I couldn't find the sites called Quasimofo, or PhenoBarbieDoll. Arse!

The book is pretty self-explanatory really. In the band sections you shouldn't need too much detail anyway. There is a bigger word count compared to my Hex Files, but even so I have had to edit, edit, edit. So I don't need to point out who has mp3's or video. Some will, some won't. (It may seem weird when I pop little descriptions by certain band names, but that is to save overall space, instead of using more words beneath the e-mail or URL. which might sometimes occupy a single line. I really do need to cram things in.) Similarly, club sites tend to be included because they have fabulous galleries. Resource sites were picked as good examples, or specialist, rather than endlessly finding dozens that were remarkably similar. The Clothes/ Business section is pretty obvious, but with more household items brought in, and the Visual Rock section, while small, is just a random taster of some of the great imagery that can be found – with some of the music being fantastic, some absolutely atrocious. Goth People sites tend to be ones where you will find good content, unless I specifically highlight the visual side, in which case go there to drool. What I didn't do was include average personal sites of Goths which are just that – purely personal. If there aren't elements pertinent to others, there's no point including them. For every site included I must have dismissed at least five times as many. Zines, Locations and Webrings are also obvious. You will also find two interviews, with the band Mothburner, and zine empress Mistress (Laura) McCutchan of Morbid Outlook, secreted somewhere. The questions are virtually identical, to ensure balance is almost maintained. The reason is not just that I wanted to stir the visual mix of the book somewhat. Laura puts the main aspect of Net-based creativity into perspective, and Mothburner are there not just because they're a great band, but because they remind us what it's all about in the first place. The main section where you can expect to encounter random craziness is Sites Of Interest, as all manner of material lurks there. Now let's have a quick point on music from Mercer Logic, before you get stuck into it all, accepting that this comes from a UK-perspective.

The success of Nu-Metal proves how Goth missed the boat. A surge of commercial activity within a scene, *any* scene, lasts five years, but leaves in its wake enough enthusiasts to sustain that scene through bleaker spells. Goth itself could hoover up intelligent Manson fans, as an example, from the metal side, who will eventually tire of his weak charades.

Sadly, British Goth bands got nowhere in the nineties. I did point out in '97 that the bigger bands were going to be coming back, and that if the then-current bands increased their activity, to benefit from renewed interest, they could then be able to use that as a springboard to interest major labels, by building an audience in indie venues, where the indie bands had been clearly stagnating. All About Eve, Bauhaus, The Mission and Nephilim did all lumber back. It was bound to happen (what else where they going to do?), but what the bigger bands did didn't matter, for this was a chance for smaller bands to boost their profile and be ready to join together, to share resources and get noticed.

If they had done, then labels would have looked to them. I had contacted many A&R people and they were interested, as some had been for several years already, but the feedback was always that while they were keen, they saw *no* evidence of any Goth bands doing *any* work, which was simply plain embarrassing.

It wasn't even really the fault of the bands, despite their insistence on playing safe within a tiny scene by mainly playing Goth Gigs only, rather having the confidence and guts to slog it out on the Indie stage. They had forgotten what it was like to compete, as though their band was actually little more than a fragrant hobby. There are notable examples that worked hard, but the majority of nineties Goth bands truly never expected to Get Anywhere. By total contrast, Cradle Of Filth didn't do that, and look where they

Goth presence, all major labels naturally look towards Rock hybrids as being the main tie-in between live audiences and sales, which is standard label *raison d'etre*. Had the Goth bands got organised during '97, then by '99 they would have been poised for serious consideration, and reaped what they had sewn. Instead none had sewing skills worth noticing.

So they've all missed out, and they're now too old, but for any new Goth bands forming in the UK (under the age of 21 hopefully) there is no need to make the same mistakes. People have to get out there and play pub gigs on the Indie circuit, as they should. UK Goth bands have to accept that they should do what 99% of Indie bands do, put all your effort into achieving impact live, to build an audience. If you impress live, then promoters – who always compare notes amongst themselves, to warn each other off duff or unreliable bands, and also therefore recommend new stars – talk to freelance journalists who regularly haunt their establishments. A&R people, who aren't terribly intuitive, pick the brains of both journos and promoters. You do well live, and *everyone* starts noticing you.

It also doesn't matter what type of Goth music you play. It is *all* relevant to create a solid scene working towards something, as you *all* benefit. The old Goths who dislike Cyber should grow up. Of course it all changed mid-nineties, as who in their right mind, especially the young, wants to hear nth generation Sisters/Neffs copyists? Of course a dance element has evolved, because that's about *enjoying* yourself. But what about the darker bands, and how come people like Placebo can do it, and Goths can't? The reason people regard Goths as a joke or well past their smell-by date, always 100% without having heard any, is because they have that idea of what was late-eighties Goth, the type of music old bores who signed them to major labels understood – the Rock ethos. But original Goth was anything but, it was bands who looked good and sounded lively, and that really is all it takes. You need to be imaginative, and exciting.

Could websites do more? Possibly, but the Net always dilutes critical impact, through its sheer variety, whereas a handful of music papers could focus attention on certain bands and scenes. But now there's only the NME, you can forget that.

Think of this, if you have been getting tetchy over what I have already said. I'm never wrong with assessments, because of what they're based upon, and my main point is this: what's about to happen in a couple of years, and why should Goths be preparing now? Answer? Come on, come on...

There is going to be a *void*.

Nu-Metal will falter, as it already is, and become sterile, and so there *will* be a void. There always is. Labels will need to fill that void to maintain the momentum they themselves have recently built up around

live bands. In two years time they're going to be looking around, hoping to see great live bands, who are part of an identifiable scene, because that makes it easier for them to push their new signings towards an existing audience. So if Goth bands start to create a worthy and dramatic impression over the next two years, you can expect to see some signed and taken seriously – which will have a beneficial knock-on effect, for various reasons, within the Goth scene for a decade to come. Those of you who feel that mainstream exposure of Goth is a disaster, think again. If it hadn't have been for the late-eighties boom, it would have been harder for many bands to survive the nineties. We all need to see it happen again.

Bands need to realise what works, and work *together*. If they become prospects they'll make a fortune. Their ability to increase people's awareness of Goth will also mean smaller bands (mainstays of the current scene) will also benefit from further sales, and when it all dies down again, towards the end of the decade, the scene will be in a far healthier state than it is now, with the small bands still capable of easy financial survival and regular releases, which is then good for the rest of us. It is a circle and cycle that becomes self-sustaining. If nothing happens in the next few years the scene at the end of this decade will be tiny, as people consistently drop away, as they always do. So instead of some people complaining that my books popularise a scene, think instead about your own attitudes and how small-mindedness can be what kills it all stone dead!

The key to this is *life*. People go to gigs to be excited. We need bands who are young, energetic, abrasive, visually sleek and wild. The dreamier side of Goth is what people listen to at home. Bands who are lovingly pretentious or softly romantic can't expect to really get anywhere, but those with the noise and the poise, the pose and the clothes, can.

Do you honestly imagine that 90% of the Indie kids who go to gigs wouldn't be altogether more impressed by Goth bands who display vitality, than the mind numbing well-meaning mush they encounter on a weekly basis? Of course they'd be interested, but they won't know until you educate them. Going to an Indie gig these days is like stumbling about in a bad, sluggish dream. In the eighties, when nearly all successful Indie labels had a Goth band, or two, they weren't signed because the labels were taking a risk, or admired their music, but because by playing live and exciting people they clearly had an audience that large quantities of records could be sold to. The reason they built up their big followings wasn't because a huge Goth audience already existed, but because they played at 'normal' venues, where everyone got a chance to see them, and became fans.

This isn't rocket science. (Sudden bizarre image of Goths building rockets in back gardens!) All the catalytic elements are already here, you simply need to exploit the situation and, as with any art form, if you're not prepared to give it your all, you won't get noticed, which would be fair, because you wouldn't deserve to be.

And this book? It shows what's out there. Look at how the Visual Rock bands have done what they've done. Follow their lead. And as for me, my plans are explained on the very last page. For the time being I have said too much, been too unkind... and you should be thankful for that.

MICK MERCER, 2002.

(The beautiful statues seen in this section are by the awesome British sculptor Philip Jackson. I was lucky enough to be living near Chichester when he had an exhibition within the Cathedral grounds. I hope you like them as much as I do.)

All photos © Mick Mercer

Pete Murphy. Photo © Stéphane Burlot

Bands

45 GRAVE
www.geocities.com/Area51/Dreamworld/4975/
dcancer.htm
Archive, with updates on members'
current projects and good discog, but
no history and only three pics.

A NEW JANUARY – ELEC
www.anewjanuary.com
info@anewjanuary.com

A PERFECT CIRCLE
www.aperfectcircle.com
This includes fan photos, Q&A sessions
with band, exclusive community
goodies, exclusive t-shirts, advance ticket
information, tour diaries and photos,
audio messages from the road, exclusive
songs and videos, member-only chats
with APC, footage from behind the
scenes, band artwork, poetry, and stories
and an online newsletter.

A PERFECT CIRCLE
www.aperfectcircle.org
contact@aperfectcircle.org
This is incredible. As unofficial sites go
I have seen more depth but never better
visuals, and massive content, in terms
of variety and quality. Even simple
ideas, like getting people to send in
reviews of any dates they see on a tour,
give an interesting overview. Divine
gallery. Also:
www.angelfire.com/me2/boywonder1/perfect.htm

A SORROWFUL DREAM
http://asorrowfuldream.cjb.net
asorrowfuldream@bol.com.br
Brazilian Gothic Doom, in English.

KARLING ABBEYGATE
& THE MONKS OF LOVE
www.comstockrose.com/karling
myface@yahoo.com
Dark Pop band with English singer,
resident in the States it appears and
compared to a sort of Bjork/Kate Bush
hybrid. Fantastic site, with the best
gallery selection I've seen from a band
and cute bio details.

ABIGOR
www.infernalhorde.com/abigor
hellbound_legions@hotmail.com
Sorry fellas, but Satan doesn't exist.
Get back to your D&D.

ABNEY PARK
www.abneypark.com/new
info@abneypark.com
A stunning site.

ABSURD MINDS – ELEC
www.absurdminds.de
info@absurdminds.de

ABUSE – ELEC/NOISE
www.underground.sk/abuse
durajka@istropolitana.sk

ACCESSVIRUS – ELEC
http://sweb.cz/accessvirus
accessvirus@seznam.cz

ACCLIMATE – DARK AMB/IND
http://community2.webtv.net/Acclimate6/PotatoCog
Acclimate6@webtv.net

ACT OF CRUELTY – ARCHIVE
http://home.nordnet.fr/~mgalvaire/bioe.htm
When you click on the photo link you
may be surprised what you see.

ACTION DIRECTE
http://home.talkcity.com/lyricln/actiondirecte/
intro.html
adirecte@hotmail.com
They call themselves a shockwave EBM/
Ministry-style collision with Nitzer Ebb.
Entertaining site, as they cleverly stand
for everything, and for little, doing so
with whirling passion. But they don't
wear cardigans. Once in a while it would
be nice to see some Industrial types
sitting in a deckchair, or smoking a pipe,
instead of looking inscrutable or chest-
beating, don't you think? That said, one of
them is wearing a feather boa in a pub.

ADAM ANT
www.adam-ant.net
webmistress@adam-ant.net

This is the official site and it's a beauty,
with all the depth and visual allure you
could desire. Totally up to date news,
plenty of good features, and sensational
pics ('Fetish For Ants' is divine). Also:
MARCO PIRRONI
www.marcopirroni.fsnet.co.uk
Often wonderfully acerbic at times, Marco
is usually up to something, and there is
always wonderful info here about his new
projects, including new bands he's writing
with, clothing, and good pics. This site
does go down for updating sometimes,
but it is regular and interesting.
http://clubs.yahoo.com/clubs/uaafc
http://eveandtheapes.freeweb.supereva.it
http://home.earthlink.net/~plink/ant.html
http://home.earthlink.net/~ultravox/adam.html
http://members.madasafish.com/~adamant
http://members.tripod.com/T_sa/aant.htm
http://nomusic.hispeed.com/ants/index.html
http://tinpan.fortunecity.com/eltonjohn/802/
adamant/index.html
www.antmusic.fsnet.co.uk
www.geocities.com/antics1999
www.geocities.com/Broadway/2418/adam.html
www.geocities.com/cartrouble_ohyeah
www.geocities.com/Hollywood/Hills/9585/adam
ant.html
www.geocities.com/SunsetStrip/Palms/3678
www.geocities.com/TelevisionCity/Studio/8022/
aata.html Also, not forgetting... (no
matter how hard we try)...
http://home.earthlink.net/~vscottjxxx/index.htm

ADAM ANT – ANT LIB
www.geocities.com/antliberationfront
Great unofficial Ants resource. Forum
gets interesting, and sharply critical in all
the right ways. There is a wealth of Ants
material here, especially all the reprints of
the Fanclub magazines. Make sure you
check out the developing history arm at:
www.geocities.com/adamanthology

ADFINEM
www.adfinem.co.uk
Synthy boys doing well, dull site.

ADRENALINE
www.adrenaline-official.co.uk

Carling Abbeygate

disclaimer@adrenaline-official.co.uk
UK Solo Goth artist Alan Shenton.
Nice site.

ADVANCED META-METAPHOR OF A PAGAN
http://advancedmeta-metaphorofapagan.net
haj@goc.liquidweb.com
Ambient and gloomy, this is weird
Japanese. English available.

ADVERSUS
www.adversus.de
Abgesang@adversus.de

ADVOCATUS DIABLO
www.advocatus-diaboli.net
service@advocatus-diaboli.net
Tons of info, only let down by no real
gallery.

AENIMA – OFFICIAL
www.aetherial.org
Aenima@aetherial.org
A fine site, with good bio and profiles,
excellent news, discography, great live
photos, fan art, nice 'behind the scenes'
anecdotes, brisk faq.

AESCULAPIUS SEPULCRA – IND-AMB
http://artists.mp3s.com/artists/243/
aesculapius_sepulcra.html

AETERNITUS – GOTH-METAL
www.aeternitas-online.de

info@aeternitas.info
Good, info-packed site, in German, with
fine gallery selection.

AFACT – SYNTHETIC CYBERWAVE
http://afact.de
info@afact.de

AFTER FOREVER – METAL GOTH
http://afterforever.cjb.net
www.aforever.syntonic.net/index.php
information@afterforever.com
www.geocities.com/melodic_metal_fanpage/after
forever/index.htm
andre@afterforever.com

AGALLOCH – METAL DREARY
www.theendrecords.com/html/agalloch.html
oakenthrone@hotmail.com

AGATHODAIMON
www.agathodaimon.de
sathonys@agathodaimon.de
Metal Goth, which doesn't interest me,
but the site itself is a stunner. A lot of
Metally ones have that offhand, austere
manner – as in, 'Be satisfied with what
we give, mortals. We, the Rock Gods
have spoken and...oh, hang on, I think
my mum's found my wank mags!' – but
this has a friendly touch, and looks
great.

AGHAST VIEW
www.geocities.com/phaseknox

AGHAST VIEW – BRAZILIAN IND
www.geocities.com/SunsetStrip/9430
ocaso@planetcds.com.br

AGNES POETRY
www.agnespoetry.com
info@agnespoetry.com
Very distinctive, almost a shock to the
system!

AH CAMA-SOTZ – INDUSTRIAL/RITUAL
http://users.skynet.be/ahcama-sotz
bats.cats@skynet.be

AIMLESS
www.aimless.de

AIP
http://run.to/aip
aip@run.to
Nice Italian 'Psycho Darkwave' site.

AJO – GOTH NOISE (HONG KONG)
http://artists.mp3s.com/info/152/matetsu1.html

ALEX CAN'T SLEEP
www.alexcantsleep.com
Mad band with similar site. Band photos
and Casket Girls are slow but great.

ALIEN SEX FIEND
www.asf-13thmoon.demon.co.uk/index.html
webmaster@asf-13thmoon.demon.co.uk
A total mess, and delightful. Not as many
pics as you'd expect, but variety is cool,
and they keep the news coming. The
'misc' section has good things for fans,
including the Fiend messages. Fan
photos: www.users.zetnet.co.uk/SWILL/asf.html

ALL ABOUT EVE – UNOFFICIAL
www.goony.nl/aae/aae.htm
goony@hetnet.nl
Great jumbled site from Goony and
Frank. Not huge, but dead cool. Also:
www.geocities.com/SunsetStrip/Towers/4378/
aae.html
http://village.infoweb.ne.jp/~tjiro/index2.htm
www.judgelx.co.uk
THE BOOTH TIMES
www.polyhex.co.uk/index.htm
webweaver@polyhex.co.uk
A suitable case for treatment, Colin's site
includes his own mini-newspaper, a
shrine to Eurovision and, on safer ground,
some Eves pages and info on his cats.

ALL HOPE LOST
www.angelfire.com/pa3/allhopelost

allhopelost@hotmail.com

Long bio, in which Matthew Heilman explains how he has tried to bring together Doom Metal, Goth and Ethereal, and to stick true to the worth of the music rather than any trend-related developments. 'Above all I do this for my own well-being, and if others find something within it, I am truly honoured to have achieved such an impact' which is very fair. In between crafting these love-lorn epics he's at college, writing for Starvox *and* DJ-ing! Expect a coronary soon.

ALL LIVING FEAR

www.alllivingfear.co.uk
www.mp3.com/alllivingfear
info@gothic-rock.freeserve.co.uk

Nice basic site, but full of fun things. The news is current, all historical details listed, a diary section, loads of pics. Best of all, tons of live gigs available on CD-R at three pounds each.

ALL MY FAITH LOST – ETH-FOLK

http://spazioweb.inwind.it/allmyfaithlost
aeterna@libero.it

Sweetly attractive site for Italian band, in English.

ALL THE PRETTY HORSES

www.prettyhorses.net

Unusual grafx as you enter, with a barely dressed character gyrating ever closer. This is Venus – lead vocals and guitar, a transgender performance artist who fronts this Glam-Goth creation, who can also be found, in greater detail at:
www.prettyhorses.net/2/a/a.html.
Emily, the go-go dancer is also on:
http://gossamer.
tripod.com. Which is worth it *just* for the sensational photos in her living room. You can visit DJ Luna's at www.geocities.com/moongoddessluna and find out about her band, Lunacy X, kind of Drag-Metal.

ALLUVION

www.listen.to/alluvion
alluvion@baldandsexy.com

ALQUIMIA

www.alquimia.co.uk
info@alquimia.co.uk

Interesting Mexican woman who fuses old musics with electronics, in more than merely ethereal styles or ambient flashiness.

ALTERED STATES

www.altered-states.co.uk
smashedup@altered-states.co.uk

All relevant info with plentiful supply of pics.

ALUCARDA – NEO-CLASSICAL ARCHIVE

www.rmit.usf.edu/eee/ink19/alva.htm

ALWAYS BEWARE OF THE FULL MOON

http://members.tripod.com/%7EXpossibles/index.html
tibbiexxx@aol.com

AMADEUS INFORMATION

www.fantasiaweb.com/~amadeus

Nene (listed as soprano vocal!) and Miyu look cool. It's also a record shop

or label, so you can buy mail order, and there's chat and a board.

AMADEUS

www.geocities.com/tsurara_indies/Amadeus
tsurara@capital.net

Tsurara's page for a crazed Japanese band, synth classical as well as hard, and Miyu is descendant of a famous ninja. Nice black and white gallery.

AMBER ASYLUM

www.amberasylum.com
info@ambersaylum.com

Supernatural Web it says on the front, where a gaunt women stares at you meaningfully from behind her instrument. Comparable to Rasputina,

All About Eve © Mick Mercer

but minus the guile. Excellent, informative and fascinating site.

AMBER SPYGLASS
www.amberspyglass.net
kreep@prodigy.net
Tiny, pretty site with music, lyrics, a few pics.

AMENPILL
www.amenpill.com
amenpill@amenpill.com

AMORTEUS NOCTURNE
www.amorteusnocturne.com

AMULET – DARK RUSSIAN
www.kuzbass.ru/~amulet
andrey@alan.kemerovo.su

AN APRIL MARCH
www.audiolab-rec.com/aam
Ethereal with power, on a sad site as it's a mini archive, with a forlorn farewell note. (Redhotred have come out of it all.) Old site at: www.gweep.net/~tefler/aam

ANAHADONIA – GOTH-IND
www.anahadonia.xs3.com
Profiles, pics and art.

ANAM KARA – GOTH-PUNK
www.anamkara.de

ANDALUSIA
www.andalusia.net
mail@andalusia.net
Dark and dreamy? Nice site for San Jose band with great little galleries.

ANCIENT DRIVE – GOTH METAL
www.cs.helsinki.fi/u/mxkauppi/ad
ancient_drive@hotmail.com

AND ALSO THE TREES
http://home.freeuk.net/aatt
aatt@freeuk.com
Although it may seem like they're gone, the site reveals that they have overcome their geographical differences. '… towards the end of last year, Justin, Steven and Paul got together for some experimental sessions in the damp back room of a mechanics workshop just off the M5 motorway.'(Ooh la la!) So, never say never. It's an extremely good looking site and has a complete gigography with a similar discog planned. For much of the material they advise going to 'the

American fan site', at: www.d.kth.se/~d92-upe/AATT/aatt.html and 'Switchblade Paradise' is an *excellent* fansite, with details overload, done in a bright way. No bio either, but plenty of history, and good pics.

AND HERE I LIE – ARCHIVE
www.geocities.com/SunsetStrip/Arena/1823

AND ONE
http://user.tninet.se/~lrv954a/andone
www.andone.com/html/index.html

ANDROID LUST
www.androidlust.com
Startling and vivid site for this dark electronica bunch. Audio, bio, great photos, video, and the like.

ANGELFISH
www.angelfish.de
Interesting 'Goth' past of Shirley Manson of Garbage from her days in Scotland. Info, lyrics, even pics. Other fan sites aplenty, so dig around for some great photos. Some are Garbage/Shirley sites, but mention her past.
http://clubs.yahoo.com/clubs/angelfish
http://members.tripod.com/~angelfish77
www.afn.org/~afn60203
www.geocities.com/anotherpill/angelfish/index.html
www.geocities.com/queenhelen18
www.geocities.com/SunsetStrip/Backstage/4573/angelfis.htm
www.geocities.com/SunsetStrip/Birdland/9970/index.html
www.ruiner.demon.co.uk/garbage

ANGELHOOD – NOISE
http://members.aol.com/deadmykel/angel.html
deadmykel@aol.com

ANGELIC – ITALY
www.angelic.it
info@angelic.it
Big resource but more from a community perspective.

CRISS ANGEL – UNIQUE
www.worldofillusion.com
How amazing – he's an illusionist but has an Industrial band as well. Described by one chap as 'post-modern Houdini'! Great pics.

ANGELS DECAY
www.geocities.com/SoHo/Den/8785
scaryfilth@hotmail.com

They recommend downloading their favourite font, 'otherwise, thou may think in a righteous manner and shall allow thy head to explode into a shower of tiny semi-sharp fragments of bone and bloody skin.' I chanced it, and laughed until I stopped. Purveyors of BlaspheMetal, they have a gore-coloured site with portentous delivery. They are Lord Scary Demonique, Father Dalkiel Vladislas, Baron Modius Nox, Count Argoth Sanctus, which may well prove to be aliases. If you want cheering up, check out their photos in 'Pornographic Messiah'.

ANGELS OF VENICE – ETH
www.angelsofvenice.com
Gorgeous site is down, so stick with:
http://artists.mp3s.com/artists/90/angels_of_venicecarol_tatu.html

ANGELS WITH KNIVES – IND
www.angelswknives.com

ANGELS & AGONY
www.globalxs.nl/home/m/moonland

ANGINA PECTORIS
www.the-angina-pectoris.com
Great site, in English, German or Japanese. All info present and correct, goods news updates and excellent gallery selection.

ANGIZIA
www.angizia.com
michael.haas@direkt.at
Dark Atmospherics of a classical bent, steeped in Rock drama, from Germany. Lovely, clever site.

ANGUISH – DARKWAVE SYNTH
www.geocities.com/anguishsf
anguishsf@yahoo.com

ANHEDONIA – DARKWAVE
www.anhedonia.org
chromapolaris@hotmail.com

ANIMA IN FIAMME
www.animainfiamme.com
animainfiamme@katamail.com
Inspired site from Italian historical Goth band, mixing the Italian past and an international future, with an English site. And the Etoile Noire pics are great, which is their rockier project that lets them explode.

ANIMAD VERSION
www.animadversion.org/bio/index.htm
animadversion@dogma.org

ANIMUS EX MACHINA – METAL GOTH
http://artists.mp3s.com/info/3/flaw.html

ANITA HACKSAW
http://members.aol.com/anithaxsaw/index.html
Goth electro. Ish. Nice sprawling bio
and pics.

ANOTHER TALE
www.another-tale.de
anothertale@gmx.de
Big site for German Rock-Goth band,
and lovingly detailed.

ANTHEMON
http://anthemon.free.fr
anthemon@free.fr
French Doom-Goth band with English
available.

ANTICHRISIS
www.antichrisis.de
Brilliant site, for a band big on
colourful Goth atmospherics, livelier
and more direct than a hollow Doom-
Goth tag allows. Huge bio and sporadic
bursts of madness – Autograph
section?!! Favourite whisky charts???

ANTIGONE
www.onr.com/user/locke
antigone@onr.com
Quiet site for quiet Goth. Lovely little bio.

ANTISISTERS – RUSSIAN GOTH IND
http://artists.mp3s.com/artists/136/anti
sisters.html

ANTOINETTE'S HEAD
www.geocities.com/applevenus666/AHEAD.html
applevenus@xtra.co.nz
Gothic pop from New Zealand, with
cheery minimalist info.

ANUBIS
www.world-of-anubis.de
bandanubis@gmx.de
Not the Mexican greats but some hairy
German Goths with a good site.

ANUBISZ – GOTH-DOOM
www.anubiz.de
j.erkelenz@anubiz.de
Seriously detailed site, in German,
with massive rank of live galleries, and

Apoptygma Berzerk. Photo © Stéphane Burlot

seeing the guitarist playing in a Scream
mask is very funny.

ANUNA – CELTIC ETHEREAL
www.anuna.ie
info@anuna.ie

APHELION
www.aphelion.dk
aphelion4@mindspring.com
Interesting band, tiny site.

APOCALYPSE THEATRE
www.theblacklist.com/apox
Email apoxtheatre@aol.com
How to do a site quickly, but with
panache, humour and just enough

visual difference to make the visitor
sit up and take note. Really clever,
with strong impact – and Goth with a
sense of humour is A Good Thing.

APOCALYPTICA
www.apocalyptica.com
Dark cellists. Debut sold 350,000!
Hardly Goth, but they fit.

APOCRYPHO – DARKWAVE ELECTRO
www.newbijou.com/harsh.html

APOPTYGMA BERZERK
www.apoptygma.eu.org
apb@wegotguns.com
It's official, big and clever, and

personalised too, with excellent news, an interestingly brief tour diary, but no real gallery. Random fansites:
www.apoptygma.de
www.berzerk.regio.net
horke@regio.net

APRAXIA – IND DANCE
www.xenograph.com/apraxia

ARC GOTIC
www.arcgotic.go.ro
arcgotic@go.ro
Gruftie origins for Dark Romantic band from Romania who sing in English and French. Fascinating insights, detailed history.

ARCADIUS – THE WAVE
www.acardiacus.de.vu
AndreasvonWave@addcom.de
Very dramatic photos, with falcon and sword, but while info exists, it's in list form.

ARCANA – MEDIEVAL
www.geocities.com/Paris/Rue/5130/arcana.html
arcana@algonet.se

ARCANTA
www.arcanta.com
arcanta@zworg.com
More lush medievalisms, but with a male voice.

ARGINE
www.argine.net
arginex@libero.it
Interesting Italian band claiming post-Punk influence and electronic handling, to create neo-classical atmosphere.

ARIEL – MOOD
http://listen.to/ariel

ARISE FROM THORNS
www.geocities.com/SunsetStrip/Underground/6953
siouxxxi@aol.com
Very interesting band on the softer side of Goth, but people who also have a hankering for some Doom Metal in a side project. Extremely sweet bio where they fall over with astonishment that anyone likes them.

ARKHAM ASYLUM
www.btinternet.com/~arkham.asylum
Boring. Links to label and Yahoo club.

Ataraxia by Livio Bedeschi

ARMAGEDDON PROJECT
– IND-ELEC-GOTH
www.armageddonproject.com

ART MARJU DUCHAIN
www.geocities.com/japanesechannel_s/amd.html
Only details available for mad Japanese Goth band.

ART OF DECAY & LD50 – EXP/EBM
http://users.pandora.be/aod_ld50

ARTICA
www.articaweb.it
albcas@tin.it
Quality Italian Goth.

ARTROSIS
http://artrosis.rockmetal.art.pl

DANIEL ASH
www.danielash.org
rdrees@psychobaby.com
Big, detailed coverage of solo material, plus Bauhaus, Tone On Tail, L&R. News and message board.

ASHENGRACE
http://personal.riverusers.com/~ashengrace
Ethereal Darkwave Goth they insist, and there's reasonable news, plus some extensive gallery shots.

ASHES YOU LEAVE
www.ashesyouleave.org
band@ashesyouleave.org
Doom-Goth-Metal. Excellent site, full of info, with good imagery.

ASK EMBLA – GOTH IND
http://home.no.net/askembla
askembla@c2i.net

ASP
www.schwarzer-schmetterling.de/de/flash/preindex.htm
ASP@schwarzer-schmetterling.de

ASRAI
http://listen.to/asrai
starvin@kabelfoon.nl
Pretty cool, lively Dutch Goth.

ASSEMBLAGE 23
www.synthetic.org/a23
Everything you'd expect from name and URL but I liked the counter (You are failure number...).

ASTARTE
www.escape.ca/~koshka/astarte
koshka@escape.ca
Canadian Dark Ethereal, supposedly. I couldn't get it working.

ATHAMAY
www.athamay.com
Phil@athamay.com
Back after 5 years. Pics, audio, info. Very neat.

ASTHAROTH – MEXICAN BLACK METAL GOTH
www.geocities.com/SunsetStrip/Arena/3614/astharoth_hpE.htm
lord_astharoth@hotmail.com
They look like Kiss after a rough night down the pub.

Ataraxia by Livio Bedeschi

JAY ASTON
www.jayaston.com
Lovely little site with his personal gig diaries, plus a little history, some nice images, news, merchandise and Radio Jezebel.

ASTRAL GREY
www.astralgrey.com
astralgrey@astralgrey.com
Small and unintentionally dingy site for Goth-Ethereal boys.

ASTRO VAMPS – ARCHIVE
www.geocities.com/sunsetstrip/lounge/5356

ATARAXIA
www.ataraxia.net
pando@misterweb.it
Look, it's the best band in the world again! They're so cool, and although this site doesn't live up to high visual standards you might expect, there is a ton of info, plenty of regular news updates in excellent newsletters, and gig details, a battery of archive reviews and interviews, and some of the loveliest photos you'll see anywhere. 'Reflections' is also a lovely touch, where they analyse

their main influences. Also, info:
www.fluxeuropa.com/ataraxia.htm

ATRISMIGHT
http://listen.to/artismight
Jan-Helge.Bergesen@go.enitel.no
Norwegian Goth-Electro band with a sense of atmosphere but also venomous attack. Small site, pleasantly filled. Tiny gallery – but they look great.

ATROCITY
www.atrocity.de/indexeng1.htm
webmaster@atrocity.de
A sporty little site by German Metal Goths. Nicely illustrated.

ATTRITION
www.attrition.co.uk
info@attrition.co.uk
Can't ever keep a good man down and Martin Bowes is no exception. This Dark pioneer has a weighty site, in terms of detail. Doesn't seem too keen to share personal, inspirational details, or have a good gallery but that's no problem.

AUDIO PARADOX
www.audioparadox.com/index.html

AUDIO VIRUS
http://artists.mp3s.com/info/216/audiovirus.html

AUDRA
http://audramusic.com
audra@audramusic.com
Moody Goth with a poppy sensibility, and little suffocating gloom. Good site, great gallery, plenty of news. Also:
http://clubs.yahoo.com/clubs/audrastwofrailhands

AUDRA & THE ANTIDOTE
www.theantidote.net
audra@theantidote.net
Compared to a cross between early Blondie and the Rocky Horror Picture Show, or 'campy lounge', which has to be interesting. Cutely dizzy site.

AUDRA REALM – OLD FANPAGE
www.geocities.com/audrarealm

AURORA – FAN PAGE
www.aurora.dti.ne.jp/~satokasa

AUTO MOD
www.auto-mod.com
webmaster@auto-mod.com
The biggest long-running name of

Atrismight

The Awakening

Japan-ese Goth history even though they're hardly Goth now. Huge site offering everything imaginable to fans, with mega-links to previous members' new activities.

AUTUMN TEARS
www.darksymphonies.com/autumntears
Only a label site, but Autumn Tears are Goth Rock and awesome with it.

AUTUMN
www.autumn-us.com
autumn@autumn-us.com
If someone ever tried an archive site they'd have fun. Seven vocalists!!! Lovely little site with cute news, info, and galleries.

THE AUTUMNS
www.theautumns.com
Very attractive and interesting fan site with good news and galleries, which neglects really to tell us anything about them.
www.deveratwins.20m.com/autumns

AUTUMNAL BLOOD MOON
http://artists.mp3s.com/artists/199/roy_adams.html
darkvalleyrecords@yahoo.com

AVARITIA
www.avaritia.net
info@avaritia.net
Excellent new site from interesting

Goth band with a Passion Play link, having good bios, photos and news.

AVOTOR – Dark Elec
www.lucidworks.co.nz/avotor
avotor@hotmail.com

AVRIGUS
www.avrigus.com
simon@avrigus.com
This is a very attractive site but each section loads separately and it's a bit pathetic when you have to wait to get the e-mail address, and then have to return to the homepage. Links broken all over the place. Nice pics, all six of them.

THE AWAKENING
www.awakening.co.za
ash@awakening.co.za
Good site from South Africa's most influential Goth band.

THE AZOIC – Dark Elec
www.nilaihah.com

AZRAEL – Goth Elec
http://artists.mp3s.com/info/144/azrael1.html

BABYDOLL JOHNSON – Elec
www.babydolljohnson.com

BABYLON HOR – Goth Elec archive
http://members.aol.com/Palechylde/hor.html

BABYLONIAN TILES
www.babylonian-tiles.com
hipdeathgoddess@webtv.net
Lovely, personable site. All the detail and news, nice galleries. Plus:
www.geocities.com/SunsetStrip/Club/6510

BACKWORLD – Maudlin
www.backworld.com
backworld@aol.com

BAD SECTOR – Dark Ambient
www.bad-sector.com

JULIE BAKER – Folky
www.juliebaker.com

BAMBOO CRISIS – Ind Darkwave
www.tonezone.com

BAPTIST DEATH RAY
www.baptistdeathray.com
bdr@baptistdeathray.com
A wild man who claims he's somewhere between Big Black, Pixies and NIN, with a strange site. Hear his rants, read his thoughts, and yes, he has his own take on Christianity.

BARE WIRE
www.eristikos.com/barewire.html
info@eristikos.com
Lots of details scattered about give a full picture, but no current info and hardly any visual distraction.

BAREFOOT CONTESSA – MOODY
http://members.madasafish.com/~indie500/bchome.htm

BASQUE
www.basquemusic.com
basque@basquemusic.com
Future classical from Ethereal duo. Informative site.

BATALION D'AMOUR – GOTH METAL
http://robert.wsi.edu.pl/damour
damour@rockmetal.art.pl

BATTERY DOMAIN
www.batteryinflux.com
Archive details, then links to all new projects, of which there are many interesting ones.

BAUHAUS
www.bauhausmusik.com
I always assumed that because they were one of the few great bands that split up way before their time, that with their solo work not exactly taking off, although clearly at an acceptable level for them, a Bauhaus reformation would enable them to exploit the slipstream caused by the Manson boy, propel them to million-aire status, and would then be an occasional biennial thing, leaving them with constant publicity, and sufficient funding for any solo endeavours they desired, as well as getting the respect they deserve. Instead they saw it as a holiday, but then they always were a bit complicated. A tremendous site, but lacking many pics, and the bio details are skimpy. Great letter from Fiction Records in the 'Exclusives' section. Fan sites:
www.ne.jp/asahi/jaywalk/love/index.htm
jaywalk@mcn.ne.jp
Japanese fan's Bauhaus site, with all the spin-off bands – even Dali's Car. All pics, a cute experience.
http://nav.webring.yahoo.com/hub?ring=bau&list
www.bauhaus.8m.com
www.cs.cmu.edu/~visigoth/music/bauhaus/index.html
www.geocities.com/Area51/Crater/6703
www.thegauntlet.com/bauhaus.html
www.waste.org/bauhaus

BAY LAUREL
http://fly.to/baylaurel
thelaurel@hotmail.com
Darkly adventurous site for Swedish Gothsters.

BEAUTY OF ASHES
www.beautyforashes.com
info@beautyforashes.com
A very attractive little site for a band who admit Cure influences.

BEAUTY KILLFEST – IND METAL
www.killfest.com

BEBORN BETON
www.bebornbeton.de
Massive, and highly informative.

BEGETS OF AUTUMN
http://members.tripod.com/~begetsofautumn/index.html

BEHIND THE SCENES – GOTH ELEC
www.behindthescenes.de
fred@behindthescenes.de

BEL CANTO
www.foreverland.de.
danny@ozone.de

BELISHA – GOTH
www.belisha.com
Fresh as a daisy UK stuff, but also just as weeny. Basic pics, no biog details, e-mail contact ensuite.

BELLA MORTE
www.bellamorte.com
bellamorte@bellamorte.com
Small site that makes you sit up, all alert and tingly. Totally wonderful Goth site, with cool pics. Read the stirring bios and just rave about the band. Not forgetting: http://clubs.yahoo.com/clubs/fansofbellamorte Posher version at www.bellamorte.net with the usual info, but they also add tour journal entries as they move around the country!

BELLATOR
www.bellator.org/index3.html

BELTANE
http://users.senet.com.au/~beltane
Friendly site for a band who place themselves somewhere between New Order and Love & Rockets. Nice info and strange gallery in which a lusty wench dances with fan held high.

BENEDICTION – GOTH
http://artists.mp3s.com/info/196/benediction.html

BENIGHTED – METAL GOTH
http://inspirationweb.tripod.com/benighted.html

BESEECH – GOTH METAL
www.beseech.net
info@beseech.net
Excellent site from Swedish band.

BETHANY CURVE
www.bethanycurve.com
sounds@bethanycurve.com
Dark shakers have trim site.

Benighted

BETROTH – Goth-Ind
http://members.tripod.com/~Betroth78/betroth
cclas@hotmail.com

BETTY'S TRASH
http://members.aol.com/trshwhore
btrash@hotmail.com
Piss Mafia? What's going on? Noisy
buggers, like a big riot grrrl's blouse.
And check '1st Stalkers', their illustrated
fan section.

BETTY X – Retrobilly
www.bettyx.com

BEYOND DAWN
www.uio.no/~thjortel/Bands/Beyond
beyondawn@sol.no
Odd site from Norwegian Darkwave
lads. Info-heavy and fairly morose, but
read press on Rock project (Inferno)
and they sound mental.

BEYOND SALEM
www.corpusnet.com/beyondsalem/
index2.html
salem@corpusnet.com.
Unusual Goth-metal from Canada, and
a good all-round site.

BEYOND THE WALL OF SLEEP
www.beyondthewallofsleep.de/index.html
jgartrock@yahoo.com
Not much here from the cool Goth band.

BISEXION 69 – unofficial
http://users.rcn.com/velvet.interport//69.html

BITTER FALL
www.bitterfall.com
bernard@pssnet.com
Dark Rock, with a bitter twist. Cool site
with news done personally, ace photos,
and fair bio.

BITTER GRACE
http://members.aol.com/BittrGrace
Kingmissile@bittergrace.com
Camera-shy Goths, who'd have thought
it! Emotionally raw boys, with a nicely
informative site, although they seem to
have slowed down of late.

**THE VOLUPTUOUS HORROR OF
KAREN BLACK**
www.karenblack.com
A total oddity with no real attempt to
explain the b-movie madness and
Horror Rock theatrics. Kembra's off to

start something new, so just enjoy a few
pics and wonder.

NICOLE BLACKMAN
www.nicole-blackman.com/bloodwork.htm
BlackmanPR@aol.com
Brilliantly absorbing site on performance
... whisper it... poet. As she loves words
there's tons of them, and some nice pics.

BLACK ATMOSPHERE
http://artists.mp3s.com/info/18/black_
atmosphere.html
No sign of official site's resurrection
at www.blackatmosphere.com, although you
can find links from there.

Blind Before Dawn

BLACK HEAVEN
– Elec-Goth-Darkwave
www.black-heaven-project.de
lucipher@black-heaven-project.de

BLACK JADE
www.black-jade.com/index.html
blackjade@bluemail.ch
Rocky with their make-up and Satanic
majesty.

BLACK OCEAN DROWNING
www.blackoceandrowning.com
info@blackoceandrowning.com

BLACK TAPE FOR A BLUE GIRL
www.projekt.com/bands/btfabg.html

blacktape@projekt.com
Friendly, informative site. Beautiful
galleries. Fan Club promo:
www.beki.com/wms/wms.html
beki@gate.net

BLACK WATER
http://blackwater.lawrence.ks.us
theblackwater@sunflower.com

BLACKFIRE
www.blackfire.demon.co.uk
webmaster@blackfire.demon.co.
Punky Metal Goth band from Bristol.

BLAKE CHEN
www.thehungryghost.com/www.blakechen.com
Was some Haunted Troubadour chap
for a while but now his modern mood
music goes under the Hungry Ghost,
but this may be a change per album, so
let's stick with his real name.
Informative site, if cryptic.

BLAM HONEY – Ind
http://netpassport-wc.netpassport.or.jp/
~wmatsuz7/index.html
Japanese Industrial.

ELLA BLAME
www.ella-blame.com
ella@ella-blame.com
Intriguing woman who has many
admirers. Good bristling site with
excellent galleries, because she has
some scary paintings on display. Looks
a right nutter actually, but when
comparisons include Kate Bush and
Nina Hagen that's hardly a shock.

BLEEDING GLITTER
http://rois.org/glitter/index.html

BLEEDING LIKE MINE
www.geocities.com/SunsetStrip/Alley/2044
hollyemmer@geocities.com
Wispy, melancholic ambient. Nice band,
dreary site.

THE BLESSED VIRGIN LARRY
www.audiogalaxy.com/bands/bvl
Messy pastiche freaks with raw power
behind them. Looks like fun. Banned
from mp3? They must have something.

BLIND BEFORE DAWN – Dark Elec
http://artists.mp3s.com/info/189/blind_before_
dawn.html
chunkygoth@yahoo.com

BLIND PASSENGERS
www.blindpassengers.com
alex@blindpassengers.de

BLIXA BARGELD
www.blixa-bargeld.com

BLOODWIRE – ELEC
www.bloodwire.com

BLOOD FOR VANITY
www.angelfire.com/co2/bloodforvanity44
bloodforvanity44@mytalk.comom

BLOOD LUST – GOTH/IND
http://members.aol.com/analog187/main.html
analog187@aol.com

BLOOD OF ROSES
– DARK KATE BUSH??
www.esunit16.com/bloodofr.htm

BLOOD RIVER – SOUTH AFRICAN GOTH
http://artists.mp3s.com/info/38/blood_river.html

BLOODY DEAD AND SEXY
– DEATHROCK
www.bloodydeadandsexy.de
band@bloodydeadandsexy.de
Colourful, mad site for noisy creatures.
English available.

BLOODY GORE
http://members.tripod.com/bloodygore
bldygore@hotmail.com
Indonesian Grindcore! Nearest I could
find. They actually refer to their sound
as 'UltraPiggyGrindsyBruitalDeath',
which means Nice Boys Who Still Tell
Their Mum They're In The Choir. A
Brazilian zine reviews them thus;
'Bloody Gore defecates in our ears 6
putrid sounds of the most insane,
nauseating and grotesque Brutal Death
Gore Grind, with extreme tendencies.
Bloody Gore vomits blood coagulated
with a very guttural vocal.' My question
is, why would anyone want to?

BLUE AND HOLDING – GOTH TRIP-HOP
www.tonecasualties.com/blueandholding.html

BLUE DAHLIA
www.blue-dahlia.com
bluedahlia@earthlink.net
As organised and composed as you'd
expect, with a superb bio, but dull
gallery. It is a good guide, and you come
away contented.

BOOLE – ELEC-IND
www.boole.org
brad@boole.org
I like this site a lot. They confess to be
immensely lazy, and then when you
check they never seem to be doing
anything other than playing gigs with lots
of cool bands? Maybe there is an answer,
because you have to visit this site if only
to crack open the galleries and pick the
first, top left. Elvis has entered the building. He's not looking like his old self.

BORGIA POPES
www.popes.com
Mad archive which zips around.

BORGESSA
webmaster@midi.com.hk
Singer from New Orleans who seems
really interesting but no site as yet. You
can find music through e-Bay usually.

THE BORIS – IND DANCE
http://members.aol.com/borisxi/Boris.html
They were The Boris Yeltsin Love XI,
but with two members leaving felt it
only decent to change. Not, you will be
astonished to learn, the most serious
band around. One EP was called
'Dracula's Teabags'.

BOZO PORNO CIRCUS – GOTH IND
www.tonezone.com

BRAINS FACTORY – JAPAN
http://plaza16.mbn.or.jp/~BRAINS_FACTORY

BRAND NEW IDOL
www.brandnewidol.com
contact@brandnewidol.com

THE BREATH OF LIFE
http://server00.gate71.be/the-breath-of-life/index.htm
breath.of.life@gate71.be
Absolutely magnificent site. I couldn't
locate the gallery but had an interesting
time trying. Superb band, superb info.

BREATHE
www.the-laughing-dolls.com
breathe@the-laughing-dolls.com
New band from Alex (Placebo Effect),
still in a far from humdrum Electro
form. Attractive site, scary photos.

BREATHFORM – SYNTHY DARKWAVE IND
http://artists.mp3s.com/artists/126/
breathform_dreamstation.html

BREATHING UNDERWATER
www.4.wave.co.nz/~west
breathingunderwater@wave.co.nz
Interesting site from New Zealand
Post-Punk/Goth solo project.

BREATHLESS
www.breathless-uk.com
jacobfleet@aol.com
This is interesting. Breathless are sort of
Goth Lite, or Darkwave Pop, having
started as bruised Indie. The bio is interesting, and charming, especially about
their first few rehearsals. Also, fan-wise:
http://members.tripod.com/~chipwich/breath
http://freespace.virgin.net/tracy.southern

BREECHDOLL – ARCHIVE
www.angelfire.com/va/phishingruven

BRICHENO BOYS
http://members.tripod.com/~Elyzium_
Succubus/index.html
Weird but sensible idea, I guess.
Keeping track of Tim and Toby with the
whole post-Sisters/XC-NN thing as Tim
headed off into Tin Star and after Toby
and Maria shelved Sunshot and did
Venus Inc. Recent reports say Toby isn't
all about composing advertising music,
at which he's successful, and there are
future plans. Tin Star are also back in
action after a lethargic spell.

**THE INFERNAL RACKET OF THE
BRIMSTONES**
www.brimstones.com
baron@brimstones.com
Eternal Surf 'n Garage Damnation

THE BRINGERS – CELTIC ACOUSTIC
www.thebringers.com

BROKE BOX – Ind Exp.
www.brokebox.com
brokebox@brokebox.com

BROKEN TOYS
www.brokentoys.net
email@brokentoys.net
Let's just say they very unusual and
worth checking out, shall we?

BROKEN HALOS – GOTH-IND
www.brokenhalos.org

BRONX CASKET CO.
www.bronxcasketco.com
Reviews suggest Metal-Goth, with

Breath of Life. Photo © Stéphane Burlot

comparisons to a doomier Type O Neg, and photos suggest you give them a very wide berth indeed.

BROTHERHOOD OF PAGANS

– ARCHIVE
www.ifrance.com/darkland/bopf.htm

BUCKETHEAD

www.bucketheadland.com/index.html
hostbot@bucketheadland.com
This is quite unlike any other site in the book. Album promised, entitled, 'Somewhere Over The Slaughterhouse'. Completely mad, inspired site based on a theme park falling apart, and sometimes uncompromising. 'In the interest of spontaneity, there is no schedule for our live performances. But if you see Buckethead setting up corpses in the rafters, you can bet there's going to be some music.' There's even a good Error 404 joke to enjoy. So take the full tour. It's a delight.

BUCK-TICK

www.buck-tick.com
Japanese band influenced by original Goth but wholly individual themselves.

BUCRANION

www.bucranion.de
post@bucranion.de

NICHOLAS BURDOHAN – AMBIENT

http://artists.mp3s.com/info/212/nicholas_burdohan.html

BURN CIRCUIT – IND-METAL

www.burncircuit.com

BURNING GATES

www.burning-gates.com
daniele@burning-gates.com
Classy Italian Goth with English available. Okay bio, some news, reviews and galleries.

BURNING ROME – ELEC

www.burningrome.com
mark@burningrome.com

DAVE-ID BUSARUS

– (EX VIRGIN PRUNES)
www.dave-id.com
Info at: www.iol.ie/~murraycp/dave-id.html

BUTTERFLY MESSIAH

www.butterflymessiah.com
hazelfaery@aol.com

Opinionated dark electronic duo with a mission, and some fascination with faeries. A fantastic little site (as in not huge), because it's a slightly different worldview. You can join the Faerie Movement and you'll also have to go a long way before seeing worse live photos than they possess. Interesting hive of industry in terms of fan art from their blessed bees. Strangely one of their 'faerie' links was evidently only too delighted to offer me the chance to watch 'hours and hours of pussy pounding Asian hardcore'. Perhaps best to try their recommended fan site instead:
www.schwarzeseiten.de/kdm/archiv/butterfly_m

CABARET VOLTAIRE

www.brainwashed.com/cv
thodson@uswest.net.

THE CADAVERS – ARCHIVE

http://members.tripod.com/~THECADAVERS

CADRA ASH

www.geocities.com/cadra-ash
cadra-ash@geocities.com
English available for interesting pure Goth band. Nice pics, little bio.

CALAVERA – DEATHABILLY

www.geocities.com/algarnett
They are there, as are many others. Cool site.

CALL ME ALICE

www.callmealice.com
callmealice@callmealice.com
You have to see this, one of the best sites imaginable. Hard Goth electronics, with a story to make your head spin.

CAMERATA MEDIOLANENSE

www.fluxeuropa.com/cameratamediolanense.htm

CANAAN

www.eibonrecords.com/Canaan.htm
One record is called 'Walk Into My Open Womb'. Thanks for that. Experimental Italian dark moodsters.

CANDY MACHINE

www.geocities.com/candymachine88
candymachine88@yahoo.com
George Earth (Switchblade Symphony) has been a very busy boy, as all the details of new material splashed on the garish front page shows.

CANDY PUSH – ELEC

www.pleasurepalace.de/cp/english/ecpstart.htm
cp@pleasure-palace.de

CANNIBAL BUFFET – IND-DANCE

www.geocities.com/sunsetstrip/stage/1006
cspotrun@xmission.com

CAPITAL

www.capital.faithweb.com
Mystic Goth from Chile. Nice pics, biog in English.

CAPRICE

www.kulichki.com/pmusic/caprice
caprice@rambler.ru
Bookish Russian band who write on faerie matters.

CARBON 12

www.carbon12.net
mail@carbon12.net

CARFAX ABBEY

www.carfaxabbey.com
cfxjohn@bellatlantic.net
Ind-Goth with rubbish site. Low on info. Try fansites instead:
http://troublebb.tripod.com/index.html
vampiregrl@hotmail.com
http://www.candelabra.org/julian
jules@candelabra.org

CARPATHIAN DREAM

http://members.aol.com/levetian
Young German Rocky Goth. Looks busy, nice photos.

CARPE DIEM – ELECWAVE

www.carpe-diem.ch
info@carpe-diem.ch

CARTARIAN DERIVATION

http://home.t-online.de/home/Christian.Meyer/cartan.htm
Christian.Meyer@t-online.de
Attempt to fuse technical Hardcore with Goth.

CASCADE – GOTH-METAL

www.cascade-music.de
This is an impressive German-only site, but with news and info crammed in among some superb photos, covering all aspects of their existence.

THE CASCADES

www.thecascades.de
www.nine66.com

Chandeen

info@thecascades.de
Cool site from interesting Goth band.

CASSIOPEIA
www.cassiopeianet.de
info@cassiopeianet.de
Very atmospheric site, with interesting
live pics of this German Goth band, but
there's no biog that I could find. Gigs
news is there, so maybe they're new?

CASUAL
www.casual-barcelona.com
Goth Rock in an eighties manner. Dark
post-Punk band Rozz fans. Site in
Spanish and Catalan, plus English.
Nice gloomy pics.

CAT FUD
www.blumix.net/estromissioni/cat-fud/main.html
Cat Fud are/were a great band. There's
a picture of them here but everything's
in Italian, so I'm stumped.

CATASTROPHE BALLET
www.angelfire.com/ca4/catastrophe/ballet.html
Eric@Public-Propaganda.de
Nice site from cool German Goth band.
Big on detail/news and great pics.

CATHEDRAL COVEN – GLOOM
www.geocities.com/~witchblaster
witchblaster@cathedralcoven.com

CAUDA PAVONIS
www.caudapavonis.com
initiates@caudapavonis.com
Dark duo from UK with bright future.

Copious info on nice site, despite no
gallery and an old-fashioned look.

CAUSTIC SOUL – IND-GOTH
www.causticsoul.com
mike@causticsoul.com

NICK CAVE
www.nick-cave.com
Never really been into Ol' Blue Lungs,
but this is an awesome site. You really
couldn't ask for anything more. Also
good fansite at:
http://home.iae.nl/users/maes/cave/index.html
maes@iae.nl

CDSOPA – GOTH-ELECTRO
www.cdsopa.sk

CELESTE NOIR
www.celeste-noir.de
info@celeste-noir.de 4

CELL DIVIDE
www.celldivide.com

CELL DIVISION
www.celldivision.ch
info@celldivision.ch
Nice bouncy site from Swiss Goths.
Cool pics, straight info.

CELLDWELLER
http://celldweller.com
cellmates@celldweller.com

CEMETERY HILL
www.geocities.com/cemetery_hill

Cemetery_Hill@vampirefreaks.com
Very young kids, studs and camouflage.
It's no good people sneering either. I
don't put bands like this down because
you don't know what they'll do, how
they'll develop. Manson may have
influenced a lot of bands to start and
they'll grow out of that bumptious
appreciation as they grow up. Slagging
bands spawned in Manson's slipstream
is as mindless as all that early nineties
babygoth-baiting, and usually done by
people scared that they may be toppled
from their perches. In which case they
deserve to see the people below arming
themselves with catapults. Culling the
fatuous is no bad thing.

CENTRE OF PESTILENCE
www.angelfire.com/indie/choronzon333
P Emerson Williams is involved, which
is cool but the site is banging on about
occult matters, and do I need a banner
ad for Anna Kournikova? I think not.

CEOXIME – DARK-ELEC
www.ceoxime.com
headaque@yahoo.com

CERVIX COUCH – DIGITAL HORROR
www.cervixcouch.cjb.net

CHAINSAWS.AND.CHILDREN.INC
www.chainsawsandchildren.com
kiddicon@chainsawsandchildren.com
Electro Metal. Site will have you
squinting it's so squashed.

CHALICE – PAGAN METAL
www.chalice.cjb.net

THE CHAMELEONS
www.thechameleons.com
Outrageously good site with all the news
as it happens (quite frequently these
days), plus an awesome archive. Fan page:
www.geocities.com/SunsetStrip/Underground/3255

CHANDEEN
www.chandeen.com
info@chandeen.com
Brilliant site for immaculate band,
between state-of-the-art Ethereal and
Portishead. Awesome gallery.

THE CHANGELINGS
www.mindspring.com/~regeana/changelings
nick_pagan@hotmail.com
Classical-ambient beauty, from a band

whose violin/viola player has the greatest surname imaginable, this is a charming site but very low on detail. Very nice pics.

CHANNEL.5
www2u.biglobe.ne.jp/~psa
Involves Nabe of Definition Master.

CHAOS ENGINE
www.chaosengine.com
http://freespace.virgin.net/goth.abilly/frontdoor.htm
It's a big site but not all sections are totally updated. (The discography is years out.) The history is very good, the bios will give you eyestrain and the galleries are truly fantastic. There is also 'Chaos branded graphics for you to beautify your world.' Ophthalmologist guidance advisory.

CHAOTICA – TECHNO-SYNTH-IND
www.chaoticamusic.com

CHAPEL BLAQUE – DARK AMBIENT
www.geocities.com/SunsetStrip/Stage/8713
fathershadow@hotmail.com

CHAPTER – GOTH-IND
http://switch.to/negative
New Zealanders, based in Tokyo.

CHARLOTTE HEAD
http://republika.pl/charlottehead
charh@poczta.wp.pl

CHARLOTTESVILLE
http://streetlightfarm.com/charlottesville/index.html
miles@streetlightfarm.com
Mellow duo with odd site. Cute pics, mini-bio/discog, wonderfully strange personal elements.

BLAKE CHEN
http://blakechen.com
Blakechen@aol.com
'The Haunted Troubadour', he calls himself, which suggests he is personally haunted by a ghost inside him, which doesn't make *any* sense whatsoever, but the reviews he has to share certainly make him seem fairly unusual and striking. Free CD is *very* cool.

CHERCHE LUNE – ARCHIVE
www.multimania.com/prikos/inde.shtml

CHERRY DEBAUCHERY
www.geocities.com/cherry_debauchery/depravity.html

cherry_debauchery@yahoo.com
Sleazy wotsits.

CHIASM – ELEC
www.chiasm.org
chiasm@chiasm.org
Good bio of Emileigh Rohn, nice personal touches, excellent photos in 'Shows'.

CHICKS ON SPEED – SHOP ONLY
www.chicksonspeed.com/tv.html

CHILDER – BRECHT/DOORS
http://childer.virtualave.net

CHILDREN WITHIN – ARCHIVE
www.childrenwithin.com
info@childrenwithin.com

CHIRON
www.gothic.ru/chiron
www.chiron.asn.au/default.asp
mrwasp@alphalink.com.au
Clean Darkwave site, in dire update crisis.

CHOCOLATE GRINDER
www.chocolategrinder.com
info@chocolategrinder.com
Very neat and clean site, introducing you to multi-faceted sounds in a Darkwave form. Gigography, archive bits, details on each CD, small gallery – very nicely posed, but motley live collection.

CHORD OF SOULS
www.chordofsouls.de
axel@chordofsouls.de

CHRISTABELLA AND THE GHOST
www.geocities.com/catg_za
catg@musician.org
One man Electro-Goth Ind project. Very new, so little content.

CHRISTBLOOD
http://christblood.cjb.net
head58m@pnet.pl

CHRISTIAN DEATH
www.christiandeath.com/news/index.shtml
Was 'temporarily' shut last I saw. Again I say... why do people *still* have to continue the Rozz (R.I.P.)/Valor debate? Rozz left – the reasons don't matter – and did his own thing, while Valor carried on, made great records, hit a fallow period after 'All The Love' but has now been back to his best for a few years. There's some good fan live pics,

plenty of music detail. What this site needs, apart from a personal tour diary from Valor – which would be superb – is a complete discography. Then again he'd probably need his own server for that! When Christian Death eventually stops the body of work left will be phenomenal. Unofficial:
www.nmia.com/~thanatos/music/xtiandeath.html

CHRYSALIDE DE L'ANGE – ARTICLE
http://membres.tripod.fr/Night04/Articles.html

CIBO MATTO
www.cibomatto.com
Okay for info, but nowt else. Fantastic fan site at:
www.damoon.net/CIBO.htm

CINDY TALK
http://chat.carleton.ca/%7Enmedema/cindytalk
They're not dead you know. All the news is here, plus semi-archive stuff and some disappointing photos – where's the live stuff?

CINEMA STRANGE
www.cinemastrange.com/cs/index.shtml
www.cinemastrange.com/nephrael/frame.html
nephrael@cinemastrange.com
Is it official? It's German-based by the look of it, with no news, but a strange live details section. Cool site regardless, with bio, galleries, online movies promised, message board. Divine Fan page was temporarily down, as part of a network, at:
www.freakyplanet.com/FreakyPages/cinema_strange/index.htm
allein@freakyplanet.com
http://reficul.cinemastrange.com
evilies@hotmail.com

CIRCLE OF DUST – IND ARCHIVE
www.dusted.com/index2.html

CIRCUM
www.geocities.com/angel_of_syn_66/Index.html
I imagine this Goth duo's site is ancient, by the look of it, but it's also cute. Makes a refreshing change from overt organisation elsewhere, and it does become like a dual personal site.

CLAIR OBSCUR
www.clairobscur.net
Superb archive.

CLAIRE VOYANT
www.clairevoyant.com

Clan of Xymox. Photo © Stéphane Burlot

cgibbens@luna-productions.com
Post-ethereal splendour. Nice little site, decent discog and reviews, okay bio, brilliant gallery.

CLAN OF XYMOX
www.clanofxymox.com
xymox@clanofxymox.com
A magnificent site which shows the band clearly understand what fans want as everything is here from past to present in superb detail. The galleries are particularly impressive with comments from those in attendance, and even greater fan contributions in the Tour reviews. If only more bands took this much care with their sites. Also: http://music.object-a.com/clan_xymox/websites.shtml
www.clanofxymox.net

CLAYMORE – CELTIC ROCK
http://members.aol.com/clayceltic/index.html
claymore@t-online.de

CLOPHILL – DARK/COLD
Site offline.
clophill@archangel.zzn.com

CLOSTERKELLER
www.closterkeller.mtl.pl
Great Polish Goth band gets excellent fan site, with bio (in good English), lyrics, news, and galleries, as well as links to other Polish pages. Try:
www.netcolony.com/members/closter/index.html

COBER
www.cober.org
cobersvb@prodigy.net
A female Radiohead? Cool, but a bit muso.

COCTEAUS
www.cocteautwins.com
Weirdly, when I accessed this I sometimes got a decent archive site, but also got a Cocteaus Yahoo! webring, listing:
http://personal.computrain.nl/eric/cocteaus
www.angelfire.com/ct2/CocteauTwins/rings.html
www.si4rockford.com/webivo

THE COFFINSHAKERS – SWEDISH NECROCK'N'ROLL
www.coffinshakers.com

COLD MOURNING – DOOM
www.coldmourning.com
Bruce@coldmourning.com

COLLABORATEUR SANCTUM – ARCHIVE
www.anet-stl.com/music/Collaborateur

COLLAPSE INTO REASON
www.collapseintoreason.com

COLLECTION D'ARNELL-ANDREA
http://rene.chalon.free.fr/caa
rene.chalon@free.fr
Your chance to find out why this band sends people weak at the knees. Basic info site, few pics.

COLLIDE – GOTH ELEC
www.collide.net
kaRIN@collide.net
A gorgeously full, detailed site with everything you need on this cool duo. Current news, mini-archive, fab gallery.

COLOR OF YOU – DARK DIGITAL
http://geocities.com/colorofyou

CONCUBINE – GOTH-IND
http://artists.mp3s.com/info/82/concubine.html

CONFESSION OF FAITH – ELEC
www.confessionoffaith.com

CONTAGION
www.pcbproductions.com/contagion/index.html
contagion@pcbproductions.com
Seriously flash, cool site, although the galleries are rubbish, but then some Industrial bands are probably best left obscured by lights.

CONTINGENCE – DARK IND
www.contingenceonline.com

COPH NIA – RITUALISTIC
www.cophnia.com

CORPUS DELICTI
www.corpusdelicti.com
This site is a wonderful archive for one of the greatest.

CORROSION
www.corrosionuk.com
www.mp3.com/corrosionuk
info@corrosionuk.com
Ordinary little site from the ex ALF Matthew, but that's understandable. At least they've tried, with some studio photos – but good God, the mixing desk and a dancing flower?

CORROSION
www.immaculatecorrosion.com
http://artists.mp3s.com/info/217/corrosion.html
info@immaculatecorrosion.com
Another lot? Temp site for American Electronica. Let lawyers commence!

CORVIS CORAX – HISTORICAL
www.corvuscorax.de

COSMIC SLUT
www.cosmicslut.com
sluts@cosmicslut.com

COURT OF THE ANGELS – DARK METAL
www.interlock.freeserve.co.uk

COVENANT
www.covenant.dk
info@covenant.dk
Great band, cool looking but sluggish site. The unofficial site has excellent bios, detail and galleries, plus good general links, at:
http://plastiq-flowers.de

CRADLE OF FILTH
www.theorderofthedragon.com/docs/index.html
webmaster@theorderofthedragon.net
You've got to be a bit weird not at least to *recognise* their brilliance even if you hate this kind of music, and Dani *is* hilarious and cool. The bio is interesting, galleries are superb, and the tour diary has their own photos. Big site, long sessions. There are a ton of unofficial ones, but the one I liked best was at:
www.cradleoffilth.de

CRADLE OF SPOIL
www.cosp.de/Cradle-of-Spoil

CRANES – FAN FORUM
www.cranes-fan.com
Cranes Mailing List:
www.xmission.com/~marysmth/inthenight

CRASH WORSHIP
www.charnel.com/charnel/bands/crashworship

CREASSAULT – IND
http://creassault.tripod.com
creassault@usa.net

CREATURES
www.thecreatures.com
Seriously cool site, which will entertain. The ones below are all pretty good, as well.
www.murkaster.demon.co.uk/noctuarymain.htm

Curse

http://exterminating-angel.itgo.com
www.geocities.com/SunsetStrip/Vine/4979/
creatures.html
Siouxsie & Creatures – Fan sites:
http://digilander.iol.it/cascade/index.html
www.mital-u.ch/Siouxsie
www.geocities.com/~emily777/SiouxsieLinks.html
www.geocities.com/SunsetStrip/1233
www.untiedundone.com

CREEPING MYRTLE – DARK MOOD
www.doldrum.com/myrtle.htm

CREMATORY
www.crematory.de
info@crematory.de
Please, Papa, may we call our band Crematory? Why, of course you must son, I think that's a splendid idea. (What is it with some bands? Crematory?!!) Gothic Metal, which claims to have an English version, but that must be humour, for which the Germans are justly famous. The site is pretty nice, in a sort of Warhammer way, with fantastic photos, excellent news, and best lyrics section I have seen any band do. And check out the merchandising, not just for a complete CD range, but the firm handling this also does other material too. Unofficial:
http://home.online.no/~rvelle/buried/
crematory/main.htm

CRESCENS COLLECTIVE – DARK IND
http://sanctum.coldmeat.se

CRIMSON JOY – ARCHIVE INFO
www.dol-amroth.de/gothic/music_crimson.htm

CRIMSON SKY FALLING – GOTH-IND
http://members.aol.com/cassiusfc/main.html
CassiusFC@aol.com

CROSSFATE
www.xs4all.nl/~forbliss/crossfate
crossfate@xs4all.nl
Pretty, brisk site for the post-Xymox boys.

CROWHEAD
www.angelfire.com/nb/crowhead
crowhead@c2i.net
'On 5th of July 99, Jol and Rym talked about their musical career, and both realized they would really like to write more depressing stuff.' I get like that sometimes.

CROWN OF JESUS – DARK EBM
www.noisemail.com/crown.htm

CRUCIFORM
www.subnation.com/cform.html
cruciform@subnation.com
Still a lush, ongoing project but this hasn't been updated to include the new album, which makes it pure archive material.

CRUCIFIX NOCTURNAL CHRISTIANS
www.sealonia.com/crucifix
crucifix@sealonia.com – or:
crucifix@darksites.com
A magnificent site from Argentinian

Goth band, with English, Spanish and French versions available. Good news, big bio, great pics.

CRUDENESS
www.crudeness.de
fanclub@crudeness.de
As a fan of outright filth I was disappointed. Tame site from longhair Goth boys, trying to prove how hard they are by posing in the snow, and keeping their jackets on. Gurls!

CRUELTY ALLIANCE – ARCHIVE
www.go.to/cruelty-alliance

CRUSH VIOLETS
www.crushviolets.com
CrushViolets@hotmail.com
Cute Goth, but hardly any content.

CRUXSHADOWS
www.cruxshadows.com
www.clubs.yahoo.com/clubs/fansofthecruxshadows
cruxshadows@cruxshadows.com
Pretty immense, as you'd expect. A fantastic news section, which manages to still retain that human feel, despite a welter of info, good history and individual bios, utterly stunning gallery selection (seemingly endless!) and good links. You can also find a brilliant ultra-fansite at:
www.bookofcruxshadows.com with essential band-related links/forums, or an old fansite, at:
www.geocities.com/BourbonStreet/2328/index.html

CRYONICA MUSIC
www.cryonica.com

THE CRYPTKEEPER FIVE
www.geocities.com/SunsetStrip/Gala/9120
cryptweb@hotmail.com

CRYPTOMNESIA – DARK TEXTURES
www.angelfire.com/de/cryptomnesia
cryptomnesia@hotmail.com

CTRL
http://analogaether.com/ctrl
American EBM band with Gothic-Ind beginnings. Cute site.

THE CULT
www.thecultnet.com/index2.html
Doggedly giving it all they've got, the site is pretty good. There's a tour diary from new boy Billy, and a surreal bio with virtually no details. The gallery is a

bit frightening though. Short-haired they look like extras from some classic prison drama. It's all looking very new, as though the past has slipped away and they're doing it all over again. Good luck to them. If they don't twat about this time they might do something. Fan archive:
www.iaw.on.ca/~jdohn/Cult.html

THE CURE
www.thecure.com
Oh go on, you know you want to. They never were a Goth band, in case it needs repeating – as the *majority* of their audience were non-Goth, if you need it explained further. Hopefully this is very much a work in progress, because when you consider what they have to put up here, the evidence is pretty banal. It's not like they ever seem to do much else, so you'd think would be packed to bursting.
Link-wise:
www.wizlow.co.uk/cure.htm

THE CUREHEADS – TRIBUTE BAND
www.geocities.com/gary_ash/

CURSE
www.curseonline.com
cursetheband@hotmail.com
Very interesting American band, who vocalist Mikaela Pearson admits move in a somewhat Creatures-ish vein. Decently updated news, cute live shots but only a tiny bio.

CURSE OF THE PINK HEARSE –
PSYCHOBILLY
www.curseofthepinkhearse.com

CURVE
www.curve.co.uk
Brilliant site for ultra-cool band. Excellent resource, and worth checking for updates, as Toni has some weird classical project on the go.

CUT.RATE.BOX
www.cutratebox.com

CYANHIDE – DARKWAVE
www.cyanhide.com
cyanhide@cyanhide.com

CYBELE
www.listen.to/cybele
cybele@superhelt.com

CYBER SPACE RESTING PLACE OF THE FLESH EATING FOUNDATION
www.fef.supanet.com

CYCLOTIMIA – POST-IND
http://cyclotimia.gothic.ru

ANNELI DRECKER
www.annelidrecker.com
snowonahotday@hotmail.com
Wonderful ongoing tribute to Bel Canto singer, with press and pics.

D'JARRA
http://djarra.co.uk

D'WOOLVE – WAVE-SYNTH
www.d-woolve.de
product303@aol.com

DACT – POST-IND
www.geocities.co.jp/MusicStar-Guitar/3006/scoop.html
k-work@geocities.co.jp
No idea, but the singer appears to be fighting someone on the frontpage. Lovely artwork in gallery.

DADDY LONG LEGS
www.daddylonglegs.de
info@daddylonglegs.de

DAEMON GREY – IND-GOTH
www.vampiresong.com

DAEONIA
www.daeonia.com
info@plastichead.com
'Progressive' Dutch Goth Rock!

DAISY CHAINSAW
www.angelfire.com/hi3/ifeelinsane
perishedinfits@hotmail.com
Brilliant site with details past and present, including Queen Adreena. Pics, discog, reviews and articles, plus covering the steps between Katie's departure and QA. Also good DC stuff on QA site at:
www.coma-pudding.com/qa/katie.html
http://groups.yahoo.com/group/gruesome

DALET-YOD – GOTH-PROG
www.dalet-yod.com

LARISSA DALLE
http://radiopenny.com/larissadalle
contact@larissadalle.com

DAMMERUNG
www.theportal.to/dammerung

DANCE ON GLASS
http://danceonglass.topcities.com
DanceOG@aol.com
Ania, ex-Batalion d'Amour, based in Devon.

DANCE OR DIE
http://dance-or-die.de
webmaster@dance-or-die.de
www.edu.isy.liu.se/~matpe960/dance_or_die

DANSE MACABRE
www.dma.be/p/ar/danse
danse@dma.be
Moody side-project of Black Metal lads.

DANIELLE DAX
www.vargol.demon.co.uk/Dax/dax.html
Biogs, reviews and pics. Nothing special. Info at:
www.geocities.com/SunsetStrip/Lounge/1110
http://kheavy.com/dax
Nice Dax fan page with full discog details and samples, which breaks the news that we shouldn't expect too much new material from Danielle as she's off to be a garden designer! Just like Kim Wilde. Also:
www.rahul.net/hrmusic/artists/ddart.html
Old, but full biog, discog, pics, reviews and album artwork gallery.
www.farrugia.totalserve.co.uk
pete@farrugia.totalserve.co.uk
Pete's home page with details about the bands what he does and the people he's worked with including Danielle.

DANGER DE MORT
www.danger-de-mort.de
contact@danger-de-mort.de
Dark electronics, with technical info and music.

DANSE SOCIETY
– LES NITS EN BLANC & NEGRE
http://personal1.iddeo.es/blancinegre
Neat bio, few pics and extras. Site also includes similar tribute details on X-Mal, Cure and The Passions. Discog:
http://slowdive.users.netlink.co.uk/Danse/index.html

DANTE'S MISSING ASHES
http://dantesmissingashes.tripod.com
londonbats@hotmail.com
You get a plea to join! This could be your chance of the small time.

DARC ENTRIES
www.darcentries.de

dontshoot@darcentries.de
Weird Goth site, in German. Looks good but when you try and read the old press items and click on them they fly away – never to be seen again!!!

DARGAARD – Elec
http://dargaard.darkwood.com/news.htm

DARK EDEN
www.angelfire.com/ny4/darkesteden

DARK SANCTUARY
www.dark-sanctuary.com
mail@dark-sanctuary.com
Now this is lovely, even though photos are poor and detail is sparse, for this French ambient solo project have blossomed into an atmospheric band. This provides enough to give you a taste, and want more.

THE DARK VIOLENCE OF BEAUTY
www.darkviolence.dynamite.com.au
Prosaic Gothabilly site from Australia, with a severe lack of news, about anything, a small bio and maybe they died, beautifully.

DARKAN – Ind-Goth
www.geocities.com/SunsetStrip/Stage/1687/Darkan.html

DARKFACE – Elec-Goth
www.multimania.com/darkface
darkface@multimania.com
It could be a French band, doing an all-round zine approach, or a zine, with some mentions of a band. Either way, the Gallery is brilliant.

DARKLING THRUSH
http://artists.mp3s.com/info/28/darkling_thrush.html
Alternative Goth-Industrial Metal for you, straight outta Orange County.

DARKSIDE COWBOYS
www.nangijala.com/dsc
dsc@nangijala.com
Truly a magnificent site with all the usual features, but luscious layout, bright bios, and an awesome gallery selection!

DARKWELL
www.darkwell.org
darkwellgothik@yahoo.com
Gothic Metal band who go down a storm on mp3.com and give a breezy

feel to their dark site. Some nice pics and good bio details.

DARKWOOD
www.darkwood.de
A nice looking site for German neo-folk artist, with plenty to show you.

DARLING DEMONIAC – Metal-Goth
www.darksites.com/souls/horror/drlingdmniac

DARLING MACHINE
www.darlingmachine.com
Post-Punk with Glam pretensions and roar power.

DARLING VIOLETTA
www.darlingvioletta.com
alifox@darlingvioletta.com
They call it the Home office, so I hope you're Angel fans. 'Darling Violetta isn't for everyone, cause what's for everyone sucks.' Shocking grammar, but you get their point. You get the little bio, the Buffy and Angel segments which are worth a peruse (Shocking Grammar II), and they're cool, as the photos testify. In court, if necessary. Galleries you'll be playing with for hours.

DAS HOLZ
www.chrom.de/home/holz
This is a sweet site, for a delicately beautiful band, with English version, and everything laid out just so, but then it's a record label site (stroll about, they have loads of good bands). Galleries are hidden in the discog.

DAS ICH – official
www.dasich.de
webmaster@dasich.de
German, English, Swiss (I think, or is that Danish?) versions. Magnificent site, a welter of detail and pretty good photos. Unofficial:
http://ourworld.compuserve.com/homepages/das_ich
wwwcse.ucsd.edu/~casanova/DasIch/links.html

DAS SCHWARZE SYSTEM
www.dasschwarzesystem.de
management@dasschwarzesystem.de
Excellent site full of details, from intense chaps.

MARGARET DAVIS – Celtic Harpist
www.flowinglass.com/princess/index.html
info@flowinglass.com
Medieval and about as ethereal as it gets!

DAWN OF OBLIVION
http://hem.passagen.se/doo
dawn.of.oblivion@swipnet.se
Neat site, with regular news, little bio, good galleries. Dramatic fansite:
www.gothic.nu/oblivion

THE DAWN VISITORS
www.socolog.be/projects/dawnvisitors
Roxane, from De Volanges in her new outfit, but there has to be a newer site than this, which stops circa '99. I couldn't find anything else. A few nice (painfully slow) pics and album details. Same at:
www.astro.ulg.ac.be/~royer/bands/dv/dawn.htm

DE VOLANGES – archive
www.astro.ulg.ac.be/~royer/bands/devol.htm

DEADBILLYS
www.deadbillys.com
deadbilly3@home.com
Gothabilly-ish. Good photos, including loads they've taken of other bands.

DEADFILMSTAR
http://deadfilmstar.cjb.net
Formerly K.N.O. Cute site.

DEAD AS ROMANCE
http://deadasromance.com

DEAD GIRL
www.geocities.com/sunsetstrip/alley/4030/main free.html
Dead site, fittingly – but check the spooky photo of Mr Klown, and I liked the idea of a ouija board-inscribed guitar.

DEAD GIRLS CORPORATION
www.angelfire.com/mt/krakwurx

DEAD INSIDE THE CHRYSALIS – Elec
www.deadinside.com/index2.htm
falloutfreaks@hotmail.com

DEAD LETTER – Elec/Exp-Goth
www.angelfire.com/md/deadletter

DEAD POETS SOCIETY
www.dunkle-sonne.de
Beautiful site from a wistful, charming band. Not many pics, but there's all the lyrics (in English), music and wonderful links page.

DEAD RINGERS
http://deadringers.stormpages.com
deadringers9@msn.com

They call themselves Ministry meets The Munsters and this line is too good to ignore: 'In the immortal words of Jim Jones, "Try it, you'll like it."' The whole site is like that, which is a boost. The galleries are amazing – a sort of Morgue & Mindy. Good woozy lyrics and a riotous spirit throughout. This is one automatic bookmarkable offence.

DEAD SCRIPTURES
http://home.t-online.de/home/m_schwartz
m_schwartz@t-online.de
This is called 'A Gothic Project', as though teacher had decided. ('Remember to get your parent's permission before digging up grandmother and utilising any ribs.') The interesting thing here is that Martin Schwartzenberg only has time to compose occasionally, being solo, and makes everything available free for download.

DEAD SEX TUNES
www.geocities.com/legion627
DeadSexTunes@aol.com
Metal-Goth-Ind youngsters with a penchant for mania. Insane manifesto-like warbling on the page, detailed bio, and some good pics, including playing inside someone's house. One is even posing in a sombrero.

DEAD SOULS RISING – ARCHIVE INFO
www.multimania.com/darkface/dsr/groupe.htm

DEAD TREE
www.deadtree.org
deadtree@deadtree.org
Restful site by solo act Rain Borlo who promises Goth with Jazz, Trip-Hop and tribal.

DEAD TURNS ALIVE
www.dtahome.net
micha@dtahome.net
Neat German EBM site. Full content, and good galleries.

DEADBOLT – VOODOO SURF
www.downinthelab.com
Wild and demented, with its pervy Vixen Vault. Stunning fanpage:
www.ixpres.com/patrick/deadbolt

DEADCANDANCE
www.deadcandance.com
Loads of links, including awesome Dead Can Dance Within:

www.dcdwithin.com which has loads of site and webring links for DCD and Lisa Gerrard. Also – Dead Can Dance Forever – www.members.aol.com/midevlman/dcd.htm – that is a good as you'd expect from someone who calls DCD 'the ultimate listening experience'. The Deadcandance links page: www.geocities.com/SoHo/7773/DCDLinks.html is a *must* for anyone serious.

DEADLY NIGHTSHADES
www.deadlys.com
deadlys@deadlys.com
Cutesy site from Australian band on the lusher side of quiet Goth. Not Ethereal, just stirring, hotly.

Deep Eynde

DEADSY
www.deadsy.com
herdeadsea@deadsy.com
Brilliant site, quite lean but keen, which unleashes a profound manifesto. 'This institution is comprised of five separate entities: academia, leisure, horror, war and science-medicine.' Or, to put it another way, sub-Metal Boy Tarts hammer their guitars. Ace photo galleries. Other info: www.deadsy.net/fram.html

DEADTIME STORIES
www.deadtimestories.com
Playfully intense Rock with programming and style. Serial killer portraits.

DEATH BECOMES YOU
www.deathbecomesyou.com
deathby666@webtv.net
Making Gwar look like The Carpenters.

DEATH LIES BLEEDING
http://deathliesbleeding.tripod.com/index.html
New band Cavea coming soon. All dlb music now on mp3 at:
http://artists.mp3s.com/artists/169/death_lies_bleeding.html

DEATH NATURE – TOUGHENED ELEC
http://deathnature.free.fr

DEATH'S LITTLE SISTER ONLINE
www.negia.net/~pandora/del.html
Final resting page for band who once featured comics writer Caitlin R Kiernan.

DECADENT AVANT GARDE
www.devianna.com
Japanese Damned site, which is also part of a Goth webring.

DECODED FEEDBACK
www.interlog.com/%7Edefcode
Ind-Elec mix, and organised. New section is huge and fizzing with excitement, which makes a change, as there is real evidence of personality here. Nice pics.

DECOMPOSING DANDELIONS
www.geocities.com/executia
torturetemple@netscape.net

DECORYAH – ARCHIVE
www.multimania.com/timlcf/deco/index.html
Basic old fansite for atmospheric Finn rocksters. Ends around '97.

DEEP EYNDE
www.deepeynde.com
fatefatal@jps.net
When the new version is up it should still, presumably, be what the old was: a lovely, lively site with cools bios, interview archive, a couple of interesting stories, live reviews with good pics, albeit a surprisingly small selection (including cute friends), good news and smart links.

DEEP EYNDE – UNOFFICIAL
www.geocities.com/RainForest/2097/deepeynde.html
Krissy's site is pretty straightforward as most links go to the official site, but there are four wonderful gig galleries here. Unofficial:
www.deathrock.com/deepeynde
Mark Splatter review, plus pics.

DEEP RED
www.deepred.com/Enter.html

suspiria@deepred.com
Good Electro-Goth site with current news, odd bio, old tour diaries, good reviews (in English and German) and most of the photos appear.

DEFINITION MASTER
www09.u-page.so-net.ne.jp/rf6/m2brain
Crazy Japanese Industrial band (regarded as the best in Japan by many) with Goth image, but not working when I visited.

DEINE LAKAIEN
www.deine-lakaien.de

DEIANEIRA – Goth-Folk
www.anti-design.co.uk/deianeira
www.livejournal.com/users/demensia
deianeira_uk@hotmail.com
Nicely personal feel to info given and great pics.

DELICA
www.delicamusic.com
Good basic site from US Alternative Goth/Industrial band, formerly The Deal.

DELICATE TERROR
www.delicateterror.com
dt@delicateterror.
Machine Rock or Hefty Darkwave? Good bio and fierce photos.

DELIEN – Ind
www.delien.com
DeLIEN@DeLIEN.com

DELIRIUM
www.delerium.com
delerium@delerium.com
You can't keep those Leeb or Fulber boys down can you? Great site, restrained but endlessly informative, with news, interviews and full discogs for all their tricky combos.

DELPHINIUM
http://artists.mp3s.com/info/103/delphinium.html
Formerly Datura.

DELTA DREAMS – TripHop/Elec
www.deltadreams.com

DEMACRETIA
www.geocities.com/sunsetstrip/pit/1054

Dark Rock African band. Looks a bit quiet news wise. Okay pics, demos and details.

DEMENTI
www.dementi-band.de

DEMONIA
http://members.fortunecity.com/demonia666/index.html
MorteViventiInc@hotmail.com
Somewhat deranged Horror Rock from LA. Trouble is, when you see a photo of some normal bloke in glasses, bearing the legend Harbinger Of Death, and learn that, 'he is the face on that invisible fear you all possess', you either question your own sanity, or just shrug happily as disbelief is suspended, hung, drawn and quartered. Their links to all sorts of Horror-related fare are wonderful, and gory colour band pics are fun.

GITANE DEMONE
www.gitanedemone.com
info@gitanedemone.com
Top quality site from awesome singer, and although the frontpage looks fairly revolting, inside things improve

Deep Eynde

swimmingly. Sadly there's no great info or galleries, but there are videos and sounds, and you see her strange art and some 'writing'. Also:
www.geocities.com/WestHollywood/Stonewall/7527/gitanepix.html
www.guavajelly.com/hollows/artists/gitane

DEONDA
http://hem.passagen.se/iapetus/New
Swedish Goth Metal with brief info, reviews and pics.

DER EISENROST
www2u.biglobe.ne.jp/%7Epsa
Metal percussion group from Japan like SPK from the eighties.

DER KALTE STERN
www.carcasse.com/derkaltestern
kalte@gothic.art.br
Brazilian band with site in Portugese or English.

DER VAMPYR
www.geocities.com/Vienna/3535
der_vampyr@svn.com.br

DERRIERE LE MIROIR
www.pagus.de/blisz/dlm/index.html
dlm@justmail.de
Wonderful German band who have had turbulent label troubles (Dion Fortune going bust), so site is in stasis, as are they. Neat bio and discog details, and fantastic pictures because they look so odd and yet so right. Galleries to die for.

LUCIEN DESAR
www.desar.com
desar@nii.net
Good, informative site from an unusual performer. Decent bios and moody portraits of him refusing to make eye contact. Interviews, news, discog.

DESCENDANTS OF CAIN
www.descendantsofcain.co.uk
e@descendantsofcain.co.uk
Nice site, with all normal details plus some good photos and some of Philippa's computer art. Try not to go near the history of Cain's descendants in their features – you could smell the RPG past before you get there.

DESERT & FORTUNE
www.desertfortune.de

Gitane Demone © Mick Mercer

DESIDERII MARGINIS
http://home.swipnet.se/desiderii
johan-levin@swipnet.se
Beautifully moody site from Swedish Dark-Ambient/Industrialists.

DESIRE
www.audiogalaxy.com/bands/desire
Old school Goth from Sweden. Strangely basic site.

DESPAIRATION
www.despairation.de
info@wintersolitude.de
English and German versions available (apart from interviews/reviews) from Goth Metal band. Big on detail, and very self-conscious photos.

DESTINY OF LOVE
www.vampires-tales.de
Jack_t_Ripper@gmx.net
Small German-only site from band inspired by vampires.

DEVIAN
www.devian.mtl.pl
Nice site for Polish (English available) Goth/Cold band. Good pics.

DEVIL DOLL
www.geocities.com/SunsetStrip/Alley/6886

Picking an artist so obscure no-one even knows what year their records were released in, who works under a state of complete ambivalence and mystery, isn't perhaps the *best* choice for an unofficial site. No access to an enigma is a bit of a problem. So, there's no real info, no pics, no sound, no news, no tour dates, no... well, you get the picture.

DEVILS GATE – DARK TRANCE
http://artists.mp3s.com/info/246/devils_gate.html

DEVINETTE
www.devinette.com
info@devinette.com

DEVOUR ENSEMBLE – DARK ROCK
www.devourensemble.com
devour@devourensemble.com

DIABOLIQUE – Goth-Metal
www.darksites.com/souls/goth/blackflower/diabolique

DIARY OF DREAMS
www.diary-of-dreams.mtl.pl
diary@mtl.pl
Official page vanished so try this Polish site 'Oblivion' with English version available at:
www.diary-of-dreams.mtl.pl – his news is better updated than theirs! Also:
www.diaryofdreams.de

DIABOLICA
www.blackwidow.4t.com
Metal band from Philippines but with excellent links.

DIE KRUPPS – DKAY
www.dkay.com
A very flash site – literally – but nowhere near as good, or informative, as it could be for a DK offshoot involving good people.

DICHROIC MIRROR
http://members.tripod.com/~Dichroic_Mirror/dichroic.htm
nocturne17@aol.com
Old fashioned site, for sweet Goth band.

DIE FORM – ELEC
www.dieform.net/dfav

DIE KRANKEN KATZCHEN – GOTH-IND
http://artists.mp3s.com/info/302/die_kranken_katzchen.html

Die My Darling

DIE KRUPPS
http://internettrash.com/users/krupps/startup.html
Excellent fanpage for the Industrial pioneers.

DIE LAUGHING – ARCHIVE INFO
http://members.aol.com/Waschelitz/die.html

DIE MY DARLING
www.diemydarling.com/index1.html
scream@diemydarling.com
Great band with decent site. News and reviews, plus good photos.
http://clubs.yahoo.com/clubs/diemydarling

DIE SYMPHONY
www.diesymphony.com
Seriously posh Ind site that will do your head in with all its features and content. Rather tense photos.

DIES DOMINI
www.cottagesoft.com/~felis/catacombs/diesdomini
felis@cottagesoft.com
Christian Goth, who leave little trace.

DIES IRAE
www.dies-irae-tempel.de
info@dies-irae-tempel.de
Basic site, with good profiles and facts. Moody pics.

DINIEGO
www.diniego.com
webmaster@diniego.com

Plenty of clear content, plus video, cool galleries. In Italian and English.

DIR EN GREY
www.tomobiki.com/wagaku/artists/deg.htm
Japanese band given Ind credentials. The point of this site is it's very descriptive and in English, with nice pictures. Also try: http://pubnix.org/%7Ewednsday/direngrey
http://www4.justnet.ne.jp/%7Eaya-satou/index.html
http://www.laamies.ne.jp/urza/dir

DIRTY BARBY – BE AFRAID!
www.dirtybarby.com

DISCIPLES OF SORROW – ELECTRO-GOTH
http://mzone.mweb.co.za/residents/slaine77/homepage.html

DISINTEGRATION – CURE TRIBUTE
www.curetribute.net

(DISJECTA) MEMBRA
www.disjecta-membra.com
info@disjecta-membra.com
Now just Membra, this was a very pretty site, currently disappeared, with a well-illustrated band history (one band member is sacked for smelling funny!), and they had great links, including other music-related sites for their previous members.

DISSONANCE
www.newdream.net/~brett/Dissonance/index.htm

DISSONANCE@aol.com
No news, sparse info but lots of music and nice images. There is also a curious link to Cat's dread-expert hairdresser, who is busy touring!

DISTORTED REALITY
www.distorted-reality.com/index.htm
info@distorted-reality.com
Hard Goth-Techno, with Martha from Deep Red. News, bio, lyrics, pics.

DIVA DESTRUCTION
www.divadestruction.com
www.clubs.yahoo.com/clubs/divadestruction
divadestruction@yahoo.com
Modern Goth par excellence. Bland news and no real details of any real sort, but saved by some stunning portraits and decent live shots.

DIVIDE BY ZERO
www.dbzero.net
band@dbzero.net
Dark Electro Rock, in Spanish with English available. Cute menu!

THE DIVINE
www.virtualdivinity.net
the.divine@home.com
Synth mayhem by the look of it. No detailed bio of band history you have to sift and pick through this lovely site from lovely boys. The warts and all diary sections of news are fantastic. Check for a band called Lacklustre.

DIVINE HERESY – DARKWAVE ARCHIVE
http://members.aol.com/seeton/dh.htm

SALLY DOHERTY – FOLK
www.sallydoherty.com

DO NOT DREAM
www.donotdream.de

DOG MACHINE – ARCHIVE
http://dogmachine.bit.com.au

DOLL FACTORY
http://artists.mp3s.com/artists/52/doll_factory.html

DOMINION
www.SUB-KULTURE.com
SUBKULTURE@Gothica.zzn.com
Biggest Philippines Goth band. URL wasn't decided when finishing the book, but they will *definitely* be worth checking out, so try both.

Diva Destruction. Photo by M Riser

Failing that, try the Goths In Asia site (see Locations).

DOWNFALL FUNERAL – ARCHIVE
http://culthero.tripod.com/downfall-funeral.html

DOZEN DOSES
www.dozendoses.com
12d@dozendses.com

DR KEVORKIAN & THE SUICIDE MACHINE
www.ddv.co.nz/drk
Top New Zealand Ind-Goth band but the site is a bit weeny.

DRAEMGATE – MOOD
www.draemgate.com

DRAGONFLY REEL
www.geocities.com/Area51/Lair/4975/dragonfly.html
gothik_ragdoll@yahoo.com
Weird, from Celtic reels to Goth ballads! Hideous site, unfortunately.

DRAGSTRIP DEMON
www.geocities.com/dragstripdemon/dsd.html
dragstripdemon@hotmail.com

Great galleries and gig reviews, all of which seem to have been The Greatest Live Events Ever.

DRAIN OF PAIN
www.drainofpain.com

DRAKENOVA
www.drakenova.com
drakenova@drakenova.com
Goth-Ind-Metal. Okay site, info-wise. Nice pics.

DRAVEN
http://draven.ch
Not the busiest Goth-Metal-Ind band in the world, with a gig every eon, but interesting little site. Divides into another for all press material at:
http://draven.raven.ch/html/index.htm

THE DRAWING ROOM – AMB-EXP
http://homepages.ihug.co.nz/~repeat/drawing room.html
krkrkrk@hotmail.com

DREADFUL SHADOWS
www.dreadful-shadows.de

webmaster@dreadful-shadows.de
Reasonably detailed site with good pics, including Gitane in the studio. Could do with more personal stuff to fill it out, but it looks nice.

DREAM CORROSION – IND/ELEC
www.dreamcorrosion.com

DREAM DISCIPLES
www.dreamdisciples.net
band@dreamdisciples.net
http://groups.yahoo.com/group/dreamdisciples
Good site for these highly regarded UK Gothsters, but needs building up, as there's very little on their past, their thoughts, even their personal biogs.

DREAMS OF THE FALL
www.dreamsofthefall.com
dreams@dreamsofthefall.com
Dark and powerful, with so-so site. Good pics and info. News is brief, but with two gigs in six months, that's understandable.

THE DREAMSIDE
www.dreamside.nl
Halfway between dcd and Ataraxia, an

enchanting place to be. Great site, mainly in English, with a few translated reviews, some brilliant photos and the usual bits.

DRIFT FROZEN – Dark-Amb
http://artists.mp3s.com/info/280/drift_frozen.html

DRIONIDE
www.drionide.nl
drionide@hotmail.com
Ex-Cruelty Alliance and dramatic. Very dramatic. Goth-Ind.

DRONE THEORY – Goth-lite
http://members.home.net/dronetheory
dronetheory@home.com

DROWNING IN DECEMBER
www.drowningindecember.de
Ash@drowningindecember.de
Basic Goth site. Looks old, but is quite new, as are they.

THE DRYADS – Dark Elecs
www.ivystone.com/dryads
itchi@ripco.com

DRYKOTH
www.drykoth.cjb.net

DRYLAND
www.drylandnet.de
andredryland@aol.com
Good site from German Goth band, with plenty of pics.

TIM DRY
www.timdry.co.uk/tikntok2.htm
tim@TimDry.co.uk
There's just no stopping some people. He used to be in Tik & Tok!!! And it's quite sweet, as he wants to remind people what they once were. Apparently it involves 'From 'Lovable Robots' into something darker and stronger. Zen Fashion Samurai and Night Club Mutants...'. It seems to be Tik speaking, treating it all as fond memories, which is nice, including thanking Numan for support, and expressing gratitude to Tok. Genuinely emotional, really. Also honest. 'And if any enterprising Promoter out there would like to offer the two of us a large amount of money and incentive to reform – we'll be there like a shot!' And the story doesn't end there, as he ends up working with Beki Bondage, and the singer out of Sailor, right up to his current projects of Dante

Something and a recent project of Baudelaire poems! His bio also makes for good reading. Even nabbed himself a part in *Return Of the Jedi*! but I hate *Star Wars*, so let's move on.

DRYLAND
www.drylandnet.de
andredryland@aol.com
German Goth site, big on info and fair galleries.

DUAL EDEN
www.geocities.com/Wellesley/Garden/1987
nebulamusic@geocities.com
Ambient soulful women, with disappointingly tiny site.

DUCT TAPE PUSSY
www.angelfire.com/indie/ducttapepussy
DollyGagger@webtv.net
The bassist is called Stella Lugosi, and that's good enough for me. The site is a mess, but the galleries are cute. Dolly Gagger has two personal sites. 'Glitter Gutter' at http://community-2.webtv.net/GlitterGutter/GlitterGutter/ has some great pics, albeit somewhat pervy (sound of readers knocking things over to get at their computers) and very little else. 'Rotting Dollhouse' is a tidier version of same.

DUST OF BASEMENT
www.dustofbasement.de
Sven@DustOfBasement.de
Bubbly German Gothsters. Great bio, fabulous pics.

D.U.S.T.
www.diricci.freeserve.co.uk
DUST@wasp-factory.com
UK Goth hopefuls with breezy site, neat bio and pics. Great *attitude*.

DV8
http://tinpan.fortunecity.com/lifeforms/880/dedlife.html

DVAR – unofficial
http://dark.gothic.ru/dvar
shadow66@mail.ru
Enigmatic Russian band, slightly Sopor-like. Read the detailed review, which is surprisingly enthralling and wonder at the mystery of it all.

DWB
www.deathwatchbeetle.com

Little is revealed about the music, apart from soundtrack plans, as the site concentrates on design, with portfolio and cards.

DYED EMOTIONS
www.dyedemotions.com
randomsoul@dyedemotions.com

DYING TEARS
www.dyingtears.fr.st
dyingtears@yahoo.com
Crazy band with some bizarre influences.

EASTGOTH – Goth-Metal
www.eastgoth.de
webmaster@eastgoth.de
Minimal info but good pics.

ECHOCELL – Dark TripHop
http://artists.mp3s.com/info/119/shaved.html

ECLYPSE CLOSE
http://eclypse.close.free.fr
French Goth band of some standing, with detailed history. Starting from a dark Goth stance and growing progressively friskier and electric as the nineties passed away, this is an interesting band. Impressively atmospheric live photos.

EDEN
http://dangermedia.com/eden
seaneden@ozemail.com.au
Sean Bowley, master of softly compelling Goth from Australia. Attractive galleries, but considering what he does this feels light.

EDGE OF DAWN – Dark TripHop/EBM
www.edgeofdawn.de
mario@edgeofdawn.de
A remarkable looking site, but there's little there except a lot of reviews.

EERIE STYLE WAVELENGTH – odd
www.geocities.com/eerie_style_wavelength

EINSTURZENDE NEUBAUTEN
http://neubauten.freibank.com
Being built, so try old site at:
www.berlinbabylon.de
or, among fan sites:
www.geocities.com/Tokyo/Club/3903/EN/index.html
www.neubauten.de

EL DUENDE
www.geocities.com/el_duende95

Einsturzende Neubauten's Blixa Bargeld. Photo © Stéphane Burlot

Oscar Herrera (ex Black Tape For A Blue Girl).

ELEGIA
www.hpo.net/users/elegia
elegia@hpo.net
Weighty, interesting site from great band. Everything you expect, and should want, which includes a wonderfully varied gallery.

ELEMENT – ELEC
http://papabyrd.com/element
elementinfo@aol.com
According to the bio, 'Element still plays and tours extensively to this day with revolving members'. To each their own.

ELEND
www.geocities.com/Athens/Oracle/4019/frames.html
bruzz@atsat.com
A duff site for an amazingly poised and beautiful band who take ethereal into new areas with mighty compositions. Choral mania!

ELESDE – ELEC
www.nucleo.de/elesde
elesde@post.de

EMBRACE OF BRANCHES – DARK-FOLK
http://embrace-of-branches.nm.ru
embrace@nm.ru

EMERGENCE
http://emergenceband.com
webmaster@emergenceband.com
Good site, in development. *Brilliant* written touches throughout.

EMMA CONQUEST
http://listen.to/emmaconquest
t.hatch@virgin.net

THE EMPATH – ELEC
www.empath.f2s.com
The_EMPATH@01019freenet.de

THE EMPIRE HIDEOUS
www.empirehideous.com
Interesting tribute site for a band that may never quit permanently. The bio is fascinating, and the galleries great fun. Lots of info here on a classic and unpredictable Goth band. More at:
http://tvcasualty.com/hideous

EMPIRIA
http://empiria.cjb.net

lacrimabilis@hotmail.com
empiria@hotmail.com
Two Italian and one English site, but confusing. Something new appears to be emerging, called Apocalypse Woman? Citing Joy Division, Bauhaus, Lacrimosa, Sopor Aeternus... as influences.

EMPRESS IN THORNS
www.thorns.sphosting.com
mjhutchings@ozemail.com.au
Very decent site from Australian Metal Goth foursome, with very good bio and profiles, and mental gallery.

EMPYRIUM
http://empyrium.darkwood.com
info@prophecyproductions.de
Where At Night The Wood Grouse Play is the official title, which is rather Dancing Did-ish. Looks like a bolder version of gloomy Neo Folk in the offing. Nice site, charming pics, very good interviews.

THE ENCHANTED
http://sinisterweb.co.uk/enchanted
Actually Pagan Metal but I liked the cheerfully detailed personal nature of the site.

END – Death/Black/Gothic
www.end-music.net
end-music@gmx.net
'Home of the depressive band', apparently.

ENDEZEIT – Darkwave EBM
http://artists.mp3s.com/artists/158/fritz-x.html

ENDLESS
www.endless.de
endless@t-online.de
Sprawling mess of a charismatic site, packed with info.

ENDORPHINE – Visual-plus?
www.endorphine-inc.com
Beautiful site. They look a 2002 Japan, with the design specifications of an Electronic experience. Great photos.

ENEMY
www.enemyonline.com
contact@enemyonline.com

ENGELSSTAUB
http://engelsstaub.de
info@engelsstaub.de
They may be back, it's just they haven't made it clear.

ENGINES OF AGGRESSION – Ind
www.enginesofaggression.com
eoa2002@hotmail.com

ENIGMA – archive
www.enigma-archives.org.uk

ENSANGUINE – synthy
www.ensanguine.com
info@ensanguine.com

ENTRAR – Ind
www.infocultura.com.br/unbrall

ENVARLA – Doors/Prodigy?
www.envarla.de
envarla@t-online.de

Estampie

EPISTEME – Ind/Exp
http://hem.passagen.se/episteme

EQUINOX OV THE GODS
www.welcome.to/thespectralgarden
thespectralgarden@welcome.to

EROS NECROPSIQUE
www.erosnecropsique.f2s.com

EROSIS
www.erosis.org
erosis666@aol.com
Satanist leads trio in Electro nightmare.

EROTIC CHANT
www.ampcast.com/search/band.php?id=6290
Basic info page on Sweden-based band led by Lebanese singer Plasticgrl. Sounds great. Looks cool.

ESCAPE – Goth-Ind
www.carpemortem.com/tumor

THE ESCAPE – archive
www.the-escape.de

ESION – Electro Rock
www.esioncentral.com

THE ESSENCE – Goth archive(s)
www.geocities.com/Paris/LeftBank/8026/
essence/essence1.html
www.terra.es/personal/lovekraft/Essence/
essence.htm
www.xs4all.nl/~essence

ESTAMPIE – Historical
www.estampie.de
management@estampie.de
A very interesting, and attractive site from a band who specialise in genuine recreation of medieval music. Includes Sigrid Hausen (Qntal), so it's quality. Full of detail, and invigorating, matched by typically good label details at:
www.chrom.de/bands/estampie/est_home_e.html

THE ETERNAL CHAPTER
www.carpemortem.com/eternalchapter
eternalchapter@hotmail.com
Total Goth, from South Africa. Fairly empty site.

ETERNAL JOY
www.uio.no/~oysteisj/eternaljoy.htm
eternaljoy99@hotmail.com
Goth-Wave from Norway. Good looking site, with nice detail, with bizarre bios

asking their favourite sexual position. ('HongKong-Chinese', gasps one) and weird 'live' gallery shots, plus lyrics, tiny news. Great cartoon in 'stuff', and you sign their guestbook 'or die'. The police have been informed.

ETERNIA
www.eternia.net
webinfo@eternia.net
Impressive solo Goth project from David Quinn, a man with an intriguing musical past that is only hinted at on this site. Enjoy stormy modern Goth here and wonder what else he'll come up with.

ETHER CLINIC – DarkAmb Goth
http://artists.mp3s.com/info/120/etherclinic.html

ETHODIUS
www.ethodius.com
ethodius@gatecom.com
Ethereal-experimental. Brief bio, attractive landscape photos.

EVA O
www.peoplejustlikeus.org/Music/Eva_O.html
Weird interview. As in WEIRD!!!!!!!

EVANESCENCE
http://listen.to/evanescence
An unofficial website for self-styled Greatest Band In The History Of The World... seems a leetle short on content. And realism.

EVEREVE
www.evereve.net
havoc@evereve.net
Nice site for Goth stalwarts. Good fan stuff, cute game, sturdy news section.

EVIL MAJICK – Noise
www.angelfire.com/ny3/EvilMajick

EVILS TOY
www.evils-toy.de
Enjoy the splendour of the Electro-nutters. Fun site with bright impact. Also try: http://users.pandora.be/geivaerts/evilstoy and www.sealonia.com/evilstoy which both have live shots.

EX NIHILO – Elec-Wave
www.sealonia.com/Ex_Nihilo

EX-VOTO – archive?
http://members.aol.com/exvoto69/index.htm
exvoto69@aol.com

Patchy, pretty site for classy Goth-Synth outfit who seem quiet of late. Nice pics.

EXOVEDATE
www.exovedate.com/exovedate_hello.html
webmaster@exovedate.com
A Canadian band who delight unwittingly with the details revealed. 'Madelynn hates raisins. Don't even come *near* her with a raisin. Fans may send her cash or PVC.' Loopily attractive site where you scroll down one page and link to whatever takes your fancy. Something about this band seems nice, and they have an all bulletins request for news on the whereabouts of one member!

EXPLIZIT EINSAM – Darkwave
http://members.aol.com/explizitei/nsam.htm
explizitei@aol.com

EZRA STONE – Goth-Metal archive
http://hometown.aol.com/nytecaller99/EZRASTONE.html

EYE KANDY – Synthcore
www.eyekandy.net
actionent@hotmail.com

F.D.K. – Goth-Punk
www.angelfire.com/nv/fdk1
fdk26@hotmail.com

FADING COLOURS
www.fading-colours.mtl.pl
Lovely site for the Goth band going a bit Darkwave or EBM as they flutter fiercely in the heat. Utterly magnificent, as you probably know. Very good news and live info, fabulous biography, article archive, useful shop and some sensational pics. Are we happy? Bleedin' delirious, mate. Early info (Bruno The Questionable) at: www.terra.art.pl/dadamusic/bruno/

FAERIES BONES AND VASELINE – archive
www.geocities.com/southbeach/breakers/2164/
Interesting self-professed dark 'fag' trio, with depressing lyrical fare.

FAIRIES FORTUNE
www.chrom.de/home/fairies
Label page for alternative project of Sleeping Dogs Wake.

FAITH AND THE MUSE
www.mercyground.com
info@mercyground.com

An exquisite site for a lovely band. Biog is great, detailed personal biogs with their early band photos are awesome.

FAITH ASSEMBLY
http://faithassembly.com
mark@faith-assembly.com
Great site for wonderfully moody band with a well-illustrated history, newsletter service and sounds. A touch austere.

FAITH & DISEASE
www.operation-glam.com/faith
bb23@pacbell.net
Cool semi-official site with good all-round details up to '97, then news to 2000. Excellent photos *and* flyer collection.

FAITHFUL DAWN – archive
Page seems to have vanished in the Outlet move to www.outlet-promotions.com, so keep an eye out. It will re-surface.

FALLEN 019
www.fallen019.com
Fallen019@aol.com
Very interesting Goth-Ind band with awkward site, producing eyestrain. Plentiful images with hints of musings to illustrate their dark intensity.

FALLEN HARLEKIN – Dark Synthy Pop
www.fallen-harlekin.de
info@fallen-harlekin.de

FALLING JANUS
http://members.aol.com/falljanus/fallingjanus.html
fallingjanus@compuserve.com
For such a good band this is rubbish! Four sections, no real bio or any historical perspective of achievements and desire. Few pics, discog.

FALSE FACES – Goth-Punk
www.falsefaces.fr.st
kergan@fr.st

FANGBOY AND THE GHOULS
http://fangboyandtheghouls.com
Splatter-mess type layout, with Fleshead Chronicles that tips its hat to Daniel Ash as an influence and wisely applauds Daredevil. All have journals, and good galleries.

FATAL BEAUTIES – Elec-Goth
www.angelfire.com/ms/fatalbeauties/index.html
fatalbeauties@hotmail.com

Fear Cult. Photo © Cyndee Arroyo

FEAR CULT
www.fearcult.com
fearcult@aol.com
Straightforward site of cool band
featuring Matt Riser, who was doing the
Synth-Goth thing while many were still
growling like Nephilim-infected wilde-
beest. News and latest photo updates
before you even enter the site, and keep
going through the main photo archive
for lovely black and white portraits.

FEAR FACTORY
www.fearfactory.com
Very lively and swish, with mad Fan Club.
www.fearfactoryfanclub.com
official-fanclub@fearfactory.com

FEARvLOATHINC – IND
www.johnnychrome.co.nz
johnny@johnnychrome.co.nz

FEINDFLUG – ELEC
www.feindflug.net

FETISCH
www.fetischmusic.com/fetisch-new

FICTION 8
www.fiction8.com
info@fiction8.com
Longstanding Goth-Elec-Ind bunch with
a site that tries hard. Cute pics.

FIELDS OF THE NEPHILIM
www.fieldsofthenephilim.co.uk
info@fieldsofthenephilim.co.uk

Under dreaded construction, and
looking gloomy. Links are rubbish.

FIELDS OF THE NEPHILIM – UNOFFICIAL
www.nephilim.co.uk
Pretty mega-site as these things go,
and you get the news from the
malfunctioning band via press releases.
It will probably *always* be better than
the official site. Big archive and plenty
of links. Also try:
http://obscure.org/~vlad/lyrics/nephilim.html
www.d.kth.se/~d93oja/fields_of_the_nephilim.html
www.geocities.com/SunsetStrip/6019/fotn.htm
www.geocities.com/SunsetStrip/Basement/7280
/fields.htm
www.nephilim.mtl.pl
www.spiraldrain.freeserve.co.uk
www.spookhouse.net/angelynx/nephilim/neph.html

FIERCE CULTURE – IND-ELEC
www.fierceculture.com

DANIEL FIGGIS
(BINTII – EX VIRGIN PRUNES)
www.danielfiggis.com

FILTH
http://artists.mp3s.com/info/139/philth.html
Dance styled Goth mixture.

FINGER PUPPETS
www.finger-puppets.fsnet.co.uk
smile@finger-puppets.fsnet.co.uk
Shite name, fun site. Nice details,
character throughout, and an
unmissable gallery.

FISHTANK No. 9
www.fishtank1.com/f9

FLAMING FIRE
http://flamingfire.com/flamingfire_new.html?

FLESH FOR EVE
www.vampiretechnology.com/fleshforeve
fleshforeve@hotmail.com

FLESH FOR LULU
www.fleshforlulu.com
info@fleshforlulu.com
Back, with one of The Revs involved,
which is cool. Great fan archive:
www.geocities.com/SunsetStrip/Backstage/
2604/index.html

FLESHFIELD – ELEC-EBM
www.inception-records.com/fleshfield
ffieldgirl@aol.com

THE FLESHPEDDLERS – ELECTROPOP
www.geocities.com/thefleshpeddlersmusic
fleshpeddlers@juno.com

FLEUR
www.gothic.com.ua/fleur.htm
Ukrainian band in the modern classique
mould. Wonderful photos. Love the one
of her asleep under the piano.

FLOODLAND
www.floodland.org
Very busy, feature packed site for total
Goth band with good history.

FLOWERS OF SIN – PICS ONLY
www.sanctuary.ch/report/SanctuaryMeeting/
FlowerOfSin.htm

FLUORESCE
www.fluoresce.u4l.com
fluoresce@fluoresce.u4l.com

FORNEVER
http://go.to/fornever
autumnal@hotpop.com
Ind-Elec-Ethereal solo project of Joshua
Heinrich. Big site, info galore.

FORNIX
www.fornix.tv
nasty@deepbeat.com

FOUR FLIES ON GREY VELVET
– ARCHIVE
http://members.tripod.com/~Braingel/4flies.html
Horror-Rock.

FRAGLEN
www.fraglen.com
contact@fraglen.com
Very unusual site for American Goth duo who call themselves Euro-Goth? 'Our Music is spiritual alternative with a Gothic European style. We provide thought through a medieval mindset for modern living. Energy exists in the unseen realm. The invisible is happening.'

FRANK THE BAPTIST
www.frankthebaptist.com
baptistf@aol.com
Not as dozy as you might think.

FRANKENSTEIN
www.mercyground.com/frankenstein/index.html
frankenstein@mercyground.com
William Faith on guitar. Sense of fun to this Horror/Deathrock which is preferable to Manson and chums. Was down, temporarily.

GAVIN FRIDAY (EX VIRGIN PRUNES)
www.gavinfriday.com

FROLIC
http://listen.at/frolic
frolic@projekt.com
Ethereal Goth on Projekt. Pleasing, effortless, very little in the way of bestiality, pleas for deforestation or clown costumes.

FRONTLINE ASSEMBLY (ETC)
www.mindphaser.com

FROST
www.mok.com/frost
frost@mok.com
New band, compared to Nephilim, fittingly cool and sombre.

FULL FREQUENCY
http://members.aol.com/gonzorcrds/fullfrequency.html

FUNERAL CRASHERS
www.funeralcrashers.com
Funeralcrash@antisocial.com
One time home of Mark Splatter but now cruising along in fine fettle themselves. Deathrock band with brains that work.

FUNHOUSE
http://cherryfields.nu
kiss@cherryfields.nu
Evil Blast Goth'n'Roll, allegedly. News, pics, info.

FUNKER VOGT
www.funker-vogt.com

DIAMANDA GALAS
www.diamandagalas.com
This wasn't fully working, so in the meantime try the brilliant all purpose site: www.brainwashed.com/diamanda or enjoy the scary photo at: www.levity.com/corduroy/galas.htm or complete links: www.geocities.com/SoHo/7773/DiamandaLinks.html

GAIAS PENDULUM
http://members.tripod.com/gaianet
gaiaspendulum@yahoo.com
Colombian site (with English). Goth band formerly known as Afflicion and

Mel Garside © Mick Mercer

Violet Gothic. Nice site, devious imagery, album details and full lyrics, with very unusual live photos.

GAIL OF GOD
www.gailofgod.com
info@gailofgod.com
A brilliantly captivating, highly original site. Crisply and clearly navigable and *exciting*, because you never know what else will appear. Really good live photos, the history well covered, and they seem to have moved from Doom occult to Dark Ind but in a charismatic manner.

THE GALANPIXS
www.thegalanpixs.de
contact@thegalanpixs.de

THE GARDEN – ARCHIVE
www.amz.com/bands/TheGarden

GARDEN OF DELIGHT – ARCHIVES
www.geocities.com/SunsetStrip/Club/9623
www.garden-of-delight.mtl.pl/

GARDEN OF DREAMS
www.gardenofdreams.com
A little bit Cure, a little bit Suede.

MEL GARSIDE
http://website.lineone.net/~steve_laurie/SKFront.html
Nice site by Steve Laurie, building the details up as and when they become available. Great press archive, full discog of Zu, Tabitha Zu and Mel, and will include details of Mel's new band, Our Lady Of Miracles. Yahoo! Group: http://groups.yahoo.com/group/Sick_on_Words

GENE LOVES JEZEBEL (JAY ASTON)
www.genelovesjezebel.com
Nice site with news about Jay and ex-members, a busy board, fan fun, gallery, press, video vault and discography.
GENELOVESJEZEBEL.NET
www.genelovesjezebel.net
astonmanagement@earthlink.net
Michael Aston site with all the news pics and downloads you could want.
GLJ POOH UK
www.gljpooh.co.uk
A quite *amazing* fansite by Pooh for the '81-'85 period. A vast adverts/flyers section (60+ items) is nothing compared to the photo gallery. I have never seen anything this detailed for any band. The biography is amazingly detailed, as is everything here.
THE JEZEBEL PAGES
http://members.tripod.com/thejezebelpages/index.htm
Nice fansite devoted to all members of GLJ. Well worth your time, for the lovely photos, backstage and live. Also: http://clubs.yahoo.com/clubs/genelovesjezebel

GETAH
www.duatiga.com/Getah
gothvamp@cbn.net.id
Goth band from Jakarta with very pleasant site. Goth in so much as they have an 'uncompromised musical style influenced by Jane's Addiction, thrash metal, and traditional Indonesian music, the self' and describe themselves further as 'a free and dark musical manifestation of the omnivorous milky fluid found in poppies and plants. GETAH delivers loud, melodic, dark and sad musical

realization of their dreams and nightmares.'

GET LOVE DEAD
www.getlovedead.co.uk
info@getlovedead.co.uk
Good Irish Goth site.

GGFH – Archive
www.adrenalin.dynamite.com.au/ggfh/main.htm
Stands for Global Genocide Forget Heaven, so expect jollity aplenty.

GHOST DANCE
www.poison-door.net/ghostdance
vicus@poison-door.net
Neat little fansite with decent bio – German only – and pics/artwork/discog. Also bigger sections on S*st*rs and X-Mal.

THE GHOSTS – Cool Retro
www.disgraceland.com/ghosts.htm
h8ual@aol.com

GHOSTING
www.ghosting.de
office@ghosting.de
Awesome. Monumentally talented Goth band, one of Germany's best by a mile. Stuffed full of things, from piquant history to droolsome galleries.

GHOUL SQUAD – Horror Punk
www.ghoulsquad.com

Ghoultown

GHOULTOWN
www.ghoultown.com
countlyle@ghoultown.com
This is mad and I love it. Wild West themes, bullet holes on pages, crazed individuals. One review calls it The Munsters meets Bonanza, another suggests Zombie spaghetti-westerns with Spanish themes and Goth lyrics. You sit there learning more and more improbable facts, just taking it in, serenely. The galleries will have you quivering with joy, and that's just their merchandising girl. The live shots are totally insane. Other names mentioned in the History are Nick Cave, Gun Club and the obvious Cramps. They hit something here, talking about the old Campfire Tales, which were usually ghostly or mythic, and there's always a shambling Gothic ethos to certain American states, so it all ties in, and this website is a genuine work of art. They've even got a comic which looks it'll be half Preacher, half Scout.

GIRLPOOL – Synth-Ind-Goth
www.geocities.com/SunsetStrip/Palms/2012
I think this is old, but the www.thegirlpool.com didn't work.

GL-OK
http://mygroup.boom.ru
Russian Gothic Rock. Nice profiles, galleries and downloads.

GLACIER
www.best.com/~glacier2/index.html
glacier2@best.com
Formed by Daniel James, ex-Tel Basta. So although brand new, worth keeping an eye on straight away.

GLAMPIRE
www.glampire.com/home.html

GLASS – Gothy Punk
www.waste.org/%7Eglass
glass@waste.org

THE GLASS ASYLUM
www.angelfire.com/il/glassasylum
Ethereal Goth poetess.

GLIMMER – Archive
www.angelfire.com/or/98glimmer
mrclemmer@yahoo.com

GLITCH – Elec
http://members.aol.com/juxtaposal/glitch.htm
glitch.digger@mindspring.com

GLOOMSTAR
www.geocities.com/gloomstaronline
GloomStar@aol.com
Ethereal Goth with fertile imagination overload. Very interesting, despite horribly clichéd and self-conscious photos.

THE GLOVE – Archive
www.geocities.com/SunsetStrip/Mezzanine/7165
mintcure@geocities.com

GOD EXPERIMENT – Goth-Noise
www.god-experiment.de
m@god-experiment.de
Industrial Goth Metal with trim site, where one fan describes them as 'Horror and shit in the pants!'. Charming.

GODCENT – Dark Ind
http://artists.mp3s.com/info/196/godcent.html

GOD'S GIRLFRIEND – Archive
www.geocities.com/SunsetStrip/Studio/9616/mainframe.htm

GOD'S OWN MEDICINE
www.gods-own-medicine.mtl.pl
gods_own_m@hotmail.com
Fine site for new Polish Darkwave band. Brief, but cool pics.

GOETHES ERBEN
www.goetheserben.de

erbenpost@hotmail.com
I don't wish to appear absurd here but it does amaze me that more German bands don't have English versions available. It's not difficult and would probably treble your audience. This site has everything, including a massive gallery. Fanclub: www.multimania.com/goetheserben – lovely site for great band. Some superb live photos. The rest is in French, but the newsletters are pretty regular.

GOLIATH
http://members.tripod.com/Bryan69666/index_m.htm

GOSSAMER
www.idrecords.com/gossamer
adagio@idrecords.com
New Wave Old School Gothic Swirly Death Pop? Have they missed anything out? A ravishingly attractive sound, and an interesting site, in that there's hardly anything here. Band bios that Sherlock Holmes would have trouble noticing, some reviews, a bit of info, and a few tasteful pics.

GOTEKI
www.goteki.fsnet.co.uk
goteki@goteki.fsnet.co.uk
Endearingly odd site, with colourful stories and some cute pics.

GOTHIC LOVE TRIP
www.geocities.com/crushedangels/GothicLoveTrip.html

GOTHIC SEX – OFFICIAL
www.bloodfetish.com/bloodkind/gothicsex/menu.html
Spain's finest. Dark site, good bio and pics/vids.

GOTHICA
www.geocities.com/gothicahomepage
gothica@tin.it
Interesting site, in English, on Italian Goth moodists, and has a section of Myths that is rather enjoyable.

GOTHMINISTER
www.gothminister.com
tom@angel.no
Interesting Norwegian character with mysterious site. Goth will save your life, he says, like it did his. It can make you a better person.

Goteki

SMILE, THE FUTURE IS NOW!

Goteki
WWW.GOTEKI.COM

GOTTERDAMMERUNG
http://listen.to/gotterdammerung
amphitryonsatir@hotmail.com
The noisy boys are back. Basic with good historical detail and images.

GRACE OVERTHRONE – ELEC-GOTH
www.thegauntlet.com/graceoverthrone.html

GRAND FISH/LAB
www.lab.uzu-maki.com
Lightly morbid and maudlin Japanese band.

THE GRAVEYARD FARMERS
www.thegraveyardfarmers.com
http://clubs.yahoo.com/clubs/graveyardfarmers laboratory
Rockabilly band with traces of Blues, Punk and Horror. Cool site, big gallery.

THE GROUPIES
www.thegroupies.net
heidi@cubase.net

GRAVITY KILLS
www.gravitykills.com

GRAYSCALE
– UKRAINIAN IND-ELEC-GOTH
www.nomorecolors.com/english/index.html
grayscale@gruppa-t.com

GREEN GRASS GOBLINS
http://artists2.iuma.com/IUMA/Bands/Green_Grass_Goblins

SIMONE GREY – ARCHIVE
www.white-man-killer.com/wire/bare_wire.html

GREY EYES GLANCES
www.greyeyeglances.com
info@greyeyeglances.com
What a charmer! You get the band section, fan reviews, a very interesting bio. Named after a Poe poem.

GRIM FAERIES – TRIPPOP
www.grimfaeries.com

GROOVIE GHOULIES
www.groovie-ghoulies.com

suggestions@groovie-ghoulies.com
Fun site, packed with bits, apart from good live pics.

GROPIUS
www.gropius.org
www.skinny.net
Crazy dames, on weird and chaotic site, with cool gallery.

JONAS GROTH
www.jonasgroth.com/index2.html

GRUP EXPERIMENTAL TEATRO GOTICO
http://members.tripod.com/~teatro_gotico/portal.html
teatro_gotico@hotmail.com

GUGGI (EX VIRGIN PRUNES)
www.guggi.com

GUGONIX – AMBIENT
http://artists.mp3s.com/info/125/gugonix.html

GUNK
www.envy.nu/gunk
Punk + Goth = Gunk, they say and promise excitement soon. In reality it should be Puth, or Gonk, neither of which sound particularly inspiring.

GUTTERSTAR – ARCHIVE
www.angelfire.com/or/gutterstar

HAGALAZ' RUNEDANCE
http://go.to/hagalaz-runedance
Ex-Aghast. Pagan tribute to the old ways of Germanic people. The band is very sweet, news is almost a diary, and gallery shots are nice.

HALL OF SOULS
www.hallofsouls.de
hallofsouls@hallofsouls.de
Rather timid site with atrocious gallery but plenty of detail.

HALLOWTEENS – ARCHIVE
www.geocities.com/hallowteens

HALOBLACK – ARCHIVE
http://members.tripod.com/~sixteenvolt/Haloblack.htm

HAMLET MACHINE – JAPAN
www.sol.dti.ne.jp/~kibun/hamlet

HANZEL UND GRETYL – ELEC
www.grumpybat.net/nephrael/frame.html

THE HARLEQUIN – IND-ELEC
http://artists.mp3s.com/info/164/catalystt.html

HARUHIKO ASH/EVE OF DESTINY
www.interq.or.jp/tokyo/eve
eve@tokyo.interq.or.jp
Revered Japanese Goth musician with some details, but the site hasn't much on it yet. (Main emphasis on his Club Eve.)

PJ HARVEY
www.pjharvey.net
Lovely site, let down by poor bio, and selective gallery. Unofficial:
http://members.it.tripod.de/~pollysize/index.htm
http://members.tripod.com/~RidofMe/INDEX.htm
http://nav.webring.yahoo.com/hub?ring=sweetgirl&list
www.angelfire.com/yt/pjharvey
www.geocities.com/SunsetStrip/Underground/5190/dryecstasy.html

HEADROPS – ARCHIVE
www.geocities.com/SunsetStrip/Alley/8399/headrops/framed_news.htm

THE HEADSTOPS
www.theheadstops.com
Formerly Italian classical Darkwave act Ephel Dùath.

HEAVEN FALLS HARD – GOTH-ETHEREAL
http://artists.mp3s.com/info/143/heaven_falls_hard.html

HEAVENWOOD
www.terravista.pt/Guincho/2265

HEDNINGARNA
www.cabal.se/silence/nyhedning/index.html

HEDONE
www.hedone.art.pl
werk@hedone.art.pl

HELEVORN – GOTH-DOOM
http://usuarios.tripod.es/helevorn2
aboutangels@hotmail.com
Attractive Spanish site with English available, poetical biog and full details. Won-derful pics don't expand, as something has vanished.

HEREAFTER AND NOW – GOTH-METAL
www.ofdarkness.de/hereafterandnow/site/frameset.htm
bmarcob@web.de

HIERONYMUS BOSCH – DARK AMBIENT
www.clubbizarre.co.nz/bosch
bizarre@ihug.co.nz

HIM
www.heartagram.com

HIROSHIMA MON AMOUR
http://hma.freeweb.supereva.it
antcampa@tin.it

HOG HAUL VALENTINE – IND/GOTH/BLUES!
http://artists.mp3s.com/info/227/hog_haul_valentine.html

HOLLOW HALO
www.geocities.com/d1ssembl3

HOLLYWOOD MORGUE
www.hollywoodmorgue.com
webmaster@hollywoodmorgue.com
Alice meets B-52's. Supposedly.

HOLY COW
www.holy-cow.cc
COW@holy-cow.cc

THE HORATII
www.the-horatii.co.uk
Good news if they're getting organised, and the photo used *suggests* they're going to be a subversive Indie band, which is okay as well. They were the single most talented UK Goth band of the nineties and quite how they never understood that by playing Indie venues and working on getting journalists on their side they would have got somewhere, and been seen as a *far* superior Suede, I'll never know. They could still do it but they'll have to change the way they do things and maybe the mournful UK Goth approach to tantalising media has left its mark. This site has been inoperative since April 2001 so 'coming soon' seems hollow, but they are meant to be recording again which is great news.

HORROR SHOW
http://home.earthlink.net/~steveskeletal/horrorshow.html
HorrorShow@disinfo.net
Deathrock-Goth. Amazing galleries. No bio?

HORRORFIEND
www.geocities.com/horrorfiend_2000/home.html
horrorfiend@horrorfiend.com
Looks fun but is painfully slow. Make a drink while it loads.

HOWLING SYN
http://listen.to/howlingsyn
synner_musik@hotmail.com
Metal-Goth-Medieval from Canada.
Straightforward site but attractive.

HUMAN DRAMA
www.humandrama.net
Vast site, with a true sense of what fans
need, part info resource, part archive.
Immaculate galleries. Tribute page:
www.deathndementia.com/humandrama/index.
shtml

HUNGRY LUCY – GOTH-TRIPHOP
www.hungrylucy.com/news.phtml
contact@hungrylucy.com
Goth TripHop is nothing new, but it
does seem right that it should finally be
giving Ambient and Ethereal a run for
its money. Bio is fascinating, pics are
okay and good links

HYDRA
http://hydra.uhome.net
www.geocities.com/die_direngrey/Hydra.htm
Dir En Grey band who look like an
anime version of a punky Sigue Sigue.
The men all tend to look very feminine
if that's a clue.

HYPNOSIS
www.hypnosis.cjb.net

HYPNOS PROJECT – TECH-GOTH
www.hypnosproject.com
fred@hypnosproject.com

I VISCERA – GOTH-IND
http://members.aol.com/_ht_a/iviscera/index.html
iviscera@aol.com

I WILL I
www.myownpocket.com
Stars of the 'Beneath The Tides' comp.
Shambolic site of various bands and
info. A few cool photos.

ICON OF COIL
www.iconofcoil.com
info@pluswelt.de
Seriously boring site.

ICONOCLAST – DARK ELEC
http://iconoclast.home.dhs.org
makethempay@killdevil.com

IDÉE DES NORDENS – DARK EXP
www.chrom.de/home/idn/index.html

IDIC – ELEC
www.idicproductions.com
theband@idicproductions.com

IGZORN – GOTH-METAL
http://igzorn.de

IKON
www.ar.com.au/~storm/ikon
storm@ar.com.au
Australian Goth legends.

ILLUMINA – ELEC-GOTH
www.illumina.org.uk
illumina@illumina.org.uk

ILLUMINATE
www.illuminate.de/indexeng1.htm
inmove@aol.com
German Goth. Cool detail, but seriously
crap gallery.
Markus Nauli – www.irrlicht.ch
Daniela Dietz – www.talesofsorrow.de
Joern Langenfeld – www.sonnengott.de
Fanpage – best of the lot:
www.illuminate-fanpage.de

THE ILLUMINATI – ELEC-IND
http://artists.mp3s.com/artists/151/the_
illuminati.html

THE INCHTABOKATABLES
www.inchtabokatables.com/material/flash/start.html
Deutung@aol.com
Bet no-one gets that name wrong when
they're dealing with promoters!

IMAGEN MUERTA
http://orbita.starmedia.com/~imagenmuerta

IMAGINARY WALLS – GOTH/GLOOM
http://hem.passagen.se/thewalls/main
Imag_Walls@hotmail.com

IMMACULATA
www.immaculata.net
stellamagna@yahoo.com
Cool stuff from highly visual Elec-Goth-
Ind band.

IMPRESSIONS OF WINTER
www.iow-music.de/IOW_e.htm
webmaster@iow-music.de
Almost academic-looking site for
German Darkwavers. Attractive – if
brief – gallery and bio.

IN ARTICULO MORTIS
www.inarticulomortis.cjb.net

Edmonton Goth band with odd
Rockabilly addiction. Was down
temporarily, or so they claim.

IN ETHER – DARK AMB
www.geocities.com/in_ether
inether@in-ether.com

IN EXTREMO – HISTORICAL
www.inextremo.com

IN GOWAN RING
www.bluesanct.com/bands/igr
ingowanring@bluesanct.com
Historical-inspired Minstrels/Goth

IN MEMORIA – ELEC-GOTH
www.inmemoria.fr.fm
French band, French site. Nice pics

IN MITRA MEDUSI INRI
www.inmitramedusainri.com
info@inmitramedusainri.com
Large, detailed site from excellent Goth
band. German only, and the galleries
are dreadful.

IN MY ROSARY
www.pagus.de/blisz/imr/index.html
imr@pagus.de
Very orderly, pleasing site, in English.

IN STRICT CONFIDENCE
www.instrictconfidence.com
info@instrictconfidence.de
News, music and tremendous galleries.
Great band history and press, with
interesting layout.

IN TENEBRIS
www.disrupted.org/~tenebris
tenebris@disrupted.org
Pretty Goth site, with nice illustrated
reviews charting their development.

INCULTUS
www.angelfire.com/de/incultus

Impressions of Winter

Inkubus Sukkubus

Inugami

INDUCING PANIC – METAL GOTH
www.angelfire.com/oh/panic7

INFERI AMORIS
http://inferiamoris.dreamhost.com/band/
index.php
webmaster@inferiamoris.dreamhost.com
Attractive site from imaginative
German Goths.

INFINITY'S END
www.infinitys-end.de
corvus@infinitys-end.de

INFLAME RESOLUTION
– SYNTHI-GOTH
www.inflameresolution.de
inflameresolution@gmx.de

INFORMATIK – IND
www.sinless.com/informatik

INKUBUS SUKKUBUS
www.inkubussukkubus.com
tony@inkubussukkubus.com
Hmmmm, the new site is a vast
improvement on the mouldy old one
but for such a great band, with
interesting personalities, gorgeous
songs, such live energy and visual
charm, with so much to write about
on a site should they so choose, this is
still a bore. Yes, the info is there, and
some pics, but this should be a real
feast and not some enforced diet. It's
not like the world is overrun by IS
sites. Unofficial:
www.inkubus-sukkubus.co.uk
pyromancer@inkubus-sukkubus.co.uk.

Lively and light on its feet as you whip
between sections. The writing's all a bit
Pagan-infested RPG fan and gushing,
but that's okay because they're so
damned enthusiastic, and they fill the
site with vivacity.

INSCAPE
www.inscape.de

INSIGHT23
www.insight23.com

INTERVOX – NOISY DARKWAVE
http://artists.mp3s.com/info/114/intervox.html

INTO DARKNESS FURTHER I FALL
www.angelfire.com/rock/bangkok
About St James of Into Darkness.

INTO THE ABYSS
www2.pair.com/abyss
abyss@pair.com
Impressive site from high quality
Goth-Psyche band from Greece
andGermany. Excellent in-depth details
and fine gallery.

INTRA-VENUS
www.intra-venus.co.uk
iv@nightbrd.demon.co.uk
Basic site for Mark (ex-Suspiria) and
Apollo. Quality Electro-Goth.

INUGAMI
www.geocities.co.jp/Hollywood-Kouen/3043
Japanese band, with English, live
details, sale of items, downloads and
the full range. They look very strange.

INVISIBLE LIMITS
www.invisible-limits.de
info@invisible-limits.de
Synthy, without a doubt. Very detailed
site in places, with a great bio, and
sections offer English versions. Also has
a wonderful Gallery selection.

IRONY OF FATE
www.irony-fate.de

IRRLICHT – DARK ELEC
www.irrlicht.ch
info@irrlicht.ch

DAVID J
www.davidjonline.com
Odd. He wants DJ bookings
(aviddj@nctimes.net) – fair enough, and
the site has a press archive as well as
details about his art exhibitions.

JACK FROST – GLOOM
www.jackfrost.at

JACK OFF JILL
www.jackoffjill.com
Hailing from Florida, the band comes
out like a children's puppet show with
Exorcist overtones. Kind of Punk level
Kiss, which does have its relevance.
Great photo gallery, even though they
look strangely dowdy onstage, plus fans'
live pics, and old flyers. I also like the
fact one of the girls is called Agent
Moulder. Site includes details of Scarling.

THE JACKALOPES
http://hop.to/thejackalopes

moshawrex@aol.com
I thought you might like to see their saucy front page image and right clicked to be rewarded with 'Hands Off, Fucker'. Looks like a Cramps and Misfits meltdown. That is a good thing.

TYREAH JAMES
http://internettrash.com/users/spookychics
gothstar@bellsouth.net
Formerly of Three Ton Gate. Woman with a troubled past moving in a Doom-Elec direction. Fine site, taking the bio sections seriously.

JANE DOE
www.janedoe.com

JANNE DA ARC
www.janne.co.jp
Pretty site for Japanese band with discog, live details, Fan Club.

JANUARY – DARK POP
www.nullpointer.com/january
zoofy@concentric.net

JANUS – WAVE-METAL
www.schlafendehunde.de

JE$US LOVES AMERIKA
www.jesuslovesamerika.co.uk
jesus_loves_amerika@hotmail.com
UK Gothlings, of a darkened electric heart. Clever site, or so they think. Fast becomes a minimalist bore.

JEKYLL SWITCH – IND
www.jekyllswitch.com
info@jekyllswitch.com

JENN VIX
www.jennvix.com
UmbrellaMusicCo@aol.com
Oh come on, this woman lists The Avengers, Malcolm McDowell and The Prisoner among her favourites, and when you see her musical tastes you know you have to get interested. Primarily a soft-depressive acting solo, she's getting uppity now. Surely she can get some decent photos? Help her out someone, if you live in Providence. Also looking for people to play live, which seems a problem.

JENNIFER HOPE
www.jenniferhope.com
Ethereal, with a very precise site.

JERK – DARK IND
www.jerkmusic.com

JESSICA'S CRIME – IND-GOTH
http://jessicascrime.cjb.net
deadgoddreaming@hotmail.com
Easy-going site. Trim bios, nice gallery archive.

JESUS FIX
www.jesusfix.co.uk
Nice basic UK Goth/Indie site. Shite bio, good news, decent photos.

JOY DIVISION
www.csclub.uwaterloo.ca/u/sfwhite/joyd.html
I'm not listing loads of links, because you can access most through this. Often you can find good eighties-related links as well.

JUDITH
www.asthetik.com/amphion
judith@asthetik.com
Just put up, but all the requisite sections are there for this class band.

JU-JU BABIES – ELECPOP
www.electricdreamsclub.com
stix@jujubabies.co.uk

JUTE
www.juteband.com

KAFTSMALL
http://drive.to/da_boys
Sweden's Horror Punk band. Not updated recently. Hardly scary pictures.

KALI YUGA
www.kaliyuga.org
http://artists.mp3s.com/artists/86/kali_yuga.html

swampwizard@kaliyuga.org
Baton Rouge Goth band, and I quote: 'The band's music evokes images of dead ex-girlfriends, the decaying relics of humanity and heathen idols commingled beneath the anoxic mud of the swamp.' As it should be...

KATATONIA – DARK METAL
www.katatonia.com

KATSCAN
www.katscan.co.uk
theband@katscan.co.uk
Ah, those Goth Gangstas. Putra-Chic behind them, they have a good site. It's the zippy tone to the writing that helps, and a sweet layout. Lyrics, reviews, great gallery, wallpapers.

KEN-ICHI
www.ken-ichi.uni.cc
Japanese chap with a great little site with big diary (all in Japanese) and cool photos. Great gurly Goth-Punk look, and the giveaway? In the links he checks Hanoi Rocks... so be careful!

KHASM – GOTH/DEATH/DOOM
http://browser.to/khasm
twgprod@aol.com
More Cradle/Moonspell than anything. Totally hideous.

KIEW – DADESQUE INDUSTRIAL!
www.kiew.org

KILHI ICE
www.kilhiice.cjb.net or www.kilhiice.de
label@codemusic-eu.com
Dark electronics with panache and guitar power. Japanese duo Tara Chan and Uni, with English version, lots of info, and great galleries.

KILL SWITCH KLICK
www.iregular.com/kskpages.html
Immaculately detailed site for Industrial greats.

KILLAROO – DARK METAL
www.killaroo.com

KILLING MIRANDA
http://killingmiranda.pair.com/main.html
km@killingmiranda.com
A site as cool as the band, and looking better than most. Modern Goth, going up a notch.

Katscan – Maxi + Martin. Photo by Caroline Bird. photoshop by Mr Diablo

KINDRED SPIRITS
http://hem.passagen.se/lurid/KS/kindred.htm
kindred.spirits@telia.com
Swedish Goth site with a bizarre sense of fun. Odd layout, not much news or details.

KISS THE BLADE
www.kisstheblade.net
kisstheblade@kisstheblade.net
Precocious Goth band with site both impressive and functional. News is updated monthly, and the gallery is tiny, but there's a superb archive, where you find more pics, discog, interviews and history.

KISSANDRA GAIA'ROIS
www.angelfire.com/va/realvamps
Interesting individual, offering acoustic Goth, with all the instruments played by her. Daughter of an opera singer, so no timid squeak.

KITTENS FOR CHRISTIAN – INFO
www.dirtbox.com/home/index.htm

KITTIE
www.kittie.net
'Kickass Metal', but undeniably cute.

KLEEN
www.kleen-la.com

KLIRRFAKTOR – EBM-IND
www.klirrfaktor.de

KMFDM
www.kmfdm.net

KNORKATOR
www.knorkator.de

KOMMUNITY FK
www.deathrock.com/kommunityfk
kommunityfk@hotmail.com
Not really a great site for such an inspiring band but I daresay it will develop. Has good info, pics and flyer archive. A band worth taking very seriously, because Patrick Mata has what it takes.

KOMU VNYZ
www.komuvnyz.gothic.com.ua
fedunvitaliy@hotmail.com
More Ukrainian Goth, in English.

JOHN KOVIAK
www.angelfire.com/la/koviak

KOYLE – Acoustic
www.fly.to/koyle

KQDELIRIUM – Darkwave
http://artists.mp3s.com/info/235/kqdelirium.html

KRATARKNATHRAK – Goth-ish Elec
www.angelfire.com/electronic/kratarknathrak
newdarknessrec@lycos.com

LIV KRISTINE
www.livkristine.de

Liv's commercial side, moving away from Theatre Of Tragedy and being a little demure minxy thing doing Ethereal Goth pop. Nice detail, good live pics and slutty promos.

KRUMMEN MAUERN
www.geocities.com/sunsetstrip/underground/8452
Brazilian Goth archive.

KRUSAFIX
www.krusafix.com

KUBIK – DarkPop
http://listen.to/kubik
kubik03@ibm.net
Dark Indonesian pop. They look cool, and there's good info.

KUROYURI-SHIMAI
www5.airnet.ne.jp/lisnoir
Recommended as a Japanese deadcandance.

L'AME IMMORTELLE
www.lameimmortelle.com/entry-s.asp
info@lameimmortelle.com
Classic Electro-Goth, in a stylish site. Excellent bio, full news, lyrics, tour reports, live pics. Fansites:
http://lai.LifeEndsDark.com
www.tears-in-the-rain.de
www.voiceless.de

LA CAPA NOSTRA – Mexico
www.geocities.com/SunsetStrip/Venue/3363/capa.html

LA FLOA MALDITA
http://home.t-online.de/home/audion-x/lafloa.htm

LA MORTE
http://members.dencity.com/lamorte

LA SOLITUDE – ARCHIVE
http://home4.swipnet.se/~w-44991/lasolitude

LA'MULE
www.lamule.com

LACRIMAS PROFUNDERE
www.lacrimas.de
mail@lacrimas.de
Doom-Metal-Goth done in a brilliant, interesting and friendly way. They write about themselves in such a way that you know they love what they're doing and

haven't got some portentous sense of egomaniacal importance.

LACRIMOSA

www.lacrimosa.com

In truth there isn't much here beyond a discography and glorious photographs, tied in with releases rather than any chronological gallery. Well worth a look, but also try the label site at: www.hall-of-sermon.de to glean more info. Fansites:
www.ontika.net/gizmo/lacrimosa (ends '99)
www.unlacrimosa.jan.notrix.de
www.dator.com.mx/lacrimosa
www.stolzesherz.de
www.tiwoli.de

LACUNA COIL

http://rml.com.lb/4lacuna.htm

LADY MORPHIA

http://ladymorphia.tripod.com
LMorphia@aol.com

LAND

www.landsite.net
Beautiful site for French moodsters.

LAND OF THE LUNATIC CANDY CREEP

www.geocities.com/SunsetStrip/Stage/5970/index.html

LANTERNA

http://web.lanterna.tv
h-frayne@uiuc.edu
Solo project of Henry Frayne (Moon Seven Times).

THE LAST DAYS

www.thelastdays.co.uk
tld@thelastdays.co.uk
Pretty empty at the moment, but *very* pretty.

LAST LAMENT

www.last-lament.com
info@last-lament.com
Cool band, attractive site. Impressive photos.

LE AME D'ORPHEE

http://spazioweb.inwind.it/lesangdorphee
lesangdorphee@katamail.com
Italian band with a penchant for eighties Goth influences, have a smart tiny site available in Spanish, Italian, English, French and German, which must be a record.

LEGENDARY PINK DOTS

www.brainwashed.com/lpd

Unbelievable archive from LPD. All the current activities are covered, but it's the body of evidence that is compelling as everything appears to have been thought of, including ex-members' projects. Also:
http://bermudes.univ-bpclermont.fr/~wildwest/lpd/index.html

LEIAHDORUS – ETHEREAL

http://artists.mp3s.com/info/147/leiahdorus.html

LEICHENWETTER

www.leichenwetter.de

LEISURE HIVE

www.geocities.com/leisurehive
leisurehive@hotmail.com
Goth explorers with mystifying site. Fair news, live and release details.

LEITMOTIV

http://members.xoom.it/leitmotiv
lieunoir@hotmail.com
Solo moody Goth man. Proper news updates, but no bio, just sweet pics of him and his daughter.

LELIO RISING – GOTH POP

http://artists.mp3s.com/info/235/lelio_rising.html

LENORE

www.lenore.ws
Individual biogs, thoughts, nice galleries, release details and one of my favourite opening messages: 'Thanks to all who came out to the Blind Pig on May 11 to see Lenore (except for Jamie, you stupid fuck)!' Alternatively you can go to www.thepurplegang.com, which also appears to be the homepage of TPG records.

LES JOYAUX DE LA PRINCESSE

http://drugie.here.ru/ljdlp

LESTAT – ARCHIVE

http://members.aol.com/srrandolph

LETZTE-INSTANZ

www.letzte-instanz.de/flash.htm
fanclub@letzte-instanz.de

LIBER-PARVUS-PICTURAE

www.liber-parvus-picturae.de

LIBITINA

www.libitina.demon.co.uk
libitina@libitina.demon.co.uk
All the info and music is included, with excellent pics, but personalised info would give it heart.

LIGA – INDIE/DARKWAVE

www.ii.uib.no/~olev/liga

THE LIGHT BEYOND – SYNTHY POP

www.geocities.com/SunsetStrip/Disco/6078
rozkh6aj@mail.prf.cuni.cz

LINIENTREU

www.linientreu.net
Very posh, dark corporate Pop.

LISA GERRARD

www.lisagerrard.com
Great site with all the info, historical textures, sound and images your heart could desire.

LITURGY OF DECAY – GOTH-METAL

www.multimania.com/liturgyofdecay

Killing Miranda

bass@runbox.com

Interesting site, in French. Don't think Rock God type of Metal, we're into atmospheric territory. I know it's a stupid thing to say but the blokes do look *very* French. Informative site with historical detail and various updated live photos.

LIVEBOY DEADGIRL
www.liveboydeadgirl.org

LOCURA – HEAVY DARK POP
http://artists.mp3s.com/info/225/locura.html

LONDON AFTER MIDNIGHT
www.londonaftermidnight.com
info@londonaftermidnight.com

As awesome as you would expect, with one of the best news sections you will find anywhere, a ton of historical data, superb photos and the usual forum/fan stuff. You can't be unhappy about this, although I'd like to see a tour diary/journal type thing because they've always had a nice personal touch about them. If you haven't encountered their music before then visit this site before any others. Fan Pages:
http://clubs.yahoo.com/clubs/londonafter midnight
http://members.tripod.com/WolfSmoke/ londonaftermidnight.html
http://nav.webring.yahoo.com/hub?ring= londonaftmid&list
www.come.to/londonaftermidnight (Japanese site)
www.datasync.com/~aladdin/lam.htm
www.geocities.com/beautyandpassion/main1.html
www.geocities.com/midnightconfessions1
www.violentacts.cjb.net

LORD HYPNOS
www.geocities.co.jp/Hollywood-Stage/5010/ index2.html

LORD OF ACID
www.geocities.co.jp/MusicStar-Piano/5050/ index.html

Praga Khan's theatrical Dark-Techno-Rock band. Big site which seems to have gone quiet, manic photos, great interview archive ('In Japan there was this guy who offered me a lot of money to have sex with his dog'), news, tour details and guestbook.

LORIEN
www.darkpassions.com

Poland's Dark Rock masters. Very good Polish fan site at: www.lorien.warka.pl.

LOST BELIEF – ARCHIVE
www.lostbelief.de/sathom/lostbelief.html
Looks very dramatic. Excellent galleries.

LOST FAITH – GOTH-METAL
www.lostfaith.co.uk
lostfaith@hotmail.com
Metal Goth in the UK, but a nice site with plenty of pics to entertain.

LOST GOAT – SATAN'S LITTLE HELPERS
www.lostgoat.com
lostgoat@hotmail.com

LOST SIGNAL – IND-ELEC
www.lostsignal.com

LOTUS
www.lotusband.com

LOVE & ROCKETS
http://loungebunny.net/lnr – brilliant!
Also try:
www.geocities.com/SunsetStrip/Booth/6088/ enter.html
www.wwnet.net/~paisli/l&R.html
www.angelfire.com/on/darknymph/page5.html

LOVE IS COLDER THAN DEATH
www.lictd.com
What a poxy site! Looks delightful, obviously, but it's info on seven albums and nothing else at all! Label info pages:
www.metropolis-records.com/?artists/ loveisco.html

LOVE LIKE BLOOD
www.love-like-blood.com/index1.html
mailbox@love-like-blood.com
Mega-organised site from classic band. News is okay, bio rather slim, but there is a huge historical back-up in chronological order of personnel info and galleries, promo and live.

LOVE SPIRALS DOWNWARDS
www.lovespirals.com
Arty, in a nice way but essentially empty. Fair news, little detail.

LOVELESS LOVE
www5.plala.or.jp/lovelesslove/title.html
kame_kame75@goecities.co.jp

LOVELIESCRUSHING – POOR ARCHIVE
http://sciborg.uwaterloo.ca/~jjvenkit/llc/llc.html

LOW SUNDAY
www.lowsunday.com
Dark Pop-Rock, signed to Projekt. Also:
http://lo.pc.ri.cmu.edu/tamara/lowsunday.

LUCID DEMENTIA
www.luciddementia.com
amazingdiva@chickmail.com
Dark Electro gone bonkers. Hilarious live gallery.

LUCIFER – THE FRONT DOOR
http://akasaka.cool.ne.jp/worldend1/ contents-e.html
It's in English, so the story emerges of a woman impressed by New Wave, by London and New York, Positive Punk and then Goth, and here she is, all scintillating. You can even join their Fan Club. It is a bit hard to follow because she has used some translation software. As an example, when making it clear that images are not be copied unlawfully it says, 'An image on this web site and the transcription without notice of text are refused hard.' So, you get the idea. Apparently she did 'In A Flat Field' for a Bauhaus tribute, which completely slipped by me.

LUCYBELL
www.lucybell.cl
info@lucybell.cl

LUCYFIRE
www.lucyfire.com
Very accomplished site for Rock-Goth Johan Edlund of Tiamat. 'Gobsmacking Gothic Rock' according to them.

LUFTWAFFE – ELEC
www.killkorps.com

LUPERCALIA
www.lupercalia.it
claudia@lupercalia.it
Looks like a quality historical-flavoured Italian Goth band to watch out for. Stunning photos.

LUX INCERTA
http://mapage.noos.fr/luxincerta
agonederochronde@yahoo.fr
Atmospheric Goth featuring Anhydre and Agone, ex-Synoptia.

LUX SOLEMNIS – INFO 1998
http://members.aol.com/agentuno/death/ LuxSolemnis.htm

London After Midnight. Photo © Stéphane Burlot

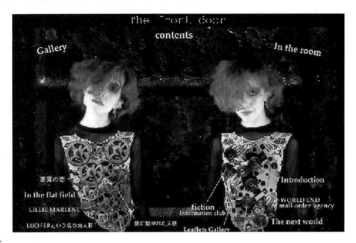

Lucifer

Malice Mizer

LYCIA – ARCHIVE
www.lyciummusic.com
info@lyciummusic.com
A good archive it is too, despite lacking many photos, with all info in place, and links to all their current offshoot projects. Trusty, cool fan site and list: http://lycia.darkspire.net.

LYRIC
www.lyric.net
lyric@lyric.net
Annoying site from Electro-Ind French band who sing mainly in English. Obviously, they can try and be as stern and explosive as they want, but one of them is called Cyril.

M-LUH – AMBIENT DANCE IND
www.thineeyes.com

MACABRE – GLOOM ARCHIVE
www.adrenalin.dynamite.com.au/macabre

MACHINE GUN KELLY
www.machinegunkelly.com
mgk357@machinegunkelly.com

MACHINES OF LOVING GRACE
www.geocities.com/corven.zain
mlginfo@emerald.net
Not as ugly as your average hard Ind-ustrial Joes, and a touch more humanistic in their approach to this busy site.

MAD PSYCHO BABYS – JAPAN
http://page.freett.com/madcats/index.htm

MADDER MORTEM
www.maddermortem.com

mail@maddermortem.com
Norwegian Goth-Metal with lively site.

MADRE
www.madre.de
contact@madre.de
Top quality Goth, back and bubbly (formerly Madre del Vizio) after a break. Fair site.

MAGENTA
www.katode.org/magenta
Anders (Apoptygma Berzerk) and Vilde doing dark pop and looking a bit Army Of Lovers.

MAGICKA – GOTH-IND
www.magicka.net
magicka@magicka.net

MAINFORM – ELEC-IND
www.mainform.de
mainform@technologist.com

MAJICKA
www.magicka.net
magicka@magicka.net
Detail-ridden site from Norwegian Dark Electro-Rock band with clear Gothic empathy. Fine news and bio, good reviews, and there's live info, but miniscule 'gallery'! Access it through 'Contact'.

MALAISE
www.malaise.net
malaise@malaise.net
Goth-electrics, with a smart site that sometimes manages to baffle. Good bio/news.

MALDOROR
www.geocities.com/Broadway/Balcony/2661
maldoror.dark@mailcity.com
Good site from Mexican Goths, but not in English. Nice pics.

MALICE MIZER
www.malice-mizer.co.jp/top.html
This appears to be official so it's pretty amazing it doesn't have an English version, considering how this band could appeal worldwide. There is a lot of info, in Japanese. One point: they often give you a band members birth date (not year) on Japanese sites, plus their blood type. What's that all about? I also couldn't find a gallery anywhere, which is criminal. One of the best looking bands music has ever known *must* have a prodigious gallery buried here somewhere – or maybe they're being capitalist pigs, by depriving people on account of them having photo-books and magazines available? Fan sites:
www.geocities.com/SoHo/Studios/3507
http://members.home.net/malice-mizer

MALOCHIA
www.malochia.com
malochia@chello.nl
Dutch Goth-Ind-Elec with verve and style. Fine galleries and info. Also: http://members.nbci.com/malochia/malochia.htm, which may be older, but starts serving up great pics straight away.

MAN(I)KIN – IND-EBM
www.manikin.force9.uk/signpost.htm
manikin@manikin.force9.co.uk

MANDYLION
www.mandylion-studio.de

MANIFEST VISION – ON HOLD
www.manifestvision.com

MANNEQUIN PORN
http://members.aol.com/princezznoize/
mannequinporn
mannequinporn@yahoo.com
Aunt Jackie from Betty's Trash is here.
You may not get the Goth link if you
like the dreamier side of things, but
there has always been an appreciation
of tacky bluster, and they sure have it.
The site is rubbish, but so cheery.

MANTUS
www.mantus.de
vollmond@mantus.de
Interesting soft Goth atmospherics.
Plenty of plans, lots of detail.

MANUSKRIPT
www.manuskript.co.uk
questions@manuskript.co.uk
Sadly small site for excellent band.
Bio tiny, photos few, info is sparse.

MARA'S TORMENT
www.corpusnet.com/torment
torment@corpusnet.com
www.geocities.com/setlack/mara.html

MARBLE FLOWERS GARDEN
www.geocities.com/marbleflowersgarden
dreamlands@angelfire.com
Brazilian Dark Wave, with English.
'Times are changed. Our olds
prophetize, our children dream.
The dead are talking.' A beautiful,
informative site. Nice gallery too.

MARILYN MANSON
www.marilynmanson.net
www.angelfire.com/il/promqueen13
Bowie tribute band.

MARIONETTES – ANDY'S
www.fortunecity.com/silverstone/healey/405/
marionettes.html
triumphdolomite_uk@hotmail.com
Nice fan attempt with cool front and
antique innards. History stops
mid-nineties – and have you ever seen
such unflattering photos?

MARTYR COLONY – SYNTH-IND
http://home.columbus.rr.com/martyrco

martyrco@hotmail.com
'Holy crap! We're taking our time
updating this thing!' And that was nine
months ago.

MARUTA COMMAND
– ELEC-DEATH-IND
http://listen.to/maruta

MAUDLIN ASH
www.maudlinash.com
info@maudlinash.com
Subtle Dark Rock, formerly Divinity.
Pleasant site, tiny bio, crap pics.

MAUVE SIDESHOW – ARCHIVE
www.sonarchy.org/archives/mauve.html

THE MAYA29 – FUNNY
www.maya29.freeserve.co.uk
maya29@maya29.co.uk

MAZOII – IND
www.mazzoii.com

PEPPER McGOWAN
www.peppermcgowan.com/cgi-bin/intro.cgi

MDFMK
www.mdfmk.net
Very dramatic and bold from Elec-Ind
barnstormers. Glowering screens
and pot-luck section was fun, and
everything is there, in a spirited fashion
despite being supposedly steeped in
Techno-gloom. Also:
www.geocities.co.jp/HeartLand-Suzuran/9162/
picture.htm

MECHANICAL CABARET
www.mechanicalcabaret.com
roi@mechanicalcabaret.com
Brilliantly playful site from the ditsy
Roi. The curtains swish back and forth
every time you click one of the little
knobs at the bottom of the page. Roi
knows his place. 'Onstage I handle the
singing and mincing about' while
pretending to help the spikier Tobi, who
creates the meat of their supercharged
pop-Industrial-Electro, or whatever they
call it this week.

MEDIAEVAL BAEBES
www.mediaevalbaebes.com/index2.htm
Excellent news because it even involves
history. Good bios, but they don't really
tell you much about the band and their
ideas, so enjoy the galleries, then

mooch away. Also:
http://eden.vmg.co.uk/baebes
www.mediaevalbaebes.co.uk/biography.htm

MELODROM
www.melodrom.de

THE MEMPHIS MORTICIANS
www.memphismorticians.com
ThanatoidGliscoene@MemphisMorticians.com
Horror Rock or Gothabilly, 'Serving all
your post-living needs since 1813'! Witty
sections: Viewings – upcoming gig news,
Pre-needs counselling – you can write to
them, Eulogy – previous gigs, with flyers,
Bereaved – news of record, Post-mortem
Portraiture – gallery, Business associates
– links, legal – links to actual funereal
organisations and brilliant testimony:
'At first I was horrified when I thought
the Memphis Morticians had lost my
mother's body after taking her to their
mortuary just hours before. I was
informed by one of their courteous staff
that her body hadn't been "misplaced", it
was actually "hidden" from me as part of
their new-fangled grieving system they
had learned while in the big city. These
guys are way ahead of the times!'

MEPHISTO WALTZ
www.mephistowalz.com
walz@pacbell.net
Looks great but has virtually nothing
there.

PAUL MERCER
http://ghosts.8k.com
paul@changelings.com
No relation. You'll normally find him
glowing in The Changelings. Ghosts is
a Neo-classical Ethereal solo project.

THE MERCY CAGE
www.melodyfallen.cjb.net
http://homepages.ihug.co.nz/~mkwood
mercycage@hotmail.com
New Zealand's premier Darkwave act,
a duo who have produced a detailed site
of news, lyrics, and info, but there's
also weird musings, as well as equally
interesting bits about their more
acoustic project called Melody Fallen
(claimed influences include The
Headless Chickens, a wild band Ostia
once turned me onto).

THE MERCY CHURCH
www.ultrachamber.com

mercychurch@iprimus.com.au
Funny site for the perky Techno boy, in
that he hasn't much to offer in the way
of putting his band in context, but then
has a huge section on some film him
and some mates were extras in, and a
big link to Asylum 7 clothes.

MERGATROID
http://mergatroid.cjb.net

MERLONS – ARCHIVE
www.venue.de/merlonslichter.de
andreas@merlons.de
Goth character. Info is all there, despite
haphazard layout.

MESH
www.mesh.co.uk
www.mesh-fg.de
trustyou@mesh.co.uk
Excellent Electro-prod site. Fan:
http://newrose.com/mesh
www.devision.de/mesh, www.mesh.dk

THE MESSENGERS
http://xy.faithweb.com
KamelaLise@aol.com
We are the puny insects according to
this Ind duo with wild hair. They are
the mighty spider. To prove a point a
spider and insect wander about the
page. The spider looks unwieldy and
dull, while the insect is scooting about
all over the place, so *we* are superior in
every way! Be alert – they claim to be
part of a larger collective called the
Apox Matrix, and there is a link which
is meant to take you to the Apocalypse
Theatre, but doesn't. What can it all
mean?

MESSY
http://artists.mp3s.com/artists/103/messy
_.html
www.angelfire.com/ri/flowerpot/index.html
jocelyn@elekktra.net
Kevin Haskins of Bauhaus, Doug de
Angelis of Peter Murphy's band, and
Jessika of Jack Off Jill, who don't seem
to be doing anything any more.

METHEDREAME – ARCHIVE
www.users.globalnet.co.uk/~meth
methedreame@meth.globalnet.co.uk
This seems unusual, being a mixture of
band site and other literary/poetical
projects, but all the news is hideously
old. Archive pics.

METUS MORTUUS – DARK AMB
www.stud.ntnu.no/~johnnyso/Metus.html

MIASMA
www.miasma-online.com
English version available. Decent bio,
plus good galleries.

MIDNIGHT MASQUERADE
www.beseech.net/projects/midmas

MIKAELA
www.bway.net/~mikaela
The seriously interesting Mikaela, who
does Murder Ballads, songs of lost loves
and hope eternal, often as solo gigs on
autoharp, before startled delinquents in
grim venues. She's also in the band
Curse. This page details gigs, and links
to www.lampos.com/mikaela.html, an
info page only with a download, and
you might find details of her 'Spiderlily'
project and EP, which is pure class.

Mikaela

MILITIA CHRISTI
www.decadancerecords.it/militiachristi

MINDSCAPE
http://home.t-online.de/home/buckrogers
BuckRogers@t-online.de

MINDSHAFT
www.mindshaftrock.com
don@mindshaftrock.com
Goth-Prog is a frightening notion, but
these seem sensible. Chaotic site.

MISSIONARIES FROM OUTSIDE
http://missionaries.nm.ru
dodheim@comset.net
Russian Goth band with endearing
history and great pics.

MIRA
www.mira.nu
mira@mira.nu
Typical Projekt signing in one sense,
although dark pop more than the tautly
stretched ambience gang.

MIRANDA SEX GARDEN
www.geocities.com/SunsetStrip/Street/6392/
miranda.html
everburning@yahoo.co.uk
Nice 'official fan' site, with seven paths
to choose, which go through past and
present. Being in direct consort with
the band means there are some
excellent photos. Archive article at:
www.mute.com/mute/msg/msg.htm

MIRIAM
www.decadancerecords.it/miriam
miriam@decadancerecords.it
Excellent Italian Darkwavesters site,
although small. Properly updated news,
with lyrics, bio, two mysterious pics,
downloads, blah.

THE MIRRORMEN
www.mirrormen.de
info@mirrormen.de

MISANTHROPE
http://misanthrope.darkriver.net
I thought it was a scene from Monty
Python when I first saw their band
photo. Tech-Metal to have you worrying.

MISERY
www.geocities.com/love_and_misery
alain.ter.schuur@hetnet.nl
Goth-Ind-Elec from Holland. Site looks
cool but lacks depth.

MISFITS
www3.alpha-net.ne.jp/users/vivi/Misfits.html

MISNOMER
www.misnomer.co.uk
ElectroPunk with dark twists.

THE MISSION
www.themissionuk.com
wayne@themissionuk.com
Not only packed with news and

current info, but done in a smooth and interesting manner. Add to that a mass of past glories, done again with great style, and it's a hell of a site. I expected something a bit grubbier somehow, but it's seriously swish. Also:
http://hem.passagen.se/joes4803/mish.html
www.cenedra.com/mission.htm
www.psychotica.net/evb/mish

MISTLE THRUSH
www.mistlethrush.com
band@mistlethrush.com
A very cute site. Loads here but everything still seems spacious, which is fitting as the space-rock element is there.

MISTLETOE
www.music.ne.jp/~mistletoe/frames.htm
mistletoe@music.ne.jp

MISTRESS OF JERSEY
http://users.skynet.be/mistressofjersey
Belgian Sisters tribute band. Maybe they're all in their mid-forties, essentially unpopular and miserable too?

MISTRESS X – GOTH-IND ARCHIVE
www.mistressx.net
info@mistressx.net

MISTS OF AVALON
www.mist-of-avalon.com
mist.of.avalon@swipnet.se
News and fan stuff, great pics, decent press supply, with interviews and reviews, but no bio. Fan:
http://hem.passagen.se/themistofavalon and www.fortunecity.com/campus/physics/152/mist.html.

MODUS OPERANDI – DARK INDIE
http://artists.mp3s.com/info/177/modus_operandi_ii.html

MOEV
www.musicmaniac.de/moev
mail@musicmaniac.de
This is nice. There's not a lot there, for a synthy band with a long stop-start past, and I'm sure he'd welcome some contributions from other Moev fans, but it's got the right spirit somehow. He's even excited by the fact they've got three reviews up! The history is there, with a cute little interview and discog.

Mists of Avalon

MONSTER IN YOUR CLOSET
www.geocities.com/monsterinyourcloset
mail@monsterinyourcloset.com
Angry young things, furious at mp3.com and rightly so. The bastards! (He said, knowing nothing about it.) And you don't need to pay for an enema, just check out the gallery. Goth Ind types you don't want to get close to. Their photographer must have been acclimatised in warzones.

MOONDUST – GOTH-METAL
www.moondustpage.de
christoph@moondustpage.de
New band, smart site, nice pics.

MOON FAR AWAY
www.gothic.ru/mfa
results_ark@hotmail.com
Medieval-inspired spiritual Goth from Russia, with English version. Nice detail, but curious approach to gallery. A picture of an old rowing boat?

MOON FOUNDATION – AMB-IND-ELEC
www.moonfoundation.co.uk

MOON LAY HIDDEN BENEATH A CLOUD – ARCHIVE INFO
http://drugie.here.ru/achtung/moonengl.htm

MOONCHILD
www.moonchild.purespace.de

susandiavollo@yahoo.de
Innovative female Poppypower-Goth, they claim. (Two of them are male!) They also applaud their debut album as being 'the best Moonchild album, ever!' much info on the site, it has to be said. Nice photos.

MOONSPELL
www.moonspell.com
moonspell@moonspell.com
If only *all* big bands could do this. A totally thrilling site. Right from the start where there are some strange musings from each member clickable on the band pic, to the detailed biog... even the discog seems enthralling. News is updated and well written. 'Net Releases' allows anyone, including the band, to spout off. There's a lovely tour diary of the US trip. 'Walk Of Infamy' is a brilliant idea, introducing or explaining the influence certain writers have had upon the lyrics. In 'Left Hand Path' they sometimes share recordings of bands they they've met on the road, which is cool. On top of that there's the usual board, list, lyrics, and audio/video, naturally, but great, great galleries. The only crap element is the 'Virtual Interviews' idea, which evidently ended in '98. I suppose the main impression you get is the band are *genuinely* interested in their site rather

than regarding it as a natural must-have promotional tool. Fansites:
http://sinpage.boom.ru
http://student.dei.uc.pt/%7Egomes/moonspell/indexo.htm
www.geocities.com/SunsetStrip/5701/moon.htm
www.geocities.com/SunsetStrip/Alley/8499
www.moonspell.art.pl

THE MOORS – Pagan Trance
http://drawbridge.com/music/moors

MORBID POETRY
www.morbidpoetry.de
morbidpoetry@morbidpoetry.de
An elegantly dour site, from class band, and I loved it. Sebastien's long history is charm personified, as we feel his pain over the endless disruptions, but maybe *don't* share his enthusiasm for doing Aerosmith covers in his spare time. It's a totally up-to-date site, teeming with life and the whole site is invested with character so even the galleries, which aren't actually much good, suddenly take on extra resonance. Weird.

MORBUS KITAHARA
www.morbuskitahara.de
mail@morbuskitahara.de

MORE
http://utenti.tripod.it/More_band/mainen.htm
more@getnet.it
Ah, it's Gianmarco Bellumori from Blooding Mask, who were an interesting Goth band in Italy. Still operating in emotionally moody areas but boring site, unfortunately. Bio, three pics, two dates, e-mail.

MORENDOES
www.gothamnights.com/morendoes
jesteins@hotmail.com
Puny history from cool Norwegian Goths, but there's okay info/news generally and some good pics.

MORFIOUZ
www.morfiouz.com
morfiouz@hotmail.com
Goth-Techno-Ind. Plain site, as solo projects often are, with a touch of bio, release details. Nice 'free music/fight hunger' campaign details.

MORGANA'S KISS – Goth Metal
www.morganaskiss.com

morganaskiss@hotmail.com
Beautifully artistic little site. Nice pics, personalised feel.

MORGION
www.morgion.com

MORPHINE ANGEL – Archive
www.angelfire.com/tx/morphineangel/mainmenu.html

REGEANA MORRIS
http://artists.mp3s.com/info/210/regeana_morris.html
regeana@mindspring.com
Regeana (The Changelings), in solo project mixing Jazz with Ethereal.

MORS EX MACHINA
www.mors-ex-machina.de
morsexmachina@lostbelief.de
Nice creepy site but no idea what they're like. Seems Goth-Electronic, and lively. Plenty of info, but only a few pics, which is a shame because there's something unusual about this pair. Their album is about Charlotte Corday, the woman who killed Marat.

MORS SYPHILITICA
www.morssyphilitica.com
info@morssyphilitica.com
Beautiful site, to look at, with things to intrigue, but not too much detail which is irritating because these are interesting people. The music speaks for itself is one argument for such enigmatic handling of their work, but I want facts and revelations, dammit. Wonderful pics. Now signed to Projekt, so you'll probably find more details there, news-wise.
Mors Syphilitica/Requiem In White – unofficial:
http://dark.gothic.ru/primrose
http://members.tripod.com/~Maudelyn/mors.htm
http://djfurie.tripod.com/mors/index.html
(Above includes Order Of The NCs).

MORTHERN VLADE ART – Deathrock
http://perso.worldonline.fr/morthemvladeart
morthemvladeart@worldonline.fr
Highly artistic site for Deathrock-tinged atmospheric compositions by duo. One is an artist, so the gallery takes on a different meaning, plus there are oblique newsy references, and a decent bio. Label info:
http://pandy.nexen.net/morthem.php3

MOTHBURNER
www.geocities.com/mothburner
mothburner@yahoo.co.uk
'Gothic Darkwave Blues from Cornwall' they say, and they could be right. I worry about this site. It's a poor reflection, and yet accurate. They're a great band, so it would be nice to find something that emphasises that. On the other hand, they'd don't really give a toss, so the scruffiness fits. There's a tiny bio on each, a mission statement, and details on their releases, a children's hospice project, and their personal witchy beliefs.

Although the UK scene is now so small after such a decade of declining impact that no-one, internationally, pays it any great heed, we do still have great bands. The smallest and most unusual of these *is* Mothburner, a couple of wry witches based in quietest Cornwall, manipulated by their shrewd dog, the svenagli, Bark. What is different about Mothburner is that while Shirin and Finn (otherwise known as Nothing) may entertain realistic dreams of making music without it being the financial struggle they current endure, they have no interest in making it big. Even making it medium might prove too much. They make the music because they have to, and here is a duo who gleefully hurl out Leadbelly, Dogs D'Amour or Massive Attack as prime paramours of the ear. Mothburner make quite startling music on a shoe-string, present it as beautifully as they can, and somehow it sounds like time-less Goth, but superbly modern Spartan music. This isn't the only reason they get the coverage they do in this book. They have no malice towards other bands, they are way off to one side and know nothing of in-fighting. They have humour, grace and ideas. They're what it's all about. The songs have totally artistry, and they exude sweet bemuse-ment. Anyone who likes emotionally vivid fare, with strong, unpredictable guitar will find them very interesting. Let us talk to this pair of bastards!

Have you ever received similar inspiration/satisfaction from other scenes/interests than with Goth?

Shirin: 'Mainly the things that can also be tied in with the Goth thing, such as Pre-Raphaelite art, wild landscapes, myths and legends, ruins, sacred sites, the sea, and witchcraft (nature based, soothing, healing, and a way to focus all my positivity and weed out unnecessary negativity).'

Having experienced the delights/ frustrations of a band, how did you approach putting Mothburner online? Did you have a plan/concept that differed in any way from what you'd been doing?

FINN: 'Doing a website was basically approached in the same way that we approach everything else: With very little in the way of resources it had to be done as simply as possible. I'd managed to get myself onto a part-time media course, which gave me access to computers and the net, and part of the course was a multimedia unit, so I was able to put the site together in my college time. (I got a distinction by the way!) We don't do the mp3 thing, partly because we don't have access to the software and partly because we don't like them! I strongly believe that low-tech is the way to go, the 'cutting edge' doesn't work half the time, whereas tried and tested stuff will only work better as the hardware gets more powerful. For instance, after investigating 'Streaming Audio' (i.e., internet radio) and finding it to be a major faff, I found out that it was much easier to put background music on a webpage and it sounded better, loaded faster and you don't need any temperamental software plug-ins. So I did that and it works...'

Has it changed the way you've had to structure your life?

FINN: 'Structure?! You're having a laugh!'

What have been the good and bad points that emerged, that you couldn't have anticipated?

SHIRIN: 'We don't get nearly as much post, which I hate! And I get left out of many of the e-mail communications that come through from contacts of ours as they tend to often be ongoing conversations that don't involve me. Good stuff? Well, I like it when we get e-mails from teenagers from across the globe with witchcraft worries, makes me feel useful!'

Mothburner: Shirin and Finn

Women dominate the net in a way that is not evident in other scenes? Why do you think that is? Is that necessarily connected with Goth itself?

FINN: 'I think that women tend to communicate and network more than men do, which is what the Internet does very well. It also allows sub-cultures to grow and involve people in a way that hasn't happened as much previously. For instance, with Punk, very few people got to actually join in, but the net allows people to connect with others with similar interests and build a scene for themselves no matter where they are in the world. I did read something once that called Goth the "first feminised music genre"; I'd say it's definitely less "blokey" than most others. (That's one of the things I like about it!) It does seem that when women get interested in something they want to share it, whereas males like to keep things to themselves.'

The Net has propelled Goth forward, which is a Good Thing. What would you like to see happening next?

FINN: 'Less homepages by confused American Manson fans going on about Satan! They're really not helping anyone...'

A lot of idiots actually dislike the fact I write about Goth, because they'd prefer it remains obscure, evidently not bright enough to realise it's everywhere you turn! Do you think Goth will explode shortly, or has anything, like the Metal impact of Manson helped subdue it?

SHIRIN: 'Being cool and obscure and underground merely translates as meaning that you're always poor, have to live in a damp house which you can't afford to heat in winter, which means that you get ill all the time and only manage to rehearse a handful of times between about November to February. It also means that you can look forward to a life stacking shelves or cleaning toilets, while you spend all your small amounts of free time slogging around trying to persuade people to buy one of your demos. And failing miserably because you can't afford to produce CDs (and failing miserably even if you do get CDs done. Resulting in ever more extreme poverty...). No one wants to be Steps, but there must be a middle ground somewhere. I can't say I'm anticipating a massive Goth explosion to suddenly turn music on its head (although I could be wrong, I often am...), but I do feel that it could spread its feelers out ever wider, thus influencing people by stealth. For me, this would be preferable to an overt surge in Goth trendiness, if only from a longevity point of view, I don't want to be part of a blink-and-you'll-miss-it blaze of publicity – well, not unless I could be right at the head of the very first wave of bands, anyway!'

You don't do the journal thing. Why?

FINN: '"2nd August 2001. Got up late, cos I've got some time off college, felt a bit fed up. Went to library and checked e-mail. Watched *Neighbours*. Shirin went out to see her gran, I stayed home, played me guitar a bit (very loudly!) and dyed my hair. When she came back I took the dog out... SNOOOrrrrrrrrrrr..." That's basically most web journals I've seen! That plus a whole load of existential angst, but that's what the music's for...'

What would you identify as the most important development within Goth over the past couple of years? What is the main thing that has interested you? (I'd imagine it is something, whether on or off the Net, that is also then reflected on it).

SHIRIN: 'Do you know I haven't the faintest idea?! We're very much out of the loop geographically, and as such have quite a tentative role within any kind of "scene". We don't know what's going on half the time, and it doesn't worry us unduly, we just get on with what we're doing, and, much to our surprise, other people seem to be taken with it, too. Many of my tastes are about 800 or so years out of date, so I'm not the best person to ask about present day developments!'
FINN: 'Digital modelling amp simulation and drum machines that can be Doktor Avalanche and a Bodhran at the same time...'

Without going all profound or arty-farty on me, it seems self-evident that you two feel compelled to make music, even though, as with most Goth bands (any other smaller genres) you know there are no real chances of commercial glory. So how does it make you feel, especially if you compare it to a time when you weren't making music. What does it bring to your life?

SHIRIN: 'Music has been such a major force in my life in one shape or form for so long now, that it's hard to remember what I felt like before that, to be honest. I started attempting to write my own songs about 12 years ago, but before that I was almost obsessive about tracking down and digging out new music that would get the juices flowing, and then I did loads of fanzine things, which then led neatly on to me wanting to make music myself. I think that the creative process itself is extremely cathartic and

almost soothing in a way, when a song's finished I tend to feel pretty sapped of energy, but I also get a real sense of satisfaction and completion. When I was younger, I would never have believed that I would ever be able to write songs or sing at all, I was always the kid in the class voted the shyest and quietest, so I like the fact that I've been able to emerge from my shell, even if just a little bit. Also, foolhardy though it might well be, I refuse to give up entirely on the possibility of one day being able to make some kind of living from music, I don't want to be putting out home recorded cassettes forever – it'll just do for the time being.'
FINN: 'I'd been trying to do various haphazard creative things for some time before I finally plucked up the courage to pick up the guitar... I failed my school music exams by trying to invent Ambient Industrial music (although I didn't know to call it that at the time!) on some crappy Casio keyboards when I should have been studying my composers: although even at that point I was using the limited capabilities of school level technology to try and create atmospheres and sounds rather than actual tunes... I wasn't particularly into Rock music at the time, I felt that the future of music definitely belonged to boxes that went beep, and of course I am now outraged to find that I was right! I actually have my ex-boss at my job that I hated (and eventually got fired from for having inappropriate dress sense!) to thank for my first forays into guitar playing; he sold me his old classical acoustic for a tenner, and I was shocked to find I actually picked it up quite quickly! Six months later I managed to save up for a cheap third-hand stratoid and a tin of black paint, and the rest is history... It basically came along at that point in my life that many confused young males reach where most of what I tried to say came out as "Nnnnnyyyyyuuurrrrrrgghhhh!!!!!!" And the ability to transfer that feeling into notes is unbelievably freeing.'

Being witches, what does music bring that witchcraft doesn't? Please be specific if there is an actual answer. Do the two fields have particular satisfactions?

SHIRIN: 'Witchcraft for me is purely and simply a way of life, it doesn't bring

the obvious rewards, emotional or otherwise, that perhaps the music can, but it gives me a sense of my small place in the universe and therefore strengthens my resolve and sense of purpose about almost everything I might do. I had already been forming my own beliefs and ethics long before I realised that Witchcraft matched them almost word for word, I didn't set out to get into Witchcraft, I found my way to it without any kind of plan or pre-formed idea as to what I was looking for – in fact, I wasn't looking for anything at all.'
FINN: 'Music is a very effective way of expressing things without having to work through the clumsiness of language. (Like that sentence!) I think that witch-craft comes from the same place, in that it's about tapping into parts of your self that you wouldn't otherwise have access to, or even think about, and using that to relate to the world around you. I find it very difficult to explain what I believe as far as the whole Pagan thing goes, because to put it into words just sounds too simplistic, it's very much back-to-basics no messing about way of looking at the universe when you strip it right back, and that's what I like about it!'

Some Mothburner tracks always sound very fragile, and some noisier tracks haphazard. Given that you have limitations imposed due to finances, how clear can we the listener be that this is the intended effect/approach?

SHIRIN: 'You can't!! Well, not with the louder songs, anyway. For the most part, we do like the feeling of fragility that often comes across with the gentler tracks, but when it comes to the loud songs our recording limitations rarely give us the sounds we really need to do our ideas justice. We do like a live, spontaneous sound, but we have no way at present of achieving the balance and tone that the louder songs demand, and until we can use an actual studio, there's not a great deal we can do about it...'

This lo-fi ethic, which clearly ensures you can do cassette releases as long as you want, and create whenever the urge hits, brings up one other point. You are way off to one end of the Gawth spectrum. Primarily vocals/guitar makes your sound unusual anyway, but when was the last time you heard someone else and went 'oooh, similar!'

FINN: 'Very rarely! We're more likely to hear stuff that we think we could maybe play alongside, but not necessarily Goth bands. I often hear a guitar tone or a rhythm that inspires me to fiddle with me gadgets, but it might well be on a song or by an artist that I don't particularly like! I think maybe we've only managed to sneak into the Goth thing by accident; if we were blonde and dressed in blue denims I can imagine us being considered as an English equivalent of that whole Alt.Country thing that comes out of Austin, Texas. Those bands are a kind of raw country with a gothic (small 'g') slant and we're doing a similar thing with a more folky tone. Although I don't want to do that whole cliché of "But we're not a Goth band!" I'd say we were more a band with Goths in, which is almost the same, but not quite.'

Leaving the lo-fi thing aside, this whole vocals/guitar approach makes you weirdly primitive. What's that all about, and are you now so primitive you're Ultra-Modern?

SHIRIN: 'I dunno, I just write what comes into my head... Mind you, we did get a letter recently that said as much, so who knows? It's not an especially trendy way of working these days, so we do end up standing somewhat alone, even though that was never our intention initially. Like I say, I'm not much of a planner when it comes to the songs, what usually happens is that I'll suddenly get a burst of creative inspiration at about 3 in the morning, and I'll sit down with the guitar until I've got it all out of my system, then I'll take myself off to bed bleary eyed sometime around 5am...'
FINN: 'Primitive good. Machines bad. We decided that Goth music is a direct-line descendant of proper old blues and traditional Mediaeval music (they mainly used pentatonic scales and didn't approve of major chords), and that does give you a way of working that's very pure and liberating. I think Shirin's always written like that, but it has come through more now since we stopped trying to be a Rock band.'

Bit of bass in the mix this time round (new demo 'All Is Quiet'), did it make you wobble with excitement?

SHIRIN: 'Oohh, it was lovely! Our sleek new addition to the band, "The Tempest", who took over from Shiphrah when she finally rolled over and gave up the ghost on us, comes equipped with this strange setting called "bass", so we thought we'd try it out... We genuinely don't want bass most of the time, we're quite happy with the stripped effect of just the guitar, drums, and vocals, but occasionally songs just scream out for it, and when they do, now they can have it.'
FINN: 'It certainly makes the floor wobble! It's only one note though, so don't get too excited...'

The guitar is getting growlier and lower, the vocals have taken on a distinctive, insistent quality. Are you consciously aware of how you are developing?

SHIRIN: 'Not while it's happening, no. The only aspect I'm more aware of is my voice, I'm always pushing myself as far as I can with it, and I take my self-training pretty seriously, so naturally I can see when I've managed to write a vocal melody that goes beyond what I might have managed in the past.'
FINN: 'I spend a lot of time fiddling around trying to get my little black box to sound like something old and full of hot valves... Before "All Is Quiet" all I had was a distortion pedal, so it was either "Loud" or "Quiet" and I'd just hit the guitar as hard as possible on the loud bits. I'm very aware that I'm the accompaniment rather than the lead instrument and I try hard to be a bit more subtle and compliment Shirin's voice rather than fight for space. Guess I must be maturing or something... Dammit!'

Lyrically it's easy to get a flavour or image, but never the whole story. It's not even like there always is story, just glimpses. Where is the common ground in what's being done?

SHIRIN: 'As with the rest of the song-writing process, the lyrics are, more often than not, spontaneous and relatively unlaboured. Often songs will come together over time, with scraps of

lyrics being jotted down on even scrappier bits of paper, and then meshed together when there's enough to be going on with. This means that at the beginning, there might be no link at all between all the different parts of the lyrics, but somehow, by the time it's finished, they seem to fuse together and make up a whole new picture. It's often a veiled picture, fully open to interpretation by the listener, and it's very likely to mean something different to everyone who hears it, but I like that quality, I don't actually want people to know the minute details of what's going on in my head! Some songs will be more clear-cut than others, but again, if that's what comes out when I pick up the pen, then that's what will eventually become the finished song.'

I've wracked my fevered brain again and I can only think you share similarities with PJ Harvey. If you had to outline how you want to be seen, how is it?

SHIRIN: 'Well, we're certainly happy to be linked, however tenuously, with PJ Harvey, but there are a few other artists that we would hope wouldn't be too appalled at the prospect of being listed alongside us, people such as the aforementioned Mazzy Star and Queen Adreena, and maybe Kristin Hersh and Cat Power. Even perhaps Mark Lanegan and Madrugada. We don't claim to sound exactly like these artists, and nor would we wish to for we see no need for copyists, but we would like to be seen as sharing some kind of common mood or atmosphere with them, albeit expressed uniquely through our own style of writing and playing. We also feel a strong affinity with the recording ideals of the likes of The Blind Boys of Alabama and Kelly Joe Phelps – clearly we sound nothing like them, but their emphasis on stripped, live, raw, and therefore speedy recordings, makes them kindred spirits of ours whether they like the thought or not.'

It wouldn't take much for people to think you're pretty weird. Does this happen a lot when people do buy your stuff? Do you get the impression they are seriously into your stuff, or they find you strangely, almost endearingly, enigmatic?

SHIRIN: 'Cheeky git! No it does not!! The people who buy our stuff would appear to be blessed with an inbuilt sense of taste and an appreciation for the unusual and challenging. And not in a bad way, either, they tend to be disillusioned with the bulk of what's currently available to them, so when they come across our stuff it really hits home. We've noticed that people seem to either really love our songs, or else they hate everything about them, there's not too much of a middle ground, but that's fine by us – I don't set out to be confrontational, but I can accept it if people don't like what I'm doing.'

Throughout the songs on 'All Is Quiet' you repeat an earlier trick of never boring the listener by endlessly repeating passages in a song. In fact some are almost abrupt. Reason?

SHIRIN: 'Because that's just how things pan out sometimes, I know I keep banging on about it, but I genuinely don't plan out a song before I start to write – perhaps I should, but it's not how I do things. When it comes to playing the song with Finn for the first time, we'll go over each section individually and then gradually pull everything together, which is where the final arrangement starts to take shape, so it's at that point that we'll find out just how long (or otherwise) a song will end up being. It's a very natural and unforced process.'
FINN: 'I hate to say it, but it's that Blues thing again: say what you need to say and then stop! Also one of the rules of Punk Rock, I am led to believe...'

I think you have an actual problem with endings. 'My Little Girl Comes Home' sounds wonderful, but the ending is shocking!

SHIRIN: 'MIAOW!!! Ask Finn, final musical details like that are his department... Bear in mind also, though, that our demos are rehearsal demos, we don't often have access to the mini disc recorder, so when something gets taped that's often the only version we'll have to work with, should we wish to do anything with the song later. Apart from anything else, we don't have the luxury of things like foot switches, so we have to wait until the last notes have

died away before either of us can get to the drum machine to turn it off – it's a long way from being an exact science!'
FINN: 'The ending's not that bad! In an ideal world it would probably go on a bit longer and fade out, but that's not being in a studio again. One day I will get a volume pedal and a foot switch for the drum machine, but until then, well at least you can tell it's live!'

That song and 'Banish The Chill' are very modern in outlook, when it would be easy sometimes for people to see you as old-fashioned. Do you yearn for the bigger studio experience to make things harder and starker?

SHIRIN: 'We can't get the sounds we want and need with what we've got at home, and there's no way of balancing

the sound across all the instruments when you've only got a mini disc recorder to work with. We lack even the basics, such as guitar amps, monitoring, proper reverb, and our bizarrely L-shaped room is a nightmare for coping with feedback and for just getting a halfway decent sound. Getting anything usable onto disc is a major undertaking, and we can never get clarity across the board and emphasis where it's needed most, it's always a compromise, no matter what we do. Saying all that, though, even when we do get to use a studio we still want to keep our live sound as much as possible, we'd probably record primarily live and just add tones where (if) needed afterwards, we have no desire to layer and polish everything to death, you lose the heart and soul of a song if you spend too long agonising over every tiny detail. We're not

Pete Murphy. Photo © Stéphane Burlot

machines, and so we can't be flawless all the time, and frankly I get bored by computer perfect music, it just doesn't do it for me.'

There's actually no real evidence of 'witch stuff' in the songs, or none than a non-witchy like myself can pick up on. Any reason for this?

SHIRIN: 'Mainly because we never had any desire to be a Pagan Band – we're just a band who happen to be Pagans. The witchcraft is relevant in as much as it's part of what makes us who we are, but it was never the reason for us to do music and so I see no point in writing about it continually. I have no problem with people knowing about it, but there's so many things I need to get out through the writing that I would never limit myself to just the one topic.'
FINN: 'Actually "Banish the Chill" is our Beltane song – it came out of one of our regular "we need to find an old traditional song about..." conversations, but it's quicker to write your own...'

On your 'Likes' section on your site, you like so much of the same stuff it's eerie!

SHIRIN: 'Spooky, innit?!! Saves on arguments, though...'

And that's Mothburner. Remember the name, explore the shockingly basic site and have a listen to the music. They have something musically others don't, and these days that's rare and important.

MOTHER DEPTH
www.pp.htv.fi/etolvane/md
This never opened for me once despite several visits.

MOTHRA
www1.zzz.or.jp/dgrmgr
Formerly Longdreamdead. Industrial Cold Chaos band from Japan. That's about all I could glean, except that they've played the Bull & Gate!!! Bio, music samples, video film, news, discog or terrible photos.

MOULIN NOIR
www.moulin-noir.com
anders@moulin-noir.com
You have to read the bio, which has a hilarious encounter with Swedish A&R

monster among the factual history of this man's long involvement with New Romanticism and the darker, softer side of emotion. A very interesting site, with psychotic gallery.

MUDVAYNE
www.mudvayne.com
mudvayne@earthlink.net.
Site looked nice but nothing worked.

MULD – MOODY IND
http://artists.mp3s.com/info/176/muld.html

MURDER AT THE REGISTRY
http://134.169.31.96/rs/murder
t.stach@tu-bs.de
Powerful little buggers who here explain why they have that penchant for noise, because Punk and Goth share roots. Nice the way they leave the bios and history and influences short, but it makes for a pleasing whole. I wonder if I should slag Nova Tekk off again, or whichever bunch actually put out the Hex Files CDs? They had Volume 3 all ready to go, without my involvement, then must have checked the contract again and realised it couldn't be released unless I agreed with it. So they ask, I say no, and... it's released before you know it! Okay, and...*relax.* Back to the site review, where we find a ludicrously small gallery overrun by mp3's and there's lyrics, which I never read – bit like Spoken Word albums which I never listen to. (If someone came round your house talking like that, you'd throw them out.) Which means, now the results are in, this is a site which is a pleasure to visit. It doesn't tire you out, and it doesn't answer all your questions. Such as... why is this the *only* site in the world to have the news and links in one shared section?

MURDER OF CROWS
www.murderofcrows.net
jaye@murderofcrows.net
Goth, with emphasis on enchanting Rock. Decent news, bio, good photos.

PETER MURPHY
www.petermurphy.org/index_k.html
hina@petermurphy.org
Good grief – an intro which is actually *interesting*? Who would have thought that was ever possible, but they've achieved it here. The site is stunning throughout, with everything you could

want, except something like personal tour diary? FANSITES:
www.angelfire.com/music2/petermurphy
www.geocities.com/glampixiex/mercyrain.html
www.kiwi-media.com/murphy

MUSLIMGAUZE
www.pretentious.net/Muslimgauze
muslimgauze@Pretentious.Net
This is sad, with the death of Bryn Jones treated beautifully with the tributes from those who knew him best. All related info is included.

MY DYING BRIDE
www.mydyingbride.org
webmaster@mydyingbride.org
An excellent and tidy site for the Goth Metal chaps with good profiles and band history, with a decent gallery – particularly the massive live selection – and release rounds-up, well updated news. Also:
http://republika.pl/mydyingbride
http://sh55k01.jvb.tudelft.nl/html/mydyingb.htm

MYRIADS
http://come.to/myriads
x_Myriads_x@hotmail.com
More Goth than Metal, and looser with the atmosphere, this site is a relaxing place. Big bio is dull, but gallery diverting.

MYSSOURI – DARK ROCK
www.myssouri.com

MYSTERIAN – MOODY GOTH
www.infernalhorde.com/mysterian
mysterian_@hotmail.com

MYSTRAL TIDE
www.mystraltide.com
Ambient and medieval inspired Goth/Darkwave/Industrial solo project based in Japan. Nice site in English, with Japanese and German versions planned. (Also at: http://artists.mp3s.com/artists/141/mystral_tide.html). Bleak imagery really doesn't work on cheery approaches, which leaves the bio/news a touch neutered. Ivan Bullock's solo Darkwave rumblings will impress, and he's planning German and Japanese (being based in Tokyo) versions soon. Imagery isn't his strong point, but there's good detail here.

9XDEAD
www.ninexdead.fsnet.co.uk/welcome.html
ninexdead@yahoo.co.uk

'Alternative Rock'? Site is basic, but it *will* get better.

N.U.T.E. – Dark Elec
http://creassault.tripod.com/nute/index.html
nutenz@usa.net
Nothing Under Total Electronics.
They're Darkwave-friendly, and this
site is info-laden with good news and
excellent photos.

NAAMAH – Goth Metal
http://naamah.rockmetal.art.pl
kalisz@rockmetal.pl

NABAKOV PROJECT – Pop Noir
www.geocities.com/theNabokovProject

NAEVUS
www.naevus.co.uk
naevus@naevus.co.uk
Not madly detailed, but enough.
Very polite.

NAKED MACHINE
www1.ocn.ne.jp/~naked
Japanese Goth'n'roll. mp3s galore.

NAMELESS CULT
www.namelesscult.com/wounds.shtml
staff@namelesscult.com
Wild-looking Japanese Goth Metal band,
or 'self-torturing' as they describe it. A
few weird gig galleries, under 'Scars'.

NAOTO
www.geocities.co.jp/MusicStar-Drum/7562
Typically mystifying Japanese site, with
crazy links.

THE NARCISSUS POOL
www.razorbladebeat.co.uk
cissies@btinternet.com
Bright and brash, from the Electro-Goth
nutters, boasting average news and
general info with smart pics. Bad bios.
Use the 'Trash' section.

NEAR DARK
www.near-dark.de
email@near-dark.de
Big Goth-Rock site, excellent galleries.

NECDUM ERANT ABYSSY
http://perso.wanadoo.fr/enzo.concept/abyssy/
default.htm

NECROFIX – Elec
www.musiclab.net/necrofix
necrofix@mindless.com
Wonderful site, only let down by
excellent pics but no thumbnails.

NECROMANTIK SUNSHINE
www.necromantiksunshine.com
info@necromantiksunshine.com
Precocious Deathrock charmers – simply
called Goth-Electro by others, influenced
by classic early-eighties sounds. Not
much content yet and they daren't show
photos lest we vomit into a bucket.

NECROPOLIS
www.gothic.com.ua/necropolis.htm

THE NECRO TONZ
www.necronom.com/dallasgothics/necro/
default.htm
Scary lounge music of Goth variety,
described somewhere as being music by
dead people, played by people who should
be dead. Or something. The site details
how they were en route to stardom one
night when a tragic accident ensued.
Later, beneath a full moon, they rose
again. 'There are karmic debts to be paid
and music to be made before these souls
are allowed to finally rest in peace.' Oo-er!

NEEDULHEAD
www.needulhed.com
info@needulhed.com
Ind characters with very enjoyable site.
Plenty of news and archive details. The
'Adventures' section takes Bill & Ted
onto another level.

NEGATIVE FORMAT – Trance
http://home.tampabay.rr.com/nf
alex@negativeformat.com

NEKROS – Dark Rock
www.nekros.co.nz
mailto:info@nekros.co.nz

NEKURA – Elec-Exp info
www.nothinginside.net/nekura

NEON ELECTRONICS
http://neon.grmbl.com
Formerly one half of The Neon Judgement, Dirk Da Davo has remodelled this
confusing site, where the irritating design
makes you rage as you learn of the old
boys still doing his stuff. Plenty of info.

NEPTUNE CRUSH
www.neptunecrush.com

Glam meets celestial, which fits. Cool
band, wild site. Unofficial:
http://jove.prohosting.com/~tygrlli/html.

NERO & CRISTALLO
http://afterhours.w3.to

NERV
www.dogma.org/nerv01

NERVOSA
www.nervosa.blis.co.uk
nervosa_the_band@hotmail.com
Fizzy Goth-lite popsters, very quiet on
the news front. Photos aren't bad.

NEUREPUBLIK
www.neurepublik.com
info@neurepublik.com
Synthpop with Dark Wave entrails.
Con-vergence stars, and somewhat
secretive.

NEURMISON
http://neurmison.org

NEUROTIC DOLL
www.interq.or.jp/silver/neu/index01.html
Featuring a member of Madame
Edwarda, one of Japan's most famous
Post-Punk/Goth bands.

THE NEW CREATURES
www.thenewcreatures.com
TNC@TheNewCreatures.com
Truly classy Goth but not a site that
does them justice. News has dried up,
and there is little bio detail, and just
some cool pics, but... just to put all this
into perspective if you read the guestbook one of the band offers a chilling
narrative of his experience of the
September 11 attack, which happened in
front of his eyes.

NEW DAYS DELAY
www.newdaysdelay.de
newdaysdelay@aol.com
Stunning little site in the works.
Beautiful design!!!

NEW MODEL ARMY
www.newmodelarmy.org
wwwsubs@newmodelarmy.org
Huge, *quality* site.

NEW TRIAL
www.newtrial.de
info@newtrial.de

Nightwish

THE NEW YORK ROOM

www.iserv.net/~nyroom
nyroom@iserv.net
Ethereal/Ambient doing Old/New with
female vocals. Where do *all* these women
come from? Does anyone actually know?
How often have you found yourself in
conversation with someone who has
even once said, 'I have quite an interest
in singing this quasi-classical material'?
I've never met one, yet they turn up
everywhere. There are loads of singers
here. Makes for a fascinating bio. Good,
detailed site. Everything is interesting.

NEW FANGLED BLACK

www.geocities.com/newfangledblack
www.livejournal.com/users/gothicfhantasy
newfangledblack@hotmail.com
Formerly Floating Fhantasy. Mad site
where you pop bubbles to reveal the
contents, and they look weird. Demo,
Mistress Rabbit ('inaudible nicotine
vocals'), Spook, Alex G and Charles are
shrouded in mystery. The live journal
belongs to Mistress R who unfortunately

says 'kewl' a lot and regards Manson as a
stunning icon of modern day creation.
Alex G has a terrible site at:
www.angelfire.com/goth/fhantasy.

NEWLYDEADS

www.newlydeads.com
nervous@newlydeads.com
Sinister, sleazy Goth. Nice.

NIGHTWISH

www.nightwish.com/english/tarjabio.html
emppu@nightwish.com
Mega 'Power Metal Goth' from
Finland, whose albums go gold. It's a
magnificent site too, with excellent bio
and profiles, high quality promo and
live pics, plus wallpapers actually worth
considering. Fan sites:
http://members.tripod.de/Zementente
www.followthewishes.com – being revamped.
www.informatik.uni-freiburg.de/~frauenho/nw/
nightwish.html

NIHIL COMMUNICATION

http://artists.mp3s.com/info/93/nihil_

communication.html
Dark Ambient solo artist who greets
you with a photo straight out of
America's Most Wanted. I don't want
you getting all scared, so perhaps it
would be safer to start with the more
anodyne.

NIN

www.nin.com
Got to loathe that loading. Very artsy
fartsy but exclusive downloads are the
plus. And: www.nothingrecords.com Or:
www.nin.net
www.nineinch.com
www.nineinchnails.net
www.nineinchnailsnews.com
www.thefragile.com
www.theninhotline.net
www.theninhotline.net/halo99

NINTH CIRCLE

http://artists.mp3s.com/artists/50/ninth_
circle_us.html
How does a band this good not have a
fine site?

NO COMMENT – Synthpop
www.nocomment.de
mail@nocomment.de

NO PERCEPTION
www.noperception.de

NOCTAMBULANT GRIMNESS
http://go.to/grimness

NOCTURNA – Doom-Metal-Goth
www.geocities.com/SunsetStrip/Pit/3356/index.
html

NOCTURNAL EMISSIONS
www.earthlydelights.co.uk
nigel.ayers@virgin.net

NOCTURNE
www.nocturne.cc
info@nocturne.cc
Dark Industrial, with added flair, and a
cool site, full of current news/info, and
very good lyrics. Bio is rubbish, and the
gallery is small (odd, when they look good
live), plus downloads, board etc. Great
link – check out the Lobster Magnet!

NOIR – Darkwave Elec
www.kurzasoft.it/noir
noir@blu.it

NOISE SHOCK – Ind-Noise
www.prolapse.org/noiseshock

NOISEX
www.ant-zen.com/noisex

NOISE SHOCK – Ind-Noise
www.prolapse.org/noiseshock

NOSFERATU
www.nosferatu.fsworld.co.uk
admin@nosferatu.fsworld.co.uk
Decent site where the poor new boy gets
his profile pushed down the masthead,
but there's bio stuff, a smattering of
pics, news and discog for the diehards.
A touch sterile.

NOT.APPLICABLE
www.notapplicable.org
courtnee@notapplicable.org
Intriguing electronics artist who is
already doing an astonishing amount of

work with others. Site's a bit weird,
because there's little personal info.

NOT BREATHING
www.notbreathing.com
wdave13@qwest.net

NOTHING HUNGER – Dark/Exp
www.mediatrixpublishing.com/nothinghunger
greatdevourer@hotmail.com

NOTHING INSIDE
www.nothinginside.net
nothing@nothinginside.net
New site from the Darkwave darlings,
including their own label so chaos was
reigning when I visited. They appear to
have signed a band called Mice In Tights.

NOTRE DAME – Horror Metal
www.geocities.com/notredamelegions

NOVA – Melancholy Electronics
www.angelfire.com/nv2/nova/index.htm
mailtonova@libero.it
Five Victorian nudes as icons, with the
most eye-wrecking FAQ ever, plus some
sweet pics. It's all very clever.

NOVA-SPES – Synthy-Darkwave
www.novaspes.com
management@nova-spes.de

ALEXANDER NOX & THE HOLY LORE
http://artists.mp3s.com/artists/125/the_holy_
lore.html
theholylore@yahoo.com
Italian Goth with a sense of the
dramatic, but their own site is down,
meaning you may miss the eccentric
bio, little galleries, ex-member info,
news, and human rights section.

NOXIOUS EMOTIONS – Ind-EBM
www.noxious.com

NUIT D'OCTOBRE – archive
www.hugo.ch/groups/ndo

THE NUNS
www.nyrock.com/the_nuns
mistressjennifer_@hotmail.com
Fetish-Goth performers with a sense of
irony and wit. Small site, with no gallery.

NUX VOMICA – Ambient 'Soundart'!
www.auricular.com/nuxvomica
nuxvomica@auricular.com
Terse, sombre stuff, packed with info.

Nocturne

NYMPH FAITHEST – DARK ETHEREAL
www.algonet.se/~nymph

OBERON
www.oberon-online.com
oberon@online.no

OBLIVIA – DARK ELEC
www.oblivia.com
info@oblivia.com
Moody, and attractive, with a fresh site
to match.

DIANA OBSCURA
www.dianaobscura.com
diana@dianaobscura.com
Cool Ethereal Goth cello-led band.

OBSC(Y)RE – DARK POP
www.obscyre.de
Detailed fansite at:
www-user.tu-chemnitz.de/~jea/obscyre.htm

OBSEQUY
www.geocities.com/SunsetStrip/Stage/8314/
home.html
Scarlock@yahoo.com
Scary hairies with keyboards, sampling
and bass. Well stark.

OBSESSIVE DOLLS
www.epsilonrecords.com
obsessivedolls@epsilonrecords.com
Details for them (no official site as yet)
are here, which also includes Ambre
from Synoptia, but was being revamped.

OBSIDIAN VOICE – DARKWAVE
www.obsidianvoice.de

OCASO
www.geocities.com/SunsetStrip/9430
Brazilian Goth archive.

OCTOBER TIDE
http://212.186.198.26/feelmysorrow/october

ODOR OF PEARS
www.odorofpears.com
diana@odorofpears.com
What some might regard as Dark
Electro-Goth band turns out to be 'a
music, multimedia, & performance art
group.' Coo, what? Pretty poor site, all
squashed in, but good info here. Three
galleries at top.

OF ONE MIND – ELEC ARCHIVE
www.angelfire.com/tx/ofonemind

OMEWENNE – ETHEREAL GOTH
http://omewenne.com
Interesting woman with unusual site.

OMNIBOX – EXP
www.omniboxnet.com

ONE FOR JUDE
www.oneforjude.fr.st
oneforjude@netcourrier.com

ONLY FLESH
www.tbns.net/onlyflesh
evolhed@yahoo.com
Very impressive, inventive site.

ONMYO
www1.neweb.ne.jp/wa/onmyo-za
I could be wrong about the name as
this is Japanese only. Whoever this band
are they look *seriously* Goth.

ONYRIA
http://onyria.cjb.net
Onyria@arrakis.es
This is lovely, with a seven-year history
of the band all laid out smartly, in
English, with good pics. They go from
Goth to Coldwave, with a touch of
Metal and are only just working on the
début CD!

OOMPH! – ELEC-METAL
www.oomph.de

OPHELIA
www.geocities.com/bandophelia
bandophelia@yahoo.com

OPEHLIA'S SWEET DEMISE
http://ophelias-demise.indiegroup.com
ophelias_demise@hotmail.com
Only very basic details and okay pics.
Tends to be wobbly.

OPIUM
www.geocities.co.jp/HeartLand-Suzuran/8051
Japanese Goth Yukino's off-shoot from
Zeus Machina, and other work which
goes back to 1985.

ORANGABELLE 5
www.angelfire.com/ny3/orangabellefive/index.html
gothgirl@berk.com
Julie Johnson and Fornever's Joshua
Heinrich. Julie also does the 2 Witches
website in America, and Grave Concerns.

ORBIS PICTUS
www.orbispictus.net
info@orbispictus.net
Pleasantly bright site for Dutch light
Darkwave group. Good lyrics, delightful
links and fine galleries.

ORCHARDS & VINES – DARK POP
http://orchardsandvines.com
contact@orchardsandvines.com

ORDINARY PSYCHO
www.ordinary-psycho.com
info@ordinary-psycho.com
It's a good site, from unexpected
characters with a new approach.

ORDO EQUITUM SOLIS
www.sinope.org/oes

Not Applicable

oes@sinope.org
A mega-site in all departments.

ORDO ROSARIUS EQUILIBRIO
www.erebusodora.com/ore
Sex Goth Magic with some highly
evocative interview segments, and stark
galleries. Rather dry as a site, with an
interesting intellectual edge.

ANJA ORTHODOX
www.anja.pl
closter@pro.onet.pl
Big dramatic site for Anja (of
Closterkeller). In Polish only, but there's
some *wonderful* photos here.

OTHER DAY
www.otherday.de
info@otherday.de
Dead basic, but cool pics.

OTTO'S DAUGHTER
www.ottosdaughter.com
jacqueline@ottosdaughter.com
Ace site from cool Goth-Elec-Ind
experience with lots of content and
some seriously mad photos and art – a
sort of Crouching Tiger, hidden Drag
Artiste. Brilliant journal as well, where
they lay into dozy promoters at crappy
venues the way you know bands want to.

OUR MUSEUM
www.ourmuseum.com
michael@nutopia.com
Ingenious site, and very attractive.

PAIGE
www.theblacklodge.com/paige
paige@theblacklodge.com
Dark Ethereal doesn't quite cut it when
they admit to influences such as Billie
Holiday, PJ Harvey, the Smiths, the Cure,
Pixies, Portishead, Bjork, Cocteau Twins,
Radiohead, David Lynch & Angelo
Badalamenti, and Bauhaus. They're out
there, *gloriously*. The site mysteriously
vanished shortly before I sent this manu-
script off, promising special news soon!

PAIN AND ITS RELIEF
www.disrupted.org/~painair
Unfortunately dark and basic site from
interesting band.

PAIN FETISH – ELEC-IND
www.ensanguine.com/pf
nephilim@painfetish.com

PALE BLISS
http://geocities.com/pale_bliss
Palebliss@hotmail.com
Quite new Goth dirgey, and see the
cheeky mare smoking her cheroot.

PALE CURVE – SYNTH-DARKWAVE
http://artists.mp3s.com/info/15/palecurve.html

PALE RIDER – ARCHIVE
www.palerider.demon.co.uk
Allow me to quote, about a tour with
Marilyn Manson and Hole. 'I refuse to
work with that ludicrous woman and
that over-sexed peacock a second longer.
"Here," he (Alexander Crowe) said,
removing his artificial hand and
throwing it at the double M "have that

Ordo Rosarius Equilibrio

wank you so desperately want and leave
me out of it!" This was followed by one
of those perfectly preserved moments
in time where nobody moves a muscle
and you can hear the proverbial pin
drop.'

PANIC ON THE TITANIC
www.paniconthetitanic.com
info@paniconthetitanic.com
Semi-archive. Quite decent detail.
Interesting pics.

PARA BELLUM – RUSSIAN GOTH
http://come.to/parabellum

PARALYSED AGE – ARCHIVE INFO
www.ferret.com/discs/empire.htm

PARIS BY NIGHT
www.parisbynight.org
parisbynyt@aol.com

PASSAGE – GOTHPOP-COLDWAVE
http://passage.free.fr
passage@free.fr

PASSION PLAY (UK)
www.passionplay.co.uk
pplay@globalnet.co.uk
A nice site but surprisingly small.

PASSION PLAY (USA) – DEAD
www.geocities.com/sunsetstrip/backstage/9460

PATH OF ALLYSON – DARK POP ARCHIVE
http://ogm1.freeyellow.com/poa1.html

PATHIAN
www.pathian.co.uk
contact@pathian.co.uk.
Friendly site of solo Darkwave project,
with nice faq and good news.

PAZMOOT
www.angelfire.com/sc/bleak
pazmoot@hotmail.com

PENIS FLYRAP
http://home.earthlink.net/~pgrella/Flytrap.htm
FlytrapHorror@hotmail.com
Classic Horror band, with Dinah
Cancer at the helm. Plenty to read, and
most of it beautifully written, plus
awesome images.

PENUMBRA
http://underwater.free.fr
penumbra_gr@post.club-internet.fr
underwater@free.fr
A temporary site for the Opera Goth-
Metal band, with more info supposedly
at: http://hidden.ifrance.com. From heady
days practising in '96 with a synth,
soprano and oboe, as is so often the case,
they have evolved into something huge.
Weird story, but nice site. Great pics.

PERDITION – DOOMY
www.perdition.com

ALVAREZ PEREZ – CZECH
www.rest.cz/alvarez
Short and sweet site (English available)
for interesting Dark Rock.

PERFIDIOUS WORDS
www.perfidiouswords.de

infoservice@perfidiouswords.de
Very neat SynthPop but site being
worked on.

PERISH
www.perishonline.com
perish@perishonline.com
Electro Goth from Leeds with cool-
looking site. Very sparse but all the
info you'll need, as well as some nice
personal insights.

PER SOMNIA
www.inconnumedia.com/persomnia
per_somnia@inconnumedia.com
Nice little site with pics in 'Performance'.

BRENDAN PERRY
www.brendan-perry.com
Not fully formed yet, but decent news
and monthly newsletter.

PERSONALITY CRISIS – GOTH/PUNK
http://artists.mp3s.com/info/220/personality_
crisis_uk.html

PETROLEUM
www.petrolmusic.com
info@digital-vinyl.com

THE PHANTOM COWBOYS – UK
www.phantoms.dabsol.co.uk/news.html

PHANTOM CREEPS – VOODOO PUNK
www.templeofdin.demon.co.uk/creepshome.htm

PHANTOM TRIBE – EBM
www.phantomtribe.com
ashram@phantomtribe.com

PHANTOMS OF FUTURE
www.phantoms.de
info@phantoms.de
Seriously strange proto-Rock, with
mental galleries.

PHYSICAL DAMAGE
www.physicaldamage.de
'Hell was full, so we came back.' EBM
with attitude.

PICTURE MOMMY DEAD
– HORROR RAP ARCHIVE
www.geocities.com/hauntedhood
Rumoured DarkHop/Goth-Gangsta band.

PIHR
www.pihr.co.uk
band@pihr.co.uk

Perfidious Words

Interesting duo, we shall all be intrigued
by, and oh look – Paul Broome! (That's
my way of saying it's bound to be good.)

PIKER RYAN'S FOLLY
www.pikerryan.com
pikerryan@pikerryan.com
Strange and compelling Indie Noir
band with fulfilling site. Remind me of
The Galley Slaves in a way. Great lyrics,
like a fully conscious Pogues.

PILORI
www.pilori.com
Very sweet and neat for texture-ridden
duo.

PIVOT CLOWJ – IND-GOTH
www.angelfire.com/vt/pivotclowj

PLACEBO
www.thebsh.com
online@thebsh.com

THE PLAGUE
www.margotday.com/plague.htm
margot@margotday.com
Margot Day's site which needs some
modern bio details and news updates.
Gig reviews, galleries etc. We know
she sounds good, so let's have it all
fleshed out.

PLATFORM ONE
www.platform-one.com
Platformi@aol.com
Synthy Darkwave band with a problem

about pushing themselves. Nice pics, tiny
details.

PLAY DEAD
www.waste.org/~winkles/playdead/index.html
A very good, informative fan site.

PLEUROMA
www.pleuroma.com
pleuroma@pleuroma.com

HELGA POGATSCHAR – HIST/AV GARDE
www.chrom.de/home/pogatschar

PRAGA KHAN
www.pragakhan.com
Mad dance, spanning genres. Great site
with magnificent galleries.

THE PROCESS
www.geocities.com/chromewhore
processedmusic@hotmail.com

THE PROCESSOR – DARKWAVE
www.tonezone.com

PRODUKT 13
http://home.tampabay.rr.com/produkt13

PROFANE GRACE
www.infernalhorde.com/ProfaneGrace
www.geocities.com/Paris/Rue/5130/grace.html

PROFESSOR PROTON & HIS ROBOTS OF DEATH
www.geocities.com/professorproton
karloff@midwest.net

PROJECT 12:01 – Darkwave
www.project1201.com

PROJECT DARKLANDS
www.project-darklands.de
Nice Darkwave-Elec fanpage.

PROJECT DONIS
www1.omnitel.net/donis
istic@yahoo.com
Neo-folk/Ethereal from Lithuania.
Basic, but pleasant site. Odd pics!

PROJECT PITCHFORK
www.pitchfork.de
Big as you'd expect. Huge gallery, detailed
bio, poll, list, forum, board. US Fan Club:
www.angelfire.com/band/thepitchfork
Fan sites:
corpsdamor@aol.com
DunkleRose@gmx.net
http://come.to/pitchfork
http://privat.schlund.de/t/tilman
tilman@thederan.com
webmaster@pitchfork-online.de
webmaster@project-pitchfork.de
www.mr-vino.de
www.netcolony.com/members/corpsdamour
www.pitchfork-online.de
www.project-pitchfork.de

PROPAGANDA
www.propaganda.de/index.html
mabuse@propaganda.de

PROSAIC – Ind
www.deprogrammed.com/prosaic

PSY DOLL – Post-Ind
www.psydoll.com
psyber@psydoll.com
English available for this Japanese band
site. I'm not sure what they're on about
in their explanation, but the bit about
the police seeking out forms of
anti-major label activity is curious.

PSYCHE
www.psyche-hq.de/psyche.html
Excellent site for Electro duo. Decent
gallery, smart info.

PSYCHIC FETUS – Horror Rock
www.ravenworldwide.com/cultof.htm
info@ravenworldwide.com

PSYCHIC TV – Archive Info
www.ambient.on.ca/hound/htopy.html
www.brainwashed.com/tg/genesis.html

PSYCHOPHILE
www.psychophile.freeserve.co.uk
mathew@hook8.freeserve.co.uk
Nice basic site from the Brightoneers.
Okay pics, and good to see a Rogue's
gallery for previous members. Biog shows
how long they've been going and how lazy
they originally were. (2000 was manic for
them, with a whole eight gigs.) Lucy was
once in a band called Verity Turnip?

PSYCHOPOP
http://psychopop.org
contact@psychopop.org

PSYCHOTICA
www.psychotica.net

PULCHER FEMINA
http://decadancerecords.it/pulcherfemina
pulcher@decadancerecords.it
Dark Electronic Italian duo.

PUMALIN – Ethereal
www.pumalin.net
info@pumalin.net

PURE DRAMA
www.puredrama.com
ryan@puredrama.com

THE PURITAN DEATH SQUAD
http://darkspot.org/pds

PURITY CRIES – Metal-Goth
www.puritycries.co.uk
puritycries@hotmail.com

PURR MACHINE – Hard Ethereal
http://home.earthlink.net/~purrmachine
purrmachine@earthlink.net

PUTRA CHIC – Archive
www.surgikill.co.uk/putrahub.htm
putra-chic@surgikill.co.uk
They came from Nekromantik,
Narcissus Pool and Sneaky Bat
Machine, to conquer the Earth. Then
they didn't, which surprised nobody.
This was a sweet tribute. Seems to have
vanished at the surgikill site now they
have their Squid/Katscan alliance going.
Tell them to bring this back!

QNTAL – Info
www.chrom.de/home/qntal

QUEEN ADREENA
www.queenadreena.com

info@queenadreena.com
The official site, and beautifully
designed. Everything you could desire,
from images to sounds, live dates,
movies and taxidermy, but be patient.
It will load when it wants to, but it's
worth the wait. Unofficial:
www.coma-pudding.com/qa/katie.html
Coma's excellent site, with full content.
A little work of art.
Queen Adreena – Somnambulation
www.geocities.co.jp/MusicStar/2683
Fantastic site, offering all Queen
Adreena info, with details, discog,
wallpapers, images and a section
equally as good on Daisy Chainsaw.
www.queenadreena.co.uk
http://clubs.yahoo.com/clubs/queenadreena
http://uk.clubs.yahoo.com/clubs/queen
adreenasplace

RACHAEL'S SURRENDER
www.surrender.com
rachael@surrender.com
Ethereal Gothic Darkwave say they, in
a confused state, admitting they're Goth
in other people's eyes. Odd-looking site,
like a publishing firm info page. To
elucidate further they have written a
myth which is beguiling but more
confusing still.

RADA & TERNOVNIK
http://rada.rinet.ru
rada@rinet.ru
'An English version of this page exists
(barely)' they say, which is sweet. Dark
Folk without the pomposity or any
dodgy politics by the look of it.

RADICAL USURPER – Classique
www.radical-usurper.com

RADIO INVISIBLE – Very Odd
www.geocities.com/SunsetStrip/Stage/7558

RADIOACTIVE FLOWERS – Weird
www.ky.net/raf

SHANYNN RAIGH – High Quality Elec
http://artists.mp3s.com/info/219/shanynn_
raigh.html

RAIN – Metal Goth
www.frozenrain.ch

THE RAIN DREAMING – Prog-Goth
www.geocities.com/theraindreaming
rainmkr01932@seagoth.org

THE RAINE

www.theraine.com
Tiny LA Goth/Ethereal outing.

RAISON D'ETRE – Ind Ambient

http://fly.to/raison.detre
Site also includes details of side-projects. Attractively done, if chilly.

RAKIT – Ind

www.rakit.net

RAPTURE

http://members.aol.com/loki265l/index.html
Beautifully quiet site, in need of updates, for interesting mood band. Nice arty pics, poor bio, and links to personal pages.

RASPUTINA

www.rasputina.com
Old page:
www.angelfire.com/la/LolitaLand/Rasputina.html
You'll love their bio, or you will be tried in a court of lore. It's all so casually clever and inspirational it makes other bands seem like snails. The 'lost souls' section actually had me crying! Check out the Wild West hookers in the portrait galleries, plus there are beauty tips and jokes to be had elsewhere in this amazing site. You'll piss yourself, which maybe isn't the best recommendation.

RASPUTINA

www.envy.nu/concubine
ginger06@aol.com
This is one of the best sites you'll ever find, which goes way beyond anything a normal band site or fan sites manages. It's so perfect your walls crowd in nearer to glimpse the screen. You'll laugh, you'll howl, you'll shoot the manager of your local record shop in the head and terrorise his family for not stocking their records. Rasputina, in full glorious detail. Every section of this site is a serious treat. The writing will charm, as copious images burst your head because they look so weird, like they've escaped from a 1880 boarding school. Site down for revamp but must return, if there is any justice in this world. Also, e-group:
anyoldeactresses-subscribe@egroups.com
http://intothemoonlight.net/rasputina/
http://members.tripod.com/~Baby_Fox/corsetier/cellohome.html
www.angelfire.com/ca2/XOXOJANE

Julianne Regan © Mick Mercer

www.angelfire.com/ca3/calamities
www.angelfire.com/va/Rasputina
www.geocities.com/soho/nook/4429/index.html
www.geocities.com/SunsetStrip/Stage/6047/rasput.html
www.members.tripod.com/~corset_strings/rasputina/links.htm
http://clubs.yahoo.com/clubs/rasputina
http://clubs.yahoo.com/clubs/candykisses
http://clubs.yahoo.com/clubs/welcometotheforest
http://clubs.yahoo.com/clubs/mylittleshirt waistfire
http://nav.webring.yahoo.com/hub?ring=ra spring&list
RASPUTINA – unofficial 'Home of the Goths'!
www.geocities.com/SunsetStrip/Stage/3388/
Long dead but worthy because it has a layout which makes your eyes retreat inside your head, plus there's some weird content; a throwaway line here or there, some well-intentioned but useless gig reviews, and an interview with a nice line about a pickled herring,

THE RAVENS

www.the-ravens.co.uk
info@the-ravens.co.uk
London Gothy boys? Great flyer collection and some decent pics (I'm assuming the drummer's on medication – if not, do *not* approach!), but they need a bio.

RAW NOVEMBRE

www.iol.ie/~kevrawn/raw-novembre/index.htm

Rhea's Obsession

Not much going on for this band since '98? Few pics, small bio.

JAMES RAY
www.users.zetnet.co.uk/jspackman/music/jray

RAZED IN BLACK
www.razedinblack.net/Pages/razed.html
razed@razedinblack.net
Brilliant site from the addictive Ind-Electro-Goth boys. Cool history, news, video games, movies, galleries – probably the best selection you'll ever find a band providing – and good links. Also:
http://razedinblack.tripod.com/sacrificed/frames.html
ultraspank@bombdiggity.com
www.geocities.com/SunsetStrip/Basement/9873/raz.html
mizartiay@yahoo.com
www.geocities.com/SunsetStrip/Cabaret/8541

THE RAZOR SKYLINE
www.razorskyline.com
Three Cure fans from Seattle in Electro-Goth-Ind explosion. Nice site. Good in depth, but stingy in the gallery department.

RAZORBLADE KISSES
www.razorbladekisses.com
Cute, but virtually nothing there.

RAZORBLADE MONA LISA
http://bluewomb.com

REBIRTH – DARK CLASSICAL
http://brainwashed.com/godspeed

RED LORRY YELLOW LORRY –
ARCHIVES
http://members.tripod.com/~rlyl
www.abbta.se/rp/live/red.htm
www.hff.gu.se/student/marc/relo
www.multimania.com/goth/lorry.htm

REDEMPTION – IND GOTH ARCHIVE
www.geocities.com/SiliconValley/Lakes/1796

REFLECTING SKIN
– ETHEREAL WORLD
www.reflectingskin.net

JULIANNE REGAN/AAE
www.julianneregan.net/index.html
The Candy Tree is one of the best fan sites – as well as being the official site for Julianne – that it is possible to find. Everything is here, in an *exceptional* labour of devotion. Don't expect any trenchant criticism or an accurate overview (other than the honest words of Julianne), because when it comes to fawning this site could re-stock the New Forest.

REGENERATOR – DARK ELEC
www.regenerator.net

REJECT TWIN
www.clubbizarre.co.nz/reject-twin
maat@lucifuge.com
'Vampire Slut Cyber Rock'?

RELIQUARY
www.reliquary.org
info@reliquary.org
A side project from Paris Burning.

REMANENCE – AMBIENT
www.remanence.org

RENOUVEAU THRASH – DARK METAL
www.angelfire.com/zine2/rt/rt.htm

REQUIEM
www.martnet.com/~kevin/requiem.html
Electro-Ind. Link to Kevin's site:
www.martnet.com/~kevin/kevin.html

RESTUS
www.rock-mexicano.org.mx/restos
restos@yahoo.com
Mexican Goth band or, as they prefer, Rock Visceral.

RESURRECTION EVE
www.geocities.com/SunsetStrip/Stage/1687/resurrectioneve.html
resurrectioneve@optusnet.com.au

THE RESURECTION MARY
www.geocities.com/SunsetStrip/9617/marypage.htm
Kentucky Goth band with a yearning for the Deathrock style, with basic site.

REVENANT
http://artists3.iuma.com/IUMA/Bands/Revenant
narcissuswept@mailexcite.com
No surprise that this artist and musician finds solace in this activity after his background. Hands up how many have had their Step-Dad shoot them and their sister? (Whaaat???!!!) Just Gonzalo Herrero then? Thought so.

REVERSE WORLD
www5.plala.or.jp/ReverseWorld
Japanese site, opens up to display Latin incantation and candelabra, and there's a big gallery which shows they're Goth not Visual but some of the links have the name Guilt involved which makes me think that's their name. Can't be sure!

REVOLUTION BY NIGHT
www.revolutionbynight.com
band@revolutionbynight.com
Nice to see they're still going, and getting all tooled up for modern sounds. Good site with well-balanced info, but no gallery.

RHEA'S OBSESSION
www.spiderrecords.com/rheas
rheas@sympatico.ca
Nice spread of reviews and interviews plus a large scope for photos which doesn't come off with far too many arty ones being obscure. Also, Russian Tribute: www.geocities.com/russian_rheas

VICKI RICHARDS
www.vickirichards.com/vicki.htm
Ex-Black Tape For ABG.

RISE AND FALL OF A DECADE – ARCHIVE
www.in-scene.com/rafoad/indexgb.htm

RIVULETS
www.rivulets.net
Dark Ambient of some promise.

ROME BURNS
http://www.darthstoo.com/romeburns
angelica@robogoth.fsnet.co.uk
Even the invented bios save the funniest lines for last. Cool Goth with a sense of style that comes naturally. Make sure you follow the link from Simon's bio to 'Bibliophile'. Good writer, and quite mad. Woeful galleries, saved by cute wedding shots.

ROMOWE RIKOITO – DARK FOLK
http://music.gothic.ru/russian/romowe_e.htm

ROSA CRUX
www.rosacrux.com
rosacrux@rosacrux.com
Amazing French band with tribal symphonics, and visuals on an epic dark theme and scale. Awesome records available... plus badges. A band that does badges! And resin or plaster works of art. Three different types of gigs/performance are available if booking the band, which they explain on their website so that promoters have the right idea.

ROSE CHRONICLES –
ETHEREALARCHIVE
http://erika.cityhunter.net/rosechronicles/main.htm

Rosetta Stone © Mick Mercer

Nice and informative tribute, with a page on 'similar bands'!

THE ROSE OF AVALANCHE
www.geocities.com/~jamesparton/home.htm
webmaster@roseofavalanche.com
Really good fan site dedicated to unearthing everything.

ROSEMARY ASYLUM – SOON
www.rosemaryasylum.com

ROSETTA STONE
http://wherever.stcatz.ox.ac.uk/hidinghole/interview.html
Actually an interview about now-ish, from Hiding Hole, but... makes for an interesting read. Why did you make that announcement at Whitby and 'abandon all Goth'? 'Because the scene in the UK is a joke... I can view it even more objectively now.... and I was right to leave... the hypocrisy and inconsistency that ensued as a result of my departure was unimaginable – the logic of some 99 percent of those I've left behind now sickens me. This may seem overly self-righteous of me to say (even by my standards) but unfortunately you weren't privy to how self-righteous some sounded on hearing the announcement of our split.'

ROSIN COVEN
www.rosincoven.com
justin@rosincoven.com
Pagan Lounge Music? Fair enough. Excellent site from the mental collective who suggest 'Edith Piaf does the cha-cha with Charles Mingus, Eric Satie tangos with Sun-Ra, and Kurt Weil broods over Doris Day.' Classic photos/invites section.

ROZSHA
www.rozsha.com

RRRRRRR
http://artists.mp3s.com/info/250/rrrrrrr.html

KARI RUESLATTEN
http://home.online.no/~torleift/kari
http://members.it.tripod.de/pazuzu
http://vavonia.tripod.com/kari.html
http://win.cea.ru/~romshish/music/kari
www.geocities.com/SunsetStrip/Backstage/2076

6AM ETERNAL – IND
http://artists.mp3s.com/artists/153/6_am_eternal.html

S-PRETTY PETS
www.s-prettypets.com
When you're greeted by a cartoon of a boy walking a dog you wonder, because the site is Japanese, whether you've followed the wrong link but inside there's a poor quality gallery and you think they're downtrodden Visual, only to hit the Live report section and find a series of fantastic live pics.

S.P.O.C.K. – ELEC
www.subspace.se/spock
Thrilling bio, bizarre, and you can download a special calendar.

SABOT – DARK ETHEREAL
www.nullpointer.com/sabot

SABOTAGE

www.sabocon.de/sabo.htm

They're noise bastards, with a sweltering rhythmic blast, but it's the artwork I know you'll love whether you like the music or not. The work of Mauro Chiarotto (www.sabocon.de/chiarotto.htm) is *incredible* and melts in your brain.

SABRINA

www.sabrinamusic.com

Jserip@aol.com

Gothic Pop woman who, we learn, will hold you in her arms, and break your back. Not to be trusted! Even the trees in the excellent outdoor portraits are running away.

SACRED CONFINEMENT

www.geocities.com/SunsetStrip/Studio/4582

sc69@geocities.com

Goth-Ind, with tiny site and nice (slow) pics.

SAD PARADE – Elec

www.internettrash.com/users/parade/parade.htm

SAINTS OF EDEN

www.metech-recordings.com

info@metech-recordings.com

Ind-Goth. Detailed site, apart from pics.

SALON BETTY – Archive?

http://members.aol.com/salonbetty/salon.html

Modern, murderous kitsch and crazed Rockabilly – à la Cramps and B-52s.

SANCTUARY – construct

www.sanctuary.pwp.blueyonder.co.uk

SANDRA SCHLERETS

http://dos.al.ru/sasalinks.htm

Personal site of singer formerly with Dreams of Sanity, now with Siegfried.

SANGUIS ET CINIS

www.sanguisetcinis.de

sec@sanguisetcinis.de

Mad strobe effect when loading sections and you have seizures galore. It is an amazing site for this stunning Goth-plus band so don't miss out, just hide behind the sofa from time to time.

SAPPHIC ODE – Ind-Metal

www.sapphicode.com

SARAH JEZEBELLE DEVA

www.jezebeldeva.com

pyrael@oz-online.net

Dark chanteuse finally gets justified fan treatment. Bit of a bladder problem in the opening sequence but this is an immensely detailed site with archive areas galore. Utterly superb, with biog, tour diary, pics, all sorts of commotions. And if you think she looks scary, check out the Webmaster. Psychotic, even when relaxed!

SATAN'S CHEERLEADERS

www.satanscheerleaders.com

rubylamb@satanscheerleaders.com

http://clubs.yahoo.com/clubs/thesatans cheerleaders

You've got to love this site, dedicated to Squad 666. 'The Satan's Cheerleaders are quite active in the "black" arts of Shameless Self-Promotion.' And it

Satan's Cheerleaders

shows. This is so funny, and cool, you just want to see them with whatever band they're cheering. Bios, 'stats' and superb galleries for each girl. Cute history, excellent news. Lucy Fur, Priss E Bitch, Vixin Nixin, Katnip, Trixi Stix and Lucky Dukes, we salute you. Not a band, no, but so what?

SAUCY JACK AND THE SPACE VIXENS

www.spacevixens.co.uk/start.htm

SAVIOUR MACHINE

www.saviourmachine.com

www.members.tripod.com/~athanasios

www.legend.de

THE SCARLET FIX

www.thescarletfix.homestead.com/enter.html

thescarletfix@yahoo.com

Ex-Meridian, but site suspended. Homestead's new rules.

SCARLET SOHO

www.scarletsoho.da.ru

SCARY VALENTINE – Ind Dance

www.scaryvalentine.com

ContactHB@scaryvalentine.com

SCHATTENTANTZ – Ruralists

www.schattentantz.de

SCHONE MASCHINE

www.schonemaschine.com

SCHWARZ

www.diezukunftistschwarz.de

SCIENCE & HORROR

http://welcome.to/scienceandhorror

Self-professed Black Sheep of Gothic Rock is one guy and his gloom. Interesting chap, it has to be said. Old site.

SCISSORKISS

www.scissorkiss.net

info@scissorkiss.net

SCISSORPRETTY

www.scissorpretty.com

info@scissorpretty.com

Dark Goth-Indiepop from Australia. Cute site with very good pics.

SCREAM AGE – Elec-Ind

www.scream-age.live.com.au

Scream_Age@yahoo.com

SCREAM SILENCE

www.screamsilence.de/frames.htm

German Goth, with brief news, decent pics and nice links.

SCREAMING DEAD

http://artists.mp3s.com/info/19/screaming_dead.html

SEASIDE SUICIDE – Dark Rock

www.seaside-suicide.com

webmaster@seaside-suicide.com

They look too genuinely dark to be Visual Rock.

SEASON OF MOURNING

www.seasonofmourning.com

info@seasonofmourning.com
Attractive moody band. Basic site, but nice pics.

SEASON'S END – GOTH-METAL
www.seasonsend.batcave.net
upyourend@hotmail.com
Interesting site for new-ish band, with good bio, details, and nice use of photos.

SEASONS OF THE WOLF
http://members.aol.com/SeasonsOfTheWolf
SeasonsOfTheWolf@aol.com
www.geocities.co.jp/MusicStar/6458
Progressive Gothic New Age Metal no less, in operation since 1988.

THE SECOND SIGHT
www.secondsight.de
info@secondsight.de
Soft Goth. Select non-Flash version if you don't want to be gnashing your teeth. Go gnash someone else's.

SECOND SKIN
www.secondskin.net
Deceiving Goth site, which looks okay but there's little info, dead gallery.

SECRET DISCOVERY
www.secret-discovery.de
webmaster@secret-discovery.de
No-nonsense Goth attack from Germany, which ended in 2000, but they keep the site as tribute to what they did and plan to link to solo projects. There's a warm feel to this, not mournful or cold, and seriously great galleries. They're looking for any pics or recordings of gigs people have to expand it further which is nicer still.

SECRET-SECRET – SYNTHPOP
http://secret-secret.com

THE SECULAR
http://home.san.rr.com/thesecular
Seem more like Punky modern Rock but Goth-ish by their own preference. Funny site. Not much there but it moves you naughtily about.

SEELENSCHREI – GOTH-METAL
www.seelenschrei.com
webmaster@seelenschrei.com

SEELENFEUER
www.seelenfeuer.de
seelenfeuer-club@gmx.net
Good site, plenty of info, good pics, and if

you get compared to Goethe's Erben that can't be bad. Axel looks a bit of a headcase.

SEIJ MINUS AC – ETHEREAL
http://geneofcube.net/seijminusac

SEIZE – LABEL INFO
www.alice-temple.demon.co.uk/seize
Very basic. Info and gallery.

SEPHIROT 2001
www.sugizo.com
This is an imaginative swirling site with as much info as any fan of this chap (Sugizo from Luna Sea) could want. Looks a bit soft and pop-starry!

SEPTEMBER
www.septemberband.com
Clever, if slightly twee, site for lugubrious mood merchants.

SEPULCRUM MENTIS
www.sepulcrum-mentis.de
Marty@Sepulcrum-Mentis.de
Great site for true Goths ('Come on people, how can some of you wear badges with Nazi symbols, where people looking like we do would have been among the first to go, 60-70 years ago? This is ridiculous.') Mega info and gallery. Also:
www.geocities.com/Area51/Vault/6692/
sepulcrum.html but beware the missing pages in the bio, and find a smattering of info, with scary pics.

THE SEQUEL – GOTH METAL/ROCK
www.thesequel.de
webmaster@thesequel.de

SERAPHIM SHOCK
– HALLOWEEN GOTH/METAL
www.seraphimshock.com
cedward69@hotmail.com
This is a good, fast site, bulging with disgraceful details and news.

THE SERPENTEENS
http://members.aol.com/alphamayle/open.htm
Goth-Metal mavericks who put on the 'Superhuman Monsters' show which looks a laugh. Check out the odd bio and gallery.

SEVEN 13 – THEATRICAL
http://coven13.com/index3.htm
SEVEN13Rep@aol.com
Formerly Coven 13. Good site for info.

SEVENTH DAWN – SOON?
www.geocities.com/gogmagod/7thdawn.html

SEVENTH HARMONIC
http://freespace.virgin.net/seventh.harmonic
seventh.harmonic@virgin.net
Like a mini-supergroup of UK ethereal. Or not, but this is a charming site, with characters writing, rather than anything bland.

SEVENTH IMAGE – ELEC-IND
http://artists.mp3s.com/artists/95/seventh_image.html

ANDI SEXGANG
www.andisexgang.com
info@andisexgang.com
Good but curious. Cool artwork by Andi, good news, discog and release details (CDs are dead cheap!), and cool pics, including a blue suit Florida drug-runner look. I wish there was some attempt to put things in chronological order, to provide a personal narrative. It would make more of his achievements. Fansites:
http://cloviscompany.tripod.com/andisexgang.html
Seems down, but never had more news than the official, despite a more cohesive look visually. Dave Roberts has a point when expressing some spleen here. There isn't much about the band as a whole, is there? Personal differences may well mean Andi doesn't extol the virtues of others on his site – why should he? – but fans need to take the widest perspective.
www.sexgangchildren.com
This has history and a wider variety of pics (Look, there's Terry, Rob and Dave!)
www.geocities.com/SoHo/Cafe/7106
stickytot@aol.com

SEX WITH LURCH
www.geocities.com/SunsetStrip/Concert/7585
sex_with_lurch@hotmail.com
Now be mindful of the fact this is only semi-official, which is a lovely distinction, and yes, these LA oddities are a bit mad, admitting to a slight Bowie, Cramps and Surfer influence. 'More coming soon!' they proclaim. That was in 1999.

THE SHADOW CABINET
www.theshadowcabinet.com
mail@theshadowcabinet.com
Sinuous modern Goth from San Jose. Site is filling out nicely.

www.sepulcrum-mentis.de
THE OFFICIAL WEBSITE

SHADOW DANCE – ARCHIVE
www.dlc.fi/~tammika

SHADOW LIGHT
www.tragickrecords.com/shadowlight
john@tragickrecords.com
A good Seattle Goth band highlighted
well here on a detailed site. Moody gallery
and great bio. Josie Nutter played for
them, under the name Wednesday.

SHADOW PROJECT – ARCHIVE,
NATURALLY
www.members.tripod.com/~Shadow_Project
Basic facts ('News Flash... Rozz
Williams, still dead...'), discog and some
good Rozz pics. The section 'Valor Ate
Christian Death's Balls' isn't working.
Nor are the Rozz links.

SHADOWDANCE
www.shadowdance.de

SHADOWHOUSE
www.shadowhouse.co.uk
webmaster@shadowhouse.co.uk
Informative site, with unusual and distinctive visual offerings. Goth duo,
recordings only, but the site takes you
around their house and 'estate',
whereby you see all manner of weird
and inviting offerings. The menu is in
the form of a map, of a house and
surrounding properties, even the dog's
kennel. All mad as hell and fun to play
with. They also have good history
section and news.

SHADOWLAND – GOTH METAL
www.shadowland-m.de

MARK SHIET
http://members.aol.com/MARKSHIET/
moon.html
Info on the unfortunately named man's
solo project, Moonlight Trance, away
from Sleepy Hollow.

SHIMMER 3 – MOPEY ETHEREAL
www.shimmer3.com
shimmer3@earthlink.net

SHOTGUN WEDDING
www.prairienet.org/shotgunwedding
Ex-Moon Seven Times, with mental
site. Click a cartoon, which represents
each song, then click the magnifying
glass to bring the tale to life, often
unpleasantly.

THE SHROUD
www.theshroud.com
shroud@lightspeed.net
Hands up who doesn't like The Shroud
– so that the marksmen can see you?
And what's with the delay? This lovely
site is way out-of-date with no galleries
or depth. Old site still creaking in the
wind at www.psnw.com/~shroud.
An Oldish fan site also exists at:
http://members.tripod.com/%7ERasputina_
2/shroud.html
http://clubs.yahoo.com/clubs/theshroudfanclub
THE SHROUDETEERS – www.shroudeteers.com
khel@fallingdream.net
Ultimate fan sites with all the community
gubbins that goes with it. Brilliant.

SIDDAL
http://siddal.home.pipeline.com/siddal.html
siddal@pipeline.com

SIELA
www1.omnitel.net/siela

SIGUR ROS
www.sigur-ros.com
Great site from fascinating artist. Love the
tour diary. The interviews and reviews
will have you comprehensively charmed.

THE SILENT AGONY
www.thesilentagony.com
pierre@thesilentagony.com

SILENT TRISTERO – ELEC
http://artists.mp3s.com/info/132/silent_
tristero.html

SILENTIUM
www.jamsankoski.fi/silentium

SILKE BISCHOFF
www.silkebischoff.de
Wilfully perverse German Goths who still
don't understand why people didn't like
them for choosing the name of a girl shot
dead in a famous hostage tragedy. They
look plug-ugly, so naturally they're all
highly stylised, a la fetish photos, and the
live shots are dark to hide their revolting
features – a reason they use so many
pretty girls in their artwork. The site itself
is clever, concise and detailed. Also:
www.drakkar.de/Home/E-Wave/Silke_Bischoff/
silke_bischoff.html

SILVERASH
www.silverash.net
webmaster@silverash.net
Official site for great looking Chinese
Goth band. Nice pics and details of
fanclub.
http://akasaka.cool.ne.jp/worldend1/index2.html
http://member.nifty.ne.jp/haus_der_luege/
lucifer/menu.html
http://village.infoweb.ne.jp/~bruna/lucifer.html
www.h3.dion.ne.jp/~worldend
Good search thing:
http://edge.ee.tokushima-u.ac.jp/urls/word/
g/o/thic.html

SINISTER APOCALYPSE – GOTH METAL
http://tinpan.fortunecity.com/tricky/168/
index.html
sinisapoc@hotmail.com

SINO
www2.odn.ne.jp/re-build
Home of this small Ind/Electro outfit
and re-build records.

SINS OF LUST
www.sinsoflust.com
Interesting US Goth band with
reputation for intense delights. Great
photos.

THE SINS OF THE BELOVED
www.tsotb.com
mail@tsotb.com
Wonderful site for Goth-Metal band with
serious staying power. Nicely informative,
easy on the eye, but with plenty of
substance. Massive links section.

SINTZ
http://sintzproductions.com

SIOUXSIE & THE BANSHEES
www.vamp.org/Siouxsie
Excellent site, and the rest are found here:
www.geocities.com/~emily777/SiouxsieLinks.html

SIRENS OF TITAN
www.rahul.net/hrmusic/artists/sotart.html
Synth-generated ethereal with medieval
concerns from female duo.

SiS GOTHIC WAVE
http://sis-gothicwave.de.vu

SISTER ADORE
www.sisteradore.com
Aislynn8@aol.com

S*ST*RS OF M**CY
If you are genuinely Goth, or have a
serious appreciation of it, and you buy a
Sisters record, still run a Sisters site, or
would consider paying to see him live
can you claim to have *any* self-respect?
He accepts that it is Goths who provide
him with his money, but he wants
nothing to do with the scene, so it's time
to give what he wants. Ether silence. Total
blackout. If you run any website containing Sisters references, why not remove
them? As he so clearly doesn't want
anything to do with the scene, it shouldn't
want anything to do with someone like
him. Eldritch has left the building.

THE SISTERS OF MURPHY
www.thesistersofmurphy.com
Tribute band who probably aren't off to
sunny Spain. The only regret, other
than the pathetic state of their hero(es)
is that the original covers band who
inspired them were Sister Sludge,
which is such a better name.

SIX PAST SEVEN – IND-AMB
www.sixpastseven.com
info@sixpastseven.com

THE SKABS
www.skabs.com
New York Goth-Punks with Electro
element. Jumbled bio and nice pics.

SKELETON CREW
www.multimania.com/skeletoncrew
Well regarded dark metal.

THE SKELETAL FAMILY
http://tinpan.fortunecity.com/floyd/616/index
.html
skeletalfamily@fcmail.com
Aims to be a fully-fledged Skeletals site,
as they report reformation rumours.
Discography:
www.musicmaniac.de/bands/skeletal/index.html

SKIN CAGE
www.skincage.com/kozfear.html
He reckons 'cacophony is the divine
language', so be prepared.

SKIN CURTAIN – METAL-GOTHISH
http://skincurtain.tripod.com
Hefty site. Not my cup of tea, but then
I prefer coffee anyway.

SKIN DOT
www.skindot.net

SKY CRIES MARY – ARCHIVE
www.wcug.wwu.edu/~cames/scm/scm_home.shtml
Christopher Ames has done a pretty good
job of filling this archive site. Nice pics
dotted in among a lot of serious info.

SKYRABIN – DARKAVE
www.skryabin.gothic.ua
Good bio and news/details, plus big
gallery sections.

SLAVE CRADLE
www.idrecords.com/slavecradle
slavecradle@idrecords.com
Not much to report as they build up the
band line-up, apart from their promise
to make you understand their motto, 'a
bad man, feeling worse'.

SLEEPING DOGS WAKE
www.cling.gu.se/~cl5pwall/sdw/sdw.htm

SLEEPING PICTURES
www.disappointedvirginity.co.uk/sleep

marc@disappointedvirginity.co.uk
UK neo-folk of the darkest persuasion.

SLEEPLESS – ISRAEL GOTH ETHEREAL
www.sleeplesscd.com/resize.html
info@sleeplesscd.com

SLEEPY HOLLOW
http://members.aol.com/Sleepyholw/
shmain.html
sleepyholw@aol.com
Powerful atmospheric elec from long-
running band. Cool site. Looks posey
before you get in but you have to admire
their courage at including early pictures.

SLEPT DOLL
http://nightaffair.net/doll
No info, just music and discog.

SLICE GIRLS – ARCHIVE
http://members.aol.com/_ht_a/isisslice/
myhomepage
http://vampyria555.tripod.com/slice.htm
Parody band of Horror actresses.

SM:)E
http://syncon.devildance.com

SMALLCREEP – IND
www.smallcreep.com
Excellent and genuinely interesting
site with a huge amount to explore,
and one section of the site, River City,
will introduce you to Gareth Bouch's
writing.

SMALL GODS
www.smallgods.com.au
Bats everywhere, opening onto a mental
site about an Australian band who claim
to have been Glam-Goth guttersnipes.
Masses of material available. Weird site.

SNAKE RIVER CONSPIRACY
www.repriserec.com/src

SNEAKY BAT MACHINE
http://liquid2k.com/sneakybat/index_flash.html
Fairly hollow experience, truth be told,
if you expect band-related matters.
History of the Death Dance, and some
nice pictures of friends.

SNOG
www.cyberden.com/imcc/html/aboutus.html
Must be good if they're appearing at
Convergence. Worth a look, as it comes
over like some subversive ad agency.

SODA ASH
www.scifilullaby.com
Quality darkpop with Ind roots showing? Clear info and good visuals.

SOFIA RUN
www.dennydaniel.com
solacex@aol.com
There's a lot more about Denny's design work than the band, due to construction.

SOL INVICTUS
www.mindstorm.com/~waxy/wserpent/SOL.html

SOLITARY SINNERS – Elec-Darkwave
www.solitarysinners.com
solitarysinners@yahoo.com

SOMBRANCE
www.sombrance.com/home.html
feedback@sombrance.com
Dirge Pop, on new site.

SOMBRE SERENITY – Dark Metal
www.ofdarkness.de/somberserenity/index.htm
stefanbotz@gmx.de

SON OF RUST – Ind-Elec
www.1201.com/silicon

SON OF WILLIAM
www.control-tower.com/berzerker/sowdex.html
berzerker@primary.net
That URL doesn't work at present, so they should be upgrading. If they keep the contents I saw you'll not want to miss this, so search for them elsewhere. Interesting site from globetrotting 'band'. Nice bio, but the top award goes to the crazed galleries which have them coming on like an anime version of Christian Death! Are they throwing knives at a bloke on a revolving board?

SOPOR AETERNUS
http://soporaeternus.de
Amazing site, with quite extraordinary pics of Anna-Varney. I never knew he/she was a she/he, or something else entirely, and you know what? It makes nothing clearer anyway. There are also some very deep interviews and very little actual detail or facts about the artist. It's very odd and totally captivating. Unofficial:
http://saturn-impressionen.fw.nu
doodziel@as-if.com

SORROW
www.piskidisk.com
webmaster@piskidisk.demon.co.uk
Interesting site with many separate pages for Rose McDowall, principally Sorrow, but also Spell (Boyd Rice) – see www.mutelibtech.com/mute/spell/spell.htm – and the 'official' Strawberry Switchblade page, which is crap. There are nice Switchblade pics at 'Since Yesterday' – www.algonet.se/~akeen/strawberry/index.htm.

SOUL WHIRLING SOMEWHERE
www.soulwhirlingsomewhere.com
michael@absolutemotion.com
Attractive, but in a pretty, minimalist style there isn't much here yet. Nice pics.

SOULGRINDER
www.torget.se/users/d/Django/index.html
soulgrinder@hotmail.com
Popular Gothlings with tough sound deserving of more than a basic site that is good, but the detail is lacking.

SOY FUTURA
www.soyfutura.homestead.com
soyfutura@juno.com
Darkwave oddball, with brief info and cosy pics, plus their own Woman Of The Month, which actually include some nice portraits. The site has a crappy but very jolly feel that makes you want to find out more about this character, and being a Homestead site does feel like treacle.

SPACE REMAINS
http://members.tripod.com/~spaceremains/index.htm

SPANKING MACHINE
www.smdungeon.com/sys-tmpl/door
Oh dear. Puns galore on this site, but no message board with a joke about 'submit'. I daresay they'll get round to it. Electro-Goth-Fetish-Ind, which you could predict. If you're into fetish stuff you might get a laugh out of the photos, and if not don't bother as they're a bit tragic for the rest of us. The links will of course take you places that squeak.

SPASMODIQUE
www.spasmodique.de

SPECIMEN
www.snadra.de
snadra@snadra.de
The site is currently down, but don't take that as a bad sign. The basic info is there, and when Snadra has more time I think
it will bounce back. I certainly hope so because it's an excellent site, which is really interesting. Some people didn't like the look, but that's no problem. It's the content that counts. Also:
www.jungle-records.demon.co.uk/bands/specimen.htm

THE SPECTREMEN
www.members.tripod.com/~theSpectremen/index-2.html

SPF1000
www.spf1000.net
David@spf1000.net
Their site is a shambles, with nice pics, but no info. In fact they're far more interested in praising everyone else and promoting other people's sites and activities, which is really sweet. The 'Friends' galleries are stunning.

THE SPIDER HOLE
http://artists.mp3s.com/info/163/the_spider_hole.html

SPIRAL OF SILENCE
www.spiral.yucom.be
the.invitation@skynet.be
Tragedy-tinged bio gets you depressed, but then you look on the bright side and realise that the people making this music have been involved with Goth one way or another, creatively, for over ten years and they're still going for it.

SPIRITUAL-REALITY
www.spiritual-reality.de
Nice little site from dark Electro band gone quiet of late. Excellent galleries.

SPITKISS
www.spitkiss.com
http://clubs.yahoo.com/clubs/spitkiss

SPLINTER – Ind
www.redrival.com/splinter

SPRINGBOK NUDE GIRLS
www.nudegirls.co.za
Hang on, it's a load of crappy looking blokes!

SPY SOCIETY99
www.premise.com/ss99
spysociety99@hotmail.com
Myke Hideous and a new project that won't ever be what you expect, or regular.

SQUID
www.squid616.com
info@squid616.com
A delightfully wayward site from those perverse Industrigoths. Images are great, the news section is updated regularly and it all has a really friendly feel.
http://clubs.yahoo.com/clubs/devastatedegenerate

SQUIRREL NUT ZIPPERS
www.snzippers.com
I know it's a duff name, but Jani of the Dead Curves rates them and obviously has really good taste. The photo archive suggests they're certifiable.

ST EVE
www.st-eve.net/sitev04
Confusing site from 'events' group. Gabrielle Penabaz has much of the 'Danielle Dax' about her, crossing genres at will yet remaining a sharp and decisive individual. Stylish gallery, if slightly Whore Of Satanesque.

STABBING WESTWARD – ARCHIVE
www.angelfire.com/fl/DarkestDays/index.html
www.geocities.com/SunsetStrip/Studio/6993/StabbingWestward

STAGEFRIGHT – ARCHIVE
www.geocities.com/SunsetStrip/Mezzanine/3877
I don't know why I got to this, or what they are, as this old site has several pages not working, but one of the occasional vocalists was a fifties supermodel, and Warhol factory fodder. Interesting, but bizarre.

STALE BREAD
www.carcasse.com/stale
stale@zipmail.com.br
Top Brazilian Goth band with neat but tiny site in Portuguese and English.

STAR INDUSTRY
www.starindustry.be
management@starindustry.be
Goth-Ind stars of the moment with efficient site. Good basic historical nuances, and news, with no photos.

STARE – ETHEREAL-GOTH
http://artists.mp3s.com/info/14/stare.html
Here's a band nobody has a bad word for.

STAY FRIGHTENED
www.geocities.com/SunsetStrip/Backstage/3924/index.html

stayfrightened@yahoo.com
Ethereal Dark Ambient, strangely quiet recently, and the site is awful.

STENDHAL
www.stendhalnoise.com
xStendhalx@aol.com
Cool site from modern Ind band. Good flyer archive, video and galleries.

STG
www.12inch.com/stg.html
Bodybag@12inch.com
Back in action, so this can do with an overhaul. All the original info here, along with REwire, UMag and Idiot Stare adventures.

STIMILUS RESPONSE
www.stimulus-response.f2s.com

STOA
www.stoa.de
www.wormfood.com/music/stoa
info@stoa.de
Very attractive site for classically-inspired German act, with decent details considering their last site got wiped out. Lovely pics.

STONE 588
http://home.earthlink.net/~ipsofacto/s588.htm
ipsofacto@earthlink.net
They're a really good band so it's shame to see the site's a right old mess. Nice bio, all squashed up, and they've got some really lovely pics to play with and incorporate.

STOP THE CAR – ARCHIVE
www.isoc.net/mau222

STORMY VISIONS
www.stormyvisions.de
webmaster@stormyvisions.de

THE STRAND
www.strandland.com
band@strandland.com
Ind with uplift. Not just great profiles of the band and everyone concerned with the band but good news, weird stories. Avoid the poetry, as always, and hunt for some amazing trading cards instead, as well as lyrics with stories behind them. Gig details also incorporate very strange ideas.

STRAWBERRY SWITCHBLADE – PHOTOS
http://home.earthlink.net/~cinka/strawberry

http://key.ors.colostate.edu/stswdisc.htm
http://members.internettrash.com/switchblade

STRIPPER – EX STUN
http://website.lineone.net/~neilash/STRIPPMENU.htm
neilash@lineone.net
Latest news, and details of how to buy old Stun releases and gawp at a few pics.

STROMKERN – WAVE/EBM
www.stromkern.com
info@stromkern.com

STRUCT
www.struct.org/main.web
struct@struct.org
Cutely compact, from American SynthyGoth-Ind foursome with almost matching Little Sense Lost hairdos, visible in nice galleries.

STUN – ARCHIVE
http://hem.passagen.se/harlot/Stun.htm

SUBMERSIBLE – Dark Trancey
www.geocities.com/SunsetStrip/Backstage/3930
blackpiano@yahoo.com
Lovely site. Very interesting, bios, detailed bits and bobs.

SUBWAY TO SALLY
www.subwaytosally.com/intro.php
Bendable German Metal, intelligently done. Beautiful site. Arty, but efficient. Fansite: www.sallysjuenger.de

SUCCUBUS
www.succubus.ch
wbbs@gmx.ch
Swiss Goth-Metal but a mix of Baroque and Synth influences churning away. Fine site, with good history, great gallery. English version available.

SUDDENMOOD
www.suddenmood.ch
Nice looking site but no English.

SUICIDE COMMANDO
www.geocities.com/~scommando
Electro men with side projects including Toxic Shock Syndrome. Very crafty site, with endless info. Never less than clear, with great pics.

SUICIDE SANCTUM
www.users.qwest.net/~pveits/suicide.html

SULPHER
www.sulpher.co.uk
Super-slick site, which for an Ind site is quite easy-going.

SUN FOR SUPPER
www.sunforsupper.de
Poppy Goth crossover.

SUNDAY MUNICH
www.kyan.com/sundaymunich
sundaymunich@kyan.com
Pretty, like a speckled fifties perfume ad, but not much here of any depth, though there are some absolutely *stunning* images in the gallery. Look at Mr Bluehead!

SUNLESS
http://inconnumedia.com/sunless
sunless@inconnumedia.com
Ross from Per Somnia.

SUNSHINE BLIND
www.sunshineblind.net
nowhere@sunshineblind.net
This promises some great personalised tales, with attitude, as the band bounce back from bad times with labels to reclaim their existence.

SUNTERRA
www.sunterra.org
sunterra@lion.cc

SUPERHALO
www.superhalo.com
superhalo@superhalo.com

SUSPIRIA – ARCHIVE
www.dunmani.demon.co.uk/suspiria
And Jon Beast is there in the pics!

SWANS OF AVON
www.swansofavon.com
info@swansofavon.com
Winsome side of the Rock element. Magnificent array of photos.

SWANS
www.swans.pair.com
This really is what you call a true archive site, with the press and lyrics and galleries, really in depth, plus you can find out about all releases and there's a collectibles section – and boy are they expensive.

SWARF – ELEC-GOTH
www.swarf.org.uk

Deeper then some, frothier than others. Cute site, fairly low on info. Small gallery.

SWEEP
www.sweep.nu
sweep@c2i.net
Synthy-Goth with a cute site. Nice and neat.

SWEET VENUS
www.sweetvenus.co.uk
info@sweetvenus.co.uk
Subtle Goth-pop attuned to calmer elements but also with powerful edges. Nice site, but virtually no pics – which is weird because Angela must look good live, and the boys can hide in the distance – just 'visuals' which could be anything or anyone.

SWEETIE
http://users.aol.com/oscill8prod/sweetie.html
Dark TripHop, with ace vocals, so why this site is such a load of rubbish God knows.

SWITCHBLADE SYMPHONY
www.angelfire.com/yt/deadpaperdoll/dead
paperdoll3.html
www.geocities.com/SoHo/Den/7121/Switch
blade.html
www.night-sky.net/switch
www.onewingedangel.com/serpentine

SYLT – ARCHIVE
www.crimson-dragon.com/sylt

SYMPTOM
www.geocities.com/SunsetStrip/Amphitheatre/
6934
symptom@usa.net

SYNOPTIA
http://listen.to/synoptia
Dead band. Links to new projects available, but hopefully this lovely site, with attractive details, good galleries and info will survive as a testament to a good band. English available.

SYNTHETIC
www.syntheticdomain.com
synth-etik@synth-etik.com
Formerly Synth-etik. Darkwave-plus, with all the EBM-Ind elements, all of which you can discover on a user-friendly site with trim bio and good news. Nice little gallery.

SYRENS
www.fridge.co.za/New%20Syrens
helgard@fridge.co.za
South African Gothettes, gone acoustic. Jolly, sparkling tiny site with mini-bios.

SYSTEMSYN
www.systemsyn.com
Classy Goth-Ind-EBM site, with an icy visual sterility that gives way to some nice info and wonderful pics.

3.0 – ELECTRO IND
www.netherworld.com/~blaze/first.htm
They look interesting and are here to save the world.

3SKS
www.3sks.com
windraven26@webtv.net
Seattle's mighty Tri-State Killing Spree, which runs easier off the tongue than 3SKS! Lovely sight, with excellent bios, good lyrics supply but sod all photos.

T-SEQUENCE – ELEC
www.geocities.co.jp/MusicStar-Drum/9395/index.html

TABIA
www.geocities.com/SunsetStrip/Stage/3218
'Hiatal difficulties... come again soon...'

TAGISMAR
www.tagismar.de
Info@tagismar.de
Goth EBM band whose photos will have you interested, as the singer appears quite mad. Basic site, but bulky.

TANQUAM
http://tanquam.studio.ru
extreme-music@usa.net

TANZWUT
www.tanzwut.com
management@tanzwut.com
Post-modern Ind German band with
nice site, but motion made me queasy.

TAPPING THE VEIN
www.tappingthevein.com
info@tappingthevein.com.
Sassily lush band, very interesting and
busy little beaverers. Fantastic gallery
pics by 'Bishop'.

TARANTELLA SERPENTINE
www.tarantellaserpentine.co.uk
Solo poet/artist with crazed dance
infusion. A real character. Excellent
concept photos and jumbled musings.

TEAR GARDEN
www.theteargarden.com
Very posh site, but somewhat
minimalist still.

TECHNOIR – COLD ELEC
www.technoir.de
steffen@technoir.de
Very nice photos and a decent history.
At least they're human.

TEL BASTA – ARCHIVE
www.best.com/~glacier2/telbasta/index.html

THE TEMPLE OF MISERY
www.templeofmisery.com
templeofmisery@angelfire.com
Ohio Ind-Goths who could safely
audition for any Highlander film by the
look of it. Quality, info-packed site. Fan
art? Now there's a weird idea.

TEMPLE OF RAIN
www.angelfire.com/mb/templeofrain
Something wrong here. You wait for
ages and then a beautiful site appears,
fully loaded. Then the screens simply
alternate and whenever you press anything, or sometimes nothing, off you go
to mp3land where the details work, and
they look seriously cool.
http://artists.mp3s.com/info/36/temple_of_
rain.html

TENEBRE
www.tenebre.com
tenebre@inbox.as
Goth Horror Metal band, which had a
competition for fans to write a story
about why one member left the band –

and you do need to read the winner's
reply! The site itself is disappointing.
Very clean and smart but after a
dramatic frontpage the innards are like
any other site.

TERMINAL BLISS – MOOD
http://cobal.org/terminal
terminal@xnet.com

TERMINAL CHOICE
www.terminal-choice.de
Christian.Arni@terminal-choice.de

TERMINAL READY
http://terminalready.iwarp.com

TERRA BELLUM
http://artists.mp3.com/info/245/terra_
bellum.html
Goth Metal Vamp Rock.

TERRANIGMA (EX-NERVOUS SYSTEM)
www.geocities.com/nervoussystem_main
ECastilla@starpower.net

TEST DEPT – ARCHIVE/LABEL INFO
www.obsolete.com/testdept
www.invisiblerecords.com/bands/testdept

TETHERED ROSES – ARCHIVE
www.geocities.com/SunsetStrip/Disco/1080

TEXYLVANIA
www.hipmagazine.com/texylvania/texintro.html
http://artists.mp3.com/info/197/texylvania.html

THADDIUS X – IND-ELEC
http://members.tripod.com/thaddiusx
thaddiusx@yahoo.com

THE 3RD & THE MORTAL
http://home.nvg.org/~thomasr/mortal
thomasr@nvg.org
Pretty dull and standard. See fan sites
instead:
http://win.cea.ru/~romshish/music/mortal
www.geocities.com/SunsetStrip/Lounge/5910/3rd.htm

THE 69 EYES
www.poko.fi/69eyes
the69eyes@hotmail.com
Finnish Goth'n'Roll, which is actually
what the scene needs more of to pull it
out of a rut and get some media
exposure. Great site finds the band
involved with the ever-genial Nikki
Sudden – one of life's true gentlemen –
for some reason. Fan page:

www.the69eyes.org and www.webvampires.com
webmistress@the69eyes.org

THE ALPHA CHILD – IND-ELEC
http://members.aol.com/thealphachild
thealphachild@aol.com

THE ALTAR
http://homepages.ihug.co.nz/~thealtar
thealtar@hotmail.com
New Zealand Goth, with emphasis on
Rock, and a well-thought-out site.
Interesting biog, good gallery.

THE ANCIENT GALLERY
www.theancientgallery.de
Fairly lacklustre, apart from
gallery.

THE ARMS OF SOMEONE NEW
– ARCHIVE
http://info.comm.uic.edu/arms

THE AUDIENCE IS LISTENING
www.audienceislistening.com

THE BEAT OF BLACK WINGS
http://fly.to/blackwings
Blackwings@t-online.de
Nice site from Goth band who also
worryingly claim a certain progressive
influence.

THE BLACK WATCH
www.theblackwatchmusic.com
J'anna Jacoby (ex Black Tape For A Blue
Girl). Lovely site. Not Goth-ish but
funny galleries, and they certainly seem
interesting.

THE CHARNEL HOUSE – DARK POP
(ARCHIVE?)
www.geocities.com/SunsetStrip/Venue/2291
thecharnelhouse@hotmail.com

THE COIL OF SIHN
www.the-coil.com
Their opening page includes a short
note – no reproduction without
permission. That's a bit beyond their
domain, surely? What they do or are
escapes me.

THE DOUGLAS FIR – MOODY POP
www.thedouglasfir.com/index.html

THE DRYADS – DARK ELECS
www.ivystone.com/dryads
itchi@ripco.com

THE ENDLESS STILL – Ethereal
www.symbiod.com/theendlessstill

THE ESSENCE EMBRACED
– Metal-Goth
www.the-essence-embraced.com
mail@the-essence-embraced.com
Nice site, bit basic on info but this is
new.

THE ETERNAL AFFLICT – Archive
www.chrom.de/home/tea/index.html

THE FACES OF SARAH
http://thefacesofsarah.classicalgothic.com/
info@TheFacesOfSarah.com
Organised UK Goth band with press
pack (other bands take note!), news,
biog, downloads, pics etc. As a band
they play traditional venues, and their
name gets around more. (Other
bands, take note!) About the only
negative thing you can say is that
their t-shirt, and logo generally, is
pathetic. Looks like a venue logo. It's
a very organised site, with things
filed away for posterity, so you can
have a good root around and not get
arrested.

THE FAIR SEX
http://vr.dv8.net/main1.html
This is the Van Richter label site (home
to Aggro-Ind artists). TFS are popular
Electro-Ind, with Goth feel. Bio here
and loads of music stuff.

THE GHOST OF LEMORA
www.geocities.com/theghostoflemora
theghostoflemora@homail.com
Cute but basic site. Everything
straightforward and in its place for fun
Goth. Witty bio, naff pics, everything in
virtual shorthand.

THE HOUSE OF USHER
www.the-house-of-usher.de
thou@the-house-of-usher.de
Big site for quality Goth.

THE INSANITY OF ERIKA
http://members.aol.com/JustSpiffy/Erika.html
Imaginary UK Goth-Ind archive. Also:
http://members.aol.com/JustSpiffy/Ellen.html
where there's decent links lists.

THE LANGUAGE OF ORCHIDS –
Ethereal archive?
www.geocities.com/Paris/Metro/3986

THE LAST DANCE
www.thelastdance.com
tld100@thelastdance.com
I like the way their separate heads
suddenly float about all over the page,
or did. It's a clunky old site, despite a
mass of content, but great fun and full
of character. There's not many sites I
took so long going through for
pleasure. Join the Fan Club, wonder
what the weather reports are for, gawp
at lots of cool and interesting photos
on this site, which are worth the wait.
Submerge yourself in reviews and
interviews.

THE LAST DAYS OF JESUS
http://lastdays.host.sk
thelastdaysofjesus@yahoo.com
Bratislavan Goth band with cool site.
Decent info and superb galleries.

THE MACHINE IN THE GARDEN
www.tmitg.com
tmitg@tmitg.com
Rather odd site from awesome band.
Big news, with reviews/links, but the
biog is sketchy, and there's a small
selection of lyrics. The galleries are
superb. They're an intriguing,
intelligent pair.

THE MIRROR REVEALS
www.middlepillar.com/mpp/mpp997
http://artists.mp3s.com/artists/135/the_mirror
_reveals.html
http://groups.yahoo.com/group/the_mirror_
reveals
mirror@middlepillar.com
Class band, featuring Kit ex-Unto
Ashes. Pure quality, emotional material.

THE MONARCHS OF EDEN
www.home.earthlink.net/%7Ejessejamison
www.latexkiss@hotmail.com
Jesse, something of a Rozz fan, and
formerly of Minneapolis cover band
Vampyre, with a new, ultra-basic site.

**THE MOON LAY HIDDEN
BENEATH A CLOUD**
www.fluxeuropa.com/moonlayhidden.htm

THE MOON SEVEN TIMES
– great archive
http://web.irridia.com/M7x/index.html

THE MOURNING AFTER – archive
http://themourningafter.hypermart.net

THE MURDEROUS MISTAKE – Elec
www.the-murderous-mistake.de
band@the-murderous-mistake.de

THE NIGHT ETERNAL
www.thenighteternal.com
thenighteternal@hotmail.com
Ethereal Goth with poor photos, short
bio, and a few reviews.

THE OLD DEAD TREE
http://theolddeadtree.free.fr
Undercon when I was there but French
and English versions available for these
majestic moodmongers.

THE ORDER OF AZRAEL
www.theorderofazrael.co.uk
info@theorderofazrael.co.uk

THE ORDER OF THE FLY
www.theorderofthefly.com
ralphierepulsive@hotmail.com
Truly barmy photo selection from gigs,
which you won't want to miss.

THE PIASS
www.geocities.co.jp/MusicStar/9609
Matching bright red hair, leather mouth
guards – what more do you want? No
idea what they're like, but does it matter?

THE REALM OF TRISTANIA
www.tristania.com

THE SEPIA – Elec
www.the-sepia.co.uk
info@the-sepia.co.uk
Very arty, but reasonable info.

THE SOIL BLEEDS BLACK
http://users.erols.com/tsbb
yamatu@erols.com
Classy Goth-Medieval, with a nice site,
but lacking in just about every department. You think they'd be capable of
something truly sumptuous, but it feels
cold.

THE UNNECESSARY REVOLUTION
– dead?
http://revolution.corky.net

THE UNQUIET VOID – Dark Amb
www.fortunecity.com/marina/skipper/1583

THE WAY OF ALL FLESH
www.boreworms.com/gwen/twoaf
webmistress@wayofallflesh.org.uk

Nice and revolting, in a cute way. Long history, the way you'd like people to do them, shocking photos.

THE WEIRD TALES
www.geocities.co.jp/MusicStar-Drum/5730/top2.htm

THEATRE OF ICE
http://theatreofice.com

THEATRE OF TRAGEDY
www.theatreoftragedy.com
band@TheatreOfTragedy.com
Now this is what you call a site! From a good history of the Norwegian Goth-Metal stars on, with individual bios, to the mass of news, with old press, the full froth of fan involvement with polls and discussions to a fantastic gallery of different subjects, it dazzles. I would advise all bands to check this out to see what a remarkable job they have done.

THEATRE OV IDIOTS – Elec-Ind
www.angelfire.com/electronic/theatreOVidiots
anal-ventriloquist@rescueteam.com

THEATRES DES VAMPIRES – Metal Goth
www.theatres-des-vampires.com
necros.box@flashnet.it

THEE DIMESTORE HALOES
www.angelfire.com/punk/haloes
Chaz, King of Cool! Intrepid explorers only.

THEE MISFIT TOYS
www.houseofvirtue.com/theemisfittoys.html
patrick@houseofvirtue.com
Basic Goth info page with discog.

THESE CRIMSON DREAMS
www.alice-temple.demon.co.uk
tcd@alice-temple.demon.co.uk
Crap site for cool band. Is this an old site or was it always this dull?

THEY KILLED FRITZ
www.theykilledfritz.com
fritzweb@worldnet.att.net

THINGS OUTSIDE THE SKIN – Horror
www.outside-the-skin.com
things@outside-the-skin.com

THIRD TRACK MIND
http://3trackmind.com

Abbey Travis

toni@3trackmind.com
Funny site from Australian Techno-Goth-Ind somethings.

THIS ASCENSION
http://thisascension.com
Relieved to move from Tess to Projekt, with re-issues galore, this is an informal but pristine site. Fine pics, good news, if sporadic, and you need to click links there to see other galleries that don't occur in the main menu. Also:
http://clubs.yahoo.com/clubs/thisascension
http://members.nbci.com/druoo
www.thisascension.net

THIS BURNING EFFIGY – info
www.gravenews.demon.co.uk

THIS MORN' OMNIA
http://home.planetinternet.be/~tmo601/ie4/normal.htm
info@hegira.be
This is mad! You wait for loading and then there's this walking stick you

pick up to drag over icons to get into sections, but there are hardly any there so while I appreciate the effort, it's an anti-climax. Some Electronic concept.

THIS VALE OF TEARS
www.tvot.be
tom@tvot.be
This excellent band is back after a silent spell. Only a bio, and some good photos.

THORN APPLE – Goth/TripHop
www.batteryinflux.com/thornapple/index.html

THORNS OF THE CARRION – Doom Goth Metal
www.geocities.com/SunsetStrip/Amphitheatre/1362
bloodthorn@excite.com

THORNS
www.thorns.com.br
Huge site. Lots of music, as Thorns is a band, but also news – from Hitler's sexual secrets as revealed by CIA, to

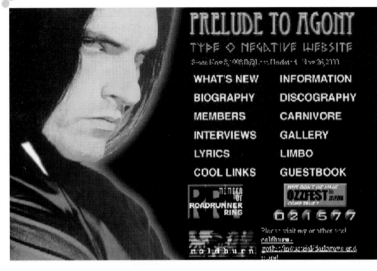

Vlad The Impaler, Michael Stipe and Beethoven. Truly, the whole world is here. Pics of local gigs they organise (Gothic Rave). There's chat, there's astrology, there's links galore. *Fantastic.*

THOUSHALTNOT
www.robotgodlabs.com/tsn
Darkwave – or Experimental Ind, Goth and Synthpop. Formerly Thou Flaming Minister! They don't look old enough to vote.

THRIVE – ARCHIVE
www.spiderrecords.com/thrive

THY VEILS
www.thyveils.f2s.com
thyveils@innocent.com
Impressively informative site for synth meets medieval composer. Another variant on modern classical which people will have to accept is a serious modern statement.

TIAMAT – OFFICIAL
www.geocities.com/Vienna/Strasse/3040/tiamat.html
Fan archive, ending '98.

TIN STAR – UK
www.tin-star.co.uk
TIN STAR – USA
www.tin-star.com
Vastly superior to UK site.
www.tinstar.org.uk – fan site archive.

TONES ON TAIL
www.angelfire.com/va/kut/index.html

www.geocities.com/SunsetStrip/Palladium/2479
www.gothic.net/~skot/tot

TONGUE DEPRESSOR – UBER GOTH
http://artists.mp3s.com/info/240/tongue_depressor.html

TOOL
www.toolband.com
management@toolband.com
Once you're actually in, past the drab homepage, it's worth it. They have tried – successfully – to make an attractive site, dark but not gloomy.

TORS OF DARTMOOR
www.mukkelpumusik.de/torsofdartmoor.htm
and, supposedly: www.printed.de.vu
rutger@knuut.de

TORSO-FICTION – ELEC/EBM
www.torso-fiction.de

TORSION
www.torsion.net
mythdmnr@aol.com
More than acceptable site for new-ish Goth-Indists, with neat bio, good gallery, plenty of news updates and links.

TORTURE BY ROSES – DARK AMBIENT
www.torturebyroses.cjb.net
info@mediatrixpublishing.com

TOTAL TRAGEDY
http://listen.to/totaltragedy
:totaltragedy@telkom.net
Very interesting Indonesian band with a sound called Romantic Goth Shadow, a

Metal hybrid. Good site, in English. Great pics. Unofficial: http://totaltragedy.cjb.net/

TOYAH LINKS
www.users.globalnet.co.uk/~wamphyri/wam150~1.htm
If you really don't know that Toyah was a catalyst for people in the very early Goth scene you can trawl these site and some of the pics will give you an inkling. The 'Sheep Farming' album was actually *way* ahead of its time.

TRANCE TO THE SUN
www.trancetothesun.com
trancetothesun@hotmail.com
'Well, occasionally we will perform and the promoter for the gig will for some reason refuse to pay us in full. So what we do is take them prisoner. Later, we perform ritual sacrifice in an inconspicuous location. This pleases the Gods and assures that there will be excellent vibes whenever we hit the stage.' The judge didn't regard that as extenuating circumstances, but these darkly hammering dream-dance darlings won't be messed with. Cute site, if a touch empty. Luckily, the interviews should enthral, and the photo galleries more than make up for any dietary nausea, especially when you hit Ingrid's art because she has a real talent.

TRANSUM – IND
www.transum.com

ABBY TRAVIS
www.abbytravis.com/framesets/abby.html
http://clubs.yahoo.com/clubs/abbytravis
abby@abbytravis.com
Why, she looks divinely debauched. Site is wonderful, because she puts a lot in, there's a sense of the unexpected, and everything informs and intrigues. She's gliding through Torch territory, the way Melinda Miel once did. Galleries are a treat.

TRE'LUX (TINA ROOT EX SW SYMPH)
www.trelux.com/index-nonflash.php3
What an irritating disaster of a site! And for all it's prettiness there's very little there beyond three downloads.

TRISOMIE 21
www.geocities.com/Athens/Parthenon/2111/t21.html
French Goth-Ind with quite the messiest site imaginable.

TRISTIANA
www.geocities.com/SunsetStrip/Garage/8211/
index.htm

TRODDEN EMBERS – DARK AMBIENT
http://artists3.iuma.com/IUMA/Bands/Trodden
_Embers

TROIKA
www.thetroika.ch
troika@thetroika.ch
Swiss Goths with reasonable site, but
nothing in great depth.

TRUCIDO
www.mystraltide.com/Trucido
http://artists.mp3s.com/artists/211/trucido.html
trucido_@hotmail.com
Endezeit and Mystral Tide, combined.
Intense EBM.

TWELTH OF NEVER
www.twelfthofnever.com
Beautiful site from coolly-inspiring band
who mix the moody elements of Goth,
Ambient and Ethereal into a cohesive
whole. Lovely details and pictures.

TWO WITCHES – FRENCH SITE
http://twowitches.cjb.net
TWO WITCHES – AMERICAN
www.angelfire.com/wi/twowitches
Best site of them all, with plenty of
history and review/interview well
organised.

TYPE 14
www.type14.com/home.htm
fdrpromo@enter.net
Okay news, brilliant galleries and no bio
details whatsoever. Now, is it just me, or
are their choices for 'Mistress Of The
Month' scarier looking than the band?

TYPE O NEGATIVE
www.typeonegative.net/home.html
webmaster@typeonegative.net
A very good official site with bios and
photos well covered. There are fan pics
of their cars with a Type O theme! Input
section has food fan stuff, and the Tour
section has some rewarding tour
diaries. Merchandise is pretty boring,
but they claim there'll be auctions soon.

TYPE O NEGATIVE
www.music.ne.jp/~type_o
Very attractive and detailed Japanese fan
site, by Asako (she of Coldburn). Info,

biogs, interviews, gallery, links. Other
good fan sites:
http://members.aol.com/daveburger
www.angelfire.com/ri/typeoneg/negative.html
www.geocities.com/~glycerin/typeo.htm

UGO SYNAPTIC MISFIRE
www.cortidesign.com/samples/synaptic

ULTRANOIR
www.angelfire.com/pop/ultranoir
ultranoir@thevortex.com
Mopey, posey boys make dark,
atmospheric pop. Good photos.

UMBRA ET IMAGO
www.umbraetimago.de
info@umbraetimago.de
Completely mental, as you'd expect. In
German, so if you're a witless oaf like
me just sit back and gawp at the
galleries. Fan site: www.darkweb.de/spirit

Umbra et Imago

UMBRALL DO INFERNO – IND
www.infocultura.com.br/unbrall

UNBOUND – ARCHIVE
http://unboundmusic.hypermart.net

UNFRIENDLYS
www.unfriendlys.com
Dark Punk. Great site.

UNHOLY WAR
http://unholywars.homestead.com/menu.html
Mad dark band, with revolting photo
sections planned. Satanic, etc. Gosh!

UNIFORM RED
http://artists.mp3s.com/info/214/uniform_red.html
Deadeye Spindle from Dead Ringers
plus the delightful Ooky Spooky in
two-pronged, fork-tongued Punk alert.

UNIVERS ZERO
www.cuneiformrecords.com/bandshtml/univers.html

UNKNOWN NATION
– COOL ELEC-IND-GOTH
www.unknown-nation.de
info@unknown-nation.de

UNLIGHT – MOOD
www.unlight.de
Unlight@unlight.de

UNTO ASHES
www.untoashes.com
unto_ashes@gothic.net
Cool Goth-medieval band, admitting
strong dcd influences. Very good site full
of detail, if rather dour look. Excellent galleries, in depth. Bio, reviews, interviews.

UNTOTEN
http://members.tripod.de/Untoten2000/
index.en.html
sonicmalade@transmedia.de
Highly regarded German moody
Vamp-Goth, from a band who have
also moved on to writing comics as
well. Nice news, photos, Fan Club/
newsletter details, and some of the
artwork by Greta Csatlos is stunning.
I can only assume that the lack of any
personal info is intentional.
Old site: http://members.tripod.de/Untoten
Two pictures of some Satanic game
(sorry, meaningful worship) going on
with three women reverently fondling
a skull.

UPBEAT DEPRESSION – NOISY
http://artists.mp3s.com/info/13/upbeat_
depression.html

USARIAN – ELEC-WAVE
www.usarian.de

USHERHOUSE
www.lensrecords.com/uhindex.html
lens@lensrecords.com
This guarantees a great visit because of
the lengthy history, and nice photos.

UZZIEL
www.uzziel.de/uzziel1_engl.html
German Goth band, in English. When
they started it was explosive. 'A cup of
coffee was made, and every single
neuron worked as an asthmatic steam-
machine.' Then they calmed down. Very
basic site, with a few drunken pics.

VACLAV – STRANGE SOLO
www.vaclav.net

VALENTINE DC
www.vdc.uni.cc
Japanese band. Middling. News, profile, Discog, Links.

THE VAMPIRE BEACH BABES
www.vampirebeachbabes.com
vampirebabes@hotmail.com
The Vampire Beach Babes, undisputed pioneers of the Gothic Surf movement, are boldly taking Gothic music to a place that it has never been before. The Beach!

VAMPIRE NATION – ARCHIVE
http://members.tripod.com/~vampirenation/fortify.html

VAMPIRE STATE BUILDING – TEXT
www.zentralnerv.de/reports/ZNHP000097.html

DAVE VANIAN & HIS PHANTOM CHORDS
www.rawk.org/vanian
www.damned12.freeserve.co.uk/p1.htm
http://groups.yahoo.com/group/Phantom Chords

VANITAS
www.vanitas.at
Vanitas@vanitas.at
Austrian Death-Gothic. Very brief bio, everything up to date, photos are good, reviews, music, lyrics, merchandise, board etc. A job well done.

VAST
www.geocities.com/nexus92k

VAUXHALL (NZ)
www.vauxhall.co.nz
vauxhallunder@hotmail.com
Fan Club: http://clubs.yahoo.com/clubs/officialvauxhallfanclub
Fan-friendly site with decent news updates, a decent variety of pics. Lyrics, but only to six songs for some reason. The links section guides you to where you can download mp3, or videos of interviews, and even the band just jamming.

VEER CHASM
http://members.aol.com/veerchasm
veerchasm@aol.com
Sub-Ind Electro-Goth. A bright site but precious little info, or even a decent-sized gallery which is a shame because they look cool. Interesting band.

VEGASPHERE
www.vegasphere.com
vegasphere@hotmail.com
Dark elec, with some fabulous moves here on a very cool site, so let it load.

VEIL
http://members.aol.com/veilweb/veilpage.html
Dark Rock, as in ROCK – listing Kiss, Banshees and New York Dolls as influences: and as long as it's not Kiss

Violemt Fix

later than 'Destroyer' that's okay. I have a theory about bands, and how the fifth album is usually the last great one. Happened with Alice, happened with Kiss (whose first albums – and I realise you don't give a toss – were when they simply stuck together everything they'd learnt from Iggy, the Dolls and Alice, and sensibly kept it within four minutes a shot, with a shout chorus – perfect recipe for success.) The site includes a great Halloween gallery.

ALEXANDER VELJANOV
www.chrom.de/home/veljanov
Deine Lakaien.

VELVET ACID CHRIST
http://the-revolution.net/vac
This is what should happen with more bands, where the fan site is made the official one, and this is an absolute beauty. The depth of the archive-in-process is highly satisfying and with the rants, the forum, the interviews, the

news...the only thing missing is an expanded gallery of live shots, but what's already there is pretty good.

VELVET VIOLET
http://velvetviolet.tsx.org
velvetviolet@onebox.com
Cute Goth-Ind site. Brief details, fan stuff, press and music. No pics.

VENUS FLY TRAP
http://website.lineone.net/~venus-fly-trap
venus-fly-trap@lineone.net
Also the home of Alex's 'Bizarre' fanzine, and Spiral Archive, a mail-order music service. Not all the pages work first time, but the VFT discog is there, early band history is partially covered in an old interview... with later releases given their own jumbled sections. Last time I tried it this was down, as lineone are crap.

VENUS VIRUS
www.venusvirus.com
nosborn@venusvirus.com
Moody Darkwave with ambient leanings. Okay news, decent galleries. Low on info or perspective.

VENUS WALK – INFO
www.subnation.com/venuswalk
venuswalk@yahoo.com

VIA MISTICA
http://viamistica.rockmetal.art.pl
mistica@alpha.net.pl

VIANNA'S MUSIC CHILD PROJECT
www.nefkom.net/m.ulm
m.ulm@nefkom.net

VIDI AQUAM
http://go.to/vidiaquam
rsnikita@tin.it
Italian Goth with bio/profiles, lyrics... all in Italian, plus a few nice pics.

VIOLENT FIX
www.violentfix.com
ViolentFixInfo@aol.com
Plenty of updates, good news, truly excellent photos, and flyers.

VIOLET ARCANA – ELEC-AMB
www.violet-arcana.com

THE VIOLET DAWNING
– DARKWAVE DUO
www.disrupted.org/~darkages

darkages@disrupted.org
Site with tiny bios and news.
Previously at:
www.darksites.com/souls/goth/violetdawn
http://artists.mp3s.com/info/62/the_violet_
dawning.html

VIRGIN BLACK – PROSAIC METAL
www.listen.to/virginblack
virginblackoz@hotmail.com

THE VIRGIN PRUNES
www.virginprunes.com
A lovely fan site with all the relevant
areas covered, and asking for any submissions of gig experiences or pictures.
They cover the where-are-they-now
aspects by going through solo careers,
and pretty good news updates, plus
there's a fine archive building. I'm quite
surprised there aren't loads of Prunes
sites, as their mystery and madness
endures rather than lessens.

VIRUS: SEASONS LEE
www.geocities.com/seasons_leehk/hom.htm
Seasons_Lee@hotmail.com
Hong Kong! A chap from the band Virus
who, unusually for a band person, keeps
a diary online, and the site deals with his
songs, there's a cool gallery (why has he
got a blue chin?), discography, history, live
news, guestbook etc. The usual, but it's
nice to see someone in a band doing it by
themselves. And Seasons Lee himself
would like to say this: "Formed in 1992,
Virus desires to promote the goodwill of
Gothic Rock in Hong Kong. They appear
in a variety of band shows all these years.
Their unique image and music style
attract the attention of band sound lovers.
In 1994, Virus released their first album
(Vague Elegance), which was appreciated
and responded favourably. In fact, the
music of Virus does not only restrict to
Gothic Rock, but is injected a strong
sense of individuality of its own to make
a brand new Gothic Rock happen. With
the changes of team members, Virus'
music incorporates new elements other
than Gothic, resulting in new surprises
for their audience. Their favourite bands
are The Cure, Bauhaus, Sisters Of Mercy,
Japan, Christian Death, Cocteau Twins,
Siouxsie And The Banshees."

VIS MATRIX – INDIE-GOTH
www.vismatrix.com
info@vismatrix.com

VISIONS OF PASSION TORTURE
www.passiontorture.com/index.asp
Fascinating bio, with some nice pics of
this tortured bunch. It draws you in, but
there's no real news as the project is on
hold. Could be good.

VLAD
http://members.aol.com/grimdirge/vlad.html
vladdirge@aol.com

VLAD & THE DARK THEATRE
www.tdt-euro.com/tdt/default.htm
Seriously weird site about a film
composer, Scott Vladimir Licina, who
is also a very talented artist.

VNV NATION
http://vnvnation.com
info@vnvnation.com
Smart site with excellent news – in
English – and exclusive mixes, plus
full discog. They may be cold Electronic
bastards, but their passion, to communicate, comes through well with the
amount of info, and there's a good
media stock. Shockingly bad live
galleries but then these bands are
always fairly crap looking, have you
noticed? That's why they do music like
this. Hide behind things.

VOCAL ART BERLIN
www.citoma.de
wolz@citoma.de
It's Christian Wolz alone, popular and
working with many others as well as his

own work, which involves improv and
experimental, so be careful.

VOLITION – ELEC-IND
www.hevanet.com/livewire

VOMITO NEGRO
www.geocities.com/Paris/Jardin/3892/bands/
vomitonegro/index3.html
Are you sitting comfortably? 'Black
vomit' – a phenomenon that arises in
the last stage of the disease yellow
fever, when the patient throws up his
putrefied intestines and ultimately dies.
Started off as old school Ind (SPK etc)
but have increasingly moved towards
more involved synth work. The site
itself gives a few hints, but is quite
basic. Pics are okay but all their press
reprinted here is over ten years old.

VOODOO DOLLIES
www.voodoodollies.com
Fan Club for Michael Aston's GLJ.

VOODOO SEX STUFF
www.voodoosexstuff.com
voodoo@voodoosexstuff.com
'In their spare time, Voodoo Sex Stuff
enjoys cross stitching, imbibing alcohol,
horticulture, meditation, painting, and
generally screwing with people's
minds.' Mainly establishing themselves
through mp3 exposure these nutters
will hold your interest. Anyone who
does a song called 'Dead Paper Bag' has
got something.

Virus

VOTIVA LUX
www.votivalux.com/news.html
Click on Output and you can control
the mad pulsing colours with your
cursor. Get it dead centre and they slow.
I'm assuming this is the same cool
band I got onto one of the Hex Files
CDs but who knows?

VOYAGE
www.geocities.com/SunsetStrip/Arena/2873
fishgirl@freemail.hu
Dark Dance-Pop. Brief bio, pics, news
and discog, in English.

VOYTEK – Elec-Goth
www.dallasmusic.com/voytek.html

VULGARAS
www.vulgaras.homestead.com
thevelocity@evilemail.com
Totally wild girls, and isn't Militia a
brilliant name anyway? Not Goth but
their tastes impinge, and they have
theatrical natures, every last woman
and transgender goddess one of them.
Links will take you to places you
might not ordinarily go. Temporary
suspension, due to Homestead.

VX – cool Ind
www.vxmusic.com

FREDERICK WALLIN
www.algonet.se/~fredwa

WAILING WALL
www.wailingwall.net/Main.htm
Dramatic arti-Goth, but quite a sketchy
site.

WATCHERS ON THE STORM
– dark solo
www.geocities.com/watchers_on_the_storm

WATER SEEK
www10.big.or.jp/~kkws

WATERGLASS
www.m.wake.btinternet.co.uk
waterglass@hotmail.com
A lot of people don't even think they
exist, but the full story here explains
their torturous history and the rest
of the site is filled with pleasing
diversions. It looks drab, which is the
last thing they need, but it's being
re-done even as I key this in, and 2002
could be a big year for them.

WAVE AFTER WAVE
www.waveafterwave.com
moonbeem@ix.netcom.com
Good Goth site with amusing bio and
lying news. Nice photos (of psychiatric
patients, I presume?), links, lyrics,
'quotes'. It's small but certainly has
character.

THE WAX MUSEUM
www.thewaxmuseum.bc.ca

WEAPON X – Metal Goth
http://artists.mp3s.com/info/2/weaponx.html

WEAVE – Ind/techno
www.weave.xs3.com

WEISSGLUT
www.weissglut.de
German-only site with particularly
weird menu, shows some dramatic
images, of something, like otherworldly
Ind. Tried the fan site – www.weissglut-fan
basis.de – which shows stocky men and
synths. That's Ind.

WEJDAS
http://saule.pit.ktu.lt/alt/wejdas

WELCOME TO THE POND
www.breiner.com
Web designer who also has cool photo
section, showcasing travel, gigs, and
Womad. In the gigs you'll find GLJ,
Cult, Then Jerico etc.

WELLEERDBALL
www.welle-e.de

WELTENBRAND
www.mos.li/weltenbrand.htm
Decent site, with five pics of the band
outnumbered by six of shoulder-baring
strumpet singer Simone. Their solitary
link goes to a guesthouse in Switzerland!

WENCH
www.wenchmusic.com
wenches@wenchmusic.com
Promising elegant destruction, we meet
Frances Byrne, solo electronics artist
who creates sacred sounds. They
discontinued their Hardcore Haute
Couture but are proud to announce
they still have t-shirts and thongs!

WENDY IS STARING AT ME
www.wendyisstaringatme.com

A compassionate Goth Ind band who
urge visitors to vote for them at some
contest because 'our guitarist has not
won an award since he learned to stop
piddling in his bed ... it would mean so
much to him...' We don't even know if
he has stopped, so why should we?
And then... 'We're not sure if you can
call us a Goth band, because Cory
actually has talent which is an
immediate disqualifier.' Owww!

WESTWERK
www.westwerk.com
nightmare@westwerk.com
It could be language thing but when
they have an 'epitaph' instead of a biog,
that looks ominous. Cute Goth pics.

WHISPERS IN THE SHADOW
http://home.t-online.de/home/Dreams.Never.
End/whispers.htm
info@wod.de
Cheap and cheerful, which is a blessed
relief sometimes from the dark prosaic
approach of most sites. This is bright
and bubbly, bold and half-arsed. Lads,
don't have a section for your equipment,
it implies you're muso-bores rather than
creative artists. Whenever you meet
someone in a band who wants to talk
about their instrument rather than
songs or music you know they'll never
get anywhere. No soul, see? Far more
detail at:
www.demonware.com/wits/index.html
And the site at:
www.mos.li/whispers.htm a mistake?

WILD STRAWBERRIES
www.strawberries.com

JOACHIM WITT
www.joachimwitt.de
One of those sites that look adorable
but doesn't fulfil, except the photo
'book' which contains very odd
images.

DAVID E. WILLIAMS – Dark Psyche
www.davidewilliams.com
DEWms@aol.com

ROZZ WILLIAMS
http://rozznet.com/dir
info@rozznet.com
Rozznet is the official site and totally
wonderful as you probably expect. There
is everything here. Recently revamped

Rozz Williams. Photo © Stéphane Burlot

with a cool blue glow, and includes the stirling work of John Collins, who did Rozz Williams + Family. Stunning.
http://members.aol.com/Alpheratz9/rozz.html
http://members.aol.com/emmaleen/rozz.htm
http://pages.prodigy.com/graveside/rozz.htm
www.angelfire.com/goth/RozzWilliamsMemorial
www.best.com/~ezurich/rozz.html
www.geocities.com/Area51/Nebula/8721
www.geocities.com/rozz94
www.geocities.com/scrooncy/index.html
www.guavajelly.com/hollows/artists/rozz

www.hallucinet.com/asylem/coven13/cov9_21.html
www24.brinkster.com/velix/index.html

ROZZ WILLIAMS – 1334 THEATRE
http://members.spree.com/sip/rozzwilliams/rozz.htm
Big Rozz tribute site, in current state of flux, with good Rozz, CD, Shadow Project and PE content, plus Gitane and Mephisto Waltz. Spree have been ditching people left, right and centre so while this is gone you may want to

search for it by title. I'm sure something this good will reappear.

WILLOW WISP
willowwisp.com
WWisp@aol.com
Goth-Metal mania, with basic bio and really big photo archive.

WINDS DIED DOWN – CYBER IND
www.mok.com/electro/winds
winds@mok.com

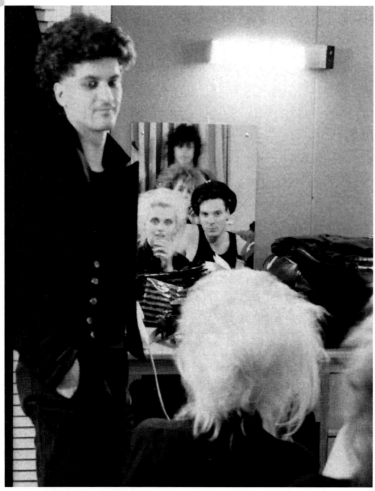

X-Mal Deutschland © Mick Mercer

WINGS OF DESTINY

www.wod.de
Wings@t-online.de

A band and a booking agency, which is different, representing many interesting artists from Attrition, Cruxshadows and Fading Colors to Ikon, Twilight Garden and The Dreamside – each with their own section and details. Fabulous news section. The info on Wings Of Destiny themselves is okay and there's some sweet pics but they tend to be rather overshadowed by the organisation.

WINTERMUTE

http://home.austin.rr.com/mstemen/winter-mute

'Welcome to a place', the dramatic screen goes, '[where] Sound meets Vision, Reality meets Imagination, where Nature meets Man.' No, man is part of nature, so all allegories and metaphors crumble. Fine archive piece.

WINTERLAND – Darkwave

www.winterland.co.nz
info@winterland.co.nz

WIRED REMORSE – archive

http://members.tripod.com/WiredRemorse/songs.html#Discography

WITHIN TEMPTATION

www.within-temptation.com
karianne@within-temptation.com

Very good site with plenty of history and modern events, pics, community spirit, and art gallery. (Be sure to check 'miscellaneous'.) Fan archive (pre-Within Temptation):
www.angelfire.com/wi/enlightment
www.geocities.com/tribushome/Within.htm.

WOLFSHEIM

www.wolfsheim.de
mail@strangeways.de

The official home of the wonder boys with plenty for fans and good press archive, vast galleries, including some unbelievably hopeless, sweet promo shots. They look like they're bunking off school for the day!
Fan:
www.geocities.com/SunsetStrip/Pit/2600
Up until 1999 this seemed to be going great guns, then Elizabeth's work stops. Nice resource up to that point, minus any really good pics.

WOMB

www.geocities.com/womb_hang
womb_hang@yahoo.co.uk

Strange yellow photos, short bio, lyrics and links – and that's yer lot.

WONDERBOOM

www.wonderboom.co.za

WORLDEND ENTERPRISE

http://akasaka.cool.ne.jp/worldend1

Great site, covering what I think may be Chinese Goth acts, Drugstore Romancia, Lucifer/Fiction (Lucifer Luscious Violenoue is a female singer to be reckoned with). There's profiles, galleries, and press reviews. Enthralling but enigmatic.

WRITTEN IN ASHES

www.writteninashes.com
bludsukr@earthlink.net

WYKKED WYTCH – Metal-Goth

www.geocities.com/sunsetstrip/palladium/6334

X MARKS THE PEDWALK

www.x-marks.com

X-MAL DEUTSCHLAND

www.poison-door.net/xmaldeutschland
vicus@poison-door.net

Great fan site with excellent range of photos, history and discog in German only.

XANDRIA – Goth-Metal Lite

www.xandria.com

Clothes – and Goth-related Businesses

A.T.H.E.R.O.
www.stardusted.net/athero
Was Gothic Hair Of The Month site, but is now general hair care and products.

ACCENTUATE
www.accentuateyourlook.com
Accoutrements and oddments. Jewelry, clothing, pet accessories and gifts. Small selections but interesting.

AETERNITAS
www.aeternitas-undergroundfashion.de
Another excellent German site offering Goth and fetish crossover items. Fairly surreal galleries.

AFFECTIONATELY YOURS
www.affectionately-yours.com/gargoyles.html
Gargoyles, wedding gifts, artistic household items.

AGE OF BEAUTY AGE OF HORROR
– CLOTHES
www.geocities.com/Paris/Metro/3691/lost/enter.html
Ophelia designs. Beautiful dresses, with elegance clearly in mind.

AISLING GOTHIC STORE
www.aisling-gothic-store.de
Clothes and boots from Germany.

ALCATRAZ GOTHIC
www.alcatraz-gothic.com
Clothes, medieval armour, fangs, and gifts – including scary jewelry and cute gargs.

ALCHEMY
www.alchemygothic.co.uk/html/cata.html
Famed the world over. What may have once seemed like some Heavy Metal or D&D spin-off has blossomed into a Godsend. Their stuff clearly isn't as good

*'Dark Angel'. Photo © Stéphane Lord.
Model: Frances Hardy*

as small specialist firms, but you can get pretty much anything here and there's much more in the Curiosity Shoppe that just their goods, because you can get involved, sifting for links of various genres, submit artwork or use their weird dictionary. Was briefly down.

ALICE AUAA
www.alice-auaa.co.jp
High-class Japanese clothes site, with a few very cool pics.

ALTERNATIVE TAILOR
www.namazuya.com/shop
Japanese designs by Hideki Ohno. English details.

AMERICAN-CELTIC MARKETPLACE
www.amcelt.com/amcelt2000/index.asp
Anything from crosses to birdbaths, with a Celtic imagery theme.

AMPHIGORY
www.amphigory.com
A bit of jewelry, but mainly hair and makeup.

ANGEL DEVIL
http://members.aol.com/angelspoon/index.html
Weird one-off dolls and bears.

ANGEL OF FASHION
www.fashionangel.com/linkpages
Huge fashion directory.

ANGRY YOUNG AND POOR
http://angryyoungandpoor.com
Punkgoff.

ANTIQUE DRESS
www.antiquedress.com
Amazing site with stuff from the early nineteenth century onwards.

APE LEATHER
www.apeleather.com
A few 'Gothic' items, probably the same Punk ones but with bats attached.

Might suit Manson fans looking for a chunky accessory.

APOTHECARY FAIRY
www.apothecaryfairy.com
Handmade natural skincare products. Plenty to interest, and a monthly newsletter.

ARKHAM DARK ARTS
www.arkham-darkart.co.uk
Very interesting site offering Lovecraft-related stuff, and a great Gothic section, plus Goth toys – including brilliant Goth dolls. There are some really lovely items at this site and they're not expensive either.

ART-OF-DARK
www.art-of-dark.de
Big German shop with boots, hardware (statues etc), comics and books, Cybergear and a fantastic Goth section. Nice jewelry in the section regrettably called 'Schmuck', and loads of coffins with the pointed tops.

ASYLUM 7
http://home.iprimus.com.au/jerrim/asylum/index.htm
Australian shop with unusually Techno-Goth gear approach to corsetry. An excellent site. You may be sore if you miss this, especially as they do one-off items.

ATELIERT
www5a.biglobe.ne.jp/~torikago
No real idea what this is but I like the way a feather starts drifting around after your cursor, and there are some lovely photos of a nice Japanese Goth girl (Torikago?) in a hat (click 3rd item down beneath word TOP on left menu) and she's got more of these blue roses which seem very popular, more of those spooky dolls, plus various clothing items, so I guess the girl makes all these. Fantastic earrings!

ATHENA CLOTHING
www.athenaclothing.com

Top: Photo of Monica by Curse. © Atrocities
Right: Photo of Rambriel by Curse. © Atrocities

Rather excellent PVC and latex site, for those who like to go squelch.

ATROCITIES

www.atrocities.com

Magnificence at every turn. This is my favourite classic Goth clothing site, for those who prefer their elegance subtly understated, or ornate. No tat, no tack. It hadn't been updated for a while, so I asked Kambriel about it, and her name. 'Your inquiry as to the origins of my name is rather sweet... and I'm happy to explain to the best of my ability. It's all rather a mystery really ~ when I was young, it seemed to be whispered in my ear one evening whilst I was sitting alone thinking, and I have been going by this name and creating artwork under it ever since. I am actually also planning to introduce an offshoot from Atrocities called 'Kambriel ~ Betwixt Today and Timelessness' for my more one of a kind, ornate designs like the ones I've created for Monica Richards... I should have an introductory website for this line up soon at: www.atrocities.com/kambriel 'In regards to our website update, it's nothing that will change things dramatically, we're just going to re-vamp a bit, improving the quality of the photos a bit, and introducing some new designs. Basically just the things we *should* be doing. The overall feel though shall remain, as we view the progression of the website much as we do the progression

of our designs. There shall be a continual growth and development, but the new inspirations will evolve comfortably and naturally from that which is there already.'

ATTITUDE CLOTHING CO.

www.attitude.uk.com

Site looks initially wanky but turns out swanky. Nice female Gothic section, firmly rooted in lush romanticism and not expensive by any means. Blokes are foppish, but nice Pecci shirt to help us forget the frightening bondage ensembles. Interesting accessories, including see-through PVC wristbands.

AVALON CLOTHING

www.geocities.com/Athens/Aegean/6782/

framep.html
(See 'Spheres Of Avalon' – Goth People.)

AVANT GARDE – Silver Jewelry

www.silver-thailand-shop.com

Check out the Kama Sutra rings and finger armour, even the nail rings. Neat ankhlets for less than a tenner!

AXFORDS

www.axfords.com
Classic corsets.

AZRAEL'S ACCOMPLICE DESIGNS

www.azacdesign.com

It's that funny Batty woman again, which is understandable as it's her company! She pops up everywhere. 'Azrael's

Accomplice is dedicated to bringing beautiful Gothic clothing and accessories to Goths all over the world.' There's even a little link to her Battycam here. The photos aren't artfully posed, but being straightforward seems a more natural touch, there is also a nice mixture between old and new, and no quibbling over the quality – obvious – and price, decent. (Obviously the bloke stuff isn't much cop, but that always happens. No one has found a way to use Napoleonic or Crimean cavalry jackets etc – something cool, rather than plain foppish and gurly.) A couple of nice touches are the fashion show gallery, and the customer's photos. That's validation, and this is a truly great site.

AZSTARELLE
www.geocities.com/jaditelefae/shop
Shop for candles, herbs, witchy things, art prints, scrolls etc.

BABY, THE STARS SHINE BRIGHT
www.babyssb.co.jp
More classy gear from Japan, with a weird interest in Victorian underwear which has followed in the wake of Visual Rock, as has this boarding school Lolita style. Maybe Rasputina should base themselves there?

BAD ATTITUDE BOUTIQUE
www.badattitude.com
Adult themed site. Perv Noir.

BAD KITTY GEAR
www.badkittygear.com
Cat toys and backpacks.

BADCATS
www.angelfire.com/rock/badcats
Cool, a handmade pillow (faux fur, satin, velvet) site, including pillows made just for cats.

BATGEAR BEYOND
www.elektronikproductions.com/batgearbeyond
Good site of links for good stuff, with weekly updates. Sites are listed by selection. This means the quantity of products that they sell, and has nothing to do with the quality of the site. It isn't a vast site but there is lot of links from all areas.

BELLE DE LA NUIT
www.belledelanuit.com
One definitely to check out. Small range

of garments, with a variety of pics for each one, which is good. Main thing here is the Goth Household accessories. Vases, décor, clocks and watches, figurines, picture frames, jewelry, candle paraphernalia, perfume bottles. Truly compelling, even when they're copies.

BERT AND BUD'S VINTAGE COFFINS
www.vintagecoffins.com
I guess there's a market for everything, and this site is a blast! You can get kits for God's sake! And check out the coffins section, and the 'whimsical' designs in particular. Fantastic. Bert and Bud are an odd couple, but they do make exceptionally good crematory urns and pet coffins too, even some t-shirts – but, please... think of some snappier lines! Better still, people should e-mail them suggestions.

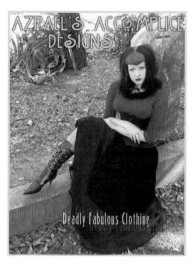
Deadly Fabulous Clothing

BINDI PAGE
www.bindishop.com
It's the decorative Hindu item that is placed just above the middle of the eyebrows. Mega range here.

BLACK ALICE
http://ha4.seikyou.ne.jp/home/Belial/alice.html
Japanese occult supplies, so you can seem cooler than your friends.

BLACK DRAGON FASHIONS
www.blackdragonfashions.com

BLACK FAIRY WINGS AND FAIRY COSTUMES
www.denyse.com/users/blackfairy
Okay, now I'm scared. There are people who actually wear these things. Not

dorky in any way, but still weird. The children's Tattered Pixie Skirts I can see, because kids like that Peter Pan/Narnia route, and, okay, horns are back 'by popular demand', but it's the wings. Dragonfly wings? Beautifully made I have no doubt... but where are people wearing these? (There was a www.blackfairy.com site but I think that went down.)

BLACK LODGE – DESIGN A GOTHIC FASHION DISASTER KIT
http://blodge.tripod.com/goth_fashion.swf
This is fun, as you change the outfits to make the model look ever weirder.

BLACK ROSE – GOTH JEWELS
www.gothjewels.co.uk
Really great jewelry selection of every main type, but also... flasks, belt buckles, tankards, chess set, lighters and t-shirts.

THE BLACK ROSE
www.blackrose.co.uk
One of the biggest, but certainly not the most attractive. The prices aren't high but the quality is mid-range at best, and some is downright tacky in a fetish vein. Even the photos are naff. Don't be put off though, as the variety will please, and it's not expensive, it just doesn't begin to compare with American shops.

BLACK SUNRISE GOTHIC JEWELRY
www.blacksunrise.com
And accessories. Massive site of goodies, including stunning rings, cool claws and okay t-shirts (been there, fuck that).

BLACK WIDOW
www.blackwidow.nl/index_all_eng.htm
Dutch shop offering jewelry and accessories, with English version.

THE BLADE SHOPPE
www.bladeshoppe.com/garg.html
Swords, gargoyles, art, crosses, t-shirts.

BLADES AND BEASTS
www.bladesandbeasts.com
Fantasy figures, plus interesting chess sets. Check this brilliant site out and root about in Skulls & Skeletons. Fantastic ashtray and clock for starters, all ridiculously cheap.

BLEUGIRL DESIGNS
http://home.earthlink.net/~bleuxiola/enter.html
Quality shirts, aprons, bumflaps,

bloomers, headscarves, with an auction element, plus message board. Cool pics.

BONE CHURCH GOTHIC CLOTHING
www.jeannienitro.com/BoneChurch.htm
Fantastic looking quality dresses for about $250, which is still cheap, bargains in the sale, and if nothing else there's gorgeous photos.

BONE CLONES
www.boneclones.com
Proper replica skulls and skeletons of humans, animals, fish and birds. Not tacky at all. In fact...wow! Anthropology department stuff, as they do casting of the expected material, but also fossils. A Neanderthal skull for $200? Extinct creatures. Sabretooth Cat skeleton kit. I would say it's the dog's bollocks, but they've probably got some of those somewhere too. Six-foot tall skeleton for $2500, but it's the others which amaze.

THE BONE ROOM
www.boneroom.com
One for 'Natural History Buffs', although you can buy genuine human bones here! I hope that most people's interest may lie in the fossil section, some of which can he had for as little as $2.00. (No sign of the elusive Eldritchius Calamitous.) Somewhat bizarrely they trumpet the fact that hyaenas are 'our speciality!' Cheaper, when it comes to bigguns, are the fossil and bone casts, with a rib as low as $2.00, and let me just say that here you will find the weirdest jewelry section in the world. One of the more conventional offerings are earrings, such as 'clusters of Thai iridescent green beetle wings. Very elegant', at $20.

BONEHEADS
www.serioussilver.com/boneheads.html
Skull jewelry, obviously, and... jaw-dropping at times. The Council Of Skulls bracelet just makes you giddy. Sure it's nearly $300, but it's perfection. Other stuff comes in at more normal prices – sterling silver rings for about £20 are good. They have other jewelry too, including boring biker stuff (when isn't it?) and Gothic offerings, where bats and vampires predominate. The variety is endless – Flames, Animals, Reptiles, Aliens, Oceanic, Faery.

BONNY DOON
www.science-art.com.au/sculpture.htm
Sculptured gargoyles and 'grotesques'.

BOOGIEMAMA
www.boogiemama.com
Hair extensions. Great little galleries.

BOOKENDS AND CANDLEHOLDERS
www.erinet.com/grandio/bookend.html

CANTARA
http://home01.wxs.nl/~cantara
Dutch shop catering for the Vamp crowd, but with clothing and jewelry (mainly Alchemy) too. Photos are interesting.

CASTLE CANDLES
http://castlecandles.com

Weird ones. If you're into hot wax these are worth a look.

CASTLE VON BUHLER RECORDS
http://cvb.drawbridge.com
Home of Glitter-Glam Countess and her dancers, The Princesses Of Porn, Sirensong and The Moors.

CATACOMBS RECORDS
www.cottagesoft.com/~felis/catacombs
New Christian Gothic label.

CATALYST STUDIOS
www.moritorium.com
Oddly clumsy site from this Seattle firm. Sections on Stonework, Housewares, Prints, Artefacts, Books and Accessories. Gallery is also good, especially the unusual but very distinctive work of Jason Soles.

CATASTROPHE CLOTHING
www.catastropheclothing.com
Currently a small range of gear designed by Jody but they look excellent so you ought to keep monitoring this site.

CAT'S MEOW CLOTHING
www.catsmeowclothing.com
Far more imaginative than most and decidedly cool. These are less showy, more relaxed, and probably more stylish if truth be told. Modern with a hint of Barbara Stanwyck's daughter about it all. Jewelry will make you wee with delight.

CAVEAT EMPTOR
www.cecostumes.com
Historical costumes from New Orleans, and modern Goth too.

CELTIC JEWELRY
www.gryphonsmoon.com
Huge site with quality goods, including for all Buffy & Angel fans more Claddagh material than just rings. Everything looks good, and is very reasonably priced.

CEMETERY SURPLUS
www.cemeterysurplus.com
Ashtrays, candleholders, clocks and gargs, but also odd wall reliefs, some fantastic skulls, and... cool business card holders!

THE CHAMBER OF HORRORS HALLOWEEN COSTUMES
www.chamberofhorrors.com
Clothes, masks, prosthetics to make you squirm and... Baby Stinky. Some of the costumes are so cheap (under $20) it's ridiculous, and they go right up to professional movie gorilla outfits for over $5,000. But watch out... they have clowns!

CHAOS A-GO-GO
www.chaosagogo.com

CHEEKY MONKEY
www.cheekymonkey.darkwave.org.uk/index.shtml
Superb shop involving Jo Hampshire. Nothing over a tenner and great stock. Some good import material available.

CHIC OR SHRIEK
http://succubus.net/chic
There are chic (site, hair, fashion, persona, make-up) reviews, and shriek reviews. Trouble is, a site gets a bad rating because someone's hair is bad!

It's one thing to tell us a site is a nightmare to navigate or even get into I to, but some of this is petulance. On the plus side they do introduce you to some real treats. Mind you, they go out of their way to offer hair and makeup tips too. They're not all about cruelty. After a while you realise the spite doesn't really feature, so you'd be a twat to miss out. Temporarily closed after 11 September. Hope it pops back soon.

CHOCOLATE EMPORIUM HALLOWEEN GOODIES
www.choclat.com/Halloween/halloween.htm
Cute sweets.

CITY MORGUE GIFT SHOP
www.citymorguegiftshop.com
'Welcome to the best place for Gothic, mortuary, forensic and death related gifts.' Absolutely. Totally weird site. Gifts include celebrity death certificates, Munsters memorabilia and 'collectables' which include some great toys. The 'floaty eyeball' key ring looks nice. The 'nodders' are garish and divine.

CLEOPATRA
www.cleorecs.com
For e-mail click on staff button. I've made it fairly clear how much I believe Cleopatra have been more than an important force in US Goth before, so I needn't repeat that. The site isn't very good, in terms of detail on bands, but there is clear news and recent releases plus vast catalogue. Only thing missing is an artists directory. Site is reasonably interesting about film video DVD, and new labels, especially as they do Glam and HipHop but...Stardust and Goldmine will bring us the classics by

Billie Holiday and Ella Fitzgerald. Yesssss! And *please* don't forget Josephine Baker, who was punk before Punk and Goth before Goth. There must be some great live recordings to put out.

CLUB BIZARRE
www.clubbizarre.co.nz
New Zealand label of Industrial, Gothic and Experimental music, importers and distributors of music, but also with a good stock of NZ artists.

CLUB GOTHIC
www.clubgothic.com
Big selection, but a fairly scrappy site.

COFFIN SHAPED GEMSTONES
http://members.home.net/mordaunte3/coffingems/gems.htm

COLOUR CONTACT LENSES
www.eyecolor.com
Some of the designs are okay but can you believe they don't have a gallery of suitable models wearing them?

A COOL BREEZE
www.ideco.com/fans/index.html
Fans.

CORPSES FOR SALE.
www.distefano.com
What do you get for the person who has everything? How about... Lady Die? Seriously. $650. You can even choose skin colour, hair colour and state of decay. A separate manual ($19.95) explains how to put lights in the eyeballs or cables to make the mouths open. For those of you on a tighter budget, but seriously disturbed nonetheless, there are always the mummified head ($245) or severed arm ($125). Or, cheapskates, a detached eyeball with optical nerve plus household fly loitering, for $21.95. $18.95 actually gets you a rather fancy reproduction of a Salem witch Death Warrant though, so it's not all weird.

CRESCI JEWELRY
www.cresci.co.uk
Excellent stuff – especially the rings – and quite unlike the majority of sites.

CRUELLA
www.cruella.ca
Montreal shop, self-titled as the Quebec Gothic Sanctuary, with Lip Service line

plus everything else. No mail-order but check out the site to see the photos. It's a gorgeous place. (Temporarily down.)

THE CRYPT CLOTHING COMPANY
www.cryptclothiers.com
Goth clothes you'll find elsewhere, Alchemy jewelry, Northern Lynx chain mail, Eden adult section, Kick shoes, cool Lip Service and serious all-purpose stuff, fine gurly tees, and some nice accessories sections, including stained glass.

THE CRYPT
www.the-crypt.de
Very good, big German site with clothes of Gothic and Fantasy with decent leather. (Incidentally the men look even sillier than normal, if that's possible!) Jewelry, candles, horror, books, good links and Buffy posters.

CUSTOM FANGS
www.whiteharbor.com/vampfangs/show.cgi/coffinmates/onlinestore.html
Online store with advice on customising fangs, and fantastic gallery of Natasha Epperson photos.

CYBERDOG LTD
www.cyberdog.net
Seriously dramatic site, verging on OTT, as the space journey each time you select a new item gets boring. The Virtual Shop is the only thing worth really looking at. Lovely bright trousers, jackets, skirts, t-shirts (including light), tops and accessories plus...well, music – except there isn't much, just a Top Ten of CDs, but then that's Cyber. Plenty of style, very little content.

DARK 13OOTIQUE
www.dark13ootique.com
Unusual jewelry, well worth a visit.

DARK ABODE
www.darkabode.com
For the disturbed child in us all, apparently. So how does that fit with advice on candles, crackle finish and shelves again?

DARK AGES DARK DREAMS
www.darkages.de
Welcome to the other side, it purrs. A German site with lots of decent Goth gear plus all-purpose outdoor stuff, shoes and boots, good jewelry and some accessories (mirrors, candleholders,

skulls, home decorations etc) – as well as a second-hand section.

THE DARK ANGEL
www.thedarkangel.co.uk
Not a huge range but a reasonable price – red cross standouts among some excellent bodices – for what is good quality and a decent service too. Swatch, etc.

DARK BAZAAR
www.dark-bazaar.com

DARK BEAT – UK LABEL
http://ourworld.compuserve.com/homepages/darkbeat

DARK DELICACIES
http://darkdel.com
Store with books, vampyre, gifts (good gargs and candle lamps – check out the circle of cats!), jewelry and t-shirts.

DARK EMPORIUM
www.darkemporium.co.uk
UK online store. All the usuals, including Alchemy. High quality skulls, jewelry, plus replica weaponry (!), candles and candelabra, lamps, burners, nice time-pieces, houseware, accessories (gear knobs!), etc – even 'drinking' (glasses, flasks, bottle-openers, goblets, tankards). Clothing is pretty poor (bandanas?) although t-shirts are quite nice. Resin sculptures – the Fossil Angel and Fossil fairy are *brilliant*, and rank figurines. A truly excellent site, which also has its Gothic Literary Opus, which you can contribute towards, and it's like those old RPG books, with choices at the end of each section.

THE DARK ENTRY
www.darkentry.com
This is nice, with only a small range but some are great, some are cute. Clothes, footwear, t-shirts, plus a music section – well, GWAR vids, if that counts.

DARK GARDEN
www.darkgarden.net
Fantasy outfits of general dreaminess look. Also has another site at: www.darkgarden.com that specialises in bridal wear, corsets and accessories.

DARK REFLECTIONS DESIGNS
www.darkreflectionsdesigns.com
Beautiful work. Mirrors, casting, frames etc.

DARK SIDE MASKS
www.darksidemasks.com
Oh, no, this is absolutely *amazing*. Just go there.

DARK STYLE
www.darkstyle.de
German Goth gear, small catalogue.

DARKLAND MUSIC
www.darklandmusic.com
Good mail-order/online.

DARKLAND OF TEARS
www.ifrance.com/darkland
Mail order distribution from France, with chat and forums sections, but very little news, and not having an English section when they have a good reputation is a seriously lost opportunity, but this does seem a small operation.

DE LUIDSPREKER
www.deluidspreker.de
Big music store of new and second hand items to do with Goth, Wave, Ambient and Industrial. Thousands of items, updated monthly.

DE MALLE HEKS
www.malleheks.nl
Wild Dutch shop, I think, with no pics. Beautiful site though!

DEAD ELF GOTHIC
www.deadelfmusic.com
American Gothic and Industrial music mail-order.

DELICIOUS CORSETS
www.deliciouscorsets.com
Very impressive site. Tasteful, elegant.

DESIGN TOSCANO
www.designtoscano.com/mktg/index.html
Great statues and similar for the garden.

DESIGNER DIRECT ARTISTRY
www.designer-direct.com
Serious site for interior design extras. Cherubs, plaques, gargoyles, historic Egyptian Art, angels, lions, bookends, candlesticks, statuary, religious art and Gothic to Christian Gifts.

DESIREE COSTUME HIRE
www.yellowpages.co.nz/for/desiree
New Zealand. Fetish, fancy dress, props, fangs etc.

DEVIANCE
www.velvet.net/~deviance
Latex demon, bat, fairy and garg wings, jewelry, corpses, skeletons and props. The wings look surprisingly good, and I guess at $500 the corpses are cheap, but it's the skeletons you want. They look great for $150.

DEVIANT CLOTHING
www.deviantclothing.co.uk
Cute site, with Goth/fetish/Cyber stuff.

DIABOLIK
www.diabolik.ca
Lovely site for Montreal Goth shop, with astonishing photos, and a big range of handmade quality clothes, brilliant jewelry, corsets and chain mail, and accessories. I guess you can e-mail for details as no mail-order is mentioned.

DIVA A GO-GO
www.operation-glam.com/diva
'Make-up tips for spooky kids.'

DIVALUXE
www.divaluxe.com
Synthetic hair pieces. Beautiful galleries.

DIVINITY
www.d-e-designs.com/divinity
Mail-order Goth clothing and accessories. All their own designs. Lovely site, good photos.

THE DOME
www.the-dome-clothes.de
Big German clothes site with some great photos.

DORK STORE
www.kovalic.com/sales/sales.html

DRAC-IN-A-BOX
www.dracinabox.com
Big range of clothes and goodies, with decent pics and even some info on photographers and models.

DRAGONHEART
www.dragonheart.nl
Dutch centre of medieval goodies.

DRAGONS GARGOYLES AND GIFTS
www.dragonsgargoylesandgifts.com
Good quality. Unusual chess section.

DRAGONS N STUFF
www.dragonsnstuff.com
Incense burners, dragons, gargs, skull pipes, etc.

DREAMS OF ARAFEL
www.dreamsofarafel.com
Jewelry, scents and pentacles.

DRESS UP JANICE
http://members.tripod.com/bluehead/kiss/java/janice.html
On-screen diversion.

DYSPHORIE
www.dysphorie.com
Parisian record shop site covering Goth, Doom, Black Metal, Electro, Thrash, Grind etc. Swift search, and their stock is very big.

EDEMONIUM
www.edemonium.com
French shop of scary things and Goth subjects, which include some incredible items for around the home.

ELF FANTASY
www.elffantasy.nl
Lovely site from a Dutch shop specialising in products, but also the stories behind their inspiration. Goblins, elves, games, gargoyles etc. (Heated garden gnomes!!!), board and card games, unicorns, roleplay, re-enactments, wizards, trolls, you name it. Virtually everything which ever looked like a Metal roadie is here. Fabulous stuff.

EMP MAILORDER
www.emp.de
Big German mail order service with English section, and it isn't just music and videos, but posters, band merchandise, jewelry, flags, masks, and a sales section.

EMPYRIA GOTHIC
www.dragonheart.nl
Dutch Goth clothes and piercings?

ENIGMA FASHIONS
www.enigmafashions.com
4 different collections of great dresses, with cool pics, plus a bridal section and jewelry/accessories. Top notch stuff.

ENTER THE GRUE GALLERY
www.gruegallery.com
He describes how he got into designing stuff, computer or models, and then you get to see them. Great skulls, dead cheap, body parts and bullet holes. Where else can you get a severed finger key ring (a snip at $5)?

EPSILON
www.epsilonrecords.com
Good label site with interesting bands, and info.

EQUINOXE
www.conk.com/world/equinoxe
Home of sorts to House of Usher and Cream VIII.

EYESCREAM JEWELRY
www.eyescreamjewelry.com
Very interesting jewelry designs, especially the dragonflies which are a lovely shape, even if looking very little like any dragonfly you've ever seen. Also very good bat selection in metal/glass. Per-haps best of all, some stunning bracelets and equally intriguing headpieces.

FAÇADE – Make-Up
http://home.flash.net/~monsters

FAIRE PAIR TIGHTS
www.tightsgoddess.com
'Making people pettable,' is a brave claim, when we're talking about re-enactment fans, but there you go!

FAIRYGOTHMOTHER
www.fairygothmother.com
Fetish and Goth gear. Pretty tat, and some glorious creations, with vibrant piccies.

FAIRY WINGS
www.faeriecreative.com
Unique designs, of faerie, dragonfly and feather variety with amazing pics.

FALLEN ANGEL
www.f-angel.demon.co.uk
Nice looking site, with a small selection of quality items.

FANTASYVA
www.fantasyva.com
Go to the 'Exotic Gifts' section and check out Gravely. Who in the right mind wants that? Weird shop, so take a leisurely look.

THE FEDERATION
www.thefederation.co.uk
High quality Goth and fetish gear. Nice bright site, shame about the clothes.

FETISH KITTEN
www.fetishkitten.com
'Fetish Kitten is the largest guide to online Goth and fetish retail sites.' Links galore on the following categories: tops, corsets, skirts, trousers, dresses, shoes, hair care, jewelry, accessories, cosmetics, lingerie, fetish, costumes, toys and household.

FIFI MAHONY
www.fifi-mahony.com
New Orleans boutique, with wigs, cosmetics and accessories (cases, bags, clips, gloves, horns).

THE FITTING ROOM
http://members.aol.com/fittingrm
Quality corsets from America. Possibly the world's only site to suggest you 'click on a grommet for information'.

FLAMING ANGELS
www.flamingangels.net
Some *very* nice items, somewhat obscured by the unnecessarily fussy design of the site, so worth persevering with. Handbags as well as clothes. Excellent quality pics.

FLUEVOG
www.fluevog.com
Shoes. For men, women and angels. Some cool, some vile.

FLYING GARGOYLE
www.flyinggargoyle.com
Gargs, angels, cowboys... you name it.

FOREVER IN BLACK
www.foreverinblack.co.uk
For people who want to stay in more. Gothic clothing, jewelry and roleplay. Is this Vagabonds stock? Seems very similar.

FUNDRESS
www3.justnet.ne.jp/~fundress
Amazing Japanese outfits.

A FUNKY SHOE AND BOOT
www.geocities.com/bbbwwwkat
Also 'Sleaze Attire', which may come in handy, who can say?

GAIL'S GOTHICS
http://members.nbci.com/gailsgothics/index.htm
They say it's cheap, and they started because they were sick of seeing stuff that was too expensive, and hard to find – so they make their own. 'We started with ceramic gargoyles and branched out to candle holders, incense burners, lamps, scented gift caskets & candles and many other interesting things. Everything we carry is hand-crafted by Louisiana artists.' Don't be put off by how tacky the site looks, because what they have for sale is genuinely excellent. Spell Kit looks nice, offering good old reliable New Orleans voodoo!, the Bat soap seems divine, and the boxes are nice. 'The Hostage' is indescribable. (This vanished with a surfeit of nbci activity, so do expect it back, and maybe search elsewhere for them.)

GALLERY SERPENTINE
http://galleryserpentine.com
Australian fashion site with underwear, capes, doublets, skirts, tops, dresses, PVC, t-shirts and there's an Alsatian modelling a corset!!! Great pictures. If you're into the Victorian style or some mix and match this place is pretty special. Look at the skull print cincher, whatever that is. Gorgeous.

THE GARGOYLE ANNEX
www.legendgiftshop.com/legendgift/gargoyleannex.html
Big New Agey place. A few gargs.

THE GARGOYLE SANCTUARY
www.gargoylestatuary.com
Very nice selection, especially the goblins.

GARGOYLE SCULPTURES – ARK 9
www.ark9.com
Impressive work, of a limited edition nature, at amazingly cheap prices.

THE GARGOYLE STORE
www.stonecarver.com/sculpture.html
Some very distinctive work, and reasonably priced.

GARGOYLE STATUES
www.gargoylestatues.com

A pretty wild selection here. Definitely worth seeing.

GARGOYLE STATUES
www.panpipes.com/gargoylestat1.htm

GARGOYLES CLOTHING
www.gargoylesclothing.com
Very nice Goth clothes, of all types, plus hosiery, purses, bags. The usual flouncy rubbish for men who want to look like something out of a Robert Louis Stevenson epic. Nicely extravagant capes and... angel wings! Great tapestries and bedspreads in the Gothic Décor section, along with gargoyles, candle holders, incense burners, ashtrays, coffin boxes and rugs. Bondage, boots and jewelry too.

GARGOYLES LTD
www.gargoylesltd.com/gargoyles
Small range of gargoyles and statuary, but high quality and reasonable prices.

GARGOYLES STATUARY ENTRYWAY
www.gargoylestatuary.com
You've got some seriously brilliant pieces here. The Jester shelf is a touch alarming!

GAUTHICA COM
www.gauthica.com/e_shoppe_main.html
Art (pleasant), photos (weird), music (empty), merchandise (empty!), links (tiny).

GHOULIE BABIES AND GLAMOUR VAMPS
http://members.eisa.net.au/~lady
One-off dolls by Lady Nemesis, and... Ghoulie Keyrings or Gardening Ghouls. Very cute, sometimes mad, and very cheap, although they are all renovated toys. As little as US$12 (although this is an Australian site), which is about what, eight quid? For a unique item? 'Any faults or damage they may have incurred in a previous incarnation only adds to their ghoulish charm and is always mentioned within their description. Due to the fact that all of the Lady's children are 100% unique and one of a kind, this site will be updated regularly as new babies are created. Ghoulie babies come with an aged paper scroll to tell you a little about their lives. Glamour Vamps come packed in their own coffin.'

GIFTS AND BEYOND
www.gifts-and-beyond.com/catalog/gargoyle.htm

Loads of different sections here. Not big on detailed studies, but there are some attractive things, and the gargs are quite jolly.

GIRLGOTH.COM
www.girlgoth.com
'Spooky goods for the masses.' They style you and there's some great before and after photos to gawp at.

GOLD
www.cd-gold.co.jp
Goth, Punk and Rock CD shop in Japan. I was clicking blindly away and the first thing I found was a mention of Ausgang, which cheered me up. No idea how to order, but find someone Japanese and you're laughing. They're not only home to surely the biggest Billy Joel bootleg collection in the world but many other bands. (Not that you heard that from me.) Plenty of good Goth material on show.

GOOD GOTH
www.goodgoth.com
Hair dye, clothing – t-shirts, vinyl and vegi leather, hosiery, dresses and good gowns – stickers, shoes, skulls – Werewolf and Gentleman are worth seeing – jewelry, cosmetics, scents, etc.

GOTH CENTRAL
www.gothcentral.com
Ha! They even have a text files service! And... this is a great site. T-shirts, books, jewelry, tarot, Celtic, radio, chat, links, bulletin board, horoscopes and mp3. The Jewelry is good, although I backed out of the Death section when I saw it had 'Speculum' listed in the contents! Ace book sections, by genre and author.

GOTH PROPS
www.dagonbytes.com/spencers/gothprops.htm

GOTH ROSARY
www.gothrosary.com
Nice designs, plus site also has the unusual pic in the gallery where she's used a cemetery statue as a model for her wares. Cute key rings and dirto cheapo.

GOTH-ISH PATTERNS
www.toreadors.com/tlb/patterns.html
Patterns, naturally.

GOTHCARD 2.0
www.gothcard.de

English version available on cute German e-mail Goth postcards.

GOTHIC ARTS
www.gothicarts.com
Handmade cherubs, angels, gargs (Compu-gargs are fabulous!), lions, friezes, plaques, bookends, big urns, ironware, pewter ware etc.

GOTHIC CANDLES
www.gothic-candles.com
Custom made, scented or un. Thing is, ones like the owls are so lovely who could bear to burn them? And the titchy ones are under $2.00!!! They have a huge range of candles, and they're all beautiful, all insanely cheap, and they even have ones for seasonal themes, or birthdays, valentines day, xmas, father and mother's day, parties etc. Vast badge line too. An *essential* site.

GOTHIC CATALOGS
www.geocities.com/SunsetStrip/Alley/4888/catalogs.html

GOTHIC CREATIONS INC
www.gargoyles.org
'Gothic Creations, Inc. carries an extensive selection of gargoyles, "Greenmen", grave images, architectural elements, tapestries, jewelry and much more.' That includes extravagant tapestries, which you have to see, beautiful selection of gargoyle books, and I know what you're

Gothic Candles

all wondering. Greenmen? Allow me to look smug for a moment, only to then admit I wasn't sure either. In this instance it's a version of gargoyles, like a pagan-ish symbol of regeneration. Remember 'Green Man And The March Of The Bungalows' by The Dancing Did? Remind me to sing it you some time.

GOTHIC DESIGNS
http://freespace.virgin.net/debi.lysaght/gothik designs
Really good Celtic and Medieval bridal wear, plus jewelry.

GOTHIC DESIGNS
www.gothicdesigns.net
Bastards! They coax you in deeper with talk of stunning Tiffany-style lamps, and then not only aren't they ready yet but they'll be fairly pricey. (Not hefty, but you'll need to be dedicated.) This is another one of those sites you *have* to see, and not only because the work is wonderful but it may be one of those areas where it makes you realise something you've been missing. Ordering a made-to-order glass panel isn't going to be at the front of most of our minds, is it? When you see them you'll start planning. It's not only glass. An 'Ammo Box' purse? Statuary columns? Metal castings (check out the Gothic clocks) of all types and what might be lovely pill boxes.

GOTHIC FIGURINE COLLECTIBLES
www.phoenixorion.com/phoenixorion/gothic2.htm

GOTHIC INSIGHT
www.gothic-insight.co.uk
A small selection in each category, but not bad. Cool pendants, gross t-shirts, decent buckles, odd tarot choices, t-shirts, earrings, and flags? Flags!!! Actually, they're okay, as are the flying bats for the wall – and check out that Furie Goblet ('Skulls').

GOTHIC JEWELRY AND GOTH BLACK ROSE JEWELRY
www.gothicrose.com
Whoa, these are gorgeous!!! 'Black Rose jewelry represents a new product in Gothic fashion, utilizing Black Jade & The Blood Red rose in vampire & gargoyle styling.' The black rose in a bottle pendant is amazing, and only $13.90? In fact there is a whole series of flowers in these odd vials. These are the best jewelry item I have seen on any of the

sites. Also odd wedding ideas, cool bats... and you will spend ages gawping at their incredible Victorian section (click on 'Legend' on left hand menu). So far ahead of all the other sites it's incredible.

GOTHIC SCULPTURES

www.shartlesculptures.com/gothic.html
Small, basic but quite sweet traditional pieces.

GOTHIC SCULPTURES

www.angelsandearthlythings.com/sculpt.html
Huge array of gargs, griffons, wyverns etc.

THE GOTHIC SHOPPE

www.thegothicshoppe.com
Hair care, cigarette holders and cases, artwork, jewelry, music and books. All pretty nice, and the jewelry is excellent.

THE GOTHIC STORE

www.spidersreach.com

THE GOTHIC T-SHIRT COLLECTION

www.ensg.u-nancy.fr/~cognot/tshirts.html
Ancient Kensington market site. Nostalgic designs.

GOTHICA STUDIOS

http://gothicastudios.hypermart.net

GOTHICS NATURE

www.gothics-nature.de

GOWN OF THORNS

www.gownofthorns.com.au

GRANDIO

www.grandio.com
Gargoyles, dragons, and the usual stuff, but with one notable oddity. Check out the Flap Cats – cats with wings!!!

GRAVE NEWS – LABEL

www.gravenews.demon.co.uk

GREY STERLING'S SELF-SERVICE MORTUARY

www.geocities.com/Wellesley/2779
Little links list to auctions, make up, clothing, dye, nail polish and advice tips.

GYPSY MOON

www.gypsymoon.com
For more than just the stick-thin as some are available in 'bountiful sizing'. All romantic stuff, which looks good, and the photos are unintentionally amusing.

HAUNT MASTERS

www.hauntmasters.com
Halloween specialists. Great fun site. Brilliant quality and variety, for low prices.

HAUNTED HEADSTONES

www.hauntedheadstones.com
Incredible!!!!! Wooden copies of gravestones, based on old designs from cemeteries. Read the 'History' bit, because this guy is really cool. His garden sounds fantastic come Halloween. Kids in the area must be thrilled. Basically, these must be the *ultimate* decorative item for the home. One of my favourite sites in this book.

HEEBEEJEEBEES

www.heebeejeebees.com
PVC, custom clothing, makeup, jewelry etc. Pretty standard but they have a great little range of t-shirts.

HEIDI

www.aros.net/~viverra
Artist, jeweller and seamstress. Only jewelry visible.

HELLO KITTY

http://store.yahoo.com/sanriostore
If you like the Hello Kitty site you can buy these, pretending they're presents for younger relatives, and then give them something shoddy instead at the last moment. Love the Goth penguin.

HEXED

www.hexed.net
PO Box 7875, Huntingdon Beach, CA 92615, USA. Deviant clobber. Note: 'Hexed Industries does not condone being flogged by an ugly nun'. The site is an ad, albeit a funny one – so you have to send an SAE, 'and see if you don't get something strange in the mail'.

HEXENKESSEL

www.hexenkessel-herford.de

HORROR GENRE WEB STORE

http://spidersreach.com/
Figures, t-shirts and the like.

HOT TOPIC

www.hottopic.com
People get really pissy about this place but it's effective, isn't charging extortionate rates and there's usually

something of interest so why moan? The accessories are okay, and it brings CDs into places they might not ordinarily appear. Wish it happened in the UK. Hot Topic for larger sizes at: www.torrid.com

THE HOUSE OF ILL REPUTE

www.geocities.com/FashionAvenue/Mall/3538
More attractive classics, with some modern minxy wares thrown in. Lovely site but if they want to get taken seriously then ditch geocities for gawd's sake! PVC backpack (Clothes & Jewelry) – with bat wings to give your shoulders such a cool look – is a classic, but would be even better in leather.

HOUSE OF LILLITH

www.houseoflillith.com
Goth, clubwear, fetish, corsets, accessories, beauty stuff. Pretty new, so building the site and range up, but it's quality stuff, with nice pics.

I SPY GRAPHICS

www.ispygraphics.com
T-shirts, stickers, art and comics.

I'M DERANGED

www.imderanged.com
Brilliantly unpredictable site, updated several times a month. Lots to admire.

IMPALER IMPORTS

http://members.tripod.com/Imported-Impaler/index.html
Novelty and collector items from Romania.

INDIEtective

www.indietective.de
Another big German mail-order firm, and they seem cheaper than the others. Has English version.

INFA ROT

www.infrarot.de
Biggest German music mail order? Probably. It's *sensational*.

INKUBUS HABADASHERY

www.inkubus.com
Goth clothes and accessories. 'Lip Service, Jeannie Nitro, Atrocities, Cookie Puss, Catherine Coatney, Shrine, Serious and others. Jewelry from Marche Noir, Alchemy Gothic, and others.' A lovely shop in South Florida (the area's premier

shop?) with its online capabilities, offering a variety of clothes.

INTERNATIONAL WENCHES GUILD
www.wench.org
This is a resource for wenches, of the historical variety, and has a direct link to www.virtualfaire.com – which has the clothing and extras you could possibly require for entering into this separate reality.

INTERNET UNDERGROUND
www.internetunderground.com/index.php?ParentID=37
Ever-expanding fashion sites list.

IPSO FACTO
http://ipsofacto.www7.50megs.com
Genuine Goth store. Clothes for Goths, fetish freaks etc. Not made by them, I don't think, and they include stuff by Jeannie Nitro, Terri King etc. Nodding Goth Girl toy is sweet. Dunno about Nunzilla!

IRRIDESCENT VEIL DESIGNS
www.shadows.addr.com/store
Very small range of goods for men and women but it looks good.

ISIS ENLIGHTENED
www.isisenlightened.com
Jewelry, with many bargains to be had, plus one-of-a-kind Barbie dolls.

IVY GOLEMS & GARGOYLES
http://stores.yahoo.com/ivygargoyles

IXION LUXURIA
www.ixionluxuria.nl
Dutch site. Seems to do Gothic décor – doors and whatnot, but also film/multimedia stuff.

J.C. CREATIONS
www.jc-creations.com
Amsterdam. Big range of corsets and lingerie. Strange galleries.

JACQUELINE'S GOTHIC VEILS
http://gothicveils.hypermart.net
Skirts, purses, pillows, chokers and head stuff.

JEANNIE NITRO
www.jeannienitro.com
She is one of the greats, and this is a charming site of Goth, fetish and accessories. This is the home of some of the gear which turns up on other sites half the time. Lovely photos. Big mixture of goods.

JEKATEX
www.jekatex.nl
Dutch firm with small straightforward range, but well organised site.

JUNIPER MOON
www.geocities.com/FashionAvenue/Catwalk/7878
Gothic Designs of Distinction, they claim, and they do seem distinctly uninteresting, unless you're into veils, because that's their speciality. The red is eye-catching. Beyond that I'm blank.

JWH STUDIO STATUARY
www.jwhstudio.com

KAMALA'S PERFUMES
www.kamala.com

KIMBERLEE TRAUB
www.voicenet.com/~eeek
Very nice and distinctive ink illustrations. You'll have seen some of her work on Morbid Outlook. Now you can buy prints original and they're not expensive, so you're well advised to see this.

KINDRED SPIRITS
www.kspirits.co.uk
Top end of the market and a fascinating site, as Jema Davies is a serious designer. One-off commissions, as well as doing TV and film orders. Great pics.

KITTENS GARDEN
http://members.fortunecity.com/paintress/index.htm
Kitten's personal site and some bargains in the Goth auctions. Kitten's a naughty Dutch girl, who then censors her pics, designs gowns, which are well illustrated in a home setting, and has a great auction selection.

KRYSTAL & STEPHIN
http://home.pacbell.net/krystlyn/index.html
Do jewelry and items associated with Renaissance Faires.

LA MODE BAGATALLE
www.lamodebagatelle.com
Historical patterns for sale, concerning Artistic Reform Teagowns. Yes, *all* life is here! They also have 'Fine Books for the Discerning Vintage Fashion Enthusiast'.

ANDRE LASSON
www.andrelassen.com
Based in Amsterdam, Andre does *amazing* sculptures – check out the skeletal cutlery! – plus divine jewelry, and intriguing furniture – chairs, beds, gates, cabinets. Work of exceptional beauty.

LEANASHE CHAINMAIL
www.leanashe.com
Great site featuring beautiful work, divided into hand decorations, tiaras, necklaces, brassieres and accessories.

LEATHER MASKS FROM THE MERCHANT OF VENICE
www.angel-mask.com/index.html
Apparently this is surreal and otherworldly elegance. Don't know about the elegance but they are strange and oddly beautiful.

LEMON SPREAD
www.lemonspread.com
Very unusual Australian shop, which has some Gothic Art and action figures. Extraordinary jewelry.

LIKE A CAT
www.likeacat.com
Jewelry and crafts. A lot of it, as they reiterate endlessly, is about Pentagrams, but the new section, Gothic Sanctum will definitely be of interest. 'Band Of Skulls' looks a bargain at $30, and what's the 'Armor Penis' all about? Secretive 'poison rings' and 'potion bracelets' are cool.

LINEA GOTICA
www.linea-gotica.it
Goth and S&M mail order.

LIX
www.lixonline.com
From Champaign, Illinois, with Clothes, including fetish, events details, which they specialise in organising at clubs, or sometimes in-store events. Decent clothes, incredibly tacky (intentionally) horror t-shirts. Nice local links.

LUNA AND SOLARA MASK MAKERS
www.maskmakers.com
More captivating weirdness.

M&A MUSICART
www.ma-musicart.com
'We know what's Goth for you,' they proclaim. Label site.

MADAME LE GOTH
http://communities.msn.co.uk/MadameLeGoth
Vamp, fetish, men, women and Catastrafiend (the Cumbrian live event). Mainly fetish and vamp stuff, plus lots of pics of the ever-smiling Sharon who designs them. Well worth a quick look.

MADE WITH HUMAN HANDS
http://darksidesunny.hypermart.net
Gothic Gifts, including occasional one-offs. Very nice variety. Dolls clocks, toys, figures, dolls, candles, jewelry, swords etc.

MAGIC
www.magic-wonderland.de
Plenty of clothes, and accessories, with updated news section. Click on InternetShop, then wait until loaded.

MAJYUTSUDO
http://eyes.iris.ne.jp/majyutsudo/index.html
Japanese store, apparently for wizards and witches.

MAKE YOUR OWN COFFIN PURSE
www.phobe.com/coffins
Cute. Explicit directions on how to.

MAKE-UP WHORES!
http://glamourgirlies.com/makeup
Serious site. Reviews, tips etc.

MANIAFOBIA
www2.ocn.ne.jp/~mania

Luxurious dresses, which look like they're about £200 a pop, but startling quality for the price. Also seems to be a model agency and fashion design shop thing, with beautifully stark design.

MANIC CLOTHING
www.manic.co.nz/home.html
T-shirts with cool retro.

MARCHE NOIR
www.marchenoir.com
Dramatic hand jewelry and wristbands. Rather odd, and some 'stone' jewelry.

MARTZ MAILORDER
www.martz-mailorder.de
Another epic German music mail-order outlet.

MASKON
www.maskon.com
Female latex masks.

MASKS BY MORGAN
www.masksbymorgan.com
Mad, as you'd expect, with some extravagant Goth designs.

MASKS BY WENDY KLEIN
www.bajema.com/wendykleinmasks
Now *these* are surreal and elegant, and just a little bit scary.

MASQUERADE MASKS
www.goblinart.com
A delightful site, with more than just masks, having puppets, and some gorgeous galleries, strange paintings and a drawings, a six foot elephant's head and, strangest of all, a model of Eccles, the famous Goons character! It's still weird, but at least this is more playful than some fetish offshoots. Sadly there aren't many puppets, because they're fairly bizarre.

MEDIATRIX
www.mediatrixpublishing.com
Run by Michel of (Disjecta) Membra, this label has interesting Goth-Ind hybrid material, and good links for the NZ Goth scene. Also has a station: http://mp3.com/stations/mediatrix/

MEDIEVAL AND RENAISSANCE GIFTS
www.silkandstone.com/products/garburner.html

THE MEDIEVAL SHOP
www.soil.org.nz/tms/intro.html
Jewelry, armour, books and costumes.

MEPHISTO'S MUSE
www.redmeltdown.net/muse/index.htm
Keep an eye out for this one, it looks good. Nice little site where she does unscented candles to save those with allergies, but can also do them smelly. The 'Celestial Moon' candle is beautiful, and most of them deserve a second look. Even better... 'Right now I'm only selling candles, but soon I'll have dresses, cloaks, capes, corsets, purses, jewelry, afghans, pillows, etc.' Yeah, well you should be adding plaster statues to that, oh dozy one. Site is here but range is currently unavailable, whatever that means.

MESCHANTES CORSETRY
www.meschantes.com
Corset firm offering custom-made service. Nothing tacky.

METAMORPHOSE TEMPS DE FILLE
www.metamorphose.gr.jp
Very nice Japanese clothes. Site may appear confusing – I thought it was a sweet shop! – but stick with it.

MIDDLE PILLAR
www.middlepillar.com
Mega-serious site, with a huge array of music. Second only to Nightbreed. In fact probably bigger, but there is a lot of 'esoteric' releases here which sometimes veer more towards New Age territory. Be patient, it's a slow loading cronky old thing, but the Search and Find Similar facility works well.

MIDNIGHT MUSE
www.midnight-muse.com
Clothes, jewellery, artwork of the lush Victorian/Pre-Raphaelite, fairy dimension.

MORGANA
www.morganaclothing.co.uk
Big all-purpose site, with Gothic just one section among loads of fetish, bridal, PVC club, Punk ... so adequate, as you'd anticipate. Handy if you live locally, in Yorkshire, but too small otherwise. Decent outfits and unintentionally amusing photos. The blokes look seriously deranged. Shoot you Sir, indeed.

MORGEVE
www.morgeve.4t.com
Fassion and make-up tips zine.

MORRA FASHION
http://dark.gothic.ru/morra
Lovely site with *very* interesting photos of outfits, as these are genuinely different, but this is a Russian/English site and the English wasn't functional.

MORTICIA'S ATTIC
www.morticiasattic.com
Big range, from the usual clothes, clothes, capes, bondage tat, some of which is hers and she's clearing it out. Books, bags, purses, CDs, gloves, hosiery.

MUSIC NON STOP
www.musicnonstop.co.uk
Calls itself, quite reasonably, The Alternative Music Store, and contains an impressive array of material from Goth, Ind, EBM and varied Elec fields. Records, mags and tickets.

N + H HOMEPAGE
www.kh.rim.or.jp/~yungoni/na+h/index.htm
Japanese clothes and jewelry designer. Look for Map, click on N+H block and you're in a site for clothes and accessories, much of it lovely, which is actually a woman's stall in a market. The accessories, as you would except for Japan, are detailed and beautiful (apart from the Jesus and Mary lampshade!). The only problem is ordering, but I'll leave that one with you. For stuff which hasn't sold out check 'What's New' first.

NAIADI
www.naiadi.com
Little Italian fashion catalogue, and very nice too. Just moved to above URL. Expect delays.

NECROMANTIQUE
www.necromantic.net
Well worthy of a lingering visit through all their wares – clothes, jewelry, furnishings, literature and 'morbid curiosities'.

NEHELENIA DESIGNS
www.nehelenia.de
Christina Dettmers does stupendous Goth and Vintage designs. Site has English and German versions. Serious quality and great sections – Gothic

(corsets, skirts, dresses), Movie Costumes (she will make what you see in the photos), Renaissance – Mercantile 1500-1600, Le Boudoir 1730-1790, Regency Pavilion 1799-1820, Period Brides, Gentlemen's Parlour. The costume events photographs are *wonderful*.

NEW YORK CARVER
www.newyorkcarver.com
Beautiful site with stone carvings to buy, but also historical matters too.

NITEWEAR
http://isidis.kasei.net/~nitewear
Chainmaille jewelry, plus beads and waves.

NOCTIFER
www.noctifer.de
German mail order site, offering English version and handling clothes (skirts, dresses, tops, blouses, coats and robes) along with veils, PVC gear, gloves and tights. Alchemy products, cheap jewelry and cosmetics. Also... plush bat pets which may well appeal, being rather exclusive, and some statues which include delightful pocket dragons.

NOSFERATU
www.goth.co.za/nosferatu/nosferatu%20index.html
The leading fashion outlet in South Africa. Handmade outfits, at remarkably low prices (unless I can't use the international currency converter properly.) Nice galleries.

NORTHBOUND LEATHER
www.northbound.com
Well known leather experts – with pretty much everything here you could desire – and a rudey site, so be warned, or encouraged, depending on your depravity. Mostly plus points, only let down by laughable belts and the shock that their leather jackets are a bit poncey.

NOVA TREASURES
www.novatreasures.com/catalog1572.html

NOVUS – THE GARGOYLE STORE
www.gargoylestore.com
I loved these. Charlie Cigar is really cute! Some, like Roswell, who is asleep, are enchanting, but others *are* quite

grotesque which a lot of firms tend to neglect. Winged cats again as well, which is nice to see. Prices are good too, considering their size.

NRG
http://plaza14.mbn.or.jp/~nrg
Japanese handmade leather goods. Great bags.

OPTICAL DILLUSIONS
www.dillusions.com
Smoking blends, plus tons of standard jewelry and related Goth/Vamp/gargoyle goods. Picture frames, action figures, statues, t-shirts, dragons, 'alternative psychedelic liquids' (lettuce opium???). Particularly impressive ashtray section.

THE ORIGINAL SIN CLOSET
www.originalsindesign.com
Period or fetish costumes. Obviously quality goods, but site is rubbish. You can see virtually nothing, so you're better off contacting them by e-mail (angldst@originalsindesign.com) to see what they can do.

THE OUTSIDER
www.tccorp.com/Merchant2/merchant.mv

PAF
http://gothik.nu
Great online music catalogue.

PAF RECORDS
www.pafrecords.com
Cheap-ish Goth, Industrial and related styles on CD.

PANDORA'S FUNBOX
www.pandorasfunbox.com
Corsets, bikini, fetish. Tiny selection, but displayed in a cheery fashion.

THE PALE COURT
www.netwalk.com/~loki
Romantic clothiers. Gothic, wedding and re-enactment specialists. Top quality handmade to order.

PENELOPE'S WEB
www.penelopesweb.com/gargoyles.html
Gargs, wizards, faeries, Merlin etc. Gallery pics aren't very big.

PENNANGALAN – GREAT BOOTS
www.pennangalan.co.uk/boots/index.html

PENTAGRAMME
www.pentagramme.de
Seems Occult/Satanic/Black Metal stuff, and mainly jewelry – including dragons and bats – of all descriptions, and not expensive.

PIERROT
www.netlaputa.ne.jp/%7Epierrot-
Great Japanese site, be it an online store or shop promo, offering clothes from Marble Visible, Kazuko Ogawa, Classic Lolita. Mille Fleurs, Victorian Maiden, Atelier Boz and Oh LaLa. Some of it's really classy.

PLASTE+ELASTE
www.plaste-elaste.com
German store with good, if small, Goth range. Nice pics.

POE'S ATTIC – VICTORIAN MOURNING JEWELRY
www.poesattic.com
More books than actual jewelry and it's an acquired taste because these are almost ugly. The reference books look interesting, and you can get a gravestone rubbing kit, which could prevent you just naively rubbing yourself frantically against them. That way leads to incarceration.

PROJEKT
www.projekt.com
That latter day 4AD. The modern world. Store – be careful here as there's new and old. Look for the bar top right, and check out the Darkwave while you are there for the distribution they offer on tons of brilliant material, including a few interesting magazines. News – nicely detailed and still friendly.

PUIMOND
www.puimond.com
'Progressive corset design' from a top designer, with more variety than usual.

PURE BLACK DISPLAY
www5.ocn.ne.jp/~gothic/gatepage.htm
Japanese site which features a few pieces of attractive Goth jewelry and fashion accessories, although what most people will probably want is the top the model is wearing!

PURPLE RAVEN
www.purpleraven.com
Faeries, mermaids and sea serpents,

Raven Eye Gothic

magickal wands, dream pillows, mohican forest bears, darkling wear and dragons. I won't spoil the surprise, and besides, I'm too cynical for cute things.

KATY QUINN
www.katyquinn.com
Already well known for her clothing work in Australia, and the Vanitas Empire activity in Camden, Katy is now resident in Whitby and still forming this site (to be up and running shortly before this book appears), focussing on clothing designs, but also with solo art and design, plus paintings, photography and even sculpture. Bound to be *top* quality.

QUINNSTER
www.quinnster.co.uk/hair
Interesting site about hair styles and all involved.

RAGDOLL WEAVE CO.
www.ragdolly.net

Brilliant pics in the gallery of this detailed hair site.

RAVEN EYE GOTHIC
www.raveneve.com
Jewelry of charm and distinction, according to me. The 'Ultimate Gothic Chain And Enamel Cross Choker' takes some beating.

REDHAZE
www.redhaze.com
Mainly Punk or rave gear, but hair dyes and cosmetics may suit. The best section is the wristbands, as they actually do good ones. Belts aren't bad.

RELIGIOUS SEX
www.religioussex.com
Posh frocks, lovely gloves and sleazy stuff. Some of the men's stuff is actually great, or maybe it's just the models aren't so dopey as usual? This is a great

A Rose Ad Mortem

site that doesn't really make enough of itself, but the customer's photo gallery is really good.

RESIST MAILORDER
www.resist.de
Small mail order specialist. Lots of neo-folk.

RESURRECTION
www.resurrection-rec.demon.co.uk
Excellent London record shop, label and mail order service.

ROISGARDEN
http://roisgarden.com
Attractive clothing line. Small at present but quality corsetry and historical stuff with Goth line planned.

ROMANTASY
www.romantasy.com
Corsets.

ROOM 13 – San Diego
www.room13.com
Intentionally garish shirts, stickers, hats, skullptures. Band links.

A ROSE AD MORTEM
www.rosemortem.com
A stunning online catalogue of Goth clothes. Gowns, skirts, tops, corsets. Fabulous photographs anyway, whether you want clothes or not, and I was thinking these were cheap, like £70 for a gown, but it's dollars, which is even cheaper! It's also unintentionally hilarious, where the bloke in the shirts

looks such a wet git. A maternity and children section too, which is good, with seriously happy toddler who hasn't yet learned how to scowl!

ROUND TWO CORSETRY
www.roundtwocostumes.com/corsets
A popular site. Renaissance era corsets? A huge selection of those, plus their costumes gallery which go from what the pre-burlesque girls used to wear when dancing in wild west saloons to Pokemon.

SACKCLOTH
http://browser.to/sackcloth
Impressive Sydney site. Corsets, dresses, frock coats, one-offs. Funnily enough some of the photos, which are all impressive, of the woman with orange hair actually work as generally cool portraits.

SAINTS AND SINNERS
www.collide.net/saintsandsinners
This is absolutely wonderful – a series of cases made by Karin from Collide. Antique silver, beautiful designs, and at $40 that's cheap! Nice unified feel to the designs yet they're all clearly different. If you don't love these I'm calling your parents. They're entitled to know they raised philistines.

SALES FROM THE CRYPT
www.thecrypt.net
'Home of the Oxford Gargoyle range and the Bone Zone, where you will find handmade skulls, gargoyles, babewyns, mirrors, candleholders, and assorted objects d'art, as well as a unique range of Celtic knotwork jewelry and Runes.' Babewyn? Shelf-perching beasts, apparently. Nice Bone Zone for skulls in plaster, and authentic gargoyles in repros of medieval styles.

SDL DESIGNS
http://sdldesigns.com
Amazing medieval outfits, slightly different approach to Goth wear, and some Fantasy outfits which are almost a mix of the two.

SEKTOR 1
www.sektor1.com
Cyber fashion and music.

STEVEN SEVERIN
www.stevenseverin.com

SEXY FOOTWEAR

www.sexyfootwear.co.uk

More or less a trash-free fetish site. Yes the underwear side of things looks a bit naff on this site (which also has wristbands and suchlike) but the shoes are quite amazing. Women's only, but works of art most of them.

SEXY SHOES

www.wildfree.com/hotfoot.htm

Thigh-highs galore, and your up-market slapper Light Up Shoe, popular with porn models everywhere.

SHADOW CLAD

www.shadowclad.com

Used Goth gear flea market.

SHADDOW DOMAIN

www.shaddowdomain.com

Okay – showergel 'Transfusion' bags? Now that's cool, actually. A brain jelly mould? Getting the picture? They do conventional crap for round the house too, switchplates, mugs, magnets, but it's the little things which please – a skull journal, some nice runes, Angel Snot ('A jasmine-scented, pearlescent substance that you can squish and stretch. Just don't wipe it on the back of the couch.') Also a small section called 'Trashy Wench Productions' which feature one-off items.

SHADOWS

www.shadowclad.com

A site of used/nearly new Goth clothes and accessories. Excellent site. Buy and sell, with decent sections on most areas of women's clothing, but not with many items because I'd imagine the turnover is swift. Also... stuffed with bargains. These are cheap. Book section just started.

SHADOWSPHERE MAILORDER

http://shadowsphere-mailorder.de

Well, it's all in German, it's big, there appears to be a lot of Black Metal, magic and satanic dribblings, plus a big Gothic section of a discussion nature. And a big Fledermause thing, whatever that is.

SHERRIDAN CELTIC GIFTS

www.smsmith.com

Celtic jewelry, prints and stationary.

SHINANAI

www.angelfire.com/stars/shinanai

'Deliciously Unusual 3-D Food Sculptures.' I'm not joking, and the menu of sections is enticing 'Creating A Dead Baby For Alice Cooper, Severed Penis For Shoyo of E.Z.O.' Accompanying photos will make you wish you hadn't eaten earlier.

SHRINKING VIOLET: PANDEMONIUM ONLINE

www.shrinking-violet.co.uk

Brilliantly colourful site for clothes.

SILKS AND VELVETS

www.yosa.com/catalog.html

Luscious variety and quality. Corsets, gowns (fantasy, wedding, renaissance, historic) and Gothic/geisha section. Kimono pics are awesome, elsewhere the designs are let down by cutesy illustrations.

SIOUXSIE & THE BANSHEES

www.vamp.org/Siouxsie

Excellent site. Also regularly updated: www.untiedundone.com

www.geocities.com/~emily777/SiouxsieLinks.html

SIREN

http://clover.forest.net/siren/main.html

Ah Siren, the site which loads slower than Alfred the Butler.

SIX FEET UNDER

www.haas.berkeley.edu/~tmiller/sixfeet.htm

'Ever wish you could make your own clothes but didn't think you had the time or skill? I have put together instructions for making easy garments geared for beginning sewers that can generally be completed in one day. Never again will you be subjected to the tyranny of modern fashion!' A D-I-Y Guide to Gothic Fashion. It's not a big affair, just Full Skirt, 'Morticia' Skirt, Renaissance shirt, and Pirate shirt. Back to the tyranny of fashion we go then.

SKIN FIT – JAPAN

www.ceres.dti.ne.jp/~kyoei

Japanese fetish site with big lycra, rubber, PVC and leather section, with the occasional nurses' outfit or choker.

SKULLS/SKELETONS

www.evolutionnyc.com/IBS/SimpleCat/Shelf/ASP/Hierarchy/09.html

The expected stuff, as this is scientific, but also books and prints, and fossil cats, but also genuine fossils, when they have any, medical kits, toys, shells, minerals, meteorites. I was thinking how nice the Dimetrodon was, when I realised it cost $8,700. One of the dinosaur replicas goes for $25,000. You could buy me for less!

THE SMOKIN' DRAGON

www.smokindragon.com/gargoyles.htm

All manner of craved trinkets, characters and other gifts.

SOMETHING SPOOKY

www.somethingspooky.com

You're going to love this, so do as they request and be patient while it loads, because it is well worth the wait. The site has gone down, but I don't believe this is anything other than a temporary blip. These six weird girls and token boy run a fun site, hope to sell photos of themselves and add some personal items in with the general products. (Good news for Tick fans.) They offer jewelry, original art and some 'spooky' items. Some are just plain daft, and all the more desirable for it (see the Classic Monster bracelet as a great example). Most jewelry is actually Vamp-related, so you may find the art by Dead Dave more interesting – and the Red Skull *is* awesome. Even if they sell that they should keep the image there. The 'spooky' element is, perversely, a normal range of dresses, cloaks etc including one-off items (purses/bags) plus some weird little devil musician figures. This is a *seriously* unpredictable site so you should find returning each month uncovers new evidence of things to intrigue. They also do Conventions, so don't say you haven't been warned.

SPECTRAL CREATIONS

www.spectralcreations.com

Ah, more divine individual stained glass objects, especially the mirrors, but you need to be quick as they seem to sell out of everything. Mesmerising items.

THE SPELL SHOP

www.thespellshop.com

'I will take you into a Magickal Realm where you can tap into and use this energy to create change and bring into your life whatever it is you desire.' Blimey! There are spells and supplies to buy. You can even Send A Spell, for

Saints and Sinners

$18.00, although I saw no mention of any money-back guarantee.

SPIDER'S WEB – SPOOKY BOUTIQUE
www.spookyboutique.com
This is adorable. The funniest site I've encountered, which feels chaotic in a cool manner. You'll definitely approve. Great postcard designs, the lovely Batsie game, good clothes, plus skimpy lace or PVC trash, and nice range of gloves, tights, shoes, adequate leather, hair dye, wigs, tiaras, boas, sunglasses.

STAR OF SOLOMON
www.wink.ac/~star/enter.htm
Japanese magic supplies.

STARKERS
www.starkers.com
Custom corsetry and romantic clothes, with a chat section. Lovely stuff all round, including bloomers for the brave. Once again, photos worth a visit alone.

STORMY LEATHER
www.stormyleather.com
Leather gear, mostly pervy, but virtually everything you could think of, or want.

STRANGE BOUTIQUE
www.redmeltdown.net/strange
Dark Shop webring.

SUNSPOT DESIGNS
http://apocalypse.org/pub/u/hilda/ssdcat.html
Brilliant selection of bracelets/ankhlets, chokers, earrings/earcuffs, pins, rings necklaces/pendants, and 'strange things'. Fabulous stuff, including the occasional one-off. Missing this site would be plain daft.

T. KUNITOMO
www.s-incjp.com/fas/tk/ttk.html
Japanese fashion collection. Not hardline Goth, obviously, but certainly attractive.

TART BLOSSOM ACCESSORIES
www.tartblossom.com
Anime hair for real people. Wild stuff, with mental wigs!

THE TASTE OF NEW ROSES
www.gothic-order.de/hauntedstore
A haunted store, apparently, from Germany. Seriously intense gargs, and... gurgle... Goth schneekugeln, which are those little glass things with a dioramic scene which you turn upside down and it snows. They look incredible and they're only about £20 (well, 60DM). The 'Monster' one looks fantastic and there's graveyard scenarios too, one with a bat taking off. Strange toys and puppets, horror masks which wouldn't scare a butterfly, odd carvings, nice skulls, and decorations which are quite scary. Totally *brilliant* site.

TATUMIRAGE
www.tatumirage.com/catalog.htm
Stockings which would be an acquired taste.

TEMPEST DESIGNS
http://badger.cx/tempest
Hand-crafted coffin-boxes.

TENEBRAE
www.tenebrae.com

Parasols, and they are divine. Some are umbrellas really, especially the seriously cool vinyl one.

TERRI KING CLOTHING
http://terrikingclothing.net
A big site, with less clothes than expected. Some are inspired, some silly, some cool, some bizarre.

TEUFELSKUCHE
www.teufelskueche.de
This is too big to try describing. Huge German clothing site. Great upgraded bondage kilt type stuff in among the Goth fare. If you can't find something of interest here you simply aren't trying.

THREE JANE 3
www.angelfire.com/ga2/ThreeJane3/index.html
Weird and interesting. New toys made from old broken ones. Cyber babies, BorgBies, Hell Dolls and Destroyed Dolls. None for sale due pressure of artist's work, but check the galleries.

TOOTH FAERY
http://zombie.horrorseek.com/vampires/toothfaery

TOXSIN
www.toxsin.com
Standard clothes, but unintentionally scary/funny photos.

TRASHY DIVA
www.trashy-diva.net
Vintage clothing. Pure class, with seriously cool content.

TRENCH COAT
www.inet.ca/trenchco/index.html
Matrix-obsessed coat site.

TRISHA STARR – HAIR
www.trishastar.com

T-SHIRT HELL
www.tshirthell.com
'Where all the bad shirts go.'

T-SHIRT KING
www.tshirtking2.com
This is funny. Search for t-shirts and see some wondrous items available. Hardly any cool names, but lots of genres.

TUSCANY TRADING
http://ttcgifts.com/

This is presumably for war game re-enactment types, but there is a gargoyle section or indoors and out which are okay, and very cheap. Pirate hats and flags... and just the place for that replica crossbow!

TWILIGHT ATTIRE
www.twilightattire.com
...'course it's corsets.

THE ULTIMATE GAROGYLES FIGURINES AND GIFTS
www.camelotgifts.com/gargoyle-catalog.html
They are very good but some are a little too cartoony, in a naff way. The majority are excellent, so have a good root about. Lots of variety.

ULTRASCHELL
www.ultraschall-mailorder.de
Message board, news, search, downloads, links as well as a big music mail-order section. In German. Nice layout, so you can also look through a second-hand and rarities section.

UNDERBELLY NIGHT GALLERY
www.underbelly.net
Not a huge range. Women's clothes are impressive but as usual men's stuff is blousey nonsense. The accessories are great – parasol anyone? The Egyptian jewelry is strangely clumsy, except a bargain silver scarab pendant at $20!

UNDERGROUND ARISTOCRACY CORSET COLLECTION
www.bway.net/~sbasu
Six very high quality designs by Shumit Basu.

UNDERGROUND SHOES
www.underground-shoes.co.uk

UNITED DESIGN GOTHIC SCULPTURES
www.raysmart.com/udcgotp1.html

URBAN GOTHIC NET
www.urbangothic.net
There are various collections of jewelry (nice rings, crap Voodoo section), plus Gothic Night bedroom attire, although that was being updated when I visited.

UTERO
http://homepage2.nifty.com/dollxxx/index.htm
Clothes from Japan. Whether one designer actually is called Jane Marple is open to question, but the quality isn't.

This is cool stuff, for gurlies only. JM, Masaki Matsushima and 'Other' create great work. Amazing jewelry.

VAGABONDS
www.vagabonds-clothing.co.uk
Cheap and cheerful, and quite gutsy. If you're a playful slut. Don't even think of taking the men's stuff seriously. The Punk stuff is good, in terms on bondage gear ('Juke' 1-3, 5-6 are crap) so check that out. Bags, boots and hosiery are standards.

VAMPIRE COSMETICS
www.vampirecosmetics.com/index.cfm
Eyes, lips, nails. Very cool site.

VANITAS
www.vanitasempire.co.uk
May not be up and running yet but this will be quality, due to the people involved and their history, so keep this bookmarked and check back.

VEGETARIAN SHOES
www.vegetarian-shoes.co.uk
Obviously an essential site for many. Shame there's no artistic designs in the boot department, because those would obviously be seriously popular.

THE VELVET GARDEN
www.velvetgarden.net
'The Velvet Garden is a site where Goths can buy or sell new & used Gothic clothing, music, books and accessories. It is like a large online Gothic Yard Sale!' It's not an auction site. You name a price, if one isn't already stipulated, for what you see and either the seller agrees or not. It's compelling viewing, if you know what I mean. Clothes, accessories, videos, CD, books. Brilliant.

VENUS
www.venusclothes.com
New and used 'full-figure' clothing (size 14) and up, including the Myth Demeanour line created just for them, although there's only four dresses right now. Considering how popular a site like this could be it is annoyingly cronky, and the pictures are uninteresting.

VERMILION GATES
www.vermiliongates.com
Tres posh firm offering great things –

what about the Gothic Gift Box? 'Each box includes: gargoyle, scented soap, scented votive candle, velvet cloth and glass gemstone marbles & pair of earrings in velvet pouch (earrings optional).' Only $20!!! Nice clothes, but they're letting their stock go to concentrate on the gift market. They also do chokers, soaps, and some jewelry.

VERSAND DER KLEINEN HEXE
www.gothickeramik.de
Unusual Goth ceramics site, which also includes powders and potions by the look of it. The ceramics are often really fantastic, so take your time, there's a lot to see.

VERSATILE FASHIONS
www.versatile-fashions.com/index.html
Corsets to costumes. High quality and huge range, including mags, vids, blahhhh.

VEXX ONLINE – FETISH-GOTH
www.vexxthem.com

VICIOUS VENUS
www.pout.com.au/viciousvenus
Fetish, PVC and well-known for corset designs.

VICTORIA COSTUMIERE
www.victoriacostumiere.com
Bridal or theatrical events clothing. Small range, top class.

VICTORIA LOUISE, MERCERS
www.fred.net/stull/victoria.html
Mercers? What a site! Go here and nowhere else (etc). Actually it's a bit weird. Mercers were dealers in fine cloth (unless my parents lied to me), and this site has that olde worlde feel, intentionally. It's historical costume patterns and the like. Not only that but... 'Victoria Louise is please to announce their upcoming Victorian buckram bonnet workshop.' Hurrah! They also do bridal veils, feathers and flowers, storage products (special paper etc, which some people ought to start considering if they have bought a lot of ornate clothes over the years), plus ribbons and brocade. Lace, millinery stuff, all sorts of fabrics, hoops and petticoats, buttons, dyes, threads and parasols. They bring honour to the name.

VICTORIA'S GIFTS
www.victoriasgifts.com/gargoyles.htm
Gargs are just the start. All sorts of weirdness, and obvious Victoriana.

VICTORIAN CHARM JEWELRY
www.vcharm.com
Themes are Bridal, Celtic, Wiccan and Gothic. All are excellent.

A VICTORIAN ELEGANCE
www.victorianelegance.com
Antique and Victorian clothes, jewelry and accessories. This is another amazing site that simply has to be seen and explored, and what they call antiques often relate to classic Bette Davis type forties and fiftiess stuff. Don't miss the amazing hats. Equally incredible selection of purses and compacts, shoes, hatpins, shoes, perfume, sewing items and magazines. For true connoisseurs.

VICTORIAN GOTHIC COUTURE
www.vicgothic.com
'High quality Corsetry, Gothic, Club, Evening & Dark ware for Men & Women.' Australian site. Very nice coats. Women's stuff is all good and the men... well, would you believe it? All designed to make you look a prize pillock.

VICTORIAN MAIDEN
www.victorianmaiden.com
Great Japanese shop. Wonderful photo section, and the catalogue throws up some really interesting stuff. Then all you need is a Japanese friend to help you order. Mainly clothes, and good quality, but with a few choice accessories including odd mirrors and their own firescreens!

VICTORIAN TRADING COMPANY
www.victoriantradingco.com
Perfect site for unusual gifts, and quality throughout. Replica jewelry. Bedroom and bathroom furniture and fittings, linen and lace, prints, desk accessories, hatpins, lamps, sewing bits, business cards, garden ornaments, kid's things rugs. Go there and luxuriate.

VINTAGE BUZZ
www.vintagebuzz.com
Retro classique.

VIRUS
http://members.tripod.com/~accw/virus.htm

Some pretty wild print designs here from this New Zealand shop.

VISABELLA MYTHIC CLOTHING
www.visabella.com
Two different catalogues online, and both very interesting. Hardly heavily Goth but very attractive. The small Dance In The Dream line offers great simplicity. It just looks so smart.

VITAL REFLEX
www.ukgargoyles.com

VIXENS AND ANGELS
www.vixensandangels.com/shoes.html
Boots and shoes, with tiny vegan section. Much admired by the Denver locals. Shoes, boots, body jewelry, jackets, suspenders, hair dye. Blah. Fairly average and therefore cheap, but good depth.

VOID
www.void-clothing.co.uk
This is a very nice site, even though there isn't a huge range. Some Goth, some fetish with nothing unusual, apart from UV accessories.

VOLLERS
www.vollerscorsets.co.uk
Big traditional corset firm. Large range, attractive, quality. Far more sophisticated than the average fetish style.

VOODOO DOLLS
www.folkart.com/~latitude/voodooshop/dolls.htm
The genuine article: a really intriguing selection of images. Even if you don't want to buy one it's just interesting to see what they look like. Some are as basic as they come, while others are really bright and dramatic. In fact you might buy one just because some are so cute, and how strange is that?

VOODOO DOLL'S FETISH RESOURCE
www.vodudoll.com

VTU
www.vudutuu.com
Voodoo Dolls 'with political umph', it seems, and they come with a clear plastic face so that you can insert the photo of your choice. Creepy.

WAISTED
www.waisted.com
Corsetry site by designer Susan Brownlie,

which goes into great detail on how to make them, and I can't imagine you could find a better resource. Nice little gallery.

A WARDROBE IN TIME
www.awardrobeintime.com
Well! It's a map of a house, which you move through, and it introduces historical themes. Antechamber – intro, Library – books and a Links search, gallery – pictures, obviously, Great Hall – music (avoid!), and a very interesting thing about dice games, Kitchen – historical recipes, and finally the Garderobe, where you can find their catalogue of clothes and accessories, which are as good as this site.

WASP FACTORY RECORDINGS
www.wasp-factory.com
A mini-guide to their interesting mixture of bands – including Chaos Engine, Arkham Asylum, D.U.S.T. and Swarf.

WAVE-GOTIK-WELT
www.shop.wave-gotik-welt.de
Absolutely mega German site for clothes and jewelry.

WELCOME TO URBAN DECAY
www.urbandecay.com/home.html
Top quality skin, hair and nail products.

THE WELL DRESSED WENCH
www.midnightgarden.com/costume/medieval.html
Baroque, Byzantine, Arthurian etc. Huge medieval site, with great links for enthusiasts.

WICKED – LAS VEGAS
www.angelfire.com/nv/wickedgoth
Vegas trash store par excellence with wings, hats, bags, clothing, jewelry, boots, makeup, body-jewelry, retro chic, the works.

WINGS AND ROSES
www.wingsandroses.com
Custom clothing, with true style. Not typical Goth, but Victorian varieties, Renaissance and Regency outfits. Chinese jacket is nice but you'd think lots of Goth designers would have caught on about how cool that Chinese style is, particularly in dark shiny colours. But that's designers for you. All frothy, less inclined for sleekness.

WONDERLAND
www.wonderlandcd.com

Arkham Dark Arts

Stunning Austrian mail order site, offering CDs, jewelry, odd fantasy figures, household accessories, gargs, postcards, smart writing paper (well worth seeing) and t-shirts, with news and strangely dull links section.

WYRD SHOP ONLINE
www.wyrdshop.com
Hey, you ain't so weird. 'The world's largest online occult and craft store.' Maybe it is? They also have a Problem Page (probably 'I believe this occult stuff works, yet I have no friends') and a nice Book Reviews section. I'm just scrying out for attention, so I looked at the site and God, it really is enormous. The occult powders look cool – Follow Me Boy (no thank you!), Money Drawing (you probably end up receiving pictures), Mojo Wishing, Jinx Removing etc. The jewelry

is disappointingly plain, but the book section is vast, whether you're serious or just a deluded mystical type. I'd recommend the medieval fortune charms.

WYSTERIA
www.wysteria.co.uk
Clothing for the 'plus' sizes, for the VoluptuGoth. Dresses, hosiery, tops, skirts and corsetry. Not a big range but well presented. Good photos.

XTRA
www.x-tra-x.de
Germany's biggest Goth fashion outlet, if I'm not mistaken, with a good Lifestyle, section boasting news and music. Four mail order catalogues also available. The clothes section is absolutely enormous, with the photos are nicely tinted. Some of the bondage

bits are also relevant and you will find under 'shirts' the best t-shirt section anywhere on the Net. Accessories include wristbands, jewelry, body jewelry, incredible 'Deko' section of statues and objects, bags, tights, cosmetics and extensions. Miss it at your peril.

YARUBA
www.yaruba.com/acatalog/Yaruba_Gothic_Eclectica_6.html
Goth gifts – skulls, pendants, bookends, clocks, lights and Celtic War Dogs.

YESTERDAZE
www.yesterdaze.co.uk
Small shop in Devon offering range of clothes and gifts. No gallery.

YOU KNOW WHAT I LIKE
www.avecor.com

Le Bal Des Vampires. Photo © Stéphane Burlot

Clubs

666 – SPAIN
www.interocio.es/666
Divine photos, fun flyers.

ABART – ZURICH
www.abart-music-club.ch

ABYSS – MELBOURNE
www.abyssnightclub.com

ALBION BATCAVE – NEW YORK
www.albion-batcave.com

ALCHEMY – DC
http://alchemy-dc.com

ALCHEMY – NEW YORK
www.geocities.com/~althea-/alchemyclub.html
Galleries from the Goth night at
CBGB's, but also more details:
www.cbgb.com/gallery.html

**ALL YOUR AREA 51 ARE BELONG
TO US** – UTAH
www.gothics.org/submersion/club.html

AMERICAN GOTHIC PRODUCTIONS
– USA
www.americangothicprod.com
Chicago site of Scary Lady Sarah,
offering details of Goth, Industrial and
Fetish events. Great site – Past
Performances is links to performers.
Club thumbnails accessible at bottom
of 'Nocturna' page.

THE ANARCHISTS' COCKTAIL –
TORONTO
www.anarchistscocktail.com

ANGELS – PLYMOUTH
www.angelsclub.freeserve.co.uk
Nice mix of personal pics, club shots
and events.

AREA – JAPAN
www.jin.ne.jp/pig/area

ART BAR – COLUMBIA, US
www.artbarsc.com/goth.html
Bright and breezily detailed site, with

some beautiful – and some quite
strange – pics of the locals.

ASCENSION – EDINBURGH
www.ascension-edinburgh.com/index.html
New, good-looking site with news,
merchandise, gallery and chat.

ASSIMILATE – SF
www.sfgoth.com/clubs/assimilate

ASSIMILATION – CAMDEN
www.assimilation.org.uk

ASYLUM – BIRMINGHAM
www.geocities.com/spookyuk
Very large site for club formerly known as
The Shriek. Includes details of activities
in Coventry, and plenty of mad photos
and board. Zine is still in development.

ASYLUM – LONDON
http://web.ukonline.co.uk/asylum
Christian Goth club at the Intepid Fox.
Busy site with plenty of info, including
live events held at Gossips. Nice pics.
I started drinking at the Fox in '77 and
it reached its first heights during the
late eighties when the Lightning Strikes
were based there. You could revel in the
sight, most evenings, of a heavily
tattooed doorman turning businessmen
in suits away with the classic line,
'You're not coming in dressed like *that!*'

ATOMIC CAFÉ – AUSTIN
www.atomic-cafe.com
But that gives way to: www.internet
announcements.com/randall/ where you
read the horrible news about Randall
Young Goodwin, and the wonderful
article written by a friend after his
death. Very moving.

B IS FOR... – NEW YORK
www.decadence.net
'Byzantium is an alternative to the
stereotypical dark music club
environment. A thrilling blend of
lounge, clubnite, art collective, and
speakeasy.' And currently homeless.

B72 – VIENNA
www.b72.at

BACKLASH – BAY AREA
www.spilledink.com/backlash

BARBIE'S BLOODRAVE – DUTCH
www.barbiesbloodrave.com
Club site, with great photos and flyers.

BAR PHONO – LEEDS
www.barphono.com/index.html
Very well organised but not immense
content, especially with the photos.
Cute Halloween galleries but slightly
different photos at:
www.barphono.com/blacksheep

BAR SINISTER – HOLLYWOOD
www.barsinister.net
The galleries are absolutely *superb* and
go way, way back.

THE BATCAVE – BRISBANE
www.guildmedia.com.au/batcave

BEDLAM – GLASGOW
http://fp.bedlamcorp.plus.com/home.htm
Great galleries hidden at bottom of
history.

BELFRY – MELBOURNE
www.bluevelvet.com.au/belfry
Excellent site with brilliant photos, plus
old flyers, including themed nights,
plus bands.

BERLIN – CHICAGO
www.berlinchicago.com

BIO DEF ADELAIDE
www.users.bigpond.net.au/biodef/blasphemy
.htm
Club with different nights, events, DJ
lists, feedback, a smattering of reviews.

BLACK MACHINE – BOURNEMOUTH
www.gothicsouth.freeservers.com

BLACK MAGIC NIGHT – DUSSELDORF
www.black-magic-night.de

BLACK ORCHID – Sweden
www.wetdrea.ms/black-orchid
Sixteen galleries of lovely people pics.

BLACK SUNDAY – Gelnhausen
http://vnv.4xtc.de

BLACK VEIL – Leeds
http://groups.yahoo.com/group/BlackVeil
Monthly at the Adelphi. Also puts on
bands from outside the UK.

BLACKOUT – Rome
www.blackoutrockclub.com

BLONDIE – Chile
www.blondie.cl
Strange site, with Goth and Techno
crowd shots, plus Debbie Harry and
Garbage galleries.

BYZANTIUM – NY
www.nycgoth.com/homepages/byzantium

THE CALLING – Cambridge
www.thecalling.darkwave.org.uk

CAMERA OBSCURA – USA
www.room29.net/CameraObscuraFlash.htm
American club site with lovely staff
details and great pics.

CARNAGE DREAM – Paris
www.mlink.net/~bdv
Parisian Goth-Vamp Party organiser.
Good staff bios and great gallery, but
that's Stéphane Burlot, so no surprise
it's awesome.

CARNIVALE – SF
www.sfcarnivale.com
Fantastic pics.

CARPE NOCTUM – Bradford
www.geocities.com/gothvodka
Scrappily fun site, with funny pics.

CATACOMB – DC
www.obscure.org/Catacomb
http://groups.yahoo.com/group/Catacomb
Five nice galleries, and they do their
own shirts.

CATASTRAFIEND – Cumbria
www.geocities.com/twiggygirl4169/Family_Album.html
Great photo gallery. Happy shiny people.

THE CAVE – Frankfurt
www.the-cave.de

CAVE CLUB – Stockholm
http://web.darkside.nu/grottan
Huge photo selection, including from
their predecessor, Eclipse.

THE CAVE OF SATYR – Amsterdam
www.geocities.com/thecaveofsatyr
Beautiful site, with stunning flyers, and
cute galleries.

CELEBRE NOIR – N. Carolina
www.celebrenoir.com
Excellent pics, plus message board.

CEREMONY – Boston
www.ceremonyboston.com
Small site, nice pics.

CEREMONY – Pittsburgh
http://ceremony.pghgoth.com
Nice pics, history, DJs, games.

THE CHARNEL HOUSE – Newcastle
http://members.lycos.co.uk/thecharnelhouse
Beautiful photos.

CHELSEA – Wien
www.silverserver.co.at/chelsea
Weird. I find pics of TV Smith and a
page on British football!

THE CHUCH – Denver
www.the-church.com

THE CHURCH – Dallas
www.thechurchdallas.com
Brilliant pic selection.

CHURCH OF MADNESS – Reading
www.sogoth.net/~cofm
'It is basically a free pub night... sometimes mysteriously empty... sometimes
mysteriously full, but always very mysterious,' whispers Gwilym, about this successful long-running weekly Goth night.
The site is lovely. Just enjoy the writing
and the ideas even if you don't go. Pics:
www.geocities.com/mistresskittyk/church_or_
madness_pictures.html

CLUB ANTIQUITY – California
www.clubantiquity.com
Club currently closed, with no news of a
move, but the site is lovely and the huge
selection of galleries will surely satisfy.

CLUB ANYTHING – Milwaukee
www.geocities.com/clubanything
New Club Anything and old Sanctuary

photos. *Don't* click the Goth link, your
screen freezes.

CLUB ASYLUM – Tucson
www.clubasylum.com

CLUB BIZARRE – New Zealand
www.clubbizarre.co.nz/index.html
Reviews, news, board, and fantastic
collection of old flyers and photos.

CLUB CYBERNETICS – Japan
http://shibuya.cool.ne.jp/c_cybernetics

CLUB GROTESQUE – Stavanger
www.checkpoint.no/clubgrotesque/cindex.html
Events, gallery, board.

CLUB HERESY – Limerick
www.oddworldz.com/heresy
Currently homeless, but adorable photos.

CLUB LUMINAL – San Diego
www.clubluminal.com
Live shows details and reviews, nice
pics, radio, interviews.

CLUB METROPOLIS – Copenhagen
www.club-metropolis.dk
Club with a preference for Industrial.
Nicely informative. Large selection of
photos from gigs (some Goth) available
to view, with links to the bands.

CLUB NOIRE – USA
www.clubnoire.com
Lovely new site. Seriously beautiful photos.

CLUB SACRAMENT – Alabama
www.clubsacrament.com/sIndex.html
Really wonderful photos. Angel's Attic
is worth a visit, top right, as it's a
regular journal and dead friendly.

CLUB SLUT – Ottawa
www.fetishgoth.com
Only Fetish Goth club in Ottawa. A few
pics available.

CLUB XANTH – San Diego
www.clubxanth.com
A few cute, or weird, pics.

COMMUNION –US Archive
http://w3.one.net/~hyperace/Communion/index.html

CONSPIRACY – Arizona
http://hexmedia.net/conspiracy
Nice, if tricky, photos.

THE CONSPIRACY – DC
http://theconspiracy.net/main.html
Old, but goodies under 'Events',
especially for Covenant fans.

CONTAMINATION – BIRMINGHAM
www.contamination.org.uk
Now D_K but no page available.

CONTEMPT – NY
www.contemptny.org/frames.html
Nice site, awesome pics.

THE COVEN – HOBART
www.angelfire.com/electronic/coven
Hobart (Australia) club with News, DJ
stuff, a nicely creepy selection of photos
from the various special club events,
Radio, and an e-zine which welcomes
contributions – short stories, poetry,
articles and message board.

CYBERAGEVOODOO – TOYKO
http://cyberage.tripod.co.jp
Industrial Gothic club in Tokyo, based
at Paranormal (Paranoia Café). Brief
site. Map, playlist and BBS.

CYBERIA – ALABAMA
http://darkdj.w1.net/cyberia
More wonderful photos of contented
patrons.

CYBERPOLIS – NOTTINGHAM
www.geocities.com/cyberpolis_uk
Must join: www.clubs.yahoo.com/clubs/
cyberpolis to view pics.

DARK CITY – TRONDHEIM
http://darkcity.goth.no
Small but lovely site with great photos,
and good links.

DARK CLUB – COLOGNE
http://members.aol.com/darkclubcologne

DARK ENTRIES – BRISBANE
http://darkentries.pasdex.au/history.php
Bubbly site, with galleries, journal, links.
Of special interest is the History Of
Brisbane Goth, with pictures and
interviews with those involved in the
scene of the eighties, and coverage of new
international bands, as well as interviews
with people from the current scene.

DARK PARK – GELDERN
www.darkpark.de
Neat site, but dark photos.

DARK TRIX – BASINGSTOKE
www.darktrix.com
Highly detailed club site. Cool pics, and
excellent all-round detail.

DARK WAVE NIGHTS – MONTREAL
www.finalcutmedia.com/dark_wave_nights/
index.htm
'Heresy nights are the soundtrack to
the new religion. So tear down the
church of your previous gothic club
experiences and prepare yourself as
best you can...' Totally demented club
with some sci-fi theme on top of Goth
news, features, forums and a hint of
insanity. A great experience, if slightly
bewildering. The club photo section
promises to be good when they've
finished it, as it will cover previous
incarnations dating back years. The
sad fact is, they're not updating
regularly enough.

THE DARKEST SERENADE – OHIO
www.angelfire.com/music/darkestserenade
DJ collective. Pics only, with links to
current events.

THE DAWNING – CHARLOTTESVILLE
www.disrupted.org/~dawning

DE INRICHTING – AMSTERDAM
http://come.to/deinrichting
Flyers and moody photos.

DEATH GUILD – SF
www.deathguild.com
Excellent site, especially the photos.

DEATH MACHINE – BIRMINGHAM
www.contamination.org.uk/dm.html

DECAY – KANSAS
www.idir.net/~daveys/urban.html
Cute photo archive.

DER KELLER – PERTH
http://derkeller.gothic.net.au
No dancefloor gives the club freedom to
play music people enjoy listening to,
and they have a broad range. This is a
lovely site because it introduces the
characters involved. Really nice
galleries, but feeble links.

DISSOLUTION – SHEFFIELD
www.gothtarts.co.uk
Good Sheffield guide, of Goth Tarts
extraction. Local info, mailing list.

DISSONANCE – LUTON
http://uk.clubs.yahoo.com/clubs/
dissonancedarlings

DOMINION – PERTH
http://dominion.iinet.net.au/dom800600.htm
Magnificent site which acts as a general
repository of Perth-related activity.
Stunning range of pics.

DOMINION – DUBLIN ARCHIVE
http://dominion.gothic.ie

DOMINION – BERGEN
www.dominion.no
Straightforward club site, with sumptuous, plentiful galleries and discussion.

DOORNROOSJE – NIJMEGEN
www.doornroosje.nl/index2.html

THE DRILL – WELLINGTON
http://darkhabit.co.nz/
Worst club page in existence?

DUNA – BRATSILAVA
www.duna.sk
Photo archive and illustrated pizza
menu, which gave me a shock when it
suddenly appeared!

EISENLAGER – OBERHAUSEN
www.eisenlager.de
Some pics (more coming at
www.mcqueensix.de) plus webcam.

ELECTRIC DREAMS – LONDON
www.electricdreamsclub.com
Really good photos, plus an archive
section with interesting eighties links.

ELECTROTRIBE – LEICESTER
www.electrotribe.co.uk
Photos under 'Tribe'. Great flyer
collection, lovely overall look.

ELIZIUM – ABERDEEN
www.elizium.net
http://uk.clubs.yahoo.com/clubs/elizium

ELVIRAS – London
www.elviras.co.uk
No pics, or any real info whatsoever, but lovely frontpage, so I don't suppose much happens.

ENDLESS NIGHT PRODUCTIONS – New Orleans
www.endlessnight.com
www.xorvia.com
'Xorvia was founded in 1999 by Todd Sabretooth to create a new type of ever changing club environment mixing the *fetish, goth/industrial, vampyre, medieval fantasy and modern primitives* genres which we call "dark fetish". Xorvia uses the mediums of art, performance, nightlife, music and fashion to create a world which exists between fantasy and reality.' Truly mad photos.

ENDORPHIN – Leicester
http://homepage.ntlworld.com/highnoon/Endorphin

ENERGY ZONE – Italy
www.energyzone.it
Brilliant site flyers, gig nights and people, well-featured in galleries.

EUPHORIA – New Mexico
www.unm.edu/~yaura
A nice, if slow site. Photos are good.

EURYDICE – Strasbourg
www.goth-eurydice.fr.st
Goth-relevant bar. Slight info.

EVE THE NEW CHURCH – Tokyo
www.interq.or.jp/tokyo/eve/clubEVE/club evemenu.html
Regular monthly Industrial/Darkwave/Electro club in Tokyo, which also includes Salon de Electro Eve, and fortnightly night Black Veil (or Club Sabbat) organised by a local occult Shop. Not all the links on this site work but it's very interesting.

EX+CUTE – Tokyo
www.ex-cute.com
A real find. This is more like it. There are a lot of bits here – including ace links. Click next, and head straight for gallery. Then you will find a block at the top, click on each section to reveal brilliant photos of Japanese Goths, and it's evidently true what they say. Women are from Venus (www.ex-cute.com/exb-31.htm/http://www.ex-cute.com/exb-35.htm) and the men *are* from

Mars (www.ex-cute.com/exb-29.htm). Suza and Afeffesis have an amazing site. I think there is film on here too.

EXILE – Bath
www.drischmi.dircon.co.uk/exile

FANG CLUB – LA
www.fangclub.com
Absolutely phenomenal array of galleries dating back eons. Treat yourself.

FANGS – Birmingham
www.happy-goth.co.uk/pear
Friday Night Goth Shite. Mad archive, may be down.

FIRST AVENUE & 7TH STREET ENTRY – Minneapolis
www.first-avenue.com
Monthly Goth club inside a haunted ex-Greyhound station.

FLAG PROMOTIONS – London
www.ecom-uk.net/flag
Main London promoter since Nemesis ended, utilising various venues (underworld, Gossips, Mean Fiddler, Garage), and a club night at Gossips.

FLEX – Wien
www.flex.at
Lots of pics, usually conventional acts.

FULL TILT – London
www.electricballroom.ndirect.co.uk/fulltilt1.htm
Legendary London night with brilliant galleries, especially the Dave Edmond section.

GARGOYLE LOUNGE – California
http://members.aol.com/gothmusic
Ongoing archive, with nice band pics.

GOSSIPS – London
www.gossips.co.uk
Been there since the dawn of time so deserves a historical section. The lack of photos is absurd.

GOTHAM – Amsterdam
www.gotham.nl
Gothamsterdam, to give its full title, a club event run by one mad DJ and two members of Xymox. Good galleries for Gotham 1.

GOTHAM NIGHTS – Norway
www.gothamnights.com

Brilliant selection of photos of people and bands from different events.

THE GOTHIC THEATRE – Colorado
www.gothictheatre.com
Madly posh and informative.

GRAFFITI – Vienna
www.graffiti-hardrock.com
Big galleries. Lots of Rock, but the pics are okay.

THE GRAVEYARD – Newcastle
www.the-graveyard.i12.com
Newcastle club, in a place called Scotland Yard. Now *that's* creepy! Info only.

GRUIS – Utrecht
www.acu.nl/gruis
No photos, as it's a bi-monthly event, but they have reviews which may interest.

THE HAVEN – Northampton, MA
http://hamp.hampshire.edu/~cbkF94
Great photos.

HELLRAVER PRODUCTIONS – Toronto/NYC
www.hellraver.com
Club and gig details, with Industrial and Techno a speciality. DJ/band bios.

HERESY – Coventry
http://get.to/heresy
Old photos on the info page.

HIDDEN SHADOWS – USA
http://hometown.aol.com/ldymonette/index.html
A production/events company that fuses several styles together. It's a clumsy site but worth it, because there's some great pics, and it's all a bit mysterious. The party photos are wonderful, and crazed. I don't even know whereabouts in America it is. There must be loads of Lexington Avenues.

HYBRID – Derry archive
http://hybrid.gothic.ie/

HYMNEN AN DIE NACHT – Bochum
www.hymnen-an-die-nacht.de
Bit messy but fun, with some good pics.

INFEST – UK festival
www.infest.org.uk

INSANITORIUM – Colchester
www.insanitorium.fsnet.co.uk/index/indexx.html

Le Bal Des Vampires. Photo © Stéphane Burlot

It's got great pics, but they're from Whibty. Interesting local info.

THE INTERNATIONAL GOTHIC CLUB LISTING
www.vamp.org/Gothic/clublist.html
Handiest guide of its sort, although tons of links are dead.

KEROSENE – DUNDEE
www.kerosene1.co.uk
Goth, Metal and Ind by the look of it. Not a huge site but regular galleries are very nice.

KITCHEN CLUB – SOUTH MIAMI
www.darkdoors.com/thekitchen
Lovely site with great galleries.

KORSAKOFF – HOLLAND
www.korsakoff.nl

KRYPTA GOTHIC NIGHT – ROME
http://spazioweb.inwind.it/jungleclubroma/diegus.htm
Club site with amazing sections, including band photos – from Ataraxia 2001, to Virgin Prunes in colour from

1984, etc. Awesome treasure trove. Also DJs, architecture and people. You *must* see this.

LA FETE TRISTE – ANTWERP
http://users.skynet.be/LaFeteTriste

LABYRINTH – DETROIT
www.bleakhaus.com/resgoth.html
Magnificent gallery, mainly of the staff.

LAST EXIT – HOLLAND
www.lastexit.nl
Visually arresting site, with clear details on past and future events, and a *fantastic* selection of gig photos in the gallery.

LE BAL DES VAMPIRES – PARIS
www.baldesvampires.net
(See also Carnage Dreams).

LE RAT MORT – PARIS
www.6emedimension.net/ratmort
Weekly Goth evening in Paris basement bar, with Goth, Industrial and Electric music, and special themed nights. Nice relaxed galleries.

LEGEND'S WEB – RALEIGH, NC
www.legends-club.com/home/navigate.html
Photos includes the Miss Prissy Patio contest.

LEGION OF DOOM – LAKEWOOD
www.thebelfry.net/lod

LELAND CITY CLUB – DETROIT
www.lelandcityclub.com
Apoptygma pics in Club links.

LES CAVES DU MANOIR – SWITZERLAND
http://isuisse.ifrance.com/caves-manoir
Flyers and Photos in 'Archives', lower left.

MADAME SATA – BRAZIL
www.madamesata.com
Sao Paulo club with a big site currently in development.

MALEDICTION – READING
www.sogoth.net/~malediction

MANRAY – CAMBRIDGE MA
http://manrayclub.com
Very cool, well-respected club for various types of music, but with info

only, as the gallery is an awful disappointment.

MATRIX – Bochum
www.club-matrix.de
Gig pics and scary party pics, including rubber nuns.

MEGIDDO – Wien
http://members.teleweb.at/megiddo/default.htm
Warning issued before entering gallery and 'Femdome' as there's Fetish content.

METRO – North Florida
http://members.tripod.com/~drinkslinger

METRO – Chicago
www.metrochicago.com
Takes forever. Worthless.

METROPOLIS – Portugal
http://more.at/metropolis
Portuguese Industrial club with DJ profiles, playlists, CD recommendations and some photos of the building when it's empty rather than with customers! Typi-cally Industrial when you think about it.

MIDIAN – DC
http://clubs.yahoo.com/clubs/midiandc

MINX – Holland
www.luxus.nl/totum/minx/index.html

THE MONASTERY – Wien
www.monastery.at
Austrian club site catering for different forms of music (each with their own handy section).

NEAR DARK – Southampton
http://communities.msn.co.uk/nEARdARK

NECROSCOPE – Coventry
www.necroscope.gothere.uk.com
Cute history, odd picture/video gallery! Developing nicely.

NEUROTRAUMA – N.E.
www.neurotrauma.co.uk
They organise events from Whitby to Scarborough etc. Small news and band bit, mainly there to push the mailing list.

NEVERMORE – Perth
http://dominion.iinet.net.au/nevermore
Cute, with pics related to the work they put in, specifically... designing banners.

NEW WORLD CHURCH – CT
www.newworldchurchonline.com
Pics still not up yet. Nice rubber nun in gasmask frontpage!

NIGHTCLUB ICON – Cinci?
www.nightclubicon.com
Different and amusing.

NIGHTMARE – Nottingham
http://uk.clubs.yahoo.com/clubs/nightmareclub

NOCTURNE – Philadelphia
www.ferret.com/nocturne

NOIR – USA
www.ferret.com/noir
Love the address, just love it, because we don't have this in Britain. They can calmly claim 'between Walnut and Locust' and not even realise how cool that is. So no pics, just like Nocturne, but they sneak in anyway.

NU-BILE – Plymouth
www.nubile.fslife.co.uk
Dead but with archives pics and future plan. Cool links.

NUMBERS – Houston
www.numbersnightclub.com

ONYX – Denver
www.onyxdenver.com/onyxopening.html
Good Halloween shots.

OSBCURE CITIES PROJECT – Italy
www.obscurecity.com
Promotion for various events in Florence and Milan, plus DK Grethel's own mysterious section.

THE OTHERS SIDE OF THE DUCK – Gladbeck
www.palmportal.de/darkduck

PARANOIA CAFÉ – Japan
www.paranoia-cafe.com
Club run by Watanabe of Definition Master, with huge yellow eyeball above its entrance, and its own fortune teller (www.t-pos.com/shirley) and make-up artists, so you can have a bullet-hole in your forehead! Special theme nights, highly regarded for its contribution on the Industrial and EBM side. www.paranoia-cafe.com/paranormal.htm takes you to their Paranormal Nights section, with club details, schedule, flyers and bbs.

PENGUINS – Plymouth
www.darkfire.freeserve.co.uk/penguins
Nice site, pics are enormous.

PHIL MARRIOTT – Portsmouth
www.philmarriott.com
DJ with detailed if dull site, but includes journal (not updated regularly).

PSYCHOBURBIA – Virginia
www.project2501.com/psychoburbia/default.html
Nice 'denizens' portraits, plus reviews section coming.

QXT – New Joisey
www.dellamorte.net/qxt

RELEASE THE BATS – California
www.deathrock.com/releasethebats
Temp page while they change URL.

REPENT – Anaheim
www.repentclub.com/2000/sepoo.htm
They have pictures, and lots of them – although club shots aren't even all up by a long way – including some brilliant Gitane spiky and redhead shots, Cinema Strange, Deep Eynde, Crush Violets, This Ascension...you name it. *Excellent* site.

REQUIEM – Newcastle
www.requiem.i12.com
It was being done when I visited but it's going to be a classy little site, you can tell.

THE REQUIEM – SF
http://therequiem.com
Stunning gallery selection.

RESURGENCE – Portsmouth
www.scathe.demon.co.uk/resframs.htm
Cute site within the main Scathe site, giving plentiful visual evidence of the club's regular nutters, as well as a growing flyer archive, a mini Goth history, and the Pete hairstyles. Look at the photo of him and his Furby and ask yourself one simple question. Which one would you ask to mind your pint?

REUNION – Atlanta
www.gothicknights.org/reunion
A few, beautiful photos.

REVELATIONS – Richmond, VA archive
www.thecoppermine.com/revelations.htm

REVELATIONS – Melbourne
www.revelationsnightclub.cjb.net

Attractive and detailed site with great pics.

REVERIE – CAMBRIDGE, MA
http://reverie.fsck.com
Weird photos.

REVOLVE – BERSKHIRE
www.gothdaze.co.uk/revolve
Organise various gigs. Good on info,
plus flyers and photos (hopefully).

RITUAL – SYDNEY
http://ritual.ar.com.au
Very good site with nice photos (including holiday snaps!), DJ links, the works.

SACRAMENT – HAMBURG
www.sacrament.de
German Goth party organisers. Cute
galleries.

SANCTUARY – LAS VEGAS
http://home.earthlink.net/~isolate9/sanctuary.html

SANCTUARY – SACRAMENTO
www.clubsanctuary.net

SECRET ROOM – ALABAMA
www.secretroom.net
Seriously weird pics.

SHEBEEN – VIENNA
www.shebeen.at

SHRINE OF LILITH – SF
www.sfgoth.com/clubs/lilith

SINISTER ZONE – FRANKFURT
www.sinister-zone.de

SLIMELIGHT – LONDON
www.slimelight.com
http://clubs.yahoo.com/clubs/theslimelight
Site by DJ Steve with details on DJs and
the club. Steve's personal journal is okay,
and the info is informative, but the best
bit is the Angel-Islington game where you
try and prevent Manson, Britney and
some beer bloke entering the club by lobbing explosive CDs. It's curiously exhilarating seeing Manson detonate, but Not
Very Loving. The photos are just press
things, and links are dull. The 'official'
Slimelight site is www.slimelightlondon.com
but isn't anywhere near as interesting.

SMART CAFÉ – WIEN
www.smartcafe.at
Fetish café. Strange galleries.

SPANK – BRISTOL
www.spankpromotions.co.uk
Fetish but with Goth and Ind also.
Great gallery, which is quite disgraceful.

SPELLBOUND – DUBLIN
http://spellbound.gothic.ie

SPIDERS – HULL
www.arachnophilia.net
Brilliant site which highlights staff and
customers, including archived galleries.
I, like a fool, have mentioned this
elsewhere by accident. Arse!

SUBZERO – WIEN
www.subzero.at
Big flyer gallery.

SYNTHETIC – BELFAST
www.thesynthetic.co.uk
www.sexshoppingandquantumphysics.com

TANZ DER VAMPIRE – MUNSTER
http://members.tripod.de/TdV
This could get good. Only '95 and '96
started in the flyer archive at the
moment, but they're building that up
well, and just one pic in gallery!

TANZDEBEIL – SWEDEN
www.movinghands.net/tanzdebil

TENEBRAE – LONDON
www.tenebrae.freeserve.co.uk

THE 13TH CHILD – PHILADELPHIA
www.the13thchild.philly1.com

Didn't find pics but this is a nice, busy
general site.

THE CASTLE – FLORIDA
www.castle-ybor.com

THE FORGOTTEN – ARIZONA
www.inconnumedia.com/theforgotten
Best club gallery found so far, even if
the quality isn't totally swish.

TOTENHANZ – RAVENNA
www.ngdm.org
Mad site for Italian club in a museum.

U-HALLO – GERMAN
www.u-club.de
Photos of performances (Test Dept)
and flyers.

U4 DISCOTHEK – AUSTRIA
www.u4club.at
Photos actually at:
www.conny.at/flash.html.

UNDERLAND PRIVAT – MIAMI
www.underlandprivat.com

THE UNDERWORLD – HOUSTON
www.underworldnightclub.com

VAMPIRE PARTY – ANTWERP
www.vampireparty.com
Seems to have no photos, but includes
reviews.

VOGUE – SEATTLE
www.vogueseattle.com
Page upon page of photos from
different nights, many of them
utterly disgraceful, you will be pleased
to learn.

VORTEX – SYDNEY
http://vortex.ar.com.au/main.html

WAKE – LA
www.bubastis.com/Main.htm
Theda pics, and *brilliant* gallery.

THE WENDYHOUSE – LEEDS
www.thewendyhouse.org
Superb site with some very nice pics,
and the flyer collection is fantastic.

ZWISCENFALL – GERMANY
www.zfall.de
Good pics from several Pagan Love
Songs events.

Locations

AAA – ASSOCIATION OF ANNOYING ALCOHOLICS
http://crimescene.org/~aaa/mainpg.html
Amusing site by Canadian drunks with many interesting diversions, including a guide to good (i.e. they sell alcohol) local bars in Toronto.

ABELARDE SANCTION – BRIXTON
www.hixnet.co.za/home/abelarde
This is one the weirdest sites you could hope to find.

ALABAMA GOTH
http://groups.yahoo.com/group/bamagoth/

ALBERTA GOTHIC IND EVENTS
www.virulent.org/cangoth/ab/index.html
One of series of thematic sites around Canada. Updated regularly with clubs, gigs and events. Guides to shopping, tourism.

ALBUQUERQUE SOMETIMES
www.unm.edu/~gryffyn
All that is Goth in New Mexico. There was once this seriously cool woman called Bev, killing time as secretary at *Melody Maker* (and a far better writer than most of them there) who ended up studying fencing – among other things – in Albuquerque, and before I lost her address I learnt that this is the hot-air ballooning capital of the world. No mention of that here, but there's club details, events, old gig reviews, and from a tourism perspective they do sell themselves well. 'We have ice caves, volcanoes, hot springs, atomic bombs, miles and miles of gypsum-sand dunes, UFO's, and bat-filled caverns.' ('Hello, I've come about the bombs.') Amusing shopping guide, some decent reviews, and if you get bored go to:
http://groups.yahoo.com/group/nmgoth

ANDY'S CHIGOTH PAGE
www.emsphone.com/chigoth
This is a sparkling set of links to things

'Nostalgia'. Photo © Stéphane Lord.
Model: Fannie Langlois

commonly known in Chicago, but also more personal sites, new radio stations and computery wibbles.

ANGELDUSTRIAL – BOSTON
http://angeldustrial.com/angel
Big on detail, with lists galore, radio info, great galleries and a myriad of Ind links.

ANN ARBOR GOTHIC
www.aagothic.com
News, chat, forum, classifieds etc. Not much happening, and their band link section is just weird – nothing local and a tiny, arbitrary selection of big names. The news is good, and their first artist David has some great work.

ARIZONA GOTH
www.azgoth.com
Great pics, good links. Plenty of life.

ARIZONA GOTHS
http://clubs.yahoo.com/clubs/arizonagoths

ARTEFACT LA LAITERIE
www.artefact.org/index2.shtml
Strasbourg news of clubs and gigs.

ASIAN GOTH BLIND FORTUNE ORG
http://asianvisigoth.cjb.net
Was bringing up awkward porn popups, so be careful.

ATLANTA
http://clubs.yahoo.com/clubs/atlantaangelgoths

ATLANTA GOTHIC NET
www.atlantagothic.net/atlanta_index.htm
Excellent guide. All the club, gig, shop info relevant, and spruce links. Loads of great pics but the skating wins every time.

AUSGOTHS – AUSTIN
www.ausgoths.org
A resource guide or Gothic Hipsters, be told! Great guide to places to eat, drink, watch and hear. Good events, lovely galleries, piercing info, reading, museums. Outdoors, indoors, modern, historical, human, afterlife. All strife is

here. And...they have a Book Club, but no bands!!!

BATCAVE – FLORIDA
http://clubs.yahoo.com/clubs/batcaveentrance

BAY AREA GOTHS – USA
http://clubs.yahoo.com/clubs/bayareagoths

BELGIAN DARK ALTERNATIVE MUSIC DATABASE
http://users.pandora.be/stefannelies/bdamd/
Big on news and reviews, with good detail in scene links.

BENVENUTI NELLA MIA MAGIONE – ROME
http://spazioweb.inwind.it/ankh
Rather old but well-intentioned Gothic Rome site, with English version. Good guide to clubs, pubs and shops, as well as tourist advice, and without anything of a real Roman scene to discuss, there is a nice set of links to Italian bands.

BIRMINGHAM UNI GOTH SOC
www.happy-goth.co.uk/gothsoc
Not much news, or updates. Just a few cute pics.

BLACKMAIL – SOUTHAMPTON
http://groups.yahoo.com/group/blackmail
'For all the Southampton Goth Commandoes.' Small but getting insanely busy.

BLACK COLLAR LUNCH
www.blood-dance.net/goth/bcl/index.html
A DC-area meeting place for people with their lunch hour free.

BLACK KOBZAR
www.blackkobzar.newmail.ru
Ukrainian Goth-Apocalypse site.

BLACK LODGE
http://members.tripod.com/~blodge/index.html
Old West Yorks society thing, with Guide To Being A Goth, board and nice gallery.

THE BLACK PAGES – DENMARK
www.goth.net/~anaesthetics

BLACK PLANET

http://blackplanet.frostbitten.org
'Blackplanet is a discussion list for Chicago's Goth/Ind/etc/etc community. Out-of-towners curious about Chicago are welcome; be warned, however, that this list is high-volume and can get very... hm... chatty.'

BLEEDING EARS – AUSTRIA

http://members.chello.at/bernhard.hansbauer
Gigs, clubs, features, weirdness. Quite a mad little site actually. Tons to see and be bewildered by.

BLEEDING EARS PRODUCTIONS

www.bleeding-ears-productions.net
Either this is the newer version or a separate entity within their company. It's flashier. More events, reviews, forums and loads of nostalgia for their earlier events with flyers and pics, plus malfunctioning gallery

BODY PERVE SOCIAL CLUB – CANADA

www.bodyperve.com/bodyperve/gallery/gallery.html
A really lovely Canadian fetish thing, photo-based (including a comical Wolverine – well, I hope that was the intention!) and great flyers. Instead of being all posey, they've made it colourful.

BORED TO DEATH: C7 – NEW YORK

http://bored.todeath.net/c7rescue/c7rescue.htm
Run by Goths worried that C7 activities aren't/weren't up to par and hoping to give visitors a cool time regardless.

BOSTON

http://clubs.yahoo.com/clubs/gothsofboston
andmass

BOSTON AFTER MIDNIGHT – ARCHIVE

http://sinister.com/~purp/netgoth

BRANDEDCREED'S CHAIN – SOUTH AFRICA

www.geocities.com/brandedcreed
Disappointing, other than his revelation he's a pyromaniac. Dominated by Alternative and 'Progressive' (sic) Rock.

BREMEN

www.gothicscene.com/XBremen

BRIGHTON GOTHS

www.srl.clara.net/bgoths/bgoth2.htm
http://groups.yahoo.com/group/Brightongoths
For Goths in Brighton and Sussex

generally. Doesn't want endless profundity and says, 'suffice to say, the Goth "scene" is about more than just a night in a club, so hopefully this site will work to reflect that and keep together the other threads that seem to have become unwoven of late.' Lists clubs and pubs, has one tiny gallery, message board, links to local bands, shops and the take-your-luck Cobwebs section.

BRITGOTH

www.britgoth.com

BRITISH COLUMBIA GOTHIC/IND

www.virulent.org/cangoth/bc/index.html
Good resource, updated well.

BROOKLYN GOTHIC

www.brooklyngoth.com

BRUMGOTH

www.darkwave.org.uk/~bex/BrumGoth/Introduction.html
http://groups.yahoo.com/group/BrumGoth
Mailing list, discussions, Brum-bias. Offers links, and chance for free club entry. Must be a member. They admit it's quiet, and in places not overly interesting, but has Events listings, links to personal Brumgoth homepages and the chance to get in free to The Haunted Fishtank club. Very well written, open-minded approach with its details. Also has a snotty attitude to vampires, which I liked.

CALGARY GOTHS MAILING LIST

http://groups.yahoo.com/group/calgarygoths

CAMGOTH2000

www.cambridge.darkwave.org.uk/camgoth
Cambridge scene, with link to Calling club (www.thecalling.darkwave.org.uk), and some good galleries of locals (apart from the impromptu Buddha impersonation), and local events. Posher 2001 version also available.

CANADIAN GOTHIC EVENTS

www.virulent.org/cangoth
Link guide to Canadian areas for Gothic and Ind doo-dahs.

CANADIAN GOTHIC WEBRING

http://nav.webring.yahoo.com/hub?ring=canada
goths&list
'A ring for Canadians who consider themselves to be Gothic in nature.'

CANAL TRANS – ARGENTINA

www.canaltrans.com
Boards and chat on music and literature.

CANGOTH MAILING ARCHIVES

www.neverwhen.net/cangoth

CARCASSE – BRAZIL

www.carcasse.com
This is *magnificent*. Extremely attractive, in Portuguese, boasting a whole range of Goth music literature and nightlife entries, with great links.

CARPE MIDWEST

www.carpemidwest.com
Party people. BOG Productions' own promotions (and nice galleries), plus lots of local events from clubs to gigs and gaming, their own marketplace, and DJ Empress Alyda's (she of the unconvincing snarl) impressive history.

CATCH v.2.0

www.crackho.com/~vixen/main.html
Houston events totally up-to-date, rants and a lively journal, and tons of brilliant pictures, including weird nudes which may well be worth avoiding.

CHAMPAIGN-URBANA MIDNIGHT ASSEMBLY

www.searstower.org/cuma
Illinois Goths and Inds who clearly feel the need to be a separate entity. Meetings and social gatherings galore. Forums.

CHAPEL OF SORROWS – CHARLOTTE

www.accessnode.net/~eldritch/chapel.html
Old, but a few links work.

CHARLOTTESVILLE GOTH

http://groups.yahoo.com/group/charlottesvillegoth
eGroup. 'For the dark damned section of Charlottesville. We lurk in the shadows (or at the mudhouse) and attend the dark sad lonely cold dawning. Party on. And poop.'

CHELTENHAM

www.custodian.com/nam-vets
The Nam-Vets page is a mini-melting pot of anything that takes their fancy. Searches galore on traditional matters, News service (!) as well as local events and there is huge links list on this site. Some of the member websites are long dead, but the Chaos Engine chaps are there looking funny.

CHICAGO GOTH
http://clubs.yahoo.com/clubs/chicagogoth

CHICAGO GOTH-IND DISCUSSION
http://groups.yahoo.com/group/blackplanet

CINCINNATI
http://clubs.yahoo.com/clubs/cincinnatigothic

THE CITY OF CHURCHES
www.users.on.net/placebo/church_index.html
Nice guide to Adelaide. Club info but
little going on, or links. They admit the
scene there is dying and they're trying to
keep it afloat, and asking for contributors.

CLUB CYBERNETICS – JAPAN
http://shibuya.cool.ne.jp/c_cybernetics
More Ind-related info from DJ Vector
in Japan.

COFFINZ – ARIZONA
www.coffinz.com
A guide to the 'heaviest' bands in the
State. Pretty boring.

COLORADO NET GOTHS
www.gothic.net/~anri/co-goths
Guide is good for clubs and shops,
profiles of local Goths and music links
are fine. Club at:
http://clubs.yahoo.com/clubs/coloradonetgoths
WEBRING: http://welcome.to/co_goth

CONTAMINATII – WEST MIDLANDS
www.s-mart.net

CovHeReTiCs – COVENTRY
http://groups.yahoo.com/group/CovHeretics
Big list.

CRISPY'S GOTHIC PAGES –TULSA/DENVER
www.geocities.com/sunsetstrip/mezzanine/9678
He invites you to see what happens when
you get trapped in the bible belt. Easy,
your waist looks heavenly. Mainly odd
looking photos, especially in the Big Book-
o-Goth with hundreds there, and radio.

CRYPT OF CHOKEN
www.torget.se/users/k/kjaken/main.html
Southern Swedish Goth guide.

CT NETGOTH – CONNECTICUT
http://members.tripod.com/~ct_netgoth/index.html
Very small, very dead.

CULTURBUND – GERMANY
www.culturbund.de

Party organisers. Very pretty classical
site, with details of upcoming events,
and wonderful, illustrated accounts on
previous soirees.

CymGothic – WALES
http://groups.yahoo.com/group/CymGothic
'Trapped up the valleys surrounded by
White Sheep and townies? Then join
the Black Sheep of the Dark Pits. Find
out here where all the other Welsh
net-goths are (in England probably) and
discuss vital issues facing the Welsh
Gothic scene today.' Bit of an attitude
visible? Small, and not busy.

DALLAS GOTHICS
www.necronom.com/dallasgothics
Homepage of e-mailing list of
Cyber-Gothics. One local venue is,
somewhat bizarrely called Bar Of Soap.

DANCING FERRET – PHILADELPHIA
www.ferret.com
Goth/Ind. Nice events page with links –
and an amazing array of features listed
bottom right. You've also got Dancing
Ferret, the label, and Digital Ferret the
store, available here, plus the quarterly
Vampire Ball explained, as well as links
to clubs Noir and Nocturne. This is
classic stuff.

DARK ANGEL & EROS – WELLINGTON
http://darkangel.co.nz/darkangelhome.php
Club and gig nights in New Zealand.

DARK ANGELS – LA GOTH-IND
www.geocities.com/SunsetStrip/Palms/1746

DARK ALABAMA
www.darkalabama.com
Decent local info and great galleries
(Art/Photography/People). Wonderful
design all round. Hauntings section is
interesting.

DARK CALGARY
www.darkcalgary.com
This is another great site, with events
and location details aplenty and some
excellent reviews/features with superb
photos.

DARK COLOGNE
www.darkcologne.de

DARK CLEVELAND
www.darkcleveland.com

DARK DREAMSCAPES – OHIO
www.ohiogoth.org/seph
I like this guide a lot. Neat personal
touches everywhere. Jennifer's personal
area includes some seriously sweet
galleries, then there's recommended
websites, plus some of her friends
(plenty non-Goth), and in the Goth
category of the local guide there are
tons more brilliant pics to peruse.
Brilliant local links of artists from all
areas, and 'The Black Market' is the
perfect guide to all local merchants.

DARK ENTRIES MEDIA SITE – TORONTO
www.dark-entries.com
'Dark Entries – Toronto's best source for
news and information on the Gothic,
Ind and Dark Alternative Scene. Want
to be updated weekly with an e mail of
the newest events and information?
Join our mailing list by sending a blank
email to:
dark-entries-events-subscribe@egroups.com'
Totally on the ball news items. Wonderful
club and events section catering for
all genres, magazine section with
interviews. Wonderful review section, of
records, live and club events. The whole
site has a scintillatingly united feel.

DARK FIRE – S.W. ENGLAND
www.darkfire.co.uk

DARK FRESNO
www.darkfresno.com
Community section, club/event news
and local links.

DARK HAPPENINGS
www.wildhunt.org/dh
Small site with a few local pointers,
people links and photos from the
Champaign/Urbana area of Illinois.

DARK LIGHT – SOUTH AFRICA
www.darklight.co.za
Very high quality South African site,
suddenly changed to a club promo page!

DARK ROOM – BRATISLAVA/SLOVAKIA
www.multiweb.cz/darkroom
I don't actually know what language this
is in (Czech?), but there's also a German
version. It's only a small site, updated
regularly, with a tiny guide, forum and
guestbook. Nice gallery of gig pics (inc.
Xymox and C. Death) in the area, which
clearly don't happen often.

DARK SIDE OF NEW ORLEANS

www.blood-dance.net/~nolagoth

Formerly The NO Gothic Guide, so you know what's here – clubs, shops, cemeteries, events, tourism. Misha's site is exquisite, and just makes you want to visit the place more than you already should. The events guide is well updated, the cemeteries and tourist section is ace, and the links are interesting. Totally superb.

A DARK SPOT IN THE HEART –
COLUMBUS, OHIO

www.darkspot.org

Bright and briskly covers gigs, clubs, shops, and local band links.

DARK ZONE – SPAIN

http://usuarios.tripod.es/sandman

Good guide to Spanish activity, although links tend to be international.

DARKLIFE PORTUGAL

http://darklifeportugal.freeservers.com

You can play battleships on this site! Or look at the very nice galleries from their sporadic events. There isn't a great deal of Portuguese content listed, unless I didn't find it. Of the Portuguese zines mentioned, only one worked, as e-mail. Still, it looks lovely and they're working on it all the time.

DARKWAVE – PHILLY

http://groups.yahoo.com/group/darkwave

DC FREAKS

www.dcfreaks.com

This is already a divine site. Plenty of events, people and mad, mad photos.

DE KAGAN KALENDAR

www.kagankalender.com

Live and club happenings in Belgium and Holland, written in Dutch.

DENVER BY DARK

www.noire.net/denver

Brand spanking-ish new site with all the requisite detail, done in a nicely styled downbeat manner – and there's more at: http://noire.net/hemlock – if you survive the scary bloody opening! After that it's very, very interesting, even though I couldn't see the full page. I also like her explanation: 'it suits me and it's based in town. That's really why, but also: it's all girls, which I like. It's not

self-consciously and ostentatiously gothy-gothy, which trait I despise with passion. It is all about substance. It is not commercialized or linkwhorish or pretentious. I feel comfortable here.' The site is actually a little too clever in parts, because there is much here to enjoy and you have to keep fiddling, but she has a sizzling style and the diary is a delight.

DESERT GOTHS

www.geocities.com/Athens/Atlantis/4882

Lubbock, San Antonio, Austin details, a small but charming gallery and sub-scription. I like sites like this because of the cosy feel, plus they've done some interesting things with their links, particularly Art.

DETROIT

http://clubs.yahoo.com/clubs/detroitgoth
technoindustrial
http://clubs.yahoo.com/clubs/detroitgothic
industrial

DORDRECHT GOTHICS

www.clubs.nl/community/default.asp?club=
dordrecht%2Dgothics

DUTCH GOTHIC

www.dutchgothic.org

Cool and enjoyable wap-friendly site, with News, Events, brilliant clubbing guide, music, articles, poetry, art, galleries, nice members section, and excellent Links.

EAST TN GOTHIC

www.knoxvillegothic.homestead.com/kgs.html

Forum, The Gate (poetry and prose contributions), IRC and Links (where you find the real local info). Weird gallery.

EdG&R – EDINBURGH

www.eusa.ed.ac.uk/societies/edgar

Edinburgh student union Goth & Rock society, and while it gives people there a reasonable guide to what's around them there isn't much else, a sure sign of lazy members.

ELIZIUM – ABERDEEN

www.elizium.net

Part Aberdeen Goth community, but also open to everyone, with good links to other like-minded ventures.

EMPIRE OF DARKNESS – GERMAN

www.empireofdarkness.de

ERBA DELLA STREGA

www.erbadellastrega.it

Very attractive Italian Goth community and zine with a huge amount of work gone into it and fantastic results. Forum, chat, newsgroup etc. Nice features and reviews (with good live photos), plus links that are beautifully laid out and described. There are also brilliant galleries, but the whole thing is awesome because there is much here. A lesson to virtually all other sites.

ESOTERICKA – BATON ROUGE

www.esotericka.org

Little links plus pics at the bottom.

FIN.GOTH – FINLAND

www.fingoth.net

Excellent site wth all-round resource, events and history.

FLORIDA

http://clubs.yahoo.com/clubs/floridagoth
http://clubs.yahoo.com/clubs/floridagoths
http://clubs.yahoo.com/clubs/floridiangoths

FLORIDA NET GOTHS

http://nav.webring.yahoo.com/hub?ring=flagoth&list

G.U.N.Z. – NEW ZEALAND

http://gunz.nitro.gen.nz/gunz-info/Contents/
index.htm

A truly wonderful history of New Zealand Goth, but mainly all recent news and developments easily available. All the bands, places and individuals, done in such a bright, involving manner. I think this is the best national site for Goth that there is. You will not be sorry you visited, and it's so well-written you will also be happy to sink into the tales of bands you have never even heard about. Done by The Preacherman and Tim, this resource covers all aspects of dark arts and music in New Zealand, breaking it down into subjects and areas. It is superb throughout.

GATEWAY – CANADA

http://gatewaycentral.cjb.net

Good Canadian Goth pics from parties.

GEORGIA – USA

http://clubs.yahoo.com/clubs/georgiagothiccouncil
http://clubs.yahoo.com/clubs/gothicgeorgia

GERMAN GOTHIC

www.germangothic.de

Newer than most German sites but better looking, and already building smartly.

GERMAN GOTHIC BOARD
www.nachtwelten.de/cgi-bin/Ultimate.cgi?action=intro

GERMAN RING OF GOTH
http://nav.webring.yahoo.com/hub?ring=goth ger&list
'A Webring for German-based Gothic pages. If you are German or your site is in German and your site is about the darker moods in life then this is the ring for you.'

GINO'S BLACK BERLIN
http://home.t-online.de/home/gino.foerster/gbbh.htm

GNARK – GERMANY
www.gnark.com
Party animals, with events details and an absolutely brilliant photo archive.

GOFFBEAT – WARWICK UNI
www.goffbeat.co.uk

GOTBLACK.COM
www.gotblack.com/profiles
Arizona Goths – a mini-resource in itself, with good menu searches and profiles.

GOTH GRRLS
www.gothgrrls.org
Initially Detroit-based mailing list, but now anywhere.

GOTH GUIDE TO CORNWALL
www.onthewire.org.uk/page5.html

A GOTH GUIDE TO AMSTERDAM
www.onthewire.org.uk/page4.html
UK perspective, and very small, and old.

GOTH IND DANCE CLUBS –
WASHINGTON DC
www.geocities.com/SunsetStrip/Underground/7737
Dead, but archive-worthy nostalgia.

GOTH.NO – NORWAY
www.goth.no
In Norwegian.

GOTH MILK
www.ossuary.net/~hazard/gothmilk.html
Trying to start a Wisconsin area webring.

GOTH TWIN CITIES
www.geocities.com/Athens/Forum/1059/goth twincities.html

Looks messy and dull but actually sift through the lists and there's plenty of local content and cross-genre links, but far too many corpses among them.

GOTHENBURG – SWEDEN
http://hemsidor.torget.se/users/k/kjaken/agenda.html

GOTHIC AGE – ITALY
www.energyzone.it/gothage/gothage.htm
A sub-section of the main Energy Zone site (www.energyzone.it), which also has Metal, DJs, forums etc. GothAgeArt has English, German and Italian versions, and photos. Good links.

GOTHIC BC – CANADA
www.gothic.bc.ca/default.htm
Mainly an enormous set of photos from various places, with mailing list details and plentiful links. I loved it. Also:
http://groups.yahoo.com/group/GothicBC

GOTHIC BOSTON.ORG
www.gothicboston.org
Great site, with arts, clubs, fashion, shops, bands.

GOTHIC BRAZILIS – RADIO
http://stations.mp3s.com/stations/120/gothic_brazilis.html

GOTHIC CHICAGO
www.gothicchicago.com
It's big, and it's clever. Events, monthly feature on local outlets, good live reviews. Interviews. Movie reviews, brilliant gallery collection, mega clubs, eating, and shopping info, tourism and the annual Funeral Party event. The only real let-down is no big section on Chicago bands.

GOTHIC CITY MONTREAL
http://members.tripod.com/~altmtl/gothic.html
Montreal forum, alternative grrrl of the month, social gathering links, fetish sites, zine link, along with macabre/horror sites and literature. It's an old site but it's been updated.

GOTHIC-CITY
www.gothic-city.de
All-round German info.

GOTHIC COMMUNITY
www.gothiccommunity.de
Magnificent resource for forum and interaction, stations, charts and news. Amazing!

GOTHIC CONNECTION – MUNICH
www.gothic-connection.f2w.de
Brilliant guide, as big as you'd expect.

GOTHIC DC
www.blood-dance.net/goth/dscene.html
Dead now, but some links remain and I like her comments on DC itself.

GOTHIC DENVER
www.geocities.com/SoHo/Studios/1896
Old, with friends, board, chat, art, events.

GOTHIC DETROIT
www.gothicdetroit.com
A few events and club details plus links.

GOTHIC FORUM BERLIN
www.gkl.de/aheim/gothforumberlin
News, forum, chat and all Berlin events.

GOTHIC FUNERAL
www.geocities.com/vampiric_pain/goth.html
OR www.gothicfuneral.4mg.com
This looks like it's from Mexico, Chile and Argentina, mixed, although run by the same person. It's nice and detailed, with good events and pages on music, vampire, literature and film, with chat, radio, forum and a gallery, which was dead when I visited.

GOTHIC GREECE
www.gothic.gr
Nice community site for Greek Goth ebm Industrial types in Greece. Decent club and shops list but no links and no bands whatsoever!!!

GOTHIC HOLLYWOOD
www.darkart.net/Prynne/hollywood.htm

GOTHIC IE
www.gothic.ie
Irish resource, not fully completed but old-ish details available.

GOTHIC IN CINCINNATI
www.geocities.com/BourbonStreet/3482/gothncin.html
Excellent guide to local shops and events, with tiny focus on Cinci Goths themselves.

GOTHIC IND SOUTHEAST
http://members.aol.com/Veneficium/gotindsthest.html

GOTHIC MICHIGAN
http://airmitt.tripod.com/gothmenter.html

Guide to Ambient, Experimental, Ind and Gothic.

GOTHIC MICHIANA - Michigan
http://groups.yahoo.com/group/gothicmichiana

GOTHIC MISSOURI WEBRING
http://nav.webring.yahoo.com/hub?ring=gothmoring&list

GOTHIC NET – Australia
www.gothic.net.au
Big and brilliant, with separate city sections for Adelaide, Brisbane, Canberra, Hobart, Melbourne, Perth and Sydney; each section showing events, club details and local shopping as and when relevant. Big netgoth list of people, by state. The worst thing is that about half of all links are dead. Why don't people check what's happening with their sites?

GOTHIC NEW ORLEANS
www.geocities.com/SunsetStrip/Studio/4483/gothnola.htm
Nice dead site with usual points of interest for visitors. Clubs, shops, music, cemeteries etc.

GOTHIC NORTH EAST – UK
http://uk.clubs.yahoo.com/clubs/gothicnortheast

GOTHIC NUT – Newcastle
http://clubs.yahoo.com/clubs/gothicnut

GOTHIC PAGES – Dutch
http://gothic.pagina.nl

GOTHIC PLANET
www.upink.com
Gorgeous Denver community site. Plenty of forum stuff, reviews, links and all, but first check out the quite magnificent galleries.

GOTHIC SEATTLE – archive
www.sea-goth.com

GOTHIC SOCIETY OF NOVA SCOTIA
www.geocities.com/Athens/Acropolis/3678/
It got suspended, so this has even older details. Still some lovely photo sections.

GOTHICSTATECOLLEGE – Central Pennsylvania
www.gothicstatecollege.com
Huge new resource, concentrating on

Goth and Ind, with added interest by features and good columns, with forum/chat etc.

GOTHIC.NU
www.gothic.nu/index.php
Swedish Goth thing, with separate sites for the webmasters (www.gothic.nu/ego and www.gothic.nu/m) showcasing design work and photos. The majority of the site is Goth/EBM news, reviews and interviews, in English. Very detailed and informative with good community relations.

THE GOTHIC WORLD
www.multimania.com/babble/gothic/gothic.htm
Looks great. In English, with a list of favourite bands gallery has fantastic pictures – really excellent – of the woman responsible, plus her friend. With a list of French places, mags, and decent links already it will be a great site when it's finished.

GOTHIQUES – Canada
http://groups.yahoo.com/group/gothiques

GOTHIQUE FRANCAPHONE
www.ringsurf.com/netring?ring=wrgothfr;id=1;action=list

GOTHLING – Twin Cities
www.gothling.com
More Twin Cities info, with the usual contents. Sprucely done... with the kind of layout many should follow, being attractively subtle, but so easy to use, with some really good photos, from a variety of events – gigs, picnics, clubs, and locals, offering the best monthly round up of shots you'll see anywhere. Good links and all-round local info with store and radio coming. They also select a good link of the week. The week I double-checked they were highlighting a firm called Dark Passage, a firm which helps archaeologists with serious sight problems, by providing specialist flashlights!!! These people *care*.

GOTHS ANONYMOUS
http://gothsanonymous.tripod.com
Articles – literature, poetry, comics, film, music, events in Holland, and their community.

GOTH IN ASIA
http://gothinasia.cjb.net
Gerard Bumanglag runs this and it isn't

fully developed yet but it will be essential, because we all need a site about Goth in Japan, China, Singapore, Hong Kong, Philippines etc. Should be properly operational at some time in 2002, but meantime he already has pics being submitted from Japan, Korea, Singapore etc, with reports from the Philippines, good links starting, along with profiles. If you have an interest in Goth overall you really need to check this out. Good band stuff is appearing already.

GOTHCHESTER USA – Rochester
http://gothic-rochester.com
Re-vamped site, and growing nicely.

GRIM SOC – S. Glamorgan
www.grimsoc.co.uk

HALIFAX GOTHIC – Canada
http://clubs.yahoo.com/clubs/halifaxgothicscene

HAMBURG EGROUP
http://de.groups.yahoo.com/group/schwarzeshamburg-newgoth

HELIX – UK
www.pennangalan.co.uk/Helix
There was a time when this was a seriously useful UK resource, since replaced in importance by darkwave.org. Still half-decent gig and events info.

HELLBANE – Brisbane
www15.brinkster.com/hellbane
Guide to Goth/Darkwave in Brisbane, and very good it is too with events, updates, messages, topics, links, fantastic gallery section, city guide, music and literature.

HELL'S CANYON GOTHIC
http://hcgothic.iwarp.com

HELTER SKELTER – Southern Germany
www.helter-skelter.notrix.de
Party organisers. Details, cute pics.

HERE ARE THE PICTURES – Canada
www.angelfire.com/emo/farm/main.html
Gigs and vast galleries from The Gateway.

HOUSTON GOTHIC IND FETISH
www.gauthica.com
This is brilliant, with a large Goth sections covering usual outlets but also inviting poems, prose, theories etc. There are detailed section all over this site and some particularly good,

regular galleries accompanying most of the events they've been announcing, and a whole visual section where people can post their own material. Quite exceptional.

IBERIAN BLACK ARTS
www.iberianblackarts.cjb.net
Iberian_Black_Arts@yahoo.es
Excellent Spanish Goth and Metal site, with English. Lovely photos of some woman called Morgana, and all sections are very detailed. There is also a huge Black Metal/Doom/Pagan Rock section.

INCY'S GUIDE TO GOTHIC LONDON
www.the-dreaming.demon.co.uk/londonguide.htm
Harmless nostalgia and much of it is still relevant as it was a sizeable piece of work.

IND GOTHIC UNDERGROUND NIGHT
www.sexandbooze.com
DJ playlists and nice pics from events, around Ohio.

INSIDE PORTALS – BATON ROUGE
www.geocities.com/inside_portals/index.html

INTO THE NIGHT
http://gothicchicago.com/scary.html
Scary Lady Sarah's events, and local guide, which offers a personal selection and sometimes suggests why you may enjoy her links.

IOWA
http://clubs.yahoo.com/clubs/gothiciowa

IRISH GOTHS
http://groups.yahoo.com/group/iegoth
Small group but messages aplenty.

KANSAS CITY GOTH
http://members.tripod.com/~kcgoth
Far more than I expected. Postcards, Wiccan, articles and KC cemeteries among the expected standards. Small, but nice galleries.

KANSAS CITY GOTHIC WEBSITE
http://members.tripod.com/~kcgoth

KATATONIE FRANCE
http://splyit.free.fr
Parisian guide to bands and clubs, with flyers and galleries to look through, and there's a Goth and Metal crossover thing going on. There is a

Mel and DJ Scary Lady Sarah. Whitby Festival, November 1999. Photo © Olga Kalantzi.
www.nef-blue-pages.com

Goth Culture/History section, well laid out, and interesting covering literature, music and cinema. Nice general galleries, of pics and art.

KC GOTHS
http://groups.yahoo.com/group/kcgoth-indus
Events, nice gallery and local places named, but little detail.

KENTUCKY
http://clubs.yahoo.com/clubs/gothgirlsof
kentucky

KITSAP – WA, USA
www.hadaverde.com/kgoths
I haven't the faintest idea where Kitsap County is (WA = Washington?), but they have regular events, and there are some lovely galleries here as well as member profiles – Pyxie: Favorite time of day: 'When I kick the kids out the door for school.'

KIWI GOTHS – NEW ZEALAND
http://communities.msn.co.nz/KiwiGoths

LAS VEGAS
www.altvegas.com/goth

LAS VEGAS GOTH
www.angelfire.com/goth/vegas
Good guide with gallery, bookstores, clubs and links, even acting!

L'ETOILE NOIR – GERMANY
www.etoile.de
German gig guide, but also with excellent live/club photos from some.

LE CIRCLES DES SITES FRANCOPHONE
http://nav.webring.yahoo.com/hub?ring=franco1998&list
'Bienvenue sites du monde entier, si ton site est écrit en majorité en français alors tu peux te joindre à nous. Sites pour tout les groupes d'âges. De 7 à 77 ans sont les bienvenues. Sites pornographiques s'abstenir svp.' Exactly!

LEICESTER GOTHS
www.leicestergoths.fsnet.co.uk
Tiny local scene guide, with some charming pics of their adventures.

LES NOIRES
www1.inetservice.de/LesNoires
Small but sleek German site with

forum, links, written contributions and galleries of photos and artwork.

LEXGOFF
http://homepage.ntlworld.com/highnoon/Lexgoff
An attractive site, with little other than events details.
http://groups.yahoo.com/group/lexgoff

LEXGOTH.COM AND LOVING IT!
www.debecker.net
Board with a relaxed, spirited feel.

LIBERTINE/LONG ISLAND – USA
http://clubs.yahoo.com/clubs/libertine

LONDON (SLUTS)
www.twisted.org.uk/sluts
Biggest list going. Details:
http://toybox.twisted.org.uk/mailman/listinfo/sluts
'In closing we'd just like to add that if you leave we'll all think you're a wuss.'

LONG ISLAND GOTHIC
http://clubs.yahoo.com/clubs/libertine

LOS ANGELES GOTHIC-IND NETWORK
www.lagoth.net
Big set of clubs, events, shopping, talk and radio sections. Vast profiles section, and great local band links.

LOS ANGELES GOTHS
http://clubs.yahoo.com/clubs/losangelesgoths

MACABRE
www.macabre.net
Selection of dark sites in France.

MANCGOFF
http://groups.yahoo.com/group/mancgoff
Group that took off from where the old site died. 'This is a mailing list designed to share information about shops, gigs, clubs and people in the Goth scene in Manchester, United Kingdom.'

MANCHESTER NET GOTH
www.grimoire.8k.com/netgoth/index.html
Site aiming to chart a swelling in local activity, until it gave up in 2000. Still some good gallery shots of Whitby 99.

MANITOBA GOTHIC/IND EVENTS
www.virulent.org/cangoth/mb/index.html

MARITIMES GOTHIC/IND EVENTS
www.virulent.org/cangoth/mar/index.html

MARYLAND
http://clubs.yahoo.com/clubs/marylandgothhangout

MEMPHIS
http://clubs.yahoo.com/clubs/memphisteengoths

MICHIGAN
http://clubs.yahoo.com/clubs/gothicmichigansingles

MIDLANDS – UK
http://groups.yahoo.com/group/tainted
Small-ish but very busy. For locals or regular visitors, and can get you discounts in local shops.

MID-WEST AFTER DARK
http://mwafterdark.tripod.com/gothIND.htm
The site was in a mess when I saw it, but that should be okay now. Old links with nothing separating Goth or Ind to give you decent guidance. Very few events.

MIDNIGHT BLUE
www.lava.net/~asylum/midnightblue.html
Hawaiian Goth community page with brief sections on the scene there, mainly club details, plus a Ghost Walks tour. Couple of links for Razed In Black, their biggest band, hefty ordinary links, plus local zines.

MILGOTH – MILWAUKEE
www.goetia.net/m_goth.html

MILWAUKEE GOTHS
www.milgoth.org/index.html
Black clothes, warm hearts they say, soppily. Nice site with projects, news, reports and interesting galleries.

THE MILWAUKEE GOTHIC COUNIL
www.angelcities.com/members/gothcouncil
www.geocities.com/milwaukeegothiccouncil
http://clubs.yahoo.com/clubs/milwaukee gothiccouncil
Very unusual, as this apparently coexists with a bi-weekly hour-long cable TV show, and the site owner also is an attorney who successfully defended the local Goth club owner against bizarre defamatory charges by the council. A small clubs and shops guide, radio, TV, events, links, sites of the month and even the weather.

MISERY'S CHAOS – COLUMBIA, MISSOURI
http://goths.mu.org
More than cute with clubs/events, town guide, and music.

MONTREAL'S GOTHIC SOULS
http://go.to/gothicmontreal
Cool site, in English or French, explaining what the Goth scene there is like, and the type of Goths involved – Ind, Glitter, Victorian, Black Punks, Vampires, Fetishists, Wannabes, Modern, Manson Knights, Goth Raver and Hyper Techno Goth – as well as giving you the low-down on clubs and shops, plus a Goth tourist guide. I shouldn't bother rooting around in the Virtual area as you can never link back properly. Magenta's journal could be interesting, as she's painfully honest in it, but I think she gets too miserable to take that too far.

MORBID KIWIS
http://groups.yahoo.com/group/morbid-kiwis

MSP – MINNEAPOLIS
http://heavyboots.com/mspgoth
Great profiles list, and a huge local resources and guide section, but this site has more dead links than any I have encountered.

A MURDER OF RAVENS – FLORIDA
http://members.tripod.com/~a_murder_of_ravens/index.html
Nostalgic old site for Florida society, or maybe it just seems that way. Did include a guide to the scene, no longer working, but also local people, artists and musicians in a cool way.

NAIADI & ROSA SELVAGGIA
http://utenti.tripod.it/NIKITA65/linus-html
Italian party events, with own zine site at www.naiadi.com

NASHVILLE GOTHIC
www.angelfire.com/tn/goths/new.html
Nothing too much happening. What gets me is that regional guides don't realise outsiders visit, seeking info. There's not even an illustrated guide, and – worse – for such a small site, the fact some links are dead shows that no-one maintains it. If you don't have much current action, why not put together historical archive pages, showing how the scene has developed? If well researched and illustrated with photos, it's going to interest everyone.

NCGOTH.COM
www.ncgoth.com
Not much action. Decent club details.

Where it scores is its 'cool sites'. Check their past recommendations you'll be happy enough, and their Fashion List section at: ncgoth.com/gothfashion/index.html. That gives links to plenty of cool sites.

N.E. GOTH – NEWCASTLE
http://toybox.twisted.org.uk/mailman/listinfo/ne-goth

NEGATIVELANDIA – SPANISH
www.geocities.com/Area51/Lair/3559

NEOGOTHIC – ITALIAN PARTIES
http://members.xoom.it/NGothic

NET GOTH FRANCE
http://netgoth.free.fr/index.html
Chat, forum, Newsgroup, Portal and good European gig news.

NETGOTHS.COM – ARIZONA
www.netgoths.com/msie.htm

NEW ENGLAND DARKSIDE WALKERS – USA
http://clubs.yahoo.com/clubs/newengland darksidewalkers

NEW JERSEY
www.eclipse.net/~andybran/index.html
Andy and Brandi's site, which is very jolly and has a clear No Fangs warning, to avoid discussing people who cram plastic into their mouth and defy logic by suddenly declaring themselves interesting. Big clubs and events news, lots of links and photos galore, with galleries going back to 1997.

NEW JERSEY EVENTS
http://www.netlabs.net/hp/drx/njevents.htm

NEW MEXICO
www.darkflower.com/abq
The Land Of Entrapment? Eh? A straightforward local hotspots guide, plus people.

NEW YORK
http://clubs.yahoo.com/clubs/gothicnewyork

NIGHT NEWS – EDINBURGH
www.nightnews.net
Like a mini-zine/guide, with local news of interest, plus music and club details, and the galleries are fantastic!!!

NIGHTROOM – GERMANY
www.nightroom.de.vu
Forum mainly, but also news and events.

NIGHTSHIFT – UTAH
www.geocities.com/SunsetStrip/Palladium/4035
Brian Warren, who does this site, also has a link to his journal, which is an easy read. But Brian, do us a favour, stop beginning entries with the word 'Well'. Driving me mad. So up to date gig, radio and club details, and some local people/band links.

NIHLISM – HAMPSHIRE
www.dvilution.com/nihilism
Brilliant site. Cyber version of Take A Byte, cool gallery, funny, and very sarcastic, guide to Gothspotting in their area, from their hugely modern perspective, as well as How To Make Punk Music. (Well, it made me laugh.) They may be squeaking in tongues but they do so very smartly. Goth ringtones – what's that all about?

NYC Goth

NINE WHILE NINE – IRELAND
www.personal.dundee.ac.uk/~gsgibson

NJ GOTH
www.netlabs.net/hp/drx/njgoth-l.htm
Very no-nonsense, and straight to the point, with all the various locations of general interest scooted into one long list, site history in another, music, and member profiles, but this can't be the main one surely? It said construction but felt archaeological. The members pages still have things.

NOLA-GOTH ORG – NEW ORLEANS
www.nola-goth.org
Updated news, good features, but the mailing list has way too many dead links. The best part is the Sites, where you can check out some seriously interesting personal pages.

NONSINEINVIDIA
http://nsi-online.tripod.com
Portuguese site which is trying hard to highlight Ind music, and it's a decent start but when they haven't a section of Portuguese links of which they feel proud, they're up against it.

NORTH CAROLINA
http://clubs.yahoo.com/clubs/gothicnorthcarolina
http://groups.yahoo.com/group/rtpgoth/
www.stowy.net/music

NORTH GOTH MAILING LIST – UK
http://toybox.twisted.org.uk/mailman/listinfo/north

NORTHERN NEVADA GOTHICS
http://groups.yahoo.com/group/nnvgothics

NORTHERN GOTHS – UK
http://toybox.twisted.org.uk/mailman/listinfo/north

NORTHWEST GOTH SCENE – USA
http://clubs.yahoo.com/clubs/northwestgothscene

NORTHWEST INDIANA
http://clubs.yahoo.com/clubs/nwingoth

NORTHWEST UNDERGROUND
www.network54.com/Hide/Forum/22474
Ind, Goth and experimental in the Pacific Northwest. Smothered with technical data and offers, like a mini-web resource, this also has local music links, which are marked mainly by the absence of Ind, Goth or anything remotely experimental.

NORVAGOTH
www.norvagoth.net
Norfolk Virginia area (plus Tidewater?) and a really cool site, with a distinctive layout. Horrorscopes, cemetery guides, events, resources, shopping, good music links and a superb gallery section.

NORWAY
http://home.no.net/cmisje
Under construction. Old galleries at: http://home.no.net/cmisje/gallery2.html

NYC EVENTS
http://anon.razorwire.com/events

NYCGOTH
www.nycgoth.com
Magnificent, naturally. Huge clubs and events details available for a thriving

Le Bal Des Vampires. Photo © Stéphane Burlot

Charming guide to all things local, with a lovely 'Scrapbooks' section. Can't understand why more guides don't have that. Big music section, thing to do, and recommended websites. This is my favourite regional guide.

OKLAHOMA
http://clubs.yahoo.com/clubs/gothicoklahoma
http://clubs.yahoo.com/clubs/okgoths

ONTARIO GOTHIC/IND EVENTS
www.virulent.org/cangoth/on/index.html

OREGON
http://clubs.yahoo.com/clubs/oregongoths

OXGOTHS
www.oxgoths.darkwave.org.uk
The Oxford Goths page, obviously, with event details, shopping, an excellent gallery where you get descriptions, and links. Disappointing, considering how nice this looks, that none of them have yet decided to write anything about Oxford's Goth past and/or present, or anything, really.

P. GOTH – PARIS
www.multimania.com/etlesgoths
It's meant to be a guide to Parisian Goth but both entry points I tried linked me straight to academic Islamic study pages!

PENDUL – ROMANIA
www.pendul.f2s.com
Imaginatively done Guide to Romanian underground culture. Nice galleries.

PENNSYLVANIA
http://clubs.yahoo.com/clubs/pennsylvaniagoths

PENNSYLVANIA
www.piga1.com
It's almost Transylvania, when you think about it. News, profile, lists, board, events, gatherings, top tens, and stunningly great links. It looks deadpan, but bulges with life.

PERTH ORDER OF GOTHIC SOCIETIES
http://dominion.iinet.net.au/pogs

PHILLIPINES GOTH
www.philmusic.com/zine/news/2000/05/053100_goth/index.htm
This hasn't really taken off yet, but it's a

hotspot. The intro section alone can enthral, and there's lists aplenty. Guides to bars, cheap hotels, the works. It doesn't seem to be updated, and must have moved on but the central info here is fabulous.

NYCGOTH – NEW YORK
www.neitherland.com
Clubs, events, shopping. Boys Are Dumb, toys, candy, widely varied image gallery, library... and so it goes on. Massive and compelling.

NZ GOTHBOARD
www.SLi.net.nz/cgi-bin/gothboard/ikonboard.cgi

OBZINE – PHILADELPHIA
www.obzineonline.com
Online news for local scenes.

OHIO
http://clubs.yahoo.com/clubs/gothohio
http://clubs.yahoo.com/clubs/ohiogoths

OHIO GOTH
www.ohiogoth.org

pleasant, informative site, which should be big by the end of the year. Or look for Subkulture instead.

PHILLYGOTH
phlaux.candiedangel.net/phillygoth
Good local guide, especially the locations.

PITTSBURGH
http://clubs.yahoo.com/clubs/pittsburghgoths

PITTSBURGH DARK MUSIC RING
http://nav.webring.yahoo.com/hub?ring=pghdarkmusic&list

PITTSBURGH GOTH
www.pghgoth.com
Another brilliant guide with everything you'd expect, except my cursor suddenly became some little bloke's head and it was seriously disturbing dragging that around! So clubs, gigs, irc, weekly rant, profiles, bands. Top class.

POLISH GOTH
www.goth.art.pl/webring/lista.html

PORTLAND
http://clubs.yahoo.com/clubs/portlandmetrogoths

PORTLAND IND GOTHIC (PIG)
www.sonic-boom.com/pig
Events photographs. This is a brilliant selection of photos from different events, from sporting excess (the Sneerleaders at Casketball are cool), to simple birthday celebrations. It loads slowly, so go off and make a meal, and revel in the delights when you return. Class stuff.

PRAIRIE DARKNESS MAILING LIST
http://groups.yahoo.com/group/prairiedarkness
'This is for Western Canadian and northern US Goths to get together and chat, to plan events, and to vent. This list will help to bring it all together for Prairie Gothics!'

PVGOTHLIST
www.coldcircuit.net/pvgoth/index.php3
Huge profile list of people, with pictures, news and rants.

PURGATORY – FLORIDA
http://goth.viciousangel.net

QUEBEC GOTHIC/IND EVENTS
www.virulent.org/cangoth/pq/index.html

RAGNAROK – S. GERMANY
www.ragnarok.de
Party organiser. Usual details. Some rather stern flyers, and links.

RAVEN MOON – ALBUQUERQUE
www.angelfire.com/nm/ravenmoon
New Mexico action. Cute photos, big music detail in bio manner, good links.

RED GOTICA
www.redgotica.8m.com
Excellent site which links together all Latin American and Spanish speaking Goth action, specifically in Mexico, Colombia, Uruguay, Argentina and Spain. Which sounds great but it's long dead and most of the links go nowhere. However, some cool pics survive.

REQUIEM – NEWCASTLE
http://clubs.yahoo.com/clubs/requiem

RISE OF THE GOTHS
http://homepage.uibk.ac.at/homepage/csac/csac4598
German site, part magazine, part guide with events covered and a great gallery.

ROCHESTER (JUST RESTING)
http://rochestergothica.vectorstar.net/

ROCK GOTHIC ANIMATION STRABOURG
http://goth.ifrance.com/goth
Mad intro!!! Then on with a Strasbourg guide of places to go, no local bands of merit, fashion, seriously weird galleries and decent links.

ROSE NOIR GOTHIC – HOUSTON
www.angelfire.com/tx2/rosenoir
Redundant looking mailing list, with extra sections for profiles, dead events, webrings and merchandise. Some profile links still work.

RUBBER SNAPS AND OTHER CONFECTIONS – S. FLORIDA
www.geocities.com/SunsetStrip/Balcony/6809
Personal-ish with some very nice photos, then links on Ind and fetish scene.

RUSSIAN GOTHIC PAGE
www.gothic.ru
Truly superb site, with English version, on bands, art, literature, cinema, community. Those involved are heavily into the scene, organising events and DJ-ing.

There is a big links section and a section on Russian bands. News, features and reviews (with translations), merchandise (their own CD and video releases). Scroll down the mighty main news section which also lists events and updates you can encounter some galleries.

SACRAMENTO DARKREALM
www.geocities.com/sac_darkrealm

SAKATCHEWAN GOTHIC/IND EVENTS
www.virulent.org/cangoth/sk/index.html
Good guide and local resource.

SALISBURY GOTHIC
www.geocities.com/jaditelefae/salisgoth
Nice site for local Goths who meet up monthly, run by Jadith Faery (Azstarelle – see Goth Sites and Clothes) plus growing sections on Goth, shopping and fashion. No events pics?

SAN DIEGO GOTH-IND
www.sdgoth.org
Various mailing lists, coffee outings, clubs, events, local bands.

THE SANCTUARY
www.sanctuary.ch
Mega-site from Switzerland, covering the scene there as well as Sanctuary events, and the full community bit. Reviews and magazine section, good news, and a general vibrant feel. There's the usual links, plus a Culture Guide to various cities. Quite magnificent, except the DJ lists haven't been updated regularly.

THE SANCTUM – IRISH
http://pub78.ezboard.com/bthesanctum91648

SCHRIE
www.informatik.uni-bremen.de/~goecke
Bremen guide. Big review archive, club/gig dates. Basic.

SCHWARZES HAMBURG
www.schwarzes-hamburg.de
Another spectacular German site.

SCOTGOTHS
http://clubs.yahoo.com/clubs/scotgoths

SCOTLAND
http://toybox.twisted.org.uk/mailman/listinfo/scot

SCOUSEGOFF – LIVERPOOL
http://groups.yahoo.com/group/scousegoff

SEATTLE
www.josienutter.com/seagoth

SEAGOTH.ORG
www.seagoth.org
Very impressive for an area guide, with a seriously intelligent view of all the traditional community aspects of Seattle itself, not just the scene – which it covers brilliantly, too, plus link to all members. Blah blah...

SEATTLE'S CHILDREN OF THE NIGHT
www.operation-glam.com/seattle
www.darkflower.com/abq
Bustling site with even more colourful investigations into local creativity. Club reviews, bands, webring, radio, board.

SF GHOULIES
www.sfghoulies.org

SFGOTH – SAN FRANCISCO
www.sfgoth.com
As big as you'd expect, with details galore and huge member section – yes, I could have phrased that better – but surprisingly mouldy band section.

SHADOWS OF CHARLESTON
www.angelfire.com/sc/Emptygrave/index.html
Nice old site for South Carolina. Personal rather than detailed.

SHEFFGOFFS – SHEFFIELD
www.darkwave.org.uk/~gothtarts/sheffgoths.php
Dissolution club link, and Sheffield scene.

SHROPSHIRE FREAKS
http://uk.clubs.yahoo.com/clubs/shropshirefreaks

SIDESHOW
www.sideshowmag.com
Colorado promoter of dark music, with upcoming event details and a few interviews.

SITE GOTHIQUE FRANCOPHONE
www.ifrance.com/gothic
Great French guide, with shops, music, forum, lovely galleries, CD reviews, Literature and Netgoth chat.

SLOW BURN – ITALY
www.slowburn.it
If I see a link for a site in Italy, what do I think, if I decide to visit? I think maybe I'll find out about Goth in Italy. What I obviously don't need is to find links to bands in Germany or America. Nor does anyone in Italy, come to that, seeing as there's no Italian descriptions. This isn't just an Italian thing, it happens in virtually every country but it seems to me that in the nineties (as Japan did in the eighties), Italian Gothic has been too apologetic and lacking in confidence in the past and this site follows that trend. An e-zine formerly known as Under The Black Rose zine (and a brilliant one at that) only it hasn't been updated for three months when I visited but the new and reviews mainly concerned music from outside Italy. Why don't they believe we can find their bands interesting, and why isn't the main section about current and past Italian bands? The country that has Ataraxia should be inspired, but would rather contemplate the S*st*rs? What's going on? Although currently down when I double-checked it's bound to be up again because this is a truly interesting and lovely site, which should be proud of its own music and start publicising it.

SOBE GOTHS – MIAMI
http://come.to/sobegoths
Lovely site, presumed dead but there's plenty of pictures to appreciate, and a charming 'tributes' section that was about Goths who had left the area, who they thought highly of.

A SOUL LOST IN THE LAND OF SORROW
http://olivier.sabot.free.fr/Gothic/Gothiceng.html
French Goth site with literature, cinema, music, rituals of death, lovely cemetery and castle galleries.

SOUTH AFRICA
www.goth.co.za
If it isn't ancient, it's boring.

SOUTH CAROLINA
http://clubs.yahoo.com/clubs/gothsnfreaksofsouthcarolina

SOUTHWEST GOTHS
www.swgoths.org
Mailing list for Goths in Texas, New Mexico and Okalahoma.

SOUTH WEST GOTHS – USA
www.swgoths.org
Looks old, nice archive photos.

SOUTH-WEST GOTH – UK
www.swgoth.freeserve.co.uk/front.htm
Proper site that contains lists but also Swot's On, Area Guide (and this is a big area) plus a fairly scary gallery. Nice links.

SOUTHERN GOTH
www.angelfire.com/ky2/southgoth
Southern clubs list. (Message board is kaput.)

SOUTHERN GOTHIC CAM PORTALS
www.io.com/~batty/camportals.html

ST. LOUIS
http://clubs.yahoo.com/clubs/gothsofstlouis

ST LOUIS GOTHIC
www.impure.org/stlgoth
Events etc plus local bands. Lovely galleries.

STRANGEGIRL PRODUCTIONS
www.strangegirlproductions.com
Fetish, costume and music vents in Tulsa, with cool pics and DJ profiles.

STRAYLIGHT – HULL
www.straylight.karoo.net
Odd site with Spiders club info, and guides to good coffee places.

STUTTGART-SCHWARZE
www.stuttgart-schwarz.de
Another huge German resource done with a personalised feel and cute graphics.

SUBKULTURE – PHILIPPINES
www.subkulture.info
Run by Doi Pollas, and covering the scene, this may become a seriously organised events and label site run around the scene there and their main band, Dominion.

THE SWITCHBOARD – CA
www.subnation.com/switchboard
Big details on South Californian area from the excellent Subnation, with clubs and bands and huge resource ambience.

SYDNEY GOTHIC – AUSTRALIA
www.goth.org.au/sydney
This is section of the stunning Aether Sanctum (see Zines), but I felt it was worth mentioning because it's a great guide to Sydney activities, with news, reviews, archives, interviews and DJ profiles.

SYRAGOTH – SYRACUSE
www.moonkids.net/syragoth
Shops, links, poetry.

TALLAHASSEE GOTH
www.envy.nu/tallygoth
You have to visit this great site if only to see the Gothic Football League photos in the People section. There isn't a lot but it feels strangely fresh compared to most.

TENNESSEE
http://clubs.yahoo.com/clubs/gothsintennessee

TEXAS
http://clubs.yahoo.com/clubs/dfwgothicscene
http://clubs.yahoo.com/clubs/houstongothic

THY KINDRED – PHILIPPINES
www.geocities.com/thykindred
Interesting site for Goth in the Philippines, with message board for news and reviews, plus seriously cool photos.

TORONTO GOTH
www.toronto-goth.com
Huge quality site with all the local info and community content you'd expect.

TORONTO IND GOTH STATION
http://stations.mp3s.com/stations/129/toronto_IND-goth.html

TULSA GOTHIC
www.tulsagothic.com
Suddenly recharged, with nice content and good photos.

UK.PEOPLE.GOTHIC
http://groups.google.com/groups?hl=en&group=uk.people.gothic
Top quality Goth chatter within the UK. Many interesting threads develop into weighty discussions, but also lots of frivolity. Many hefty contributions from Michael Johnson and the occasional curtsey from Sexbat.

UKRAINIAN DARK SYNDICATE
http://members.tripod.co.uk/old_monks_saga
Site covering Darkwave and Ind projects.

UKRAINIAN GOTH PORTAL
www.gothic.com.ua/ua/main.htm
Good site offering promotion in Ukraine for Goth bands. Send them your CDs and they review them in English, and also play them in clubs and sometimes arrange gigs for visiting bands. Reviews are good. This site is quite a huge resource for the area, and endlessly informative. I didn't understand it but they have all the sections expected and a big list of local Goth and Darkwave bands. Mp3 and video. Bottom right hand side of page activates links to lovely gallery section and translated areas.

UTAH
http://clubs.yahoo.com/clubs/gothicutah
http://clubs.yahoo.com/clubs/utgoth

UTAH GOTH MAILING LIST
http://utahgoth.net
As with everything else linked to Utah's Goth scene this is attractively and thoughtfully done. All the necessary member details, including a few pics from past events. 'Just be forewarned that we're all a little jumpy since half the state wants to throw us in jail and/or wash our souls clean.' Yes, but so do I, although that's simply because I have the flu as I'm doing this entry. Nothing personal. Currently down.

UTAH GOTHICS
www.gothics.org
There is something very sweet-natured about the Utah scene, and I find it refreshing. This is a local programme to help in the community! Cast all scepticism aside.

VANCOUVER GOTHIC
http://groups.yahoo.com/group/van-goth

VIENNA – CURRENTLY DOWN
www.astro.univie.ac.at/~feli

VIENNA GOTHIC CAFÉ
www.gothic.at
Beautiful Austrian site. All the usual local guide info, plus a magnificent illustrated reviews section on gigs and festivals, plus forum and links.

VINTAGE GOTHIC – STRATHCLYDE
http://communities.msn.co.uk/VintageGothic

VOICES IN THE DARK
www.geocities.com/Athens/Agora/7257

Old site, but still with interesting Savannah info.

WASHINGTON DC
www.obscure.org/~lady-k/gothcult
Small and nice, with some dead kinks.

WESSEX
www.valinor.freeserve.co.uk
Very odd! A gaming and astronomy kind of thing going on.

WHITBY GOTHIC WEEKEND
www.wgw.topmum.co.uk

WHITBY – PHOTOS
www.darkwave.org.uk/whitby
Unlike Convergence, where I had to search to put together a bigger list than official sites had, this is a pretty comprehensive guide to all known Whitby pics. Anyone who has some should contact them pronto, especially the early events.

WINNIPEG GOTHIC
www.nightshadepromo.com/winnipeg.htm
Although it says there's a vibrant scene, the guide can't offer much beyond a few locations of interest, clothes and record shops. Pretty dramatic painting at top of page.

WNYGOTH – BUFFALO
www.wnygoth.com
Fair to say this isn't busy, with no updates in six months, so they may have moved elsewhere and eluded me.

WRIT IN WATER
www.serve.com/diavolo/grave
International memorials to the dead.

WYOMING GOTH MAILING LIST
http://come.to/WyomingGoth

XHPONOZON
www.xhponozon.com
Interesting German site of party/events organisers who prefer somewhere scenic. Shame the galleries are so insubstantial.

YORKSHIRE GOTHIC
http://swift.northtower.co.uk/gothuk/main.asp
Big selection of scary pics.

People

0DIVXO
www.empire.net/~savage
Antique Jen archive, but snow pic is weird.

1 GOTHMAN WELCOMES YOU
http://members.home.net/laydbac70/1gothman
Long bio, nicely done, plus pics, poetry, artwork etc. He forgets to give his name and could do with less apologies about living in Iowa. He also worries about what the Goth Persona means exactly, claiming to have spent his whole life working that one out. No, not your *whole* life.

13AM
www.13am.net

21ST CENTURY DIGITAL BOI
http://21stcenturydigitalboii.com
Dutch boi. Mainly pics.

8MM
www.xsynthetic.org/8mm
Dave is a witty and enigmatic character. Site looks great, journal is lively, cool pics.

A GOTHGURL'S EXPERIMENT
www.gothgurl.com
Gothgurl is really sweet and remodelling this brilliant site after a while away. It's arty, there's a nice gallery selection, with a lovely wildlife theme as well, and cemeteries in New Orleans. It's amazingly interesting, and strangely soothing as you try and track down the elusive girl. The alphabetical brief lives section is brilliant, j is for Joy Division, k is for 'my kickass shoes'. Future plans include more photography, also featured in the regular journal, and poetry, with a grittier, Industrial look.

A.T.H.E.R.O. – HAIRDO ARCHIVE!
www.stardusted.net/athero

ARABELLA ABADDON
www.crucified.com/angylfaerrie

'Protection'. Photo © Stéphane Lord.
Models: Frances Hardy and Rose Cleaver

ABANDON ALL HOPE YE WHO ENTER HERE
www.gothic.net/~imperia

ABBERLAINE
http://abberlaine.tripod.com
Some excellent writing here, horror, erotica, non-fiction.

ABSENTIA
www.velvet.net/~absentia

ABSINTHE HOUSE (DOWN?)
www.hadaverde.com/absinthe
Personal site, and the walking stick in The Study is awesome. Cute Convergence pics, some links to sites with details on brain-melting absinthe itself... and one of the best sets of fashion links you'll find.

ABSOLUTION: NMB
http://uk.geocities.com/nmb666
Good writing and art.

ABSOLUTION
– VICTORIA'S GOTHIC PAGE
www.threethirteen.net/absolution
Nice site, pretty bubbly. Brief bio of Victoria Gwaed, for it is her from Antimony & Lace. Journal 'Dreamcage' – detailed, and regular. Pinkbat and Bartok (great cats both) get a section The Vanity Gallery. Some brilliant photos of her as well, plus good writing. She has a view, she has something to give, which is what separates this from the majority. (See: Night Of Black Glass later in this section.)

ABSOLUTION 2000
www.geocities.com/absolutionfairy
Art, writing, pics.

ABYSINTHE AND THE DEMON DREAMER
www.geocities.com/SunsetStrip/Cabaret/6305/main.html
Homepage from Hawaii with fetishy stuff too.

ACERBITY
www.acerbity.org

ACHIEVE THE WARHOL LOOK
www.acidkiss.org/~tragic
Makes you smile initially, but disappointing overall. Journal shows character.

ACONITE
www.darkwave.org.uk/~aconite/index.html
Looks lovely, but beyond some excellent portraits, there isn't really anything here. It's a site promo for her modelling work.

ACTIUS LUNA AND THE SILENCE OF GLACIERS
www.cirratus.org
Beautiful site. Slightly mystical.

ADAMNATION
www.geocities.com/adamnation
Big design portfolio section, short stories, reviews, heroes etc.

ADDICTIVE
www.angelfire.com/goth/tkrazie6969

MARTIN ADIL-SMITH
www.madilsmith.fsnet.co.uk

ADOR CHARMING
www.bandchannel.com/ador
Personal, from Bozo Porno Circus man. Galleries amid dementia.

ADRENACHROME 9'S NIGHTMARE
http://msnhomepages.talkcity.com/AquariusAve/adrenachrome9/Adrenas-Lair.html
Big bio, pics (wonderful, but too big to load quickly), history of Goth, Billy Idol and Joan Of Arc.

ADVANCED META-MORPHOR OF A PAGAN
http://geneofcube.net/advancedmeta-metaphorofapagan
Well, it's very dark and arty with more links than you can handle easily. Interest-ing but without much of a personal touch.

ADVENTURES IN AVERYLAND
http://members.aol.com/_ht_a/feything/AdventuresInAveryland.html

Avery Louis – writer, model, keyboardist and a sort of Warhol throwback.

ADVENTURES IN STACYLAND
www.angelfire.com/fl/raineyslair
You have to admire this. She has denounced Goth, and gives her reasons, but she still does Goth stuff. (It never stops, unless you're a weirdo, because it *can't*.) Really nice photos, and *frosty* opinions, rants and memories all tied into one uncompromising bundle – so she makes it interesting.

AE
www.tgyouth.org.uk/~aoife

AESTHETIC DEVIATION
http://deviblue.tripod.com/
Very cute, with lots on crossdressing, transvestism, transgenderism and transexualism.

AGOGO138'S HORROR BUSINESS
www.geocities.com/agogovampira/main.html
A strange girl, with okay pics... but the art – check that out! She makes gravedigger dioramas in her room, out of papier mache!!! I approve, don't you?

AGONY A HO-HO
www.manifest-angel.com/medusa

THE AGONY & THE ECSTASY
http://elisabat.netgod.net
Very interesting, although enjoyable may not be the word. Nice pics with great captions – 'me staring at my food in New Orleans 1997' – and frightening article about Congenital Multiple Osteochondromatosis which she suffers from, ending with, 'Now that I'm no longer on welfare, I no longer receive free medical care, so I won't really be able to follow up on my tumours anymore. A retail job doesn't pay for multiple x-rays and surgeries. I also suffer from Chronic Fatigue Syndrome and Clinical Depression. Isn't life grand?' You want to get a job in England, we have a thing called the National Health Service, which you might be able to avail yourself of. (Just forget to mention any health problems when applying or arriving, and then profess blind ignorance as you visit a hospital, saying how you felt it had all gone away.) Great cat pics, with the especially roguish Jynx, a few Goth links, plus Sekhmet.

THE AGONYZER
www.chaoticgenesis.com/agonyzer
Logan L Masterson is his name, 'poet, artist and storyteller'. It's a cool site.

AH, SO YOU FOUND YOUR WAY
www.velvet.net/~daednu/Index2.html
This is a really sweet, old site. Goth wedding, plus Vow renewal ceremony two years later, a brief Goth Shopping trip. A few cute pics, and the Temple Of The Hat section, which appears to be the biggest, is charming.

AHH, THE FIRES OF HELL
www.angelfire.com/nm/gothina/index.html
Fairly bland musical tastes but she's certainly wittering on about stuff gamely. Loads of photos, usually playfully slutty. (Nice smoking pics!) Probably models a lot, but says she's working on screenplays.

AKILLIANNA'S DARK LAIR
www.geocities.com/akillianna1
Well-intentioned dramatic layout, of the old-fashioned variety, which is old hat now. Some lovely photos, plenty of links, chat, oddities, and writing/poetry.

ALAYNE'S PAGE
http://hometown.aol.com/mariadimension
Goth Lite, from a woman with wide-ranging musical tastes, and... wrestling. Has her launch.com station, journal and cam, which is worth avoiding, as it shut me down!

ALEUSHA
www.aleusha.com

ADRIAN ALEXIS
www.icehouse.net/alexis
Interesting and strange personal site. Wild photos.

ALISSA THE POET
www.geocities.com/alissathepoet/home.html

ALL BAD CHILDREN ARE DENIED HEAVEN
www.angelfire.com/ny3/deniedheaven
Reverend Charles goes on a bit but that's okay because he does it with kitsch style (he plays in three bands, Molly Ringworm, the Lice Girls and the more serious Dark Eden). Nice photos of him and his mates.

ALL YOUR BASE ARE UNBEKNOWNST TO US
www.unbeknownst.org
Elysibeth does a good gallery, her journal is rubbish and doesn't work anyway. Her auctions are okay which makes for a reasonable mixture.

ALLEINGELASSEN
www.alleingelassen.de

ALSION OAKLEY (NEE GARDNER)
www.custodian.com/alison
Nice and basic, but with lovely photos.

ALTHEA'S PAGE
www.geocities.com/-althea-
Looks old, but it's just basic, with details of her gig and club activities, and some *fabulous* photos in her galleries.

ALYYSS IN WONDERLAND
www.alyyss.com
Okay, the photos are strange, don't care what anyone says. (I refer to the blonde sixties Star Trek hair and wings! The others are cute.) There's a journal but I don't see why anyone expects anyone to read them really. Friends might find them useful, but enemies find them even more useful. Unless somebody is a particularly good writer there is no point even looking at them. It's usually misery and regret.

AMAZON BITCH'S SEX CAULDRON
www.amazonbitch.org
A semi-fetish, proto-music woman with strong attitudes and a nicely agitated style. The journal may not be regular but it's spirited.

AMBIENT NEUROSIS
www.dork.com/raavyn
Good looking site, with a few too many listy bits, but nice journal, sweet pics.

AMELIA G'S LAND OF TEXT
www.blueblood.net/amelia
Old but interesting, involving more than Blue Blood. Pics, fiction, details.

AMERICAN GOTHFATHER'S DEN OF INIQUITY
www.geocities.com/americangothfather/home.html
This is clever, with its front page, and falls away slightly because it's obviously old, but any Goth site which includes Willow pics gets my vote.

AMERICAN GOTHIC

www.angelfire.com/wi/Soultear/index.html
Site apparently dealing with supernatural
things people fear, plus the weather.
Nicely shambolic pics of Meg and
friends, and some strange topics –
Black Plague, Satanism, Apocalypse.
Journal has nice touches.

AMIDST THE THROES OF PERLEXITY

http://www.fadedmoo.com/spellbound/
Creatures/Siouxsie fans will like this,
so will Faery folk or Louise Brooks fans.
(If you don't know he she is, you ought
to find out.) Looks brilliant and
disguises well the fact there should be
a lot more content.

AMNIISIA..NIINA

www.amniisia.com/niina/index.php
Interesting thoughts and cool pics.

AMPHETAMINE LOGIK

www.livejournal.com/users/logik
If you want another cool view of the
Canadian scene you won't do much bet
then this DJ, who points out some of
the faults of those in the scene, and
what is involved in the work he does.
Nice writing style, informative but
relaxed, and often *wildly* amusing.

ANASTASIA'S LAIR

www.anastasiaslair.com

ANATHEMA INFINITUM

http://netjunk.com/users/ashen_alar
Er, a well meaning girl, with a short bio,
pics and poetry bit, some links to
explanatory Goth pages and a flyer done
to help reverse negative images and
ideas about Goth. Nice idea but I can't
imagine many people reading it and
going, 'Oh no, I have been such a fool!'
Perhaps her Meaning Of Life section is
more important, along with Theological
Discontent.

AND SHE WILL SHIMMER LIKE STARS

www.velvet.net/~darkjuli

AND SOMETIMES SILVER (DOWN?)

www.envy.nu/nakiakasu
Sole member it seems of the Goth
Grannies webring. 'My name is
Nakiakasu. It means "weeping into the
night".' Erratic random thoughts
journal, some lovely drawings worth
seeing. Regina Mewlancholia

splashpage, and Little Miss Scaredy Cat.
Also an online Cat's cemetery/shrine.

ANDREW

http://209.35.175.209/andrew/zbegin.htm

ANDY & CAT

http://cybergotho.tripod.com
Not much to see here, except for an
entertaining essay on Goth used as part
of an MA, plus a few pics.

ANGEL OF DEATH

www.geocities.com/gabaod
Personal section, plus Wiccan matters.

ANGE DE LA MORT PHOTORAPHY

www.dogma.org/angedelamort
Not much here yet, but some nice live
pics by Angela M Bacon, to give her
true name away, of Attrition, Autumn,
Dies Irae, Faith & The Muse, Glass, I
Parasite, The Creatures and Trance To
The Sun. Copies can be purchased.
Don't forget to see the page about her
because there are four lovely portraits
there.

ANGELIC DESTINY

www.angelicdestiny.com
Apart from the bit where she offers to
give pointers on websites it's the usual
ego thing, although the journal is fairly
lively. Six webcam variations? Six???!!!

ANGELTHING

www.angelthing.com
Portfolio of twelve beautiful photos.

ANGELUS ERRARE

www.angelus-errare.com

ANKAVANKA

www.ankavanka.com
This is sweet, which doesn't mean it's
anything unusual, but because she has
translated from Swedish into English it
has that lopsided charm.

ANONYMOUS IMPULSES

http://nightsvision.net/nighty
Oblique bio, the journal is good, and
this has a nice honest feel to the
emotional side plus... diabetes. (Did
you know that elderly diabetics are
forbidden to cut their own toenails?)
Great face, eyes, glasses. Web cam
shots are *ace*. Photos, Art and cheeky
Gifts.

ANOTHER WASTE OF SPACE

www.darkmaru.com
Really lovely pics, and the diary was
okay, then stopped because she'd been
slagged off by idiots over her pics,
presumably because she isn't some
egotistical waif with a cam obsession.
Luckily there are normal people who visit
her guestbook, and I hope it will all be
back up now.

APOCALYPSE

http://welcome.to/the_apocalypse
Little music section, as well as fonts and
WWF!

THE ARCANE HARVEST

www.arcaneharvest.com

ARE WE NAUGHTY?

www.impure.org/naughty
No, merely misguided. Supposed to be
alluring and maybe sophisticated, but
people like Pandora and Shae look
either gormless, droopy, or both,
because of poor angles and *atrocious*
picture quality. Weird!

ARE YOU SAD YET? NO?
THEN COME ON IN

http://ennui.20m.com/
Ennui also does Evil Furby Inc. This
site is sparse, and bleak.

ARIA'S WEB

www.geocities.com/aria_black/Aria_Web.html
Weird links, nice pics.

ARLEODS CASTLE

www.dol-amroth.de
Gothic roleplay! I'm saying nothing.
Mind you, some nice pics can be
found.

THE ART & PHOTOGRAPHY
OF NATASHA EPPERSON

www.natasha-epperson.com
Amazing photographic work, and
interesting art in different styles. Even
photos of her, looking a bit mad. You
won't get bored here, that's for sure.

ART AND SUFFERING

www.angelfire.com/oh3/sharp/index.html

AS LONG AS THERE IS A PROMISE...

www.treasurehiding.com/miasma
Stunning, visually, nice photos and
cliquey links.

ASHER
http://domestic1.sjc.ox.ac.uk/~ahoskins
Cute pics.

JACKIE ASKEW
http://freespace.virgin.net/jackie.askew
Jackie, novelist and perky character, has
details on her work with extracts from
the SunDown SunRise novel, as well as
an interview, but plenty of photos of
bands – PIL galleries abound – including
some of her own (Pauline Murray, Very
Things, Purple Things, Ghost Dance,
Pete Murphy, Cave, Einsturzende,
Almond etc).

ASHLAR
www.shocking.com/~ashlar
Seems to update annually, and has
ditched all his writings. The pics are
okay but everything else is too brief.

ASHURE ONLINE
www.ne.jp/asahi/ashura/fan-club/TOP/A_01.html
Hardly Goth, until you realise how
strange it is. Another one of these
Japan-ese dancers, with her own Fan
Club, and an amazing array of 'Official'
pictures, with Josephine Baker-like
costumes. There's a prophecy/
divination section.

ASTRA0
http://astrazero.cjb.net

**AT HOME WITH THE
GOTHIC TOYBOX**
www.angelfire.com/goth/asphyxia
Check out the bit about her, the
happyskull girl from Chicago. Great

gallery. She also has a Razed In Black
page, one for James O'Barr, humour
(yeah, right!), personal lists, Endgarden
(cemetery pics), her collection of odd
toys, music bits, including photos, and
'Art?' (No.) Great fun throughout.

ATTACK!
http://antigirl.nu
Lip gloss assassin – when it hits you
feel no pain – and unnervingly bright
for 17!!! NIN and Portishead fan,
blogger finds interesting topics aplenty.
Glam babe's portal as she winds
herself around on her bed. There's an
antigirl mafia webcam portal which is
invite only.

ATOMIC CHERRY
http://atomic-cherry.net

AUTO EROTIC MANIPULATION
www.angelfire.com/or/Kristy
Vague journal, interesting art and
excellent portraits.

AVIVA'S DARQUE MINDS
www.angelfire.com/id/Dethnita/enter.html
Aviva is dead sweet, and there isn't
much here, apart from lots of midi files,
and links to her friends' sites. The bio is
tiny, but you'll like it.

**THE AWFUL EMTPYNESS
INSIDE ME**
www.angelfire.com/mb/awful

AZAZEL'S WORLD
www.geocities.com/Tokyo/Island/1737
Member of Asian Goth Clan. It's

actually rather boring, and dead, but
the webrings work in places.

AZRAEL
http://web.tiscali.it/azrael

AZUREANGEL
www.azureangel.com
Art, journal.

BABYDOLL
www.geocities.com/glitterrain138/index.html
Just a few nice pics.

BABYDOLL9MM
www.geocities.com/babydoll9mm

BAD BAT
www.badbat.net
Photographer in Switzerland. She looks
great, and funny, and has examples of
tons of great photos here.

BAJEMA'S WEB
www.bethalynne.com
(www.bajema.com should be the new
domain)
This is seriously high quality despite
soppiness and self-importance in some
of the writing. In many ways this is
actually one of the best in-vogue mini
empires you'll find out there because
there is true quality to her work, and
there is a visible thread, which makes
sense across and between the sections.
It is still annoying to see how much
lightweight froth is introduced into
people's journals, as though they think
they are conjuring up great art (it's a
journal, you're *not* a novelist!), and
there's that weepy, sub-mystical feel to
some of the journal here, as though it
was anything more than upmarket
fiction from a women's magazine for the
over-fifties. Mills & Boon for a new generation would be quite fitting on some of
these sites. Where is the granite jawed,
steely-eyed man most of these women
seem to want to find? (He's probably out
strangling children with his bare hands
even as I speak.) Anyway, there's art and
thought, and a world full of inspiration
gone into this, through its many layers.
Just take a break from the saccharine
mushy parts from time to time.

MICHAEL R BARRICK
www.mbarrick.net
This is a must-see. Not only is he

extremely amusing in both cartoons and journal, and throws in for no real measure a theory about wearing black and drinking coffee, but his photo galleries are *huge*!!!! He's also a weirdo sculptor.

BAT GLITTER
www.geocities.com/demonblossom
Bustling, smartly laid out site. Weird pic layout.

BATGRRRL
www.batgrrl.com
Michelle, who also runs the Carpe Mortem label (www.carpemortem records.com), home to Gossamer, Delien and Stare, so you know she's sharp. Beautiful photos of her and friends, utterly brilliant cat pics, long bio.

BATHORY HOUSE
www.angelfire.com/la/bathoryhouse/13.html
Bats everywhere. Vampy.

BATHORY'S ENTRY
http://bathory.batcave.net

BATHSHEBA'S MIASMA
www.geocities.com/bathsheba1.geo
Good site offering its own mini-directory to Goth clothing, corsets etc, and has some stunning examples of unusual cemetery photos. Being an odd girl she naturally links corsets and cephalopods under the same 'Constriction' section. Smartypants.

BATHTUBGIRL
www.bathtubgirl.com
Perky Kim deserves to be a star. 'At the BTG loft, we do seven shows a week (yes, out of our bathtub) with several different themes; Bedtime Stories, Weekend Outlook, Acid House Saturday night, and Church of Love. Our production team is featured in the Open Gallery. I also have my own line of bath salts and oils. Besides thoroughly relaxing you, these special oils and salts will bring out different attributes based upon the blend you select.' This is a sparkling site stuffed with verve and imagination. Weird New Age stuff, a sweet journal, cool graphics. You can sometimes watch her having a bath, there's the cam archive, lots of links to other cams, including other Goth gurlies and music promotion. Hope it's odd enough for you.

THE BATTERY
www.angelfire.com/goth/nephthys

BEAUTIFUL MADNESS
www.24.brinkster.com/madnessofone

JENNIFER K. BECHKOFF
http://members.tripod.com/~bechkova/Bechkoff.html
Weird. Poor man's comeback to a Goth gurl who dumped him for a richer guy. He puts this up to irritate her in case she was ever to search for her own name. It isn't insulting in any way, which is fine, in fact it's a doomed romantic fable.

A BED OF BLACK ROSES
www.atlantagothic.net/helen

BEEZELBUB
www.beezelbub.org

BEHOLDING EYES
http://award.mysterious-eyes.com
For men and women with 'mysterious eyes'. This cropping of the portraits avoid the usual simpering poses. It's interesting. Miss Nutter actually seems stern.

THE: BELFRY
www.thebelfry.net
Attractive site from Batty, with personal design and club details. Not much in it yet, as it seems new but very smart.

BELLE CYBERGOTHIQUE
http://hem2.passagen.se/atropab
From Sweden, in English, a divine little site, full of photos, including the story of her hair, told through pictures.

BEM'S FRAMES
www.bempire.com/main2.html
Some interesting pics of the Dutch scene in here among the huge galleries.

BETWEEN HEART AND MIND
www.geocities.com/betweenheartandmind/heartandmind.html
Frances has a beautiful site in the works, but it's only just begun.

BEWARE THE FAERIE GONE BAD
www.angelfire.com/mi3/thefaeriegonebad

BEYOND THE BLUE
www.geocities.com/SunsetStrip/Diner/7913
Poems and eclectic photo mix – from Depeche to Dark Arts festivals and Hare Krishna. And wrestling? (What *is* going on?) Lfetish – which may be the name she's chosen – looks like butter wouldn't melt, she's so charming, and she likes all things wild. You can never tell. In fact it's discoveries like this site, which keep you going as you trawl through another few hundred totally typical ones.

BIEVENUE A L'ENFER
http://decemberx.diaryland.com
I have a feeling I saw this on a site elsewhere, but this a tragic, depressing journal of a woman trapped in some hideously draining relationship. If anyone is thinking of helping to lift someone's spirits, I would say this woman needs advice and support more than others.

BIOMEKANIK
www.angelfire.com/ca6/xerephina

BITCH GODDESS OF BLOG
www.sarahsmiles.com

THE BITCH IS BACK
http://zowwie.net

THE BITCH'S PAGE
www.geocities.com/SunsetStrip/Floor/9639/geohomepage.html
Poems galore, but also nice friend gallery.

BITTER FRAME:
A LIFE IN WORDS & PICTURES
www.bitterfame.com
This is amazing. You will love it, unless you have never enjoyed reading so much as once in your life.

BLACKNIGHT
http://members.aol.com/thedarksouls

BLACK DAISIES
www.blackdaisies.com
Cute Gothlies with multi-coloured hair in strange video game-esque, nerd-friendly (nerdy in a good way) situations and presented in different galleries – Goth, Sci-fi, fantasy. The bio is 'just another girl, nothing special', although she looks cool and has mauve hair. This is the girl behind the great Gothbabies site, currently available through:
http://blackdaisies.com/gothbabies/

BLACK PAGE FOR A GOTHIC BANSHEE
www.resort.com/~banshee/Gothic/gothic.html
It may look duff when you get there but

there's nice thoughts as mini-essays, and hardly the rants he suggests. Plus... 'learn to waltz'!

BLACK LIPSTICK STAINS DOT NET
www.blacklipstickstains.net

BLACK ROSE & BLUE WITCH
http://members.tripod.de/BlackAndBlue
Two German Goth girls and their disturbed friends.

BLACK SHEEP – VEGGIE GOTH
www.geeeing.com/veggiegoth/text/frame.htm
Done by the girlbehind www.geeeing.com/mire and this is good, with advice, and info. Easy classification? 'Veggiegoth, n. a goth who doesn't eat or wear anything that once had a face.'

BLACKSILVERPURPLE
www.blacksilverpurple.net
Live Psychophile pics in Observe.

BLACK SUNSHINE
http://blksun.sinfree.net/

BLACK VLADJA
www.kiss.to/blackvladja
Art, fetish pics, digital.

BLACK WIDOW'S WEB
http://blackwidowsweb.org
Fetish model. Great photos, but I only saw the free gallery. You pay for the naughties.

BLACKENED PEARL
www.angelfire.com/tn/am/index.html
Would you call this a 'rant'?: 'I saw Depeche Mode play on Monday in Atlanta. It was so fun! It was good to see a band perform that I was into when I was a kid (and I still am into them very much so). Hopefully they'll tour again one day.' Is that it? Luckily there are a load of lovely pics of Andrea, so enjoy those instead.

BLANK INIFNITY
http://rancid.custard.org
Offers sage advice – 'Never rub another man's rhubarb.'

BLESSED SINNER
www.blessedsinner.com
Shame about the coarse persona, because the humour soon tires which takes away from the fact the journal entries can be interesting. Good pics.

BLOODLETTING
www.geocities.com/SunsetStrip/Stadium/3151
Vampy girl archive. Nice pics, regardless of quality, and lots of Bloodsucking stuff.

BLOOD ROSE'S DOMAIN
www.goth.net/~blood_rose/main.html
Very ornate, with literature as a subject, and everything is charming. Sections give a clue: Polite Society, Drawing Room, grotto, etc. It isn't even full, but there are lovely photos, and an exquisite effect. Also includes an account of her disenchantment with Gothic.net and how and why she introduced her own message board.

BLOODY LOVE
www.ninetombstones.com
Dramatic little personal site. Cam, diary ravings and reviews.

BLU
http://members.aol.com/ashton343/art.html
Artwork from Blu, which should interest anyone. Old, but interesting. She is the Editor of the excellent Starvox zine, updates the Atlanta Gothic photo galleries, helps out at the Glitterdome club and if you want some seriously brilliant cat pics try www.starvox.net/credit/blu.htm

BLUE
www.emote.org/fixate

THE BLUE CITADEL
www.velvet.net/~benton

BLUE PERIOD – BECKY
www.blue-period.fsnet.co.uk

BLUEMOONGLOW
www.geocities.com/me1178

BLUEGYRL'S PLACE
http://mypages.blackvoices.com/bluegyrl
Creator of A Darker Shade Of Pale, Allegra has some nice pics so far, but is clearly building this up.

BLUEROSE
www.geocities.com/Paris/Metro/5154
Cosmetologist with poetry and pics.

BLUTFROST (BLOODFROST)
http://members.tripod.de/BLUTFROST/flash40/final.swf

Very arty site, with photos of Gothic Women, Fantasy Art, paintings, poems.

CYNTHIA BOHRN
www.livejournal.com/users/synax

BOO
http://boo.mordea.com/

BOOM
www.narcissistic.org/pekoe
i_will_be_responsible_for_the_death_of_your_idol@hotmail.com
Pic of fluorescing cuddly toy. And a warning: y'know, they look all soft and cuddly. But one false move and they'll hurt you, and everyone you care about. Then you can see some of Alice's photos which are shockingly bad. The rudimentary paintings and drawings are better but the worse scans I have ever seen. She writes, a lot, and it's brilliantly written. *Brilliantly.*

THE BORDERLAND
http://golachab.tripod.com

BORG WORLD
http://members.aol.com/borgnyc/index.html
A two girl DJ team and their site, worth visiting just to see the photo of Charlie the cat in a 'skinny' moment.

THE BOX OF DELIGHTS
www.kilireth.freeserve.co.uk
Interesting, because here's a Classic Goth taking on Cyber Goth, and while neither will ever win it's good to see the subjects tackled, whether she's ranting or not. Also stuff on comics, roleplay, Pagan matters. Links galore, often for serious subjects.

BOY GOTH
www.boygoth.com
Nola DJ with nice personal site, and great photos in his Media section, especially from the Crow bar where he works.

BRAT GLAM – GOTH MODEL
www.manifest-angel.com/glam/TheBratPrincess

BRATFINK
www.bratfink.net
Decent journal, nice pics. Artwork may be up now.

BREATHING UNDERWATER
www.breathingunderwater.net
Girl. Cam. Journal.

BRIAN'S EVIL EYE
www.geocities.com/brianseviteye
Busy personal site where he details gigs he's been too. Mainly Rock, but excellent little galleries from Whitby, festivals, parties, gigs and Blaises.

BRIANNA'S INFERNO
http://come.to/BriannasInferno
A magazine, of sorts, with open and dazzlingly honest personal insight and links to many True Crime type sites, which implies she has a thing about revenge and morbid curiosity generally. Successful campaign to get paedophile out of her neighbourhood will have you cheering, and there's lots of art and poetry slopping about.

THE BRIDE WEARS BLACK TONIGHT
http://nocturna.net/bride
Quite cool, with some writing that may appeal. Nice links.

POPPY Z. BRITE
www.poppyzbrite.com
Very compact, and almost coy. Quite charming.

ISABEL BROADFIELD – CLOTHES DESIGN PORTFOLIO
www.geocities.com/pinktetsuo

BECKY BROCK
www.manifest-angel.com/dizzy

BROCKENHEXE – WITCHY
www.brockenhexe.de.vu

BROKEN-WINGZ
http://broken-wingz.net

BULLETS
http://bullets2.tripod.com
Some pics, including Sneaky Bat Machine.

STEVE BURNETT'S SITE
www.webslingerz.com/sburnett
Top marks for the lemur pic, and Rasputin confession.

THE BURNING TIMES
www.bway.net/~eliane
Great old pics.

BUT YOU LIED
http://spiderbyte.org

CAFFEINE PTERODACTYL
www.envy.nu/angelface69

CALEEPSO'S HAUNT
www.geocities.com/FashionAvenue/Salon/2619

CAPTAIN STERNN'S DIGITAL DIARY
www.darkangels.net/sternn/index1.asp
It's certainly very dramatic to get in. He runs Dark Angels.net and he gives good quotes: 'I drink beer and play video games. Like God intended for engineers to do.' Fun gallery – all the stars with the DJ – and he can certainly rant.

CAPTURED
www.devlbunny.com/captured

CARADOC
www.cynage.com/raphael

CARMILLA'S ROOM – SPANISH
www.geocities.com/deadcarmilla

CAROLIINAN MUAILMA
www.goth.net/~caroliina

CARPE AETERNUM
www.carpeaeternum.com

CASEY J'S PAGE
http://members.tripod.com/~cacey_j/index.html
It was meant to be a doll's page, of the rag variety, but it's old, and some links no longer apply. However, good writing remains here, and cute photos.

CAT BLACK
www.din.or.jp/~catblack
Japanese site. There's some music by Takeshi Kobayashi and hints that fashion lurks here, but I never found it.

THE CAT'S MEOW
www.kittikity.com

CATACUMBA DEL MONJE
www.geocities.com/CollegePark/Classroom/6575
Mexican matters, from a man despairing of Goth's evolution. Good local info.

CATERPILLAR GIRL
http://hometown.aol.com/caterpillargirlx/caterpillargirlx.html
Basic site at present, with details of her and her Jasper.

CECILFRAU'S HOMEPAGE
www.geocities.com/Area51/Labyrinth/8512

Nice site doing the old 'House' thing with sections as rooms.

CELESTIAL OVERLOAD
www.psychokitty.net/jolie

CENOTAPHE'S MAISON DU GOTHIQUE
www.geocities.com/cenotaphe
It's old, it's sweet and there's some cheery photos.

CESADA
www.cesada.de
Top quality photos of people, places and bands, plus German poetry.

CHAOS
www.geocities.com/Athens/Atrium/9688/index.html

CHEZ BRAT
www.bratling.org

CHINESE GOTH
http://osagecon.missouri.org/~dauphine/chinese_goth.html
Don't get too excited, because this is a bit weird. Surreal might be the better term. 'I use the term "Chinese Goth" since my tastes are oriental and I hope to relate some Chinese customs and myths that roughly parallel those in the western "Gothic" world.' You tell 'em mate! Discover tarot with Chinese characteristics, link till you puke, ask Scott about the Chinese navy, read Chinese Gothy Stories (very odd), and wonder what the hell is going on?

CHOOSE YOUR PATH
www.davidbowie.com/users/sarahmonster
Strange site, without real clarity but the writing is certainly enjoyable and imaginative.

CHRISTIAN GRIGIS
http://depwho2.mw.mediaone.net/cgrigis
Nothing actually here except for a nice mixture of live photos on the following: Apoptygma Berzerk , Black Tape For A Blue Girl, Brendan Perry, The Change-lings, The Cruxshadows, Das Ich, Dead Voices On Air, Die Krupps, Faith & The Muse, Gravedance, I Will I, Judith, Legendary Pink Dots, Mors Syphilitica, ohGr, Siddal, Sunshine Blind, Switch-blade Symphony, Tapping The Vein, This Ascension, Underflowers, Unto Ashes, Vendemmian and Voltaire.

CHROME ZONE IN POWDER PARK
www.io.com/~batty
Batty comes up with more cool stuff on her site. Okay so the Dullasschick Network ad pops up, but you can ignore that. Her journal is spirited, the bio is cool, the photos are really sweet, like some weird *Revenge of Gone With The Wind* fashion. The usual Fan Club nonsense crops up. (Why is this happening? What kind of saddoes fall for this stuff?) I mean she, like Josie N, is very distinctive, so you can see girls being inspired to be like her... but some of these sites behave like the protagonist feels they're a filmstar. Except there is no filmcrew. At least Batty's is tongue-in-cheek and an extension of what normally occurs on the site, which is plenty, although it would be nice to see her writing about more subjects, because she handles it well and has things to say. If nothing else you'll love this site for the photos. Few people look cooler.

CHURCH COTTAGE WHITBY WEB SITE
www.ppot.fsnet.co.uk
There are loads of great Whitby pics here, but Simon also has the Devonshire and Leipzig. Excellent quality throughout.

CHURCH NOT MADE WITH HANDS
www.kittenlady.com/goffhockey
Nice personal site with writing and weeping, all ordered into relevant sections, but no actual hockey, which was pity, as that could have been surreal.

CHURCH OF FRITZ
http://homepages.paradise.net.nz/church_o
Lewd site with cutely depraved photos, including great portraits. A mad mission, with a nice sense of humour. Examine 'The Other Stuff' at your peril.

RENE CIGLER
www.renecigler.com
Serious site for artist/sculptor/designer.

CINFUL AND SELFISH
http://liquid2k.com/cinner

CINNER
www.cinner.net

THE CIRCUS TEST
www.geocities.com/star_god
Zizza's site has a painfully honest

journal. Extraordinary stuff. Also try the Asian Pride Brigade link on her front-page and you'll end up travelling through some strange sites.

CIRRATUS
www.cirratus.org

Chrome Zone in Powder Park

CJ
www.geocities.com/cj_goth

CLARAMYNE THE GOTHIC BUTTERFLY
www.geocities.com/SoHo/Lofts/8264

CLAUSTROPHOBIA – UK
http://members.tripod.co.uk/Phobik/home.html
A personal site where Jaidn decides to try and keep to a habit of spending five or ten minutes a night writing 'crap' for us to enjoy. Why thank you, kind sir. The journal is actually kind of weird, and worth following, because there is a saga unfolding of will he/won't he get one of his play scripts produced, and the different types of responses he receives.

CLINT CATALYST
www.purpleglitter.com/clintcatalyst/index.shtml
This is a very enjoyable site, outlining all Clint's current writing plans, of various types, and including in-depth coverage of his work. Plenty of charming pics as well.

CLUELESS
http://neuraloverload.com/clue

COFFIN MATES
www.gothic-life.com
Classy ads! Men/women, men/men, women/women etc.

COLEFAXIA
www.geocities.com/bourbonstreet/quarter/6946

JIM COLEMAN
www.geocities.com/taoist_goth
From the Dark Trix club to Taoist teachings and his novel, you may enjoy a brisk visit here. Seemingly loses credibility points, on anyone's credometer, for photos of his old house (but check out the toilet), and photographic memories of a rugby tour (trust me – don't go there!), but makes up the ground with his car, and then goes into credit for having a cat called Basil Rathbone.

COLUMBINE'S LABORATORY
www.geocities.com/CollegePark/Classroom/6575
Was once a full and fizzy site no doubt, but now looks antique.

COME INTO THE HOUSE OF SHAME
http://hometown.aol.com/fairyflesh/FairyFlesh.html

THE COMPLEXIITY OF CLARITY
www.hell-flower.com/clarity/home.html
An intelligent, expressive young woman, Autumn has put a lot of time into this. It's a shame her 'Thoughts' sections are so brief because I believe here is someone who can write really well. (The following example, written when she is 17, and referring to something from years before – 'I was going through a few papers under my desk and scribbled on one of them was: "I am not a woman. I am the over dramatized synthetic version of a little girl"'. I think there's some meaning to that.) Pics are funny.

CONCUBINE
www.concubine.net
A pierced Ashly with a hilarious journal. Some good photos.

CONCUPISCENCE
www.jadephoenix.com/concupiscence
This is a cool little site with nice photos,

a few surprises and a very thoughtful enjoyable journal.

CONFESSIONS OF A DISCO BITCH
www.disco-bitch.net
Lovely and unusual looking site for what still has the modern-day-plague form of layout, with excellent artwork (truly), very interesting writing and yet perversely *awful* poetry! Great photos.

CONFRONTED FEARS
www.godlikeproductions.com/confrontedfears/main.htm
'The art and creativity of Madilyn Chen'.

THE CONTAGION SPREADS
www.virulent.org
Run by Siobhan of the main Canadian links resource, and this includes some personal ramblings and scary photos of friends.

CORINTHIAN (DOWN?)
www.geocities.com/WestHollywood/9762
Irritating woman! You start reading about her life since leaving Girlpool and understand immediately that here is someone who can narrate stories naturally and with a lovely, light style. Then you click on words and it's poetry!!! You can really write, what are you playing at??? Some serious Goth pics too.

CORPUS UTERI
http://members.tripod.com/~dyonisia/front.html
Subtitled 'A Woman Lost', this is a disappointingly slim site for a woman who DJs and is a swing fanatic. The lovely galleries make up for it.

CORVUS CORAX
www.zowwie.net/corvuscorax
Unusual and charming diversion.

CORY
www.geocities.com/SoHo/9094
Very serious, studious looking site, with endless tracts on religion, and a bit on science and monarchy. Like most Christian Goths, there is an awful lot on Christianity and hardly *anything* on Goth. What there is of the latter is interesting and well explained.

COWBOY'S BLOODY CORRAL
www.geocities.com/BourbonStreet/Quarter/9018/index.htm

THE CRIMSON KNIGHT
http://members.tripod.com/~thependragons/crimson.html

CRIMSON MEI
http://hometown.aol.com/morbidpic

CRIMSON SPARKLE
www.crimsonsparkle.org
www.crimsonsparkle.org/weblog

CRUX/LASHED
http://un.openvein.com
Sky and Jen's cute photos of each other, odd digital image galleries, links and a very dramatic but ultimately pointless exercise called 'stir'.

CRUXSHADOW CHIC
http://geocities.com/CruxshadowChic/CruxshadowChic.html

CRYIN4THDETHOFM-HART
www.members.tripod.com/Madori6666/madori6666.html
'Greetings to my fellow creatures of the night... As you creep through the coils of my head... keep me close at heart.' What the Hell are you on about woman? There's an evil contest, one of the candidates being Angela Lansbury. Personal details, cute pics, reviews, ideas, thought... general weirdness? Quite interesting, actually.

CYBER CENTRAL
www.suspiria.karoo.net
One South African guy's change from old Goth to Cyber, with a seriously entertaining array of galleries.

CYBERBAT
www.djcyberbat.com

CYBERCZARINA
www.retrofutura.co.uk

CYBERGEISHA
http://members.aol.com/adrianna99

CYBERTRONIC
www.cybertronic.fsnet.co.uk

CYNTHETIK
www.angelfire.com/electronic/cynthetiksex
This girl knows Shadow the cat. I'm impressed. She's very cute actually, a diminutive terror. Starr is her name, the all webamatic, all dancing girl. Find out about her and her friend Melanie and their S&M adventures. Atrocious grammar, but she has a nice gallery and good links.

DAEMON CHADEAU
www.geocities.com/dchadeau

DAGGER IN BLACK
www.geocities.com/daggerinback

DAMN DA-NESS
www.angelfire.com/my/leather
Odd little site, especially the images. No different to many others but it feels good.

Clint Catalyst

DAMNIT
www.geocities.com/glittermeow/Damnit.html
Was awesome, but now gone.
Returning soon in its Goth Bible way.

DANCEFLOOR TRAGEDY
http://members.aol.com/vonsuhl
Mathew is definitely an old school
Goth, who bemoans the state of
things, particularly his own life,
which he opens up on in a very frank
manner.

DARENZIA'S TASTY
DEATHROCK MORSELS
http://darenzia.2y.net
Darnenzia's site is one huge photo
experience, with wonderful shots of
her, but also some great pics by her, of
bands, places, people and animals –
and this really does include the best cat
selection I've seen.

THE DARKAMBER DRAGON'S DEN
http://home.no.net/damber
This is great, being a big mix of old and
new from committed Norwegian Goth.
A *lot* of personal info, poems, great pics,
and plenty of interesting Goth links,
including classic antique ones. She
obviously adds to this regularly making
it a very pleasant experience to go
through.

DARKLING'S CRIME OF FASHION
www.liquidgothic.net/darkling

DARKPOOKA
www.darkpooka.co.uk

DARK ANGEL
http://move.to/da

DARK CELL v.3
www.darkcell.com
This is a bit weird. Dark Cell calls his
partner Milady, which always makes me
heave, and then there's site religion,
some links and a journal, which is
where things pick up because his
honesty makes it *very* interesting.
There's another reason to go – for the
stunning portraits of a woman called
Charity. Don't bother with 'rooms'
photo menu, they're actually pictures
of rooms!!!

THE DARK DAHLIA'S HOMEPAGE
www.geocities.com/SunsetStrip/Exhibit/2404

DARK DAVAZ
www.geocities.com/dark_davaz
Nice pics and writing with a fetish for
dominos.

DARK DESIRES
http://rain.fanspace.com/index.html

DARK DJ-OMAC
www.mindspring.com/~rmiller1

DARK DREAMS
www.geocities.com/~evangelene
Occult, creepy, links, music, photos.

DARK ENTRIES
www.geocities.com/haloglitter/index.html
Some hot dame (Halo Glitter?) who
gives brief personal details, shows some
Cinema Strange and London After
Midnight photos she's taken, and offers
decent 'linkies'.

THE DARK NIGHT OF THE SOUL
www.thedarknightofthesoul.com

DARK PRODUCTIONS
http://dark.ecesis.org

DARK REFLECTIONS
http://falx.tripod.com
Could get interesting, but fairly chaotic
right now.

DARKROSE'S PLACE
http://communities.msn.com/DarkrosesPlace/
gate.msnw

A DARK STAR SHINES
www.shadow-within.com/darkstar

Personal, well Gothic, great pics, but
too brief.

DARK TOWER
www.geocities.com/DarkTower_us/index.html
Aynastasia and her weird art and sweet
photo galleries, containing many a
magnificent image.

DARKE DREAMS
http://users.indigo.net.au/darke

DARKEST FAERIE
www.geocities.com/darkestfaerie
Shawna here, with a nice site which
also links to the local Graveland Inc site
which promotes the Goth club she's
involved with. (Also see Annabel Evil.)
Lovely pics, a few obsessions, and
excellent journal at:
www.livejournal.com/users/annabelevil where
she pulls no punches and reveals how
small the Kansas scene can be.

DARKNESS WITHIN
www.webrox.net/tasha
Look at the shameless hussy! Nobody to
blame but herself is she catches cold.
The prime thrust of her site appears to
be the galleries, and I'm sure you will be
pleased to know that there are outdoor
shots that are, well... memorable. Then,
just to confuse further, the feminist
essays will be there to bend your brains.

DARKSIDE OF THE MOONHILLS
http://homepage.mac.com/fantasma
Another of these bizarrely moody or
capricious Japanese strippers!

THE DEAD BIRDS
http://fly.to/thedeadbirds

DEAD.FISH
www.deadfish.org.uk

DEAD FLESH
www.deadflesh.org
Cenobite, and her crazy world. Plenty of
good pics, average art and personal site
proper: http://deadflesh.org/fem revealing
her horror and Clive Barker fascination.

DEAD INSIDE
www.lytha.btinternet.co.uk

DEAD ROSES
www.angelfire.com/ca/venuslove/DeadRoses.html
'Cheeziest' wrote this off, so there has

to be something good about it, and there is: the excitement when a link to a Bauhaus archive site takes you straight to one for Britney Spears, or another for Nick Cave which turned out to be someone's fav-ourite fishing stories. People are encouraged to leave stories about relationships and all matters of the heart. There is also something odd about 'Willow Tree Chil-dren' – which I'd never heard of before.

DEAD ROTTEN
www.agitated.nu/~rotten

DEADLY CURVES – JAMI
www.deadlycurves.com
Super-cool model Goth girl with a taste for the Swing era onwards. Nice galleries, brilliant links selections, plus merchandise.

DEATH BEFORE DISCO
http://home.swipnet.se/annagrau
Beautifully artistic site from someone's personal world which hasn't even got beyond the first sentence in creative terms. One to refer to around the time you get this book, I hope. It looks very promising. Nice style.

THE DEATH OF GLITTER
http://hometown.aol.com/boredbatty/enter.html

DECHILD
http://dechild.com.ne.kr
This is a Visual Rock fansite I think, and if you click on costume play and explore you get three amazing galleries. These people are having *fun*.

DEFINITIVE GOTHIC GALLERY
www.geocities.com/definitivegothicgallery
3 bois, 24 girls. Hardly definitive, but doesn't have all the usual faces.

DELABANE
www.geocities.com/delabane

DELICATE TERROR
http://geocities.com/chinadesade
China's journal is good, but sporadic. Bio is okay, nice pics. She has plans for the site, and she's smart, so this could get good.

DELYVERENCE
www.geocities.com/delyverence

Small site, but I really like the way she gets huffy and puffed up in her rants.

A DEMENTED MIND
www.geocities.com/gothic_usagi
Old style. Bio, pics, poetry.

DEMON JESTER – PICS/POEMS
www.geocities.com/demoniqua

DES BLUTENGELS GRUFT
http://members.tripod.de/Jennie_3/index.htm
German site with a ton of Grufti material, plus writing and photos.

DESCONCIERTO
www.geocities.com/desconcierto_uk

DESESPOIR
http://members.tripod.com/%7Ebechkova/desespoir.htm
Ancient site but 'I've kept it online as a sad sort of document, like the ratty old teddy bear you can't seem to throw away, even though you know it's an embarrassment.' Since when was a childhood bear an embarrassment? (I'm still rather proud of mine.) Weird bloke! Pics are quite cute.

DESIRABLE MADNESS
www.blackglass.org/ladyd
'Hahahahaha!! I have a web cam now! You shall all tremble at my mercy.' Why would anyone tremble at someone being merciful?

DESIRE
www.impure.org/pandora
PandyDandyCandy@hotmail.com.
Big bio and then a selection of

charming but repetitive photos from webcam.

DESIRE/GLAMWHORE
http://glambitch.net/glamwhore

DESOLATE GRAY
http://halteq.com/nyx
This is different. Got nice pics, but as you wade in deeper you find Randilyn's obsession with reptiles also conjures up unusual raptor fiction. If you're into reptiles there are good links here, which will be more beneficial than aimless web searches which tend to give you shop lists.

DEVIL BUNNY
www.devlbunny.com
Jae, Pacia, Kat and Rapunzel: all have their sites through this with journals and pics. Very sweetly done, but nothing major. Jae's journal is detailed, Pacia's pics are lovely, and if you want you get 'sweetest perfection' (a Pacia Fan Club!), and Elite Gothic Angels.

DEVILISH
www.nadiasix.net

DAMIEN DEVILLE
www.damiendeville.fsnet.co.uk
He of Nosferatu, with his home page and own studio and remixing services details.

DEHD DOLLY'S HOMEPAGE
www.dehddolly.cjb.net
Just seriously weird photos.

DEX DREAMWORLD
www.angelfire.com/stars/dexhexsex

It's Swedish Paulina, with her tales of domestic bliss, tattoos, and if you see Trashcan click on it, because that's scary. A great photo, of her and her mates, and a small gallery of clothes and jewellery she's made, although there's no clue that these are available. Excellent cat photos.

DI DI'S DOMAIN
www.ranere.com/di/didi2.htm
Good photos and art.

DIGITAL DREAMS
www16.brinkster.com/digitaldreams

DINDRANES GOTHNICITY
www.geocities.com/Athens/Troy/5187/gothcity.html
'If you're Gothy and you know it, clap your hands.' Lovely site, which includes the ever popular 'Gothic Entertaining'. What spooky music to choose, decorations, food etc. If you really want to make Spider Guts Cake, or Wormy Apples, look no further. This is journey's end. You can also find Goths In History and Make Your Own Kimono. Old, but interesting.

DISFUNCTION
www.disfunction.net.tux.nu
Mansonesque 'Euronymous'. In his journal, which isn't terribly interesting, as it revolves around too few things, he has flashes of real inspiration, which is weird for someone who admires Lavey, so maybe there's hope for him. (Lavey reminds me of Crowley – a total wanker who claimed to have power, who claimed to have influence, which obviously explains how he ends up broke, a pathetic laughing stock. Lavey gave off that conman feeling. A clue: if it looks like an ugly oaf, it IS an ugly oaf.) Site is generally ambitious too, but comes off as a depressing experience.

DISHMOP
www.dishmop.net

DISSOLVED GIRL
www.dissolvedgirl.net

DITCHKITTY
www.ditchkitty.com
And just when you're despairing of finding any good writing one day this comes along with some impassioned, well argued pieces. Not many of them,

but as the photos show she could quite easily pass for one of these doe-eyed girls with no imagination despite their visual flair, but this feels good. News links! Good pics, and common sense. Fresh air.

DIVA'S DELIGHT
http://members.tripod.com/~diva2000/index.html

DIVINE CORRUPTIONS
http://exquisite21v.com/corruptions/index.htm
Jhaesayte. Personal site with bio and rants but broken frames galore. Also try Exquisite 21:
http://exquisite21v.com/me.htm.

DIVINE INADEQUACY
http://peekaboo.mordea.com

DJ ABSINTHE MINDED
www.esotericka.org
The site is actually called Esotericka but the name is a joke which had me chortling for ages. Baton Rouge news abounding, and it's a good read in places. Where else are you going to find a Virtual Maths page? The gallery is a must-see as there's lovely pics of friends.

DJ ADMORTEM
www.atlantagothic.net/rosemortem
Cute site of Atlanta DJ, with bio, and playlist/band section to show what you might be able to request, and nice photos.

DJ ANNABEL EVIL
www.angelfire.com/goth/annabelevil/main.html
Details of where she playing, great pics.

DJ BATTY
www.thebelfry.net/index2.html
Good updates and thoughts.

DJ BLACK BADTZ
http://users.telerama.com/~beep/djblackbadtz.html

DJ CARRIE MONSTER
www.geocities.com/carriemonster_99
'Oh yeah and you don't have to tell me what a bitch, dork, whore, loser, etc that I am. I am fully aware thank you!' I never said *any* such thing! Brisk site, but with details of where she's spinning (whether that involves records, drink or unnatural acts I leave to your imagination), so there'll always be up-to-date info. The galleries are *great* fun.

DJ DARKNESS – SEATTLE
www.angelfire.com/wa/AgingDarkness
Guide to various events and sites involved where he appears.

DJ EPINE
www.livejournal.com/users/dj_epine
Michelle, crazed Canadian DJ, is a constant source to me of good cheer and information. She doesn't keep this up to date constantly, and the live journal seems to be a victim of its own success lately, meaning you can't always gain access, but she does always have lively insights into the Goth and Industrial scene there, in which she is a charismatic player.

DJ ETERNAL DARKNESS
www.angelfire.com/wa/AgingDarkness

DJ FEMME FATALE
www.dogma.org/visionshift/femmefatale.htm

DJ FRIGHTNIGHT
www.djfrightnight.de

DJ HORN – GERMANY
www.djhorn.de
Check 'bilder' at bottom left.

DJ JOEY
www.djjoey.com/joeyframes.html
Nice brisk site with good galleries and 100% truthful bio.

DJ LAZARUS
www.djlazarus.com
Clubs may come and go but this bloke's site will probably always have links to new places which have visuals.

DJ MIRKO
http://djmirko.dissected.net

DJ RODENT – SYNTHBOY!
www.greg311.com/dj-rodent
Lots of pics from Californian activity.

DJ SACRIFICE
www.sunflower.com/~angenoir

JANE DOE
www.angelfire.com/ca/janedoe13
Unusual art and good pics, although the journal is *very* girly.

DOLL RIOT
www.doll-face.org/dollriot
Rocky girl, amazing pics.

DON'T PUNT THE KITTEN!
www.assimilating.net
I should think not! Cool, with brief contents done in a hi-tech way.

JUNO DORAN
www.junodoran.com
Many stunning photorealist art pieces, with classy portraits in the archive.

DR X
www.netlabs.net/hp/drx
Mad site which is a mini resource, and trumpets proudly its eighties links.

DRAMA CIRCUS
www.burningsoul.com/circus
A sweet looking girl and clearly troubled but battling back through these highly distinctive sites, but there's too much spread all over the place.

DRAVEN'S DOMAIN
www.geocities.com/draven_1980/index.html
Very cute personal site from Scott, which needs more detail.

THE DREAD REVEREND
www.geocities.com/sxoidmal
More mild-mannered than his intro suggested. Mad pics of people, fizzy writing.

THE DREAMING EYES
www.thedreamingeye.com
Seriously good paintings and photography by Alice Egoyan. Love the hippos, and don't miss Lily's Pages.

DREAMING OF FAITH
www.discarnate.com/dreaming

DREAMS OF GLASS
http://nitescence.net/dreams

DRUCIFER
www.drucifer.co.uk
Personal page included within his business site for Drucifixion at www.drucifixion.com, so yes, it's smart looking. Nothing too interesting but a pleasantly relaxed personal site.

DYONISIA
http://members.tripod.com/~dyonisia
Gothic Beauty Tips For The Health-Conscious (one so far), thoughts and a quite wonderful gallery. Also provides useful tips of places to visit in the South of America.

Ebon Bliss

DYSFUNCTIONAL BEAUTY DOORSTEP
www.geocities.com/dysfunktionalbeauty/db.html
Big old NM area site, with personal pics and ideas which presumably moved on somewhere else. Very messy, but fun to dig about in.

E-VILLE
www.geocities.com/SoHo/Village/7866

KEVIN J. EARLY
www.geocities.com/SunsetStrip/Arena/6477
Big, and excellent personal site with various Goth-related topics. Some duff frames but more than enough to keep anyone happy.

EBON BLISS
http://ebonbliss.darkgod.net
This is a highly diverting site from the cheeky strumpet Agony, although she seems to go with Joi in her singing persona. She can't be arsed with her journal, invites you to send in fetish pics and artwork she displays, and also links to her fetish site:
www.fetishbliss.com

ECHO AND DESCEND
http://mandra66.tripod.com

THE ECHO SIDE: DEATH
http://broken-wingz.net/echo

ENDE NOIR
www.endeneu.com

EIDOLON
www.eidolon.co.uk
Mainly work-related and tech, but fantastic variety of Goth photos, because James Payne has a talent for it.

ELASTIC DREAMS
http://members.aol.com/elastikxdreamz
Excellent photos of the saucy mare and hey boi, but the journal is pretty annoying – this sucks, that sucks, *everything* sucks. Zzzz.

ELECTROCHEMICAL
www.geocities.com/Paris/Bistro/6225

ELEMENTAL VIOLENCE
www.elemental-violence.co.uk

ELENA GNOME
www.angelfire.com/oh/elenagnome

ELESHA'S DIARY OF WISDOM & BOREDOM
http://leech-peach.diaryland.com

ELIXXIR
www.elixxir.net
Nicely crazed woman, with some really great pics. She also has something wild going on at:
http://pub48.ezboard.com/balexia42434

ELIZABETH'S DARK CASTLE
www.nether.to/elizabeth
Very dark Metal transgender chick with board and portal.

ELLIS IN WONDERLAND
www3.justnet.ne.jp/~elellis_fan2
'Keep watching me. I exist here on the net, with a little bird on the shoulder. In Japan we have a saying that a soul resides inside a doll. I am a doll. My existence is so free that no one knows what I am thinking. My existence is so vacant that I am able to become anything. Such a mysterious world of cyber-doll, this is Ellis in Wonderland. Peep, peep, chirp...' A Japanese site of Cosplay. Where the true masters (mistresses) of the genre ought to be. There is also a fascinating written insight given into what an 'Idol' represents in Japanese youth culture. 'Many people asked me what is the real purpose of my site. This site is not a step to be a model or an actress. I have already experienced a fashion model, but I do not continue the job. I do not want to be a professional actress, either. My present interest is to create words and poems in English. I started uploading my poems and words in my Japanese site. But I am not a native English speaker; it is a very tough job for me to write English sentences! The purpose of this site is to scatter cute-and-intelligent virus inside the human brains all over the world. I am a silent-warm-cute-kawaii-angelic-cyber-doll terrorist to destroy your brain and imagination from within, softly. I have already......started existing inside your brain and imagination. This is the real mission of a cyber-doll.' As well as her bio there is also The Life And Habits Of Budgerigars, and she likes Pizzicato Five, who some people find naff but I think are charming.

ELVIRA
www.elvira.com

ELVYRA: Mistress Of The Dark
www.penddraig.co.uk/elvyra

ELYSIAN WAVES
www.freakpride.com/ladyk
Nice personal site with excellent portraits, lots of updates (mainly about Gurly awards won), with sections on faerie, Wicca and Goth.

ELYSIUM (down?)
www.virtue.nu/elysium
Very attractive site, Pre-Raphaelite heavy, with ornate journal style, unusual fiction and a few good pics.

EMILY – Lil Punk Rock Girl 6
http://lilpunkrockgirl6.tripod.com/Emmy2.html
Cute page from young Goth with attitude. Pics and rants.

EMOTION IS DEAD
http://tbns.net/missstarbright

EMPIRE DOWN
http://empiredown.com
Certainly honest: 'As my twenty-first birthday approaches, I find myself sinking more and more into depression: mainly because I envisioned myself doing much grander things with my life than working for minimum wage at a fast-food restaurant. It seems that serendipity alone will not provide me with worthwhile employment, and thus, I feel that I am a degenerate. Also, I have an enormous and painful carbuncle upon my nose. Someone in this world must have advice to offer me.' Check in and see how he's faring. Send ointment. And then, when I double-checked, I found this: 'My girlfriend left me today, thus validating my belief that I am not a winner in the game of life. With my newly-gained privileges of age, I hurried to a bar to wallow in self-pity, drowning my loss with "White Russians." And thus my new life as an insane, filthy vagrant begins. Look for me mumbling nonsense and vomiting upon myself at a streetcorner near you.' Poor bastard.

EPHEMERAL PULP
www.geocities.com/veronicaclay
Great journal from an excellent raconteur.

EPITOME GIRL
www.epitomegirl.com
Brilliant site with ideas a-go-go, fiction, pics, food, film, music, games, all done in a stylish, provocative manner. A bona fide classic.

ERESHKIGAL'S CRYPT
www.geocities.com/Area51/Shadowlands/7175

ERICA
www.geocities.com/esoif001
Cute. Flowers, Gothic novels, gardens and pics. She could easily do the whole camgirl thing but she's a bit too smart.

ETAMNANKI
www.geocities.com/etamnanki77

ETERNAL BEAUTY – THE USUAL
www.envy.nu/etnlbeauty

ETERNAL DEATH
www.darkhosts.com/eternaldeath

ETERNITY – RPG-ISH
http://fullpsy.tripod.com

ETHERMITE
www.geoworld64.freeserve.co.uk/flash.htm
Great and unusual personal site, with plenty of personal details, but also a club, Innvervation, in Northampton (not included in clubs, as he was starting it, but returning almost immediately to live and work in Birmingham) as well as a great collection of photos.

EUDAIMONIA
http://julie.blar.org

EUPHORIKA
http://erika.cityhunter.net
I love this, as Erika makes her photo captions so funny (see both Black Halos sections), in a surreal, but delicately prim manner, and she has a mini-tribute to the disbanded Rose Chronicles.

EUROPE IS OUR PLAYGROUND
http://pretention.net/greycat
Nice way to show off her sites, plus a few pics, and a dull journal.

EVAN
http://home.att.net/~BabyHuey36

EVE
www.livejournal.com/users/angelheart

Eve's journal is pretty lively and very regular. I'm glad I don't have her life.

EVE GHOST
http://members.tripod.com/Eveghost
Lovely mad site, with its Ekklectik zine, containing nothing, some Gene Loves Jezebel links (?) and a little something on The Gemini Saints, an ambitious book/ online saga about the history of a band.

EVECHAT'S GRAPHIKARTS
www.evechat.ca
Montreal artist wild woman with a penchant for all things romantic pre-Raphaelite and gothic. The portfolio galleries are well worth your time, but you must let them fully load before exploring, and close down before re-entering each section. Journal is in French. Also Yahoo! Club – Les arts graphiques.

EVERYTHING IN ASHES
www.geocities.com/Paris/Parc/4107
Nice pix, okay fiction, one excellent piece of artwork ('Innocence Obstructed').

EVIL GRAPHICS
http://evilgraphics.com
It was free grafx to use, but it's more Caroline's site now, with only a few pics and a faltering journal, which is very odd as she looks really good and writes well. Strange how some people go all modest.

EVILYN
www.livejournal.com/users/evilyn13
Evilyn ('no Anthrax, please') writes the best live journal I have seen for the social side of things. This is no spoilt brat, just a very warm and witty woman. Her observational touches can be brilliant and the photos are always cool. This is a treat *not* to be missed.

EVISCERATE YOUR MEMORIES
http://datura.org/memory

EXOTERICA
www.velvet.net/~cheshire

EXPERIMENT WITH TEARS
www.darkside.nu/fabienne
Smart fetishy site which invites you to 'peek inside my drawers', with journal

and pics. A brilliantly quiet little site full of excellent writing. She apologises for poor English, being Swedish, and then it's *all* very well written. She hates having her picture taken and has looks most Goth girls would die for. There are nicely dour journal entries, and good ideas and thoughts interspersed. Excellent, basically. 'Goth – a misunderstood subculture. Vampires, blood, Metal, bad makeup and teen angst is not Goth. Goth is style, class and good music. It's a shame that so few people understand this.'

EYELINER JUNKIE
www.angelfire.com/goth/Storm

EYES OF A FALLEN ANGEL
www.darkflower.com

EZIL.ORG
www.ezil.org.uk

...FAERIE POISON
www.darksites.com/souls/goth/pinkfaerie
Cute site actually, considering the topic and theme, which normally leaves me slightly dumbfounded. Nice bio, and some of the pics are *fantastic*.

FAITH IN NOTHING
www.geocities.com/euthanasia8

FAKE HAIR – DOWN
www.thepanthera.de
Dramatic extensions of Panthera, shown in the gallery, who gives you a little insight into her life, in German or English.

FALLEN ANGEL
www.gefallen.net
Nice pics, including bands in Germany.

FASHIONABLE NIHILISM
http://fashionablenihilism.com/newprog.html
Melanie's site is full, with poetry, kinkiness, pics, journals and chat.

FAT
www.fatgoth.freeservers.com

FEAR IN MOTION
http://user.pa.net/~skautz/
Quite peculiar, with nice ideas and imagery.

FEED.ME.NOW
www.envy.nu/feteceria

FELIS S HUMANUS
www.geocities.com/felisshumanus
Jane and Felis share their interest in roleplay and anime, some pics.

FEMME FATALE FUJINO
www.ah.wakwak.com/~fujino
Unusual site in which a beautiful! Japanese erotic dancer has galleries galore, often semi-naked. Fantastic portraits. Check this one;
www.ah.wakwak.com/~fujino/japon/pinup/ishikawa_21.htm
There are even paintings people have done of her. I found this via a Goth site, but it *is* confusing. The 'Idiocy' section, as an example, has various stripping sequences, although the 'Dead Lock' portraits are conventional again, and she's definitely Goth ('Stand' is a fantastic pic). The 'Darkness Malia' set is equally brilliant. When you click on 'Body' you enter some sort of stripping archive, which is bizarre. Some is normal fetish type stuff but some is mind boggling, with photos you'd get from plays. In fact there are so many galleries, and 'reports', I believe she's doing these in clubs where fans take pictures and review her, which makes sense as it is done in a fetish Glam Goth spirit with a group of five girls, as though it were a gig.

FETISH KITTIES – OF THE WEEK, ETC
www.geocities.com/Paris/Louvre/2612/fetishmain.html

FIESTY
www.angelfire.com/extreme2/fiestyssoul

FIONA – DOWN
www.niceboots.org.uk/fiona
Loads of pics, and lively journal:
www.livejournal.com/users/zoo_music_girl

FIONA'S DARK CORNER
www.lacrimosa.net

FIRE IN CHAINS
http://fire_in_chains.tripod.com/welcome

FIREDRAGON
www.blar.org/firedragon
Okay, 'Penis poetry'? Old journals (quite fun) and nice photos.

FISHES AND FETISHES
www.murkworks.net/~lena
Magick Pagan, disorders, writing.

FITS OF THE ABSOLUTE
www.geocities.com/~emily777
Poetry, great pics, art. New site is
Ephemeral Pulp.

FLAWED BODY
http://blackglass.org/influx
Verse, pics, activism.

FLESH FAILURES
www.geocities.com/manufacturedtears
Vernice with tattoos and art. Nice moody
feel to it all.

FLUFFY DAVE
www.fluffydave.com
Brilliant, fun personal site with ace pics.

FLUFFY GOTH
www.geocities.com/madbobmcjim

FLUPSY666
www.geocities.com/flupsy666/home.html

THE FLY TRAP
www.geocities.com/Vienna/Choir/5654

FOLLOW ME OR GIVE ITALL AWAY
http://skinwalker666.tripod.com

BRIAN FORGE
www.drelub.8k.com
Founder of Arizona Goth club.

FOULED VISIONS
http://members.whatthefuck.com/outzider
Looks good, balancing nice pics with
dull journal.

FRAGILE MUSE
www.fragilemuse.org
Expect to see a ton of sites emulating
this look. It isn't the first, but it makes
sense.

FRAGILE SIN
www.badasschick.com/fragilesin
Good quality galleries from rude
woman! Writes well, but we don't get
enough of that as the journal is bitty.

FRANCESCA DANI
www.francescadani.com
Italian Cosplay fanatic. Cute galleries.

MAGDA FRANCOT
www.magda-francot-art.com
Oil paintings. She may not be in Anne
Sudworth's league – not even close –

but this is a cool site. She explains the
process of painting a portrait – showing
you the actual stages – and you can
even commission her to do your
portrait. Some if it reminds me of the
Victorian travelling painters, who would
paint you against a preordained stylish
backdrop regardless of your image, the
same way photographers would set you
against a background.

FREAK
www.operation-glam.com
Athena's cool domain, so explore at
your leisure.

FREAK'S CORNER – Katie
http://freakscorner.2cuk.co.uk

FROM THE SHADOWS
www.fromtheshadows.com

FROZEN ROSE
http://frozenrose.cirratus.org
Beautiful site.

FUCK GUILT
http://sia.wasteland.com
Immense journal, lovely photos.

FUH-Q
www.fuh-q.com
Bloody hell, what a life! She tells it like
it is, to show you can survive anything
and take heart. Brave of her. This is a
million miles removed from the posey
trash most cliques are peddling.

FULL OF STARS
http://fullofstars13.homestead.com/home.html
Tiny info, nice (slow) pics.

FUNERAL IN CARPATHJIA
http://au.geocities.com/crystal_jade_au
Well-done site for all you vamperoids.

FURIOUS
http://hells-fury.gothicunderworld.com
Naomi/Jez/Jezebell/Jezzy – self-
professed domain slut, so there's links
to many projects. Fairly average.

GABRIELLE
www.geocities.com/flupsy666/home.html
An enjoyable hotchpotch of a thing,
with weird September 11 experience.

THE GARDEN GATE
http://faerygarden.8m.com

Faery/Goth stuff with a tinge of
religion? All told, it's a bit odd.

A GARDEN OF NIGHTSHADE
www.butterflymessiah.com/nightshade/
garden.html
Robert from Butterfly Messiah,
'musing'.

**GASOLINE DREAMS (GLAMOUR
CHILD)**
www.grumpybat.net/danielle
Webcam, journal, Christine Danielle's
bio, projects, friends etc. Too much
spread thinly, but beautifully done.

GavYn
www.livejournal.com/users/typicaldream
NJ Goth, who styles himself as a
God-like figure. It's a chaotic affair.

GEM – GREAT GALLERIES
www.gothgems.f9.co.uk

GEMMY'S PLACE
www.gemmyc.freeservers.com
Model, with portfolio, but duff frames,
which tends to defeat the purpose.

GEMINI
www.gemini.scriptmania.com

GENERATION VEXT
www.vext.co.uk
Okay, this bloke is definitely weird, but
the Tiffany elegy is a real treat.

GENGOTH
www.gengoth.com
Intentionally for Manson Goths.
Nothing worth bothering with yet, but I
expect there are plans, because she has
dirg.net as her personal page, which lists
eight other sites. All of it would fit in
one, but that's the current trend I guess.

GEORGIA
http://members.aol.com/Circes116

GIGERVOLF
http://members.aol.com/DrewGiger/
Gigervolf.html

GIRL GONE MAD
www.girlgonemad.com
Shellee's brilliant site has expanded to
be a web-resource guide of things she
think could help people with their own
sites, plus poetry (yeeks!), and art links.

GLAMOUR
http://undenied.org/glamour
Liked it. Brief writing and cute pics.

THE GLAMOURPUSS'S CLOSET
http://glamourpuss.ihateclowns.com

GLASS FAERIE
www.glass-faerie.net

GLIMERENA STORM – FAERIES, ETC
www.geocities.com/Glimerena

GLOWINTHEDARKBAT
www.glowinthedarkbat.com
Very nice photos, strangely pointless
journal.

GODIVA'S WEBSITE
http://216.156.148.174
Live tarot cam?

GOOD GIRL'S GRAVEYARD
www.angelfire.com/me/sjgothpage/index.html
Nice site, with details of him, pics of
friends and his fiancée, plus some art.
Interesting letter from Sean Brennan in
the general area marked 'trash'.

GOTH FETISH
www.geocities.com/gothfetish
Not much here yet apart from some
lovely photos.

GOTH FRONTLINE
www.gothfrontline.de

GOTH GALLERY
www.angelfire.com/goth/gallery

GOTH INDEX – ARCHIVE
www.geocities.com/sunsetstrip/villa/3145/
gothindex.html

GOTH NUDISTS
www.egroups.com.hk/group/GothNudists
No sniggering at the back, thank you!
(That's my job.) 'Are you also a Wiccan
or Pagan who practices skyclad? You're
welcome too! Come on, creatures of the
night – *get naked in the crypt*!' Pass.

GOTH REALITY
www.envy.nu/gothreality/Main.html

GOTH STALKER HAVEN
www.dirtygoth.com
A bit strange, with poems,
weight-obsession and good photos.

GOTHBOY
www.nanospace.com/~gloss/gothboy
Weird, but funny. ('Love' is good.)

GOTH-BOY
www.goth-boy.com
Croydon's Chris, self-confessed former
trendy, has a sweet site, full of expected
things of which only Gothemian
Rhapsody is unusual. The music
elements are Cradle Of Filth and
Metallica!!!

GOTHCHIP
www.malk.demon.co.uk

GOTHFAERI'S BOUNCY KASTLE
www.geocities.com/RainForest/Vines/2010

**GOTHGIRL'S GOTHIC/INDUSTRIAL
MUSIC**
www.angelfire.com/me/GOTHGIRL
Whoa, this is a big site filled with Goth
and Ind stuff from a girl who is
obsessed with that and writes for Black
Monday and Sideline. There's features
and reviews, but she also dabbles with
Horror/Vamps etc. so there's masses to
plough through.

GOTHIKA
www.sinsoflust.com/mystery

GOTHIC BARBIE
www.geocities.com/hellgoth666

GOTHIC ELF
www.angelfire.com/ne/RapperNP/gothicelf.htm
Jamy is only 14, living in Holland.
What you lose on the poetry you gain
in the pics.

GOTHIC GIRL
www.gothicgirl.com
Gothic, Wiccan, Pagan with Magick,
text/voice chat, art galleries, etc.

GOTHIC GRAPHIX
www.gothicgraphix.net
Goth site of art and music bits from
talented artist Rolando N Matos.

GOTHIC KITSUNE'S ARTWORK
www.angelfire.com/wa2/gothickitsune
Galleries of Manga-management,
personal stuff, good art and
photography, all in a bubbly way, and
the club photos, featuring Stacy's butt
are wonderful.

GOTHIC MECCA
www.geocities.com/Elizabethia
Brilliant site with the personal material
done in an inviting manner, but music
only dotted through it. Fantastic photos,
but hardly a Gothic Mecca!

GOTHIC MODEL GRIM TRAGEDY
www.mcs.nl/photo/gt

GOTHIC PREACHER XANGA SITE
www.xanga.com/home.asp?user=GothicPreacher
Excellent journal affair (with reviews
spin-off) with seriously cool creepy
stories.

**GOTHIC ROCK STAR AARON
PROCTOR**
http://kiss.to/gothrockstar
The next degeneration.

GOTHIC SHARK
http://home.talkcity.com/SweetheartLn/
gothic-shark
'I'm a male Gothic bi-sexual vampire
that cross-dresses and likes to party.'
And in that one sentence he seems to
have involved just about everything!

GOTHIC WEDDING
www.psychocatstudios.com/wedding
This is cute, the story of Donna Clancy
and Ryan Goertz, wed in 1997. Let's
hope it didn't end in tears. They're
probably both out whoring as you read
this. One will be involved with a gun-
fight with police, the other will seduce a
politician, and that leads on to blackmail. Oh, glory be! This serves as a
reminder of more innocent times.

GOTHLAND
http://pc-62-31-185-155-wv.blueyonder.co.uk/
homepage/index.htm

GOTHSIDE
http://members.dencity.com/smclean/index.htm
Sean Mclean's site, where he shows off
mainly his fiction, his band Zaranyzerak,
with mp3 links, and covers other bands
that take his fancy. Fairly weird.

GOTTES CAM: THE COMEDY OF PAN
www.fetisha.net/gottestod
Deep but witty journal, writings and
bio. Cool pics.

GRAVE DESIRES
www.angelfire.com/goth/vammp/index.html

GRAVESIDE TERRORS
http://pages.prodigy.com/graveside
Todd's site may look rubbish, but delve deep and there's a mass of cemetery photos.

GREATER DARKNESS
http://homepages.ihug.co.nz/~malefic/greaterdarkness
Looks big, but isn't. Belonging to DJ Malific Malificent, longtime Goth supporter of NZ scene, this showcases people involved in the DJ community and the events they're involved with, and some good pics.

GREY MOMENTS
www.greymoments.com
Detail-intensive site. Plain but easy layout, brief but regular journal, stacks of bio facts and many excellent photos. Nothing out of the ordinary, which doesn't seem right, but it just hasn't any central *thrust*.

GRIMALKIN'S LAIR CROSSROADS
www.mindspring.com/~micah-ra
Old School, but just bio, a few class pics, and nice links.

GRIPPEN
http://geocities.com/grippen

GUTTER GLITTER
http://cybergeisha.org/psycotia

GWEN'S ALTAR
http://members.optushome.com.au/djgwen

GWENDOLYNN
www.gwendolynn.net
I really liked Gwendolyn's site. She has a sparky feel to the writing, and her ideas make everything work so well, meaning it actually reads as good as it looks. The journal could with much longer entries, and I don't know why but the pic of her and two friends, Jackie and Adam, where Adam looks awfully white, is one of the best I've seen on personal sites. She also has some nice gig pix but displays hardly any, the taunting swine.

SAM GYSEMAN
www.sgyseman.demon.co.uk

H-CHAN'S COSPLAY
http://cosplay.girlsofanime.com/cosplaygirl

Offical Grumble Bat

(and don't you forget it!!)

Great site from Heather, a girl in the comics world herself, so you'd expect ultra-style, and you get it. Makes Cybergoth sites look really lame. Tons of great photo as she pretends not to be some representative of Hot Bitch central.

HAIRDRESSER ON FIRE
www.angelfire.com/nm/unklenardi/index2.html

THE HALLS OF POLIDORI
http://hometown.aol.com/vamppolidori/Polidori-index.html
Includes a big set of visual Whitby memories.

DAVE HALO 1
www.halo1.freeserve.co.uk
Idiot boy gives us virtually nothing, when he writes and presents ideas very well! The tiny Meeting piece is the sort of thing that leaves you wanting more. Hopefully he will provide it.

THE HANGING GARDEN
www.thehanginggarden.net
Bryony's attractive site lacks depth, but has very good photos.

HAPPY G:oJTH
www.happy-goth.co.uk
Big pic array.

HAVEN OF LOST SOULS AND FALLEN ANGELS
http://pathway.mine.nu/Narasha/

HE MADE ME CLEAN, SQUEAKY CLEAN
www.angelfire.com/ca/reticence/index.html

HEATHERIFFIC
www.mercurous.net/heatheriffic
Smokes like Bonnie Parker!!! Cool pics, big site, mainly cam-related. Journal is lively but hardly thrilling, and oh God... why do people do this 'Dreams' thing?

HEDONISM ON THE DARK SIDE
www.dark-reign-society.de
The most bizarrely-designed personal page. Menu takes up three quarters of the page and just stays there. The Goth band/visual stuff you select opens in the very top left hand corner only, where you have to scroll around trying to find it all. The work of a madman! In German.

HEIDI
www.geocities.com/SunsetStrip/Floor/9639/geohomepage.html

HELEN-LOUISE
www.livejournal.com/~baratron

HELENA
www.targum.net

HEN WINTER KILLS
www.mindspring.com/~dethcherub

HERE COMES BRIDEZILLA!
www.cris.com/~jeniphir/wedmain.html

HEXENE – DAVE
www.dmh.org.uk

HEY! YOU WANNA SEE MY TITTY?
http://hometown.aol.com/sickout77

HI IHR SUBEN
www.beepworld.de/members6/reboc

HIGH PRIESTESS OF THE TOILET DUCK
www.sub-rosa.com/lamotte/indexold.html

HIPSTER SLUT
www.livejournal.com/users/hipsterslut

HOLLOW MEN
www.geocities.com/who_are_you_now

THE HOME OF THE PSYCHONAUT
http://psychonaut.nu
Amazing. This bloke, who seems more into Metal, but has a Nephilim fixation, travels the world, seems to be a cellist and has...wait for it...an image database, with a search facility, of 7000 images!!!! Mini-journal, all with image folders. And one section on his site, labelled Musketeer. This, it transpires, is a 'restricted area for those of you who feel like a musketeer'. Oh, one of those!

HOME SWEET HAUNT
http://users.bestweb.net/~cherylb

HOUNDSTAR
http://fragilemind.net/she

HOUSE OF GLAM
http://members.aol.com/SkyCries/hog.html

THE HOUSE OF RED COMETS
http://club.pep.ne.jp/~tsugio.m
Taizo, Japanese Goth DJ, who has here his own dance company. There are unusual photos if you look carefully.

THE HOUSE OF THE HOLY
www.angelfire.com/la/nephil

HOUSE PANTHION
http://hometown.aol.com/ldymonette/index.html
Game-playing gal with lovely, lively pics of friends.

HUMAN VOICES WAKE US AND WE DROWN
www.lhabia.com/kore
Poetic journals, taut novellas, plus quality photos.

HUMILITY WORN VANITY
www.geocities.com/erzule
This is mad, and she's certainly different. It's a mess, but a beguiling one.

I AM A ROSE
http://devlbunny.com/Jae

I AM AN EVIL PRINCESS
www.angelfire.com/ca4/jackiism
Jacklyn is going for an all-encompassing person/music/friends/topics sort of thing. There is something rather jolly about the whole process, which is nice. She lets off steam in her journal, and she has sweet pics of her friends. The only problem is that it isn't too subjective, and I quote: 'My all time favourite band now and forever is Marilyn Manson.' How do you possibly know that being impressed with shrewd genre manipulation by Manson will last *forever*?

I AM SHE... MISS HIP DEATH GODDESS
www.angelfire.com/ak/hipdeathgoddess
It's Bryna of Babylonian Tiles. Details and pics.

I AM UBER-GEEK. FEAR MY WRATH
www.armory.com/~kamio
Excellent photos buried in what must once have been a useful site.

I AM YOUR MANIC QUEEN OF DEPRESSION
http://home.talkcity.com/headbangershwy/katylina/index.html
Actually she seems really jolly and unaffected. Tons of nice photos.

ICE PRINCESS
www.sit.wisc.edu/~camott

THE ICE QUEEN COMETH
www.theicequeen.net
'I'm a geek,' admits the Fairy Godmother. 'Very cool, but a geek.' Well pardon me while *I* make an admission – which chills me to the bone – but I got through her poems without shuddering once, and I never read poetry! Good writing and all her friends seem to be blokes, which is unusual.

ICICLE – NICE PICS
www.icicle.34sp.com

ILLEGIBLE CITY
www.celiablue.com
Pics, poetry, videos.

ILLOGIC
http://illogic.net

IMAGE CIRCUS – ART/PHOTO/WRITING
http://expanse.onslow.dyndns.org/imagecircus

IMAGE IS EVERYTHING
http://come.to/Violencia

IN A CUBE 2001
www.cmrcx.nu
Excellent site with a smidgeon of art, but mainly blessed with great short stories, and a wonderfully imaginative journal.

IN A STUPID ASS WAY
www.califia.org

IN DARKNESS BRIGHTNESS FALLS
www.alexander.cx

IN GOTH WE TRUST
http://angelfire.com/tx3/Ingothwetrust/index.html

IN SANITY'S SOLITUDE
http://members.tripod.com/DedOdette/insanity.html

INADEQUATE
www.nocturna.net

INDEX OF MIRANDA
http://digilander.iol.it/davidx

INGENUE
www.infragmented.net/ingenue

ANNE INNES
http://folk.uio.no/annei
She's clever, this one. I like the bio being announced as, 'The personal and egocentric part of my homepage, showing off how clever I am and how extremely interesting my life is'. She certainly writes about life, job, clothes-designing, rats and with good humour. There are weird photos of her doing historical roleplay, and Whitby.

INSIDE THE RAIN
www.angstfire.com/~deviance

INTERNECIO
http://spideypimp.tripod.com
Attractive site, with a lot of Labyrinth, RPG and Bowie going on.

INTRIGUE
www.angelfire.com/tn/seven777
Sporadic poetic journal entries and a few very nice pics.

INVALID LITTER
http://livejournal.com/users/silvermind
Journal from woman who does Violet Ray and Silver Factory Sites.

ISOBELLA
www.geocities.com/Paris/Chalet/7898
Mainly naughty poems from stunning woman who has an RPG thing going on.

JADED OLD GOTH
http://jadedgoth.homestead.com
Huge site with plenty to roll about in. The journal can be wonderful. ('Who will take my weakened carcass to a mid-priced hotel, bathe me in luke-warm water, towel me off gently and put me in a full length silk gown, afterwards tucking me in with cable running while I fitfully doze?') Best

section is Suburban Gothic (http://suburbangothic.com) which is *seriously* funny and elsewhere she obviously includes a journal. She drools about men, and other critters. She has a cam and a page about her, subtitled Pretend You're Interested. This gets ten out of ten, no problem. And then the homestead problems began, so look on: www.livejournal.com/users/suburbangothic/ for details.

JAI TRASH
www.geocities.com/jai_trash/jai.html

JANINE
www.angelfire.com/ab/polargoth/index.html

JANSIC
http://pages.eidosnet.co.uk/~jansic

JASMIN6777
www.geocities.com/jasmine6777/ankh_enter.html

JENNE'S TCHOTCHKE
www.geocities.com/goth_muse

JENNIE'S PLACE
www.triffid.demon.co.uk/jennie
Fascinating. Interesting personal details, with her writing and clothes design plans, but with problems at home everything is in the balance. She has many interests, with sections explaining them, or decent links. If nothing else initially, just read her personal history, which is a magnificent piece of work in itself.

JESSA
www.geocities.com/Paris/Maison/4786/Jessa.html
Not her site anymore, really, but this is a perfect example of how many individuals involved with the moaning side of Goth are scum. It simply doesn't matter what her site looks like, whether you like her poems or her photos. The venom that spews mindlessly from the individuals who gleefully taunt her in her message book is disgusting. Why not send those who have left their e-mail addresses some similar material. Check out how few encourage her in any way but just launch themselves into some fascistic witch hunt, based on their feelings of deluded superiority and disgraceful cowardice. Any normal human being would have avoided the 'Cheeziest' morons slating her site, read the content of her poems, seen she has self-esteem problems and left well alone. Not so the pompous cretins who scuttled over there to lash out, but... the supreme irony here? Jessa obviously stopped doing this site as result of these verminous visits, but the likes of Morticia (wow, she sounds imaginative!) haven't even got the intelligence to realise.

JOANNA
www.livejournal.com/users/joanna_theobald

JOSIE NUTTER: GOTHIC ANIME GIRL
www.josienutter.com
Fantastic site, with odd bits like her RPG section, local Seagoth stuff, sewing, superb gallery and an excellent bio. Live journal is fairly poor, which is a surprise because she writes with verve, but there's precious little detail. Goth section is Seattle, Convergence memorial and Clothes. Also expect her drooling over hubby, and annoying Sadass Chick popups.

JOSH AND KATE'S WEDDING PAGE
http://members.tripod.com/~kate_and_josh/main.html

JYNXX – HERE THERE BE GOTHS
http://users.aol.com/jagority/jynxx333.html

K LUC
www.longhaireddude.com/longhairvegan
Long-haired Japanese surfboy in make-up or something. Well Gothic, and with a sleek and stylish site. Quite a dramatic little journal going.

KALIYUGA
www.geocities.com/Athens/Oracle/6315

JEROEN KANTERS
www.angelfire.com/goth/reptile

KAT TRAP
www.jynxkat.org.uk

KATE – CINCINNATI
http://members.aol.com/fishie1416
Basic personal site, vaguely updated with lots of fish content.

MICHAEL J KEATING
www.celticdreamscapes.com
Designer of Celtic imagery.

KEIRAN
www.twisted.org.uk/cgi-bin/twistblog.cgi?action=none

KELL
http://geocities.com/kell1744/darkside.html
Poetry and fiction from dark character.

KELLY
www.boreworms.com/kelly
Mainly mini-journal site for Kelly, from The Way Of All Flesh.

THE KETTA'S LAIR
www.angelfire.com/in2/thekettaslair/index.html
Nice personal site, worth it just for the pics because Lauren and her mates look so cool, in such a casual manner. Ataraxia fan though, so she's bound to have that extra touch of class.

KEV36663
www.kev36663.digitalgothic.com
Mind you don't step in any poetry and this is interesting, because he has a cute live photo section of bands buried away, and the Interesting Stories, although

they appear to have been written too quickly, and are poorly presented, can be funny and remind you of the whole drink/travel/gigs equation very well. A site to spend time with.

KITTEN
www.bruised.net/kitten

KITTENLAND
http://communities.msn.co.uk/Kittenland

KITTY RAIN
http://psychokitty.net

KOLLIQ
www.geocities.com/kolliq

DIANA KOU
http://dianakou.tripod.com
'As one could clearly see, I have greatly based 3/4 of my pages on the Three Lights/StarLights of Bishoujo Senshi SailorMoon. My love for these genuine characters, although one in particular – Seiya Kou, has inspired me to cover all regions and aspects of the creation and background of such, seeing as how I maintained pages on the Anime and Manga versions, as well as Theatrical Musical.' It's a serious site, but you can link out to find her costumes.

KREDO
http://poligon.bptnet.pl/~kredo/construc.htm
Polish site, although the English version should be up by now. Check out the galleries, including some of the *spookiest* cemetery pics imaginable, and a huge collection of interesting, somewhat surreal art on a fantasy, Goth and occult themes. Site wasn't working second time I checked, so e-mail for details. You'll *love* the pics.

KRISTOFF
www.kristoff.com/mypage%20
The man behind PunkAssGear, obviously, and there isn't much here apart from that and links, other than a load of photos.

KROLOCK
www.geocities.com/krolock_nl
Nice site, venturing onto Gothic, Ghost, Vampire and as well as personal details. Jekyll & Hyde, Jack The Ripper, Were-wolves, Self-Injury, Depression, The Flying Dutchman, The Wandering Jew, Pirates, Highwaymen, Sherlock Holmes. Not all sections were quite finished but it's looking really good, with excellent galleries.

KYRSTEN KINSELLA
http://members.tripod.com/~modELLE
Model. One pic left.

L'EAU
www.rosegardenofwhores.com/leau
Visually stunning but ultimately dull Hellebelle site.

LA DURATA E L'ERIDITA DI
www.angelfire.com/mn2/energy2323
Poetry, writing, pics.

LADY BATHORY & CEREMONY PRESENT (DOWN?)
http://home.ici.net/~rpollock/index.html
Interesting homepage of talented writer/designer.

LADY CONSTANCE
http://members.tripod.com/lady_constance
Old school with plenty of historical research and interests. The apprentice embalmer (!) has a beautiful site, full of choice material. Manson fans can enjoy the railway shot in the galleries. This is long dead, or between-updates, but I liked it.

LADY UNICORN'S REALM OF FANTASY
www.therealm.free-online.co.uk

LADYBIRD'S PAGE OF PERGOTH*ISH*NESS
http://uk.geocities.com/ladybirdintheuk
Alice's site is fun all round but not heavy in depth.

LADYHAWKE'S NEST
http://fly.to/ladyhawkes_nest
Bio, design portfolio, a few lovely pics of bands, cemeteries, portraits and horses.

THE LAIR
www.angelfire.com/co3/thelair
Gallery, poetry and resume.

THE LAIR OF THE PAINTED ONE
www.niceboots.org.uk/lan
A great series of photos from Goth and personal events.

LAIR OF THE WHITE BOY
www.idrecords.com/aran
Personal page of a Gossamer member.

LALANDER
www.lalander.com

THE LAND OF GAJA
www.angelfire.com/me3/gaja
The Edward stories are quite nice, as are the pics.

LARA-GOTH
www.lara-goth.com

LAST KISS
www.acidkiss.org/~lkgirl
Buzzy site with good pics, including bands and a sparky journal ('I just love how some men, especially the ugly grimy looking ones, just have the balls to sit in front of you on the subway and stare at you like you're dinner. Am I suppose to find that charming?'). Good content throughout.

LAURALAND (DOWN?)
www.envy.nu/bellepain
Quietly inspired and quite daft.

LEGION
www.choronzon.com/legion

LEMONADE'S ADDICTIONS
http://members.tripod.lycos.nl/lemonade_addict/index.htm

LEMON YELLOW BLACK
www.crackho.com/~vixen

LESTAT DE LIONCOURT
http://win.cea.ru/~winter/lestat.htm
Homepage of a curious chap. Vamp content, but links are interesting.

LET IT FINISH LOADING BEFORE YOU CLICK
http://internettrash.com/users/orgyfans

LET'S GET LOST
www.synaesthetic.net/~saraicat
Normal details and nice pics but the writing has a serene observational quality you might go for. ('My Dad is singing Clash songs right now. My cat is sitting on my feet. I'd like to go back to bed.')

LETHE
http://internettrash.com/users/lethe

LIA'S PAGE
www.geocities.com/SoHo/Lofts/6490/
Fuzzy_can_spew_can_u.html
Art and photos.

LIBRARY OF RAIN
www.library-of-rain.com
Spanish site, with Goth section
and forum, plus a few lovely Whitby
pics.

LIFE WITH RATS
http://hometown.aol.co.uk/cyberratty/
myhomepage/pet.html
Dark Rose has a Goth bit too, but
mainly her favourite pets, so her live
journal is also intriguing:
www.livejournal.com/~gothrose

LIFT YOUR VOICE
http://disillude.com

LIGHT BULBY
www.angelfire.com/ut/lightbulby
Oh this is good! Funny pics, but not
many, so concentrate on good, varied
writing (I didn't go near the poetry –
doctor's orders) and some excellent art.
Don't miss it.

**LIKE A SCREAM BUT SORT
OF SILENT O**
www.sfgoth.com/~fayth

LIL TO ALICE
http://lil.to/alice

LIL TO VISUAL
http://lil.to/visual

LILIN-CHILD
http://members.home.net/wirfunkeln

LILITH MY STORY
www.geocities.com/liorahchanah/lilith

LILITH STABS
http://community-2.webtv.net/deathwish
barbie/COUNTESSLILITHSTABS
Horror actress? I've never heard of
her, but straight away in the News
section all becomes clear, 'See me in
the July issue of Prick magazine.'
I'll ask down the newsagent, but I'm
not overly optimistic. *Twenty-four*
lovely galleries!

LINDSAY CAM
http://offcentre.net/cam

LINDZE
www.lindze.com
Click on circular items if in doubt
and words appear. Be patient with
loading. The Lilith Cosplay pics are
brilliant. I don't know much about
anime, as it was only a passing interest
for me in the eighties, but that didn't
deter me. These are wonderful pics on
these sites of brilliant, imaginative
women. A hundred times more
interesting that Goth Cretin Of The
Week stuff. Sexy stuff in hentai
costumes. Lists dislike of being eaten
alive by ice weasels, and we all know
what that's like.

**THE LINE BETWEEN OBSESSIONAND
LOVE IS THIN**
www.dainty.net/serendipity

LINZI
www.gothgrrl.freeserve.co.uk
As well as her normal site there is
the side-issue of 'Campaign For
Long-haired Men'. Otherwise it's loads
of pics.

THE LION'S DEN COSPLAY GALLERY
www.sailorjamboree.com/lions_den/
lions_den.html
More odd people dressed up in
improbable costumes. Great fun.

LIQUIDDREAMGIRL (DOWN?)
www.jacksonville.net/~hdm/
Interesting, with nice cat pic, and good
photography generally.

LISTLESS
www.livejournal.com/users/sujet

A LITTLE SLICE OF LIFE
www.gothcafe.com/~kristie/index.shtml
Very cute site of Kristie and her son,
with a few sweet pics (her mum looks
cool!) and band links.

LOA'S LAIR
www.llamacom.com/~lightquencher

LOCO 4 RAYNE FOSS ROSE
http://homepages.about.com/wickedgoth/
loco4raynafossrose

LONAMID
www.lonamid.de
Brilliant outdoor photography, and
excellent Goth and Cats selection.

LOOK WHAT THE KITTY DRAGGED IN
www.angelfire.com/ca4/HereKittyKitty

LORD PLAGUE
www.lordplague.co.uk

LOTUS ROSE
www.geocities.com/SoHo/Cafe/4428/lotus.html
You think this will be ego-mania and in
fact he has Pre-Raphaelitie imagery and
empathic poems, alongside Poe, and
lots of risky photos. Also some very
original, and at times quite horrible
writing which should impress all but
the surliest.

LOVE IN VEIN
www.violeteyes.org/jessicka
Cute cam pics, but avoid the inane
journal.

LOVE.LESS
http://love.less.as
Writing, artwork and photography.

LOVER ME
www.virtue.nu/loverme

LUCIER WILD
http://members.fortunecity.com/aschkan/
Hemsida.htm

LUCRETIA – FLOCKING MIST
www.angelfire.com/on/lucrecia/front.html

LUCY – CUTE PICS
www.cradle13.fsnet.co.uk/index2.html

LUCYLLE'S LAIR
www.geocities.com/SunsetStrip/Palladium/2381
Nice roomy site of art and music.

LUSIVE
www.darkhosts.com/lusive

LYLLITHS LABYRYNTH
www.geocities.com/sunsetstrip/palladium/2381/
main.html
Included as a tedious period-piece
where you can't get anything quickly, as
you 'move' through the house. Site has
content of worth but it's the route.
Zzzzz.

ELAINE LYON
www.uboot.com/u/ElaineLyon

LYTHA
www.lytha.btinternet.co.uk

LYTHIUM'S BOOK OF SINS

http://devoted.to/lythium

Nice attempt at fiction here, although some aren't finished, cool gallery and a journal which doesn't help her relationships, I wouldn't have thought. If people know you have a site they know you have a journal – or someone who knows both of you may tell the other. (Just a tip there.)

M.A.I.N.F.R.A.M.E.

www.gothic.net/~elexa

M.Y.D.O.W.N.W.A.R.D.D.E.S.C.E.N.T.

www.geocities.com/SunsetStrip/Vine/1106/index.html

MACBETH'S MEMORIES

www.angelfire.com/ak/Ladymorg

MACKIE

http://mackieweb.cjb.net

Nice pics, and the poor bugger lives in Ashford. As a Stanwell boy I pity him.

MADAME ARCHEL

http://4z4thoth.k4d4th.org/~rachel

Great looking woman does nice site with masses of photos. Good bio with rantings and excellent photos, with good cats and even the UK! 'New!' she announces, 'I am the author of a bi-weekly column hosted by Coffin Mates. www.gothic-life.com/aesthetic/aesthetic.html – check out my articles on various aesthetics issues, including makeup artistry, cruelty-free beauty finds, and cost-cutting tips for all people... not just Gothy types. New music project! I have started a cross-country collaboration with Barry, formerly of Mephisto Walz, on his solo project, Bari-Bari.'

MADELINES ATTIC

www.gothicsociety.net/Madeleines_Attic/index.htm

Warning: contains artistic nudity. (That should keep people out!) Pink-haired forensic scientist with vibrant pics for you to see. And that's all, not that I expect she gets many complaints.

MADEMOISELLE POXY

www.breatheme.com

Includes Soapboxx, the all-women art collective, run by demure DJ Aileen.

MAEVE

www.gothic.net/~maeve

MAGPIE'S AERIE

www.otherwonders.com/magpie

Good pics and writing.

MAKE ROOM FOR SARAH

http://vassun.vassar.edu/~sachen

MAJOR STRANGENESS AHEAD...

www.angelfire.com/nb/nanofaerie

... pass at your own peril, says Nanofaerie, but it's just the usual, which is odd, as the biog is good, and should just be the start, but it peters out thereafter.

MAMABAT'S REALM

http://home.earthlink.net/~mamabat

Great pics.

MARALILY'S HOME ON THE WORLD WIDE WEIRD

www.thevision.ws/maralily

Photos and writing.

MARCEL DE JONG

http://marceldejong.com

Gothic artwork, and the word is *Wow!* Go drool.

MARIANNES REPUTE

www.divinedata.net/empress

Only a few pics, but nice – especially the cats.

MARIBOU QUEENSEX

www.angelfire.com/me3/DaBrat/index.html

MARIRENE

www.marirene.com

Few pics, tiny facts, mini-rants, and corsets.

MARTIN

http://home.swipnet.se/alvpojken

MASOCHIST

www.geocities.com/masochist_nz/mainpage.html

Strange NZ woman with entertaining writing, forums, cool links and pictures on girls, guitars and cemeteries.

MATRIXCRAWLER'S HOME

www.go.to/matrixcrawler

MAXMIN

http://home.earthlink.net/~mxmn/index.html

Lovely pics and serious work on the Council Of Nicea.

MONIKA MAYER-KIELMANN

www.geocities.com/BourbonStreet/2536/welcome.htm

LAURA McCUTCHAN

http://mfadt.parsons.edu/~lauram

It's the genius behind Morbid Outlook. Here you can find a visual resumé of her technical and artistic skills.

MEDUSA – A GALLERY

www.envy.nu/medusas

Bit weird. HelleBelle and Jhaesayte pics, included alongside Linda Evangelista, some other super model, Nicole Kidman and Jennifer Lopez, which all seems rather crass. A few pics of 'web divas' Aszo and Theda are included, who blow Helle and Jhae out of the water anyway, so at least it's not an ego thing, and there's some weird introductory blurb about the power and look of Medusa.

MELANCHOLIA

www.melancholia.com

Beautiful NZ Goth site, with Nekros's Goth Pages incorporated. Music, art, architecture, cemeteries.

MELANIA'S PAGE

www.rit.edu/~mlg0910/mel.html

Nice pics, clothing ideas.

MELODY'S DOMINION

www.gothic.net/~malady

Nice bio and fantastic photo section.

MELVIRA'S MUSINGS

www.angelfire.com/me/melvira

I'm sure she won't feel annoyed if I point out this is a crappy site, because it does look slack, and the photos are thin on the ground, but the writing has *serious* potential, and you'd be pretty weird if you didn't enjoyed some of it a lot. She has real talent. In many ways that's probably why the site itself doesn't look amazing, because it doesn't have to, but it's far too dark and old-fashioned.

MEOW: ENTROPIC ECCENTRICITIES

http://meesha.is.veryweird.com

This will be good when it's fuller, so keep an eye out.

MERCATUR
www.mercatur.net
Pretty dull, but with her plastic surgery coming the journal might get gruesome. Has a more meaningful hair site: http://hair.mercatur.net.

MERCUROUS: THE GHOSTS INSIDE ME
www.mercurous.net
Hideous, actually. She writes about her pet praying mantis, and describes its food thus: 'He was kind of large but just as ugly, grotesque, and vile as any other odious grasshopper.' She gets a kick out watching it eat crickets, getting off on their *fear*! Then the mantis dies because she hasn't the intelligence to feed it properly! Witless moron.

MERKAVA
www.livejournal.com/~merkava
He also has:
www.geocities.com/merkava_2501_temp

METAPHORIC
http://glitterkitty.net/shyangel

MIASMA
www.gothic.net.au/~miasma
Very cool.

MICHELLE'S WEB EXISTENCE
www.michelle-maulsby.com
If she looks like a nutter she probably is. Nice site, *very* good galleries, and as she likes Big Black and Twin Peaks that's really no surprise.

MICHELLE
www.rosegardenofwhores.com/main.html

MICHELLE
www.geocities.com/Athens/Forum/1059/mich.html
Genuinely weird tribute site!

MIDNIGHT
www.geocities.com/gothic_bi_girl/Midnight.html
Determinedly minxy, with art, writing, pics galore and cats.

MIDNIGHT CONFESSIONS
www.geocities.com/midnightconfessions1
Marisa's bio, cute pics and art.

MIDNIGHT DREAMER'S REALM
www.geocities.com/SunsetStrip/Limo/6150
Very detailed personal site.

THE MIDNIGHT GARDEN
http://members.tripod.com/~raaberao

MIDNYTE
www.midnyte.net
Photos (lovely black and white statuary) or LifeSexDeath (personal pics, including club shots).

MIND OF A CHILD
www.geocities.com/Area51/Hollow/3899/index.html

MINIGOTH
www.darkwave.org.uk/~minigoth
Great photos.

MINTCURE'S DESCENT INTO MADNESS
www.geocities.com/SunsetStrip/Palms/1552
Bio, fonts, themes and Cure pics.

MIRAGE
http://illusion.ubiquitous.nu

MIRAN KIM
www.geocities.com/SoHo/Gallery/1586/darkart.html
Comic art of the dark variety, on a dead site.

MIRANDA'S PLAY YARD
http://miranda.darkmotive.com
Lovely pics.

MISERATI
www.geocities.com/whoreofthedead

MISS BEHAVIOUR
www.missbehaviour.org.uk
Looks great, okay pics, warm and bubbly journal.

MISS BLOODY KISSES
http://hometown.aol.com/MissBloodyKisses/index.html

MISS MARDI GRAS
www.missmardigras.com/index.html
Mental as everything, with cool pics, and stories, which must be read. The cat-pill equation is so funny I was crying.

MISS PISSHEAD
www.paralytic.org.uk
Lovely site with plenty about alcohol, but it's the pics you'll enjoy best. Tons of funny shots, of Goth interest, plus

the news that will terrify the world, the formation of Gothic Handjob.

MR ED'S BANSHEE ALCOVE
www.banshee-alcove.org.uk
Bloke's a complete nutter, so as you have pick your way through the various sections expect to find a heap of pics from all over, and the music he did with Cabal and as Mr Ed.

MISTER SISTER
www.geocities.com/SunsetStrip/alley/4935

MISTRESS BATTY
http://angelfire.com/journal/mistressbatty
Brilliant photos – from a different Batty. Sadly bowed to pressure of morons and stopped her journal. This is pretty light-hearted but anyone who doesn't like it must be a stone-hearted creep.

MISTRESS KATE'S WORLD
http://kiss.to/mistressk8
Cool personal site as she isn't restricted in her tastes, rating Jill Scott alongside VAST. Busy diarist, nice pics and the site is very nicely varied about her own obsessions.

MISTRESSKITTY (KAT)
www.geocities.com/mistresskittyk
www.iblametheparents.20m.com
www.livejournal.com/~mistresskittyk
send_chocolate@hotmail.com
Club (Malediction) info, personal stuff and some nice pics.

MISTRESS RAVEN'S DUNEGON
www.angelfire.com/va/MistressRaven21

MISTRESS VON SATAN
www.geocities.com/mistress_von_satan

MIZAR
www.geocities.com/mizar_vienna/index.html

JEANNIE MIZEL
www.ceeba.co.uk
Interesting personal site, with its quest for the lost toy zebra, cool (slow) pics and a Rufus Sewell adoration page, plus design portfolio.

MNEMONYSS
www.geocities.com/Area51/Corridor/8660
Old site for some Vamp-inspired woman, hence the weird name. Nice

'Two Stiffs'. Illustration © Marcel de Jong

photos but she has the Dark Night Of The Soul site now.

MONKEY MISSING – FOUND SHAVED
www.pacificneotek.com/pd

MONOLOGUE AT 3AM
www.geocities.com/nephthys79

MOONCOW
www.ludd.luth.se/~mooncow

MORBID LUST
morbid.mordea.com

A MORBID PAGE
www.angelfire.com/me/rhi/goth.html
Also known as Rhiannon's Morbid Toilet, which is good. Brief bio, unusual pic approach, and the journal is lively at:
www.livejournal.com/users/devotchka138

MORBYD
http://morbyd.cjb.net

MORGANA'S LAIR
www.angelfire.com/ma2/ladymorgana13
Nice bio and a lot of lovely pics.

MORPHINE ANGELS' TEENAGE DREAM OF SHANGRILA
www.geocities.com/SunsetStrip/Cabaret/9163

MORPINE BABY
www.acidkiss.org/~morphinebaby
Cool, without trying, but too brief, apart from the mad writing. She looks like Buffy's sister Dawn, all grown up!

MORRIGAN NET: DANIELLE NI DHIGHE
www.morrigan.net

MORRIGAN'S TEARS
www.darksites.com/souls/goth/bantrobel
Bantrobel's site is good. Don't believe me? 'As a side note: my Mom and Step-Dad recently logged onto my site and left me an interesting message in my guestbook (now deleted) condemning this site and all sites like as "cesspits of evil".' So – must be doing something right. Interesting bio, strange photos, and a brooding Gothic soap opera.

MORTE DE ANGE
http://mortedeange.homestead.com/hell.html

A Morbid Page

MOSTLY BLACK
www.mostlyblack.co.uk
Antony Johnston's design site. Interesting comic details with dark themes.

MOTHER SUPERIOR'S HORROR PICTURE SHOW
http://members.tripod.de/MotherSuperior/Kittyline.html

MUK3
www.muk.btinternet.co.uk
Nice pics.

MY BLURRY EYES
http://members.nettrash.com/darktress/darktressopening.html
Tiny personal site about someone called The Darktress, with poetry, gallery of friends, a tiny tattoo section and some very odd Pagan links.

MY DARK STAR
http://peekaboo.mordea.com
More than just a Suede site, by the girl who did Jaquoranda fanzine which was excellent. Busy with slick post-pop kitsch, mad photos and slightly naughty. Forbade entry last time I tried! Weird.

MY HORNS KEEP UP MY HALO
www.glass-faerie.net/horns

MY TRISTESSA
www.mytristessa.net

MY WORLD – PORTLY DOG
http://paul_liverpool.tripod.com/myworld

MYKE AMEND
www.geocities.com/mykeamend

MYSKHA MALDOROVNA MYCHKINE
www.livejournal.com/users/myskha
It's her journal and she'll cry if she wants to. It's in French.

MYSTERIOUS EYES
www.mysterious-eyes.com
Daniele (Obsucria) is fascinated by eyes, which explains this site. Webcam, tiny musings and charming award winners (see also 'Beholding Eyes').

MYSTICAL VIOLET
www.mysticalviolet.net
When Erica Alayne writes, she sometimes doesn't stop, which makes the journal nice. No dribbling mush.

MYSTRESS PRYNNE
www.darkart.net/Prynne/prynne.htm
Nice bio from a woman who'll probably be grieving over the news that Sisters Of Mercy only want her for her money. Funny bio, her house (see Goth House – Sites Of Interest), and a cute section on the Costumiers Guild. What's really weird is, she looks cool, but the photos are dreadful, apart from her favourites, the saucy slut!

MYWORLD
www.geocities.com/irishtexan79/myworld.html
She has a Yahoo! Club called Bite My Butt.

NAGAL'S WEB DOMAIN
www.howie9.freeserve.co.uk

NATHALIE'S CORNER
http://nathalie.alien8.org.uk/
Awesome cat photos, and Louis Wain pic.

NATURAL GOTH OF THE MONTH
www.angelfire.com/goth/naturalgoth
As opposed to seriously disturbed Goths having sex with lay preachers in the open air, and singing lullabyes loudly to the police who are trying to separate them?

NEAL OKAMI
www.angelfire.com/pa3/LordOkami/index.html

NEBULA
www.geocities.com/area51/nebula/7007
One pic, written scraps.

NECROMANTIC
www.necromantic.net
Brilliant site. Looks murky and sensual, has sections on road trips by and for Goths ('Darkened Paths'), Lilith du Pavot's own interesting but lazily maintained journal and nice pics, plus 'The Ethereal Fjords', her dead parrot's space, which is pretty weird. Good jewelry promised, and Serpahim Productions bowling along soon.

NEF. BLUE PAGES
www.nef-blue-pages.com
She takes great live photos, from various sources, and you're bound to find something to satisfy your hunger – Xymox, Creatures, Horatii, Faith & The Muse, G-L-J, Mesh, VNV etc. The festivals section is particularly good, and 8thWGT is the place to find *amazing* Ataraxia shots. Tons of Whitby shots, and her 'Personal' section is excellent too.

NEKOI'S CABIN
www.ceres.dti.ne.jp/~nekoi
Funny little site from Japanese Goth, with profile, music, art and cinema items.

NEKRODOMOS
www.nekrodomos.clara.net
Clockwise and Cyberkitty shows personal sides. Good pic variety and personal info.

NELLIEWHERE
www.geocities.com/whatisthespowage

NEPENTHE
http://cs.smith.edu/~sdavis
Bio, brilliant pics, with breezy journal, and diverting Slut zine. Very pleasant.

NERIANA
http://members.tripod.de/Neriana
German Goth and Pagan bits.

THE NETSLUT NETWORK
www.synthetik.net/slut

NET.VIKING.23
www.kuci.org/~sdoljack
Hilarious and very sweet journey

around a town filled with mad people. It's not in English but it's so charming nothing matters. Just stroll around the weird town of fantastic creations.

NEUROSIM
http://neuroism.net
Nice gallery and big on effort generally.

NEVER NEVER LAND
www.mstinkerbell.com
Cute personal site with pics, wedding, and pictures on the Tinkerbell theme.

NEVER'S SPOOKY DREAM HOUSE
http://never.blogspot.com

NEVLA
www.geocities.com/nevla

THE NICEST PART OF HELL
http://members.aol.com/firebug053/nicehell.html

KALI NICHTA'S PAGE OF CRAP
www.sfgoth.com/~kali
Some interesting fiction here, alongside poetry and filmfan stuff.

NIGEL'S CRAP WEBSITE
www.gothic-subway.freeserve.co.uk/welcome.html
Starts with a warning dialogue box – 'This site is best viewed by turning your browser off altogether' – and it improves steadily from that point on.

NIGHT OF BLACK GLASS
www.threethirteen.net/glass
Victoria's artwork showcase. Good canvas, basic paper and clichéd digital. One interesting aspect of her, currently closed, is the webcam, where she lets you watch her working on a piece.

NIGHT SHIFT SISTER
www.geocities.com/nightshift_sister

NIGHTMARE GOTHGIRL'S LITTLE GRAVEYARD
http://hometown.aol.com/nitemaregothgirl/myhomepage/auto.html

NIGHTMARES ARE BEAUTIFUL
www.geocities.com/SoHo/9596/Ginger.html
Some very good writing and wonderful pics.

NIK
www.geocities.com/swede7304

NITESCENCE
http://nitescence.net/body.html
It's the Tristesse Blanche woman again.

NOCTURNA
www.nocturna.net

NOCTURNAL DIMENSION
http://get.to/nox

-NOIR+ANGELIQUE
www.geocities.co.jp/Milkyway-Orion/9991
There's a no-response BBS where you leave thoughts, wishes, poems. There's a dark and fantastic greeting card which I couldn't see. Visit sitemaster zAkro's residence, download some nice roses, and a whole separate cybercity complex.

MATTHEW NORTH
www.geocities.com/SunsetStrip/Underground/4968
Member of All Living Fear and Corrosion, who doesn't mind us knowing about his Dr Who fixation, a Blakes 7 technical forum, and even old televisions and video recorders! Decent pics of The Mission aren't enough to stop us shrieking 'weirdo!'

NOT A PRETTY GIRL
http://viciousangel.net/belisima

NOT HERE: v4
www.not-here.f2s.com

NOT IMPORTANT
www.flannery78.freeserve.co.uk
Very swish site for Cybergoth Kaine.

NOTHING LEFT
www.nothingleft.org

NOTHING...BUT PAIN
www.angelfire.com/wi/gothboigod
He doesn't look well, but he's got a Rozz tribute.

THE NUMBING AGENT
http://johnnypaella.tripod.com

NYX, GODDESS OF THE NIGHT
http://nyx13.tripod.com
Excellent writing, however brief.

O TEMPORA
www.carter-stephenson.freeserve.co.uk

OBLIVIAN
http://members.tripod.com/Viscera_Brood

OBLONGISM
http://theoblong.iwarp.com

OCELLUS PLUMAGE
www.geocities.com/ocellus_plumage/
index2.htm
Only some good fiction and an
avalanche of cam stills.

**ON MY WEAK BODY LAYS
HER DYING HAND**
http://emote.org/mydarksky
Self-confessed cemetery-obsessive in
the Philippines (also responsible for
Thy Kindred site), which is fine by
me. Nice journal, and fabulous
photos.

ON THE SHORES OF HELL
www.total.net/~uriel/testgold.html
Certainly artistic as hell, this is a visual
treat with cool writing and rants,
sometimes. The majority of sections
seem empty unless I'm too dim to
fathom the mystery. Are all Montreal
Goths this strange?

ONE HAIRDO AWAY FROM HELL
http://rois.org
Brilliant site from a woman with
rants and self-designed fonts to share,
links to her clothing site, poetry,
fiction, photos, her band, sewing tips,
role-playing.

OOH LA LA!
www.disgraceful.org/~x

OP HET JUISTE PAD
www.viola.nl

OPIUM
www.geocities.co.jp/HeartLand-Suzuran/8051
Yukino's (Zeus Machina) personal site.

ORIOLE
http://oriole.ubiquitous.nu
Mazy journal with links off.

OTHER VOICES
www.temoto.co.uk/hollowsound
Brilliant! I mean it. Ain't nothing here
but them journal entries, but writing of
style, with wit and grace, and not
predictable in any way. A real treasure.

PAIN AND SUFFERING
http://home.earthlink.net/~shadowcat1/
index.htm

Big, big pictures of a nice woman sitting about, and some weird 'Gothed'
ones.

PAINTED REALITY
www.angelfire.com/ne/alb7
Interesting, sensitive artwork.

PALE GOTH GODDESS
http://palegothgoddess.tripod.com/pale
gothgoddess
Funny toy section.

PALESTINE
www.envy.nu/ultraluxe

PANDORA WEST ENTRY
www.gothic.net/pandora
Dedicated to Christa Faust, Poppy Z
Brite, Caitlin R Kiernan and 'The
Furies' with pics, plus reviews and
interviews.

PANDORA'S PALACE
www.madbastard.com/pandora
Pandora's photographer goes by the
name The Bastard In Black. There are
many seriously wonderful photos here,
especially the cemetery shots. You may
also find the paintings for sale at the
very bottom of the page interesting. Her
art is the central focus of the site.

PARADOXIA
www.plasticandy.net/001

A PARALYTIC SILHOUETTE
http://verotika.org
Cradle Of Filth meets Sylvia Plath!
Spectacularly bleak poetry, art
appreciation and some *very* good
galleries.

PARASITE LOST
http://fly.to/parasitelost
Some great pics, especially the
'Rhapsody' section.

PARIS IS BURNING
http://darkling.parisisburning.com

THE PARLOR
www.sff.net/people/Daniel.Dvorkin/index.htp
Daniel's interesting site, in which he
has bits about him, his partner, and
pets, but also expounds upon his
musical tastes, and how they happened
upon him, plus there's the first signs of
his writing being something he should

develop further. Having been in the
military and experiencing a different
type of life it's a shame there isn't more
of how many other people he met in the
military also shared his interests. No
way of telling how modern it is.
Definitely worth a visit.

PATHWAY TO THE LITTER BOX
www.geocities.com/Paris/7022
Cute antiquity with nice pics

PATINKA
www.patinka-online.de

PAUL
www.rock-god.freeserve.co.uk
Paul from ALF and Corrosion, looking
rather Tim Roth in his carefully edited
front-page pic (he wishes!), but be
prepared for full and frank Star Trek
confessions.

PEACHY
http://batwinged.com/random
Lovely, *lovely* photos.

**PENANCE & LIGEIA'S GOTHIC
WEDDING**
www.penance.net/other/other.htm
Aw, bless! Fabulous pics. They even
managed to get some good cemetery
pics while on honeymoon. Now *that's*
dedication.

THE PENTAGRAM
http://w3.one.net/%7Emorlock/morlock
Man who has nude art shots of himself
for sale.

PEOPLE ARE STRANGE
www.goth.net/~stranger
Interesting standard Goth page.
Good bio, writing, endless poetry, and
rant.

PERKY GOTH PLANET
www.angelfire.com/goth/PerkyGothPlanet

PERSEPHONE
www.geocities.com/kittynscratches

PERSEVERANCE
www.angelfire.com/weird/feeling

PERSONAL EPHEMERA
www.mindspring.com/~belladonna
Nice site, if not bursting at the seams.
She's poorly right now, with depressed

status stamped all over her imaginatively written journal.

PERSONAL SPACE
www.geocities.com/SoHo/Easel/3884/profile.html
Alrey, once of the Philippines but now in Australia, is moaning that he doesn't know how to do profiles. He tells us he's in a band called Rue Morgue ('neo-medieval avant garde darkwave'), his links are mainly about Nietzsche, and there's some poems, so watch out.

PHORQUE'S PHAGE
www.schizoid.com/phorque

PHOTO JOURNAL
www.virtue.nu/yakkityyak
'My life is pointless and petty but at least I would have been able to share it.'

PHTH
www.columbia.edu/~ll216
Lisa's purely personal site is old, different and therefore interesting. Shame it isn't big.

PINK ANDOROID
www.linkclub.or.jp/~fei
Lovely site from Japanese Goth girl Fei. I don't understand it but she may be in Malleus Maleficarum, or a club DJ.

PIT OF CSE JTHE
www.goth.net/~csejthe

PIXIE GLITTER
www.virtue.nu/pixieglitter

PLANET 13 GRAPHICS
www.bleakhaus.com
This wasn't, as I expected, the band Shadow To Ashes but Brian Necro, DJ and multi-talented guy. Personal site, showing off his work and will someone please take a cricket bat to his head until he agrees never to praise Merchant Ivory films again? Thank you. Not a real cricket bat, obviously, but one you will lovingly shape out of small ferns, glued together with lark spit. I didn't see any grafx, so it isn't finished yet. There's a microscopic gallery (very sweet) and some mad astrology.

PLEASURES AND WAYWARD DISTRACTIONS
www.angelfire.com/fl2/auntiepatsy

Site brimming with happiness, having just celebrated the birth of their new child. Pics, bad poetry and a fondness for wrestling.

A POISON'S SHADOW
www.geocities.com/area51/nebula/6049/main1.html

POP TARANTULA
www.poptarantula.com
Interesting animation planned from this web-design couple, and nice photos. Their cat called Poe is worth looking out for.

ALICIA PORTER
www.gothics.org/alicia/profile.html
Friendly site – avoid the poetry, and there's hair dye advice via the gallery.

PORTRAIT OF A LIFE IN PERMANENT CRISIS
http://permacrisis.net
Brilliant photos, web design and journal.

PRETENTION
www.pretention.net

PRETTY PRINCESS POOP
www.geocities.com/prettyprincesspoop
Alice has an individual approach, but she doesn't write much. Art and good pics.

PRETTY WHEN YOU CRY
www.gurlpages.com/circatica/Prettywhenyoucry.html

PRINCE OF GOTH
http://princeofgoth.diaryland.com

AARON PROCTOR – ARCHIVE
www.op.net/~tservo

PROJECT DENNY'S
www.p7a77.net/dennys/viewer/view-id.html
In case the page ref is no longer valid, as this is a site which is compiled continually, search the A-Z for a Denny's in Coeur d'Alene, Idaho for a nice little anecdote.

PSYBERNOID
www.psybernoid.pwp.blueyonder.co.uk

PSYCHO STORM'S GRIMOIRE
www.geocities.com/psychostorms_darkblysse

PSYCHOPIXI'S HOME
http://psychopixi.com

PSYKOGRL (+ JOURNAL)
www.psykogrl.com
www.angelfire.com/in2/psykogrl/index.html

THE PUBLIC LIFE OF J
www.unm.edu/%7Ecleverly
Life in New Mexico. Old, but interesting.

PULL ME OUT FROM INSIDE
http://colourblind.ubiquitous.nu
Interesting site by a small group of people, with thoughts and pics.

THE PVPPET SHOW
www.deadflesh.org/skinnypvp

PURPLE BITCH
www.angelfire.com/ny/PurpleBitch/index.html
This is the old site, with pictures, looking like a sulky Mel from Tabatha Zu. There are earlier shots showing her singing and playing.

PURPLE GLITTER
www.purpleglitter.com
Absolutely superb. Info ('shrines') galore on Lake, Michelle Tea, Clint Catalyst, Spider Baby and Donna Tart, plus reviews of art, films, books etc. Stylish, with sufficient depth to give one the bends if leaving too quickly.

PYRA'S WORLD
www.dreamwater.org/calanthe/directory.html
Lovely personal site, with the emphasis on life, but also stories, poems and recipes. Nice pics. I liked the stories best, especially the ones of her experiences, and the Goth observations are *very* good.

PYTHONESQUE
www.pythonesque.org
Moments of depth and profundity on various topics. Looks good too. The humour doesn't work, but she's religious, and the two things don't usually sit well. Pics are interesting. Was being upgraded.

PYWACKET'S ASYLUM
www.concentric.net/~Pywacket
Pics, himself, friends, excellent cats, and immense journal archive.

PYXIE'S LAIR
http://hometown.aol.com/pyxiewytch/page6.html

QUEENIE GRAFX
www.queenie-grafx.com
Great, inspired art and advice experience, from serious Ants fan.

QUEENO'S MIDNIGHT SALOON
www.ghoultown.com/queeno/queeno.htm
It's Queeno, Goth-ish bass devilette from Ghoultown. Personal bio, news and great pics. Look, then shop.

HARLEY QUINN
www.evilgenius.net
Ron and Nancy. They're excitable.

QUINNSTER
www.quinnster.co.uk
100 C7 pics.

RADIANT SHADOWS
www.janafaerie.net/radiant_shadows/index.htm
Faery stuff with photos and unusual 'fey cards', plus personal poetry and strange artwork from Jana. Her disenchantment with certain aspects of Goth also makes for good, if depressing, reading.

RANDOM VANITY
www.geocities.com/blake34x/vanity
'I'm a 16-year-old in Kingston, Ontario, Canada; home of limestone and very little else. I am a Goth, a Pagan, and I am gay. Seemingly, I'm not someone you'd want to take home to meet your parents.' Weird bloke, what does he want to meet my parents for? Nice pics.

RANDOMLY ACCESSED MEMORIES
www.onewingedangel.com/koneko
Looks good. Anime nut with lots of comic-related bits.

RANSOM PAGE
www.angelfire.com/ar2/Ransompage

RAPUNZELS ASYLUM
www.devlbunny.com/rapunzel
Looks good, but it's tiny.

RARABOT
www.geocities.com/rarabot/index.htm
Well-written site, with nice pics, explaining his interest.

RASHELL'S DEVILLAUS
www.geocities.com/rdevillaus
Wild woman with cute journal about bring up her child.

RASPBERRYSWIRL'S HOME PAGE
www.geocities.com/Area51/Hollow/5472
Polite sections – poetry, film, Christian and... she looks brilliant but there's only four pics would you believe? Must be the Christian thing: unconscious suppression of ego.

THE RAT'S NEST
www.superstition.demon.co.uk

RAVEN ANGEL
www.angelfire.com/pe/mysight/gateway.html
Very big, nicely sprawling personal page. Plenty of writing, photos of the shameless young strumpet and her dear ones, with a *lot* to enjoy. A decent journal is promised.

RAVEN DAMASK
http://users.erols.com/egreeley

RAVEN NIGHTSHADE
www.shades-of-night.com
Big personal site, includes the Aviary. Corvids galore.

RAVEN SKYE
www.angelfire.com/sk/ravenskye
This looks crap but it is actually interesting to go through, as there is a load of content, and many weird empty bits. Perplexing more than satisfying.

RAVEN ZANANGEL
www.stormloader.com/zanangel

RAVEN'S DOMAIN
http://web.idirect.com/~ravenous

RAVENBLACK
www.ravenblack.net
Goth-like, but it's mainly the Corvids content which will interest, if you're into birds.

RAVNAS HEXENHUTTE
http://ravna.de.vu

RAZOR CANDI
www.geocities.com/razorcandi/MyPictures.html

RAZORBLADE SMILE
www.angelfire.com/goth/razorbladesmile
Friends with moody portraits and links.

REALM OF THE DARK WYCCAN
www.waningmoon.com/realm
He may be Goth but there's also a lot of useful Pagan/Wiccan stuff here because that's a personal interest. I have ignored it as a subject in the book this time,

obviously, but you can certainly check out the links section for John J Coughlin. He says: 'There are many faces to the Dark Wyccan. People tend to know me more by my projects than my name since I like to keep a low profile.

I am the creator of CorporateGoth, the Gothic Personals, Pagan Personals, and all the other sites listed on the main page of waningmoon.com. I also wrote a book that will soon be published. I have rambled enough about me on the other pages so here I'll just throw in a few more facts about me to fill in the blanks.' Shy and frequently apologetic, he is sort of a visual cross between the Joker and wotsisname in the Matrix.

THE REALM OF THE GODDESS
www.geocities.com/isisvamp

REBEKAH
www.envy.nu/whizzer

RED ANUBIS
www.red-anubis.com
Looks fine, the writing is a little self-aware, hoping to achieve style. Too many sites, really. If Dilly pulled all the elements together she'd have a stunning site.

RED LEOPARD EVENING (DOWN?)
www.dirge.net/galaxy
Web designer, so it's nice, if dark, by a cool looking woman, who does Gengoth. Her artwork is gone at the moment but her journal is:
www.dirge.net/shadows.
The links prove more interesting than the site content itself right now.

RED VELVET HEAVEN (DOWN?)
www.velvet-heaven.net
Being re-organised, but the journal looks good, and the pics are nice.

RED @ SILVER FACTORY
www.silver-factory.net/fight/blah.html

REFLECTIVE
www.reflective.nu/ie/index.html
It's Maria, from Sweden, with a very swanky little site, crisply designed. Doesn't say much, other than Cosplay, has a smart mini-gallery, links for clothes.

REFUGE FOR A VICTIMISED MEDIA WHORE
http://dark.sinister.com/~glamboy/
Looks very distinctive, and includes unusual items and wonderful photos.

RELEASE THE BATS
http://members.aol.com/dthrck
Superb gallery of photos.

THE RELIQUARY
http://mamagoth.gothling.com
Away from Gothling.com with some int-eresting photos and brief personal facts.

RELIQUE
http://relique.net
Now 'The Loathe Of My Life' has gone, stick with this. The Belle Lettres section is well worth pursing.

THE REPROBATE – 'MONGOOSE'
http://freespace.virgin.net/g.horsman

REQUIEM FOR THE MASSES
http://silentrequiem.net
You have to follow one link to various things he does such as The Forest Whispers (personal bio, photos of self and friends, digital art, drawing, writing – which isn't bad at all, even though he admits a Poppy Z Brite influence he's no blatant copy), Kells – print design, web design and photography, plus boring work resumé.

RESPONSE:DREAM:SHUTDOWN
www.elektronikproductions.com/BeataBeatrix

THE RESULTS OF MISGUIDANCE
www.geocities.com/SoHo/Den/7121
Interesting personal site with things to mumble about, and also some great gallerics of Xymox, Human Drama, Siouxsie/Creatures, Vandals, Switchblade S and Black Tape.

G W REYNOLDS III
http://jettyman.com
Home site of Gothic novelist G W Reynolds. He looks like a closet serial killer to me. Like Laura's dad before he went mad in Twin Peaks. Cute site, because all his stories take place in the real area, where he lives, so he actual gives a guide tour of specific locations which are relevant to the books, even with little maps.

DONNA RICCI – GOTHIC SUPERMODEL
http://donnaricci.tripod.com
Bio, cam, nice pics. Has own agency for new models (www.wickedtalent.net) which should be a good way to start. Very interesting character, as sampling her diary will reveal.

RIGHT IN TWO
www.linkclub.or.jp/~rightin2
Personal Japanese site by an interesting character covering literature, music and movies, and there's Goth in there too.

ROB'S AREA
www.crg.cs.nott.ac.uk/~rji
Antique, definitely, but it keeps on featuring in search results!

ROBYN GRAVES/BANKS
www.geocities.com/robynbanks_78
Titled Insanity – I'm Glad You're Here, To Wash Away The Pain – but she's quite up. Journal is lively, everything updated at reasonable intervals. Pics are *really* nice.

ROSA MVNDI
http://members.aol.com/thessalia/rose.htm
This gives you Thesswhirled (www.gothic.net/~thessaly) with books and tarot, and Angela Carter, also personal stuff at:
www.gothic.net/%7Ethessaly/rosamundi while things are being changed from the old site. The journal-ish part ('Nonsense') is definitely interesting.

ROSANA'S HAVEN
www.geocities.com/SoHo/2721

A ROSE FOR THE DEAD
http://angelfire.com/bc/deadrose/jendex.html
Busy self-promotion. Nice pics, but the journal is tedious and there's nothing else except mates and poetry.

ROSE KINGDOM
www.h3.dion.ne.jp/~worldend
Lucifer Luscious Violenoue, the vampire again.

ROSEGARDEN OF WHORES
www.rosegardenofwhores.com
Fetish, Satanism, imagery. The bio is good.

ROWAN SPYDER
www.angelfire.com/80s/rowanspyder

Weird girl with a writing style like a Manic Street Preachers song. Nice bio and general one-liners dotted about. Superb painted portraits.

ROZI'S HOME
www.cyberkitten.freeserve.co.uk
The cattiest kitten in Britain.

ROZZ – NASTY PASTY
www.livejournal.com/users/rozz
Interesting journal from this Australian DJ, when he starts discussing nightlife.

RUAN'S REALM
www.angelfire.com/in/thenight
South African Goth-Metal fan with a ton of pics.

RUPTURE
http://straykitty.com/undulate

S TYLE...S UBSTANCE
http://garnet.acns.fsu.edu/~hlo3176/
Heather from Tallygoth with mini-bio, resume, travel pics.

S:H:A:D:O:W:C:R:O:W
www.goth.net/~anders

s3kr1t b0n3 l4ngu4g3
www.gothic.net/~squee
And after endlessly checking I'd spelt the title right you find out for yourself what this site is like! (Live journal has inspired moments, so don't miss that.)

SABELLES SANCTUARY
www.blar.org/sabellessanctuary
Good writer, with a well thought out journal, and there's rudery in the 'Fables'.

SACROSANCTE
www.sacrosancte.com
Hosts Grey Desire: Kathlea's own personal space (nice photos, webcam, prose and poetry), plus Gothic Mother Of The Week and Dark Gentlemen, both of which are recommended.

SADOMASOCHRIST
http://transfer.to/sadomasochrist

SAIIRASAURUS
www.saiirasaurus.co.uk
Lovely pics but most frames duff.

SALON BATINAGE
www.geocities.com/madylyn
Dead old site? But *cute*. Jennifer lives in Cincinnati, which is apparently controversial by reputation. She does her own line here along 'Corporate Goth' clothing strategies, lists favourite stuff, covers the Cincinnati scene, brilliant photos in 'More Than A Little Goth', tales of her adventures at loads of Anne Rice fan event parties (with links in that section other Covens Past parties), details of Cinci Goths. Lots of dead links in here but the section about what to do in Cincinnati, or Cinci as I shall always think of it now, is bound to be fairly constant, except clublife. There is a recent events update section so play close attention to that. Nice pics of the Vertigo parties, and just generally brilliant.

SALVATION
www.zowwie.net/agentaeon
Pretty good all round. Nice pics, writes with control.

SAMAEL
www.geocities.com/mossrock1
Cool and interesting art, nice cat pics, and writing. Fun character.

SANCTUARY DE LEVESQUE
www.envy.nu/midnyght
Stockpile of Vamp fans.

THE SANCTUM SANCTORUM OF CHAMAELIRIUM
www.geocities.com/Area51/Shadowlands/1636
This has some spectacularly snappy stories in it. I was entertained.

SANCTUM SATURNALIUM
http://members.rogers.com/saturnglitternglam/
This is a good one from perky Saturn. The usual photo gallery, lots of precise posing. The Art part might interest many because I think this is the biggest link section for art galleries, museums, associations and artists themselves which I have seen on a Goth site. Diversions = music, clubs, sewing, Goth, oddities (very odd, so it's worth spending time going from here), corsets, 'Saturnalian salutations' etc.

SANCTUS GOTHICA
www.angelfire.com/goth/whippy

SAPPHIRE FAERIES
www.sapphire-faeries.net

SARAH'S SANCTUM
www.geocities.com/imperatrixmundi/home.html
A straightforward site but with cute pics and art, plus interesting art and literature links.

SARUMAN
www.geocities.com/damien_mocata/index.html

SATURNA
http://home.nikocity.de/saturna/start.htm
Looks part-personal, part band site. In German. Semi-saucy photos of friends, and live pics of bands, including great LAM and Lacrimosa shots.

DAVID ALLEN SAUNDERS: DEAD BUT DREAMING
www.geocities.com/seraphsblood

JENNIFER MAUREEN SAVAGE
www.wpi.edu/~savage

SAX AND VIOLINS
www.trill.net/trill

SCABBED ANGEL
www.scabbed.angel.de.vu
Nice big personal site, German only.

SCARLET SEDUSA'S OBSESSION
www.geocities.com/scarletsedusa
Nice pics, and great band pics.

SCARLETTE
www.angelfire.com/oh4/random/index.html

SCARY BEX
www.darkwave.org.uk/~bex
Blimey, she's English and does a good site, and she wants a Harrier Jet. We have a weird one! Musings on life, cool pix, artwork, including some of her grandad's stuff, which is sweet. Awesome photo selection, especially vast array of mates at four Whitby events. Yes, it's an essential.

SCATTERGIRL
www.scattergirl.com

SCORPION'S CORNER 2
www.geocities.com/scorp2cool
This site is being revamped, so just in case it comes back anodyne, which I doubt, I want to show something he

wrote before the change, because it's important, and something everyone should consider as worth acting upon. There are *serious* points being made here, from an American perspective: 'Something is starting to reek within our subculture. I am speaking of all the closed-minded elitist FUCKS who are moving onto our turf. Walk into any Goth club and you WILL notice that it's just not the same as it was, for example, two years ago. I'm not speaking in terms of particular people, I'm speaking in terms of the general mood and atmosphere. Today, it's a feeling of "hostile territory". I see guys walking around with beer muscles, looking to pick fights. I see girls turning their noses up at any guy who doesn't resemble a celebrity. I spit on them all. I have actually had instances where I would be at a Goth club and a group of so-called "friends" would call me over just to say, "Oh, look! A black Goth!" then they would all laugh. I see no humour in this. Or perhaps it's the fact that I'm African American. I'll *never* look like Trent Reznor. Sue me. I won't even try. Whatever happened to being accepted for *you*? Based on my initial exposure to the scene I have always believed that true Goth comes from within. The open-mindedness, the friendliness, the self-expression, the acceptance, the spirit, the respect for each other, and so on and so forth. For the first time in two years I was turned away by a girl because I was black. This *never* happened to me before at a Goth club! Another time I witnessed three so-called "Goths", all drunk, making fun of one poor kid and trying to start a fight with him, simply because he was dressed androgynously. Apparently being yourself isn't cool anymore. The subculture is becoming as fake as any other. I want to beat the living shit out of any 18-year-old smartass who comes up to my face and wants to mouth off. I will NOT stand idly by and let this happen to our subculture. This is my home.' He doesn't give his name, so he's a sort of Mr Angry – check his '?????' section to understand more, but his words sear the screen. (I have given you only snippets here.) You should be impressed, and you should take note. Not too much on music but great, pointed arguments. Nice links too.

SEBASTIAN
www.sebastianstudios.com
Awesome photos that you'd be mad to miss. The disappointing thing is there's little personal stuff, but the studio quality pics are stunning. His links are very good and there's some sensible advice on where to go for photo tips.

SEBASTIAN VON DARK BLACK
www.geocities.com/sebastian_von_dark_black
A work of some individuality!

SEDUCED BY DREAMS
http://jaded.ubiquitous.nu
Nice site, but one of those with the rectangular approach. Nice journal with scattered thought sections, some okay art, a weird bit on personality tests.

SEHNSUCHT
www.sehnsucht.za.net
Bit messy, but includes Tarman, dumb superhero.

SEMJAZA'S ASCENDANCY
www.envy.nu/danadark
DJ Dana Dark, who could probably do a good Bettie Page if you asked her. There's virtually nothing here bar defective cam links and galleries, but there is a picture here so brilliant – of her as a witch – only for you to get some cretinous message from envy.nu or wherever prohibiting expansion. Your blood boils. Go and look at it anyway.

SERAPHIM WEB – FORMERLY LADYHAWKE'S NEST
www.seraphimweb.com
Robin Finnell? Photos – gifs, portraits, horses, cemeteries, still life, virtual exhibits. Web designer yet again, so this site is interesting.

SEX AND CIGARETTES
www.geocities.com/spydercvnt/sexandcigarettes.html
A site about life and its pitfalls. Allegedly.

SEX AND DEATH
www.sex-and-death.org.uk

SEX SHOPPING AND QUANTUM PHYSICS
www.sexshoppingandquantumphysics.com

Nicely mental, with good pics and writing.

SHADES OF GREY
http://ethereal.de/angel
Highly jumbled erratic journal http://ethereal.de/grey/ and idiotically small on a tasteful but fatuous layout. It's style over content.

SHADOW OF MIDIAN
www.shadowofmidian.co.uk
Nothing here, just waiting. Plans a Harro-Goff section.

SHADOWGATE GOTH CEMETARY
www.geocities.com/SoHo/Den/2836/ShadowGate.html
What sets this apart from usual X of Y boredom is they include bands! Brilliant.

SHADOWS AND LIGHT
www.dirge.net/shadows

SHAWNA
http://keki.net

SHE LIKES THE DARK
www.msu.edu/~stagnerr

SHELL
www.shellhell.homestead.com/shell.html
I think this is sweet, although if you're over 18 I can't see it being of any interest.

SHELTER FOR MY MISERY
www.go.to/nikola_gt77
Nikola Prevot's personal site of art and photography.

SHIMMERING ROSE
www.glass-faerie.net/shimmer
The usual women, shimmering.

SHORTGOTH'S HEAP OF SHIT
http://members.aol.com/djrs001

SHROUDED IN BLACK
www.kostika.com
Moody girl posing for ordinary photos, but she also takes nice cemetery stuff.

SHUDDER TO THINK
www.astral55.com/kelli

SHUDREL
www.darksites.com/souls/vampy

Mess with Fae and you never know what to expect

Sistas of Darkness

A few nice pics, downloads, covers and links from the Australian boy responsible.

SHYX
http://uk.geocities.com/shyxy
Strange 'About' page, plus statuary gallery and graphix.

SIDHE IN AETERNUM
www.butterflymessiah.com/sidhe/maiden.html
'I am a dreamweaving spider, a songstress and a faerie witch. Muse of Robert Nightshade. Our Gothic fae music Butterfly Messiah, is my part in bringing the beauty and shadows of Faeryland back to Earth.' And that concludes the case for the prosecution, m'lud.

SILENT Q
www.silentq.org
Old collection of travel diaries, and very good they are too.

SILENT WEAPONS
www.silentweapons.org

SILKIE
www.io.com/~silkie/portfolio

A good portfolio of graphic design, illustration and photography.

SIMPLY FIENDISH
www.fiendish.org
Formerly a club thing, there's currently only some great photos.

SINFUL CAT
http://community.webshots.com/user/sinful_cat

SINFUL MADNESS
www.beautifulmadness.net
Very nice touches here, with weird stories. Check out this journal! Singing for Thatcher, arguing about her mum, confessing a lust for David Copperfield.

SINNOCENCE
www.sinnocence.com
This enormous site is salacious, disgusting, filthy, perverse *and* demented. High praise indeed, and you'll see why when you visit. No surprise that this is popular, because of the vibrancy and variety. People even send autographed photos of their body parts! The central section zooms from one topic to another, and there's British stuff – villagers defending a local street

called Cowshit Lane, pictures of Prescott's left jab the day after it happened! Her changing attitudes to Goth make sense to, and she does the whole look-at-me webcam dolly thing. Message board. Video board, portals, voicemail blah blah blah. Immense is the word. Takes a while loading.

SIN'S DUNGEON
www.geocities.com/SunsetStrip/Palms/1552
Pics, sci-fi, horror, vamps, author stuff, religion occult.

SIREN SUMMER
www.angelfire.com/tx2/SirenSummer
Basic bio, good journal and huge array of nice photos posed, and fashion.

SISTAS OF DARKNESS
www.geocities.com/fae_dejavelin/Sistas.html
A few bio pages from like-minded women and Awards criteria.

SISTER SIN 7
www.geocities.com/sunsetstrip/balcony/3287

SIX SIX SIX
www.sixsixsix.de
Weird personal site from Germany, where you go round the house picture by picture clicking on paintings and walls, to be transported elsewhere, including forums and chat and I hadn't a clue what was going on. Damned clever all the same.

SIZZ'S HOUSE OF GOTHIC
www.geocities.co.jp/Hollywood/7907/index.html
Japanese Goth girl living in America but trying to help out with some explanatory links to Japan. Rarely updated, too busy partying.

SIZZILIA
www.geocities.com/Area51/Rampart/8548

SKYSHROUD
www.skyshroud.co.uk

SMILING GOTH PRODUCTIONS
www.smilinggoth.com
Loads of decent photos, some average art and writing.

SMIRK
www.angelfire.com/ks/goddessisis/index.html
Short bio, poetry but good journal.

JAMES CURTIS SMITH
www.atrous.net

SO GOOD TO SEE YOU ONCE AGAIN
www.velvet.net/~cymbies

SO VERY SAD
www.angelfire.com/de2/soverysad

SOMETHING MUST BREAK
http://angst.accessnode.net/~indigo

SOMETIMES WHEN EVERYONE ELSE IS ASLEEP... I AMPUTATE MY FACE
www.emote.org/blackacid
Don't you just *hate* it when that happens?

SONNET (DOWN?)
www.xcentric.net/sonnet
I liked this, especially the name part. 'No, that's not my real name. I don't like to give out my name to people I don't know, and for all I know you could be some internet loony.' There's only some lovely pics and wedding plans, which with her interests and studies is something of a disappointment. This isn't some vacuous sub-Heathers girl, moving about in cam city. She could do a really cool site. Keep tabs on it, it might develop.

SORCERY KID THE GOTH BOI
www.prairienet.org/~rkrause/SorceryKid
This bloke's a bit weird.

SOUNDS OF CATHEDRAL
www.soc.prv.pl
Polish DJ.

SOUNDS OF RAVEN – SATANIC
www.anti-design.co.uk/soundsofraven

SOUTHERN GOTHIC CAM PORTALS
www.io.com/~batty/camportals.html
'I accept Gothic, Industrial, Pagan, or just simply dark minded. I *don't* allow: Ravers, Mansonites, or anything that is especially preppy.' Is this just the usual suspects? No, and Sinnocence has lipstick on her nose.

SPANKYS HOUSEOF HORRORS
http://spanky.kaos.gen.nz
Brief bio of Auckland Goth with lovely pics.

SPHERES OF AVALON
www.geocities.com/Athens/Aegean/6782/framep.html
Personal pages, some lovely pics of her plus mates, Elven creations which are so good she should sell them commercially, or some astute business should contact her, and her Avalon Clothing designs.

A SPAZ OUTBURST
http://members.tripod.com/~MistressBecky/index.html
She was Mistress Becky but after e-mails from pervs and after a spanking chose Spaz instead. Nice tale of European trip, good cemetery photos, *brilliant* personal galleries.

SPIDER B
www.spiderb.com
Boris site, with all manner of DJ stuff and wonderful pics.

SPIDER BABY
www.angelfire.com/ok2/spiderbaby
Mansonette, except there is some genuine anguish in the journal and a sign of intelligence in the pics.

SPIDERGIRL
www.geocities.com/spidergirl1nonly

SPIRITS OF THE DEAD
http://tosky.iwarp.com/AGF.htm
Goth, cats, people, cemeteries and lots of alt.gothic related material. Packed site and good fun. Part of the bigger, www.eriu.com which is very cool.

SPITE, INC. (DOWN?)
http://phlaux.candiedangel.net
Excellent personal site, with bouncing baby. ('I think I have car doors for ears.' Dislikes: most of humanity.) Projects include PhillyGoth, Gothboiz and WKUR.

SPOOKYBAT
http://spookybat.net

JAMIE W. SPRACKLEN
www.geocities.com/terriblepoet
Poet and man behind the excellent Monas Hieroglyphica zine and Monas Press. Includes trim bio, poetry and... archaeology!

PATTY SPYRAKOS
www.retina.net/~sidereal/index.html
Lovely pics, and portfolio.

SQUEAKY'S DOMAIN – MANSONETTE
www.bludkitten.ihateclowns.com

STANDING ON A BEACH
www.geocities.com/delutions
Pics galore.

STATIC
http://perdition.com/static
Big Cure fan with cool attitude. 'I am Dementia. Welcome and thanks for visiting this site. You are currently visiting static, formerly known as static – I run around hysterical in dead persistent gloom.'

STE 3:16
http://matrix.netsoc.tcd.ie/~ste

STEEL GIRL
www.steelgirl.com

STEVE-O
http://communities.msn.co.uk/steveoportfolio

LYNDA STEVENS
www.geocities.com/SoHo/Exhibit/5981
Complex woman, Goth to her heart. Nice art site from Lynda, with colour drawings, great collages, some interesting trot deck designs, and once you've enjoyed the interesting bio, check The Poison Quill with reviews and interviews (also available in small print zine), of a fully International variety. The pen & ink drawings are fantastic.

STEVY'S HOME PAGE
www.kilireth.freeserve.co.uk/index1.html
Very pert Goth stuff here, particularly the Goth Wars section.

THE STITCHES MORTUARY
www.goth.net/~stvee

STRANGE AFFECTIONS
www.dirge.net/dycilla
Anima fan who enjoys saucily flaunting her legs in public. Dramatic gallery inside greengrocers!

STRANGE AS ANGELS
http://bettie_x.tripod.com/strangeasangels
Personal site with a mad edge also has interesting art sites attached.

STRANGE DAYS
www.geocities.com/SunsetStrip/6515

STRANGER THAN ANGELS
www.toreadors.com/tlb
A bustling site filled with Convergence memories, links and explanations on Goth subjects, some excellent photos throughout, and the chronology of her fashion style is interesting. (I don't think 'Costume Closet' works.) You'll also enjoy her various written inclusions, and there's a monthly update teeming with ideas.

STRAWBERRY FIXATIONS
http://strawberrys.i85.net

STRIPPED BARE – PICS AND LINKS ONLY
www.angelfire.com/zine/strippedbare

STROLLING THROUGH A STARLIT SKY
www.blood-dance.net/~yvain
Interesting Goth bit, from elsewhere, but intriguing writing by Heather Denise Barrett throughout.

THE SUBERVSIVE 11 1/2 INCH FASHION DOLLS PAGE
www.gothic.net/~theda

SUCCUBUS
www.succubus.net
Not much there yet, although she hosts Chic Or Shriek and Bitch, and they're both quality.

ANNE SUDWORTH
www.annesudworth.co.uk
One extraordinarily talented artist. Look at the works visible here (disregarding a couple of staple fantasy blemishes) and then just accept all the other art you'll find on sites mentioned throughout this book mean nothing by comparison. Anne is the real deal, the

Big Anne-Shaped Cheese. There's bits written by her about art, which are good, 'The Black Page' is drivel, but the Animals page gives good charity details, and the links are interesting. There is also a section on chocolate.

SULLEN GIRLS
http://home.bitchgoddess.com/blackdove/sullen

THE JENIPHIR SUMMERS EXPERIENCE
http://obscure.org/~jen

SWEET DREAMS v2
www.gengoth.com/gaby

SWEETBEJESUSDEMONICA
www.angelfire.com/ne/sweetbejesusdemonica
She's a naughty girl this one, so imagine all the little boys scampering for the galleries. Not much detail elsewhere, bar links.

SWIM TO THE MOON
http://swimtothemoon.cc
Mr Cool with moody pics and a very good journal. Enjoyable.

SYLENCE
http://envy.nu/sylence
Poetry, musings, nice pics.

SYNGENEIC
www.waste.org/~oriet
Looks intense. Also art:
http://oriet.deviantart.com/

SYRENEA
www.angelfire.com/ne/syrenea

SYSTEMATIK DELUSIONS
http://members.aol.com/elastikxdreamz

Brandie Doll gives good face and decent journal.

SYTH NOCTURNUS
http://syth6.tripod.com/SythNocturnus
DJ and comic artist with a basic but extremely full site with personal info but also art, vampires, and his bands Angels Of Addiction and Devigene Flux.

TALAITHA'S DISHARMONY
http://talaitha.dynamine.net
Currently studying to be a Druid, so there is much here you can learn about that, plus nice variety of pics and surprisingly drab journal.

TALKING TRASH
www.cris.com/~jeniphir
All manner of interesting things, although not many pics. Rants are interesting, with a fondness for Henry Rollins. Masses on wedding plans but not enough photos.

TANGENT
www.nettally.com/infernal
Excellent site from Tally Goth. Writes well, is never dull.

A TANGLED PURPLE WEB
www.iamnota.demon.co.uk/kari/index.html

TARA
www.blackglass.org/tara
Beautifully expressive bio.

TARIK DOZIER
www.osirisani.com
'I spend my nights as a leather, spike, and fishnet-clad, rubber chicken-wielding costumed crusader... fighting for all that's good and right in the world, along with my elite army of Goths. This, too, is my idea of fun.' You *have* to give him a visit.

TASHA
www.darkwave.org.uk/~tasha
A smattering (not the 'lots' promised) of pics, but they are by Stéphane Lord, and equally brilliant ones of Scorchy.

TEATIME
www.discarnate.com/teatime
Technically it's Betsy's Teatime, and it's divine. The fiction annoyed me. It was very good, but there wasn't much, but

SUCCUBUS.NET

it is varied, and there are plenty of pictures and abrupt diversions throughout. The individuals involved are depraved but they are thrilling. Betsy's like the ultimate glamourpuss and her diary swells with loving feelings: 2001-04-13 – 3:35 p.m 'Did you ever just suddenly become so overwhelmed with hatred for a person or a group of people that you just suddenly feel like crying? I want them to shut up. I want them to just fucking leave. I want them to die. My co-workers. I hate this. My head is fucking killing me because these worthless shitbags are just sitting around the diner, cooking bacon, of all disgusting pungent odours. It's worse than popcorn. God, I hate popcorn. My stomach is just churning and my head... My head wouldn't hurt so much if it wasn't for their fucking witless incessant yapping. Why the fuck aren't they working? Is the entire account service division in there? God!! If they're not gonna sit at their goddamn desks why don't they go home?? Why does reception have to be their fucking romper room? How the fuck am I supposed to take calls? I'm gonna puke.' Face it, she's great.

TECHNODOLL
http://ragdolly.net/ragdoll
Great little site, with tiny writing but bizarre and good galleries.

THANATOPSIS
www.virtue.nu/thanatopsis
Very pretty personal site.

THEDA BARA
http://silent-movies.com/Ladies/PBara1.html
If you don't know who Theda Bara is then you can get down on your knees and grovel with gratitude to me after visiting this, because it's going to open your eyes to what she did. Five galleries of bliss. (While you're there, check out Josephine Baker, Greatest Person of the twentieth century, and Louise Brooks who was a right little character, well before attichewed was endemic.) I grew up in the sixties, and for me it was West Ham, Daredevil, *The Avengers*, all Gerry Anderson, the Marx Bros, Will Hay, *The Man from U.N.C.L.E.* and *The Prisoner*, apart from an amazement over Josephine, and a sense of mystery

every time I saw a Theda Bara photo. When I was seven or eight I had a copy of the horizontal skeleton pics (top left, gallery 2) which I used to keep in my back pocket of my jeans whenever I was hanging round the local church yard. She was an influence

Theda Bara

subconsciously, as well as a lucky charm. I had no real awareness of *why*, she just *was*. Also:
www.mdle.com/ClassicFilms/PhotoGallery/tbara.htm
www.bombshells.com/gallery/bara/index.shtml
www.geocities.com/Hollywood/1096/bara.htm
www.csse.monash.edu.au/~pringle/silent/ssotm/May96

THEE GOTHIC LAYRE
www.netjava.com/~fl4lover
Well, you can't say she doesn't warn you. It's a huge personal site, from the soon-to-be-novelist – 'Dhampir' – and when she rails she rails, when she wails, etc. I recommend the 'Roommate from hell' section. Some rants, like religion, aren't particularly interesting, unless you've never contemplated such matters before, and who gives a toss about her favourite films? But

when she starts to lay into topics you do get caught up. Nice pets page too. Half of the world's cat population stays with her. The section on house renovation is sort of dull, but it just drags you in. I don't care about this stuff but I was still reading away quite happily. Bizarre!

THEE TAINTED GARDEN
www.geocities.com/~vinylla/2-0

THESE BONDS ARE SHACKLE FREE
http://grrlsruin.com/lunacy

THEY WATCH WITH CLOSED EYES
www.sinsations.net
Very visual, sometimes sparky journal.

THIS IS HOW A STAR FALLS
http://poetoftragedies.homestead.com
The photo gallery is really sweet, her own photography isn't bad and the journal may be too grim at times to be entertaining, but is interesting.

THIS IS MOCKINGBIRD LANE
www.mockingbird.clara.net

TICKLED PINK
www.envy.nu/xxryanxx

TINKERBELLE
www.angelfire.com/al/tinkerbelle

TINKERBELL'S DARKER PLACE
http://tinks.cheetaweb.com

TINSEL
http://internettrash.com/users/thistle
'You've never seen hipbones until you see mine,' boasts Thistle, which is preposterous, as I have, at the very least, seen my own. I expect you feel similarly cheated.

TINTED CURIOSITIES
http://michis.cjb.net
Nice photos and drawings, with weird 'Calotypes'.

TOMMY HARLOT
http://hem.passagen.se/harlot

TOMORROW'S TEARS
http://digilander.iol.it/tomorrowstears
Italian fan of The Cranes, Cure, Garbage, Julianne Regan, Suede, and

Portishead, who is well up for a spot of tape trading.

TOO FAR GONE TO SAVE
www.virtue.nu/blisterblue

TRACY B
http://speakeasy.org/~traceyb
Brilliant Cheapskates zine, which must be admired, plus corsets section, which is fairly detailed in the history and includes lot of cool piccies, some of them very odd. Like the bloke in the wig and school dress!

TRACY'S PAGE
www.haas.berkeley.edu/~tmiller
Lots of nimble Goth info, plus a link for Middle Eastern dance (or Belly Dancing, to use tourist lingo).

TRACY'S PAGE OF NO PURPOSE
www.haas.berkeley.edu/~tmiller/home.htm

TRAGIC
www.disillude.com/tragic

TRAGICALLY GOTH
www.tres-gothique.com/tragicallygoth
Ooh, cat fight! Read the 'notice'. Then wonder what the fuss is all about.

TRANCE PLANET VORTEX
www.columbia.edu/~kmc106
Nice site with dull pics but good journal and hair stuff.

TRANSCENDENCE
www.velvet.net
Great collection of photos, a wonderfully evocative journal and plenty more besides.

TRANSFIXION = RENDERS MOTIONLESS
www.darkhosts.com/neophyte
Webcam, strange photos, graphic design.

TRANSMISSION COMMENCED
http://talula.adulate.org

TRENDY BARBIE DOLL IN BLACK
http://members.tripod.com/~Ephebe

TRICELT
www.tricelt.com
Pics, kiddy journal.

TRISTESSE BLANCHE
http://nitescence.net/illusions
Beautiful French site with a few pics,

stories. Poems, lectures (just seemed to be books), statuary photos. Links to other sites – Frost Flowers http://nites cence.net/dreams/numb.html Flux – great webcam, plus archive photos – http://nitescence.net/x/. All very interesting – and it's French Canadian, I think.

TRISTESSE
http://hk.geocities.com/manahime1437
Stumbled across this when seeking Asian Goth scene info, and here she is, with her blue hair, an interest in Cosplay and impersonating a femme man from a Visual Rock band. Very odd and seriously cute

TRYSTAN AND THOMAS
www.fishcat.com
Another wedding site, with extravagant photos, but also the whole story, from the proposal onwards, where he stumps her by making the announcement in front of a hall full of people, with pictures, through to the day itself, with journal and photos. (Nothing smutty, mind!)

TWIGGY
http://gothic.nu/chuggarkjub
Gorgeous and colourful site with your attention dragged this way and that. Those Brazilian Goth girls are in evidence, as are The Ramones! Some cool personal pics.

THE TWILIGHT MASQUERADE
http://home.earthlink.net/~morpheus99

TWINKLE YELL
www.lamoon.net
Cosplay madness. I include these sites because you never know when someone Goth will start a similar thing.

TYPH'S WHIPPING STOCK
http://members.tripod.com/~mansongurl

THE UBER GOTH WONDERLAND HOMEPAGE
www.angelfire.com/goth/ubergothwonderland
He does a band, Infinite Halo. He's a Rozz fan, but calls himself Nothing. A bit like our Mothburner hero. Some nice photos of mates.

UGLY SHYLA
www.geocities.com/uglyshyla
Ugly is actually a very sweet *maniac*, and quite dementedly busy, with her fingers

in many pies. She does disturbing dolls, has one of the best scattered galleries I've seen, can genuinely paint, has shockingly bad taste in music, designs clothes and t-shirts, and you wish you had half her charm.

ULTIMA 100
www.gengoth.com/ultima
Tons of people, clearly.

THE ULTIMATE GOTH CHIC'S ABODE
http://theultimategothchic.freeyellow.com
I have no idea what she's doing. Bio buzzes with mad attitude. Anime archive link included, a few other sites. 'Spider webs and roaches, pickles dancing on my ear'?

UNDERWEAR
http://vague-inklings.net/underwear

UNNAMED
http://twinfusion.com/vincent
Pretty basic, but I think you'll find his journal interesting.

USED COFFEE FILTER
www.angelfire.com/ga/DeviAngel/main.html

V.O.I.D.
www.silver-factory.net/void

V
www.mydarkstar.com
Not much V, apart from some attractive photos, and her own general photography of bands and events. Hosted sites aplenty and a massive cam resource list.

VACANT
www.angelfire.com/ne/alb7/index.html

VAGUE INKLINGS
www.vague-inklings.net
Stunning design, beautiful content, with good journal, interestingly work-able fiction and an amazing cat face.

VAIN-EGO
www.vain-ego.com
Christopher Howell's site is basically music-free but sleek and mysterious. His Sub-Zero idea is brilliant.

VALERIE'S WEBSITE
www.zoetic.demon.co.uk
Nice site showcasing her writing, be it

erotica or music journalism, plus her art and photography.

VALESKAH'S PAGE
www.gothic.net.au/~valeskah/index.html
Ancient Australian site, with nice big old pics.

VANITY
www.digital-sugar.net/~vanity

THE VAULT
www.members.tripod.com/%7Earphalia
A site of astonishing art. I've never been one for this Furry thing per se, but this site contains *amazing* work. Anyone who doesn't go there gets 'dunce' tattooed on their face while they sleep, and if you've already had that done out of choice we'll think of another punishment, involving a lifelike Michael Bolton mask.

THE VEIL OF NIGHT
www.veilofnight.net
Morgoth's site isn't manic, but there are a lot of good photos, especially atmospheric outdoor/church shots.

VELVET DREAMLANDS
www.velvetdreamlands.com
Poetry, bag of trash, cam, sign or chat. She has some great pics of herself, in the old section, and the newest webcam shots. The journal isn't very good, and the layout is a crushed nightmare.

VENUS IN FURS
www.geocities.com/SoHo/Lofts/1789/index.html
Cute personal site which also reprints that *Details* magazine article on Goth, where the early memories are so warped you wonder what's up with the people!

VERMILLION – PICS
http://communities.msn.co.uk/VerminIn
Vermillion

VERSION MARY
www.whamizone.com/versionmary

GABRIELLA VERVAINE
http://speakeasy.org/~traceyb
Excellent writing here, not that I could navigate it well, being a dunce.

VERY FUNNY SCOTTY NOW BEAM DOWN MY CLOTHES
http://ubergoth.net

The FAQ is classic stuff, photos are good. I Whine is entertaining.

VEXEN CRABTREE'S PHOTOSITE
www.woodlandworld.com/Vexen/photos/goth.asp
Crazed personal site, with plenty of odd things, but a wonderful array of personal Goth pics

VICIOUS ANGEL
www.viciousangel.net
Domain, plus personal site: Not A Pretty Girl (http://belisima.viciousangel.net), where she is revealed as one hot dame, with a surprisingly modest amount of photos. Also doing Florida Goth Directory called Purgatory (http://goth.viciousangel.net).

VINTA GOTH
www.livejournal.com/users/vintagoth

VINYL SEDUCTRESS
www.vinylseductress.com
A model of the rubbery variety, with pics from Convergence 6.

VIOLET EYES
www.violeteyes.org

VIOLET ROSE
http://uk.geocities.com/violetsrose
Clothes and artwork. Involved with Lady-bird yahoo club, so she knows her stuff.

VIOLET TUMBLE
www.lunarpages.com/violettumble
It's like 'Rocky' never happened and Hitchcock would have approved. Just see for yourself and enjoy your bemusement. Great links.

VISIT YOUR INFINITE DREAM
http://poort.com/extreem
Naughty – but not here – fetish girl who seems barmy to me.

VOID
www.silver-factory.net/void

THE VOLUPTUOUS HORROR OF COUNTESS BATHORY
www.bathoria.com
For the true vamp freaks among you this will be a joy. Well thought out and repulsive in just the right way. The galleries are exceptional, if you're into this.

VULTURE MIRANDA
www.geocities.com/SoHo/Lofts/8231
Interesting personal details. Odd mix of pics, some cool portraits, some fetish – not all of her.

WAITING FOR EUPHORIA
www.suddeneclipse.net/leahstarr
The pics are nice but the writing is stunning. You can't get much more honest than this, and although it is often horrible, and at times inspiring, it is *always* moving.

WAITING FOR THE NIGHT TO FALL
www.digitalfae.net/salyx

WAITING FOR THE TRAIN
www.califia.org/~serenova
Very nice photos and journal with some good writing on topic like Victorian women and human rights abuses.

WALKER 1812'S LOUNGE
www.walker1812.com
Writing, photography, and musings by this odd man.

WARNING HIGH MAINTENANCE
http://torque.diaryland.com

SARA WASSON
www.people.cornell.edu/pages/spw7
Interesting, friendly and artistic site, on personal side. Rude, and seriously intelligent.

WASTELAND
http://sia.wasteland.com
Sia does Dark Perfection, and this is her personal site, with loads of artfully placed photos, and a seemingly endless journal. I don't know how she finds the time or even why. Does her own cam portal, and has others accessible, but there are print archives and live cam archives and god knows what else.

THE WAVE OF THE FUTURE
www.bmeworld.com/guagegrl
Great natural portraits.

WE GOT A WINNER!
http://livejournal.com/users/vertabreak

THE WEB OF THE BLACK WIDOW
www.angelfire.com/ego/medusa
Good personal site, with fiction and dissertation on 'The Terror Within: a

The Wicked One

Psycho-analytical Exploration of Victorian Gothic Horror'. Worth spending time here.

WELCOME TO FUSCHIA'S SECRET ARCHIVE
www.geocities.com/fuchsias_secret/index.html
Very cool Peake-inspired site. Probably a complete mystery to anyone else.

WELCOME TO FAERYLAND
www.angelfire.com/nt/uberfaerie

WELCOME TO GLAISTIG
www.mindspring.com/~glaistig

Personal site with design portfolio included, but very interesting writing (and life, although she doesn't seem to think so) in her live journal. You can also invoke a demon, or read her poetry – I know which I chose!

WELCOME TO LADY DRAGON'S CORNER OF HELL
http://members.tripod.com/~Lady__Dragon/welcome.html

WELCOME TO MY DARK ILLUSIONS
http://hometown.aol.com/rravenx/index.html
Very old and basic, but you may find

the 'Gore galleries' interesting because this is her make-up artist work section – and Blood Recipes (of the fake variety).

WELCOME TO MY HELL
www.angelfire.com/ns/adoress/index.html
Tenielle's basic site with nice pics.

WELCOME TO MY MIND (Be afraid...)
www.geocities.com/dark_paine/mymind.html
Oh hush now pet! She doesn't like people who think Blink 182 are Punk and yet she likes Manson. She's very photogenic but a trifle too aware in the

photos, You can learn all about her piercings and infections but don't go near that poetry. No, I said don't... oh God! Fortunately she makes up for these errors of judgement with great many wonderful pictures of her cats. Oh and there's the problems Only Goths Have, Why Do You Dress In Black etc from other sites.

WELCOME TO MY WORLD
www.angelfire.com/mn/DarKiosk

WELCOME TO MY WORLD
www.geocities.com/euthanasia8

WELCOME TO OPHELIA'S LOST HOME PAGE
www.geocities.com/Paris/Metro/3691
Dawn's sites with nice pics, and Colorado events.

WELCOME TO SHIN'S PLACE
www.geocities.com/digitalangelshin
An anonymous man's Cosplay site, including one character called Goth Shorty.

WENDOLEN'S GATEWAY
www.velvet.net/~wendolen

WET PAINT
http://turpentinewine.terrashare.com
Interesting mini-bio bits, beautiful photos, *very* interesting art.

WHAT'S IN REBECCA'S POCKET
www.rebeccablood.net
Huge personal/resource site, with intriguing areas on many subjects. The weblog is fantastic, as is the whole thing. You could be here for days.

WHEN ANGELS WEEP
www.blackglass.org/nimsay
Thoughtful, subdued, attractive.

WHICH WAY?
www.gothic.net/~subgirl
Turn right, and in the Gothic section you can see her Gothic Scouts Merit sash. There's lots of content here, including a Sheep On Drugs obsession.

WHISPERS
http://disillude.com/whispers

ANTHONY A WHITE
www.gothtec.com

Excellent personal site. Great pics, plenty musing.

WHO IS ANN KOI?
www.moritorium.com/koi/bio.html
A talented artist by the look of it.

THE WICKED ONE
http://thewickedone.cjb.net
Very good personal site from molecular biologist with stunning photos, weird history and tombs section, plus daffy journal.

THE WIGHT WYTCH
www.wightwytch.co.uk

WIKKID GOTHBABE
www.geocities.com/wikkid_gothbabe
Samantha, jewellery designer. Great pics of her, at club events she's attended.

WILD WINGS
www.pink-vinyl.org/meow

MEHITOBEL WILSON
www.gothic.net/~sighs
She's a horror writer and this is her little site. There's not too much to this site to be honest but then you're only going to it for info on her.

WINGS TATTERED, FALLEN
www.grumpybat.net/nephrael/tattered
Has she got a pet raccoon?

WONDERGNOME
www.wondergnome.co.uk
Looks like it could become stunning. Only Pagan chat there so far.

WORD WORDS WORDS
– A Gothic Portfolio
http://members.aol.com/Loki265n/words
index.htm
The words and work of Brent Douglas (Gossamer/Rapture).

THE WORLD OF SAYA
http://worldofsaya.tripod.com
Fantasy drama, in sections. The site is a world within a world sort of thing. Fairly soppy, but certainly well done and compelling and for fans of the genre.

THE WORLD OF VERA
www.meinehomepage.purespace.de/index.htm
It's Vera from Lost Belief and Mors Ex

Machina's homepage with photos, lyrics/poetry and designs/illustrations.

WORLDS IN THE VOID
http://falchion.cirratus.org
Fascinating little site, visually. Not much content.

WRAPPED IN LUST AND LUNACY
www.serpentine.net/orchidkiss

WRETCH
www.madsavants.org/wretch
There's a webcam, she looks charming, three links and... oh, that's it.

WRITHE
http://writhe.net

X COMMUNICATION WUMPSUCK
www.geocities.com/wumpsuck
Fantastic imagery, plus art, odd recipes, herbals, potions, etc.

XKRISTYX
www.envy.nu/xkristyx
You can always tell. First you check the photos. Then you think, 'within half a page the journal will say something sucked'. It did. Move on.

XzONE
http://xzone.cjb.net
Great site from Singapore which also has a whole host of pages devoted to other bands (L'Arc-en-ciel, Blue) and other things (Lenore, Darth Maul), with art and photos.

NICK YARAUR
www.yaruar.dircon.co.uk

YEA THAT WOULD BE THAT EPITOMYZED CHICK
http://epitomyzed.net
Jia, from Texas. Poems, random thoughts, views.

YENDRI
www.yendri.de
This is a wonderfully inventive and seriously attractive site that will have most designers dribbling out of their slack-jawed mouths, envious as hell. Personal, musical and artistic.

VENUS ZARCAS
www.geocities.com/SoHo/Lofts/8380
Cool artist archive.

Resources

37.COM
www.37.com
Saves time on searches.

ADERLASS GOTHIC LINKS (TOP 100)
www.aderlass.com/gothic-top100

AKASHA INC
www.ninemuses.demon.co.uk/akashainc/index.htm
Little art gallery, outdated gig section, nice 'hosts' bios, but things seem oddly quiet for a well-respected organisation such as this.

ALCHEMY TOP LIST
www.netcentral24.de/free/Gothic/index.shtml

ALL THROUGH THE NITE – FONTS
www.geocities.com/Paris/LeftBank/8669/Halloween99/fonts.htm

ALTA VISTA DIRECTORY
http://dir.altavista.com/search?pg=dir&tp=Entertainment/Music/Genres
Just when you least expect some results, you will find odd bands popping up, especially older ones. Once at genres pick 'Alternative'.

AMG ALL MUSIC GUIDE
http://allmusic.com
Despite its duff look this really does throw up some gems and offers a pretty handy guide. It is far from perfect, and if you hit a genre trail it will announce Dali's Car as an influential Goth act, but it's surprisingly good with basic discographies and histories, and you can easily see the most accessed requests. A fair smattering of pics to illustrate their own bios.

ANTI-DESIGN
www.anti-design.co.uk
Design site company run by Simon, but also has news and reviews. One to keep an eye on.

'Jesus Blood'. Photo © Stéphane Lord.
Model: Veronique Major

AVERSION.COM
www.aversion.com
Pretty crap search base. Hasn't heard of Seminal Goth influence Dali's Car, but it does better with Bauhaus, although the promo pic is scary, with David Jay looking a little too much like Chris Evans for comfort. Even with Rozz Williams it only gives two whole links.

BLACK HEAVEN GOTHIC TOP 50
www.netcentral24.de/free/BlackHeavenGothic/index.shtml

BLACK WIDOWS TOP SITES
http://darknetwork.hypermart.net/topsites/topsites.html

BLACKLIST TOP 100
www.damnage.com/cgi-bin/hell/rankem/rankem.cgi?action=in&id=malaise

BLOOD FETISH
www.bloodfetish.com/bloodlinks/pages
General Goth, Vamp, Ind, Horror etc.

CEMETERY IN ASHES – GRAFX
www.angelfire.com/art/detnuah/index.html

CLICK MUSIC
www.clickmusic.co.uk
Very good on bigger names as it uses Rolling Stone's site as a reference.

CLIP ART OF HORROR
www.allfreeclipart.com/horror.html

CREEP SPOOKY FONTS
http://members.aol.com/reninnc/fonts/fonts.html

DAILY DISH
www.dailydish.com
Decent news searchable over many years. Turns up nuggets.

DARK CLUB TOP 100
www.netcentral24.de/free/darkclubcologne/index.shtml

DARK CROWN
www.darkcrown.com

Another big portal. Exchange, newsletter, links, topsites and horoscope. Plus loads of section lists – art, business, music, media etc. It's growing and should get better.

DARK FEAR
www.darkfear.com
Top 66 horror and Goth sites, with list resets twice a month. Interestingly, no porn. Horror, Industrial, Satan, and Halloween – lots on that which is cool. Plus, look into the site itself more generally and you'll find paranormal anomalies, crime and punishment, bands, arts and entertainment, business and commerce, horror and blood, society, politics and religion, health and medicine: reference and resource enough for you? Nearly two thousand links.

DARK GOTHIC 100
www.netcentral24.de/free/darkgothic100/index.shtml

DARK HOSTS
www.darkhosts.com
In return from having their ads (no hardship whatsoever) they'll host you – 50mb of space. You have to deserve it mind, and apply. No hate crap.

DARK LINKS
http://darklinks.tsx.org
Very big lists for bands, zines, clubs and labels. With reviews and forum.

DARK LINKS
www.darklinks.de
This is an *amazing* resources site. Really superb, with a natural German bias. Great basic bands links list, plus magazines and radio as well as chat, forums for the German scene, with excellent clothes listings and general sites. Plus a really superb photo section that is well worth frequenting as they cover the main German festivals each year as well as individual gigs.

DARK MAGIC TOP LIST
www.netcentral24.de/free/DarkMagic/index.shtml

DARK REINCARNATION TOP 100
www.netcentral24.de/free/aratta/index.shtml

DARK SOUTH TOP 100
www.angelfire.com/tx3/darksouth/top100/index.html

DARKEST WEB
www.darkestweb.com
Formulaic search results, always amiably suggesting you try sites which they must be linked with. Only use when bored, because there are some surreal treats in store. A lot of chat or merchandising links, so you may find things of use.

DARKNESS.TV
www.darkness.tv
Boring Portal/Search

DARKSITES
www.darksites.com
General community thing with forums, galleries, reviews and features, but it seems drab. Certainly in need of contributions too.

DARKSOULS OF DESIRE TOPSITES
http://gothicrose.hypermart.net/topsites/topsites.html

DEAD TO THE WORLD
www.gospelcom.net/deadworld
Chicago's Christian Goth/Ind/Techno resource site. Dead to the World was founded under the name A Forest of Suicides in November of 1996. 'Dead to the World is a group of counter-culture Christians based in the greater Chicagoland/NW Indiana area who are interested in meeting other similarly minded people. We are not a church, or a youth group of any sort. We are simply a group of students, professionals, musicians, artists, and anyone who seeks Jesus from within typically worldly sub-cultures.' It's actually dead, I'm sure, but there's a cute Eva O interview, and Tara VanFlower, plus some interesting links.

DELIRIUM TOP 100
www.topsitelists.com/area51/delirium/topsites.html

DISCARNATE
www.discarnate.com

EMPIRE OF DARKNESS TOP 100
www.netcentral24.de/free/eod/index.shtml

FINIX ARTS GOTHIC LINKS
www.exclusiv-topsites.de/topsites/topsites/GOTHICLINKS1217K/index.html

FONTS FOR FREAKS
www.gothic.net/~tygre

FONTS & THINGS: THEMES
www.fontsnthings.com/themes/gothic.html

FREEALITY MUSIC INFORMATION
www.freeality.com/music.htm
A variety of music search engines. Some are decidedly unsuccessful – at anything! – but persevere and you'll find some handle smaller genres like Ethereal and Ambient quite well.

FURRYLAND – GRAFX
http://furryland.cjb.net

GHOST TAIL
www.sol.dti.ne.jp/~taizen
Took a while to work this Japanese site out, but go through the door and from the left menu beneath the ghost, click on Ghost Material, and then move down to the safety pins. Each of those links to a separate spooky graphic. I like the bouncing iron man.

GIFS OF THE NIGHT
www.angelfire.com/goth/Necronomicon/Images.html

GOTH TOP 50
www.gothic-auktion.de/gothicsites/in.php?site=985472265

GOTH PAGES
www.gothpages.net
Banner Link exchange plus mini-resource.

GOTHIC GRAFIX
www.fortunecity.com/victorian/dadd/283/grafix.htm

GOTHIC HELL LINKS
www.gothic-hell.de

GOTHIC NATION BOARD
www.nachtwelten.de/cgi-bin/Ultimate.cgi?action=intro

GOTHIC RIBBONS AND ICONS
www.webgurus.com/matic/gallery/gothic.html

GOTHIC SITES TOP 50
www.netcentral24.de/free/GothicMagazin/index.shtml

GOTHIC TOP 100
www.netcentral24.de/free/Gothic100/index.shtml

GOTHIC UNDERGROUND TOP 100
www.gothicunderground.de/liste/toplist.phtml?id=3

GOTHY SEARCH
www.gothysearch.de
It does work, but Rasputina 0, Rozz 1. If you're not after German bands maybe don't bother. Murder At The Registry threw up Manson, Vamp and Horror sites, plus something about the electric chair!

HALLOWEEN CENTRAL
http://rats2u.com/halloween/halloween_index.htm
Massive links resource. Worth pottering around for a while. Tons of categories.

HELL ON EARTH TOP 100
www.netcentral24.de/free/hell100/index.shtml

HORRORFIND
www.horrorfind.com
Big horror/supernatural resource, plus plenty of Gothic.

INDUSTRIALNATION TOPSITES
www.Industrialnation.de//list.php3?gate=n

INTERNETUNDERGROUND
www.internetunderground.com
Big links and darksite promotions. Gothic, Industrial, personal pages, Punk, religion stuff, Vampire, chat, people, banner exchange, Gothic postcards, message board, guestbook, mp3 streaming. Biggest and best organised outside Dark Side of the Net. As it's regularly updated, you could be here for hours and never get bored.

KAT'S MEOW
http://katsmeow.com
Grafx of a medieval, Goth and fantasy theme, free to take.

LUCIFER'S TOP LISTS
www.darkvoid.net/topsites
Yeah, like he's got time to sit around compiling them? Actually, he would have, when you think about it. Not exactly in the mould of Inspirational

Underworld Figure, so maybe he gets lonely? It's a hobby. He went through that whole Shoegazing era and found it wanting, and now he's still recommending shite without realising it. That's the true nature of damnation.

MACABRE MANOR'S COLLECTION OF CREEPY FONTS
http://macabremanor.50megs.com/fonts.html

MP3
http://search.mp3.com/bin/search
Pretty obvious. Good for info.

MUSIC FREE LINK
www.kaleidoscope-musicbox.com/music-link
Excellent Asian search engine. Takes a while to get the hang of and the results tend to come as geometric characters, but you'll get interesting stuff more than half the time, and it allows you to use most Asian search engines.

NOCTURNAL FIXATIONS
http://nocturnalfixations.org
Could be good but with dead links and no reviews there's just a handful of tracks available by Narcissus Pool, Element and Katscan. Dead journal, a few photos.

OPESYS
http://kergan87.free.fr/opesys
Superb French site. Menus right and left with left fonts, games, graphics, gifs, mp3 etc. Top right for groups and societies, wallpaper, skins, drivers, downloads galore.

PINBOARD
www.ritchies.de/webtools/pinboard.htm

ROSES ARE RED TOP SITES
www.gothic-rose.com/topsites/index.shtml

SAPPHIRE'S TOP TEN
www.sapphire-faeries.net/stt/index.html
Sapphire, bless her, picks her top ten sites of women who have an actual idea behind their sites.

SICKOZELL – GOTHIC SEARCH
www.sickozell.f2s.com/index.shtml
Another cool resource with the usual music, poetry, art, fashion, clubbing, CDs, e-zines, merchandising etc, plus a half-decent search engine for Gothic,

Medieval, EBM, Synth and Industrial, or so they claim. Rasputina – 0, Rozz – 1.

SIM GOTH TECH – DESIGNS
www.mosaicsun.com/gothtech

SMALL FONT COLLECTION
http://home5.inet.tele.dk/martyr/fonts.htm

SONG SEARCH
www.songsearch.net
Pretty good for obscure stuff.

SONIC NET
www.sonicnet.com/artistinfo
I often use this, but it's hardly infallible. Rasputina – 18 sites. Rozz Williams – 0! And when you start going through the lists there's always 50% dead links if not more, but tough titty. It still yields good results.

SPOOKY LINKS TOP SITES
www.spookylinks.com/ts/index.html

STONE CREATIONS GOTHIC THEMES
www.darkhosts.com/xvvgothicvvx/index.html
Wallpapers and links.

SUPER GOTH WEBSITES
http://supergoth.hypermart.net/topsites/topsites.html

THE BONEYARD
www.fontcraft.com/boneyard/boneyard.html
Horror & Halloween Fonts & Art.

THE DARK NETWORK
www.thedarknetwork.com
Dark... antisocial, beliefs, art, exchanges, games, general, movies, music, online shops, personals, photographers, portals, scrolls, services.

THE DARK PAGE TOP LIST
www.darkpage-toplist.de

THE DARK TOP 100
www.topsitelists.com/area51/Damien/topsites.html

THE TASTE OF NEW ROSES
www.gothic-order.de
German forum.

THEMEWORLD
www.themeworld.com
Amazing collection on all shows, sports, comic styles etc.

TOP 100 DJS
www.zorknemesis.de

TOP SITES 100 MAGAZINES AND OTHERS
www.site-creators.de/topsites/index.html

TOP TEN GOTHIC BAND LIST
http://thycotic.com/gothic

TYPE EUPHORIA – HORROR/GOTHIC
http://fonts.linuxpower.org/list_cat.php3?category=gothic-horror&title=Gothic/Horror&offset=0&range=10

UBL
http://ubl.artistdirect.com
Generally the best on bands, although obscure or new artists won't feature unless you add info. Does very well with big names, and gives similar band links to aid your all-round pleasure. So when you look for Rozz you get Eva O, Gitane, Shadow Project, various discographies, plus links to Rozz chat and newsgroups, mailing lists, e-cards etc.

ULTIMA 100
www.gengoth.com/ultima

WAVE BOARD
www.wave-board.de

WITCHES VOICE
www.witchvox.com
One cool Wiccan resource.

WITHIN DARKNESS
www.ebo.com.au/wd
Industrial and Goth search engine. Rasputina – 0, Rozz – 1 (and that was an Australian homepage of someone who mentioned liking him!).

WORLD OF GOTHICS TOP 50 LINKS
www.netcentral24.de/free/wog/index.shtml

ZERO
www.hf.rim.or.jp/~_0_/
Big member's only site from Japan with tons of links, but hardly in Japan itself, other than some big classified site where a search for Gothic only turned up an article about Paul McCartney! They do have a nice gig reviews section plus some *brilliant* club night photo reports. Big forum thing, and nice to stroll around.

Goth websites

A.G.F. DREAM CENTRAL
www.geocities.com/SunsetStrip/Palms/1629/
dreams/dreams.html

A.G.F. FASHION
http://tosky.iwarp.com/AGF.htm

A.G.F. QUOTES
www.velvet.net/~ratty/agf/quotes

A-Z NET.GOTH FASHION ITEMS
http://home.no.net/damber/gothic/
azgothfash.html
Old Sexbat stuff, on a Norwegian site
now. Yes, I could have found a different
URL but it appeared, I snared it.

ALAS – ONLINE COMIC
www.clashingblack.com/alas

ALT.GOTHIC
www.altgothic.com
List specialists, with massive
Convergence involvement.

AM I GOTH OR NOT
www.amigothornot.com
They pose and post, some seriously,
some not, and you vote. It can be *very*
funny when someone is taking the piss.

ANDROID GODDESS
www.neuroism.net/androidgoddess
'Android Goddess is an awards page for
women, based not on looks but mainly
on personality and attitude. I know how
it is to feel alienated. If you're stubborn
and stand up for what you believe in,
you're considered a bitch. Does this seem
odd to you? The "Android" part is about
the alienation, and the feelings of not
fitting in, not belonging, and not even
wanting to. The "Goddess" is because we
kick ass and don't take any shit. We're
different and are not afraid to speak our
minds, and that is goddess material.
However, if your site gives off the kind of
attitude that you don't know who you are,

*'Hidden Desire'. Photo © Stéphane Lord.
Model: Fannie Langlois*

or don't care, or are just trying to impress
people, this is when I click the delete
button.' I included that spiel because I
liked it. So we're getting away from
looks, supposedly, which is good, but it's
half the people you see everywhere else.
Mind you, that still leaves you lots to
gaze at, and I do mean a lot, particularly
the Future lists, but she claims it is
dying. Get in there and help save it!

ANTIMONY & LACE
www.threethirteen.net/lace
'Welcome to Victoria Gwaed's guide to
Gothic fashion. One of my main interests is clothing design and construction,
it's a good thing too. If I weren't a
sewinGoth I'd either be a completely
brokeGoth or a nakedGoth. This site
has ideas for entering the wonderful
world of Gothic fashion, instructions to
make Gothic clothing yourself, links to
sites Goths might find helpful for
engineering their own wardrobe, as well
as sites that will ensure you have lovely
livery to your hearts content even if you
can't sew a stitch. Of course if you can
sew, that doesn't mean you can't shop
too. Every Goth has their own fashion
sense and taste, but I hope you will find
this site helpful whatever your Gothic
bent is.' Brilliant site includes Fashion
Tips, How To Wear A Cloak, Caring For
Fetish Garments, How To Remain Goth
And Improve Your Work Prospects,
Identifying A Variety Of Goth Styles,
How To Start Building Your Wardrobe
Up, Male Goth Fashion Possibilities.
There is also a fashion gallery, reader
submissions, DIY fashion tips, paper
dolls, links and message board.

ANYWHERE OUT OF THE WORLD
www.chez.com/anywhere
It's in French and clearly done by two
girls who appreciate Gothic culture.
A weird red shape appears when you
click on sommaire and there are little
pockmarks on the shape. That's what
you click. A 'Lectures' section provides
Fanzines (Elegy and D-side), Recuils

(about dark fiction). They write about ten
pages on Elegy. Musique section: NIN,
Manson, Cure – fairly normal, except...
in other groups a high Industrial or EBM
element. They review things and provide
a link to the official sites. Similarly,
another good, quality section on Cinema,
Culture, Mode (Piercing, Clothes, etc)
Events: Soirées (Rouen, Paris, London),
pics of her out and about, Concerts and
Festivals reviews of NIN and Manson.

THE ARCHIVE
http://anton6.free.fr/archive.htm
Site, building up, with pics and articles
of many bands, including Danse
Society, X-Mal, DAF, Virgin Prunes etc.
Very interesting.

ARE YOU A DARK DORK?
www.batwinged.com/darkdorks

AS MENINAS GOTHIKAS
www.carcasse.com/gothikgirls
British, Portuguese and Spanish versions
available on this Brazilian site. This is
absolutely awesome, a stunning little
cartoon strip series of the maddest like
Goth girlings on the universe. There's
even a funny fuq (frequently unasked
questions). Pure genius, it had me
stunned and riveted. Those four girls:
Whipcunt – 'Of difficult and radix
personality, she possess a great trend to
inebriate and to arrange confusion.'
Cursed Sun – 'Marilyn Manson freaky
fan. She recently gets interest for Gothic
stuff, however, when somebody question
she define herself as "an apprentice of
the profane arts". She likes so much to
dance, but she never knows who are the
musicians.' Zille – 'When Zille is away
from Whipcunt, she writes long moody
poetry, home-brews Absinthe, and makes
new Goth and fetish clothes. When they
are together, they go out to the clubs,
scare the normal people, have explosive
fights, and have explosive sex.' Barbie –
'The sexy vamp stereotype made flesh,
Barbie find herself many times involved
in intrigues and rumours without at least

leaving her house.' Plus TrevaeDojo – 'TrevaeDojo alleges to have never used clothes other than black ones, and shows off with pride all the scars of beatings of Skinheads, and he's also pretty sure that nobody in the world is Gothier that him.' Pain – 'Pain seen to be a open-minded Cat... Used to freaky people, weird music and really sick attitudes. Anyway, reacting is not it's specialty.' You need to know it's the same idea, but the Power Goth Girls aren't even close. This is ten times better.

AT HOME WITH THE GOTHIC TOYBOX
www.angelfire.com/goth/asphyxia
Mike and Pam have a wonderfully, and fittingly, playful site, and if you're not careful they're considerate enough to direct you a Backstreet Boys site. The amount of silly things to do – other than take the Goth Baromoter test – is overwhelming, but there's *beautiful* artwork, some great photos, and good music reviews. A real gem of a site.

ATILLA TOTH
www.attilatoth.de
Nice photos, badly labelled. Brilliant Skinny Puppy in 'archive'.

AUDIAX NET
www.kelly.fr.st
Great French site. There's lots of traditional Goth material discussed and a section which clearly means they have opinions, as this is labelled 'Goth Dorks'.

AZHRARN'S GARDEN
www.blood-dance.net/hls/azhrarn
Nicely artistic grave girl personal page, with her thoughts, attitude, art. Best of all are her essays in Gothic Ramblings, which are worth your serious attention, for here is an Old School Goth whose disenchantment is on solid artistic, aesthetic and altruistic grounds. The literature covered is cool as well. I would have looked at the poetry but strange primeval forces made my head explode all over the room instead. You will not regret visiting this site. She also does some BDSM for Beginners (http://blood-dance.net/bdsm/index.html), Goth Near Twilight (http://blood-dance.net/goth/index.html) and Net.Vampyre (http://netvampyric.8m.com).

AZN
www.sevaan.com/files/krycek/azn

It's something for Asian Goths, but there's not much there yet, and no bands!

AZSTARELLE
www.azstarelle.co.uk
Hopefully interesting site done by Jadite Le Fae, who has plans for a delightful personal section, along with existing Goth and witch material she sells mail-order.

BABYGOTH
www.velvet.net/babygoth
In the old days Goths were laughed at for being young, which was bizarre, so it's a nice idea, like the Fairy Gothmother group, but as people have to be under a certain age, why aren't the members' sites checked on the list and deleted when they hit that mark? Then again why don't people with sites check their links sections and ditch all the dead'uns? It seems only polite to do so.

Gothic Baby Pictures

BAD GOTH POETRY
www.Gothic.net/~mage/Goth/poetry
This is extremely funny. Dead for now, which is fitting. At least have a look.

BATWEB
www.batweb.de
Details about nightlife related events in Germany, with pics of band members posed in cemeteries. Plus links and Batchat.

BAT WINGS AND BUTTERFLIES
http://tres-Gothique.com/wings
'Voting for someone as having *bat wings* indicates that you find them to possess dark, mysterious features, have a site of a dark or Gothic nature, and find their style of design to be mature and unique. Voting for someone as having *butterfly wings* indicates that you find them to be more cute then alluring,

their site is in the stages of emerging from a cocoon, perhaps needing a little work, care, and attention.'

BEAUTIFUL BOYS IN EYELINER
www.mydarkstar.com/eyeboys.htm

BEAUTIFUL DARK ENCHANTING GOTHIC ANGELIC BABE OF THE WEEK
http://theda.tripod.com/bdeagbotw.htm
Do you think that somewhere there is a Threatening Repulsive Clumsy Drunkard Goth Sow Of The Week? Probably not.

BEAUTY IN BLACK
www.angelfire.com/vt/beautyinblack/1.html
This is a very well done site, which almost manages to make the beauty of the week idea appealing again.

BIG BEAUTIFUL GOTHS
http://members.tripod.com/~Gothic_Chamber/bbg.htm
Must be over 165 pounds to qualify.

A BIT SQUIFFY...AGAIN
www.btinternet.com/~graham1980
Graham's photographic prowess on nights of debauch, taken at clubs.

BITCH (OF THE...ETC)
www.succubus.net/bitch
Might just be the usual cobblers, but they each have to tell a story of recent bitchy behaviour to justify their award. Some are quite funny, and some just make you loathe them, so... interesting move!

BLACK AUKTION
www.blackauktion.de
German auction site.

THE BLACK PATH
http://theblackpath.com

BLACK SUNSHINE – POETRY
www.darkhosts.com/blksunshine/poetry.html

BLOOD-DANCE BLOODSTONE GATE
www.angelfire.com/wa/BloodstoneManor
Weird site. One of those building ones with different rooms.

BLOOD-DANCE
www.blood-dance.net
Home to The Black Pages. 'To those of you out there who still look to me to provide direction, I apologise. You deserve a brighter beacon to show you the way

home. My fire isn't burning too brightly these nights. For those who just want to see where the latest gathering of shallow music & mascara whores is going to congregate... well get off your shiftless asses and figure it out yourselves. Don't let the port bang you in your packets on the way out of the server.' Zines, Industrial stuff, Goth musings and... wrestling.

BRAINS FACTORY
www.tk.xaxon.ne.jp/~davie
Japanese label who do Goth stuff from time to time. Also official archive site for a dead Goth band called Gregor Samsa, and some new music, where we are urged, 'please feel my Psycho Horror Sound'. The links are great.

BREATHTAKING GOTH COUPLE OF THE WEEK
http://members.tripod.com/~Kaitalah
Old but still sweet.

BRITGOTH
www.britgoth.com
Small and with empty sections but quite cool. 'Goth Bitch' is best.

CALIGULA'S GOTHIC GALLERIES
http://bite.to/caligula
Not many pics so far, but some great images.

CANTARA
http://home01.wxs.nl/~cantara/
Odd site with Goth, Vamp and Bowie stuff, plus many photos.

CARCASSE: COMUNIDADE VIRTUAL DA ARTE OBSCURA
www.carcasse.com
Fantastic looking Brazilian Goth site, with rare local songs in mp3 format which should interest anyone.

CARPE MORTEM
www.carpemortem.com
Fantastic Goth/Industrial label site. Nicely done, as it's also a big resource site and does hosting. Bands, Sites, Labels, Publications. News, clubs, tours, personal sites, chat, forums, mailing list. This is enjoyable to visit and could become one of your favourites.

CARPE NOCTEM
www.gothicmetal.de/index.php3
Huge resource for Goth-Metal.

THE CATACOMBS OF GOTH GORDON
http://go.to/GothGorgon

CEMETERY GIRLS
www.cemeterygirls.com
More of chosen models rather than of The Week. Was just starting, so not much to see but looks very promising.

CHAPEL OF GHOULS
http://chapelghouls.ifrance.com/chapelghouls
General music site covering dark territory from France but with English. Pretty lively and good info source.

CHEEZIEST GOTH SITE OF THE WEEK!
www.gothic.net/~wilt/cheeze
Probably the most odious site discovered – which seems dead, so let us hope it stays that way – for their preening attitude and belief that they're not doing any harm by poking supposedly harmless fun at someone's website. It is all meant to be taken *in good heart*. Well fuck that. What these *miserable little cretins* do is encourage other worm-brained scumbags to go along in a sense of cowardly camaraderie and slag off people's sites, filling their guestbooks with hateful comments, and then leave, feeling big and clever. The person who has tried to enjoy doing their site then finds all this vitriol and has to cope with it. One girl, Jessa, whose site was up for a few days, had such filth left as messages that you wonder why the people behind Cheeziest don't realise the kind of vermin they are encouraging by their pathetic antics. I deliberately visited all the sites looking for redeeming features and found that most had been shamed into closing down! They seemed particularly amused by a site done by a guy in his forties who drives a forklift for a living and turned up to work in full makeup every day. Er... yeah, so he was having *fun*, and clearly had more balls than you, you idiotic wankers? There is nothing clever about mindlessly slagging someone off just because you feel like it. It is done out of a feeling of superiority, like little office-chair Nazis. Sites like 'Cheeziest' are nauseating, and if anybody actually knows the people responsible you should criticise them for being the worthless, pointless creeps they are. People like this are *poison* in any scene, and should be ostracised.

CHRISTIAN GOTH
www.angelfire.com/ny/angelmiette
Message board, chatroom, books, poetry and Gothic Christians Unite. Supposed to have moved to: www.christiangoth.com?

CIGARETTE GOTH OF THE MONTH
www.rosegardenofwhores.com/cigarettegoths

THE COMPLEXITY OF CLARITY
www.hell-flower.com/clarity
Trim, interesting site from the woman behind The Millennium Goths project, with little journal (live at www.livejournal.com/~meerno), and various side projects.

CONCERNING THE GOTHIC SUBCULTURE
www.suba.com/~rcarrier/Goth/index2.html
Learned approach with link to faqs.

CONVERGENCE 2
http://bway.net/~slutboy/C2index.html
www.digitalangel.com/convergence
www9.pair.com/lincecum/convergence/index.html

CONVERGENCE 3
http://ativan.netdesign.net/~moses/c3
www.perkigoth.com/pictures/convergence/c3/default.asp?image=7
www.sff.net/people/lucy-snyder/c3
www.toreadors.com/tlb/c3tea.html

CONVERGENCE 4
http://bitsy.sub-atomic.com/~moses/c4/index.html
http://dispatches.azstarnet.com/zoe/1998/0828.htm
http://members.aol.com/skintwonyc/c4.html
http://whimsy.neverwhen.net/c4
www.digitalangel.com/c4
www.geocities.com/SoHo/9306/C4
www.marge-central.demon.co.uk/convergence
www.mtholyoke.edu/~dbono/c4.htm
www.tarogue.net/goth/convergence
www.tyranny.com/~raphrat/C4
www.virulent.org/converg4

CONVERGENCE 5
http://ativan.netdesign.net/~moses/c5
http://bitsy.sub-atomic.com/~moses/c5/index.html
http://home.tampabay.rr.com/krysania/convergence5.html
http://members.tripod.com/~Sarai_The_Cat/convergence.html
http://www.inviolate.com/c5/index.html
http://members.tripod.com/tww_fanfic/stories/p-t/sk_Convergence_5.htm

www.darkart.net/C5/C5.htm
www.geocities.com/BourbonStreet/8976/c5.htm
www.geocities.com/SoHo/Studios/2052/c5.html
www.neverwhen.net/c5
www.nola-goth.org/c5
www.perkigoth.com/features/convergence/c5
www.synaesthetic.net/netgoth/c5/photos/
c5007.html
www.thechateau.org/~kellin/c5
www.toreadors.com/tlb/c5

CONVERGENCE 6

http://eye-of-newt.com/nazareth/Pictures/
Happenings/00.05.28%20Convergence
http://sinister.com/~ianh/C6
www.convergence6.com
www.gothics.org/c6
www.josienutter.com/converge
www.mydarkstar.com/convergence6.htm
www.swcp.com/~celine/pics.html
www.thechateau.org/~kellin/c6

CONVERGENCE VII

www.convergence7.com

CONVERGENCE – HISTORY

www.virulent.org/converg4/past.html

CORPORATE GOTH

www.waningmoon.com/corpgoth
'The stereotype of Goths being either
unemployed or working in simple jobs,
such as mailrooms and record stores,
may fit some, but for others, especially
the older Goths, this simply is not an
option. Despite the romantic appeal of
such a "non-mundane" life, many of us
prefer the comforts that money can
provide. Perhaps we are "sell outs" as we
put fashion aside for the sake of our pro-
fession, but I like to see these "corporate
Goths" as being intelligent enough to
know when to adapt to one's surround-
ings to take advantage of the benefits the
mundane world can offer. After all, looks
alone does not make a Goth. This is a
work in progress. Your experiences are
most welcome. E-mail your thoughts,
ideas, comments, death threats, etc (to
corpgoth@waningmoon.com).' This is a *brilliant* site, with relevant sections. Survival:
'Dress in a manner that is comfortable
for your co-workers (within reason).
Compromise enough to establish a
good working relationship with your co-
workers.' Networking: 'Networking is a
must in the corporate world... we corporate Goths should stick together! Use this
area to leave your contact information and

share a bit about how you deal with being
a Goth in a professional environment.'
Professions: This is where people give
advice on how you're likely to be treated.
Fashion: What does and doesn't work.
Plus, seriously busy discussion forum,
nice galleries, and t-shirts, stickers,
bumper stickers, mugs and...lanyards (?)

COVEN OF BLACK ROSES

www.covenroses.com/coven
A little clique of Goth sites.

CREATE YOUR OWN DARKLY GOTHIC POEM

www.deadlounge.com/poetry/index.html
Brilliantly funny site, with five types
available, to prove just how shit poetry
really is. The Supernatural Violence &
Horror Darkly Gothic Poem, The Fear of
Religious Persecution Darkly Gothic
Poem, The Eternal Love of Vampires
Darkly Gothic Poem, The Black Abyss of
Righteous Hatred Darkly Gothic Poem
(defective). Using the Goth-O-Matic
Poetry Generator I chose The Feeling
Very Sorry for Yourself Darkly Gothic
Poem, making choices without looking. I
tried and so, pray silence, for... 'Devoid of
Love'. 'The night falls in a heavy, suffocating cloak, entwined are we, The salvation
for which you pine flares once, then dies,
crushed by the all-encompassing dark.
All hope must sicken and die. Your heart
desires no more. How could you tear us
asunder? Our dark emotions surround
us, crying. We are fallen.' Please, please,
up off your knees. No autographs!

THE CRIMSON KISS OF THE WEEK

www.angelfire.com/electronic/violetdome
How many hours a week do these girls
spend looking out for new sites to add
their pics to?

THE CRYPT OF MIRFEUS

http://come.to/Mirfeus

C✳B✳RG✳TH

www.cybergoth.f2s.com
Here you can meet likeminded
enthusiasts for the culture that dare
not explain its own name.

DARK-ANGELS – EROTICA

http://dark-angels.com

DARK ANGELS

www.angelfire.com/ct2/DarkAngels/intro.html

DARK ART

www.darkart.net
Truly a mesmerising experience, with a
huge selection of Convergence sites,
Dressed To Thrill, Gothcon, the Mistress
Pryne one, plus Goth House, two Goths
Invade Disneyland trips (classic pics!),
and Hallowmas. You'll be there hours.

DARK DREAMZ GOTHIC PHOTOGRAPHY

www.geocities.com/Athens/Acropolis/5855
Old Philly Goth site that fell into disuse.
Some nice band shots.

DARK FAIRIES

www.darkfairies.co.uk
Gothic Medieval Victorian and fetish
photography plus a short bio of
Stéphane Lord. One of the truly great
colour photographers on the scene, if
not *the* best! Amazing galleries to adore:
Faeries & Angels, Classical, Gothic,
Urban (you *have* to see the white taxi
pic, gallery 1), Shiny and Others.

DARK FLYER

www.darkflyer.de
Impressive German Goth community
site packed with services.

DARK LOVE AND ROMANCE

http://kiss.to/darkloveromance
Bryan K Watson's site for People,
Bands, Architecture, Statuary, Erotica.
Nearly all good. Dreamy Squid shots.
Outdoor models look restless.

DARK MAGIC

www.darkmagic.de
German Goth sites – covering bands, parties, gigs, comics, mp3, chat and forum.

DARK PRINCESS OF THE WEEK

www.geocities.com/Vienna/Choir/7032/index.html
Old, with most links dead, but nice pics.

DARK RENAISSANCE – DARK ARTISTS

www.geocities.com/SoHo/Workshop/8053/
index.html

DARK SHADOWS

www.darklust.gothic-domain.com/index.html
Great Goth photos, plus info on
Banshees, Faith And The Muse, and
Diva Destruction.

THE DARK SIDE

www.darkerside.virtualempire.com/index.html

Promises Horror Fact, Fiction and Folklore from around the world.

THE DARK SIDE
www.vamp.org
Very good site, with the Image database you'll encounter through many searches, the Siouxsie & Banshees home page, plus the Gothic page with the international clubs listings. Strangest part is the small Dark Side gallery.

DARK SIDE OF THE NET
www.darklinks.com
Although no longer the most up to date, this has to be the primary Goth source *of all time*. It has fantastic depth, and continues to be updated regularly. Carrie Carolin's site may now seem pretty drab, but it all works well and if you haven't got this bookmarked it is still essential, and by far *the* most important site in this book. News and updates service via: http://groups.yahoo.com/group/darklinksnews

DARK VOICES
http://blood-dance.net/discographies/index.html

DARKENED PAGAN OF THE WEEK
www.geocities.com/RainForest/Jungle/1420/dpw.html
Unbelievable!!! The first thing I see is another Josie Nutter set of photos!!! Looking dead charming and all, as usual, but how *does* she do it?

A DARKER SHADE OF BLEAUX
www.angelfire.com/la/Bleaux
'A surreal gothic playground?' Music – nice choice of bands and links, Poetry – loads, but I'm allergic. Vampire – boring, Rants – dreary, Gothic Topics – ah, here are well argued, beautifully written accounts of Goth and its meaning and 'Defining Goth: Origins of Modern Gothic Culture'. The real stars of this site are the funny ones. How Not To Be Goth, Goths Are Wusses, How To Live Through The Embarrassment And Torture Of Family Gatherings and Why You're Not Gothic, all by Thurmond. This man is a seriously witty and entertaining writer. I've bookmarked this so I can read his journals, and I would advise anyone of the non-Manson, snobby variety to do exactly the same. Also, cute postcards – love those gargoyles – and although it says it's an e-zine based on submissions, I think it's an all-purpose lab of brilliance.

A DARKER SHADE OF PALE
http://clubs.yahoo.com/clubs/adarkershadeofpale
A forum for Goths of any colour. 'Welcome to A Darker Shade of Pale. This club was made for people of colour of all ages, genders, and sexual persuasions who happen to be active in the Gothic, wiccan, artistic, club or vampire lifestyle who choose to enjoy life with a "darker" twist... All we ask is that you respect the other members within the club, as we respect you. Or, we will find you, attach your limbs to four separate horses, and watch gleefully as you are quartered.' Consider yourself told!

DARKEST BLACKNESS, BLACKEST DARKNESS
http://uk.geocities.com/lonelyaesthetic
A mixture of a guide to Leeds through one Goth's eyes, plus a few mini-points about Goth, the most pertinent being irritation with older Goths rubbishing what this tries to do. It isn't the greatest site you'll see, but things need time to develop, and pompous bores criticising is a hindrance. (The 'inter rivalry' section makes a cute point that these critics are probably unable to remember what it feels like to be young.)

DARKFACE
www.multimania.com/darkface
Interesting French info/zine site for Electro-Gothique. Good info on Dead Souls Rising and Digital Blood and Exitium and great Gothique Art section, along with fine galleries of French Goths out and about, dating back to 1991.

THE DARKLY GOTHIC NIGHT BEFORE CHRISTMAS
www.deadlounge.com/xmas/1998/index3.html
Very good poetry pastiche.

DARKWAVE.ORG.UK
www.darkwave.org.uk
The premier UK site, bar none, acting as it does as a giant teat for net.goth to suckle on (*and* vice versa), along with its generic sections on mailing lists, FAQs, bands, communities, clubs, shops, humour, e-zines and music downloads. There's online chat and minuscule downloads. Slashgoth too, where the topics come alive and you can rant to your heart's content about what they are highlighting or what you want to impart. Or to quote the people responsible, 'Slashgoth (/goth) aims to be a news and discussion forum for netgoths, in the style of slashdot/goth is a service provided by darkwave.org.uk, but a whole pile of people moderate and contribute to it.' It's nowhere near some American or German sites but it's by far and away the best this country has, and it grows all the time, as do the dead links. Naughty people!

DARKWAVES.ORG
www.darkwaves.org.uk
Mission, plus Goth site. Mainly pics right now.

DEAD BABIES
www.sonic-boom.com/pig
A site that covers all manner of Goth and Deathrock bands who have bitten the dust, in a graceful fashion. In German, and in need of some contributions. It also has modern reviews.

DEAD TO THE WORLD
www.gospelcom.net/deadworld
Christian Goth-Industrial site, which had its own zine, but the thing looks deserted.

DEATH BY MOONLIGHT – RADIO
www.dirge.net/fox

DEN-SORTE-HULE
http://home.no.net/sorthule
Not being able to speak Norwegian I don't know but it seems personal, yet offers a wide variety of clues as to the Goth scene in Norway.

DER KALTE STERN
www.carcasse.com/derkaltestern
Dark-ish Electro-Wave, possibly based in Brazil as it's through Carcasse, and site is available in Portuguese and English. Bio, pics, lyrics, downloads.

DER LACHENDE PROJECT
www.der-lachende-prophet.de
In German, so I wasn't sure what it was, but it contains fantastic art and brilliant band photos.

THE DEVILISH DELIGHT OF THE WEEK
www.geocities.com/SunsetStrip/Underground/1037/devdelite.htm
Dead, but you have the whole '98 archive to explore.

DOOM IT YOURSELF
http://clik.to/auntbat
Two things, one on corsets, with a few articles and pointers, but at Cheapskates a huge list of short articles about various cost-saving ways to approach making or getting things.

DREAMS AND DARKNESS
http://homepage.ntlworld.com/submu/ddv7/dreams.html
Poetry and prose, where you join The Ruined. Also features Byron and Poppy Z Brite.

DRESS THE GOTH!
www.waningmoon.com/dressthegoth

DRIP DRIP DRIP
www.surgikill.co.uk/grind/nav/satnav.htm
Otherwise known as The Surgikill Grind Alliance. Site featuring Katscan, Squid and Mechanical Cabaret.

ECTOPHILE'S GUIDE
www.smoe.org/ectoguide/guide.cgi?genre/ethereal/amber.asylum
Interesting guide with visitor comments on a list of Ethereal artists, but few links. I checked out their Ambient – same thing – but it is useful for finding intelligent descriptions.

ELAISTED
www.elaisted.com
One of those sites with galleries of arty girls pouting and preening. It is beautifully done, and the photos are exceptional quality, but certain pages jam.

ELYSIUM PLAYGROUND
www.elysiumplayground.com
A site dedicated to the Goth Community in Tallahassee, FL, but it's more than that, because it's a photographic oasis for beautiful Goth photos, all done by the Walker 1812 man who also lurks at: www.walker1812.com. He's even done all the locals as suspects holding mug shots boards. There are parties, cons, club nights, weddings, friends. It's a *magnificent* experience.

THE EMBRACE – RADIO HISTORY
http://embracecfbu.cjb.net

ENCLAVE
www.jesusfreak.com/enclave

The Christian Net Goth resource. Excellent Christian Doom Metal, Art, Community, Music, News, Library, Link. See peoples art; photos, drawings and some excellent prints by Kara Clark. Chat forum and directory. It's only in the Library you get Christian stuff: Bible passages, etc. This is why I like this site. The directory is excellent and unlike all other Christian Goth sites this is about Goth, for people who have Christian beliefs. It's not Goths going on about Christianity.

ENERGY ZONE
www.energyzone.it
Interesting Italian site with tons about bands, events and releases, with some great photos.

ERRONEOUS ASSUMPTIONS
www.Gothic.net/~mayfair/trenchcoat
More Littleton related outpourings.

ETHEREALGOTH.COM
www.etherealgoth.com/home.html
Fabulous ethereal resource. Gig list (ambitious international idea!), bands, fan clubs.

EVERYBODY WANTS TO BE A CAT
www.liquid2k.com/gothcat
It's... Gothic Cat Of The Week, including theme songs. Shadow (a 2001 winner) has her own page – www.angelfire.com/electronic/cynthetiksex/shadow.html – and the second pic is brilliant. Wonderful. Sean Brennan gets credited as being partly responsible, along with Spoonhead.

EXPERIMENT WITH BEAUTY
www.darkside.nu/experimentwithbeauty/main.html
Fabienne's X of Y site for those with good sites. Pic/link.

FAIRY GOTHMOTHER
http://groups.yahoo.com/group/fairygothmother
Gothic Mentoring e-list. 'The purpose of this list is to provide a place for young Goths to meet and meet older Goths. A great place to get advice from some of us who have been around the block a few times.' I joined this for a while before having to concentrate on the book. It was fun. No elitist idiots anywhere.

FETISH KITTIES – OF THE WEEK, ETC
www.geocities.com/Paris/Louvre/2612/fetishmain.html

THE FOSSIL DUNGEON
http://users.erols.com/tsbb/fdungeon/index.htm
This looks really promising, a label which offers limited edition CD-R releases of new Ethereal, Ambient or Experimental artists. Lovely site too.

FRED'S OFFICIAL DARK SITES MUSIC INDEX
www.freddark.net
Great bands links galore, plus a wonderful selection of photos taken live by Fred. Abscess, Collection, Corpus Delicti, Creatures, Cure, Die Form, Faith & The Muse etc. Definitely check that.

A GATHERING OF THE DIVERSE
http://communities.msn.com
Just key in the title.

GAWTH KRAFTE
www.geocities.com/RainForest/Vines/2010/GawthKrafteX.html
'In other words... this is a page for the dark and/or glittery of heart, who are tired of learning how to make adorably bubble-lettered coat hanger deely-bobs. We want some creepy crafts! Some spooky schemes! {and some perky projects, too!} There are plenty of ways to make that pink ruffle into black lace, and replace a baby blue sponged finish with black and pewter crackle. Please note: I am often using the spelling "gawth" as opposed to "Goth". This is partly because I think I'm just the bee's knees, and I can get away with it, but it's also partly because I'm trying not to lay down the gospel on what is and is not Gothic.' What is in it? Gothic decorating tips, covering a vast range of material. It is as huge as it is cute and informative.

GAWTHPALLOR
www.geocities.com/RainForest/Vines/2010/gawthpallor.html
Good grief!

GAY GOTH NETWORK
www.gaygoth.net
Horse imagery? Meet dream dates, read fiction – about a boi and a ghost he falls for.

GE
www.gothic.net/~godeater
Ancient tribute. With a smattering of nice Goth people photos in b&w.

GHETTOGOTH
www.ghettogoth.com
Great frontpage, like Vortex comics (circa *Love & Rockets*) but only small diary inside, with some good live pics. (See also Emulsion Art in Sites Of Interest.)

GLITTER GOTH 101
http://members.tripod.com/~Abracadaver
Abracadaver's Guide to Goth/Glam/New Wave/Mansonite and Otherwise Unusual Makeup . And the reason? 'After watching Ricki Lake, attending numerous Goth clubs, fan conventions, Marilyn Manson concerts, and hanging out at Denny's at 3 am, I came to the realization that a lot of people are in desperate need of help with their makeup.' Hardly authoritative, but it is simple to follow.

GLITTER WHORE OF THE WEEK
http://alittlenothing.com/glitter/razorblades

GLOSSARY OF LITERARY GOTHIC TERMS
www2.gasou.edu/facstaff/dougt/goth.html
Seriously wonderful site, with so many surprises, and historical pointers intertwined.

GO GOTH!
www.deadlysins.com/gogoth/index.htm

GOTH
www.spod.org/~pen/pen/goth.htm
The only person in the world who believes Led Zep had something to with Goth. Long since dead, but interesting, if only to see how wide of the mark people can be.

GOTH 90S UK
http://members.tripod.com/syn_thetic/syn_goth90.htm
Timothy C. (of band Synthetic) explores the evolution of the UK Goth scene over the past decade... 7237 words long.

GOTH-A-BILLY
www.gothabilly.net
Rude women, fiction, poetry, bands, cars.

GOTH AGE ART
http://digilander.iol.it/gothgeart

Brilliant Italian site that is semi-personal and others are invited to send in articles, photos, scans of art and suchlike. It just makes you want to do something.

GOTH AUCTIONS
www.gothauctions.com

THE GOTH-BIBLE
www.goth-bible.com
Hasn't been going long, but looking good already.

THE GOTH CARD
http://apocalypse.org/pub/u/hilda/ssd/gcard.html
'The Goth Card is laminated for immortality, with a pinch of stardust for luck. The back of the card says, simply, "Goth," and the front reads: This card entitles the Bearer to mope, wear black, write poetry, exhibit anachronistic taste in clothing, weep openly (even in a nightclub), smoke cloves, drink snakebite, enjoy highly emotional music, eschew the use of gender-specific pronouns, read out-of-date literature, ignore fashion, occupy large amounts of dancefloor space; and, in general, notice, describe, celebrate, acknowledge, draw, sculpt, paint, photograph, dance, and otherwise express the manifold and under appreciated wonders of Darkness.'

GOTH CAT RESCUE
www.geocities.com/Petsburgh/Zoo/2085
Apparently it's harder for black cats to be adopted! Links to cats available through shelters across the states. 'Whether because of superstition, prejudice, or simply because they blend into the shadows in the back of the cage, black cats are statistically less likely to be adopted than more brightly coloured felines. As those of you who had the misfortune to live in the rural United States in the early eighties may remember, there was a time when fear of Satanism was so strong in our land that actual mass panics and small-scale riots broke out at times. During that era, many animal shelters adopted policies to prevent black cats from being adopted on or just before Halloween for fear they would be used as sacrifices. Many of these policies are still in place, and even where they are not, certain shelters may be leery of you if you show up around Oct. 31st in full Goth

costume. Use your own judgement here. If you absolutely must have a new cat, and it's Halloween, you're likely to do better if you dress conservatively. If, on the other hand, dressing down feels like a moral compromise to you, try waiting.' What? Go there in a fluorescent sack if you have to! Just get down there and save them!

GOTH CODE 98
http://ativan.netdesign.net/~moses/gc98.cgi?_form

GOTH COUPLE OF THE WEEK
http://cybergeisha.org/couple/
Beautifully simple site, but unlike the usual 'X of' sites (of which this is the best by a mile) it usually has a delightful story of how people met, and is being written when the bloom of love is still freshest. Adorable.

GOTH GOOSE OF THE WEEK
www.gothgoose.net
Elderly geese archive.

GOTH HOUSE
www.darkart.net/house/house.htm
Extraordinary site about a house completely transformed into a Goth masterpiece. Can't say I could put up with it but if this is your style it's an amazingly detailed piece of work, and it is in the area where Theda Bara once lived, which is a serious plus, and the

Christmas pics are adorable. (See also Mystress Prynne – Goth people.)

GOTH HUNTING
www.internettrash.com/users/salatrel/hunting.htm
Well, *I* thought it was funny.

GOTH JOKES
www.geekhaus.co.uk/gothjoke
Allegedly.

GOTH NETWORK.COM
www.gothnetwork.com

GOTH OR NOT
www.gothornot.com
Like Am I Goth or Not except you need to register. Slightly more obvious in content and hardly used. Has potential, especially as it gives you a chance to establish yourself in their mini community.

GOTH PHOTOS:
Guaranteed 100% Graveyard Free
www.asc.upenn.edu/usr/cassidy/pix/goth/1.html
A brilliant selection of studio, live or portrait (social/personal/posed) photos. Don't miss this. Stunning Otto's Daughter selection.

A GOTH PRIMER
www.sfgoth.com/primer

GOTH QUOTE GENERATOR
www.brunching.com/toys/toy-gothquotex.html

GOTH TARTS – ARCHIVE
http://members.tripod.com/~blue123/gothtart.htm
Men and Women of the... last millennium.

THE GOTH TEST
www.geocities.com/SoHo/Lofts/8869/gothtest.html

GOTH TRAILER PARK – COMIC
www.gothtrailerpark.com

THE GOTH WORKOUT
http://members.tripod.com/~LadyJane69/asylum/workout.html
'I shall be the first to admit that this sounds like a cheesy idea, but noticing the increasing number of tubby-Goths out there, it is not so bad. I feel it is my duty as a health-conscious human being to bring this useful list of exercises, carefully fine tuned to the needs of the non-waify Goth, onto the web. I have included a few dietary tips to slimming down without taking crack, and a blurb about the benefits of muscle tone over the starved look.'

GOTHCON 2002
www.gothcon.com
Site for annual Goth/Industrial (etc) festival that is a benefit for HIV sufferers. If you look under Past Events there are links to loads of photo selections at the bottom. These will take you interesting places. Dana Dark's pics are wonderful.

GOTHFORALLRACES
http://clubs.yahoo.com/clubs/gothforallraces

GOTHGRRLZ ON THE NET
www.lollyland.com/gothette/index.html
There are some very lovely portraits here, as well as straightforward snaps that work brilliantly (Amandaz and her pumpkin being the best example).

GOTHIC
www.geocities.com/jungleprincess97/gothic.html
I though this might be a particularly ironic joke at first. There's nothing going on!

'GOTHIC' – WEIRD STORY
www.5thpanel.com/gothic.html

THE GOTHIC ANGELS PROJECT
www.gothic-angels.org
More post-Littleton angst and plans for 'understanding'. Perspective, people! I stopped the British papers going into overdrive in about a day, by contacting responsible journos, and I'm sure someone did the same in the States. Websites on the other hand went into emotional overdrive.

GOTHIC ARCHES
http://dearborncounty.com/gothicarches
This is a B&B near the Ohio river!

THE GOTHIC ART OF MARK BELL
www.markbell.com/gothic.htm
English, German, or Spanish. Some mad stuff going on here. Check out the hell-throne, and you'll get the Giger homage. Prints, and the less than aesthetic mugs t-shirts and mouse/rat pads but the Cloister Graveyard On Acid print looks great. Also takes you to: NecroMatrix.com - www.necromatrix.com which offers online communication with the dead no less! Quite funny. And Quad Cranium, for you technocrats: www.evor.com/Quad-C/Quad-1.htm

GOTHIC ART PHOTOGRAPHY
http://members.iinet.net.au/~gothic1/frames.html
The work of Leslie Webb, Perth photographer. Body-painted Goth girls with antlers Moody portraits. Limited edition prints (25 copies only) Single prints $150 (Australian) 16x20 inches – and he makes knives and swords, so no insults!

GOTHIC ARTS REVIVAL
www.geocities.com/SoHo/Museum/4430/index.htm
'The Gothic Revival is a project dedicated to showing the world what we are capable of. This page will have a compilation of Gothic Art and information on the History, Anthropology and Philosophy of the culture.'

GOTHIC AUCTIONS
www.gothicauctions.com/index.cgi

GOTHIC AUKTION
www.gothic-auktion.org

GOTHIC BABE OF THE WEEK
http://industrialgothic.com/gbotw
This is the mob who started a craze, and Boi of the week followed. They have a huge archive dating back to 1996. Over two million visits since then. 8,000 this week. Monumental.

GOTHIC BEAUTIES
www.geocities.com/azwrath_devine/bab.html
Girls, Girls, Girls... and their websites.

GOTHIC BEAUTY
www.gothicbeauty.cjb.net
Site awaiting Girl or Boi submissions.

GOTHIC BITCH OF THE WEEK
http://thunder.prohosting.com/~gothic/bitch.html

GOTHIC BOY OF THE WEEK
www.gothboyoftheweek.com/current.htm
'And his shall be the face of an Angel.' But not always, going on the evidence.

GOTHIC CLASSIFIEDS
www.gothic-classifieds.com/indexx.html
Radio, forum, chat, Cryptbabes, CryptBois, GC gallery – these are fantastic (leaving aside the images whipped out of my GR book). This Dodger who's in charge of the site is one talented bastard when it comes to art!!! The 'Outsiders' magazine section is interesting. Great site.

THE GOTHIC CHAMBER
http://members.tripod.com/~Gothic_Chamber
Including the Occult Shop, her online store. Crap layout belies great contents. Big Beautiful Goth, Greeting Cards, Make-overs, Personal section, with a thing about Kate Bush.

GOTHIC COURSES
www-sul.stanford.edu/mirrors/romnet/iga
This could provide further impetus and ammunition to go for a specialist degree.

GOTHIC CULTS AND GOTHIC CULTURES
www.sfu.ca/english/iga2001/index.htm
Conference, which may have gone but perhaps the site remains?

GOTHIC DESIRE OF THE WEEK
– ARCHIVE
www.batalie.com/desire

GOTHIC DISTOPIA
www.geocities.com/gothdistopia
Select Gothic community, keen to weed out the weirdoes first (or encourage them, depending on their preferences). Gallery, board etc. It's dead-ish, but pics are cute and some links worth pursuing.

GOTHIC DREAMS AND VISIONS
www.geocities.com/Athens/Forum/1059/gothicdreams.html
Strange little discursion on the shamanic nature of Goth visions, tied in here with the painful themes of buffalo slaughter. It does make sense, so have a look.

GOTHIC – EINE INNENANSICHT FUR AUSSENSEITER
www.gothicculture.de

GOTHIC FAQs
www.darkwave.org.uk/more.php?cat=FAQs
They may be general, they may be specific, but it's hard to see what purpose most serve. A bunch of them are corralled by darkwave.org.

GOTHIC FASHION
http://groups.yahoo.com/group/gothfashion
E-list run by Morbid Outlook, and so big that membership is being restricted. If you want to join you need to explain why. 'This list was created to discuss fashion from lush, past periods to the futuristic fetish. How to find and make your own is part of what this group is about.' Site with links galore:
www.ncgoth.com/gothfashion

GOTHIC FESTIVAL
www.gothicfestival.de
All the news you'd need.

GOTHIC FOR CHRIST (CHRISTIAN)
www.geocities.com/SunsetStrip/Theater/4299/index.html
One of the strangest histories of Goth ever, which suggests Goth was a backlash against colourful disco, rather than an emotional and artistic step on from Punk which had many of its original roots in gay clubs (i.e. disco!). Plus some pictures of Christian Goths who look decidedly strange.

THE GOTHIC GARDEN
www.gothic-garden.de
Fabulous photography site. Stunning statuary in atmospheric surrounds, even gargs in situ, museum exhibits, portraits etc. They are immaculate and you can buy limited edition prints. A 20x30 cm print is 24DM. That's about eight pounds!

GOTHIC GODDESSES OF THE MONTH
www.geocities.com/SouthBeach/Palms/3320
'Beautiful Gothic Women From, Around The Globe' it says here. Long dead.

THE GOTHIC GROUPIE PAGE
www.rosegardenofwhores.com/gothicgroupie
HelleBelle's site is hilarious and inventive, but also there's a mixture of truth in there, apart from missing the obvious trick. You need to book a room in the hotel where the band are staying, and then you're instantly separated from any of the lesser beings gathered and giggling outside. But this has all you will ever really need to know, and there's even a Gothic Groupie Of The Month award.

GOTHIC HELP RETREAT
http://victorian.fortunecity.com/postmodern/197/gothic/gothretreat.htm
Goth imagery advice tips and links.

GOTHIC HOLIDAYS
http://members.tripod.com/darknessw/holiday.htm
Nope, not package tours but celebrating certain days – Valentines, Halloween, Easter and Christmas. It's a breezy little guide of playful things to do. The Xmas tree ideas are cool.

THE GOTHIC INTELLIGENCE TEST
www.obscure.org/wombat/amusements/int-test.html

GOTHIC LINK WHORE OF THE WEEK
http://members.tripod.com/~Batty_Page/glw.html

GOTHIC LINKS – Germany
www.gothic-links.de
All in German and it's one of those which links to some of the sites listed within their site. Meaning restricted viewing, but it is worth persevering with, being pure quality.

THE GOTHIC LITERATURE PAGE
http://members.aol.com/iamudolpho/basic.html
Intro, Resource, Bibliography, Gothic Terms, Graveyard Poetry, Gothic Bluebooks etc, Short Stories, Course Syllabi, Critical Sources, Gothic Texts, and much more.

GOTHIC LITERATURE READ BY ROMANTIC WRITERS
www2.gasou.edu/facstaff/dougt/gothic.htm
'A list of Gothic works read by the major writers of the period 1780-1830.' It goes into detail, plus there is A Glossary of Literary Gothic Terms, which is brilliant.

GOTHIC MARTHA STEWART
www.toreadors.com/martha/index.html
Okay, we don't know her, but it's a cross between Delia Smith, Changing Rooms and Ground Force, for Goths. This site sprung from the hypothetical question: 'What if Martha Stewart was a Goth?' For the uninitiated, Martha Stewart is a phenomenally successful domestic arts champion and stylemaker who advocates an upscale but not ostentatious style of living which has a lot to do with making things yourself and finding new uses for the old, instead of just buying everything new. And so it goes on into every aspect of the home, with shopping tips, décor, wedding items, and all-round general clues and resources. It's all about The Ambience. Invaluable.

GOTHIC PALACE
www.gothicpalace.com
Nice basic site from Borgabesh Milan, who has a CD out herself, which you can get from her online shop of CDs and vids.

GOTHIC PARENTS
e-list: www.gothicparents.com
bbs: www.gothicparents.za.net

GOTHIC PEOPLE
www.gothicpeople.de
Goths Internationally.

GOTHIC PET OF THE WEEK
www.geocities.com/Paris/Salon/1384

THE GOTHIC PUEBLO
http://members.tripod.com/~gothicpueblo
Artist Daniel Martin Diaz and his interesting work.

GOTHIC RADIO
www.gothicradio.com
In a shock shift into surliness, I'm not going to tell you what this is. You'll have to guess.

GOTHIC-ROSE: INFINITE DREAMS
http://gothicrose.hypermart.net/story.html
Unusual. An interactive story where you choose what happens next. She also has three webrings going.

THE GOTHIC SANTA PICS ARCHIVE
www.rosegardenofwhores.com/gothsantapix
Pics of Goths posing with department store Santas. Very cool.

GOTHIC SCOUTS
www.gothicscouts.com
Occult fan Simone, who looks fairly scary. 'In a nutshell, the Gothic Scouts is a online community for people of the Gothic type persuasion type... thing... like that. You know. Like, yeah. Gothic Scouts Version 4.0 started officially on August 8th, 2000. We're now taking a completely different focus, moving from Gothic humour site that got blown *way* out of proportion to full Gothic community. We're now working on implementing the things that GS members have wanted to see since we first started the page, such as a full handbook, badges, more content, and other things that we aren't going to list because, well, it's a surprise.'

GOTHIC SCOUT MEMBER SEARCH
www.gothic.net/~mage/goth/scouts/memlist/search

GOTHIC SHORTCAKE OF THE WEEK
http://members.tripod.com/~LordBiran/shortcake.html
'A Shortcake is someone that is generally sweet to everyone, takes care of their friends, and goes out of his or her way to do something for someone else.' Not surprisingly this site about Goth niceties ran for precisely eight entries. Their photos remain as a testament to their good work.

THE GOTHIC SOCIETY
www.gothicsociety.net
'We will seek out those who ridicule and berate us and seek to educate them and help them see the beauty of the Gothic Culture. We will seek out those who seek to harm us both publicly and physically and teach them through patience and understanding that we mean no harm. We will educate parents, the media and the religious community that the dark world of Gothic is but a crucial part of our identity.' Good luck with that! An almighty mission. Really a lovely site, which you ought to admire, with plenty to appreciate on books, photos, art and music.

GOTHIC STEREOTYPE
www.peerlessdesign.com/gothicstereotype/gothicstereotype.html

GOTHIC TEARS
www.gothictears.com
Mainly poetry with rants.

GOTHIC THE GAME
http://gothicthegame.funonline.de

GOTHIC TOMB.COM
www.gothictomb.com
Jacqueline, the saucy mare responsible, has created a fantastic site. Loads of photos of her (nothing crude, you dirt-hounds!), and even her family. She's vaguely Buffy-like, and seems perpetually surprised by the camera, which is odd. Nice links, and there's the Gothic Tomb Shoppe:
www.cafepress.com/gothictomb
The site was down when I double-checked, but the shop wasn't so I'm assuming this was being redone.

GOTHIC TOP TEN – Nostalgia!
http://thycotic.com/gothic

GOTHIC UNDERGROUND
www.gothic-underground.com
Typically vast, thorough German site with all the interactive/community areas, plus interviews and reviews.

GOTHIC WORLD OF BANDS AND OTHER DARK STUFF

www.the-gothicworld.de/frames.htm
Big site with reviews, plenty of local scene news and interviews, all in German.

THE GOTHIC: MATERIALS FOR STUDY

www.engl.virginia.edu/~enec981/Group/title.html
More heavyweight gubbins, but easily digestible, so fear not. Introduction, Individual and Social Psychologies of the Gothic, The Female Gothic, The Gothic and the Supernatural, The Sublime and the Domestic, Gothic Drama, Annotated Bibliography.

GOTHICA – DARK FICTION

http://members.tripod.com/kailleaugh andersson

GOTHICAS AND GOTHICOS

http://clubs.yahoo.com/clubs/gothicasand gothicos
Club for Hispanic Goths.

GOTHICS GEGEN RECHTS
– GERMAN INFO

www.fortunecity.de/kraftwerk/bauhaus/149

GOTHICEYE

www.gothic-eye.co.uk
Formative stages for UK Goth resource site with decent worldwide links, although many are already dead.

GOTHIC.NET

www.gothic.net
Top quality writing on a variety of topics, including music. Site has usual chat and board, but the difference is that if you want to pay subscription you can have access to new writing by established authors first. Brave scheme.

GOTHICK.NET

www.gothick.net
Undernet IRC spin-off.

GOTHIKKA

http://gothikka.hypermart.net/index.html
Busy auction place, tons of Goth stuff. A section on spells, with ratings on difficulty! A very odd section about ghosts in her house with details and photos! A lot of it looks like shit on her film considering how bad the pictures themselves are. Need to clean your camera girl!

LucyFurr

GOTHIXS

www.gothixs.com
Clothes, chat, free classified ads, messages, bitching. New site run by The Crow, not much there. Your involvement would change that.

GOTHIC LAND

www.gothicland.com
Lovely site featuring the usual interaction, with its own radio station, plus charts, band reviews, including English versions, fashion section and really good live events gig list section and photos. Still growing and one to watch.

GOTHLIKE GOTHIC & WITHCRAFT

http://huizen.dds.nl/~gothlike

GOTH.NET

www.goth.net
Formerly in Texas and now Australia, a resource with its main troubles behind it hopefully. Small at the moment and could use some member involvement to flesh out its contents.

GOTHPUNK

www.gothpunk.com

GOTHSIDE

http://members.dencity.com/smclean
Personal site of Zaranyzerak, and his invisible friend Sean McLean, with chat.

GOTHTARTS

www.gothtarts.co.uk
Sheffield club, and I like the logo, so thought I'd mention them again.

GOTHS AGAINST HATE

www.rosegardenofwhores.com/gah
Well intentioned and therefore rather dull, this site started after Columbine, with the intention of explaining that not all Goths are homicidal maniacs. Em... I think everyone knows that! 'It has been two days since the incident and already many Goths have talked about being harassed on the street, or have been mocked, ridiculed and threatened.' Well, that comes with the territory. There are some nice contemplatative essays.

GOTHS OF COLOUR

www.angelfire.com/oh4/gothsofcolor
Run by LuCyFurr, this is a fantastic site. She started it because she was feeling slowly excluded from a scene she feels has become increasingly lax, and she has faced some reactionary morons in her time. She also makes a great point, or twenty. 'For anyone who has ever searched the net, scouring for Goth pages, I am sure you have probably been struck by the complete lack of "difference". They all look alike! Same outfits, same backgrounds, same waify, high-nosed little snots with bad poetry. Back in the day, Goth was about being different. It did not have a "code of dress" or little subcategories. It was strength in numbers, and merely helped to identify us. But that is *all* it was. It didn't become some strict code until recently (and that goes for all the branches of perky Goth, angsty Goth, uber Goth, Industrial Goth, S&M Goth as well). But, if that is the way people want it to be... so be it. Here

comes the new chapter....Ethnic Goth of Color." Several sections: What Is A Bad Kitty: Her own personal rules and calm observations, which obviously fit other beings too. What Is Goth? Yes, the usual but written well for once. From a painful perspective and a gloriously defiant one. With a neat sense of what original Goth did, compared to the sloths of today. Becoming An Elder Goth: Facing up the to the big 30. She makes this more dramatic than it need be but there's still a point. Links (including the Goths Of Colour forum board (http://pub41.ezboard.com/bg0c78071) And I love the way at the end of the contents page there is a dismissive 'oh, and about the vampire stuff' which leads into a charming rant. 'Let me say this; I do not entirely discredit this, but I (and anyone else with sense) knows that someone who claims to be 300 years old and yet doesn't have the ability to spell properly is a liar.' *Awesome* woman.

GOTHSTAPO
www.geocities.com/mangyflower/gothstapo.html
The Store For Fashion Fascists. Great site. Please understand it *is* a joke!

GOTHSTUDIA
www.tc.umn.edu/~gunn0025/studiadex.html
Archive of articles on Dark Culture.

GOTHTASTIC
www.thinks-he-can.freeserve.co.uk/Gothtastic.htm
Short, interesting part of a PhD.

GOTHWITCHES
www.geocities.com/gothwitches
Please keep an open mind they ask. I could barely keep my eyes open. Includes murky night-time pics of people outside Notre Dame!

THE GREAT BELOW
www.chez.com/greatbelow/index.htm
French Goth's site with journal, and ex-ploring literature, music and Goth generally. Not a site bulging with detail. Nice pics of her and her bloke, plus cemeteries and in one case combing the two. Currently just seems to be the photos up.

GRIMLY GLITTERY GOTHIC GHOUL OF THE BI MONTH
www.angelfire.com/fl/glitterbugnation
Great pics and loads of new people.

GRIZEL
www.geocities.com/waking_the_dead/grizel.html
Site combining details on fanzine and Warwickshire club of the same name.

HAIR!
www.btinternet.com/~quinnster1/hair/hair.html
Site about hair extensions, with Goth in mind. Very detailed.

THE HAPPY GOTH
www.thehappygoth.com
I wasn't particularly cheered by this.

THE HAVEN OF DARKNESS AND LIGHT
www.blood-dance.net/~yvain/goth
None of it worked except essay on Medieval Gothicism, which was good.

HELL'S BELLES
www.rosegardenofwhores.com/hellsbelles

HELL'S FURY
http://hells-fury.gothicunderworld.com
Another channel of the Underworld site. Pics, recommendations, etc.

THE HOUSE OF THREE RAVENS
www.disrupted.org/~hotr
New-ish, with features, station, board, etc. Needs contributors.

HOW TO BE GOTH (IN LESS THAN AN HOUR)
www.gothic.net/gothnicity
The crazy world of Gothnicity. Again, funny – 'Don't forget – genitals are great when pierced! I have a tire pressure gauge through mine and I couldn't be happier!' but there should be other sections too.

HOW TO DANCE GOTHIC
www.gothpunk.com/goth/how-to-dance-gothic.html

HOW TO SEDUCE A GOTH PRINCESS
www.macabre.net/seduce
AKA "How to seduce a Goth princess when you're an awful frog or just a vampiric old varlet. This is a new kind of Goth site. You all know the "Gothic girl of the week", "Gothic vampire of the week", "Gothic lesbian of the week", "Gothic Barbie of the week" etc... And what do you find there? Just a girl. A beautiful girl, maybe. Sometimes even a goddess. And you men always ask yourselves, "but how could she ever be my girlfriend? I love her but she's too good for me. I'm not Austin Powers!" Then you open a can of beer, looking deeply at the cold screen, and you start burping with desperate tears in your eyes. And every week it's the same. And you girls ? Aren't you tired hearing your boyfriend burp and saying deeply "Oh my Goth, she's gorgeous this week..."? So we have something new for both of you. Every month we'll invite a Goth Princess here. And reveal what we would do to try and seduce her. Of course we're not able to charm her every time. But we'll try! And always with an awesome and desperate plan. So all you guys, maybe you'll find some insane ideas here to inspire you. And you, beautiful Gothy girls, expect all the men to really try to seduce you in a different way from now on, not just buy you a drink.' (The best bits are their ludicrous attempts on Princesses they have tried so hard to seduce. Really, this *is* funny. They're mental. And their seductive powers ran out at the start of 2000 but that doesn't mean you shouldn't enjoy their labours.)

I'M SO GOTH...
www.geocities.com/SoHo/Cafe/4428/IAMSOGOTH.htm
Yawnorama.

IN PERPETUAL MOTION
www.ipmradio.com
Goth Industrial Electronic radio, although never all at once. One of the best.

INSANOSOMNIA
www3.sympatico.ca/insanasomnia
Punk Goth discussion/forum thing, in French.

INSTA GOTH KIT
http://sykospark.net/goth

INTERNATIONAL GOTHIC ASSOCIATION
www-sul.stanford.edu/mirrors/romnet/iga
Modern, weighty association. For the serious enthusiast.

JEWISH GOTHIC
www.jewishgothic.com
(Also links to Jewish Gothic Club: http://clubs.yahoo.com/clubs/jewishgothicclub)

It looks dire, which it isn't, so stick with it. There is a lot of beautiful writing here. Obviously quite an intellectual approach been taken: Architecture, Painting, Etching, Fiction, Poetry, Music, Cinema, Fashion, Sculpture, Orthography. Not much humour, but plenty of weirdness, as you'll see Frankenstein and the Golem, Jewish Vampirology, The Gothic Personality and Quiz – and they also plan something on Jewish Demonology.

KANAGAWA GOTHIC UNION
http://members.jcom.home.ne.jp/kanagoth/
Japanese site with interesting disco details, sparked into life because of the early-eighties bands (Decay, 1919, Ausgang). Also CD-Rs.

KATIE'S GOTH WANNA BE PAGE
http://angelfire.com/or/katesgothpage

KAZKI
www.interq.or.jp/rock/kazki
Very cool Japanese Goth site with emphasis on L'Arc En Ciel and Sex Machine Gun galleries – or paintings – plus a Gothic section that seems to involve illustrated fiction. Click 'off shot' for some great photos.

KEI'S NOVEL SITE
www3.ocn.ne.jp/~roserose
Japanese Goth site. It's in Japanese, but that makes the mystery all the more enjoyable.

KEMICAL.ORG
www.kemical.org
Some very nice pics, especially Absynthe Night.

KITTIE – A LAIR FOR LESBIANS GOTHS
www.angelfire.com/ca5/kittiegoth

LA NUIT OBSCURE
www.lanuitobscure.de
Great Goth site. Packed with everything you could desire, and some odd Gothic Ladies galleries – which are far more attractive than any of the sleazy sites – but the menu system is unexpected.

LADYBIRDS UK GOTHS
http://clubs.yahoo.com/clubs/ladybirdsukgoths
Club with a smart attitude. 'This is an argument free zone! Anyone being a continuous pain in the bum will be kicked out into a puddle.'

LE CERCLE NOIR
www.ultimatom.com/cerclenoir
Goth, vampiric, Metal-related, magick, occult, art, religion, etc. Absolutely brilliant French resource.

LENORE OF THE WEEK
http://lenore.mordea.com
Lovely idea but the reality is... same old, same old.

LES NITS EN BLANC I NIGRE
http://personal1.iddeo.es/blancinegre
Archives for Cure, Danse Soc, X-Mal, and Passions.

THE LITERARY GOTHIC
www.litgothic.com
The Web's Premier Guide To Gothic Literature. An amazing wealth of info. Stunning amount of authors, all with mini-bios, plenty of resource and library links, more than enough to satisfy, although maybe it's a bit too dry for its own good.

LOKI MUSIC
www.loki-music.co.uk
Didn't quite know where to put the scary looking Rev. Dr Loki, as this is part personal site, but he's a DJ, and does reviews!

LUSCIOUS BEAUTY (OF THE ETC)
www.zowwie.net/luscious/frames.html

A MACABRE GARDEN
www.dreamwater.com/sancho/macabre garden.html
Useful and thoughtful views on gardens and flowers for those seriously inclined.

MADIHA'S DOMAIN
www.geocities.com/madkins2000
'It's still about Gothism, its still gonna be dark and dreary, but will have more information to it.' Dreary? Are you sure that's right? Sheffield girl relocated to Canada but goes for the 'what is Goth?', stereotypes etc etc.

RUBY MALLACH
www.geocities.com/SunsetStrip/Towers/5411
Good live photos of Bauhaus, Alien Sex Fiend, Cure, Cramps, LAM etc.

MANCHESTER UNIVERSITY PRESS
http://catalogue.mup.man.ac.uk/acatalog/MUP
_online_catalogue_Gothic_Studies_12.html

Their new international heavyweight reference journal. A snip at £39 for three quarterly issues. Or £93 internationally. They must have devised the most expensive method possible!

MERMAID CADAVERS
www.angelfire.com/electronic/mindFvck
Into Placebo, Jack Off Jill, NIN. Some nice pics.

THE MIDNIGHT CAFÉ
www.angelfire.com/me3/MidnightCafe
Em... maybe it's just me but this is the biggest anticlimax ever? In fact, I love it!

MIDNIGHT DRIVE
www.enchantress.org.uk/index.html
Has tiny pages on Inkubus Sukkubus, Little Match Girl and Tarot.

MILLENNIUM GOTHS
www.hell-flower.com/y2kgoths
Brilliant site based on a survey conducted with Elder Goths, Baby Goths and Normals. Makes for very interesting reading. And you can still take part. http://clubs.yahoo.com/clubs/millenniumgoths

MOPEY GOTH CENTRAL
http://members.tripod.com/mopey_gawth
They say the idea is to bring laughter, as though bestowing largesse, and to show those who are mopey it is okay to laugh with you, but it's fairly boring.

MORE THAN MORTAL: FALLEN
www.morethanmortal.com
Interesting Goth domain with various sites – webrings/fanfic – of an intelligent and amusing hue.

MORKAOS
www.morkaos.com
A 'European Goth Indus Collective' which covers Austria, Czech, France, Germany, Slovakia, Switzerland and Poland, where it lists (regularly updated) gigs, parties and festival details. There are separate link sections for Central and Western Europe, and The World, which cover bands. Should have their zine element up by now, which will improve things.

MULTIMANIA
www.multimania.com/mortycyann
Canadian site, in French, with Goth advice and observations.

Photo © Lord Heathcliff. View From the Darkside @ www.chez.com/darkside

MUSIC FOLIO
http://musicfolio.com
Pleasant little round-up of reviews.

NACHT WANDLER
www.nacht-wandler.de
Big site by Regina and Susanne, German Goth girls running a big site, with features, reviews and some good live pics.

NAME THAT GOTH
www.cris.com/~jeniphir/babynames.html
Great site where people write in suggesting kiddie's names, under various genres. All suggestions welcomed. I like

Kerosene, if it's a girl, and with blokes it doesn't actually matter what you call them, as they still end up mental.

NATURAL GOTH OF THE MONTH
www.angelfire.com/goth/naturalgoth
As opposed to seriously disturbed Goths having sex with lay preachers in the open air, and singing lullabies loudly to the police who are trying to separate them?

THE NATURE OF GOTHIC
www.gothicnature.co.uk
Interesting and imaginative new label, run by David Quinn of Eternia. Already

done the Whitby comp, and many more planned. Low volume mailing list: gml-subscribe@Gothicnature.co.uk

NECROSOFT
www.gothic-classifieds.com/necrosoft
Magnificent central resource for all manner of things, in great depth. Classifieds, chat, Twilight, ICQList, Cryptbabes/Bois, GC Radio, Crypt Whispers Forum, Necrosoft Search, Necrosoft Metasearch. Art galleries: fan collections. Bands & Musicians: Goth band fanpages, Industrial fanpages. Businesses: bookshops, clothing, games: CCGs, Dark Fantasy Games, Dark Sci-Fi Games. Gothic Diversions: Dark Search, Dark Webrings, Goth Resources. Multimedia: mp3 sites, music servers, photographs, Occult & Pagan sites: Ritual Sorcery, Satanism/ Christian. Personal Webpages: General. Programs & chat: Downloads, Gothic chatrooms, webapplications. Reading materials: Dark Literature, online poetry books. Vampire sites: Vampire fanpages, Vampire pictures. Gothic Adult Sites: Requires Age Assertation.

NEMESIS – ITALY
http://web.tiscali.it/dark/dark.htm
Some nice artwork.

NEMESIS PROMOTIONS
http://www.nemesis.to
Hopefully this will remain as a fitting tribute to the work of Michael Johnson and his faithful crew, now that Nemesis has dwindled away. There's some nice photos left of the bands who played, with links. You can't blame Michael for stopping, having put so much of his personal money in, while trying to keep it independent. So good luck to Michael in whatever he chooses to do next, which so far includes writing (which he already does well at *Meltdown* magazine) and maybe even a return to DJ-ing, as he's ruling nothing out, but more intriguingly, working with his wife, Bunny Peculiar – check her out inside the Women Of Sodom site at: http://drawbridge.com/pkweb/pkweb_main/ pkindex.html – in a musical capacity, in what he suggests would realistically be Performance Art with something of an accessible charm. She wants to move away from what was fetish-like work,

and be 'weird', and Michael is only too happy to share the weirdness with her.

NET.GOTH DIRECTORY
www.legendsmagazine.net/pan/netgoth/
directory/world.htm
It's a nice old antique, which doesn't yield much... but this is where the map resides. Okay so there's no Goths in Guam or Mongolia, but apparently not many anywhere else, and why does Bulgaria link to Singapore? An epidemic of dead links, naturally.

NETGOTH.ORG.UK
www.netgoth.org.uk
The original, now eased back into regular activity. Over 8000 registered users although how many are non-UK is up for question. You can check out the map to see who's where and contact people, access information for social activities, and you're sharing all the Darkwave.org info anyway. There's a great gallery section, where the freaks come out.

NETGOTHS 2.0
www.netgoths.co.uk
A resource that evidently floundered. Approach wedding pics in Library with caution. It froze me, twice.

NEUE AESTHETIK MULTIMEDIA
www.asthetik.com
Despite the imposing title, this is a label/press site who do a very particular Goth thing. Bands involved include Judith, The Brickbats, Funhouse, Holy Cow and The Shroud. They also produce 'The Sentamentalist'. On top of that they have their conventional online store, which means you can irritate your friends after visiting by saying 'I just got back from NAM'. They'll hate you, and it'll all be your own fault.

THE NEW-GOTHIC MESSAGE BOARDS
http://pub33.ezboard.com/bthenewgothic
messageboards

NEW HALL GOTHIC KNITTING TRIANGLE
www.thelunaticfringe.f9.co.uk/chic1.htm#
You want Faux-Goth Chic? You got it. Laura, Mary and Kirstie, with examples of the outfits they create.

NIGHTBREED
www.nightbrd.demon.co.uk

Cutting back on the scale of work somewhat this site, while unwieldy, represented their awesome mail order catalogue above all else, but apparently they've stopped that. Now they will just be a label, and a shop, hopefully.

NIGHTMARE ZONE
www.gothic-order.de/nightmarezone
www.nightmarezone.de
It's those Thyssen brothers, Ralf and Thomas, an essential part of the German scene as DJs, writers, organisers. Worth it just for the galleries, but if you speak German (and, I presume, read it) you'll have a wonderful time. The zine section is particularly cool, but links are weird. Cock Sparrer? What!!!

NO MERCY
www.angelfire.com/goth/gothmercy
'For all you wannabe Goths I've given you some information on how you can become a Goth with links to shops and fashion and makeuo resources.' Blimey, it couldn't be simpler! Fashion, bands, clubs, makeup, hair, tattoos, movies, people, chat, BBS.

NO RELEASE
http://members.tripod.co.uk/thecharnelhouse
Goth band galleries, vast 'Gothic Beauty' gallery, pages on The Crow (dead) and Jewellery, animations and NIN. Slightly strange, all things considered. They also organise club nights twice a month.

NOISEBOYS
www.noiseboys.de
Interesting site covering music and art and loving X-Mal and Malaria.

NONEMORENEGATIVE
www.envy.nu/bellepain
Acres of photos, mainly from Whitby, but other cool work also.

OBSCURE BEAUTY OF THE WEEK
www.geocities.com/Paris/Jardin/5978

ORKUS CHAT
http://orkus.misantrophe.de

OUT AND PROUD GOTH OF THE MONTH
www.lifeishell.de/outproud

PERFECTLY PERFECT... OF THE MONTH
www.gengoth.com/ppg
This is a Josie Nutter one so that's more than okay, and it has a sound reason behind it. 'The Perfectly Perfect award was made to showcase and promote designers and developers with talent, personality and dedication – inner beauty as well as outer. They help inspire us to work hard on our own web projects and deserve our respect.'

PERKIGOTH
www.perkigoth.com
Radio, features, homepages, mega pic and flyer collections. This is a gorgeous site.

PERKYGOFF WORLD HEADQUARTERS
http://echo.echo.com/~magpie/perkygoff
Includes manifesto and faq, perky origin and other guides.

PHOTOS DE CONCERTS GOTHIC, ELECTRIC, DOOM
www.multimania.com/liturgyofdecay/
photos.htm
Great black and white gig shots. Sadly not that many, but an interesting selection.

PLANET GOTH
www.planetgoth.de
News, poetry, music, art.

POGOX
www.pogox.com/pogo.html
Past Out Goths Of...X. Send in pics of your mates when they're too pissed to know. This is actually funny, and, unlike other spiteful sites, allows people to get back at you.

POLISH DARKZONE
www.darkzone.mtl.pl
Links to various official and unofficial sites.

POSTCARDS FROM THE GRAVE
— E-CARDS
www.alsirat.com/postcards/index.html

POWER GOTH GIRLS
www.powergothgirls.com
Very cute, but which came first this, or As Meninas Gothikas?

PRIDEGOTH
www.velvet.net/~pryde

'The list is a national list to cover the lives of, and issues important to, gay, lesbian and bisexual people in the Gothic and Industrial scene. This does not mean the list is in any way straight-exclusionary. There are tons of regional and national e-mail lists and usenet groups, both Gothic/Industrial and queer. But there are none that cover both, and the added issues of being a "double freak". We hope to do just that, while maintaining a level of entertainment and information.'

PROBLEMS ONLY CHRISTIAN GOTHS HAVE

http://members.tripod.com/~sideways_8/problems.html
Trust me, this is cute.

PSYCHO MOTOR

www.geocities.co.jp/MusicStar-Vocal/5640
Goth and Psychobilly fan in Japan.

RANDOM GOTH LYRICS GENERATOR

www.scribble.com/dghq/gothlyric

THE REAL GOTHIC FAQ

http://anon.razorwire.com/real-goth-faq
This is really funny and a welcome antidote to the general level of boredom associated with these things. It also makes a serious point. It's there for the right reason, without being inane.

REALM OF ENCHANTNG DARKNESS

www.devoted.to/blackorchid
This is a very good personal site in that it fully explores her interests, be they Anne Rice, tarot, clothes, Goth imagery, whatever. Plus I love the magic Eight Ball which answers your questions. I asked, 'should I go to the shops now?' and quick as a flash the dramatic reply appeared 'Yes! Before it's too late!' (I was actually out of ciggies at this point.) I tried again. Are cigarettes good for me, as I have always believed? 'Don't get your hopes up.' A link to the psychic world, I'll swear! So finally, the big tester – Will Buffy and Angel actually remember they're meant to be good programmes when doing seasons 6 and 3? 'Definitely. No question about it.' God, the relief! And you get moon wanings details, radio, board (etc), plus interesting links. A lovely all-round experience.

REBECCA 'I AM NOT A GOTH' BLOOD

www.rebeccablood.net/goth.html

REFLECTIONLESS MIRRORS

http://members.tripod.com/~reflectionless

THE RELM OF DARK INSANITY

www.geocities.com/deadshadow666_69/index3.html
'Children are our future,' we are always told. Is it too late to change that? Both journal and photos are unmissable, because this is pastiche bordering on genius.

RIDE THE NIGHT – GRAFX AND SUCH

www.geocities.com/Area51/Dungeon/2511

RUBILYTH

http://groups.yahoo.com/group/rubilyth
Batty-overseen resource 'for graphic designers, illustrators and artists in general of a gothic, dark, and freakish nature.'

S-INC JAPAN

www.s-incjp.com
Fashion and music site.

SABLE INDUSTRIES – ANDY BURGESS

www.sableindustries.org
Intended to be a personal site but also highlighting quality design. As an animator and web-designer himself, Andy will be including exclusive 3-D animations based on the GloomCookie comics, set to the music of Deathwatch Beetle Repairman and Voltaire, as well as including his personal art. He doesn't want it looking like some manic corporate site as he also hopes to offer his services to others, hoping to get enquiries from the Goth fraternity, so check him out. If the site is down keep trying. These are concrete and interesting plans.

SACRAMENT

http://cgi.zipworld.com.au/~kashum/sacrament.pl?cmd=splash
Proper Goth radio show, but when I tried to read Leigh's 'ramblings'... ramblings there were none. Flyers for clubs.

SAD ANDROID

www.sadandroid.com
Wonderful selection of photographs of events, festival, shots and friends, plus sections on comics, trading cards and art.

SB PHOTOGRAPHIES

www.sb-photographies.com
Astonishing! *This is a must-see.* Stéphane Burlot's black-and-white photos are the best Goth photos I have *ever* seen, so don't be put off by the ropey front page at all. Inside you will find the best pics you have seen that are taken at clubs. Check out all of the Soirées section, every last one of them. Magnificent quality and, most importantly of all, he captures the *spirit.* The cemetery photos are equally Godlike, with the Paris section taking the breath away, which is fitting I suppose. Really cute family pics. Musically there are sections on group shots, portraits, gigs and festivals, and *all* of it brilliant.

SCATHE

www.scathe.demon.co.uk
Two sites, the Scathe Web and History Of Goth. Still clearly a work in progress, the latter is the first real attempt online to piece together the History of early Goth. There is little investigation into club culture, because you need to track down people who actually went to the damn things, but he is piecing together why people went from Punk to Goth in the first place. There's a great dates section year by year, highlighting major events which so far goes up to 82. Overall, it breaks down as Summary, Updates, Influences Movement, Subculture, Names, Bands, Fashion, Batcave... with various elements assessed: Punk, Futurist, Psychobilly, Deathrock, and you have a few images and media thrown in. It's a lot to take in. Over at Scatheweb, you get details of the different clubs he DJs at, which I've covered in the clubs section, plus some visual Whitby nostalgia. The site frontpage says 'Clubs, Goth history and silly haircuts' and it's the haircuts bit he seems to like best. Not for the faint-hearted. There are also old music reviews, a guide to Alternative Portsmouth, some DJ in-jokes and technical stuff, as well as some yearly reviews.

SCOUSEGOTH

www.scousegoth.co.uk

Odd site, home to scousegoff group, but also Perla 6 studio, Subspecies and Narcissus Pool sites, with many photos to enjoy, as well as Formula One links!!!

SHADOWLAND
www.shadowland.no
Norwegian shop specialising in Goth.

SHATTERED ECSTASY
www.geocities.com/shatteredextasy
Dreary homepage of Sin, responsible for the brilliant 'Glamour & Suicide'. Tedious journal also.

SHMENG
www.shmeng.com
Odd mini-world and community of mad folk, formerly Gothic Enlightenment.

THE SICKLY TAPER
www.toolcity.net/~frank/Index.html
This website is dedicated to Gothic bibliography. Supremely heavyweight stuff.

THE SILENCE OF DARQNESS
http://members.aol.com/darqdean/index.htm
More odd writing, things about angels, plain old Goth topics, great reprint of old Danielle Dax interview. Bits on Buckley, Jarman, Storm Constantine, cats, a few Whitby photos, a whole raft of scientific anthropological and belief topics.

THE SLAGHUIS
www.slaghuis.net
Used to be a big, well known site. Now quite small, but being worked on again. Sam Sam info, with cool photo archive going on.

SLASHGOTH.ORG
www.slashgoth.org
From netgoth.org.uk. comes the coolest news and discussions in UK.

SOMETHING WICKED THIS WAY GROWS
www.gothic.net/~malice/index.html
Epic Goth gardening site, with serious approaches to various topics around how to create particular types of gardens. This is as good as Gothic Martha Stewart. Theme gardens, and attracting certain wildlife. Ye Olde Gothick Herball Potpourri – various

Pete Scathe @ www.scathe.demon.co.uk

items and tales regarding plants, history and fables.

THE STAGLIENO CEMETERY – GENOVA, ITALY
www.agora.stm.it/A.Borgnino/fecim.htm
Beautifully illustrated historical site, with English version.

A STUDY OF GOTHIC SUBCULTURE
www.Gothics.org/subculture
Articles on music, gang rumours, depression, the vamp side of things, advice, message boards.

SUBURB GOTH
www.morethanmortal.com/suburbgoth
Webring and listy thing, with nice character and profiles.

SUNLIGHT AND SHADOW
www.angelfire.com/goth/sunandshadow
This is an attempt to 'understand' Goth, which goes... people are s ceptical, but Goths are nice, or most are. History, sources etc. Looks nice, and gives an interesting American perspective.

SUPERGOTH! COMICS
www.angelfire.com/bc/stripcentral/supergoth.html

THE SUPERSUCKERS OF THE WEEK
www.deadflesh.org/sucker
Great artwork. This site cherrypicks the best webcam shots discovered. Lots to see.

THE TAO OF GOTH
www.demon.co.uk/bat/aircrash/tab002.html
Ancient Sexbat frivolity

TAMAGOTHI – CUTE CURIO
www.gothic.net/~luvcraft/tamagothi/tamagothi.html

TEACHERGOTHS (!)
http://groups.yahoo.com/group/teachergoths
'This is a gathering place for teacher-goths... Goths who just happen to be

teachers.' And the funny thing is, they have 18 members.

THEE MOOVY NITE
www.nola-goth.org/moovy/index.html
Totally cool idea, but you'll only find out what if you see it.

THEY'RE SO BEAUTIFUL
www.blacklipstickstains.net/people
'This clique began in late 2000 and was started by Decay. She started this clique to recognize people who are fucking gorgeous on the inside. This means they: respect themselves and others, are kind, original, smart and creative, are open-minded, or, all of the above.' It's got a sense of humour too, one pic showing a bloke going, 'I'm the prettiest thing I've ever seen. God, I love myself.' Loads to explore.

A THOUSAND LOVERS CRYING
http://gomez1313.tripod.com
Gomez doesn't like Manson. You get two choices to enter, based on whether you don't like him. Express your admiration and you are directed to the place you deserve. For others there is personal info, including Car Of The Week!

TRAGICALLY GOTH
www.tres-gothique.com/tragicallygoth
'Tragically Goth is for those who have a sense of humour, and can joke about the Gothic lifestyle that we live and love. Is your dwelling dark & cavelike? Are the walls and furniture adorned with bat/spider/skull images that you've had since you were a kindergoth? Do you have more than one black cat? Did you used to have a cat that was not black but is now?'

TRES GOTHIQUE
www.tres-gothique.com
Looks like a Mini-recommendation of Goth sites, with the usual beauty stuff but site aids. Neat little news updates on sites moving too.

UKGOTHICTEENS
http://clubs.yahoo.com/clubs/ukgothicteens

THE UNDERWORLD
www.gothicunderworld.com
'The UnderWorld is basically a personal website with a business edge to it. Originally, when we first developed this site we concentrated more on personal ideas and content, whereas over time, we've branched into one of the dark-webs' newest and biggest resource-centers for all dark sites. Whether your site is Gothic, Vampiric, fetish or Satanic, The UnderWorld strives to promote it. Our only limits to promotion are sites of a lesser level of respect for other peoples' beliefs and practices, i.e., hate sites, overly and continuously bashing other sites that are merely trying to gain their public spot on the web. This is not acceptable in our books. We have many resources for you to use, and all we ask is for the required return link.' Nice idea, and quite cool. Don't bother with the search engine, it's useless, as these things usually are. 'Darkpic post' – send in or just gawp. (In sections Gothic, Vampiric, etc. Funniest has to be Satanic. Look at these losers! Actually, many pics have – as if by magic – failed to appear. Struck down? Repented? Sucked into hell?) Top 100 sites, Forums For once we even find a nice description of What Is Goth?

Photo © Lord Heathcliff. View From the Darkside @ www.chez.com/darkside

VAMP LESTAT'S GOTHIC SERVER
www.vamp.org/Gothic
Goth image database – poor. alt.gothic text files – strangely disappointing. Goth club listing – good. net Goth gallery – hideous. Resource list – Artwork, Business, Culture, Fashion, Music, People, Regional Writing, Vampire.

VAMPIRE DARK FANTASY
http://web.kyoto-inet.or.jp/people/kameno/varavara.html
Goth Site from Japan, bats everywhere. So as not spoil things, I'll just say: start clicking the menu and a symbol near the bottom of each page that appears, and you'll see odd things.

VAMPIRE FREAKS
www.vampirefreaks.com
You used to be warned that the site contains ideas and images which go against the ideology of mainstream society. I know, I know, let me in!!! Now it's straight in. It's Goth and Industrial with reviews, pics and the chat, forum, board thing. Pics are great, and the reviews are okay, and plentiful.

VIEW FROM THE DARKSIDE
www.chez.com/darkside
Dashing photography by Lord Heathcliff from France. Goth models, Dark Glamour, Moody Locations. These photos are magnificent and you'd be a fool not to visit at least once – and he does update. You can also buy top quality prints. He could do with some more models though, so anyone in France should get in touch! Or London, which he visits each year.

VIVI HOUSE
www3.alpha-net.ne.jp/users/vivi
Japanese site, which eulogises over Manson and The Misfits. In the Manson section you will see one fan's MM doll having its picture taken outdoors, along with one of Hide. There is some seriously good photography visible throughout this site.

WANNABEGOTH
www.wannabegoth.com
'The domain name of wannabegoth.com was not meant as an insult to the Gothic community. Rather, it is meant as an insult to the mass misconceptions society has regarding Goths. It's a statement against the portrayal of Goths as violent and evil. It's a statement against those who call themselves Goth and bring a bad name to the rest of the community. Wannabegoth has become a far cry from the original idea. What you'll find here is e-mail forwarding, Wannabegoth of the Month, webrings, mailing lists, and hopefully much more in the coming months." Plus, Dark Literature mailing list.

WAVE-GOTIK TREFFEN PFINGSTEN
www.wave-gotik-treffen.de/english
Seriously big German festival site. Lots of interesting info, and as it's regular always worth bearing in mind. *Brilliant* galleries.

WE ALL LIVE IN A POKEGOTH WORLD
www.pokegoth.co.uk
Forget the Pokedrivel, this site's main appeal is a series of Whitby pictures and accounts of their various weekends. Full of reminiscences like, 'meet up with the others back at the cottage and eat vodka jelly (from a brain-shaped mould).'

WELCOME TO DEADLOUNGE
www.deadlounge.com/index2.html
Relax in the Artic Chaos Gothic Offramp, get confused by Sarco's Bloodbar & Grill, and concentrate on the DeadLounge itself. Very weird world within a world. There are people in there, and they're not normal. Lethal cocktails are suggested. I was on the Dead Lounge Games Room for ages, so be careful, as you may never emerge. The Goth Dentistry joke caught me, and Sarco's didn't work, but I still had a lovely day out.

WELCOME TO GOTH TALK
www.geocities.com/TelevisionCity/Stage/9766/gtmain.html
Cable show in Florida, with transcripts etc to past shows.

WELCOME TO THE WITCHUNT
www.geocities.com/Athens/Cyprus/2703
Another snapshot in time, circa 1999 about Goth misrepresentation in the media.

WHAT IS GOTH?
www.tarogue.net/goth
Haven't the foggiest.

WHAT MAKES A GOTHIC ROLE MODEL?
http://members.tripod.com/%7Egothic_role_model/rolemodel.html
'They set a good example for others and help shed a positive light on a subculture that is normally looked upon as being "evil" or "corrupt". This page praises all those who do their best to be caring, stylish, witty, and a true example of what a Goth should be.' A few nice pics remain, most links are mummified.

WHITBY GOTHIC WEEKEND
www.wgw.topmum.co.uk/index.php
Info site for the latest developments.

WINDOW OF THE 8TH FLOOR
www02.so-net.ne.jp/~rey
Might be old, old, old. There are sections, all in Japanese, so just click at anything illuminated and you find yourself with a section of old school Goth reviews, a section on cemeteries and trips abroad, but when you click on Japanese Gothic there are photos of dolls in kimonos. Is this irony? There are also some links to Japanese sites but the weird thing is that when you reach them you really don't know what you're doing. That, of course, is half the fun.

XNETGOTH.COM
www.xnetgoth.com
Online Christian Goth newsgroup. 'Welcome to xnetgoth.com, the home of the xnetgoth Christian Goth Mailing List. But more than that you will encounter a worldwide community of Goths and other outcasts that have one thing in common: The Christian faith. This is no ordinary website, it is made up of those who walk in the shadows cast by the Light of the world. Welcome to our home.' It's okay mate, just passing...

XTREN'S GOTHIC GRRRLS
www.angelfire.com/goth/xtrensgothicgirls

YOU MIGHT BE A GOTH HICK IF...
http://ucsub.colorado.edu/~kaminssl/gothic/goth.html

YOU MIGHT BE A GOTH IF...
www.apocalypse.org/pub/u/hilda/rugoth.html
Another one of those comical lists. Be still, my aching sides...

Sites of interest

13 GRAVE
www.13grave.org
Should be site for Japanese Goth bands Shrine and The Darkcell, but when I visited it was just a mini-history.

313
www.threethirteen.net
'There is no great mission here, other than a vision to provide interesting, occasionally useful, and always opinionated dark websites for your amusement and annoyance.' You are advised to touch the web (it's a graphic) for Propaganda – can't see anything, Absolution (Victoria's Gothic Page) – her personal site, Night Of Black Glass – Victoria's artwork, Forums, and there's Fairy Gothmothers – where younger Goths can safely go to meet Older Goths, for decent reasons, not smut! All excellent stuff.

9MUSES GRAPHIC DESIGN
www.ninemuses.co.uk
Justina Jane Heslop of Whitby Dracula Society and Philip Smith. Shows the design work they do, some of the illustrations and art being well worth your time.

ABISMO
http://abismo.8k.com
Brazillian or Spanish site, includes literature and music and some Halloweeny gifts.

THE ADAMS RESIDENCE
http://welcome.to/theadamsresidence
Cemetery photo page, news on the dead Gothic Society, an awesome collection of cemetery photos. A trip to a museum exhibition about London's disposal of the dead.

ADOPT 80'S CARTOON CUTIES
http://whimsical.nu/rainbow/adopt.html

'The Spy'. Photo © Stéphane Lord.
Model: Karine Alger.

ADOPT A DARK CREATURE/THE WORLD OF SAYS
http://worldofsaya.tripod.com
You can adopt one of the creatures providing you link back to her page. They seem Elvish. 'Welcome to the World of Saya, traveller! My name's Ayana of Saya, storyteller, writer and your guide during your journey through our world.' Yep, it's one of those, but attractively done.

ADOPT A DEMON
www.1freespace.com/adoptademon/index.html
Demons to suit your computer backgrounds. Some crap, some seriously weird.

ADVENTURES BEYOND
www.adventuresbeyond.com
Promo site for videos they do, like 'America's Most Haunted'.

ALA MODE PRODUCTIONS
www.joyfarm.com/alamode
Theresa Ala Mode, photographer, who looks like a little like Lisa Left-Eye Lopez, has some great pics here for you. She also has a section called Bog Images which are feminine storylines played out in an Autumnal Bog!!! Weird portraits are worth a look.

ALISA
www.alisachan.com
Alisa's Cosplay, which is *amazing*, revealing a sense of dedication and fun.

ALMOST SATISFIED
http://lashes.ubiquitous.nu
Dazzling, with its own domain and hostees, a fairly good journal which is literal morse code in some places. Her thought pieces are okay, but it's her bio that shines.

ALTERNATIVE GRRL OF THE MONTH
http://altmtl.virtualave.net

ANALYNN
www.analynn.com
Great, mad site, although fairly coarse.

ANDREW COLLINS
www.andrewcollins.net
Good site from fascinating writer who dabbles in and deals with the darker, edgier mysteries of life. The site contains enough to have you wondering whether he could eventually reach 'Chariot Of the Gods' status. (He does seem to ignore his earlier books, which suggests he wants to be seen in a more learned light.)

ANGEL DEVIL
http://members.aol.com/angelspoon/index.html
Truly amazing. Love the 'Crackle Dolls'. All dolls are one-of-a-kind, fully jointed sculptures by Anna Puchalski. 'My main objectives are a unique appearance and the ability of movement in my "dolls as art", employing many unusual puppetry techniques. I will accept made-to-order requests, but please note, these require a modest waiting period. Take a look in the "Available Now" section for new dolls available from me or from an Angel Devil Retailer.'

ANGELIC
www.angelic.it
Radio station, plus a band section for details, mp3, audio exchange.

ANGRY JACKAL GRAPHICS – FURRY
www.icefox-studios.net/ashryn.html

ANGSTBABE
www2.pair.com/tracylee

ANGST BOY – COMIC ARCHIVE
www.ferret.com/angstboy

ANIME WORLD
www.anime-world.co.uk

ANKOKUKOUBOU DARK ART
http://art.pos.to
Weird game and graphics.

ANNALISA'S HOMEPAGE
www.geocities.com/algarnett
This is a somethingabilly page with a mass of bands I've never heard of and, in

truth, would probably not like if I did, but there are interesting names and there seems to be some crazy forties/fifties-inspired American bands who take that Lounge style and throw in death references. It's a great experience, marvelling at all these weirdos. I'm sure they'd think the same. Mega-gallery section, full of chubby men in suits or Hawaiian shirts and... good God, the Guana Batz!!!

THE ANTONELLA GAMBOTTO WEB
www.users.bigpond.com/ambrosiamoneybags/home.htm
Magnificent, interesting site from talented writer and novelist, Antonella Gambotto, who long-standing readers may have noticed in my past two books. Now firmly entrenched in Australia, and considered a serious talent, she has also taken to the Net like a blindfold trapeze artist. Nothing is too much trouble for her. Sharing her site with many friends, and encouraging salacious gossip and opinions, alongside philosophy, affairs of the heart and ecological matters, her site is both beguiling and perverse. On top of that you get her morse-code diary, and strange personal details. The bio is modestly brief, as is the use of photos. Some-times lofty, sometimes downright low and dirty, this is a wonderful place to visit.

ANYTHING BOX
www.anythingbox.com
A label using the Internet to promote what will be tech-influenced music, 'by rehumanizing the process by which

music is distributed and promoted" – it says, in a cold, anodyne manner. That's the problem. The ideas of sites like this are laudable and natural, the music is usually interesting or exciting, but the sites actually have a totally inhuman feel.

APOCALYPSE TATTOO LLP
www.apocalypsetattoo.com/apocalypse.html
Disney goes Buddhist graphics to open, and then you're into a Seattle tattoo parlour.

APRIL ATOMIC
www.geocities.com/MissAprilAtomic
Cheesecake pin-up gal.

ARGONAUT GREYWOLF
www.alienufoart.com/GhostInvestigations Photos.htm
Ghost investigations and photos. This is hilarious. I've seen ghosts and they didn't look like these whisps of smoke or camera-fogged negatives which they have decided has greater meaning. The photo that started them off was taken at Christmas and is in a family's front room. I hadn't even read the caption and was thinking some tinsel had simply drifted past the camera as the pic was taken. But no, it's a ghost, don't you see! I get all sorts of rubbish effects on my gig photos at times. Smoking causes some of them too. I don't go, 'Look... A Curved Energy Vortex!' There's loads of this sort of stuff, so laugh yourself sick. Even better is the orb phenomenon, where a bit of muck inside the camera has caused a circular mark. One person even admits they took the pic with a disposable camera. That's right, you use shit, you get crap results.

ARIANN'S SAVINI HORROR HOUSE
http://members.tripod.com/~AriannB/index.html

ARISE: AraQniD
www.arise.demon.co.uk

ART, NOISE, RNS
www.geocities.jp/lovi88669988

Very cool photo and art galleries from Japan.

THE ART OF LISA PETRUCCI
www.lisapetrucci.com
Very distinctive, like a cross between Warhol and Archie comics.

THE ART OF RAIN
www.dirge.net/rain
Startling visuals you may download and use, as long as they're not for backgrounds.

ARTEFFEX – DESIGN
www.arteffex.com

ARTIST LAUNCH
www.artistlaunch.com/songplaysrank.asp?p1=Goth
One search area is Gothic Coffee-house Pop!

ARTIST OF THE BLEEDING HEART
www.bleeding-heart.com
Grafx and Rants, with many artists represented, and lots of banners/award bits.

ARTMAGICK: Dante Gabriel Rossetti
www.artmagick.com/artists/rossetti1.asp
Just an example. Biog, with relevant links, poems, paintings (utterly amazing selection of artists and in-depth on that artist) and huge list of recommended reading. Galleries on a generic theme – Victorian painters, Victorian fairy painters – and info on exhibitions.

THE ASSOCIATION FOR GRAVESTONE STUDIES ONLINE
www.gravestonestudies.org
Massive resource, in depth for the serious admirer.

THE ASYLUM ECLECTICA
http://asylumeclectica.com
Welcome to the Asylum Eclectica (formerly Typhoid Mary's Asylum) – the only place on earth where Heinous Crimes, Terrifying Tragedies, Atrocious Occurrences, Malicious Murders, Vile Illnesses, and Whimsical Curiosities can at last peacefully co-exist. She gives us Morbid Fact Du Jour (I've bookmarked this). Malady Of The Month, plus some Sandman and then tons of 'Dark & Gruesome' links – and she's not kidding.

ATOMCAM
www.atomcam.com
Having had a rough (as in *rough*) time of it lately, this may not be the most easy-going experience. When she writes it can be very touching. A lot of it is gloop, but the stuff that is good really connects.

ATOMIC
www.atomicmag.com
Brilliant retro mag site.

THE AVENGERS FOREVER
http://theavengers.tv/forever/guide.htm
Godlike, in every way. A site you *have* to explore.

THE AVIARY
www.shades-of-night.com/aviary/index.html
Great site for photos of and myths on Rooks, Ravens, Crows, Jackdaws and Jays.

AZARIEL
www.angelicaduti.org
Nicely arty with books, art, with a gallery of smiling people. In Italian, so I haven't a clue, but I think literary appreciation figures, as Michael Moorcock seems to be honorary president of something they've organised. There's also opera and a lot of horror links.

THE BARCELONA REVIEW
www.barcelonareview.com
Brilliant site dealing with contemporary fiction, available in Catalan, Spanish, French and English. Good reviews and great interviews.

BAT CONSERVATION INTERNATIONAL
www.batcon.org
Seriously cool and interesting site. Bats magazine! Fruitbat t-shirts, education and conservation matters.

BAT DANCE
www.batdance.net
Chat room, Vamp style, animated bat greetings to send to friends, cool screensaver, and custom fangs.

BEAUTY IN DARKNESS
http://sinisterbeauty.com/ashlie/index.html
Photos by Ashlie Dawn, on a wild looking site. There aren't actually that many yet but more than enough to make it a satisfying experience, and the Hospital pics are creepy without trying.

BELA'S PRODUCTIONS
www.belasproductions.co.uk
If it isn't updated by the time you read this it's just a bright antique dream. When someone has a section captioned Bela's Lugosi's Shed (a travelling club), you know you're at the right place. Music promotions, and they also promote clothes etc. Perversely, they only seem able to boast about working with Gong at present. They appear to be selling New Age stuff too – mystical, incense, runes.

THE BELFRY WEBWORKS – FURRY
www.belfry.com
Very odd, from the mask-making to the bed and breakfast, Furry comics and Furry fascinations. A little cornucopia of...well, I'm, not sure exactly. Intriguing, whatever it means.

BELLADONNA FINE ART & PHOTOGRAPHY
www.belladonnafineart.com

BEST WITCHES
www.rci.rutgers.edu/~jup/witches/index.html
'We are a discussion of the historical witch trials of Europe and New England. We are *not* witches!'

Asylum Eclectica

BETHANY PASEMAN
www.bethanypaseman.com
Absolutely magnificent photography.

BETTIE PAGE – NOTORIOUS
www.angelfire.com/mn/NightmusiC
She is popular in most scenes, and a fair few Goth sites allude to her. If you know nowt about the saucy mare, here's a good start.

BEYOND GRANDPA
www.beyondgrandpa.com
'Within these walls lies a forgotten land... A place frozen in time, where men smoke pipes and drink cocktails 'til dawn... As you approach, exotic rhythms grow more intense. The neon glow warms your eyes and the music takes hold. Enter here, and abandon what you thought you knew about Grandpas... Do you try it? Stop! Are you 18 yet? If you're under aged, look away! It burns! Do you like to be burned?" Disturbing cartoon postcards, 'Grandpa Speaks Out', desktop patterns. A classic.

BLACK EASTER FESTIVAL
www.ensg.u-nancy.fr/~cognot/bef.html#atarax
Small photo-illustrated account of a 1995 bash.

BLACK ROSE
www.black-rose.sk
Drab photos of people in a bar, accompanied by some out-of-place fetish shots. Very strange indeed.

BLACK ROSES IN DELIRIUM
www.covenroses.com
Brian Grisham, writer and poet.

BLACK SUN
http://dark.Gothic.ru/lunophobia
Don't blame me, I only linked here.

BLAH.BLAH.SMOKE.BLAH.BLAH
www.glittersores.net/~smoker
Now I have nothing against passive smoking per se, but why can't people buy their own? 'Hi I'm using neon colours for the first time, yee hah. I think it looks good. Anyway welcome to Smoker, the clique! If you're a smoker tired of people beggin' you to stop smoking and blah please join this clique.' Give this girl a medal!

BLAR.ORG FORUMS
http://forum.blar.org

BLOGGER
www.blogger.com
'What is Blogger? Blogger is a free, web-based tool that helps you publish to the web instantly – whenever the urge strikes. Blogger is the leading tool in the rapidly growing area of web publishing known as weblogs, or "blogs", as we like to say.'

BLOODLUST UK
www.bloodlust-uk.com
Huge vamp community and resource site.

BLOODSHADOPWS – RPG PICS
www.bloodshadows.org

BLUE BLOOD – (JAPAN)
www.geocities.co.jp/PowderRoom-Rose/4424
This is probably the weirdest doll site I found as the anime influence made the variety, from Goth to Vampire, Monster to semi-Elvis, all the odder.

THE BONEGARDEN ESTATE 2000
www.bonegarden.com
You *have* to see this, it is a work of genius. The person responsible has created a virtual haunted house.

BOOKEND OGHAI
www.geocities.co.jp/Bookend-Ohgai/8943
I don't really know what this is. Click the bat and find out. The lyrics section suggests a band, and yet there are brilliant illustrations in the Treasure Room. Click on Incarnation and the menu produces many visuals to enjoy.

BOUNDLESS... NORMAL IS BORING!
www.boundless-home.de
Huge array of fantasy art. Lots of stories too. Slightly old-fashioned but beautiful quality.

BOYS NEXT DOOR
www.discarnate.com/boysnextdoor
Fanfiction from various manga, anime and video games, forum and reviews. 'How to tell if a writer has never smoked a cigarette'. Etiquette in comics yet?

Boys Next Door
a shonen-ai and yaoi site.

BRAINGOOP
www.toxicbug.com/braingoop
Artificial Environment Therapy program, via The Cancerian (now that's style) Connie. You can download her moody music, approve of her cat, enjoy occasional webcam activity, avoid the poetry and sign the guestbook.

BROMART
www.bromart.com
Truly amazing artist who has books and artwork, sculptures and toys all coming at you very soon. Check out this gallery and just drool the time away.

DAVID GEORGE BROMMER
www.cybersuspect.com
Photographer with Goth, Vamp and Fetish galleries, but also words to explain his fascination. Other artists get to utilise the site as well. Impressive.

BUFFY AND ANGEL
GOING THROUGH THE MOTIONS:
http://musical.chosentwo.com
Incredible tribute to *Buffy – The Musical*, the extraordinary episode. Also has excellent links.
TELEVISION WITHOUT PITY:
www.televisionwithoutpity.com
Just pick the show(s) from the menu. You will become addicted to the funniest reviewers anywhere on the Net. Strega does Angel, Sep and Ace do Buffy, and all three are Gods.
BUFFY GUIDE:
www.buffyguide.com
Great all-purpose, slow, Buffy guide with good database.
BUFFY CROSS & STAKE:
www.angelicslayer.com/tbcs/main.html
The most imaginative fan site with great detail, news and general verve.
THE SANCTUARY:
http://sanctuary.digitalspace.net
Best all-round Angel site – amazing details and fantastic episode reviews.
WILLOW:
The following are all Alyson/Willow-based and therefore have an almost religious intensity, all of it so richly deserved.
http://members.tripod.com/~Little__Willow
http://members.tripod.com/Little__Willow/wpwp.html
www.alyson-hannigan.org
www.chosentwo.com/girlfriends
www.hannigan.com

www.network23.com/hub/ahas
www.slayerettes.org/bbab
www.teenage-wasteland.com/willow
BUFFY/ANGEL sites, CHARACTER-SPECIFIC OR GUIDES:
http://angel-btvs.co.uk/
http://hometown.aol.com/danilynn27/bhome.html
http://rhiannon.dreamhost.com/angel
www.angelfire.com/nv/josswhedon
www.angelfire.com/scifi/Buffaholics
www.chosentwo.com/buffy
www.cityofangel.com/noflash.htm
www.efanguide.com/~amber
www.emma-caulfield.org
www.epguides.com/BuffytheVampireSlayer
www.episodeguides.com/shows/buffy/guide.htm
www.geocities.com/~angelsecrets/index2.html
www.geocities.com/Area51/1544/index3.html
www.geocities.com/Hollywood/Land/8628/themes.html
www.halcyon.com/griffee/buffy/index.html
www.harsh-light.com
www.michelle-trachtenberg.com
www.morticiasmorgue.com/buffy.html
www.nicholas-brendon.com
www.ninetozero.com/sense
www.onthefringe.org/crazy
www.pure-evilness.com/buffy
www.slayerweb.org
www.slaymuch.com
www.spikespotting.com
www.theslayer.net
www.web-glitter.com/~buffy

BUNNY CHAN'S COSPLAY WONDERLAND
www.bunnychan.com

BURLESQUE AS IT WAS
www.burlesqueasitwas.com
Hilarious modern tribute to the olde entertainment where stripping was more suggestive. Done in a beautiful style, this site is far from kitsch, and makes you realise just how crass 99% of fetish material really is. The photos of shows are brilliant, the girls sections are sweet – Bella La Ball, Kitten Kaboodle. They also hold auditions and organise events.

BURNING CHROME
www.burningchrome.org.uk
Imaginative William Gibson tribute.

BURNING INSIDE
www.burninginside.net
Loads of nice-ish girly portraits.

BURST

www.coremagazine.co.jp/burst
General promo for sub-culture magazine in Japan, with occasional Goth content.

BY THE VERY FANGS OF MALICE

www.sekhmet.org/~malice
A conceptual disaster about death, designed like a house, where every area corresponds to some death incident he wishes to expand upon.

CADAVER

www.cadaver.org

CAMILLE ROSE GARCIA

www.camillerosegarcia.com
Incredible visual feast, of artwork around children's stories, like some latter day Hans Christian Anderson, with a Nightmare Before Christmas feel. Crap bio, beautiful gallery, and prints for sale.

CAMMY FAN

www.cammyfan.com
Seems to be a comic character. There's a gallery of hundreds of girls dressed like her.

CANDYAPPLEBLACK

www.candyappleblack.com
'If you have never been abandoned, betrayed, or broken-hearted, then you have no need of this place or its stories, and this safe harbour was not created for you.' A different feel right from the start. The artwork is amazing, the story cool.

CAOINE

http://caoine.org
Can I just say this site annoys me because it was originally called The Odditorium, which was a wonderful name! Interesting looking site. Good vibrant journal. (www.precarious.org/), wonderfully striking photos available from the left hand menu of the 'exposition' section. Her own photos aren't so good, but the design and writing examples are interesting. She does a good design site for people wanting to learn:
http://caoine.org/disintegrate

CELESTIAL DUNG

www.knoxvilleGothic.homestead.com/twocd.html
Fine reviews and general outpourings from one TN character in the States.

CEMETERY COLLECTION

www.Gothic.ru/cemetery/index2_e.htm
The difference here is they're all Russian. Beautifully done.

CEMETERY CULTURE: CITY OF THE SILENT

www.alsirat.com/silence/index.html
'Welcome to the web's most extensive cemetery site. Information about cemetery symbols, epitaphs, history, consumer protection, folklore and folk art, last words, tombstone rubbing, and other aspects of mortuary culture. Also free email and postcards. Also, Enjoy The Mythology and Folklore of Death, Cemeteries as Culture, Cemeteries through Time, Cemeteries amid Society, Cemeteries in Art, Cemeteries on the Internet.' *Magnificent.*

CEMETERY MONUMENTS

http://cemeterymonuments.homestead.com/index.html
Straightforward site expressing an interest with big colour photos. Being a Homestead site it is slow, but if you're patient, there are nice shots. Unfortunately these are bright and sunny! Nice little links, and photo contributions can be sent:
adipocere@subdimension.com

CENTRE OF DESIRE ENTERTAINMENT

www.codemusic-jp.com
Unusual promotions site, with mail order and info of events, specifically Angina Pectoris, for whom they also do an official Japanese page.

CHAMELIA

www.chamelia.com
'Why are we the best? The answer is quite simple. There are beautiful Russian models, talented painters and photographers in our team. It allows us to do what nobody else can do, in such number, that you can't even fancy.' Fair enough then! Seemed to be some weird bodypainting site.

THE CHAPEL PERILOUS

www.sepulchritude.com/chapelperilous
Huge selection of interesting art and 'historic smut'.

CHEMICAL PLAYSCHOOL

www.maddycat.com
The truth? – Name: Lady Madelyne

(Maddy) Location: Houston, Texas Occupation: Makeup Artist (Special effects hair and makeup) 'I specialize in theatrical make-up and many types of hair extensions, from braids to huge hair. Photo shoots, band photos, parties, or just going out... I'm an official H.A.G. (Hateful Arrogant Goth). I'm old, I'm tired, and I *will* slit your throat.' I like the sound of her already. Gallery – pics of her, family, mates. Nice artwork, okay links. *She* comes over as really great, but there's virtually nothing here. It's not really any good saying, 'If you don't like what this page has to say, take your ass somewhere else!' Give us *more.*

THE CHIAROSCURO: THOSE WHO WALK ALONE

www.gothic.net/chiaroscuro
Horror cons, book reviews, film reviews, member profiles and brave or foolhardy attempt at writing. And Vent, where people moan.

CHI-CHIAN – COMIC

www.voltaire.net/chichian.html
It's that Voltaire bloke up to his brilliant tricks again.

CHURCH OF MARY

www.church-of-mary.co.uk
'Immaculate conception gone wrong', apparently. *Very* strange!

CHURCH OF VIRUS

http://virus.lucifer.com
Collaborative New Religion and New Aesthetik. Some people really *should* get out more.

THE CIRCLE OF DARK POETS

www.darkhosts.com/darkpoets
I quite like the image of a circle for dark poets, but there's no photographic proof, which means we've stumbled upon the

crassest of liars. The dark Poet of Scotland introduces you to his work, via his own site, and eventually the work of others. *Very* intense. 'Life is torture enough to endure. Let your mind wander now and then. You'll find you like the results.' Hush, pet.

CIRCUS OF THE BARKING DEAD
www.circusofthebarkingdead.com
'We have a new section with information on taking care of an undead dog.'

THE CIRCUS TENT – COOL
www.geocities.com/star_god/index.html

CLAN LOST SOULS
www.geocities.com/Area51/5472
It's a role-playing thing.

CLEAN.VAPID.ORG
http://clean.vapid.org

CLUB GIO
www5.big.or.jp/~gio
Japanese site, with links to bands, and club dates info.

COLD MARBLE
www.dgbn.com/coldmarble/index.html
A cute little cemetery site with lots of great photos. 21 cemeteries covered so far, plus postcards and useful links. How come none of these sites link to shops selling actual funereal products, which we could have indoors? The webcam shows the man responsible sitting at his desk. Just resting.

COMA-DOSE
www.coma-dose.net
Industrial label, presenting site in zine format but fairly unresponsive.

COME INTO MY PARLOR
www.flowersforthedead.com/tasha
'Either this page is under construction, or I'm out digging up bodies again.' She's funny, a talented artist and there's a lot here which is slightly weird, including one of the most imaginative photo galleries. You'll find some nice brief rants too.

CONFUSED – ART/PHOTOS
www.geocities.com/effigy82/index.html

A CONSPIRACY – SOLVE THE MYSTERY OF THE HYPNOTISING PICTURES
www.the-void.dk/incident/intro.html

A book about alien landings, where all the 'evidence' that supposedly remains are these few pages. Conspiracies over the paranormal, done in a delightful manner. You'll need to look at the messages section to get the most out of it.

CORVI CHRONICLE
www.azstarnet.com/~serres/corvi.html
One for the crows and ravens enthusiasts. Old, but tons of info.

COSMIC DEBRIS
www.cosmicdebris.com/all/index.html
Kitsch couture, from clothes to paper dolls, personalities and underground emergents.

THE COUNTESS NADAZDIE
http://gurlpages.com/nadazdie/index.html
The Countess, Philippines martial arts and Duran Duran, amongst others!

COYOTE'S GRAPHICS HORDE
www.geocities.com/coyotegraphics
Animals (25), Anime/manga (60), Gothic (26), Misc (70), Christian (94) – pages in brackets. Plus 24 backgrounds. A *brilliant* resource.

CREPT-IC
www.darkhosts.com/crept
'Dark' photos, but actually generally very jolly.

CROWN O' GEMS
www.gleeful.com
Very mad little poetry collections.

CRYSANIA
www.crysania.com
'Welcome to a page devoted to yaoi and shonen ai fics'... at which point I'm lost, but this is a big site, which includes a section called 'Invasion Dream'; that concentrates solely on bands, with great links and an ace gallery, lyrics, downloads and links.

THE CYBERDEN
www.cyberden.com
Music, tech, links, forums. In fact it's great fun because it's so deranged with ideas spinning off everywhere, the party animals.

THE CYBERGOTH NEXUS
www.degenerates.freeserve.co.uk
Feral Cat's site looks good, but that's the

art and for a Cyber Goth he likes NIN, Christian Death and Rosetta Stone. Broken links, even on his own band, Inoxia.

CYNICAL – WEBRING
http://souhi.com/cynical
You have to be a cynic – but not a moaner – or you can't join. There are interesting sites in here but a lot of dreary journal-based nonentitities.

CYNTHIA VON BUHLER
www.cynthiavonbuhler.com

DA5ID'S LRP PICTURES – RPG
http://home.wanadoo.nl/alamais/pics

DAME DARCY
www.damedarcy.com

DAMION A TIDD'S BLATANT SELF-PROMOTION
www.sfGoth.com/~perki
Photo collection, including club Polaroids.

DANGERMEDIA GUILD – TOPICS
http://dangermedia.org

DANIEL FUSELLO GOTHIC HORROR MOVIE SCULPTURES
www.labellestudios.com/danielfusello.htm

DANIEL MCKERNAN – ART
http://brainwashed.com/daniel

DARK ARENA
www.darkarena.com
It's a woman thing and a portal thing, leading to lots of other sites, all on a dark theme and all potentially very interesting. So many sections you would not believe. 'This is not a satanic, Gothic, Vampiric, or any other "this group only" site. DarkArena.com is open to any and all who have a taste for the dark side. This for me is a love of Dark Art. Whether it be photography, games, sketches, digital art, or oil paintings, I love dark art. Some artists have an imagination that I can't even conjure when I am sleeping much less when I'm sitting in front of a canvas or computer.'

DARK DESKTOP THEMES
http://darkwrath.org
'Here you will find the darkest desktop themes on the net, mainly themes based on dark bands and music. These desktop themes contain custom desktop wallpaper,

icons, animated cursors, sound clips, and startup/shutdown screens. All these features are sure to add plenty of dark atmosphere to your boring Windows 95+ desktop.' Tons of bands and he likes suggestions for new additions.

DARK DOORS

www.darkdoors.com

'You've reached the creative galleries of Cyn Surreal. In sharing my expression with you, all visitors are invited to indulge in the inspirations of the soul. You are invited join others in viewing or discuss or post poetry, listening to a choice of two internet radio stations, like Art of Darkness Ethereal Radio and Necrodance Industrial Radio, or simply sit back and view the images behind this quiet mind.' Illustrations and artwork are extremely basic, and the gig photos are laughable, but the portraits are *very* nice.

DARK FURR

www.darkfurr.org

Pics and topics galore, including an amateur production of 101 Dalmatians. Yep, *weird*.

DARK INK GRAPHICS

http://members.home.net/darkinkgraphics

An interesting little site for a graphic and web designer but for the time you wait, maybe it's one for the art crowd.

THE DARK INNER RING

www.thedarkerinnerring.com

A site promoting various Goth models and their sites. Stunning pics.

DARK MAGICK

www.darkmagick.com

Stories, poems, artwork, Magnus Opus and Nightwinds downloads.

DARK OR DORK?

www.darkordork.com

You know the score by now, and this is okay... but not enough dorks.

DARK PASSIONS MAGAZINE

www.darkpassions.com

It's interesting – here you can get fetish junk, jewellery, photo prints, and kid's dolls. Example contents: Deathrock – good or bad, What to do in Sacramento, Movies, A Nun Singing, Film reviews, Fetish/Goth crossover, Erotic Horror,

Introduction to Fetish, Vampire stuff, CD reviews.

DARK PENGUIN

http://relic.addr.com

A one man designer. 'Dark Penguin is a design company without a staff, without clients, and without income. Projects are directed under one vision. And displayed for the few that care.' He shows projects being worked on, which either haven't come to anything but might, or won't. Not too encouraging, but this 'Media Meatball' is still young. Fantastic coffee mug available through the store, and nice shirts. Weirdly, the mouse mat doesn't feature cute penguins, which is a tragic error.

DARK POETS SOCIETY

http://dps.intermag.com

DARK POSTCARDS

www.darkpostcards.com

DARK SYMPHONIES

www.darksymphonies.com

I haven't included many labels, but then this is such an attractive site, with a mixture of some of the more interesting Rock and Metal bands, as well as some Goth-inspired, that it may be of interest to some.

DARK THEMES

www.darkhosts.com/xvvGothicvvx/index.html

Welcome to Stone Creations & Gothic Themes Desktop themes, which are pretty impressive.

DARKE GOTHYC VAMPYR BRAYNE OF THE MONTH

www.evilscience.net/brayne/brayne.htm

Not for those of a queasy disposition.

DARKER IMAGE

http://members.aol.com/graaargh/darker image.html

Creepy art, changed each month. Some okay, some most decidedly very okay.

DARKLANDER

www.terra.es/personal2/darklander/menu.htm

Dark, death-like imagery, film and art. Bit weird, actually.

DARKNESS GOTHIC

www.geocities.com/darknessGothic/main.html

DARKROOM DESIGNS

http://darkroomdesigns.com

DARQLANDS

http://members.aol.com/DarqLands/index.html

It's ambitious, this seven-chapter web novel, and not necessarily very good, but if you fancy something to read you will find it quite involving. Part of his bigger site, The Silence Of Darqness.

THE DAVISON FAMILY WEBSITE

www.kdavison.com

Leads to a disrupted Gothic Vision site plus a Winnie The Pooh epic.

DAWN'S DANCE WITH DEATH

http://goddessdawn.hispeed.com/index.html

Joseph Michael Linsner is an artist and Dawn, the character, is The Goddess of Birth and Rebirth, Lover of Death is a Xenaesque beauty. Actually it's more of a seventies Red Sonja thing but this site has as much info and examples as you possibly bear, being a true labour of love, all done by an equally pneumatic wench name Cyndee. Why isn't she one of the models?

DAXXAMILLION – KING OF SCABS

http://oberon.spaceports.com/~daxx

Nice, stick that on your cv, and you'll have no problems! Interviews and odd news.

DEAD BABIES – COMEDY HORROR

www.thisisacryforhelp.com/db.htm

DEATH (THE COMIC)

www.best.com/~teleute

Stories, comics, toys, links etc.

THE DEATH CLOCK

www.deathclock.com

Want to know how long you've got? I have (had!) nine and a half hundred million seconds left. Best hurry, as when I double checked I was down to 928 million. Eek, but time flies...

DECADENT AVANTGARDE

www.devianna.com

Unofficial Japanese site of The Damned, with a BBS which includes Goth.

DEMONOPHONIC LTD

www.demonophonic.com

It's a label for madness, giving homes to artists who would otherwise be a danger to themselves, helping them to bring a hint of destruction to our lives instead.

DESPAIR INC.
www.despair.com
This has little do with anything – it's out on its own and quite brilliant. (Oh, they do a nice mug!) The Idiotic Insights are wonderful, and you can buy packs of joylessness.

DESTROIKA
www.industrialnation.nl/destroika
Photos of Industrial acts.

THE DEVIL DANCE
www.devildance.com
Devils, bats and skulls, dancing in a line. A link to Satandance should you need it.

THE DIARY REGISTRY
www.diarist.net/registry

DINNERLADY'S LUNCH BOX
www.geocities.com/SouthBeach/Marina/1564

DISAPPOINTED VIRGINITY
www.disappointedvirginity.co.uk
Interesting mood-Fetish photography from Marc Blackie – who is also involved with *Quiette* zine and the band Sleeping Pictures.

DISCOVER ALLURING BEAUTY
www.tres-gothique.com/AlluringBeauty
A little selection of people and sites they can link you onto. Quite sweet. 'We are looking for people who possess a rare beauty... one that can only be found in a select few... Beauty is something that emanates from the soul. Pictures should be alluring without being posed. Pictures of individuals in death poses holding flowers or exceptionally amusing poses in cemeteries will have less chances of winning. Cemeteries are beautiful places and some photographs taken within their confines are acceptable. Please submit your favourite picture URL to be used if you win the Alluring Beauty Award and let us know if others can be found on your site.'

DO RE MI
www.doremi.co.uk
Steve, of Big Bro 2, with a strange site that includes weirdoes Inner City Unit, but has a whole Glam History section you will enjoy. (Also David Devant, John Otway and Hawkwind.)

DOLL GLASS UMI
www2.odn.ne.jp/~cbb49840
Another great doll site, more odd photos.

DOLL LABO
http://dolllabo.honesto.net
Another one of these Japanese doll sites. Presumably these are for sale, but they're also so strange and compelling, like Drusilla's long lost children. There is a little visual section showing the manufacture, and there are pictures of exhibitions, which are mainly shop-based displays. It isn't just dolls, but toys generally which are available. It is all in Japanese but check out this page, with the top pic being the most important (http://dolllabo.honesto.net/rakutan/27.htm). Quite extraordinary. The Victorian dolls with black eyes are wonderful, but I'm not sure about the genetic experiment ones, where there are bears with doll faces. That's just weird. This site is a work of art and you *have* to see it.

DOLL MDA
http://doll.mda.or.jp/~naruto
Now this site is by a Lucifer Luscious Violenoue, Gackt, Malice Mizer fan, so we're getting closer to Goth territory. It's a personal collector's site with some cool pics, a BBS, info section and diary, but all in Japanese.

DOLL SITE
www.geocities.co.jp/Hollywood-Studio/4623/index.html
Another weird one. Great photos of dolls with disconsolate faces and odd mouths, although it could be links to other sites as I'm not sure what I'm clicking on and why. Still seriously interesting, and occasionally you find little outfit sections, including some Goth gear!

DOLL SPACE REMI
www.mars.dti.ne.jp/~futoyama
Another amazing doll site, perhaps more clearly laid out, with fantastic gallery and exhibition pages. Some pics are really sad too, as the dolls are posed in dioramas a bit like that Eliza Drew thing Kylie did with Cave. Drowned women. Every section here is strange and compelling with the photos of the dolls like classic paintings along the lines of Death of Marat or Victorian prostitutes. The only thing I couldn't find was a price list.

DOMAINIAQUE
www.dirge.net/domainiac/main.htm
Clique for domain owners!

DRAGON.CON BIOGRAPHIES
www.dragoncon.org/people/indexall.html
Profiles of some interesting writers and artists, with links.

DRAMA CIRCUS
www.desonika.net/ice
A sweet looking girl and clearly troubled, but battling back through these highly distinctive sites, but there's so much spread all over the place. If it was all packed into one immense site it would be stunning.

DrkAngilsEYES – POEMS?
www.geocities.com/drkangilseyes/DrkAngils EYES.html?988082503940

DROID ANNDROID
http://droid.anndroid.net
A grrrl who likes noise. Pics, ranty journal.

DUNGEON KIDS
www.dungeonkids.com/PRIMORTAL/index.html
Has artist pages, and music links.

DURHAM RED INVITES YOU TO THE SHED

www.califia.org/~toni

Only some cute photos on late-nineties website.

DX-TOHJI

www.dx-tohji.co.jp/english

A club where Japanese dancers work. The profiles include some bizarre statements.

E-WITCH

www.e-witch.com

Pagan auctions.

EDEN CELESTE ILLUSTRATIONS

www.edenceleste.com/eden-darkers

EDGAR ALLAN POE

www.Gothic.net/poe

'While I do not (and cannot) claim to be the *best* site on Poe that's in existence, I *do* believe you'll find this site to be an *excellent* starting point for furthering your studies into the man I consider to be one of the truly brilliant masters of the use of rhyme & meter, humour, and of the macabre in many of its known forms.' A *beautiful* site, with all works listed and categorized for easy access. Great links section, and a brief filmography. If you're into Poe, then start here because of the links and everything here to download happily. Or try: www.poecentral.com

EGNART'S VORTEX

www.csn.ul.ie/~egnarts/old_site

An old site about vamps, Goth and Ireland.

ELECTRIC CHAIR

www.theelectricchair.com

Quite a serious approach to the subject, even interviewing the chap who conducts executions in one state, and not forgetting...'the lighter side of the electric chair.'

ELECTRIC FRANKENSTEIN

www.electricfrankenstein.com

Soon to be an online modern horror site, which is why this Punkoid mad bunch get a mention.

EM.BRY.ONIC

www.freakyplanet.com/FreakyPages/embryonic/index.htm

A variety of photographers and some very interesting work.

EMULSION ART

www.emulsionart.net

Not much personal info. 'More input later after I develop a more conceited attitude.' Wonderful live photos, including Cruxshadows, and superb portraits.

EN 1300B JOURNAL ASSIGNMENT

http://members.home.net/tetsab

Odd writing task. Stories, all of them enjoyable, which form a whole in the author's mind.

ENCHANTED FOREST

www.geocities.com/EnchantedForest/Creek/7900

Christa's home page, in a sense. 'Hello, my name is Christa. I currently live on death row at the TN prison for women in Nashville. This webpage is my home where I live in my dreams and imagination. Hopefully, someday I will be back home with my family and friends that I miss so terribly. My mom and dad are building this page for me since I do not have access to a computer. Please be patient with us as we learn to build and make this a wonderful place for all to visit.' Lots of Edgar Allen Poe poems, with Tinkerbell zapping about above them. Christa killed someone when a teenager: that much we get, but there's no more. It's a very touching site, especially when you see the photo album.

THE END IS NEAR

www.raverbashing.com

The site sweeps from left to right, which throws you.

ENERGY ZONE

www.energyzone.it

Pretty important. Watch the popups though.

ENIGMA'S WORLD – PHOTOGRAPHY

http://members.tripod.com/~cool42_luv4u/enigma.html

EN-TRANCE

www.matazone.co.uk

Wonderful art and animations. If in doubt: www.matazone.co.uk/kitty1.html

EVASIVE

http://evasive.org

Rather an elaborate facade for what is, essentially, a journal by Kristine which just doesn't grab the attention, yet.

EVOLVE

www.angelfire.com/pe/bottled

Ladies and Gentlemen (you wish!), we have ourselves a star. This is brilliant. The writing will have you enthralled. Check out Michael Bolton's War ('He now wandered the lands, living off his own toughness, having ninja battles, and loving like only the crooner known as Michael Bolton could.') There is masses of it. He says you'll be pleased. I say you'll become addicted.

EYE CANDY PHOTOGRAPHICS

www.eyecandyphotos.co.uk

THE FABULOUS WORLD OF CORVIDS

www.pokeintheeye.com/accr.html

Crows and Ravens. More info that you can handle in one sitting.

FIGHT THE GOOD FIGHT MINISTRIES

www.goodfight.org/exposesnames.htm

Where you go to expose Bands Who Are Evil. It's seriously weird, but still has some interesting Manson stuff.

THE FILING CABINET

www.geocities.com/Paris/LeftBank/6043

Crazy, detailed, contagious writing.

FIND A GRAVE

www.findagrave.com/cgi-bin/fg.cgi

Type in your name and see if you're dead. I am, eight years ago in Springfield, Illinois. You'd think someone might have said something!

FLAWED ANGEL DIGITAL PHOTOGRAPHY

www.flawedangel.com

FLOWERS FOR THE DEAD

www.flowersforthedead.com

Personal items, C7, The Fear Project – an illustrated litany of strange phobias, plus Kiss dolls, in monthly instalments.

FLUFFY MULES

www.fluffymules.com

Fashion, vanishing style icons and opinions with cool characters, and a new perspective on t-shirts. 'Bad Ass Hard Gal T-shirts that should exist but won't': "I've Got Crabs, I Smell Of Pee, I Did The Whole Team, I Shagged Your Dad, I Just Masturbated, This Is A Stuffed Wonderbra."

FOR THE LOVE OF CROWS
www.zeebyrd.com/corvi29
Fairly self-explanatory.

FOSSIL SURGERY
www.members.tripod.com/~Lyall/index.html
Lyall Anderson has a small site on a specific interest, part of a Paleo ring.

FOTOGRAF FENRIS BIE SONIC SITES
www.sonicsites.de/fenris.html
Goth, fetish, statues photos, etc.

FRAGMENTS OF AN ETERNITY
www.fragmentsofaneternity.com
Art, chat, pics, grafx, vamps, statues, banners.

THE FRANKENBURIES
http://home.earthlink.net/~jerkrecords
The scariest band we've never heard of, allegedly. The site is a mess and takes an age, but...click on their graves on the bio page photo and you meet people who will swear the band sound like Gwar.

FROSTYLIPS
www.frostylips.com
The world of the Platinum Pimpette (Michele from Queens.) She's very funny, don't bother looking for a Goth link – it's just everything, and wonderfully mental.

THE FUNERAL GUY
www.funeralguy.com
Cemeteries, celebrity death sites, dead celebrities, bookstore, music, links. Mainly pics, with respectful details of famous dead people, and not just showbizzy types. This is tasteful and yet slightly different. Also, jazz funeral marches.

FUTURE BITCH
www.futurebitch.com
More from the talented Max Ellis, with illustrations of otherworldly proportions.

THE GARDEN OF ADAM
http://worlock.mortis.org/index.html
Books poems, gallery, broken links, cute sketches, webcam.

GARDEN OF WRATH
www.garden-of-wrath.de
All in German – art gallery, including stuff done for bands. Pretty weird.

GASHED
www.gashed.com

Site representing many mad Electronic bands.

GASLIGHT ELECTRONIC TEXT AND DISCUSSION SITE
www.mtroyal.ab.ca/programs/arts/english/gaslight
'Gaslight is an Internet discussion list which reviews one story a week from the genres of mystery, adventure and The Weird, written between 1800 and 1919.' They even have reading puzzles for eggheads. It's brimming with good old-fashioned intentions.

GGH
www.ghastlyghosthunter.com/ggh.html
Ghosthunting! Ooo-hh-ee-ooh. 'Nothing but hardcore ghost hunting.' Cemeteries – black and white at night (finally!), orbs, vortexes, ectoplasm – genuinely eerie, apparitions, thunderstorms. Pics galore of all of these, plus a few specific explorations explained. She's out there at night, with her camera, which deserves respect.

GHOST RESEARCH SOCIETY
www.ghostresearch.org
Chicago based investigations. Real and fake ghost photos – with even less awareness of camera problems. Great links section to other Ghost-related sites.

GHOST STUDY
www.ghoststudy.com
Great video clip of ghost girl in Japanese car park.

GHOST VILLAGE
www.ghostvillage.com
Pretty feeble. A community thing with people submitting their experiences.

GHOSTWEB
www.ghostweb.com
See the evidence. Or not. Depends.

GHOSTS OF THE PRAIRIE
www.prairieghosts.com
Historic tour, pictures, museum element. More of a book site than anything.

THE GHOST OF OHIO
www.geocities.com/ghosts_of_oh

GHOSTS SPOOKS AND POLTERGEISTS OF HAUNTED ONTARIO
www.darksites.com/souls/horror/hauntedont/index.html

THE GHOST STALKERS
http://ghoststalker.topcities.com
Camcorder proof on this one, as well as real and feel photos, plus ghost stories and apparently Ordshall Hall is a speciality, and recordings with site owners own haunted house.

THE GHOSTWALKER
www.ghostwalker.net
Touring the Historical Cemeteries of Colorado. Beautiful Site. Dead basic, but the emphasis is on the photos themselves, which are lovely. In colour, but they have exactly the right feel, and cemeteries in the snow... quite enchanting. Also very unusual perspectives. This person has a wonderful eye for detail and place.

GIGER
www.giger.com

GIRL UNDER GLASS
www.zowwie.net/whore
Personal site, languishing somewhat, for good reasons. It looks good.

GIRLS WITH GLASSES
www.girlswithglasses.com
Not rude, just charming.

GO INSANE
www2.justnet.ne.jp/~zep
Japanese fan, who likes Bauhaus, 4AD and a big mix of Indie.

GORMENGHAST
www.centenary.edu/~balexand/gormenghast
Brilliant, or what? It's tied in with some course or other, but for the rest of us it's fun and interesting, the architectural flow of the guided tour being something to enhance your appreciation of Gothic Literature. It's actually quite creepy.

GOT NAILS?
www.cherrytart.net/nails
Yes, I have nails. Usual women, and then some.

GOTH BUNNY
www.gothbunny.net
Goths and Furries, in Australia. Either this woman is insane, or inspired, and once you've realised she is not alone in her interests maybe you should plump for the latter. Marvel at the Goth Furry stories, study the Furry profiles, and then question your own sanity.

GOTHIC PRESS:
PUBLISHERS OF THE ABSTRACT
http://members.tripod.com/gothic_press
Er, yes. Check out the examples of their
work *before* buying a book of their
glorious vampiric tales. That is my advice.

THE GRAVEGRRL MANIFESTO
http://blood-dance.net/~azhrarn
Attitude a-go-go.

GRAVER
www.graver-industries.com

GRAVEYARDS OF CHICAGO
www.graveyards.com
The site hasn't been updated for some
time because he's been busy with Nova
Roma – http://novaroma.org – 'a Roman
reconstruction society where I have
been elected as Curator Araneae
('Webmaster') for 2001. The name I use
there is Marcus Octavius Germanicus.'
So he's obviously an obsessive of sorts
as nobody would publicly admit to
such activities, but the site's great.
27 cemeteries or graveyards covered,
with excellent photos.

GRAVEYARDS OF DIXIE
http://members.tripod.com/%7Egraves1/
index1.html
Sweet photo site of cemeteries in
Georgia. Pics are nice, including very
unusual statues.

GREY DAY
www.grey-day.net
'This domain contains adult themes.
At any given moment you could see a
naked breast or read a graphic depiction
of sex, violence, cruelty to vegetables,
etc... you name it it's probably on here.'
Very intricate, beautiful site.

GREY MATTER
http://noahgrey.com/greysoft
Multi sites hosted here, and the variety
is enthralling. You could spend a day
circling this and not get bored.

GRIM RIDES
www.grimrides.com
Grim Rides is a group of funeral car
fiends based in the San Francisco Bay
Area. Info on meets, tips on buying,
postcards to send. Hundreds of hearse
links, pics, clubs etc, and 'Grim Girls'
('These chicks could make the dead

Grim Rides

rise.') Such people are absolutely
brilliant, and crazy. 'Don't let your first
ride in a hearse be your last' © Amy
the Hearse Queen.

GRIM'S GALLERY
http://dimensional.com/~tujiro
Good art/ad/illustrations thing, but
that's all apart from nice party pics.

GRINDER
www.grindertool.com

GROUPIE CENTRAL
www.groupiecentral.com
Interesting site, when it comes to
looking back, but blurs the likes by
having wives and girlfriends of famous
'stars'. How does Justine Frischmann
deserve to be plonked in here? The
news, gossip and groupie stories will
have you entertained.

HALFMOON COMICS
www.halfmoon-comics.com

HANDCRAFTED DOLLS SITE
www.jade.dti.ne.jp/~ak-labo
Again, this is only in Japanese, but
there is a wealth of detail here about the
design and manufacture of the dolls
themselves, plus plenty of gallery pics.
The one indicated is modern in a
surreal way and these really are the sort
of things which make for the perfect
present. This site even has specific
design sections for hair, eyes, torso, feet
etc. Amazing stuff. Click on 'This is

Handcrafted Dolls Site

Blythe' for starters, as it shows the
whole process quickly.

THE HAPPY HOUSE
www.angelfire.com/nh/thehappyhouse

HAPPY JACK'S CAM TALES – WEIRD
http://dialmforagoodtime.parisisburning.com

HAUNTED MANSION
http://ghost.lib.net
Japanese-language only site covering
horror/Goth fiction, plus music.

HAUNTED OHIO
www.prairieghosts.com/hauntoh.html

HAUNTED ONTARIO
www.darksites.com/souls/horror/hauntedont/
index.html
Useful for anyone living in the area.
Interesting for a brief read as well.

HEATHCLIFF, IT'S ME (ETC)
www.treasurehiding.com
Cute, on a seriously artistic bent. (See
'Enchanted Artists.')

www.hauntedheadstones.com (see Clothes/Businesses section)

subjects.' Such as; Dark-Art Demons, General-Horror, Ghosts, Gothic, Graveyards, Halloween, Haunted-Houses, Haunted-Places, Horror-Attractions, Horror-Movies, Horror-Stories, Horror-TV Interesting-Celebrations-Customs, Magic, Monsters, Music. People, SCI-FI, Vampires, Weird-and-Unusual, Werewolves, Witches, Zombies.

HOSOJIMA – ART
http://hosojima.homestead.com

HOW LOATHSOME – STORIES
www.howloathsome.com

HUMAN SKIN
www.humanskin.net
Art site destined for a comical look at life.

ROBERT W HEDENGREN
www.nomoreromeo.com
This is top quality work. True you can see lots of recurrent themes from artists, in and around the comic world generally but so what? This is a *great* selection. He's also a fabulous writer and all round good geezer, and even has baby tee designs done, which is cool. Sometimes his style is ruthlessly modern, at other times it reminds me of European children's books from the thirties to fifties. It has a weird innocence about it. Or, as he puts it 'I am caught helplessly between two ways of thinking and drawing; one, a realistic approach with an eye on detail, and two, simplified metaphors using cartoons and ambiance.' The Pen & Ink section is a *must-see*, okay? Everybody who has this book must visit, or your book magically disintegrates within three weeks of ownership. The drawings section is small, and crap, but there are some moody paintings, and very cool Flash work. You can buy prints, which would be a very sensible investment, or send enchanting postcards. It's a lovely site.

HELLHOLE
www.herebedragons.co.uk/hell

HELLO KITTY'S TEA PARTY
http://groovygames.com/kitty
You'll either find this very sweet or go scuttling and scowling back to that Manson collection.

HEXE-THERESIA
www.hexe-theresia.de

HEXEN WITCHES CLUB
www.hexenwitchclub.here.de
German site where you can all get together and wiggle those hats about, or whatever it is that you actually do.

HIDDEN SANCTUARY – RADIO
www.hiddensanctuary.com

THE HIDDEN SANCTUARY
http://intothesky.net/darkcell/hidden_sanctuary/index.htm
Radio thing with new bands on rotation.

HOLE IN THE HEAD – PIERCING
www.holeinthehead.8k.com

HOLLYWOOD MONSTERS
www.hollywoodmonsters.com/index.shtml
There are some really great live galleries here (under 'Monsters'), as well as LA confidential leaks about who did what and where. It's got a massive club guide and leaks smart smut everywhere.

HORROR WRITERS ASSOCIATION
www.horror.org
The Horror Writers Association (HWA) is a worldwide organization of writers and publishing professionals dedicated to promoting the interests of writers of forror and dark fantasy.

HORRORFIND – CEMETERY GATES
www.horrorfind.com/flashhorror/cemetery gates4.html
Huge resource really. 'Horrorfind.com the directory and search engine dedicated to Horror, Halloween and Spooky

HYBRID
http://bluenine.cjb.net
Go to: www.redmeltdown.net/hybrid/index.htm for pics, photo and digitally affected, loads of personal details, rants. Uber Goth over-hearing the last statements about Manson and Hot Topic: '*Psh* You guys aren't Goth. I am. I am the epitome of Goth. Fear my wrath and so forth. You don't know what music IS. I listened to Christian Death when you were still listening to New Kids on the Block. When Rozz Williams died I *tried* to kill myself about 8 billion times. But then I realized I was a vampire, and the immortal can never die! mwahhhhh haaaaaa!' Advice is then given: 'Get off your whiny Goth ass and go outside and do something you enjoy, that makes you happy. Watch a funny movie. You're not hardcore just because you've seen *The Crow* and *Interview with a Vampire* everyday for the last two years.'
I loved this site.

HYPNOX PHOTOGRAPHY – PORTRAITS
www.hypnox.com

I'M A TEENAGE SCUMBAG
www.dreamwater.com/jackieblue

I DRANK WHAT ?!?!
www.idrankwhat.org
Brilliantly inspired magazine offering an intriguing view on contemporary matters.

'Patience'. © Robert Hedengren

I FEEL SICK: A WEBSITE ABOUT A GIRL
www.saucybard.com/devi/index.html

I LOVE GOTH CHICKS
www.undergroundpropaganda.com/ruenco/
gothic/gothchico2/pages/mall15.htm
Appears to be a high quality set of
photos of mildly pierced girls in sepia.

**IF I CAN'T MAKE THINGS RIGHT,
I'M GONNA DO IT MY WAY**
http://lizzka.com
Okay, a beautiful, smart but simple site,
which has acres of content, yet looks
pint-sized. She may have crap taste in
music, or strangely unadventurous, but
the rest is a joy: an extended journal,
basically, but done brilliantly. Funny
pics in the old files, and she takes a
camera with her everywhere, to
illustrate her journal.

IF LOOKS COULD KILL
www.crookedmoon.com/necrodoll
So this is Necrodoll's site, where we
find drawings of bizarre women, and
details of how these styles arose.

IMMORTELLE.NET
http://members.aol.com/crescntcem
A pictorial tour of New Orleans' Cities
of the Dead. Reviews and photos of all
the cemeteries there, with prints for
sale. It is beautifully realised with
fantastic quality pictures. And something very unusual. Virtual Views allow
you to take a 360 degree panoramic
look at some of the cemeteries.

IN PERPETUAL MOTION
www.ipmradio.com
Radio, much respected.

INANNA IN THE UNDERWORLD
www.geocities.com/mirandaraven_uk/inanna/
index.htm
Some historical epic played out with
Barbie dolls. Very weird.

INDIGO DREAMS – FAERIE
http://members.aol.com/spriggan1/Spriggans
Lair.html

INTENSITIES – THE JOURNAL OF
CULT MEDIA
www.cult-media.com
High-brow online mag with articles
about cult TV, and related themes.
Seriously interesting, I kid you not. *Buffy*,

Stark Trek, *Dr Who*, *3rd Rock*, plus books
and the deepest meaning everywhere.

INTERGOTHEN – COMIC
www.striporama.com/web/gscouts.html

**INTERNET LIBRARY OF EARLY
JOURNALS**
www.bodley.ox.ac.uk/ilej
Eighteenth and nineteenth-century
journals, where saddoes who could only
dream of webcams and the idea they
could tell us they had a bad day at work,
now have a cold, and will never ever
speak to any of their friends again.
('Life sucketh.')

INTO THE WESTERN LANDS
http://sinister.com/~purp
A Burroughs poem apparently, and an old
site, full of crap but a few sweet photos.

INTOXICATING BLOSSOMS COSPLAY
www.geocities.com/intoxicating_blossoms/
index.html
Nicole Angelique Jo is very sweet, as
she admits it's a small site because she
hasn't been into this long and can't
afford to do many costumes.

ISOLATION TANK
www2.mailordercentral.com/isotank
Mail order for all variety of Electronic
music.

IVANA FORD PHOTOGRAPHY
http://blok.org/ivanafoto

**I'VE HIDDEN MYSELF SO LONG IN
YOUR SMILE... I HAVE FORGOTTEN
MY OWN.**
www.angelfire.com/pa3/Vampryixie/index.html
Weird girl. Photos, links, poetry and
guestbook. Weird choice of pics and
captions, says 'Mike is a rather strange
kid lol... but fun to be around, although
sometimes I would love to stab him.
Fuckin Prick!'

THE IVORY TOWER
http://childlike.ivory-tower.net
Strange art, cool photos, tiny bio,
brilliant cats.

IZAM
www.izamadonna.com
A fiendishly winsome site with lots
of little bits going and flowery
graphics. I like it, and haven't a clue

what it is, apart from there's band
appearing in photos, as well as food and
objects in her room, and a clothes shop
section. I liked the dancing bunny best.

JAPONICA PETITCHAT
http://members.home.net/irrbloss
You tell me. A real name? She's like a
fantasy fairy or something, and the
links are even stranger.

JASON BEAM STUDIOS
www.jasonbeamstudios.com
This is a very attractive site that I am
sure will get even more interesting.
Pays respectful homage to his models,
there are some t-shirts, and The Store.
Limited edition prints, artist proofs and
originals all available. No prices given.
Magnificent wallpapers.

JDOLL
http://homepage2.nifty.com/jo-adachi
A sort of Dolls R Us thing, done along
the lines of all the action figure
merchandise you can get these days.
Some look mass-produced and lack any
real quality but the strange cherubs
would look good around the house.
Mind you, they're about 70 quid.

JENNY'S
www4.big.or.jp/~syara
Jenny is another Malice and Gackt fan,
and opts for the most colourful
fantastical dolls, and good links.

JERKBOX STUDIOS
www.jerkbox.com
Jerkbox & Punk'nhead comic. 'Jerkbox &
Punk'nhead are the top demonic hitmen
in Big Jack Satan's crime syndicate in
Hell! They will *so* kick your ass!'

JILTED ANGEL
www.angelfire.com/ab/jiltedangel

JUST ANTITHESIS
http://justantithesis.cjb.net
Very stylish site, of poetry and journal.
Everything about this site is good, and
trust me... the bio is great fun. She's a
cutie and she's odd.

KIN
www.kaffene.net
Excellent journal/magazine with all its
links and comments on the vagaries
of life.

KAIHAWAII

www.kaihawaii.de/home.html
German site with info on eighties and
Electronic bands and events.

KARA MAE

www.karamae.com
http://clubs.yahoo.com/clubs/thekaramaefanclub
Interesting woman, a model with over a
thousand members in her club, but
who would seriously pay $600 for a
20x30 portrait?

KATAN AMANO

www.synforest.co.jp/cdrom/sf-019
If you find the Japanese doll sites interesting, which you will unless you have your
head up a cow's backside, then you may
find this interesting. A CD-Rom of Katan
Amano's dolls. She died years ago, but
her creations have inspired many since,
and her originals go for serious money.

KATRINA DEL MAR

www.bway.net/~katrina
Very odd, a filmmaker as well as photographer, who has a film on Girl Gangs. I'm
sure some them are very intimidating but
the Glitter Girls – 'riding bikes in tight
pants. So tuff and pretty' – are on push-
bikes for God's sake! Portraits are lovely.

KAYULI HIINA

www.ne.jp/asahi/kayuli/hiina/index.html
Another one of these strange doll sites
and this one is truly extraordinary.
Check the profile, with the photos of
her work over the years as well as the
gallery. *Incredible* imagery.

KEIRSEY TEMPERAMENT AND CHARACTER WEBSITE

http://keirsey.com
I'm an Idealist.

TINA KRAUSE

www.tinakrause.com

L'UNIVERSE D'AGATHE ET ANANTA

http://agathep.free.fr
Some excellent live photos here of loads
of bands.

LACUNAE – GOTH FURRY COMIC

http://lacunae.pangaean.net

LABYRINTH 13

http://embyquinn.tripod.com
Zine on the occult, crime and conspiracy.

LARS DEIKE PHOTOGRAPHY

www.deike.de
Arty nudes, portraits, commercial work.

LAST KISS

www.acidkiss.org/~lkgirl
Journal of course. Check 'chick' and
look for band pics – including The
Misfits Bettie Page tribute
www.envy.nu/bettiestar – and Guys to drool
over, plus Twisted Clique – a group of
quality journals, Eyeliner Love Clique –
the discussion area for people who have
a thing about men in makeup –
www.virtue.nu/eyelinerlove so there's variety
throughout this stunning site.

Just Antithesis

LAUREN LIBERTY

www.angelfire.com/retro/laurenliberty
Great little site, beautifully simple in
design, with handy DIY tips, and
fantastic links.

LE FREAKSHOW 7

http://tangledcurls.org/lefreakshow
A Visual site with pics poetry and such,
basically from NIN fans.

LEFT.OF.CENTER – DOLLS

http://embyquinn.tripod.com

LELEBEAUXART

www.lelebeauxart.net

As hot ex-Mormons go, she's up there
with the best of them. Goes into great
depth about everything, has some
okayish art on display, plus Domino's
novel Jessica ('The trials and tribulations
of an overweight, unpopular, junior high
school girl.')

LENORA'S PAGE

http://lenoraclaire.com/lenora
Model and filmmaker, bust-thrusting
actress. 'I strive to make interesting, visually intense stop motion animation films,
with among other things, Barbie Dolls.'
Good luck with that. Credits Cocteaus and
Eraserhead., so can't be all mad. Check
out her fanclub for the trite messages.

LENORE

www.spookyland.com
http://home.earthlink.net/~schatten13/lenore.html
http://members.tripod.com/~AnnieDork/
DaZine/Roman.html
www.envy.nu/lenores

LENS RECORDS – ARTISTS PAGE

www.lensrecords.com/artists.html

LEXIE'S JOURNAL

http://livejournal.com/~batwinged
The girl who does Batwinged. The
journal is okay.

LILEKS (JAMES) – THE PECULIAR ART OF MR FRAHM

www.lileks.com/institute/frahm/index.html

LITTLE GLOOMY – COMIC

www.littlegloomy.com

LIVE ART

www.stellareng.com/liveart

LIVING DEAD DOLLS

www.livingdeaddolls.com
'We've passed away, now it's time to
play.' Only available through certain
outlets these are so awesome you're
probably going to want to get them mail
order. Each doll (10" tall) comes in its
own coffin, with death certificate. I
guess you have to e-mail about prices as
even the Mezco site doesn't reveal its
prices. Tower has them at $125.99 for
six different figures in a sealed case,
except you get two Sadie and two Sin!
http://clubs.yahoo.com/clubs/livingdeaddolls
http://clubs.yahoo.com/clubs/livingdeaddolls
devotees

http://groups.yahoo.com/group/living deaddollscoffintalk Plus, why not visit the Living Dead Dolls fansite, Deader Is Better: www.deaderisbetter.com

LORD HAWK'S DARK KEEP

www.darksites.com/souls/vampires/lordhawk Poetry, paranormal, vampires... blah.

LUNAR COFFIN

http://planet.gaiax.com/home/koitsukihime Another Japanese doll site but with a strange feel, including having a BBS called The Lunatic Garden.

THE LUNCH PACKET MISSION

http://missionlunchpacket.tripod.com

(MACHINE)X(SOUL) – RADIO

www.machineandsoul.com

MAGICAL WAKE – MAG

www.paranormal.de/para/MagicalWake/ magicle.html

MANIFESTEANGE METAMORPHOSE TEMPS DE FILLE

www.metamorphose.gr.jp
Huge array of clothes and accessories for dolls, with shops everywhere.

MATT BAUER – ARTIST/DESIGNER

http://members.home.net/nmb111

THE MAUSOLEUM

www.the-mausoleum.com
Promising curiosities and oddities is all very well, but can they deliver? Oh yes indeed! Gothic and Industrial downloads, plus things from Boy George to Blake's babies and Depeche Mode. Big bands link section started, with virtually no links. Forties/fifties US propaganda films. Stream horror film clips. Poseur Lounge is a modern commercial critique in a splatter method.

MAX ELLIS

www.junkyard.co.uk
Digital art wonders from Max, former singer with God & The Crazy Lesbians From Hell. You *will* be captivated.

MEDUSA KATE

www.manifest-angel.com/medusa
Brief journal, some good writing, interesting photo portraits and silkscreen prints.

MEET THE TROUPE – BELLYDANCING

www.bellydancingbyzamoras.com/troupe/guests
I'm not telling you who the surprise member of the troupe is. Visit to find out.

MEMENTO MORI:
DEATH AND PHOTOGRAPHY IN NINETEENTH CENTURY AMERICA

http://cmp1.ucr.edu/terminals/memento_mori
Nothing salacious or sick here, but a serious historical thing about early photography. Proof that death can be handled on a site in a dignified manner.

MEMENTO-MORI.COM

www.gloomcookie.com
A comic, plus rpg. Wallpapers to die for.

MIDNIGHT CARNIVAL

www.oz.net/~lotus/mcpage.htm
Interesting fiction (Bloch gets a mention) zine. John Navroth is involved.

THE MISANTHROPIC BITCH

www.misanthropic-bitch.com
Wow! 'Providing jack-off material for white misogynists since 1997.' Brilliant opinion site. This, on another high school shooting, 'If you couldn't cope with 16-year-old bullies with inferiority complexes, how do you deal with the adult world? *Oh, yeah, endless hours of vampire role-playing games.* Teenagers are obnoxious shits because that's what that stage of life is about. It's about seeing how far boundaries can be pushed, dealing with the insecurities of an ever-changing body and mind, feeling out one's place in the world and all of that other psychological development bullshit – generally a human being at its most insufferable. What would you rather be, Colby, an American nerd with a shitty personality (and access to downloadable porn) or a malnourished African with AIDS, cholera and sickle-cell anemia?' Truly exceptional.

MISS CALENDAR'S TECHNO PAGANS

www.angelfire.com/ca/MCTP

MOMO'S ROOM

www.zakonet.ne.jp/~angel/momochan/ momo.shtml
Japanese body-piercing site.

MONGOOSE – FURRY

http://mongoose.net

MOONLAB

www.moonlab.com
'Before you go to the moon, you must agree with the following: I am voluntarily choosing to enter this site because I want to see and hear the vulgar, moronic stuff that is available on this site. Dr Maad strongly supports parental controls on the Internet. If you are a parent and you want to block this site, then do it, cocksucker.'

MOONSMUSES.COM

www.moonsmuses.com
Want to pretend to be special? Here you go! Quite funny magic site, as in 'Stay for a spell' and you can't accuse them of ripping you off. 'Burnt Offerings $ Prosperity $ Kit = Parchment paper seals are powerful additions to your spells, rituals, amulets, talismans. Parchment Seals come four to a kit, all different designs but all one theme. Comes with printed "scroll" of instructions for use. Each seal is approx 5 inches X 5 inches.' Only $5!!!! "Anna Rivas Dragons' Blood Ink is Perfect for writing most magical writings." Only $7.50 for 1 oz, but I did not detect an actual list of ingredients.

MORBID FACT DU JOUR

http://asylumeclectica.com/morbid
One horrifying story every day of the year.

MORE THAN MORTAL: EXODUS

www.morethanmortal.com

THE MORTICIAN

www.themortician.net
Another death-related site, but tastefully so.

MORTICIA'S MORGUE

www.morticiasmorgue.com/vampires.html
Big! She calls it Morticia's Occult Emporium – so click on that box to see her store. There's nothing about her but the site also covers vampires, Gothic matters, Buffy and cult TV.

MOURNING SOULS

www.mourningsouls.net
Cemeteries/ghosts/webring/poetry.

MOYA

http://home.gwi.net/~changeling
Classic cat photo alert, fiction, poetry and an essay on Goth, including her attack on shoddy sites: 'And even when I *was* an idiot, at least I was an idiot

with style and class!' You can also see her moving into Spy thriller territory and sci-fi.

MOZART ROTTWEILER
http://home.computer.net/~mozart

MP3/STREAMING ETC
www.darkwave.org.uk/more.php?cat=Streaming%2FMP3%20Music

MR BIG
president@whitehouse.gov
You know, if you get bored... but mind your language!

MR HUMPUTY DUMPUTY
www16.freeweb.ne.jp/art/ryu-jing

MUNDUNGUS
www.mundungus.com
This has the maddest journal ('Noise'), which is hilarious, plus unusual fiction.

MUSEUM OF DEATH
www.museumofdeath.com
Rozz has an exhibit going in!

MUSEUM – SYNTHS
www.anz123.com/VSM/s_frame.htm

MUSIC DATABASE
http://kzsu.stanford.edu/eklein

MUSIC STAR DRUM
– JAPANESE GOTH/BBS
www.geocities.co.jp/MusicStar-Drum/5795/Bach.html

MUSICMANIAC
www.musicmaniac.de/index2.html
Useful Industrial/EBM/Electro/eighties/Synth/Goth discographies as well as sale and trade lists.

MY FAVOURITE BANDS
www.geocities.com/xxtalenaskittiexx

MY PIC
http://hometown.aol.com/pixytoy

MY WORLD: MY REALITY
www.sijun.com
Good personal site dominated by computer art, with tips and tutorials!

MYLENE FARMER
www.mylene-farmer.de/index.htm

MYSTICAL WORLDWIDE WEB
www.mystical-www.co.uk/sub.htm
Folklore, divination, crop circles, Gaia etc. The New Age approach.

NANCY KILPATRICK
www.sff.net/people/Nancyk
Nice site for horror writer, plus online writing courses! She also looks so damn cool in pics, without even trying.

NBM
www.nbmpublishing.com

NECLORD'S NECRONOMICON
www.angelfire.com/goth/Necronomicon
You might think this is a saddo site. Think again. Vast array of dark GIFs, dark jpegs, skulls and the like. Wicca and occult.

THE NECROBOTIC DANCE PARTY
www.kuci.org/industrial

AL AZIF – NECRONOMICON
www.geocities.com/SoHo/9879/necpage.htm
Is this a real Necronomicon? No, but it looks convincing, and it is *very* serious.

NECRONOMI
www.necronomi.com
Online Grimoire, under construction. Will be witchy occult oasis by now.

NECROPOLIS: XENOPHOBIAN FEAR
www.xfpower.myweb.nl
Site of a necromancer, or so he believes, with bits about wizardly, Magecraft, healing.

NEW ORLEANS CEMETERIES
www.mardigrasneworleans.com/~bigeasy/deadcity.html

NEW ORLEANS CEMETERY AND VOODOO PAGES
www.geocities.com/BourbonStreet/6157
Cemetery photos, a Voodoo section, paranormal Pick of the Week.

NICHOLAS SEIZURE
www.nicolasseizure.com

NIGHT OF BLACK GLASS
www.threethirteen.net/glass
Victoria's artwork showcase. Good canvas, basic paper and clichéd digital. One interesting aspect of her, currently

closed, is the webcam, where she lets you watch her working on a piece.

NIGHT PHOTOGRAPHS
www.fotog.net

NILAIHAH – LABEL
www.nilaihah.com

NINISTRY – JAPANESE IND
www.ne.jp/asahi/ninistry/industrial

NISHIMI
www.amy.hi-ho.ne.jp/nishimi9
I won't even pretend to know what's going on here. It's dolls, Jim, but not as we know them. They'd give Tim Burton nightmares.

NON-STOP HORRIBLE DISCO
http://glitzern.tripod.co.jp
Strange Japanese site. Goth and Rock reviews + tiny downloads.

NORTON TOPICS ONLINE
www.wwnorton.com/nael/nto/romantic/litgoth/litgothfrm.htm
Bite-sized education overview on Goth influence from then till now.

NOT YOUR NORMAL PROJECT
www.envy.nu/epindc

NOX-DESIGN
www.nox-design.com

OBJET TROUVES
www.vividinfinity.com/ac
Xanthi and D have put together a very interesting and attractive site with odd ideas and rudery flitting through each other's territory. Journals are poetic and surreal. A true work of art.

OFFICIAL ROCKY HORROR SHOW
www.rockyhorror.com

THE OFFICIAL STORM CONSTANTINE WEBSITE
http://members.aol.com/Malaktawus/Home.htm
There's masses to see here, including Storm's mini-journal about how her latest project is going, which is a nice touch. The excellent info service Inception can be reached at: Peverel@aol.com and you can join the mailing list, but you'll be too busy initially rummaging through the old book details, the art and photos (brilliant 1997 shot of her with Cleo Cordell and Freda

Warrington – 300 years ago they'd have been arrested as trollops!). In 1999 Storm goes all mumsy, but by 2001 she's in pagan relaxation! A changeable wench and no mistake. This site is endearing, and the links are intriguing. Don't miss one of the *best* cats galleries anywhere, and no, we're not talking stage musicals. (Deduct ten credibility points anyone who just over-excited then.)

OH MY GOTH! – COMIC
www.voltaire.net/omg.html

OLD BONES
www.geocities.com/BourbonStreet/6157
Gravestones, statuary, early American postcards of same, mourning cards, mausoleums, memorials. A beautiful selection of photographs taken by a variety of talented photographers. An absolutely brilliant selection of jokes on gravestones, my favourite being: In a Thurmont, Maryland, cemetery: 'Here lies an Atheist, All dressed up, And no place to go.' Superb site. Have fun, just don't drop litter.

ONE WINGED ANGEL
http://onewingedangel.com
Anime, comics, games.

THE OPTIC NERVE – ART
www.theopticnerve.com

ORANGE LIPSTICK – WEBCAM/RANTS
www.orangelipstick.com

OTAKU WORLD – KISS DOLLS
www.otakuworld.com/kiss

OUT AND LOUD
http://grumpybat.net/necrofae
Formerly Soft Whisperings. Support and advice site for gays and bisexuals. And it's a busy, busy site. If this is what you're looking for I'd say pretty much everything is thought of.

OUTLET PROMOTIONS
www.outlet-promotions.com
It's Glenn from Faithful Dawn, and chums, offering services to help bands get places. May be worth UK bands checking out.

PAPAVER'S GALLERY OF CEMETERY PICTURES
www.geocities.com/Area51/Chamber/8333/index.html

Loads of pics, including the West Brompton cemetery in London.

PARANORMAL A – Z
www.paranormalatoz.com
A simple guide from a-z of mysteries and cultish fare. You get a definition, then links to sites of actual relevance.

P.A.R.O.D.Y.
www.redmusic.com/goths/index.html
Brilliant site about how parents can detect the dangers of their child becoming as Goth. With sensible advice about give-away clues in Goth's behaviour and how to spot it. 'Writes angry entries in a secret diary (you can usually find the diary easily if you search your child's room). Has paranoid fantasies (many GOTHS accuse their parents of spying on them).' If you don't enjoy this, you're lost.

THE PASSION OF AN EGGPLANT
www.geocities.com/SoHo/Coffeehouse/8643

PERSONALITY DISORDER TEST
www.4degreez.com/misc/personality_disorder_test.mv
I'm schizoid, as well as moderately 'schizotypal' and narcissistic.

PHANTOM COACHES HEARSE CLUB
www.phantomcoaches.org
Pretty epic stuff for enthusiasts, weirdoes though you are!

PHENOMENAL WOMEN OF THE WEB
www.phenomenalwomen.com

PHOTOGRAPHY BY SNAPSHOT
www.snapshot-photography.de
Excellent photos, with band shots, often promo. Also portraits, TV, literature.

THE PHOTOGHRAPHY OF JOE HUNT
www.geocities.com/kilted_one
Lightly perv-noir moody portraits.

THE PHOTOGRAPHY OF WILLIAM SIEBERT
www.geocities.com/virginsheep

PICTOGRAPH HOLLY
www.pictograph.co.jp/pastrays/index.html
Interesting art, on a Japanese site.

PINK HANDCUFFZ
http://pinkhandcuffz.com
This is madly vibrant. Nothing to do

with Goth at all, but a livelier take on the whole clique and comment thing. Lisa's a complete nutter!

PITAXCHANGE
www.tres-gothique.com/pitaXchange
'Angelique of disillusion design is providing a new way to promote your pita.'

PLANETGRRL
www.planetgrrl.com
An irreverent look at the world through spiky female eyes, on a massive site done by some seriously imaginative and evil characters. Extremely funny, sometimes confusing (to me!) and always evolving. You'll love this, especially as the other sites are so interesting. 'Dear Planetgrrl' is particularly frank in its advice, and Life and Babe are better than the dross you find in newsagents. Jules (Ms Lovely at Big Bro 2) and Sam also do Fluffy Mules.

PLASTIC GOTHIC
www.spawn.co.kr
It's Korean, but that's all I can work out, other than Action Figures get a mention!

PLATONIC LOVE
http://page.freett.com/liyadoll
Liyarna's one and only official bisque doll site. 'Sex: man and woman mixed blood. Proof: purple butterfly in the chest. Loves: The beautiful one, doll, Gothic/Occult, Princess, the queen, prince, witch, angel, and Satan.' Yep.

PLEZ ONLINE
www.dikenga.com/plez
A saucy mare called Pleasant Gehman – writer, dancer, performer.

POISON RAIN
http://poisonrain.com/menu.htm

POPFOLIO
www.popfolio.com
Some great gig photos by Jennifer Jeffery.

PRETTY PALE
www.prettypale.com
Hand-coloured prints for sale. Lovely cemetery things, but poor portraits.

PRIKOSNOVENIE – LABEL
www.multimania.com/prikos

'Serenity'. Photo © Stéphane Lord. Model: Fannie Langlois

PROJECT Z – MAD ZINE/FORUM
www.projectzee.f2s.com

PSYBER FIELD
www.angelfire.com/ut/psyberfield
Conspiracies, prophecies, etc.

PURGED BEAUTY
http://purgedbeauty.8m.com
Talented Gothling who has forgotten
to do anything with site. It's her details,
a few pics, list of mates.
This (http://nyssadark.neckercube.com) has
something to do with her.

THE PURPLE GANG
www.thepurplegang.com
Detroit Electronics label, plus band and
collective project.

**RAKUHAKU TENSHI & BARA
NINGYOUKAN**
www.alpha-net.ne.jp/users2/maren
This seriously creeped me out, but
worth it just for doll pic on front page,
but there's more. Exhibition – click on
feathers or below and find really weird
doll photos: well Gothic, and click on
right candle for more, gallery – click
each pic to produce a weirder selection
– click the right one for the best,
including dolls in birdcages, profile –
(unless I'm mistaken you can e-mail the
dolls!) and links to strange doll world.

RAMENBUDGET
www.ramenbudget.com
Clever comic strip art site with
character interaction.

RAVEN MAILING LIST
www.rinzai.com/raven/ravenlist.html
Serious Raven enthusiasts mailing list.

RAVEN MUSIC GROUP
http://ravenworldwide.com/RMG.htm
Good site for label and live/cultural
events and publishing group. Bands –
Cult Of The Psychic Fetus, Abbadon
and Wicked Angel.

RAVEN'S RANTS
www.ravensrants.com
'Gothic Poetry and more.' Well I should
bloody hope so. 'The meanings and
intents of this site have changed over
the years, but now, it's back to where it
began… publishing, distributing works
while at the same time receiving

feedback and creating conversation
and hopefully helping or otherwise
engaging the reader. Never cry, never
smile, quoth the raven, nevermore.'
There's poems, short stories and rants.
Diary is good.

THE RAVEN SOCIETY
www.student.virginia.edu/~ravens/home1.html
Anyway… so this very morning I'm
writing this review, I was out at 7.10am
on a rare jaunt. There was no-one
around but I heard weird noises, and
when I looked up there were crows
everywhere, a crow on every chimney,
on all the houses, on either side of the
street, and they were making odd
sounds, which I believe was for my
benefit. ('What's that? You want me to
follow you?') Some were even tapping
their beaks inside the rim of the
chimney pots. Maybe this is their
band? Well they know my address,
can't they do these things in a formal
manner? Anyway, the point I'm trying
to make is that ravens look upon crows
with disdain. Probably saw the film
and thought the birds must be equally
shite. This site celebrates the work of
Poe.

READ MANGA EX!
www.geocities.com/azzorrac
Delightful cartoons. Don't miss this.

READING ROOM INDEX: GOTHIC
www.lib.msu.edu/comics/rri/grri/gothic.htm
Comic info archive, for the serious
collector/completist.

REALITY CHECK
http://cattygoths.com
I thought *Love & Rockets* was a comic,
but the girls have escaped! This is like
Cheeziest Goth site, with a slightly
different agenda, in that they go for the
innards of what is wrong with a site. I
feel sure that if someone was simply
misguided or just starting out they
wouldn't be too hard on someone and
might pass on to other targets, and
when they're taking people up on their
spelling at least there is consistency
here… but how would they know, for
example, if someone doing a site was
dyslexic? (Spellcheck doesn't help
someone in that instance.) And let's
remember, CleoCatra didn't even spot
that The Relm Of Dark Insanity (see

Goth Sites) wasn't real!!!!! They steal
people's pics and apply their own
whimsical captions and they have the
usual get-out clause: 'If you are
offended, don't come here, we don't
mind if you don't visit us.' It looks *very*
attractive, and I am sure these spiteful,
snooty little excuses for human beings
have a great time. If you are also
fatuous vermin who regard yourself as a
Higher Being, you may enjoy it too.

THE REALM OF THE DARK KISS
http://members.tripod.com/~bluehead/kiss/
kiss.html
A strange and complex world of
anime-inspired dolls, including Goth
and Sandman dolls. The more I looked,
the less I understood.

REANIMATOR
www.deathrock.com/reanimator

REBELS IN DREAMLAND
www.rebelsindreamland.com
This was coming soon, so I'm taking
this on trust, as Sophia is a cat-lover.
And, as we all know, they don't lie.

REDUX
www.redux-angel.org
Gillian Anderson fans running amok.

THE REFUGE (CHRISTIAN GOTH)
http://members.truepath.com/Wyntyr/index.html
There's lots about Christians and not
much about Goth, put it that way.

REI'S DOLLS AND SWEETS PAGE
http://home.att.ne.jp/yellow/doll/rei
Again mystifying, covering dolls but
somehow naming them after sweets
and food, with an equally beguiling and
baffling links section.

REINES DU SABATT
http://page.freett.com/liyarna
This is a sister site by the woman who
does the Platonic Love doll site. Click
the crescent moon to get in, then click
the blue links under the small red rose
and illustrations of historical figures
appear for some reason, but below
them are links to wistful doll heads.

REPETITION
http://homepages.ihug.co.nz/~repeat
Great general resource for NZ
underground music.

REVENGE LADY – 'ADVICE'
www.revengelady.com

ROBOTGIRL.NET
http://robotgirl.net
Technology and digital art mixed together.

ROCK YOU IN THE RAIN'S ARMS
www.grey-day.net/cerulean
A beautifully simple journal. Smooth design, bit light on content and depth, sad to say, although if you're a fish fanatic you'll empathise with her daily worries.

RODNEY'S WHIMSYLOAD
www.whimsyload.com
'The Center For Advanced Whimsy.'

ROMANTIC CIRCLES
www.rc.umd.edu/indexjava.html
'Romantic-period literature and culture. Romantic Circles is the collaborative product of an ever-expanding community of editors, contributors, and users around the world.'

ROMANTICISM ON THE NET
www.sul.stanford.edu/mirrors/romnet
'An International Refereed Electronic Journal devoted to Romantic studies. The peer-review system means that articles submitted to the journal will normally be considered by at least two experts in the field, one of whom is a members of the Editorial Board.' In other words don't send anything about how much you loved All About Eve. They'll send doctors round.

ROSEBLEED
http://rosebleed.home.att.net/
Open 'dark poetry' forum.

RP's GALLERY
www.abbta.se/rp/indexx.htm
This is the menu page of quality photographer RP's site, with pics of RLYL, Danielle Dax, Kastrierte Philosophen, Laibach, and Siouxsie & Banshees.

S.P.U.D.
www.geocities.com/CapitolHill/2801
Fanzine with a difference.

SACRIFICIAL SCREAMS
http://sinisterbeauty.com/sacrificial/intro.html
I had to include at least one Metal-proud site: this is it.

SAILOR JAMBOREE – COSPLAY
www.sailorjamboree.com

THE SANCTUARY 2
www.geocities.com/Paris/Palais/4183
Another Christian site, but wait... where else will you see someone discussing Disused Underground Stations? Rejoice!

SAPPHIRE FAERIES
www.sapphire-faeries.net

SARYN ANGEL
http://sarynangel.com
Beautiful portraits.

SATAKO MAGAZINE
www.satokomag.com
Extremely interesting mag-type site. Things occasionally turn up which are relevant.

SEASON OF MIST – LABEL
www.season-of-mist.com

SEDLEC OSSUARY – AWESOME
www.ludd.luth.se/users/silver_p/kutna.html

SENSORY EXPANSION MEDIA
http://users.nac.net/thread
Electronic-ish label cunningly ensures that anyone visiting goes away none the wiser about their artists because it's done in a mysterious manner.

SEQUENTIAL TART
www.sequentialtart.com/cgi-bin/cover_0401.pl
A truly fantastic and wildly absorbing comics industry webzine.

THE SEVEN DEADLY SINS & SEVEN HEAVENLY VIRTUES
www.deadlysins.com/tales/010128.htm
Berserk site about sin and The Sins, with bizarre numerology conspiracy theories, and some astonishing stories.

SAPPHIRE FAERIES

SHADOW OF THE MARQUIS
http://shadowofthemarquis.homestead.com/Entry.html
Potentially offensive literature.

SHADOWLAND – CHRISTIAN
www.geocities.com/Paris/LeftBank/1613

SHALINDRIA – FURRY
www.furnation.com/Shalindria

SHAMAKOU'S JUNKROOM – GAMES?
http://shimakou.szero.net

THE SHANMONSTER
http://shanmonster.bla-bla.com/index.html

SHIMMER'n'NIGHTSHADE
www.geocities.com/SunsetStrip/Pit/3885
Cute pics of Dutch Patti, done by surprisingly bad quality photographer.

SIDESHOW ENTERTAINMENT
www.netherworld.com/~paisli
Gig organiser who also has a large written archive.

SILVER ARTIFICE GRAPHICS
www.angelfire.com/co/SilverArtifice

THE MICK SINCLAIR ARCHIVE
http://micksinclair.com
Mick was always one of my favourite writers at *ZigZag* because of his humour – so dry and quick you never

www.spookyland.com

really knew what to expect next. Since then he has gone on to far more successful things, and his whole archive of stuff is available here. All manner of topics. If you enjoy quality journalism you'll love this.

SINFEST
www.sinfest.net

SINITHA
http://envy.nu/sinitha

SIRAGIKU
http://siragiku.virtualave.net/index2.html

SIREN SUMMER
www.angelfire.com/tx2/SirenSummer
A Goth Model. Tons of photos at fashion shows she's worked. The Blackmail ones are great. Ah, she's pondering doing a Judas Priest site! Moving on...

SITE ELECTROWEB DARKT 56
www.multimania.com/darkface/frames.htm
Electro and Goth, French style, and huge content. There are wonderfully high quality galleries with gig and club dates listings, features on bands like Dead Souls Rising and Digital Blood, plus lifestyle and art.

SKULL COLLECTION
www.d91.k12.id.us/www/skyline/teachers/robert
sd/skulls.htm
Animal skulls, the cleaning and keeping of. You can view them in 360º if you like. Mammals, fish, reptiles, you name it. What a weirdo.

THE SLEEPYTIME AND CHERRY PANDA
http://crash.to/sleepytime

SLG PUBLISHING – COMICS
www.slavelabor.com
You can also ask questions of their Mr Bob, a chimp wearing glasses.

SLUGGY FREELANCE
http://sluggy.com/d/990510.html
Comic art, ages old, including *Muffin The Vampire Baker*, which is nowhere near as crap as you might expect.

SO WHAT HAPPENS NOW?
www.broken-lips.net/~resplendent

SOMBRESLIEUX
www.sombreslieux.com
Demons, Gothic, vampires. Very dramatic site, if you can put up with all the pop-ups. It's all Art, and some is fantastic but there's quite a few faulty frames. Worth persevering with when you have half an hour spare.

SOMMEIL ABYSSE
http://noctropolis.net
Although a bit traditional for an Arbus fan, there are lovely photos available to buy.

THE SPARK.COM
http://test.thespark.com
I am 39% Slutty, just as I am apparently 38% Gay. I'm not sure how accurate the various tests may be. For example: '39 women agreed with you, and chose "Groucho Marx" as the best sex option of all time. Fact: So far, the most popular place to lick lubricated men is below the right nipple.' 44% Bastard, hurrah!

SPICE GOTHS
www.geocities.com/SunsetStrip/Studio/1721

The links on the right still work if you're feeling nostalgic and just plain spiteful.

SPINAL THING
http://free.freespeech.org/apophysis
Amazing portraits, by Richard Taylor plus design, art links and a great cat tribute.

SPOOKYLAND
www.spookyland.com
Magnificent site revolving around Roman Dirge (Lenore).

STAND BACK, CITIZEN
http://thingy.apana.org.au/~fun/agsf
'We will kick your arse and not even smear our eyeliner.' Sounds good, no? Well you can find out the hard way.

STANDOUT PRODUCTIONS – PHOTOS
www.geocities.com/uniprod/ucg.html

STEVE DIET GOEDDE – PHOTOGRAPHY
www.stevedietgoedde.com

STEVE DRURY PHOTOGRAPHY
www.geocities.com/SunsetStrip/8616/index.html
Old mucker of mine, who has bravely fought the photographic wars, and here you find some evidence of good work, plus odd Spanish touches. Bauhaus, Party Day, ASF, Wolfhounds, Gavin Friday and... er, Def Leppard! Make sure you click on the 'index' arrow inside each section.

STORIES BY DOMINO & STEPHANIE K DYE
www.lelebeauxart.net/novel.htm

STRAITJACKET COMICS
www.straitjacketstudios.com

STUDIO RONIN – ILLUSTRATIONS
www.studioronin.com

STUDY PLAN – GOTHIC PRIMARY
www.ric.edu/rpotter/gothictexts.html
I guess this is there to give ideas for your degree courses?

SUBNATION
www.subnation.com
It's the ace Demian chap, but this is the label site, which has compilations and bands like Venus Walk. For Cruciform look in bands.

SUBVERSION (UK)

www.subversionuk.com

This is going to be mixture of Punk and Goth, and will be taking as a wry look back as much as commenting on current developments.

SUCCUBUS AND INCUBUS INFORMATION WANTED

www.succubushunter.com

I'm scared shitless! Please help me! I am in hiding, all alone, terrified that they will find me! You see, I am being chased by Succubi!!! And they won't stop until I'm dead!!! I know it sounds crazy, but you must read my terrifying reports. I swear to you, it's all true. Bizarre, with photo report of evidence.

SUCCUBUS

www.succubus.net

Bitchiness, fashions and links. Very dark.

TAKE A BITE 1.0 – SEXBAT ANTIQUES

www.crg.cs.nott.ac.uk/~rji/Gothic/TAB/tab.html

Antiques, of certain charm, but haven't aged well. TAB 4:

www.demon.co.uk/bat/aircrash/tab.html

TAMAGOTHI

www.gothic.net/~skarblade

TAPES OF TERROR

www.morticiasmorgue.com/tot.html

From horror to Eurotrash to exploitation and action movies.

THERESA'S LIVE JOURNAL – EXCELLENT

http://daemoniacus.livejournal.com

THIS GUY LIVED ALONE

www.and was feeling a bit lonely.com

So he went to the pet shop to get something to keep him company. The pet shop owner suggested an unusual pet: a talking millipede. 'Okay,' thought the man, 'I'll give it a go...' So he bought a millipede, took it home, and for lack of advance preparations, made it a temporary home in a cardboard box. That evening testing his new pet, he leaned over the closed box and said, 'I'm going to the pub for a drink, do you want to come too?' He waited a few moments, but there was no reply. He tried again, 'Hey, millipede, do you want to go to the PUB with me?' Again,

no response. Disgusted by his gullible nature, he decided to give it one more try before returning the millipede to the pet shop. So he got real close to the box and repeated rather loudly, 'I SAID, I'M GOING TO THE PUB FOR A DRINK. DO YOU WANT TO COME?' 'For God's sake, I heard you the first time!" snapped the millipede, "I'm just putting my shoes on!'

THOMAS GIANARDI – PHOTOS

www.thomasgianardi.com/khm.html

THOUGHT PUREE

www.impure.org/thoughtpuree

Interesting, artistic zine.

TIME TO WAVE GOODBYE NOW

www.geocities.com/SunsetStrip/Exhibit/7589

'I think this is the last time I'll be able to do anything to this page at all. Computers don't interest me anymore at all, and besides, I have a life now. A really interesting one at that.' Ooh, get you!

TOKYO COSPLAY GIRLS

www.din.or.jp/~sowelu/cos.htm

'Thank you. Good bye!' it says by greeting. Then photos of weirdness galore are yours. Huge and fast loading site of mainly photos of sweet Cosplay fans. Very odd links as well, which means you never know what's happening next.

TOMB OF THE VAMPIRE

www.darkhosts.com/shock/tomb.html

Uploaded thrice weekly no less. Vampy woman. Site doesn't contain much other than personal stuff and brief, if startling, art, plus her own launchcast station.

TOMB WITH A VIEW

http://members.aol.com/TombView/twav.html

'Tomb With A View is a quarterly newsletter for cemetery friends, fans and followers. It is about the appreciation, study and preservation of the art and heritage in historic cemeteries.'

TOYOMI

www4.justnet.ne.jp/~toyomi_fan2

This is a weird Japanese site about this girl, and I couldn't work out what she does. It's nice to explore, because even if she's normally naughty this is chaste,

which makes it charming. Also: http://loversdesign.com/ex/ and: www.toyomi.tv for added clues, some involving handcuffs.

TV GO HOME

www.tvgohome.com

Very different!

TWINFUSION

http://twinfusion.com

Nice basic site done by Nicole Lee who claims to have been born in May 1928, in which case she's wearing well by the photo. Comics (Peep and the fab Jane are examples) and features on people such as Ginny, an LA gluegun artist, and she's a Sex Fiend fan so instant inclusion!

TWISTEDLENS.COM

www.twistedlens.com

Girls in glasses in the shower, in the tub??? Showers, Fishnet, bands (only Rock so far – Stitch, Luxt, Movement and Breach) also: www.girlswithglasses.com for more eye appeal.

UKRN

http://ukrn.topcities.com

The Unweaned Kitten Rescue Network Inc. is an Australian non profit/non government association that rescues, hand raises and then re-homes abandoned or orphaned unweaned kittens.

UNEARTHLY POSSESSIONS

www.unearthlypossessions.com

This is the bloke who does the Living Dead Dolls so it will be good.

URBAN NIGHTMARE

www.urban.ne.jp/home/nmare/index.html

Japanese site which includes a novel, a game and a diary.

VAMPIRE CONDOMS
www.vampirecondoms.com

VAMPIRE/DONOR ALLIANCE
www.darksites.com/souls/vampires/vampdonor

VARLA
www.varla.com
Music and women mag, with a difference.

VATOVEN
www.vatoven.com
Insanely colourful site from Mexico hoping to have a big band directory, with mp3 and live details.

VECTOR'S WEBSITE
http://tokyo.cool.ne.jp/vector
Industrial/EBM DJ'S site. Quite an intriguing but also confusing Japanese site. *Very* interesting Links, and he takes great photos.

VESPERI – Dark Glamour
http://vesperi.50megs.com/main.html
vesperi@aol.com
Clothes designer, photographer and illustrator, with lots of visual evidence of her craft on display. I think it's to get her noticed, but it's also a pleasure to sift through.

VIA DOLOROSA PRESS
www.angelfire.com/oh2/dolorosa
The home of that giant brain, Hyacinthe L Raven, and her small press activities of exquisite warmth and imagination. The site itself is not good, and I shall be having stern words with her about that, but the content will be *everything* you could hope for.

THE VICTORIAN WEB: AN OVERVIEW
http://landow.stg.brown.edu/victorian/victov.html
An astonishing site with pretty much anything you could want, from art to literature, gender issues, museums, history of the social variety, politics, philosophy, religion, science. One for Manson fans everywhere. Arf!

THE VIOLINS HAVE STOPPED
www.wormfood.com
Funny site, plenty of interest. Amy Stewart's – don't mention 'Knock On

Wood', although I actually loved that – hugely impressive design portfolio, plus Vladimir Thee Teenage Vampire (he's confused), and Goth Inc are well worth checking out, especially the FAQ. Mao's personal bit is great. She's sharp, likes to stare (nice pics), has good taste in links and you'll warm to her spikiness ('flap your wordhole' = Contact).

VINYL DEMON
www.vinyldemon.com
Proof someone can look cool and like hideous music!

VIOLET STORM – ART
www.violetstorm.com
Art, flyers and writing combine to form a site half portfolio, half zine.

VIOLET-RAY
www.violet-ray.net
From the Invalid Litter and Silver-Factory stable. How To Disappear (in 'Projects') is good, but the contents on each section are tiny.

VIPE.ORG
www.vipe.org
Women's issues done in a way that is fascinating, and on a par with planetgrrl, with serious and amusing easy bedfellows.

VISIONARY TONGUE
www.geocities.com/terriblepoet/vt.html
Storm Constantine's writing mag site, handled by Jamie W Spracklen.

VOLTAGE
http://voltagemagazine.com
Quarterly – free! – CD mag. Online details and Seattle links, plus address to send for mag (postage only).

VOLTAIRE.NET
www.voltaire.net
'Greetings humans,' it says. Who you calling human? He's a filmmaker, and has CDs available too. His images are awesome and the site is quite brilliant.

WARNING: HIGH MAINTENEANCE
http://torque.diaryland.com/index.html
Maybe it's Heather Spear and maybe it isn't, but this is fascinating objective fiction, with links to others who do equally brain-stretching work.

WARREN ELLIS – WRITER
www.warrenellis.com

FREDA WARRINGTON
http://members.aol.com/FredaMike
Okay, she's a cool, talented and respected writer, particularly among you vamp and vampettes, but it's nearly all about her books (a lot to consider) and very little about her! I felt miffed.

WELCOME TO BONEVILLE!
www.boneville.com

WELCOME TO GOTHIC NORTH THEATER
www.gothic-north.org
It's a theatre in Reno, Nevada. I just liked the name.

WELCOME TO HORROR LAND SPOOK HOUSE
www.angelfire.com/zine/njdevil/index.html
Hotel was closed when I went. Hopefully a virtual haunted thing.

WELCOME TO THE CATHEDRAL OF SORROW
http://members.tripod.com/~MorbidAngel_69/index.html

WESTGATE NECROMANTIC
www.westgatenecromantic.com
How cool is this site? There are icicles in your eyes. 'You are entering a website in Love with Death.... Death the Entity, the Angel of Death, Azrael.... in this Spirit's many names and incarnations, always the Great Separator of the soul from the flesh.' Well, I don't understand all this Azrael business, but anyone interested in that has to see this. 'The Original Source for Necromantic Literature and Art' it says, and it has

Visual Rock

No, these Visual Rock bands are not *strictly* Goth, but the influence of it is often easy to see. During the early and mid-eighties, Goth was so popular in Japan I even got asked to write some articles for magazines out there, only to be informed at one point that people had got then into Rock, by which they seemed to mean old fashioned Metal, and Goth wasn't so important any more. This gave me the clear impression that a lot of Japanese Goths shifted allegiance purely because of fashion. True Goths stuck with it, and that spirit has survived, as you will see throughout this book, but something weird has clearly happened out there, from our perspective.

They have a slightly different approach to genres, and while Indie has had great popularity, circa Britpop, they have also seen the main Metal side become more futuristic, cooler again, as Industrial and Club music has become hotter. Add to that the understanding and streamlining of image which the Japanese music industry has always exploited, and you have bands going all out to grab attention, looking great. (When they become a success they progressively tone it down, hoping to last and be taken seriously across a broader audience.)

This makes for some very weird sites indeed. A lot of the Visual bands do sound exciting, but many are much softer than you would imagine, like poppy Rock bands, with little intensity and overactive vocals. It is strange, and therefore fascinating. Looking at Japanese sites is also a nightmare because there are very few photos used compared with what we're used to, and you won't even find gallery sites on most fansites, because copyright law is different there and respected by the fans.

I really do recommend you start sifting through some of these. Most of

the bands look better than any European or American Goth bands ever will, they just do it so well, so the visuals of Visual are a treat. Just don't expect much in the way of great music. Have fun, and keep clicking on anything illuminated, as you never know where it will take you. Trust me, there are some *very* unusual voyages ahead for the intrepid.

Oh… and a lot of the men try as hard as they can to look like women. Then you get Cosplay sites, where it's mainly women trying to look their idols. So it's women, dressing as men dressing as women. I hope that's cleared that up.

Understandably, a lot of Japanese Goths hate the Visual Rock phenomenon as devaluing their scene, but I think they should consider that it will bring in people very young, who after a couple of years will want music of more substance – and if there's a Goth or Industrial scene there, then they stay with it. VR brings blood to the Goth scene in a big way. It doesn't take away.

Also consider the *effect*. There's lots of Hide (from X Japan) sites about a remarkable guitarist who hung himself. At the funeral, 50,000 fans turned up. 12,000 attended a wake. (Kurt *who?*)

AINSI SOIT IL
http://yokohama.cool.ne.jp/ainsi
Not sure what this is but Lucifer Luscious Violenoue from Fiction seems to be involved. Her site is at:
http://akasaka.cool.ne.jp/worldend1/index2.html

AMADEUS
www.fantasiaweb.com/~amadeus
Fairly old site, in English.

ANDROGYNOUS MINDS
www.geocities.com/SunsetStrip/Stage/2442/am_index.htm
This site introduces you to Luna Sea (dead), L'Arc-En-Ciel, Buck-Tick and Kuroyume on an interesting site, which also offers an explanation of what goes into this form of music.

AZITO
http://live.co.jp/kiyoshi
Fluffy looking VR performer.

BANG DOLL
www2.csc.ne.jp/~bangdoll

BISHOUNEN – DEVOTED TO BEWITCH
http://devoted.to/bewitch
A site with some English, and a gallery selection, plus some superb visuals. In the gallery click on the names at the bottom to go to more.

CELL No. 7
http://maebashi.cool.ne.jp/cellno7/indextop.html
Weird little site.

CLOTHOID DOLL
www05.u-page.so-net.ne.jp/zb3/at_kato
Female-led (by Youka/Rinne) Visual Rock band which makes a nice change, and this is a cool site anyway.

COLOUR ME BLOOD RED
www.geocities.com/Tokyo/Spa/5703

CRYSTAL EYE
http://page.freett.com/crystal/crystal.htm
rin-k@geocities.co.jp

D'ESPAIRS RAY
www.internet-wave.net/bi/artist/d/despairsray/data.htm

DIVINITY SHRINE
www.geocities.com/kamui_tina
Kamui from Gackt site, and there's Gackt and Malice M sections, but the

glorious thing here is the Cosplay section. Check out the awesome pics, especially the girls in black in 29.4.2001. Superb stuff. All the Cosplay galleries have pics which should give ideas for new images. As the Comic World ones are creepy horror, like Kung Fu ghost films. They're doing it far better than the lace and fetish approach.

DUE'LE QUARTZ
www.ps-company-web.com/Duele/main frame.html
Standard pretty boy Visuals.

DUNE
www05.u-page.so-net.ne.jp/rd5/shoji/dune.html
Crazy bastards!

EL DORADO
www07.u-page.so-net.ne.jp/qg7/takamaki/eldmain.htm?

GACKT SHRINE
http://talk.to/gackt
Standard stuff but good links to webrings at the bottom. Fansites:
www.angelfire.com/my/sawasdeegackt
www.geocities.com/Tokyo/Bridge/7727/regret.html
www.shallealerilla.ocatch.com/index.html (Italian)

GARGOYLE
www5.big.or.jp/~gio/band.html
General Japanese band sites. Three links at bottom lead you to various items. Band links are worth following, just for the pics.

GIROTIN
www.geocities.co.jp/MusicStar-Drum/9393/gui.html

GLAD TO BE GLAY
www.geocities.com/SunsetStrip/Arena/4919

GLAMOUR & SUICIDE
www.geocities.com/glamoursuicide
Great site for Visual Rock enthusiasts. This has sections on dozens of bands. What I love is the list at the bottom of news, showing how many bands are splitting up, or members leaving. This is more than a scene, it's a soap Rock Opera! The good thing is that some of the bands have bite. One is described as Atari Teenage Riot combined with

Cradle Of Filth. They describe the bands in terms we'll all understand, which is very helpful.

GLAM JAPAN
http://communities.msn.com/GlamJapan
Amazing selection of reviews and pics. 150 bands covered already.

GLAY ONLINE
www.geocities.com/nayuglay
Singapore fansite. Plenty of history, and some news, in English.

HYDRA – DIR EN GRAY
www.geocities.com/die_direngrey/Hydra.htm

JAPANESE CHANNEL
www.geocities.com/Tokyo/Field/4849/menu.html
Huge links list on VR bands, and it's in English. Chat, forums, fan areas, photo galleries, profiles etc. Awesome.

JAYWAVE
www.jaywave.com/index.cgi

JROCK DIMENSION
www.geocities.com/jrockdimension
Amazing site for its galleries, which include over a hundred, and often more of each band they feature. There's over 400 pics of Glay!

JROCK ROCK RING
www.crickrock.com/cgibin/webring/list.pl?ringid=jrock;siteid=255
Already 214 sites to pick from!

KAGRRA
www.hf.rim.or.jp/~angellie/key/crow

KAMIMURA
www.angelfire.com/rock/Kami
Is this another tribute to a dead person? I know a few of the main VR boys have died, and this site suggests, with some very sweet writing, in English, that they're dreaming up future scenes

involving their favourite character, not so much a What If, as a Where Now.

LA MULE
www.lamule.com

LACHESIS
http://homepage.mac.com/lachesisnet

LAPUTA
www.crunch-loop.com
Official Laputa site, in Japanese but with English section headings, plus links to a member's site, label site and fan club. They all list their favourite cigarettes except for drummer Tomoi – 'a cigarette isn't smoked'.

LES FEES MAUDITES
www.malice-mizer.musicpage.com
Malice Mizer tribute, particularly Kazuki, who died. There are many band galleries here from the scene overall (check the blue-haired angel in Shazna!) and one at least had the presence of mind to name one live event Deadstock, which is funny.

LILITH
http://plaza28.mbn.or.jp/~cyberange

LUNA SEA – LUNATIC FRINGE
www.geocities.com/Tokyo/Bay/5901/index2.html

MADETH GRAY'LL – FAN ARCHIVE
www.jahanna.net/higeki

MALICE MIZER
www.malice-mizer.co.jp
The official page of the band's best looking band? In Japanese, and no way near as good as the visual unofficial sites. How about a few dozen live photos for starters – at least then people who can't speak Japanese can still be intrigued?

MALICE MIZER – FANSITES
http://jpop.hatch.co.jp/scripts/jsearch1.pl?keyword=malice+mizer
http://malice.narod.ru
www.angelfire.com/az2/malicemizer/malice mizer.html
www.angelfire.com/indie/Corey/Malice.html
www.geocities.com/bois_de_merveilles
www.geocities.com/Tokyo/Harbor/4574
www.simcommunity.com/sc/malice/hiro7
www.webring.ne.jp/cgi-bin/webring?ring=malice;list
www4.plala.or.jp/jeunefille

Clothoid Doll

NEKOI'S CABIN – PSY DOLL
www.ceres.dti.ne.jp/~nekoi

PSYCHEDELIC VIOLENCE
http://w5.dj.net.tw/~Xjapan
Busy tribute site to X Japan.

QUAD-RU-PLETS x
www.eris.ais.ne.jp/~quad/
Japanese-only Malice Mizer site, so
stick to the weird galleries, devoid of
photos, but with strange illustrations.
Their BBS, chat and e-mail section is
also called 'Tea Party' and that's
something else girls go for in this
scene, some quaint English imagery
like the ever-present late Victoriana in
their 'Lolita' fashion style – a little bit
Alice Through The Looking Glass.

RAPHAEL
www.geocities.com/xxhanahimexx/Glorious_
Angel.html?987289402360
Unofficial. English used, for history.
Coquettish gallery with Pierrot make-up.
Some translations, of band messages
and lyrics which often work and
sometimes don't, such as, 'I don't have

interest anymore in toys which are
covered by cat,' which is pretty cool.

RAZORBLADE GEISHA
www.geocities.com/razor_geisha
This has various Visual stuff, but in
Gekko No Onna there is an attempt to
redress the balance of VR by concentrating on women in the scene, although
there is only one section ready. Takes a
while. Wait until two masks appear,
then click the left (white) one.

SOPHIA
http://jrock.pe.kr

STRIP
http://members.ch.tripodasia.com.hk/c_fish
A Gackt site, I believe. Ex-Malice Mizer
and now a keen exponent of... fishing!

TOKYO GENSOU
www.geocities.com/pserenity/jmsupport/index.
html
Visual Rock 'support page'.

TOMOBIKI.COM
www.tomobiki.com/wagaku

This is great for a well-written guide, in
English to J-Rock and Visual Rock

TRISTESSE – MANA FANSITE
http://hk.geocities.com/manahime1437
This is weird, because it's a bit of Malice
mania, but there's Cosplay where she
creates pics of her looking like Mana,
and she looks great in all her shots. All
very innocent, nothing unseemly. Plus
live stuff and her own writing elsewhere.

VARIA
http://members.jcom.home.ne.jp/varia
Some excellent pics tucked away in the
Live Reports.

VISUAL ROCK ART ENTRANCE
http://vr-art.com/rock
Mega-photography site. You *have* to see
the band galleries. All of them. It's
coming back as a member's suite soon.

YAHOO GROUP: KRANKE
http://groups.yahoo.com/group/kranke
VR mailing list that focuses mainly on
the indie bands Kein and Deadman (and
any future projects of Mako and Yukino).

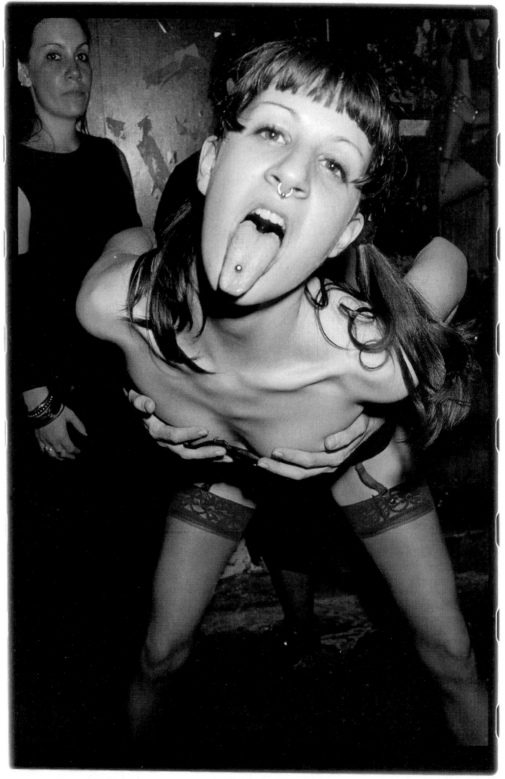

Le Bal Des Vampires. Photo © Stéphane Burlot

Webrings

A TOUCH OF RASPBERRY
http://nav.webring.yahoo.com/hub?ring=rasp
ring&list
'Where Rasputina sites unite.'

ALT.GOTHIC FASHION WEBRING
http://nav.webring.yahoo.com/hub?ring=agf
webring&list

ALT.GOTHIC WEBRING
www.saber.net/~tzabaath/altgothic/altgothic.html

ALWAYS VICTORIAN
www.ringsurf.com/netring?ring=alwaysvic;
action=list
Victorian subject matter, obviously, set
up by those nice Pale Court people.

B.I.T.C.H.
www.ringsurf.com/netring?ring=bitchring;
action=list

BEAUTIFUL DARKNESS
www.ringsurf.com/netring?ring=1beauty;
action=list;sd=98

BETTIE SCOUTS OF AMERICA
http://nav.webring.yahoo.com/hub?ring=bettie
scoutsofam&id=6&hub

BEWITCHED TEENS
http://nav.webring.yahoo.com/hub?ring=witchy
teens&list
'A webring for the members of
Bewitched Teens and Sister
Organization OntarioTeenWitch that
have webpages.'

BLACK GOTHIC
http://nav.webring.yahoo.com/hub?ring=
gothicky&list

BLACK ROSES & OTHER RARE BLOOMS
http://nav.webring.yahoo.com/hub?ring=lyciana
&list
'A ring for Dark/Goth sites with
appreciation for the finer side of life.'

BLAME INFATUATION (CURE)
http://nav.webring.yahoo.com/hub?ring=
infatuation&list

BLESSED DARKNESS
www.geocities.com/BourbonStreet/8005/
dark.html

CEMETERY PHOTOS WEBRING
http://nav.webring.yahoo.com/hub?ring=
cemphoto&list

CERCLE NOIR
www.ultimatom.com/cerclenoir/sites.htm
Huge webring site with eleven separate
sections. 'Dark & Gothique' is at:
www.ultimatom.com/cerclenoir/dark.htm

CHERUBICK WEBRINGS
AND CLIQUE DIRECTORY
www.envy.nu/cherubick

CHOKOTTOAKUMA
www.webring.ne.jp/cgi-bin/webring?ring=
akumakei;id=10;list

CHRISTIAN GOTH RING
http://nav.webring.yahoo.com/hub?ring=cgoth&list

CIRCLE OF DARK SOULS
http://nav.webring.yahoo.com/hub?ring=
darksouls&list
'This ring was specifically created to
join together quality sites that express
the enticing beauty of darkness in its
various forms, be it Gothic, vampiric,
horror, pagan, dark fantasy, or another
dark-orientation. Walk with Us and Be
Seduced...'

COBWEBBED AND SPIDER-STREWN
http://nav.webring.yahoo.com/hub?ring=
cobweb&list
'A ring for those involved in the Gothic
scene, or those who are interested in
poetry, art and the beauty of darkness as
well as light.'

THE CORSETORIUM
http://nav.webring.yahoo.com/hub?ring=
corsetorium&list

THE CYNICAL FEMME ARTISTA
http://nav.webring.yahoo.com/hub?ring=
wombat12&list

'For well-done sites of the creative and
cynical femmes and femme-friendly
men of the Web. Please be sure to read
the Applicant Instructions for more
information.'

DARK ARTS
http://nav.webring.yahoo.com/hub?ring=
darkartsring&id=1&hub
'A webring to pull together and pool
artists of a dark, Goth, dark tech,
Industrial, and alternative nature
hope-fully to eventually group showings.'

DARK EXCHANGES
www.thedarknetwork.com/portal/DarkExchanges
Webrings, portals, banners galore.

DARK HUMOUR
http://nav.webring.yahoo.com/hub?ring=18049
6440&list

DARK MUSIC
http://nav.webring.yahoo.com/hub?ring=
darkmusic&id=12&hub

DARK SITES OF THE WEB
http://nav.webring.yahoo.com/hub?ring=
fangs&list

DE.SOC.SUBKULTUR.GOTHIC
http://nav.webring.yahoo.com/hub?ring=
dssg&list
'This is a webring for regulars of the German newsgroup: "de.soc.subkultur.gothic",
formerly known as: "de.alt.szene.gothic".'

DEUS EX MACHINA
http://fly.to/edens_air

ENNUS RING OF GOTHIC
http://webring.parsimony.net/webring95/liste.htm

ESCALIER EN ESCARGOT
www.webring.ne.jp/cgi-bin/webring?ring=dark;list
Dark Japanese webring.

ETERNAL TEARS
www.webring.ne.jp/cgi-bin/webring?ring=
blackmetal;list
Japanese webring for Black Gothic Metal.

THE EVIL EMPIRE

http://nav.webring.yahoo.com/hub?ring=lilla&list

FREAKY GIRLZ WEBRING

http://nav.webring.yahoo.com/hub?ring=freakygirlring&list

'This webring is for girlz with sites with freaky, macabre, Gothic, Alternative, Heavy Metal and unusual themes, graphics, and subjects.'

FREAKYPARENTS

www.geocities.com/chibimoonlee/FreakyParents.html

FRIENDS OF GOTH

http://nav.webring.yahoo.com/hub?ring=gothicring&id=38&hub

GOTH FAERIES OF THE WEB

http://nav.webring.yahoo.com/hub?ring=gothfaerie&list

'This ring is to honour all girls (bois are welcome too!) that possess a certain magic about them. Their site must be of high quality and be of a Goth or darker nature.'

GOTH NO MERCY

www.ringsurf.com/netring?ring=goth_no_mercy;action=list

GOTH? TAKE UP YOUR CROSS!

www.geocities.com/SunsetStrip/Palladium/9494/goth.html

'Are you a Goth for Christ? Do you have a web page that expresses that? Are you a Christian Gothic band in the ministry for Jesus? Then you belong in this webring. This ring is designed to unite Goths in the Lord, help you get acquainted with other Christian Goths and get Christian Goth/Industrial band pages in one place on the internet.' Now in the interests of balance, it could be argued that I should also include Satanic webrings, but do you know, I really can't be bothered?

GOTH X OF THE X

http://nav.webring.yahoo.com/hub?ring=goffick&list

'This ring is dedicated to linking together sites that feature a Goth X of the X award.'

GOTH-IND MUSICIANS NETWORK

http://nav.webring.yahoo.com/hub?ring=gimnet&list

'The Goth-Industrial Musicians Network is dedicated to advancing the careers of bands, musicians, DJs, writers, and promoters in the online Goth-Industrial community.'

GOTHIC ANGELS: UNLEASHED AND UNITED

www.angelfire.com/fl/raineyslair/gothangel.html
Angelfire sites.

GOTHIC ARTS REVIVAL

www.geocities.com/Area51/Dimension/1594

THE GOTHIC EMPORIUM

http://nav.webring.yahoo.com/hub?ring=thegothicemporiu&id=1&hub

THE GOTHICALLY ELEGANT WEBRING

www.geocities.com/Area51/Chamber/9781/goth.html

'This is for sites that are done elegantly... Sites that celebrate what is dark and beautiful in a hauntingly seductive sense... Something pleasing to read and look at... that will interest the public... and perhaps enlighten...'

GOTHIC HAVEN

http://nav.webring.yahoo.com/hub?ring=gothichaven&list

GOTHIC LOVERS OF THE NIGHT

http://nav.webring.yahoo.com/hub?ring=6vex6hecubus6&list

'This ring is for anybody that might be in the Gothic community or might just want to get more hits on their page. Although in order for them to be accepted to the ring they *must* have some type of Gothic content in it. (e.g. what being Gothic to them is, etc...) My main goal is to unite all the Goths that are in love with someone. Those who are in love with other things though (music, art, etc) will also be accepted.'

GOTHIC NITE

http://nav.webring.yahoo.com/hub?ring=gothic_nite&list

GOTHIC ROMANCE

http://nav.webring.yahoo.com/hub?ring=romgoth&list

'Gothic Romance, a ring for people of the darkest love and who appreciate the night and what to love in it forever.'

GOTHIC ROMANCE (2)

www.webring.ne.jp/cgi-bin/webring?ring=Gothic;id=28;list

Japanese Goth webring. If you can't find quality stuff in among the Visual Rock you aren't trying. Lots of it is so strange you'll be sifting for hours.

The Wicked One @ http://thewickedone.cjb.net

GOTHIC VISIONS

www.ringsurf.com/netring?ring=gothicvisions;
action=list

GOTHIC + WEBRING

www.webring.ne.jp/cgi-bin/webring?ring=
goths;list
Second biggest Japanese Gothic
webring.

GOTHICALLY ELEGANT WEBRING

http://nav.webring.yahoo.com/hub?ring=
andromeda_ring&list
'Gothic or 'Goth' sites that are done
elegantly and with taste. This ring is for
the best of the best, the dark sites with
elegance that are worth seeing.'

GOTHS WHO LIKE VODKA

http://nav.webring.yahoo.com/hub?ring=
vodkagoffs&list
'Goths 'n vodka... Two great things
that go great together, or something
like that.'

HELL CAT

http://neuroism.net/hellcat
"This ring is for girls who have style,
sass, and class! If you're a girl who
doesn't take any shit from anyone and
knocks 'em dead with your sharp claws,
tongue, and wit, then this is the ring
for you. Guys can join too, if they love
hellkittens!"

HIDE LOVER RING

www.webring.ne.jp/cgi-bin/webring?ring=
pinkmars;list
Same as the Hide ring, in theory, but
with a more wayward selection.

HORROR PUNK WEBRING

www.theorderofthefly.com

I {HEART} MY DOMAIN

http://neuroism.net/heartdomain

INSOMNIA: THE MIDNIGHT GARDEN

www.hell-flower.com/insomnia
For people with insomnia, naturally.
Requirements? 'Think journals, life
stories, poetry, art, and other forms of
expression. I'm not very picky but I will
not tolerate the closed minded, sex
crazed monomaniacs, hatred filled
lunatics, racist pigs, or anyone I find
horridly distasteful in general. AnD
TyPiNG LikE thIS is a No nO.'

JAPANESE DOLLS WEBRING

www.webring.ne.jp/cgi-bin/webring?ring=
loveblythe;id=14;list
One extraordinary voyage starts here....

JROCK WEBRING

www.crickrock.com/cgi-bin/webring/list.pl?
ringid=jrock;siteid=manahime
Because so many of these bands will
be the modern equivalent of Japanese
Soft Metal with better imagery I
won't delve too deeply, but I would
recommend an occasional trawl
through this because you will find
interesting sites.

THE KISS DOLLRING

http://nav.webring.yahoo.com/hub?ring=
kissdollring&list
'KiSS is the Kisekae Set System, the
Japanese format for computer paper
dolls. Originating in Japan, a large
number of KiSS dolls are drawn in the
anime/manga style but there is also a
growing number in a large variety of
styles. Dress-up fun for all ages!'

LACED-UP

http://taintedangel.net/lacedup

LE ESPACE DE SOIR COCOFILLE

www.geocities.co.jp/Milano-Aoyama/1844

LES AGENDAS TRES GOTHIQUES

www.ringsurf.com/netring?ring=gothiques;
action=list

LONDON AFTER MIDNIGHT

http://nav.webring.yahoo.com/hub?ring=
londonaftmid&list

MARILYN MANSON – JAPAN

www.webring.ne.jp/cgi-bin/webring?ring=
marilynmanson;list
www.geocities.co.jp/Bookend/8641/webring.htm
You can't say I'm not all heart. Japanese
Mazza webrings.

MARION WEBRING

http://nav.webring.yahoo.com/hub?ring=
marion2&list

MERVYN PEAKE

http://nav.webring.yahoo.com/hub?ring=peake
&list

NETRING – THE UK GOTHS WEBRING

www.ringsurf.com/netring?ring=uk_goths;
action=list

NOCTURNAL SUPREMACY – CRADLE OF FILTH

http://nav.webring.yahoo.com/hub?ring=cradle
offilth&index

ORDER OF THE DARK ROSE

http://nav.webring.yahoo.com/hub?ring=
darkrose&list

OTHELLO'S REVENGE

www.geocities.com/Area51/Hollow/5472/
web.html

'Do you hate being defined by the colour of your skin and show the world day by day that you do *not* live a lifestyle like people *expect* you to on sight... maybe you listen to Industrial/Punk/Ska/Goth, maybe you're the only skater kid you know with dreads, maybe you're *sick* of Goth being defined as *pale* and *white*. Then this, my dear, is the webring for you.'

PEN AND GLASS II – Convergence New Orleans
http://nav.webring.yahoo.com/hub?ring=penandglassno&list

PEZHEADS
http://mesmerized.org/zelda
A webring thing for fans of Pez. Some heads are relevant, so don't get sniffy!

PHANTOM
www.webring.ne.jp/cgi-bin/webring?ring=phantoma;list
Japanese Goth-ish webring.

PLAYTOWN YOYO
www.geocities.co.jp/Playtown-Yoyo/5387/uindex.html
Several Japanese webrings at bottom of page.

PRETENSION
www.ringsurf.com/netring?ring=pretension;action=list

RING FOR ROCKIN' GOTH GIRLZ
http://nav.webring.yahoo.com/hub?ring=gothgirlz&list

RING OF THE DARKLING
http://nav.webring.yahoo.com/hub?ring=akian13&list

RING OF DARKENED SPLENDOUR
http://gothicvisions.veryweird.com/webrings.html
'A ring for those of the slightly more dark minded or spirited. Not evil, but the ones who find beauty and splendour in darkness and the night. There are many other rings like this one, but I want my piece in the deal.'

THE RING OF GOTH BOIZ
http://nav.webring.yahoo.com/hub?ring=boi&list

RING OF OLD SCHOOL GOTH
http://nav.webring.yahoo.com/hub?ring=gofficring&list

'This ring is intended for those who are interested in the old school Goth culture and old school fashion. If you're still backcombing, wearing your painted leather, and can remember who the "Birthday Party" are, you'll want to join this ring.'

RING OF UNITED GOTHICS
http://mitglied.tripod.de./LaFeteNoire/webring.html

RING OF WICCAN MERCHANTS
www.witchs-brew.com/webrings/merchants.html

SHADOWDANCER'S UNION
– Goth/Ind
http://k.webring.com/hub?ring=shadowdancersuni

SICKLY SWEET AND PRETTY
http://blackdaisies.com/sicklysweet

SICKENINGLY PRETTY
http://poisonrain.com/sickeninglypretty

SILVER FISH
http://ns.31rsm.ne.jp/~gackt/EasyRING/ering.cgi?mode=all
A Japanese webring of total variety from dolls to computers to music but with the emphasis on the unusual, noir and artistic. You'll have fun.

SINISTER GRACE
http://nav.webring.yahoo.com/hub?ring=sinistergrace&list

SIOUXSIE
http://nav.webring.yahoo.com/hub?ring=satbring&list

SIREN SONG WEBRING
www.crosswinds.net/~etherealmusic
'Siren Song is a webring for ethereal music sites and related styles (dark Electro, medieval, atmospheric, etc.). To join the ring, your site must be about or have a section dedicated to one or more musicians in this genre.'

SWITCHBLADE SYMPHONY
http://nav.webring.yahoo.com/hub?ring=switchblade&id=11&list

TIE + + ME
http://nocturna.net/tieme
'The idea for this webring is very

simple: gathering all (the best) webrings that have a dark theme to make it easy for those who want to join one finding the one they're looking for. I personally spent some time browsing through webrings indexes and I realized that something like this strangely still doesn't exist.'

TND NOISE IND ELECTRO GOTHIC WEBRING
http://pub12.bravenet.com/sitering/nav.php?usernum=1012613176&action=list&siteid=36467

TORUS OF GOTHIC CLUBS & DJS
http://nav.webring.yahoo.com/hub?ring=gothclubs&list

TROSTLOS GOTHIC WEBRING
www.webring.de/cgi-bin/webring/navigate.pl?page=40591&knopf=Alle

TWILIGHT OF DREAMS OR REALITY
http://nav.webring.yahoo.com/hub?ring=t_dreams&list
'Twilight of Dreams or Reality Webring is for sites containing Paranormal, UFO, OOB, Vampyre, Wiccan, Fantasy, or Unusual or Unexplained Experiences, Information, or Prose. No Satanic sites please.'

UK GOTH BANDS
http://nav.webring.yahoo.com/hub?ring=gothbandsuk&index

THE ULTRA EGOTISTICAL (AND LOVING IT) GOTHS WITH A 'TOOD WEBRING
http://nav.webring.yahoo.com/hub?ring=tood&list
'The web's first ring dedicated to those lovely and wonderful dark people (of *all* categories) with swelled heads and inflated egos. This is the place in which we may be ourselves and not have to worry about moronic comments of simpletons who attempt to get near us *file nails* Whether your site reflects your own true narcissistic behaviour or that of a chosen persona, or even if your site is humble but terribly self-centred, you will fit in just perrrfectly. Nurture the attitude, dahhhhlings!'

VISUAL ROCK
www.webring.ne.jp/cgi-bin/webring?ring=vrock;list

Zines

A SOPHISTICATED HAUNT
www.nighterror.com
Dark music, spooky things, horror and humour mixed. Reviews and rants, also comics and creepy figures.

ABOVE THE RUINS
www.abovetheruins.com
Neo zine.

AIRCRASH MONTHLY – ARCHIVE
www.demon.co.uk/bat/aircrash/contents.html

ALL ABOUT EVE
www.julianneregan.net/iss
Ink & Second Sight, a magazine written by fans, for fans, with full support of the band and including work by Julianne herself.

ALL THE SIN
www.blacklipstickstains.net/allthesiN

AMBOSS
www.amboss-mag.de
Metal + Goth from Germany. Big bugger with huge reviews section, plentiful interviews and news. Only thing lacking is a good gallery section.

AMERICAN GOTHIC
www.darksites.com/souls/goth/blackflower
Pagan, Gothic and horror short stories/poetry. Submissions accepted.

AMONG THE RUINS
www.geocities.com/soho/cafe/2815
It's that class act, Christina de Melo, back in action after a long layoff, so this could get seriously good. Plenty of old material to peruse, and her Ruination Press project looks cool.

ANCIENT CEREMONIES – PORTUGUESE
MAG PROMO
www.ancientceremonies.cjb.net

ANTICHRIST
www.antichrist.com.au
This actually is anti-Christ! Or anti-church, with articles about perverts in the clergy etc. Very strange and quite cool, with loads of satanic bilge as well.

ARC OF DESCENT
www.arcofdescent.hpg.com.br/index.swf
Absolutely brilliant Brazilian zine, with the normal features and content, but done in a bewitching manner, made wonderful by creepily surreal imagery. You don't need another language to understand the fantastic look and feel of this site. *Essential*.

ARTIST OF THE BLEEDING HEART
www.bleeding-heart.com
Art, poetry, fiction, musings.

ASPHODEL ARTS
www.asphodelarts.com
A mini-art zine where you can contribute.

ASTAN
www.astan-magazin.de
Dirty music mag? Weird.

BACK AGAIN
www2.pair.com/nlw/back/homeback.htm
This has grown! Alexander Pohle's fanzine is now a huge site covering a lot more varied musical styles than before. There are reviews everywhere, in English. It's satisfying, because it doesn't have that sterile look many big German sites have chosen.

BAT2
www.ninemuses.demon.co.uk/akashainc/index.htm
Part of Akasha, with art, bands, literature and galleries.

BEYOND MY REINCARNATION
www.geocities.co.jp/Broadway/3675/indexE.html
English version of Japanese site, which appears to be a mainly Metal, with Goth included. The links section to sites for bands and zines is immense.

BITEME
www.bitememagazine.co.uk
Excellent online version of mag with cool sections (people, films, spooky links, features) and a real sense of vitality.

BLACK HARVEST
www.geocities.com/blackharvest
EBM, Ind, Elec zine. Very bleak looking, very clean.

BLACK KOBZAR
www.blackkobzar.newmail.ru
Ukrainian Goth-Apocalyptic site, with English. Very interesting mp3 archive section. News, columns, philosophy and reviews. They have a healthy attitude to Goth out there and would doubtless appreciate some more promo stuff from bands, because there is also a fair-sized audience.

BLACK MAGAZIN
http://come.to/BLACKMAGAZIN
German and English promo site for quarterly German zine, which concentrates on info and depth and less on visuals. Nice links on site and details of their own CD releases.

BLACK MONDAY
www.lundinoir.com
Cool design, steady content – a bit of a hidden jewel. Try this as soon as you can.

BLACK SCREEN
www.blackscreen.de
Interesting, almost low-key German zine, which isn't packed, but has a variety of things, including good info on new bands, and nice galleries.

BLEEDING MINDS
www.bleedingminds.com
Jessica's site of photos, poetry, art etc. Great photos, and then read her interview at:
www.badasschick.com/webmistresses/jessica.
Don't miss Gothic Vixens either, that's quality... but it may have just vanished?

BLIND LINE
http://home.primus.com.au/taranis/index.html
Old, yes, but with weird photos.

BLOOD 666
http://homepage2.nifty.com/blood666/strange
doll.htm
Japanese Goth Horror Vampy mag.

BLOODY TEARS
www.interq.or.jp/rock/gothic
Interesting, if baffling, Japanese site
which includes some Gothic history in
terms of strange releases, along with
other styles, but does have a good little
links section which can take you to
other Goth sites.

BLUE BLOOD.NET
www.blueblood.net
Brought to you by the inspirational
Forrest Black and Amelia G duo
bringing you music, stuff, fashion,
editorial and stuff – *incredible* galleries,
great variety in content. This is the best
online zine escapade there is, bar none.
Don't waste time reading my thoughts,
go and bookmark it now.

BROKEN DOLL
www.goth.net/~brokendoll
Small zine from Western Australia, with
nice content but not much, which is
why they request submissions.

BZINE
http://usuarios.unincor.br/bzine
Horror, as in cinema, I think. Not easy to
tell, but the B may be relevant, because
there's a kitsch ethic at play. Music of
anime? Weird, but you get the idea.

CATEDRAL
www.angelfire.com/ct/catedral/interzona.html
Brazilian site with videos, good links,
especially local, and it's very well done.

CHAOS CONTROL DIGIZINE
www.chaoscontrol.com

CHAOS CRITQUES
www.geocities.com/chaoticcrit
Goth content in with Industrial, Metal,
Punk etc.

CHARLOTTE SOMETIMES
www.charlottesometimes.com
This is definitely different. Naughtiness
abounds at a site for art, fashion, music
and general rudery. Amazing photos by
Donna Clancy-Goertz, which you really
should consider, including local Goth
dignitaries, some of them clothed.
There's erotic fiction, brilliant columns
in Words, especially the rants, fashion
fixations, and a nice mix of music
interviews.

**CHURCH OF THE NIGHT
SCAVENGERS**
www.geocities.com/Athens/Thebes/9122
Art, Literature, Poetry and Music. Old,
but art is okay.

CLASSICAL GOTHIC
www.classicalgothic.com
New zine with good and clear intentions. Reviews aren't top quality but give
them time, as this has potential.

COLDBURN
www.music.ne.jp/~coldburn
Asako's brilliant Japanese music site,
updated regularly. Not much in the
way of reviews yet but very useful links
for sites in and outside Japan. You
should try those. Apparently the news is
updated daily, and there are interesting
things in the 'goodies' section. Make
sure you check out the Definition
Master gallery there, which has great
live pics.

COMA
www.geocities.com/comazine
Music, comics, art, columns, fiction.

CORPUS NET
www.corpusnet.com/rikstuff/Artwork/splash.htm
From the people who bring you the
Violet Collection and webring, a small
zine with regular updates with
interesting artists.

CORRIDOR OF CELLS
www.geocities.com/~zaraza_doom

CYBASE 23 – I N D
www.cybase23.co.uk

CYNFEIRDD
www.geocities.com/SunsetStrip/Theater/6787/
presentation.html
So it's fanzine and label, under one roof
with lots of tiny exclusive releases of
music in that whole Sol Invictus line.
Written in English and French.

D-SIDE
www.d-side.org
Promo site for French magazine of
the whole Goth/Industrial, Dark
Wave/Electro thing, as well as art and
literature, games, cinema etc. with
cover CDs.

DAATH
www.geocities.co.jp/Broadway-Guitar/2499
Japanese site which covers Rock, Metal
and Gothic. Quite interesting and I
think they welcome news from abroad,
especially England.

DAGOBERT'S REVENGE
www.dagobertsrevenge.com/index.html?rose
Magazine, but this isn't quite a simple
promo site. There's weird history
thrown in and loads of music features
worth reading.

DAMAGED TRANSMISSION
www.dtonline.net
Another great zine, offering the sharper
side of things. Features, reviews and
well-sculptured articles.

DARK CULTURE
www.darkculture.net
Recently changed from being The Gothic
Preservation Society. You will actually
need a brain inside your head for this
one. It isn't soporific in any way, because
it is one of the very best, *anywhere*. You
get quality articles here. Reviewers cover
new and old releases and include film
and other media. You also get art,
lifestyle and really enjoyable columns.

DARK DESIRE
www.dark-desire.com
Was being re-designed. Should be
luscious now.

DARK ENTRIES
http://welcome.to/DarkEntries
Wave, Gothic and Electro magazine
covering Flanders/Belgium/Netherlands.
Promo site with a little news. Some
wonderful gallery shots, going back years.

DARK FIRE
www.darkfire.co.uk
Small UK site with zine capabilities. They organise events in the south, and review those, with pictorial evidence, but there's other reviews also.

DARK MINDS
www.darkminds.co.uk
Tiny writing and art zine.

DARK MUSE – HORROR/COMICS
www.darkmuse.com/home.html
Big zine with decent features and its own art and babes section.

DARK REALMS
www.monolithgraphics.com/darkrealms.html
Mag promo, which covers Dark Fantasy in literature, art, music and cinema.

DARK SCENE
www.darkscene.at
Excellent zine of the Metally persuasion, all areas covered.

DARK VELVET
www.darkvelvet.com
Online publicity for quarterly mag on Darkwave and Goth matters by members of the University of Virginia along with people from the Charlottesville, Virginia community.

DARK ZINE
www.darkzine.net/main.html
Not really a zine in fact, but check out the Moxie graphics bit on the bottom right. His work is very immediate in its impact.

DARK ZONE – POLAND
www.darkzone.opole.pl
Attractive zine, in Polish only.

DARK ZONE – SPAIN
http://members.es.tripod.de/sandman
Good quality Spanish e-zine, hoping to create an English version soon. Seems to have stalled with not much happening. Could benefit from visitor involvement.

DARKBEAT
www.surf.to/Darkbeat
Brillantly done zine with regular reviews, clubs, events and galleries.

DARKER THAN THE BAT
www.proservcenter.be/darkerthanthebat

Big zine, with features, reviews, club, websites and radio guide.

DARKLIFE – MAG PROMO
http://darklifezine.xodox.de

DARKUS.NET
www.darkus.net
Inventive French site. Move the black bits on the spokes to select section. Goes between Goth and CyberPunk, with music, cinema reviews, Goth font downloads, moody photo galleries and weird art.

DARKWEB
www.darkweb.de
Excellent for clubs, reviews and photos.

DAS DARK-WAVE PROJECT
www.dark-wave.de

DEAD HEAVEN
www.deadheaven.de

General music, occult, philosophy, in German. Bit old, but does update.

DEADLAST MAGAZINE
http://deadlastmagazine.com

DEATH THREATS
www.deaththreats.com/deaththreats
I don't know about its claim to be the loudest e-zine, but the reviews and features are singular but very nice, especially the featured band. They welcome new writers, and it looks like they need quite a few to crank up some action.

DEATHROCK
www.deathrock.com
More than just a zine, this should be bookmarked by all. A wonderful site run by Mark Splatter and his nefarious crew. They say 'deathrock.com contains news and reviews, web pages, and complete info for Deathrock, early Goth, Gothic,

post-Punk, Goth Punk, Horror Rock, and gloom and doom.' Site naturally includes interviews, live reviews and CD reviews, plus sections. Spectres – people and bands who are dead. Invocations – the weirder death-related material. It isn't constantly updated, it's more a site which is slowly building up into a weighty oasis.

DELIRIUM
www.deliriummag.com
Excellent personalised zine that offers refreshingly varied interviews, reviews, has a good news section and is usually updated weekly. Welcome submissions.

DIGITAL ABYSS
www.digitalabyss.org
Interesting site with interests in dark reading, philosophy, Gaelic, etc. Not eclectic, but also not for dummies.

DROP SERENE
www.dropserene.com
Lithe little zine with good interviews and reviews, some interesting attempts at unusual photography and movies. Also, the editor is called Christina Q Pudding, which is charming.

DUST TO DUST
www.goth.net/~dust/main.html
Ethereal archive.

EINGANG
www.the-gothic-life.de
Odd and personalised site with nice photo menu, with an emphasis on photos and poetry/art rather than music, other than Placebo! Nice pics.

EL BESO
www.elbeso.cl
High quality art, literature and music zine from Chile. Plenty of Goth and Visual Rock. Some lovely pics (and some craps ones, admittedly).

EL LABERINTO – Spain
http://members.tripod.com/laberinto1
Dark Wave and Goth zine, but I couldn't read the brief page.

ELECTRO AGE
http://electroage.lowlife.com
Great zine, but only Industrial and Electro here... with lots of Noise and experimental, Synthpop. No Gawth whatsoever.

ELEGY
www.elegymag.com
Big magazine. This promo site looks every bit as vivacious, with huge links section, great French resources, however minimal, and big news coverage.

ENDEMONIADA
www.angelfire.com/ny3/ENDEMONIADA
A zine designed to promote women in bands, of all sorts, but darkish throughout. There's good interviews, and tiny galleries. The cutest thing is that the main staff have their own little sections, where they try and look Satanic, and Head Bad Girl, Lucifera, can't stop smiling!

EQUINOXE – mag promo
www.equinoxe-magazin.de

EXOTERIC
http://digilander.iol.it/exoteric
Very smart, Industrial, Electro and Neo Folk, but other influences exist.

FIBERONLINE
www.uol.com.br/fiberonline
Brazilian Electronica.

FLUX EUROPA
www.fluxeuropa.com
Part zine, part resource. Worth book-marking for the excellent news updates.

FUGA I
www.fuga.com.mx
Intriguing site from Mexico which mixes music, photography and comics, and there is a huge amount of everything.

FULL MOON
www.darkfear.com
Looks like an old site, for various zines, including Vamps, Jack the Ripper, Horror, Sherlock Holmes etc.

FUNERAL PROCESSION
www.funprox.com
Neo folk, Gothic, Industrial, worth seeing just for the live photo sections. Spotty reviews, fave bands explained, incredibly good links and some very odd art.

GALLERY APA – Furry
www.kendra.com/mauser

GOTH GOSSIP
www.gothtime.com
Lifestyle, when it's up.

GOTH IS GOTH
www.geocities.com/Paris/Bistro/9610/index.html
Stories, poems and reviews of what they see as classics. You may enjoy the article about Goth Club Tips. Be aware, English is not their first language. I think it's very sweet. Mind you, look at the Coven and ask the question, RPG fans, or not?

GOTH'S UNDEAD
www.carcasse.com/crisis/index1.htm
A sub-section of the mighty Carcasse site, this has pure Goth themes. Archive features, reviews and tabs, and loads of new columns by people, all in Spanish, I think. Good Brazilian links.

GOTHIC AND MORE
home.pages.at/gothic
Rather small site which welcomes submissions. Help them build their strength up.

GOTHIC ART – Poland
www.gothicart.iq.pl
Very attractive Goth site with plenty of art and photos in among other sections I couldn't quite understand, as well as reviews/features.

GOTHIC BEAUTY
www.gothicbeauty.com
Promotion for hard copy.

GOTHIC CHRISTEN
www.gothic-christen.de.vu
German Christian Goth site.

GOTHIC DIRECTORY
www.gothicdirectory.de
This looks a new take on the drabber 'Dark' resources, with bands, shops, label, architecture, fashion, chat – and it's mega-zine, which was the only real disappointment. *Everything*, in other words, but with a small central viewing area which can annoy.

**GOTHIC FAIRYTALES:
FOR MELANCHOLY CHILDREN**
www.gothicfairytales.com
Magnificent looking biannual zine. 'Inspired by old fairy tales and modern ideas, Gothic Fairy Tales for Melancholy

Children is an unnatural twist to a prevalent world.' Not much music, but the artwork is gorgeous.

GOTHIC HELL
www.gothic-hell.de
Poetry, news, and a *sensational* selection of photos.

GOTHIC LOVE
www.gothic-love.de
Not smut, more a small zine with news and art.

GOTHIC MAGAZINE
www.gothic-magazin.de
Another German biggie, which has a brilliant column by Dave Roberts (ex Sex Gang), with a very touching tribute to Rozz that you *have* to read. The rest is all in German so I'm clueless. Info, reviews, big on community, news galleries, comic, vamps, erotica, club info, their own online shop, downloads.

GOTHIC PARADISE
www.gothicparadise.com
Magazine, Goth 'stuff' – cards/gallery and odd roses, events and Forum. Also the Gothic Office – links, mainly. Very cool throughout.

GOTHIC TIMES
http://freespace.virgin.net/hazel.sex_goddess/gothicintro.htm
Fanzine site of old, with Blackpool Weekend pics.

GOTHIC WORLD
www.the-gothicworld.de/frames.htm
Absolutely brilliant German site, where the little bats drift down the page after your cursor. All the news and review/interviews you could want, tons of resource and community areas.

GOTHICS CULTURE
www.gothics-culture-ev.de
Very impressive, lovely-looking site. All in German, but the word culture isn't in the title by accident. This covers what it's all about. What it means to people, and there are lots of intelligent bios and contributions from Goths. Looks learned, but fresh.

GOTHICS NATURE
www.gothics-nature.de

News, chat. Forums, reviews, galleries etc.

GOTHISM
www.gothism.da.ru

GOTHS ANONYMOUS
http://gothsanonymous.tripod.com
Layout is pretty mouldy but the content is excellent and varied. You'd be an oaf to pass it by.

GRAVE CONCERNS
www.angelfire.com/ny2/graveconcerns
Site with a lot of potential, with plenty of good Goth and Industrial interviews and reviews, as well as the occasional article, but they could do with a few more writers to achieve consistency of quality, and would hardly sneer at any offers.

HATE THE MAINSTREAM
http://hatethemainstream.com
Another biggie with news, rants, Bettie, forums, cams, chat, archive, a fetish for unusual people, cartoon strip, good writing, downloads etc. A lack of music, naturally, unless their own, and some drab galleries, but this is about life and zest in all directions.

HAUNTED CASTLE
www.pukupuku.com/haunted
This Japanese site has just started and so far only the board and chat seems working, but it is Gothic and it should look nice by now. A second visit showed that rooms were taking shape and there were good links.

HUZZAH – FURRY!
http://huzzah.org

IMMORTALI ET MORS – POETRY AND FICTION
www.karafiat.com/iem/index.html

IN MUSIC WE TRUST
www.inmusicwetrust.com
Has tiny Goth/Electronic section

INCISION – ELEC
www.geocities.com/SunsetStrip/Lounge/3911/editor.htm

INDUSTRIAL NATION
www.industrialnation.com
Well it's just epic, isn't it? This is an inflated promo site, because there's good news and massive links.

INSECTS & ANGELS
www.bajema.com/insects/index.html
Interesting zine specialising in art and fiction.

J.A.M.
http://web9.freecom.ne.jp/~free_jam
Alternative Japanese magazine. Plenty of interviews, plus reader involvement. When you click the interview tab it sets up a photo of each interview subject so you can have a pretty good stab at getting the right type of music.

KATO'S NETZINE
www.katosnetzine.de.vu
Available in German and Spanish. Speaking neither I chose the latter, for a change. It's a nice site, mainly with reviews, but film as well, as some good gig galleries.

KNIGHTIMES DOWN
www.knightimes.cjb.net
Excellent zine with Goth and Industrial to the fore, plus their own CD comp, and radio, board, forum etc.

KORTEX – ELEC
http://kortex.n3.net

L'AME ELECTRIQUE
http://geocities.com/ameelectrique
Smart, small French zine with Electro and Goth.

LA COQUILLE FELEE
http://coquille.jeckel-dev.com
No idea – maybe a French archive-in-the-making from the person who does

LIMITED AUDIENCE
www.limited-audience.com
Fetish and fashion.

LOOP ZINE.TV
www.corecom.net/geiger/pointcast/
current.html
Goth, Industrial etc with a very
imaginative design that had me
stumped for a while. Good writing and
visuals, and overall rather strange.

LOSING TODAY
http://perso.wanadoo.fr/losing.today
Truly beautiful looking Italian magazine
with CD. Promo site to whet the
appetite, until your neighbours think
there's a rabies problem.

LUX AETERNA
http://r703a.chem.nthu.edu.tw/~maldoror
Chinese site, covering Galas, Coil,
Einsturzende, with sections for Contemporary, Pagan, Industrial, Rock etc.

MALICE
www.emote.org/gothzine

MEGALOMANIAC PRODUCTIONS
www.megalomaniac-prod.com
Absolutely bloody remarkable. English
available and the quality of writing is
excellent. Reviews, naturally, with
astoundingly good live photos, hilarious
articles in the 'way out' section, which
is modern recollection at its best, and
completely mental links. One you must
not avoid.

MELTDOWN
www.meltdownmagazine.com
Britain's best Goth/Alternative lifestyle
magazine. Promo site with full details.
All the early issues have sold out,
which is no surprise. If you live in
the UK a subscription would be
advisable.

METAL.de
www.metal2.de
Be not alarmed, for while it seems like
that would be all Metal, they've Goth in
there as well. Into The Abyss was their
main album review when I looked. It's
another massive site.

MIDNIGHT DREARY
www.dirge.net/dreary
Nice looking archive for mini-zine.

'Gothique Francophone' webring, but
I'm flummoxed. Looks nice.

LAST SIGH
www.lastsigh.com
One niche point here, is that they will
be concentrating part of their site in
future on Woman Industrial artists,
who they feel get neglected. (Well, of
course, because Industrial is the new
Rock.) They have great features and
reviews, including a big archive, plus a
live gallery going back years which isn't
massive but is interesting.

LEGENDS
www.legendsmagazine.net

Tied in with other interesting site
projects, Legends offers great features
and reviews on a variety of styles. Plus
rants, fiction, sci-fi/fantasy, you name
it. They're serious about the music, and
it shows.

LEXICON – ELEC MAG PROMO
http://users.erols.com/guerue/lexicon.html

LIFE IS MY SACRIFICE
www.kreestal.fr.st
On the Manson/Cradle tack here,
but it's looking good. Horror, comics,
and an amazing gallery, which I
presume he has collected from other
sites.

MINDPHASER – ELEC
www.mindphaser.com

MOM, THEY KEEP LAUGHING!
– COMICS/ART
www.geocities.com/SoHo/Lofts/2287/index.html

MONAS HIEROGYLPHICA
www.geocities.com/SoHo/Museum/9668
Promo site for Pagan/Magick zine, poetry zine and tape label (including a Leisure Hive/Winter/Womb compilation).

MOON
www.moon-magazin.de
I couldn't really work this mag promo site out but I think it's 'Love, Lust & Lifestyle'.

MORBID OUTLOOK
www.morbidoutlook.com
One of the classics. There is not much content compared to many, but it's what's there that counts – Art, Music and Musings. It's a *superb* experience and there's an archive part for each unit. If you haven't been frequenting it these past few years you can overdose right now. Run by Mistress McCutchan – 'She is not a dominatrix or a drag queen (as Mistress may imply), but a very silly and overly ambitious/workaholic Goth girl.'

Laura – Mistress – McCutchan is the woman at the helm of Morbid Outlook, one of the genuinely reliable zines online, as well as a designer, which you will find more about when you investigate the site properly. I wanted to talk to someone who has experience of both the old conventional fanzine and the Net also, and her answers have a light-hearted but shrewd observational clarity. Relax, and enjoy the burbling.

What inspired your interest in Goth – was it that it matched some of your personal interests, or were you reacting to something in the Goth scene itself?

'I'm not quite sure how I got turned on to the Goth scene... back then, the word "gothic" simply wasn't used. Collectively, we were just a bunch of "freaks"... after eight years of Catholic education, I went to a public high school, wore lots of black, listened to the Cure, dyed my hair black and carried a lunch box. The "underdog" always appealed to me.'

Have you ever received similar inspiration/satisfaction from other scenes/interests?

'I don't think I've ever been involved in any other scene than the Goth scene. The darker side, so to speak, has always appealed to me, and as I get older, other interests sort of fall into my lap. Like gardening – and trying to grow black and purple plants or anything sort of creepy. Or Victoriana. Or anything creative and designy. I'll bet even when I'm sixty years old, I'll be the "witch lady" of the neighbourhood that still wears all black!'

Having experienced the delights/frustrations of a zine, how did you approach putting MO online? Did you have a plan/concept that differed in any way from what you'd been doing?

'Morbid Outlook had existed as a print entity from 1992 until 1996. When I jumped on the internet bandwagon in 1995, I knew I had to learn how to make Morbid Outlook a web entity because it was simply much easier and cheaper to produce and distribute. By the end of August in 1996, I gave up the printed version completely. I was able to make a new issue every month instead of two a year!'

Has it changed the way you've had to structure your life?

for the 21st century and beyond!

meltdown
uk.gothic.alternative.lifestyle

Laura 'Mistress' McCutchan of Morbid Outlook zine.

'My significant other can surely tell you how Morbid Outlook takes up a lot of my time and energy! I spend a lot of late nights up on the computer, collecting content, "meeting" new contributors, designing, editing, and promoting. I really enjoy it because it's my baby and I want to put out an excellent zine.'

What have been the good and bad points that emerged, that you couldn't have anticipated?

'I would have never have guessed how many people read [it] and how popular the zine has grown. Morbid Outlook receives between a quarter to half a million hits a month. Readers log in from all over the States, Canada, Australia, South Africa, the UK and Scandinavian countries. On the bad side, when I get designer's block, it's really tough to "force" myself to get inspired. Sometimes I have to step away and something will come naturally in order for me to get back designing. I get really picky sometimes, and as a stubborn Capricorn, sometimes I can't let go of things. I'll get hooked on some

design element that doesn't work, try as I might.'

Women dominate the net in a way that is not evident in other scenes. Why do you think that is? Is that necessarily connected with Goth itself?

'The internet is a true democracy – very grassroots with anyone and everyone able to voice themselves! Although there are many techie guys, I think women dominate the web in that they can easily slip into the role of the voyeur/exhibitionist at any rate they please (whether very anonymously or

very openly!) And yes, the Goth scene is a very man-hungry scene, especially here in NYC! Considering that a large part of the Goth style is the fashion, it's easier to find Goth women dressing the part than Goth men.'

Nobody can have failed to notice the whole clique/domain thing with those rectangular boxes, which are done by people with Goth links. (Is there a generic term for these?) They're all done by women, and they appear to have very little reason to exist other than consistently uninteresting dream journals and a host of crappy camshots.

What can you see coming out of these that can be positive and interesting?

'The whole clique thing you're referring to is a "webring", which links up sites of a similar nature. It's not *just* women guilty of doing these! I think this can be good if you are seeking particular sites. For example, if you are looking at a webring of dark faery art or something, you'll be able to find lots of them linked up in one ring. On the other hand, like many things you'll find online, there's a lot of crap out there and it's a matter of sifting through crap to find something you really want to read/see.'

I meant the gormless sites, which aren't always in a webring, it's just a fey generic form which has taken holds recently. On the Net there is often much griping about Goth vs CyberGoth but there's very little evidence of actual Cybersites. To me those which exist often look like pale imitations of good dance sites? What say you?

'Goth vs CyberGoth sounds like just another hybridisation of subculture. In the late eighties/early nineties, no one used the word "Goth", and nowadays, people have broken down Goth into little subcategories like the PerkiGoth and the Victorian Goth, Fetish-Goth, Industrial-Goth, etc. The music and the look has gone down different roads. You can't even walk into a club without all the music sounding the same these days with that thump-thump-thumping EBM baseline. I couldn't really tell you what CyberGoth is... unless CyberGoth is synonymous with Net Goth, which is just a Goth person who spends a lot of time in front of their computer!'

The Net has propelled Goth forward, which is a Good Thing. What would you like to see happening next?

'The Net has propelled Goth forward by introducing more people to each other and making the community feel larger while making the world smaller. Now all we need to do is get more people out from behind their computers into the real world creating some live events!' A lot of idiots actually dislike the fact I write about Goth, because they'd prefer it remains obscure, evidently not being

bright enough to realise it's everywhere you turn! Do you think Goth will explode shortly, or has anything, like the Metal impact of Manson helped subdue it?

'I think that the Goth scene gains popularity or notoriety every time it pops into the mainstream or the media's eye. Like around Halloween, there's always some rag writing about the Goth scene. Or like that whole Columbine episode where those poor stupid, confused kids were mistakenly called "Goths". Or when some fashion designer includes corsetry and other designs in a given season with Goth appeal. This scene has been around for twenty something years and never really seems to be popular, it just weaves in and out of the public eye. Goth has hybridised and changed a lot since the early days! As far as Metal goes, that whole scene took a nose dive around the time grunge fully emerged. Metal is still going strong, but is more underground than Goth, in my opinion. Except, what strikes me as funny, is that some Goth music in Europe, especially in Scandinavian countries, would never fly here in the States because it's too Metal sounding. It must be a cultural thing, Black Metal and Goth don't mix here!'

You don't do the journal thing. Why?

'Why don't I do the journal thing? That's exactly the answer – Why? Everyone's got their reasons for doing a web journal. My ego, although fairly large, is simply not that big that I need to broadcast my daily thoughts. I don't even keep a personal written journal because it would become such a chore. Anytime something that's a hobby is a chore, that's when it's time to quit.'

What would you identify as the most important development within Goth over the past couple of years? What is the main thing that has interested you? (I'd imagine it is something, whether on or off the Net, that is also then reflected on it).

'I think that the Internet has had quite a big hand in helping the Goth scene grow and continue on – think of all the Net Goths out there! I also think peer-to-peer applications to share music (like Napster, LimeWire, Gnutella, etc.) has helped spread new and old music. Everyone

needs a resource in terms of finding what's new and what's good, and if you don't have the budget to buy everything you want, at least you're not being left out. What's kept me interested? My love of music, fashion, art... that's something I can't find anywhere else! Most pop culture really turns me off. Goth has always struck me as being a more intellectual and interesting scene.'

What, from a Goth perspective, would you like to see more of on the Net?

'From a Goth perspective, I want to see more content on the web! Good content! Even from a non-Goth perspective, I want content! As I mentioned earlier, there is an awful lot of crap out there – and while eye candy has it's place, I want good content! That's what will keep me coming back for more. So many personal Goth sites are just pure vanity – pictures of themselves and their friends, likes and dislikes, and a smattering of 'poetry'. That's fine among friends, but it won't keep the random visitor interested. Or sites that exhibit a lot of technical know-how with Flash and whatnot. That's great the first time around, but the tenth and twentieth time around, I don't want to sit through a bunch of animations. Content needs to come first.'

Similarly, what would you hope to see less of?

'I want less crap online! Less pop-up windows! Less crappy advertising – although it is a necessary evil sometimes, I don't want it to take over *content*!'

Considering how popular Morbid Outlook is, do you have certain ways you would like to see the site go – like some of the Dark Network or Necrosoft type mini-empires, where you run it as a business... or would you ever consider again doing a print version for a specific purpose?

'Morbid Outlook is in the process of a re-design, where it can grow into something bigger and better, perhaps an online store will be included! As far as the print world goes, I'm not interested in doing a print zine again. It was too costly and difficult to manage in the first place – it's just cheaper and easier to produce online.

suggests it's a lively entity. They welcome submissions.

NECROPOLIS
www.ladefuncion.com
Incredible imagery on this Spanish zine. It will really get you. Interviews and cultural sections abound.

NEGURA
www.negura.go.ro
Romanian mag promo.

NEO GOTHIC
http://members.xoom.it/NGothic

NEPHILIUS WEBZINE
http://crash.to/joost
Varied musical genres covered in Norwegian zine that welcomes contributions.

NEST OF SPIDER
www.chez.com/nestofspider
French site with menus for various areas – Lens, Paris, Montpellier, Rennes, Toulouse, Aix Le Provences and Marseille. They give live and soirees details, a guide to shops, and radio stations.

NEW GRAVE
http://newgrave.hypermart.net/newgrave.html
US mag promo.

NEWAVEMUSIC
www.kaihawaii.de
Eighties, EBM, Synthpop, Industrial. Lovely news section, reviews, features.

Although I do think some hardcore fans would love a printed version for their coffee table!'

Mistress McCutchan~the ethereal swirly girly~
P.O. Box 838, 128 East Broadway, New York, NY 10002-9998.
www.morbidoutlook.com

MOTHER OF DARKNESS
www.mother-of-darkness.de
Mega-resource, covering far more than Goth, but when you see it you'll understand the scope of everything involved. Everything you could want, for an all-round perspective.

MOURNING THE ANCIENT
www.mourningtheancient.com
You are warned about the site featuring nudity and about it hailing free expression, which gets your hopes up at once. It's a big site, which also

does its naughty photo CD sideline but there's plenty of music here. Interviews are good, but the reviews are strangely mundane, where pretty much everything is wonderful! You can click onto their separate site about the 'erotic' blood drinking blondes type imagery, where they sell CDs for $13, or $15 worldwide, and you get 500 pics for that, which still isn't as good as what I have planned, although mine aren't rude. It's different, but it's whether it's your cup of serpent-filled tea or not.

MOVING HANDS
www.movinghands.net
EBM-Goth-Ind-anything-Alternative zine from Sweden, in English – formerly *Totenklage* – and very high quality.

NECROGOTH
www.necrogoth.de
German Deathrock Mag promo, and something about the feel of this

NIGHTERROR
www.nighterror.com
Horror more than music plus action figures! Weird, but enthralling.

NIGHT SHADE
www.nightshadepromo.com
Impressive zine from company that also manages bands. They'll do all online promotions for bands and take a 15% cut if you're not up the task yourself or just too busy. Has features, their artist profiles, poetry, various resources, and Winnipeg Gothic, and is growing at a steady rate.

NIGHTMARE ZONE
www.gothic-order.de/nightmarezone
Great site, run by Thomas Thyssen. German only, with news, their own events, some fabulous little galleries, including some pics by Ralf Thyssen (nice festivals one, and cool Gitane), reviews galore, newsletter option and webring. A seriously reliable guide to what's out there, and what's quality.

NOCTURNAL DIRGE
www.skylord.com/nocturne
Dark Gothic Fantasy webzine, allegedly updated bi-weekly but hadn't been touched for months. Interesting content.

NOX OBSCURA
www.noxobscura.de
Neat, petite zine covering Electro, Industrial, Darkwave and Goth, with reviews, stories, and a lot of film.

OBJECT A
www.object-a.com
Gothic Industrial and underground culture. Depth but not overly angsty.

OBLIVION
www.oblivion-magazin.de
Heavy Metal, plus some Goth. Mag promo.

OCEANS OF CONFUSED DREAMS AND WANDERING STARS
www.borg.com/~lordxul
Is this it? A poem and a pic? Ambassador! You're despoiling us...

OH MY GOTH!
www.geocities.com/SoHo/Canvas/4411
Old, sweet French zine with interviews – even has a Dominion one from 1999!

– poems, short stories and graveyard photos.

OUTBURN
www.outburn.com
Quality mag promo site.

PANDORAS
www.gothic-portal.com
German Goth portal, filled with news, pics and reviews.

PAWPRINTS – FURRY
www.best.com/~lynx/pawprints.html
Okay, now I'm *very* scared!

POLARSTAR
www.polarstar.de
Mona's WebWorld is the best site of three included on this one site, offering photos, including artwork for band's record sleeves, and some interviews (in German). Polaricht is promo details for a magazine but I couldn't extract much info. Corva Verlag is... a total mystery to me!

PREMONITION
www.premonition.com.fr
Was a great site, with a super cool layout, and now a new one is being prepared. The old site is still worth it for the pics you'll find by Stéphane Burlot in the Goth section.

PROJECT INSANIA
www.insania.com

PROPAGANDA
www.propagandamagazine.net
This promo site lets you in, in detail, on latest issue's contents. Style has altered, moving away from romantic Goth to Morrissey, Siouxsie, Coal Chamber, and Genitorturers, Godhead, etc. Still as cool as ever.

PROSPECTIVE
www.prospective.nu
They were changing server so I could only canter through some electro news, but it looks the business.

PURPLE FUZZ
www.freakyplanet.com/FreakyPages/purple_fuzz/index.htm
Lots of links, very little review content, plus links to masses of clothing, divided into styles. Art and photography

is submitted. Girl, boi etc. It's a very nice compact site but would be even better with contributions, which are clearly welcomed. Move to new server may delay access.

QUIETTE
www.disappointedvirginity.co.uk/quiette
Interesting zine, for those who can walk and talk without getting confused.

QUINTESSENCE
www.swcp.com/mv/essence
Another beautifully simple site about obscure music which seems inviting rather than off-putting, which is far rarer than you'd think.

RECYCLE YOUR EARS
www.recycleyourears.com
Huge site covering Industrial, Electronica, Experimental, Neo-folk, Darkwave and a tiny bit of Goth. It's a mega-site with news, well written reviews and features, plus a decent archive, forum and a truly magnificent links section. A glorious surprise.

ROSA SELVAGGIA
http://utenti.tripod.it/NIKITA65/rs/iindex.htm

RUE-MORGUE
www.rue-morgue.com
Canada's premier horror mag. As for the website itself? Info on the current issue, some cinema news. and some basic links to sections which simply don't work!

RUINATION ARTS
http://gdn.net/~ruinnation
Art and music collective, with e-zine for Industrial, Experimental Electronica, Noise etc. Radio, publishing, own CD releases.

RUSTLINGS OF THE WIND
http://wind.xephyrus.com/impellent
Arty e-zine with authors and artists, and doubtless dreamy poets. It's well done but a bit soppy.

SCHWARZE SZENE
www.gothicscene.com
'Heartily welcomes!' they pronounce by way of a greeting, but unfortunately this site is all in German, which is a shame because it's yet another absolutely wonderful resource with review and

Blu from Starvox zine

interviews, and cool links galore – including to other equally good regional sites.

SCHWARZESEITEN
www.schwarzeseiten.de
Another superb German site with the zine only part of its whole news, archive, search engine resource. Nice pics – either outdoor Gothic themes, or all the cool live ones with the gig reviews – although the staff *do* look like they have escaped from somewhere.

SEDIR
http://seidr.woods.ru
Russian, with English version.

SEVENTH CIRCLE
www.seventh-circle.com
Massive Canadian zine/resource with excellent reviews and news, nicely varied interviews and full community projects, and competitions.

SICK KITTEN
www.angelfire.com/ego/sickkitten
Bands, reviews, interviews, desktop items, competitions, auctions, chat etc. Growing, hopefully, because it has a ranty feel anyone interested in Goth will adore.

SIDE-LINE
www.side-line.com
Brilliant magazine with online arm, including shop and CD ordering. Newsletter available, and some decent reviews and features as online specials, plus archive. True stars of the scene.

SISTINAS
http://sistinas.com
Music, Art, Literature, Film and Pale. I chose Pale, which turned out to be five crappy model portraits! It's an arty site, well-intentioned but rather stuffy.

SONIC SEDUCER
www.sonic-seducer.de
Mag promo but with news to access, and lots of small ads and reader requests, which is a nice touch others could follow.

SORDID
http://sortedmagazine.com/Sordid.php3
Quality Irish zine, Sordid being the dark side of Sorted. It's mainly reviews with some features. Good musical mix, and high standard of writing.

STARVOX
www.starvox.net
Mega-site! Brilliant articles, interviews of depth and up-to-date reviews, with vivacity, but also radio reviews, club scene, amazing galleries, contests etc. They also promote, and Blu's cat pics in the Credits section are some of the best you'll find. Click her photo, then hit the bottom of the page.

STIGMA
www.black-rose.sk/stigma

STROBELIGHT MAGAZINE
www.strobelight-magazine.de
Good live festival pics on front page, then mag promo and general news inside.

SUBURBIA MAGAZINE
www.suburbiamagazine.net
Mega Italian site with many genres covered including a very good Goth and Electronics section stuff, especially Italian, and with excellent news and reviews.

THE AETHER SANCTUM
www.goth.org.au
Dark culture 'with a quizzical Antipodean twist', which is one way to describe a mega-zine, resource site. Easily one of the best and most

reliable sites in the world. Views, fiction, scene guide, reviews, articles etc. Bookmark now!

THE BLACK GIFT GOTHIC
www.the-black-gift.de
Three choices before entering – the Mag, Culture or 'Kaufkunst', whatever that is, but they're all on the main menu anyway. Plenty of events coverage, live and clubs, reviews, poetry, some good links, and – best of all, although I'm usually biased – some gorgeous galleries. I had fun, and I don't even understand German!

THE CROBARD – FRENCH GOTH HUMOUR?
www.thecrobard.comicpage.com

THE DARK HOURS
www.darkhours.com
Looks dead but some interviews survive.

THE DARK VOYAGE
www.dark-voyage.de
Extremely attractive all-ranging Goth zine.

THE GOTHIC LIFE
www.the-gothic-life.de
Good reviews and news, naturally, but also *fabulous* photos.

THE GOTHIC TIMES
www.geocities.com/thegothictimes/homepage.html
Tiny, scabby old thing, with lovely atmosphere, poetry, vampirology and reviews, plus chat.

THE GOTHIC WORLD OF DARK MUSIC AND LIFESTYLE
www.the-gothicworld.de
Another brilliant German one with all the news, forums, links, reviews and interviews you want. Lovely layout. Little bats drift around the page in a beguiling manner, which is lovely,

not kitsch. Beautiful galleries in 'Dark Stuff'.

THE MAYFAIR MALL
www.themayfairmall.com/zine/intro.htm
Huge zine, with some Goth, part of the Mayfairmall site which is a big directory for all sorts of music-related avenues, and they do promotions work for a rock club in Newcastle. There are masses of interviews and reviews here. Easy-going, overtly enthusiastic. Have fun.

THE NEW EMPIRE
www.newempire.com
As big as most German sites and run along similar lines, but specialising in electronics, with Industrial slotted in nicely.

THE ORIGINAL SIN
http://mitglied.tripod.de/DreamsNeverEnd/original.htm

THE SENTIMENTALIST
www.asthetik.com/print/Sentimentalist/home.html
A cool, regular literary and artistic quarterly. Promo site.

THE STIGMATA
www.thestigmata.de
Fashion, events, links.

TOMB RAVER
www.onthewire.org.uk/tombraver
Old as the hills, but a few archive moments you may enjoy.

TWILIGHT MAGAZINE
www.twilight-magazin.de
Brilliant zine with news, interviews and photo-ridden live reviews.

TWILIGHT REALM
www.twilightrealmzine.com
You have to see this for her gallery which contains objects of an exquisite nature. Trust me, get thee hence! And the zine is quality too. Her interviews are direct but imaginative, as are the reviews. She has a perception about her that many zine writers don't have.

TWILIGHT ZONE
www.twilight-zone.it
Ind, EBM, Dark Ambient.

UNDERGROUND PROPAGANDA
www.undergroundpropaganda.com

Reviews, art, music and smut. Won't be interesting until bands start contacting them. At the moment it's weird, certainly, but conventional in its tastes.

VAMPGIRL
www.vampgirl.com
Book, pic of the week, music à la Goth and vamp stuff including an immense gallery selection.

VAMPIRE FREAKS
www.vampirefreaks.com
Mad comics, a love of freaks, plenty of music reviews, and the most instantly attractive element, the bulging galleries, which contain hundreds of ace portraits. I'm not into the vampire thing *at all*, so it's got to be special if I say it's a *really* good site.

VANPYRAE
http://vanpyr.ifrance.com/vanpyr
Nowhere near as predictable as you might imagine. Dark, intense, and artistic as Hell.

VER SACRUM
www.geocities.com/Paris/LeftBank/1667/info.html
Detailed site, in Italian, of classic zine, and it really is a work of great merit.

VIER – MAG PROMO
http://vier.norvagoth.net

WARDANCE
www.wardance.net
It's French, which could be useful, and English available. Mailorder and magazine. Shops, zines, links, chat. 'Zines' has lots of old interviews from the mag.

WAVE GOTHIC
www.wavegothic.de
Big again, with Metal, Gothic, Industrial and Ambient. All the usual areas are well covered. Not as big as some, but that's only a matter of time, and maybe a touch more attractive.

WELCOME TO REALM GOTHICA
www.realmgothica.com
'Sanctuary for creative Darklings.' Monthly music zine which may include a poetry feature, or interviews, with bands and writers – anyone that Naika Malveaux sees as making it in the industry. The site also showcases her

own artwork. Interesting Link Bank, and this is building all the while. Impressive.

WHAT'S GOTHIC?
www.geocities.com/gothic1997
This French zine (in English) looks like an oldie rejuvenated, as the interviews are archive material. The galleries are enchanting graveyard shots and the reviews/news seems reasonably current. I like the spirited explanation of Goth.

WRAPPED IN WIRE
www.wrappedinwire.com
Some seriously compelling artwork in the art gallery, a humour section, message board and masses of reviews – albeit in small doses, so don't check in too regularly.

WRATH
www.wrath.de
This covers all styles, and does so superbly, with a big block of interviews, tons of reviews, downloads, e-cards, and some great professional gallery shots.

X86
www.mycgiserver.com/~siusin
Hong Kong e-zine, which has interesting links to various big Asian sites.

ZERO
www.hf.rim.or.jp/~_o_/
Big member's-only site from Japan with tons of links. They have a nice gig reviews section, plus some *brilliant* club night photo reports. Big forum thing, and nice to stroll around.

ZILLO
www.zillo.de/index.html
This is *the most important Goth-related magazine in the world* and has been for years. The site is only in German, as it mainly serves that scene, but you can find archive listings of back issues, for collectors, and for German speakers there's a great news service, lots of merchandise, a forum, little sneak glimpses of articles in the upcoming issue and tour info. It's a *vast* site. The layout doesn't look good, but then the magazine never has either, until recently, so maybe this will catch up shortly? This is all about content over style. It's an absolute *classic*.

Noir

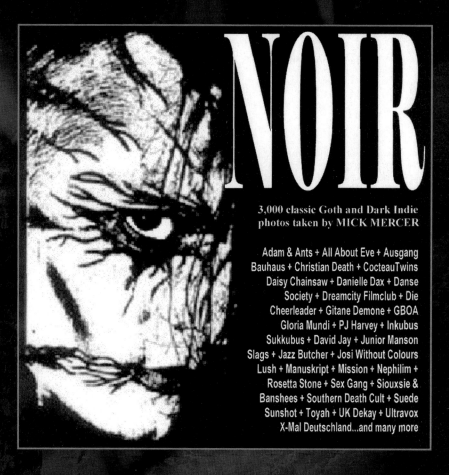

NOIR

3,000 classic Goth and Dark Indie
photos taken by MICK MERCER

Adam & Ants + All About Eve + Ausgang
Bauhaus + Christian Death + CocteauTwins
Daisy Chainsaw + Danielle Dax + Danse
Society + Dreamcity Filmclub + Die
Cheerleader + Gitane Demone + GBOA
Gloria Mundi + PJ Harvey + Inkubus
Sukkubus + David Jay + Junior Manson
Slags + Jazz Butcher + Josi Without Colours
Lush + Manuskript + Mission + Nephilim +
Rosetta Stone + Sex Gang + Siouxsie &
Banshees + Southern Death Cult + Suede
Sunshot + Toyah + UK Dekay + Ultravox
X-Mal Deutschland...and many more

ROSETTA STONE 91-95

Sex Gang Children

SIOUXSIE AND THE BANSHEES

TEST DEPT

NOIR is my first release away from books. A CD containing 3,000 jpegs of photos to which I own the copyright, from gigs and interviews – average size 14 x 10cms – they make for lovely shots when printed out. This is obviously a bargain, as it only costs £20, $30 (American) or E30, including postage, and comes with case and covers. Bands as follows:

1919, 4 Came Home, 8-Track Cartridge Family, Action Pact, Adam + Ants, Andalula's Locket, All About Eve, And All Because The Lady Loves, Angel Intercepter, Anna, Anonymes, The Arguments, Ausgang, Band Called Jeff, Bang Bang Machine, Barefoot Contessa, Bauhaus, Beef, Bible For Dogs, Big Black, Bingo, Bleach, Blessed Ethel, Blind, Blondie, Blood Sanction, Blubber, Bluetones, Blur, Bob, Bollweevils, Bowlfish, Brackenclock, Brian, Butterfingers, Butterflies, Carmines, Catwalk, Cecil, Charlie's Angels, Charlottes, Cherry 2000, CNN, Christian Death, Cocteau Twins, Cravats, Creaming Jesus, Cuckoo Club, D.A.D., Daisy Chainsaw, Dancing Did, Danielle Dax, Das Tor, Dreamcity Filmclub, Death By Crimpers, Dead Souls, Destroy The Boy, DF-118, Die Cheerleader, Die Laughing, Diskord Datkord, Doll, Doyenne, Dune Buggy Attack, Dust Devils, Gitane Demone, Echobelly, Edith Strategy, Elastica, Electric Sex Circus, Empyrean, Enrapture, Th' Faith Healers, Faith Over Reason, Fields Of The Nephilim, Flinch, Frost Flowers, Gaye Bykers On Acid, Goya Dress, Grimetime, Gloria Mundi, God & Crazy Lesbians From Hell, Gum, Headjam, Heza Sheza, PJ Harvey, Tim Harrison, Honey-lipped Divine, Honey Rider, Infected, Inkubus Sukkubus, Invisible Girls, David Jay, Junior Manson Slags, Jazz Butcher, Josi Without Colours, Judda. Kitsch, Laughing Mothers, Lean Steel, Lovecraft, Lush, Luxx, Manuskript, Marion, Martian Dance, Melinda Miel, Melt (UK), Melt (Canada), Merry Babes, Minxus, Mission, Monoland, Pauline Murray & The Storm, Nosferatu, PUMP, Pink & Black, Plastic Fantastic, Playn Jayn, Powder, Psychic TV, Punishment of Luxury, Pure Essence, Purple Rhinos, Julianne Regan, Rattlesnakes, Rosetta Stone, Sadodada, Salad, Sandira, Scarlet Fever, Scarlet In Heaven, Sex Gang Children, Sharkboy, Shoot The Joker, Siiii, Siouxsie & The Banshees, Siren, Ski Patrol, Skunk Anansie, Skyray Lollies, Slam City, Sonar Race, Southern Death Cult, Splintered, Star 69, Strax, Suede, Tabatha Zu, Test Dept, Toxic Shock Syndrome, Toyah, Tragic Venus, Trashcan Soul, Turbo & The Rockets, UK Decay, Ultravox (John Foxx), Vicious Kiss, Walk On Water, Wact, Weekend Swingers, Whiskey & The Devil, Witches, Woman, X-Mal Deutschland, Michelle Yee Chong, Zip Zip Undo Me, Zu.

These images are better quality than ordinary reprints from camera shops – and in fact just one film's worth of standard shop reprints would cost this much! Internationally, payment is by cash, but send 'registered' if you require proof I've received it, or ask in your post office about postal cash transfers. Most countries do them. Eventually I'll have Paypal and credit card capability on my website, but not just yet. In the UK, I obviously accept cash or cheques (payable to Mick Mercer). Address:

Mick Mercer, 76A East Street, Selsey, West Sussex, PO20 OBS, England.

While NOIR makes the perfect accompaniment to any of the earlier works, I also do photo CDs of certain artist from the above list, with more to come. All details at www.mickmercer.com. These CDs feature images averaging 28 x 20cms, meaning you can do the equivalent of 10" x 8" prints, on the paper of your choice. Enquiries: mercerm@supanet.com

GITANE
Black & White

Outro

GOTH GREATS

320 pics of bands, by Mick Mercer.
Some known, some forgotten heroes.

Anno Lucis + Bible For Dogs + Bod
Brackenclock + Cries Of Tamuuz + Das Tor
Empress Of Fake Fur + Enrapture + Fields
Of The Nephilim + Finish The Story + Josi
Without Colours + Judda + Lean Steel +
Manuskript + Mission + 1919 + Nosferatu +
Restoration II Romeo Suspect + Sex Bitch
Goddess + Siiiii + Southern Death Cult...

Just so you don't think I have forgotten how utterly love-ly you all are, I do have further plans. These will take off as regular releases from 2002 onwards. Obviously there's a website – www.mickmercer.com. At the time of writing this is mainly about my CD series, which is the first Goth photo archive organised anywhere in the world. Later, the site will be the place where the news of my other projects will be freshest. Here you will learn when my first three books, *Gothic Rock Black Book*, *Gothic Rock: All You Ever Wanted To Know But Were Too Gormless To Ask* and *Hex Files* will be made available on CD, as I am always getting enquiries about those. On each CD there will be a few hundred extra photos, as well as new text additions. As long as you have Acrobat Reader, you'll be fine.

There will also be regular reviews on my site. Bands who wish to be reviewed should send their CDs or tapes to Mick Mercer, 76A East Street, Selsey, West Sussex, PO20 OBS, England. Please also include full bio details and photos, as my next Goth book will be concentrating *solely* on bands and I wish to start that fairly soon, so the two areas overlap. I also wish to interview bands. All the info you can send is much appreciated. Annoying as some people may find me, they can't deny that unlike a lot of people when I say I'm going to do something I do it. It doesn't automatically appear relevant to people when I first announce something, but the idea generally gets through and via my site there'll be ideas people will doubtless copy, but I don't stop. So when I say I have plans for constant reviews and interviews, I'm aiming to have some new writing up virtually every day.

I have several archive CD books planned, constituting my 'PoseurNostra' series, which will each contain much more material than you'll find in any book. Other illustrated CD book projects include a *Best Of* (sic) approach to my other writings through the years, from fanzines, to 'professional' work, as well as my first illustrated novel, *Terror Firmer*, which will see the light of day on CD towards the start of 2003.

The other main plan is a quarterly CD release, *Justice*, which will be like my old fanzine *Panache*, but on CD, and far more imaginative and detailed. I am also currently trying to photograph every old (pre-twentieth century) church with a graveyard in the South of England. That project will take a few years to finish.

I know the majority of you always see the point of my books, and under-stand their relevance, even if you don't particularly like them personally. Whatever happens, please rest assured that this is not the end. It is not even the beginning of the end. But it is, perhaps, the end of the beginning, as I believe someone once said. So I hope you'll also at least be reasonably interested in the fact that, if this book is a suc-cess, I would like to be bringing out a book with Reynolds & Hearn every 18 months, if not less. This may not fit in with their plans, of course, but that's a rough time estimate!

And now be off with you. I plan to reacquaint myself with the concept of sleep.

Mick Mercer, long after midnight, 2002.

Danielle Dax

BAUHAUS

Rock
Garden
1980

DOLL